PHILOSOPHY: The Study of Alternative Beliefs

THE MACMILLAN COMPANY
NEW YORK · CHICAGO
DALLAS · ATLANTA · SAN FRANCISCO
LONDON · MANILA
IN CANADA
BRETT-MACMILLAN LTD.
GALT, ONTARIO

PHILOSOPHY

The Study of Alternative Beliefs

Neal W. Klausner

MILLER PROFESSOR OF PHILOSOPHY

Paul G. Kuntz

PROFESSOR OF PHILOSOPHY
AND RELIGION

GRINNELL COLLEGE

The Macmillan Company   NEW YORK

First Printing

Library of Congress catalog card number: 61-5948

The Macmillan Company, New York
Brett-Macmillan Ltd., Galt, Ontario

Printed in the United States of America

Preface

William James once wrote that " . . . philosophic study means the habit of always seeing an alternative, of not taking the usual for granted, of making conventionalities fluid again, of imagining foreign states of mind. In a word, it means the possession of mental perspective."[1] Since this statement first appeared, the temperaments, aims and methods of philosophers have changed, but the point James made is still pertinent and important. In 1876 when he wrote these lines he was protesting against theological dogmatism. At that time philosophy was largely designed by college presidents to indoctrinate students in religious orthodoxy. Today neither philosophers nor students have to submit to such pressures. For the most part we have achieved the freedom to follow an argument wherever it leads without being compelled to reject a belief or to accept one because it is official.

How should we, as James exhorts, "attack things as if there were no official answer preoccupying the field"? Certainly, as a beginning, by reflecting on what it is to believe, or to hold an opinion, in contrast to what it is to know. If we do not begin here we may become the easy victims of the irrationalities which spawn so quickly when honest criticism is smothered by dogmatic pronouncement. This is where we begin our book. We have deliberately striven to make our first chapter relatively easy and in it we consider the distinctions between belief and knowledge. Concern with these distinctions is so traditional in the history of philosophy that every major philosopher since Plato and Aristotle has marked them in some characteristic way.

[1] William James, an unsigned letter, "The Teaching of Philosophy In Our Colleges," *The Nation,* Vol 23, No. 586, 1876, p. 178.

Our second chapter makes many of these refinements available for use in discussion. We do not suggest that learning to philosophize is the same thing as learning the history of philosophy, but often what previous philosophers have said may not only introduce us to new ideas but may illuminate the problems we have dimly perceived. The past is not so utterly different from our present that we can afford to ignore its wisdom or repeat its errors. Ideas, as Whitehead put it, have adventures, and what we do now is in no small measure a fulfillment that cannot be appreciated without the insights of our predecessors.

Knowledge is generally judged to have a more secure foundation than belief and that foundation is reared not only on fact, but also by man's finest critical reasoning. Logic is therefore essential to philosophic study. We consider it unsafe to assume that students will come to an introduction to philosophy equipped with a knowledge of deductive and inductive forms. This will explain two novelties in an introductory text: historical perspective within which one deals with the problems, and logical preparation for the analysis of the relations among beliefs.

Another aim of this book is to treat fairly both the tradition of system-building and the vigorous contributions of logicians and linguistic philosophers. Two chapters in epistemology and two in metaphysics deal with the reasoned alternatives offered by different thinkers. We hope this will help the student to appreciate the great parting of the ways that bear the sign-posts, "speculative-systematic," and "linguistic-analytic."

In these and the subsequent chapters which present problems of men's beliefs about history, religion, politics, art and ethics, we have rarely taken sides among the alternatives. The alert reader will be able to detect our leanings, but we have quoted rather fully, allowing representatives of the major positions to state their own views. The later chapters demand more from the students than do early ones; an instructor may easily order them to suit his taste and may make selections of material. Each of these chapters has a section on material fallacies that are commonly alleged to vitiate the arguments. In addition every chapter has problems that encourage the student to construct arguments that he may never have been taught. These problems for thought and discussion are not merely review questions to test whether the student can reproduce a reading assignment. A brief bibliography after each chapter will, we hope, induce the student to go beyond the minimum.

Philosophy has, as do other disciplines, its own technical vocabulary. We have frequent and extended sections defining various terms, particularly when they have alternative meanings. Hence a brief definition often fails to be adequate. For this reason we have not constructed a glossary; instead an index of terms with collected page references to their alternative usages is printed at the close of the book.

We believe that difference is a significant category and that differences of belief are not only inescapable but to be cherished. We also believe that differences are to be dealt with in the spirit of a dialogue, not of a directive. Camus, in *The Fall*, has described the frightening alternative: " . . . You must have noticed that our old Europe at last philosophizes in the right way. We no longer say as in simple times: 'This is the way I think. What are your objections?' We have become lucid. For the dialogue we have substituted the communiqué: 'This is the truth' we say. 'You can discuss it as much as you want; we aren't interested. But in a few years there'll be the police who will show you we are right.' "[2]

We also believe that philosophy, broadly speaking, is the basis of the liberal arts. One falls short in understanding almost any course of study unless he knows the fundamental principles upon which the study is based. This may be said to be the philosophy of that field. But in a more restricted sense philosophy is a highly critical study in itself, whose aim is to acquire the willingness, the courage, and the facility to examine thoroughly whatever one believes. In short, it is man's most reflective effort to find the best reasons possible for holding a belief or a set of beliefs. We hope this book will present living alternatives which the student may find useful when he tries to give rational support to his beliefs or disbeliefs about man, society, God and the world. Philosophy from this point of view is impertinent. It assumes the right to ask questions of anyone who claims to have a belief or to have knowledge; this is our Socratic heritage.

We owe much to many teachers and students. Our footnotes acknowledge only published stimulation from which we have directly quoted. We are grateful to our publishers and critics who have helped us to remove errors of fact and judgment. Undoubtedly some remain. We shall be grateful to have them called to our attention. We hope that our book's central theme is true and useful in teaching. Philosophy is no mere collection of puzzles and theories, nor a carefully protected series of noble sentiments. It is coherently relevant to what men believe, deny, and doubt, and how they affirm, negate, and suspend judgment.

[2] Albert Camus, *The Fall* (Justin O'Brien tr.), Alfred A. Knopf, New York 1957, p. 45. Published by Alfred A. Knopf and Hamish Hamilton, Ltd., London.

Contents

xiv / Contents

I

Philosophy: The Analysis of Belief

I. The Problem of Definition

What is philosophy? Or, what is philosophizing? These questions with which this book begins may be the same questions asked at the close of our study. There is neither a single nor a simple reply. How we answer is important because what we do in philosophy is largely determined by what we think philosophy is. But not entirely, for we discover, in part, what philosophy is by philosophizing. However, we need some kind of orientation, or some sense of direction so we must have a tentative definition to keep us from intellectual vagrancy. One way of achieving this is to examine the structure of the word itself. But do not expect too much from this etymological study. As you will shortly see, it leads to the request for more definitions. The term philosophy is formed from two Greek words, *philein* and *sophia,* meaning "to love wisdom." This is, of course, only partially satisfactory. We are irresistibly led to ask, what is the wisdom we are to love, and how is it to be distinguished from knowledge and folly? And what does it mean to love it? But faulty as this is, it does help. At least we know enough about language that we do not confuse philosophy with mechanics or farming or sailing. True. But might not literature, art, science, and religion also make a claim to love wisdom? If so, might we not be philosophizing when writing poetry, painting a picture, searching for a hypothesis, or worshipping a god? Well, we may be, but such a broad view of philosophy fails to be useful just because it does not describe the phi-

1

losopher as such. We know this much at least from the analysis of the term philosophy: it is something one does with the "mind" not with the body. To act well is one thing, to think well is another, and the latter seems nearer the meaning of wisdom than the former. Thus far we may fairly say that philosophy concerns man as a thinker rather than man as a doer. If you are inclined to remark that thinking is doing something, then we are forced to contrast the activity of a mind while thinking, and the activity of a body while behaving. Whether these must be completely separate is a tough problem—certainly not to be considered in the first paragraph of an introduction to philosophy.

The first step has been taken. We have given the source of the term philosophy. A further natural step would be to present a few sample definitions from well-established philosophers. Although they may not agree, we can at least get some idea of what they think they are doing when philosophizing.

Let us choose three from relatively recent accounts. The first is by Josiah Royce, a great American philosopher.

Philosophy, in the proper sense of the term, is not a presumptuous effort to explain the mysteries of the world by means of any superhuman insight or extraordinary cunning, but has its origin and value in an attempt to give a reasonable account of our own personal attitude towards the more serious business of life. You philosophize when you reflect critically upon what you are actually doing in your world. What you are doing is of course, in the first place, living. And life involves passions, faiths, doubts, and courage. The critical inquiry into what all these things mean and imply is philosophy. We have our faith in life; we want reflectively to estimate this faith. We feel ourselves in a world of law and of significance. Yet why we feel this homelike sense of the reality and the worth of our world is a matter for criticism. Such a criticism of life, made elaborate and thorough-going, is a philosophy.[1]

The next two definitions are also by distinguished American philosophers. W. P. Montague said that philosophy "is an attempt to gain a reasoned conception of the universe and man's place in it."[2]

R. W. Sellars wrote, "Philosophy is a persistent attempt to gain insight into the nature of the world and ourselves by means of systematic reflection."[3]

Definitions of philosophy could be given endlessly, but these three will

[1] Josiah Royce, *The Spirit of Modern Philosophy*, Houghton, Mifflin Co., Boston, 1892, pp. 1–2.
[2] W. P. Montague, *The Ways of Knowing*, The Macmillan Co., New York, 1925, p. 3.
[3] R. W. Sellars, *The Principles and Problems of Philosophy*, The Macmillan Co., New York, 1926, p. 3.

serve our present purposes. All philosophers would not approve of them wholly, but there would probably be widespread agreement about one emphasis. To bring this out, let us review certain terms found in the definitions. They are, "a reasonable account," "reflect critically," "critical inquiry," "mean and imply," "reflectively to estimate," "criticism of life, made elaborate and thorough-going," "reasoned conception," "persistent attempt to gain insight . . . by means of systematic reflection." These words give us the clue that philosophers generally regard their work as being primarily one of thinking. Philosophy, then, is a <u>reflective enterprise</u> —the most thorough, consistent (William James said "obstinate"), attempt to answer man's perplexities by means of steady thought. But before presenting our own views of philosophy, let us look at some conceptions of the philosopher.

II. Some Alternative Views of the Philosopher

The philosopher has often been called the wise man, not because he had reached wisdom, but because this was his aim. To be a wise man or a sage meant, in part at least, that the person had attained a view of life that enabled him to arrange the demands of existence according to a scale of values such that first things came first, and everything subordinate was put in its proper place and given appropriate attention. No mere accumulation of facts, no matter how vast; no cleverness of speech; no accident of birth; no display of possessions or wealth; no brute power—none of these could be identified with wisdom, and in fact were quite irrelevant to its definition. Although it is easy to say what the wise man is not, it is difficult to say what he is. Even the wise man himself may not know. The story of the wise man in the various cultures and civilizations, how he is defined, how he lives, what he teaches, would be interesting to write, but this is not our problem. Most contemporary men, including philosophers, no longer take the ideal of the wise man seriously. The sage is contemptuously dismissed or affectionately ignored. He has been replaced by a team consisting of psychiatry, counseling, social work, and other forms of professional friendships. And the philosopher in college classrooms looks and acts too much like other men to be mistaken for a wise man. In fact, he feels a bit ridiculous if he is ever called one. Today's philosopher sees himself in a narrower (not humbler) role; his problems are more strictly defined, and his aims more easily described. But perhaps it was a sad mistake for philosophy to turn away from its ancient ideal.

Again, the philosopher has sometimes been thought of as the learned man, that is, one who has mastered the extant knowledge of his day, who speaks and writes with authority on almost any subject in any field, and who, in the passage of his life, has made original contributions to theory in science, law, politics, ethics, art, language, education, history, and so on. Few men have ever been close to this ideal—the names of Plato, Aristotle, Leibniz, Kant, all come immediately to mind, and there may be a few others.

These men possessed immense intellects, with a range and power met infrequently in the history of man, but their existence and activity affected the thought of subsequent centuries. Each spoke not only for his own day, but also for the remote future. The timeless universality of their thoughts makes them eternal contemporaries. Can they ever really be studied only as historical curiosities? Much of what they said, of course, was limited by the technical knowledge of their times, but the grandeur remains, and smaller minds can appreciate it.

But this ideal too is passing from philosophy. No man can now grasp the enormous range of knowledge, either in theory or detail, that lies stored, not in intellects or memories, but in books, catalogues, films, and journals. The reason is threefold—the field is vast, the time is short, and the man is fallible. Today it is not the learned man who has authority, but the expert, that is, one who knows as completely as possible all there is to know about a determinate and therefore manageable slice of a slice of a slice of human experience. Philosophers no longer survey all time and existence. They have lowered their sights and have tried to see more clearly a nearer target. Some are still reluctant to submit, but even they know that the human race may have had its quota of Aristotles and Leibnizes.

A third conception of the philosopher is perhaps more common among those having little or no acquaintance with man's intellectual history, though the roots of this view can be traced to post-Aristotelian thought. It is often found among laymen and is revealed in some expressions of ordinary language, for example, "he takes things philosophically." The meaning suggested is that the philosopher is one who possesses the Unperturbed Mind; who is able to rise above the minor irritations, as well as the overwhelming tragedies of existence; who has achieved a high level of unconcern about his personal history, and is able to meet life with a serenity and assurance that makes other men look like fussy little worriers. In this connection, of course, we remember the Stoics of ancient Greece and Rome; they are the prototypes of all those modern men who have learned to endure their lives with equanimity. So in popular thinking, being stoical about anything is almost equivalent to being philosophical about it. Now it is perhaps true that if a philosopher has any special insight or knowledge about the relative importance of the demands, desires, temptations, lures, pains, and joys of life, then we should expect him to order his attitudes according to the weight he gives to the multitude of interests that attract him. And it may be that the tribe of philosophers, with certain obvious exceptions, have attained a level of balance and considered dignity superior to that of other men. Such a possibility might be established by empirical, psychological research, though frankly we doubt it. In any case, we do not think there are many contemporary philosophers who take this as a mark of their vocation, or as a symbol of their attainment. They consider themselves to be men among men, whose outlook is often modified by temperamental differences or by the fortunes and misfortunes chance or plan have brought their way. And yet, if one can read between the lines of contemporary philosophy, one may see here and there a kind of nostalgic awareness of the ancient ideal of *sophrosyne*. This word, difficult to translate into English, has been said to mean "self-control at its widest." Plato wrote a whole dialogue about it. It is related to the ideal of moderation and temperance, of nothing in excess. And our modern philosopher, though making no claims to be different from other men, knows that somehow or other he is a philosopher in smaller dimensions if he lacks or derides the Greek virtue of *sophrosyne*.

A fourth view of the philosopher may also be found in the history of thought. He is sometimes said to be a systematizer of knowledge. Although he does not make new factual discoveries himself, the philosopher tries to survey the various other fields to see what ways of ordering diverse data are possible. He searches for relations, not for facts. Amid the multiplicities he believes there is a unity, missed by those who stand too close to the differences. To find the unity (or unities) one must "stand above," or transcend, the separate details. Even in everyday life, the lowliest of us may feel the need to rise above the innumerable demands of a piecemeal existence to try to bring order out of chaotic diversity—to gain perspective and see things in proportion. And at the higher levels of intellect, for example in science, separate facts are related to make a science, and various sciences may be seen to be so interrelated that new sciences are formed, such as biochemistry and biophysics. Is it not theoretically possible that if one could see far enough and deep enough one would see the Whole, the One, the Absolute? This has been the goal of some men who are called philosophers, who try to see beyond the fragmentation of life and thought, and who would rather know one big thing than many small things.

But again this ideal, or hope, is fading in many circles of philosophic activity. Some philosophers want to be more modest in their claims and therefore they reject an interpretation that suggests the philosopher is a kind of super-scientist. For them it is much better to know thoroughly and clearly one aspect of human experience than to know loosely and vaguely its entire range. One form of protest against this view of the philosopher as a systematizer of all knowledge is to be found in the next description of his activity.

The twentieth century is characterized by the notion of the philosopher as a critic of language. This has restricted the area of his thought and allowed him to make moderate claims about discovery and knowledge without presuming to be either a wise, or learned, or unperturbed, or synoptic man. Language is unquestionably a human activity of immense significance with an incalculable number of relations to other forms of experience; and still it is something narrower than the total extent of the world and knowledge. The problem of meanings, the analysis of propositions, the search for analogies, the examination of categories, all this, though difficult and demanding, seems more manageable and controllable than problems about the World, God, and the Self. This movement too has its roots in traditional philosophy as far back as Plato, and certainly in the great traditions of British philosophy represented in Hobbes, Locke, Berkeley, and Hume. Two statements from contemporary British philosophy may be taken as representative. Professor Gilbert Ryle of Oxford has written that philosophy is in the main "the detection of the sources in linguistic idioms of recurrent misconstructions and absurd theories." And the late Ludwig Wittgenstein of Cambridge wrote:

Most propositions and questions, that have been written about philosophical matters, are not false, but senseless. We cannot, therefore, answer questions of this kind at all, but only state their senselessness. Most questions and propositions of the philosophers result from the fact that we don't understand the logic of our language.[4]

And again, he writes, "all philosophy is 'Critique of Language.'"

The student's first few months in a philosophy course may lead to the kind of experience William James said was characteristic of the newborn child—it is all a "blooming, buzzing, confusion." If the blooming and buzzing subside, the confusion may remain, because it all seems to be merely a matter of words. Our generation is becoming highly sensitive to words. The popular and technical contributions of semanticists and ana-

[4] Ludwig Wittgenstein, *Tractatus Logico-Philosophicus*, Routledge & Kegan Paul, Ltd., London, 1951, 4.003.

lysts have made us aware of the powerful role words and language play in human thinking, and therefore in human affairs. Although in a sense philosophy is verbal, this does not mean that it is arbitrary or only a matter of convention as to which symbols shall be adopted to express a thought or belief. We do need words for these purposes, but the words are there to perform a duty, not to command a salute. Their duty is to help us point out, describe, and identify the discernible differences and similarities of our experience. But philosophy is not a kind of word game. Words do not belong to philosophy as chessmen belong to chess. Chessmen reveal nothing beyond themselves. They have no function in chess but obedience. A word, however, has fulfilled only a part of its duty when it has been correctly placed in a sentence. By far its most important and significant work is to call attention to something other than itself. Because words may express our beliefs well or poorly, truly or falsely, philosophers must learn to use them critically and judiciously.

Now although a contemporary philosopher, to be in fashion, must be acquainted with the techniques and literature of this new way of philosophizing, some philosophers regard it as trivialization. They are unwilling to give up philosophy in the grand manner, they want to keep alive the great tradition that produced a Royce, a Dewey, a Santayana, and a Whitehead. They are willing to grant that language analysis has been useful, but they do not accept it as the ultimate description of their tasks.

The differences of opinion in these matters have not been resolved, but the authors feel it can be said with some assurance that it is difficult to keep men, no matter how small, from trying to answer questions, no matter how big.

Finally, let us consider a view of philosophy that shall largely represent the position of the authors of this book. The definitions considered above have been useful. Although we shall not adopt them, they have helped to get us under way and we are better prepared for the construction of our definition.

We suggest that no one is totally unprepared for philosophy. By this we mean that everyone has beliefs and disbeliefs that he has tried to defend or oppose. These are about things, other people, gods, as well as about ourselves. Sometimes our beliefs accord well with those of other persons, and sometimes they do not. Sometimes our beliefs are consistent with each other, and sometimes not. Having a belief may be said to be a necessary but not a sufficient condition for philosophy. There are a number of different things a person can do with his beliefs. For example, he can enjoy them, or express them, or ignore them, or boast about them. None of this has any philosophical importance. Philosophy's primary interest is the way in which these beliefs are tested. It seeks to make explicit and precise the best reasons for holding a belief.

No philosopher can avoid the necessity of defining his terms, as we have already seen. Therefore, if we define philosophy as the critical analysis of belief, we must be prepared to make clear what we mean by "critical analysis" and by "belief." Much of this chapter deals with belief. The chapter on logic will show in part what critical analysis involves. For the present we must be content with whatever common-sense notions you have concerning these terms. It will be useful, however, at this stage, to give an illustration.

Let us suppose that you believe Mars is inhabited. You may be asked a number of questions. For example, you may be asked, "Why do you believe that?" which may be a question concerning the utility of your belief, or its motivation, or the strength of the evidence that supports the belief. Again you may be asked, "If you believe that, then do you also believe such and such?" which is a question concerning the relation of this belief to some other possible belief. Or you may be asked a very general question indeed, something like, "What are the conditions necessary for holding this belief?" This is enough for the present. When such questions are asked, the critical analysis of belief is under way.

The alert student may wish to make a point here. He knows we carry with us a whole catalogue of beliefs about relatively unimportant matters, for instance, the belief that Wednesday is the fourth day of the week, or that lunch usually comes between breakfast and dinner. Now are these beliefs the stuff from which philosophy is made? At this stage in our philosophical growth, we had better say no. Philosophy's concern seems to be with beliefs of wider scope and greater meaning for man's life than these. It is only when we become very mature and subtle that we may find a philosophical problem in the days of the week or the time of meals.

III. The Uses of Belief

We have put off defining the key term of this book, belief, because the meaning of the word depends so much upon the contexts in which it is used. It is doubtful whether there is one common essence in which all beliefs share and of which all beliefs are variations. Belief is not a concept like "animal," of which we have logical, epistemological, and metaphysical divisions, much as the animal kingdom has its classes: fish, reptiles, and birds. But belief may be said to constitute a family of meanings with certain resemblances, such as making a claim to truth, expressing degrees of certainty, and being based on degrees of evidence. To regard beliefs with the intention of judging them is philosophizing—a difficult, but necessary and fruitful pursuit of the human mind.

It will be useful at this point to look at two terms common to the vocabulary of belief. The first, *scepticism,* is used in philosophy to describe the position that denies that the human mind can obtain certain or absolute knowledge or that it could recognize knowledge as such even if attained. The second, *agnosticism,* must be distinguished from the first. It is largely a confession of ignorance and a willingness to suspend judgment. The sceptic says we cannot know. The agnostic says we do not know. The first rules out the possibility of knowledge, the second leaves open the possibility but takes no steps that might lead to the discovery of evidence. At this stage of our work, we advocate neither view but suggest a middle position that adopts a sceptical caution while energetically seeking for knowledge. Neither an a priori denial of success, nor a refusal to act is the way of a philosopher. All believing is risky. He is willing to take these risks.

Some beliefs go together, or, as we might say, are compatible. Others quarrel when brought into close association. Although some beliefs are compatible, this does not necessarily demonstrate that they are true, but it may well be an important and relevant step in establishing their truth. On the other hand, if beliefs are strictly or logically incompatible, such that if one is true another is false and vice versa, then to show the truth of one does prove the falsity of the other. They are said to be contradictories.

It is quite possible for a person to hold incompatible beliefs without having them quarrel. Usually this occurs in two situations, the first of which may be called compartmentalization. This refers to the fact that beliefs may be consciously kept apart so that their relationship to each other is unrecognized or obscured. For example, there may be geologists whose scientific beliefs about the age of the earth are incompatible with the story in the first chapter of Genesis, yet who hold to the literal truth of the Bible. Again, many of our double moral standards in politics and economics arise from compartmentalization. In such cases it is the work of philosophy to disclose the unfriendly character of the beliefs and to show why they cannot be held simultaneously by reasonable men.

The second situation in which incompatible beliefs may be held occurs when one fails to see their hostility because of insufficient analysis. Many of us are guilty on this count. It is often an extremely difficult job to get our beliefs consistent with each other, for we may be holding inconsistent beliefs without being aware of it. Again, it is the persistent effort of philosophy to examine beliefs so that they may go together. We want them to have more connection than the beads children put on a string, for, if and when we get our beliefs ordered and organized and related, we find that they tend mutually to support each other. At least this is an ideal we may strive to achieve. Thus, for example, we must deal with the problem of our beliefs in science versus our beliefs in religion; our beliefs in ethics versus our beliefs in politics; our beliefs in cultural relativism versus our beliefs in absolute and universal standards; and our beliefs in our country versus our beliefs in "one world." There is no problem, of course, if one is willing to believe whatever is demanded by any authority. In such cases it is not even permissible to suggest that there are alternative beliefs and any such claim may be immediately branded as disloyalty. But at the beginning of philosophy, as well as in its fullest development, we must insist on the right of the individual to believe independently according to the best evidence available.

Believing is a highly personal, mental activity. No one can believe for you, but it is possible to share or communicate our beliefs, which may result in a certain attitude, and may vary in intensity from utter conviction to complete disbelieving. Attitudes cannot be said to be true, or false, although it may be true that you have or do not have a certain attitude. Thus the philosopher's interest in beliefs is not interest in the attitudes that usually accompany them, for, as we have said, attitudes themselves are neither true nor false; moreover, they are not at all evidence for the truth or falsity of the belief. There is, however, a kind of consistency about attitudes that reveals something about the believer, which may be called his character or personality. But this aspect of belief is a psychological matter and has nothing to do with the logical and epistemological problems of belief.

So far in our analysis of belief, we have distinguished two elements, an act of believing, and an attitude of the believer, neither of which can be said to be true or false. But because it is the truth or falsity of our beliefs with which we are concerned, the analysis must continue. Let us use the word *certitude* to refer to the degree of intensity or conviction with which a belief is held, and the term *certainty* to refer to its logical status as truth. Thus a belief may be held with high certitude although it is logically uncertain; or it may be certain—that is, true—but disbelieved—that is, held with complete absence of certitude.

It is the question of the certainty or uncertainty of our beliefs that we must think through now. This will help us to distinguish the other elements in belief. It always makes sense to ask the question: What is believed? This is a request for the content of one's belief. If I believe that my hat is in the next room, then this is precisely the content of my belief, it is what I believe. There seems to be no limit to the possible contents of belief—anything and everything may become the content of my belief—nothing possible or actual, ridiculous or sublime, is excluded a priori from becoming the content of somebody's belief. The content of belief is, therefore, what one replies in answer to the question, what do you believe? But the reply takes the form of an affirmation, or perhaps a denial, in words. It has to be stated. You cannot indicate what the content of your belief is by nodding your head or making some other gesture—unless the question itself includes the statement; for example, you may nod affirmatively to a question such as, "Do you believe that war is inevitable?" The statement of belief is a sentence, written or spoken, that declares, affirms, denies, or asserts something. This "something" is a proposition. It is the proposition that is believed or disbelieved. It is the proposition that is common to the three sentences, "Tu es belle, ma chérie," "Du bist schön, Schätzlein," and "You are beautiful, dear."

But let us return to the belief that my hat is in the next room. So far we have seen that "my hat is in the next room" is a statement of the content of my belief. Suppose we ask now, is the proposition true, that is, is my hat really in the next room? The fact of my hat being in the next room is the objective reference of my belief—it is what my belief aims at. And the relation between the content of my belief, as expressed in a proposition, and its objective reference determines the truth or falsity of my belief. Furthermore, let us note that there may or may not be a fact that makes it possible to determine the truth or falsity of the belief. Thus the world of belief may be a richer, more complex, and more populated world than the world of fact. For example, one may believe in ghosts, or gods, or gremlins, but these may not exist.

Let us summarize our results so far. We have said that the elements of belief are as follows: An attitude, called psychological certitude; a content, called a proposition; an objective reference, called a fact; a relationship between a proposition and a fact, called truth or falsity; and the evidence that may be called the grounds of belief and which is related to one's certitude as well as to the truth value of the belief.

But now we shall consider another distinction. Philosophers and non-philosophers alike do not use the terms "believe" and "know" interchangeably. The two words have different work to do in the language; for example, it does not make sense to say I believe I am in pain. When one has a pain one knows it. Nor does it make sense to say I believe I see a red patch. When we see a red patch, we know it. To believe something suggests the presence of an attitude of trust, a tendency to accept with approval, a willingness to affirm without the ability to prove. But when we say we know something, the term is used to suggest that we could not possibly be wrong, that all the relevant and necessary evidence is in. Moreover, the term "know" also suggests that we are able to perform some act, or as Ryle puts it, bring something off. His full statement is pertinent in this connection:

'Know' is a capacity verb, and a capacity verb of that special sort that is used for signifying that the person described can bring things off, or get things right. 'Believe', on the other hand, is a tendency verb and one which does not connote that anything is brought off or got right. 'Belief' can be qualified by such adjectives as 'obstinate', 'wavering', 'unswerving', 'unconquerable', 'stupid', 'fanatical', 'whole-hearted', 'intermittent', 'passionate', and 'childlike', adjectives some or all of which are also appropriate to such nouns as 'trust', 'loyalty', 'bent', 'aversion', 'hope', 'habit', 'zeal', and 'addiction'. Beliefs, like habits, can be inverterate, slipped into and given up; like partisanships, devotions, and hopes they can be blind and obsessing; like aversions and phobias they can be unacknowledged; like fashions and tastes they can be contagious; like loyalties and animosities they can be induced by tricks. A person can be urged or entreated not to believe things, and he may try, with or without success to cease to do so. Sometimes a person says truly 'I cannot help believing so and so'. But none of these dictions, or their negatives, are applicable to knowing, since to know is to be equipped to get something right and not to tend to act or react in certain manners.

Roughly, 'believe' is of the same family as motive words, where 'know' is of the same family as skill words; so we ask how a person knows this, but only why a person believes that, as we ask how a person ties a clove-hitch, but why he wants to tie a clove-hitch or why he always ties granny knots. Skills have methods, where habits and inclination have sources. Similarly, we ask what makes people believe or dread things but not what makes them know or achieve things.[5]

Immanuel Kant distinguished three degrees between the subjective certitude of a judgment or proposition and its relation to objective validity, namely, opining, believing, and knowing.

Opining is such holding of a judgment as is consciously insufficient, not only objectively, but also subjectively. If our holding of the judgment be only sub-

[5] From *The Concept of Mind*, by Gilbert Ryle, 1949, by permission of Hutchinson University Library, London, pp. 133–134.

jectively sufficient, and is at the same time taken as being objectively insufficient, we have what is termed *believing*. Lastly, when the holding of a thing to be true is sufficient both subjectively and objectively, it is *knowledge*. The subjective sufficiency is termed *conviction* (for myself), the objective sufficiency is termed *certainty* (for everyone).[6]

In opinion we are aware that the proposition is insufficiently grounded, and that our own conviction, or as we have said certitude, is subjectively incomplete. In believing, our subjective certitude is complete but is seen to be insufficient in objective justification. And in knowledge both the objective grounds and subjective conviction are sufficient and complete. This suggests what we have been saying, namely, that between no evidence and sufficient evidence there are varying degrees of evidence, and between doubt and absolute assurance there are varying degrees of certitude.

A belief, then, may be affirmed on the basis of other accepted beliefs, for example, a belief that killing another person is wrong may be based on a belief in the validity of the Ten Commandments, which may be based on the belief that the Bible is the inspired word of God, which may be based on the belief in a Supreme and Perfectly Good Divine Being. Or a belief may be affirmed on the basis of the available factual evidence, whether or not we are able to gather the evidence ourselves. Thus we may believe that the sun is 93,000,000 miles (approximately) from the earth because we have made the necessary observation and calculations or accepted the astronomers' authority. In any case, our usual response in these cases is "I believe such and such is the case." But when the evidence is overwhelming, or conclusive, or complete and sufficient, or when we are able to perform some act of demonstration, we usually say, "I know that such and such is the case."

It is clear, from Ryle's analysis, that these two words behave in different ways in the language. But we have insisted that a belief has a content, namely, what it is that is believed, and that this usually is expressed as a proposition that may or may not be true; this is indicated when we say "I believe that," rather than "I believe in." In any case, whether we believe that something or believe in something, the test or criterion of our belief is largely what we do about it. To believe, in short, is to be willing to act on what we believe, or to draw inferences from our beliefs that also lead to action. It is said sometimes of another person, "He says he believes in God (or democracy, or free speech, or world government), but he doesn't act as if it made any difference to him." We generally expect our beliefs

[6] Immanuel Kant, *Critique of Pure Reason* (Norman Kemp Smith, Tr.), Macmillan and Co., Ltd., London, 1930, p. 646.

to be reflected in some kind of action—how we live, what we say, how we vote, and so on.

Furthermore, one must distinguish between the causes of a belief and the reasons for a belief. The former may be of interest to a psychologist, but it is with the latter that a philosopher is properly concerned. The distinction can be brought out by a number of examples. Offspring frequently hold the same political, social, and religious beliefs as their parents, not because they have reasoned their way to these beliefs, but simply due to constant association with the family in which these matters were discussed. The depth-psychologists have suggested that some of our beliefs have their source in the unconscious, and this source is better spoken of as a cause than a reason, for the unconscious scarcely ratiocinates. When primitive man dreams he is away hunting lions and then wakes to find himself under the tree where he went to sleep, this may become the cause of his belief that his soul is separable from his body and can act independently of it. If a man bets on a horse named Galloping Agatha because his favorite aunt's name is Agatha, this is certainly a cause of his belief that the horse will win—who could possibly call it a reason? Of course it may not always be easy to tell what are causes and what are reasons for a specific belief, and in any case the belief, so far as philosophy is concerned, is subject to analysis and criticism. But the analysis and criticism is largely directed toward the search for reasons rather than for causes.

IV. Alternative Ways of Deriving and Defending Beliefs

Our beliefs come to us from many sources and they are defended in various ways. One is a philosopher in some sense whenever one is willing to apply a standard for either the acceptance or rejection of a belief. A philosopher, in the completest meaning of the word, will have rigorous standards of criticism and apply them thoroughly and patiently.

A. Common Sense

One of the sources and means of defending our beliefs is known as common sense. To many, common-sense truth seems obviously true. We count on everyone to accept the statement that $2 + 2 = 4$. It is nonsense to say that $2 + 2 = 5$. But why is one statement so obviously acceptable and the other not? The reply is frequently, why it's just common sense. If we say that Wednesday is blue, everyone who understands English would call the statement nonsense, because it is common sense that days of the week are not colored objects. There are many, many beliefs about ourselves, the world, morality, religion, behavior, based on common-sense standards. But what is this standard? Is it common, in the sense of universal? Is it infallible, in the sense that it never fails? And how is the term "sense" to be interpreted? Is common sense analogous to a sense of hearing or sight? To all of these questions, a negative answer seems required. Common sense is certainly not universal, for we know there is disagreement about beliefs which are said to be common-sensical. It is not infallible, for we know that some beliefs once accepted on the basis of common sense are now rejected. And we possess no sense organ to help us distinguish nonsense from common sense.

If common sense means a judgment based on the knowledge and wisdom of normal experiences, we find reasons for accepting or repudiating a given belief. We tend to trust our common experiences because, by and large, we share similar ways of acquiring information. But having said this, we must also ask what "normal" means, and point out that even among normal men and women there are sometimes severe differences of opinion. This begins to show up the weaknesses of common sense as a source and defense of belief. The philosophical indictment of common sense is, however, much more devastating than we have indicated. It is devastating because philosophizing cannot proceed very far if its only method is that provided by what is usually called common sense. There are at least five charges against common sense, all of which point up its failure and unreliability as a test for belief.

1. It is not self-critical. Any good method for establishing a belief must be able to turn upon its results and try to see them from a different perspective or in a new light. This prevents us from sheltering error and forces us to see all the truth in any belief.
2. Common sense tends to keep its beliefs in packaged forms, wise sayings, epigrams, and so on. This means it fails to relate one belief to another, to relate beliefs with the known facts. We are aware that isolated statements do not make a science. Only when these statements can be connected or related is the great power of science revealed.
3. Again, common sense is too infrequently disturbed. It is notoriously complacent. If this is all we had to rely on, no advances in knowledge would be made, or it would come so slowly that its usefulness would be impaired.
4. Moreover, reliance upon common sense leads too quickly to satisfaction; it is too easily wearied and agrees too soon to solutions of difficult problems. The attempt to bring order and truth to our beliefs is an

exhausting and extraordinarily demanding task. It cannot be done by a mind unwilling or unable to withstand the rigors of hard thinking.

5. Finally, the beliefs of common sense are often self-contradictory. What is common sense to a New England farmer may be at odds with the common sense of a Texas oil man. We want our beliefs mutually consistent, because we commonly hold that all true beliefs are consistent, and we want our beliefs to be true.

Trust in common sense for establishing the truth or falsity of our beliefs is obviously inadequate, whatever its usefulness as a beginning. It can always be improved on by better reasoning, or more critical thinking.

But there are other ways of defending and attacking beliefs, which may be used alone or combined with the reliance upon common sense. These are sense-experience, tradition, authority, and intuition. Sense-experience is the appeal to things as they appear to us, with the assumption that things appear the same to all of us after a minimal training in observation. Tradition is the claim that the basis of a belief should be the age, sanctity, and stability of the belief in human history. Authority is the claim that some person, institution, or group of persons, constitutes the most reliable guarantee of the truth or falsity of a belief. Intuition is the appeal to a kind of "feeling" that one's beliefs are true. These alternatives must now be considered in detail. We shall meet them again in different forms as we deal with specific problems in later chapters.

B. Sense-Experience

The senses seem to be constantly engaged in reporting things in the external world. Every human being is equipped to make discoveries that will prove or disprove any belief established by sense-experience. We know by eye, ear, and touch. Here is a desk. My eye tells me it is brown and boxlike. My ear catches a dull sound when I strike the wood. To my touch it is smooth, perhaps a little cool, and certainly solid.[7] We are sure any normal person would describe it precisely in this way. Precisely? There's the rub. How precise is this description of the desk? Is it really brown? Ask the artist. And is it really boxlike? Walk around it. Look down on it. Do you not often see only the plane surface of one side? Is it really smooth? Ask the fly crawling on top. You can approximate the fly's-eye view through the microscope. Let's ask a physicist if it's really solid. The senses are indispensable, but they lead quickly to a problem not solved by sense-experience. Whose point of view will we adopt, and for what

[7] Adapted from Bertrand Russell, *Problems of Philosophy*, Oxford University Press, London, 1948, p. 8.

purposes are we framing our beliefs? We see what we see, but is it necessary to believe what we see? Do we not often believe what we cannot
see? To what extent can belief be based on seeing?

C. Tradition

Tradition is also indispensable. We could not have a civilization without
something being handed down from the past. The family is a basic institution that lives by tradition, and a child's first beliefs are set by his
parents. No one escapes some form of obedience to society. The web of
loyalties binds us together by countless threads. No one can step outside
the human race. One of the most widespread and powerful appeals is to
share the beliefs of the dominating and molding social pattern. Not even
a hermit has ceased to behave and believe as a human being—no matter
how heretical or deviant he is. To some what is "American," or "British,"
or "Indian," seems the touchstone of all beliefs. On this basis, for Americans
it seems "normal" to be filled with hope in the future, because life is good
and under certain conditions can quickly be made better. Therefore, let
desires be satisfied, and men be free to invent and to engage vigorously
in making goods more efficiently. Striving is good, and struggle is the secret
of progress. Is this pattern of ours the whole truth and the only secret of
the good life? What shall we say to the Buddhist who claims that life is
illusory in its promise of happiness? He observes that desire is the root of
misery, and he sees suffering among men. For him, striving and competi-
tion and struggle to succeed do not lead to happiness and peace and
harmony. Confronted with alternative traditions, we are driven once again
to examine the claims and evidence. The diversity of tradition leads back
to reasoning.

D. Authority

Authority may claim not only the age and sanctity of beliefs shared by
members of society, but also the dignity and knowledge of experts. Three
high authorities exist among us, continually guiding beliefs. Perhaps the
most venerable is the religious authority of the church, or the churches;
another is that of the courts and law-making bodies; and more recently,
the authority of scholars and scientists in universities and learned societies
has risen to eminence. It would be an easier and simpler task to establish
beliefs if we could accept the creeds of religion, the codes and decisions of
law courts, and the pronouncements of scientists as infallible. Why not
let the experts decide? There is great appeal in the call to the expert to
decide an issue. Some trust in these institutional authorities is inevitable,

but which authority? To what extent should we distribute our confidence among them? Which do we trust in case of conflict? And are not churchmen, justices, and scientists continually revising their decisions, sometimes even reversing former conclusions? The validity of these authorities comes in large measure from their reasoning. If the experts reason badly, we must take the consequences of error. If we trust the wrong authority, it is we who are deceived. There seems to be no justifiable recourse except to follow the argument of the experts and to weigh their evidence. Once again we are led back to reasoning.

E. Intuition

The senses conflict, the traditions are various, the authorities are not unquestionable. Perhaps none of them can be trusted. We may turn, then, to intuition, the authority of insight, hunches, feelings, reasons of the heart, and leadings of the spirit. The names are legion, and the appeal is rarely clear enough to admit precise definition. There are mystics and poets and prophets who make claims without appeal to reason, and often in defiance of what passes for common sense. To take one example, Wordsworth claims that:

> One impulse from a vernal wood
> May teach you more of man
> Of moral evil and of good
> Than all the sages can.

But isn't it most difficult to discover what we are to believe on impulse? It is even more difficult to discover what the trees teach us in springtime. Wordsworth has expressed his feeling of kinship with what we know as nature, the round ocean, and the setting sun. This conviction is not trivial, as we shall see later, but can we credit his impulse and also the impulse of another poet who is equally earnest and deeply convinced that "man is a stranger and pilgrim upon earth, seeking a better land?" Indeed Wordsworth himself shared this impulse of estrangement as well as one of at-home-ness! And so do nearly all of us at some point in our experience. Intuition seems to be subject to special circumstance, the prey of incalculable and uncontrollable mood. We may be easy victims to crazy notions if we trust even our own intuitions. The validity of intuitions can emerge only by examination. Once again we are returning to the way of reasoning.

F. Reasoning

It is the hope of those who trust in reasoning to see common sense turned critical and established as the daily norm. Tradition can be continually tested and modified. The expert whose predictions are verified can be established on the authority of his knowledge. The intuitions of mystics and poets and prophets can be selected by squaring them with what we know on other grounds.

To believe everything offered on the basis of any one or all of these alternatives would lead us into confusion in thought and action. Only reasoning, the exercise of critical thought, can assign to common sense, sense-experience, tradition, authority, and intuition, their proper roles, curtail their excesses, and supplement the defects of each.

What credentials can reason offer? Have not many inconsistencies, and falsehoods, and fragmentary pictures been proposed in reason's name? We must admit that there have been very many, yet there is a difference. Reason boldly attempts thinking free from social prejudice and personal bias. If the attempt is never completely successful, at least some approximation to the ideal is commonly achieved. How is this possible? First, by test of consistency. Second, by yielding in experiment to the weight of evidence. To reason is to reach conclusions by valid thought. Sometimes we speak of the primacy of method over conclusions. We have standards of validity that we share more generally than any particular conclusion. In logic we make clear what these are. We shall deal with logical methods in Chapter III. Perhaps, however, we should give a word of caution. Philosophy, though highly critical of the alternative ways of defending beliefs we have discussed, does not completely reject them. Its aim is to supplement, not repudiate. Where these methods fall short, there must be something to correct the failures. This philosophy, as critical reason, tries to do.

G. Clifford and Peirce on Beliefs

W. K. Clifford, in a delightful essay, has called attention to the fact that there is an ethic of belief.[8] He feels that in order to maintain his status as a man, that is, neither a god nor a beast, a person must not permit himself to believe anything and everything. The right to belief is a right to be earned. It is earned only by patient inquiry. Whenever we allow ourselves to believe without sufficient grounds we have committed a moral fault, for believing is not merely a private matter. What we believe has been derived from and is guided by the beliefs of past generations and our own beliefs will become the creative forces of the new worlds to come. "Belief, that sacred faculty which prompts the decisions of our will, and

[8] W. K. Clifford, "The Ethics of Belief," *Lectures and Essays*, Macmillan and Co. Ltd., London, 1886, p. 344.

knits into harmonious working all the compacted energies of our being, is ours not for ourselves, but for humanity." But belief is not to be had for the wishing. Every instance of belief must be preceded by a prior activity, namely, investigation and appraisal of the evidence. Unwarranted belief is not only a disease and a disaster, it is sinful.

Every time we let ourselves believe for unworthy reasons, we weaken our powers of self-control, of doubting, of judicially and fairly weighing evidence. We all suffer severely enough from the maintenance and support of false beliefs and the fatally wrong actions which they lead to, and the evil born when one such belief is entertained is great and wide. But a greater and wider evil arises when the credulous character is maintained and supported, when a habit of believing for unworthy reasons is fostered and made permanent . . . . if I let myself believe anything on insufficient evidence, there may be no great harm done by the mere belief; it may be true after all, or I may never have occasion to exhibit it in outward acts. But I cannot help doing this great wrong towards Man, that I make myself credulous. The danger to society is not merely that it should believe wrong things, though that is great enough; but that it should become credulous and lose the habit of testing things and inquiring into them; for then it must sink back into savagery.[9]

Clifford's point is finally and succinctly put in these words. "It is wrong always, everywhere, and for any one, to believe anything upon insufficient evidence."[10] But what is sufficient evidence? Here Clifford is not so clear. He will allow us to believe when expert, authoritative voices give the nod, which makes sense in medicine, chemistry, mathematics, and so forth. But who shall be the authority in religion, art, politics, and ethics? Can one "know" in these areas as one "knows" in, say, the sciences? Clifford's stringent requirements for belief are needed as a corrective in a society that is too eager to turn its wishes into beliefs, but he does not seem to make room for the element of risk in all belief. For him the risk is a shame to be avoided at all costs. The demands Clifford makes upon "believers" are so stiff that it would be difficult to distinguish them from "knowers," and there seems to be no reason for blurring the distinction language supports. Nevertheless, his aims are high and his warnings pertinent—too easy believing certainly leads to a softening of the intellect, which then becomes prey to a variety of irrational ideas.

The aim to hold beliefs for the best possible reasons was a strong motive in the philosophy of Charles S. Peirce. In an essay called "The Fixation of Belief" he considers the relation between doubt and belief. The former is

[9] *Ibid.*, pp. 344–345.
[10] *Ibid.*, p. 346.

an irritation and causes a struggle to emerge into a state of belief, which itself is a kind of preparation for action. When belief is attained the struggle ends. Another name for this struggle is inquiry. Its object is the settlement of opinion. But when opinions are settled, we may call this condition the fixation of belief.

Peirce offers four ways in which beliefs may be fixed, but they are not all of equal worth. The first he has named the method of tenacity, by which a person simply holds to a belief to avoid being disturbed and distressed by doubts, thus escaping misery and uneasiness. He does not question the belief, but protects it by systematically keeping away from all opinions and views that might threaten it. Ideally such a man is immovable, because he is irrational and cannot be reached by argument and evidence. But, of course, this method shows its weakness if the believer lets himself be confronted with the fact that other sane persons do not share his belief. His confidence in this belief will sooner or later be shaken and the need for revision will become apparent.

A second way of fixing beliefs may be called the method of authority. This is essentially the fixation of belief by the suppression of opinion. No elaboration of this device need be given to contemporary students. We all know from recent events how this malevolent instrument works. It leads not only to the loss of ideas, but also to cruelty and atrocities. One thing can perhaps be said for it. It does get things done, even if those things ought never to get done. Here too there is a major weakness. It is impossible for any person or institution to regulate and prescribe all opinions for man, nor is it possible for conflicting and opposing views to be kept out, and these will eventually give rise to doubts.

Sometimes, Peirce avers, we fix beliefs because they seem agreeable to reason, although they do not rest on observed fact. But "agreeable to reason" usually means, in this case, that we find ourselves inclined to believe because we want to believe. This is called the a priori method. It is perilously close to wishful thinking, and makes believing a matter of taste, or perhaps of fashion. No doubts are really satisfied, and the capricious elements of belief dominate. This, too, is obviously unsure ground for supporting our beliefs.

Finally, there is the method of science. Peirce states its fundamental hypothesis in the following words:

There are Real things, whose characters are entirely independent of our opinions about them; those Reals affect our senses according to regular laws, and, though our sensations are as different as are our relations to the objects, yet, by taking advantage of the laws of perception, we can ascertain by reasoning how things really and truly are; and any man, if he have sufficient experience and he reason enough about it, will be led to the one True conclusion.[11]

This is the method that starts with known and observed facts and moves to the unknown, according to certain rules. The rules constitute the practical side of logic. Here the appeal is not to need, authority, or feelings, but to the application of a method.

Peirce admits, however, that other methods are not without some advantages:

On the contrary, each has some peculiar convenience of its own. The *a priori* method is distinguished for its comfortable conclusions. It is the nature of the process to adopt whatever belief we are inclined to, and there are certain flatteries to the vanity of man which we all believe by nature, until we are awakened from our pleasing dream by rough facts. The method of authority will always govern the mass of mankind; and those who wield the various forms of organized force in the state will never be convinced that dangerous reasoning ought not to be suppressed in some way. If liberty of speech is to be untrammelled from the grosser forms of constraint, then uniformity of opinion will be secured by a moral terrorism to which the respectability of society will give its thorough approval. Following the method of authority is the path of peace. Certain non-conformities are permitted; certain others (considered unsafe) are forbidden. These are different in different countries and in different ages; but, wherever you are, let it be known that you seriously hold a tabooed belief, and you may be perfectly sure of being treated with a cruelty less brutal but more refined than hunting you like a wolf. Thus, the greatest intellectual benefactors of mankind have never dared, and dare not now, to utter the whole of their thought; and thus a shade of *prima facie* doubt is cast upon every proposition which is considered essential to the security of society. Singularly enough, the persecution does not all come from without; but a man torments himself and is oftentimes most distressed at finding himself believing propositions which he has been brought up to regard with aversion. The peaceful and sympathetic man will, therefore, find it hard to resist the temptation to submit his opinions to authority. But most of all I admire the method of tenacity for its strength, simplicity, and directness. Men who pursue it are distinguished for their decision of character, which becomes very easy with such a mental rule. They do not waste time in trying to make up their minds what they want, but, fastening like lightning upon whatever alternative comes first, they hold to it to the end, whatever happens, without an instant's irresolution. This is one of the splendid qualities which generally accompany brilliant, unlasting, success. It is impossible not to envy the man who can dismiss reason, although we know how it must turn out at last.[12]

Here we have two complementary approaches to belief. Both Clifford and Peirce have insisted that beliefs held without evidence or good reasons

[11] Morris Cohen (ed.), *Chance, Love, and Logic*, Harcourt, Brace & Co., New York, 1923, p. 26.
[12] *Ibid.*, pp. 29–30.

are dangerous, or at least obstacles in the way of communication and the community. Each in his own way has appealed to the potential reasonableness of man and sought to lift him by admonition, argument, and ridicule, to the level of his best thinking.

V. *Belief, Faith, and Knowledge: The Relations among Philosophy, Religion, and Science*

A. Belief and Philosophy

Another term in our language has a closer relation to "belief" than it has to "knowledge." It is, of course, "faith." This term seems to be nearer those instances when we prefer to use "believing in" rather than "believing that." When we say we "believe that" something, we usually are ready to, and expected to give our evidence. But when we say we "believe in," we may find it difficult to give evidence when we are asked for reasons. "Faith," at least in some uses, suggests that although there is not sufficient factual evidence for our belief, there are nevertheless reasons and causes for our holding it. "Knowledge," on the other hand, is ordinarily used when we are sure that we are correct in our belief, that is, the factual evidence is sufficient to exclude doubt, and no fact or set of facts would alter the status of the belief as knowledge.

The way we use these terms will help us see the relationships among various interests—philosophy, religion, and science. Beginning students come to their first course in philosophy with different attitudes. Some come apprehensively, fearing that philosophy will weaken their religion; others come hoping that it will support or be a good substitute for religion; still others come skeptically, having heard that the interminable discussions, so often about words, never lead to agreement or to the acquisition of a good substantial block of knowledge, such as one may get in a course in a science. Perhaps we can modify some of the attitudes if we state tentatively the difference between these human interests as brought out by the uses of the words belief, faith, and knowledge.

We have already indicated that philosophy's role is essentially that of critically analyzing beliefs in order to find the best reasons for holding or rejecting them. In this endeavor philosophy refuses to exclude any belief on the grounds that it is "sacred," "universal," or "demanded by authority." This, of course, does not mean that an examined belief is a weakened belief, nor that its examination is necessarily a prelude to disbelief. Our beliefs might well become stronger after the ordeal of thoroughgoing scrutiny. John Stuart Mill made this point emphatic when he wrote that the Roman Catholic Church

. . . even at the canonization of a saint, admits, and listens patiently to, a 'devil's advocate.' The holiest of men, it appears, cannot be admitted to posthumous honors, until all that the devil could say against him is known and weighed. If even the Newtonian philosophy were not permitted to be questioned, mankind could not feel as complete assurance of its truth as they now do. The beliefs which we have most warrant for, have no safeguard to rest on, but a standing invitation to the whole world to prove them unfounded. If the challenge is not accepted, or is accepted and the attempt fails, we are far enough from certainty still; but we have done the best that the existing state of human reason admits of; we have neglected nothing that could give the truth a chance of reaching us: if the lists are kept open, we may hope that if there be a better truth, it will be found when the human mind is capable of receiving it; and in the meantime we may rely on having attained such approach to truth, as is possible in our own day. This is the amount of certainty attainable by a fallible being, and this the sole way of attaining it.[13]

B. Religion vs. Science and Faith vs. Knowledge

Religion and science may be contrasted according to the degree of knowledge involved; "faith" largely characterizes religion; "knowledge" usually applies to science. This is generally adequate even though we do speak of "religious knowledge" and "scientific faith." The one does not absolutely exclude the other, but probably science would prefer always to exchange its faith for knowledge and, in fact, takes this as a kind of ideal. Religion must cope with the fact that some of its basic beliefs cannot become knowledge in the same sense that beliefs in science may become knowledge, that is, by experiment or inference. Many of these problems will be dealt with in Chapter X, but Cardinal Newman's point is pertinent here.

Life is not long enough for a religion of inferences; we shall never have done beginning, if we determine to begin with proof. We shall ever be laying our foundations. . . . Life is for action. If we insist on proofs for everything, we shall never come to action: to act you must assume, and that assumption is faith. . . . I can only say that impressions lead to action, and that reasonings lead from it. Knowledge of premises, and inferences upon them,—this is not to live. . . . We are so constituted that Faith, not Knowledge or Argument, is our principle of action. . . .[14]

Newman's position by no means tells the whole story, for knowledge, too, often leads to action and it makes just as much good sense to say that we are so constituted that knowledge is the principle of our behavior. In short, the fact that we are willing to act does not sufficiently discriminate

[13] John Stuart Mill, *On Liberty*, The World's Classics, Oxford University Press, London, 1946, pp. 28–29.
[14] John Henry Cardinal Newman, *Discussions and Arguments on Various Subjects*, Longmans, Green, Co., London, 1918, pp. 295–296.

faith from knowledge. And if it is insisted that we must act without any knowledge whatever, this can hardly be distinguished from rashness or foolhardiness. Furthermore, if we believe and insist that others believe, in spite of a complete absence of knowledge, this is sheer dogmatism. We need evidence for both belief and knowledge—but when we have knowledge, all the evidence needed is in; when we have belief there is still work to be done to establish it. This may be taken as one way of marking the distinction between religion and science. In the latter the possibility is open that all the needed evidence can be gained. With respect to religion it is doubtful that the evidence is ever sufficient to establish its claims to the degree that we can call it knowledge—at least not in the same sense that science can claim knowledge. This is to say that religion does not get or give information about the world in the same way that science does. "There is a God in the Universe," does not impart knowledge in the same way that "there is arsenic in the coffee" does. We know how to verify the second statement with high certainty, but no similar way is open for the first. But then, man does not live by knowledge alone. Much of the vitality of his life comes from beliefs struggling to become knowledge. Faith is often unarticulated belief. It is usually not formed into propositions but is more nearly related to attitudes.

As an instance of the distinction between belief and knowledge, in which belief is related to faith and knowledge to science, let us present the case of Louis Pasteur. He was a devout Catholic, and also a genius in dealing with problems that required evidence. The problem of fermentation was solved by the theory of germs. But the contrast between his scientific knowledge and his religious faith was extreme. On one occasion he said, "I know only scientifically determined truth, but I am going to believe what I wish to believe. I expect to meet this dear child again in another world." Pasteur did not think it proper to say he knew that his soul and the soul of the child would meet again in another world; he could not prove it; there is not sufficient evidence to establish it. And yet here was the claim that, although faith cannot be translated entirely into knowledge, it may be constituted by justifiable beliefs. But justifiable in what sense? Certainly Pasteur did not expect to explore heaven as we do a continent. This particular belief he knew was not subject to experimental verification. It could only be maintained if some other beliefs were accepted, such as the goodness of God, the trust in religious texts or ecclesiastical authorities.

Pasteur has helped us to see another distinction between "believe" and "know," that is, one may believe without evidence, but one cannot know anything unless there is evidence. Some ascribe belief to simple wish, but success in knowing does not follow from wish. Freud has certainly made the expression "wish-fulfilment" clearly useful in our language. We speak of wishful thinking or wishful believing, most often in a disparaging sense, usually to condemn an attitude that refuses to "face reality." But, of course, in one sense wishful believing is a necessary step in any creative process; without the wish to discover new worlds and the belief that these worlds can be discovered, no advance in knowledge is made. And yet, it must be emphasized that the wishing neither falsifies a belief nor makes it true, it is irrelevant to both.

The defense of faith, however, often takes another form. Even when we are not in a position to verify the beliefs of faith, it is sometimes said that they are justifiable because they are good, or beautiful, or useful. There are, for example, many positive words that have a good sound, and names of attitudes that generally express approval. There are also negative words with a bad sound and attitudes we know are disapproved because of the names we give them. For instance, a thesaurus will list the blessed words belief, trust, confidence, assurance, conviction, credit, reliance, fidelity; but the opposites have a forbidding sound: unbelief, misgiving, infidelity, suspicion, distrust, scepticism, doubt, denial, faithlessness, dissent, and so on. Of course, there are a few positive terms with a bad sound, such as, fanatic, superstitious, naive faith, dogmatist. And a few appraisal words have a good sound: critical, examined, tried and tested. Now, although the sound of a word may sway us one way or another, we should carefully guard against prejudice, remembering that the emotional content of these terms carries no logical weight whatever. It is always bad philosophy to suppose that the emotional value of a belief is evidence for its truth. And it is also poor philosophizing to resort to name-calling, which tries to condemn a belief by attaching to it a name with a bad sound, or to try to support a belief by describing it with one of the blessed words.

The problem of the relation between belief and knowledge is certainly as old as Plato. There is, he said, a difference in the objects of each, for example, our knowledge which comes to us by way of the senses is not certain; we think we know real tables and chairs when we see or touch them, but all we can safely say is that our opinion about them is such and such. The term *knowledge* should be restricted to that which we know "for sure," and the only objects we can know in this way are those grasped by the intellect, not the senses. These, says Plato, are the forms or universals. You will hear more of them later.

It is a long jump from Plato, a fifth- and fourth-century B.C. Greek philosopher, to William James, a nineteenth- and twentieth-century American philosopher, but we must try to make it. We do not want to suggest that in between no work was done on problems of belief—in fact, much attention was given to these matters, and we shall deal with them in the next chapter. Here we use Plato and James to make a point. Although Plato wishes to reserve the term knowledge for our grasp of forms and universals, he does not say that we must passively sit and wait until this knowledge comes as a gift or miraculously blooms in the person at an appropriate stage of his growth. Rather, one must prepare oneself, in short, take action, in order to receive it. The long, long years of a rigorous education serve this end. Many of our beliefs, therefore, may become knowledge if we are able to survive the ordeals of preparation. But the point is that we can do something to accomplish this goal.

Now let us turn to William James. In one of the most famous essays in American philosophy called "The Will to Believe" James defended the view that when the intellect has done all its work toward getting evidence for rival hypotheses, it may still not be able to decide which is correct or true. When this situation occurs, says James, we have a right to accept as evidence what our passional or emotional nature would prefer to believe. "We have the right to believe at our own risk any hypothesis that is live enough to tempt our will." When one refuses to believe until all the evidence is in, James calls this the rule of intellectualism, a rule he does not accept or advocate. In another essay, James insists that there are faith-tendencies in man which are his expressions of good will toward certain results. These tendencies are active and forceful, and though outstripping evidence, they lead to actual accomplishment so that things get done. In this connection he constructed a "faith-ladder" which is described as "a slope of good will on which in the larger questions of life men habitually live." The ladder has the following rungs:

1. There is nothing absurd in a certain view of the world being true, nothing self-contradictory;
2. It *might* have been true under certain conditions;
3. It *may* be true, even now;
4. It is *fit* to be true;
5. It *ought* to be true;
6. It *must* be true;
7. It *shall* be true, at any rate, for *me*.[15]

[15] William James, *Some Problems of Philosophy*, Longmans, Green & Co., Inc., New York, 1931, p. 224.

Thus, for James, <u>faith is a practical, undogmatic attitude, one of the</u> "<u>inalienable birthrights of our mind</u>." We believe not only because we may, but because we must, but this "must" is not a requirement of logic. It is a rule arising out of the practical affairs of a struggle to maintain ourselves at our best. When we are confronted by a world of diverse powers and possibilities, there are four attitudes open, one of which, says James, we must take. This is a logical must—for the alternatives are exhaustive. Either we must:

1. Follow intellectualist advice: wait for evidence; and while waiting, do nothing; or
2. *Mistrust* the other powers and, sure that the universe will fail, *let* it fail; or
3. *Trust* them; and at any rate do *our* best, in spite of the if; or, finally,
4. *Flounder*, spending one day in one attitude, another day in another.[16]

James, of course, thinks that number three is the only wise way. But may we not object here and ask why waiting for evidence means that we do nothing? Can we not search for evidence and be useful and happy, even in the search? Plato did not think that the ideal state or men's knowledge came by mere waiting; there was always something to go on, some advance being made on the way to knowledge and each new step is not merely one of trust or faith, but of knowledge—incomplete, of course, but still knowledge. James runs the great risk of identifying the *ought-to-be* with the *is*, and also of permitting men to believe too soon, that is, when the grounds are insufficient. Moreover, this view could mean that we might become satisfied with half-hearted research so that belief actually becomes an obstacle on the way to knowledge. But at least James has drawn our attention to the role of beliefs in our lives, and in particular how they affect the believer himself. Beliefs may make his life richer, more satisfying, better, both for himself and the community. If they secure these effects, James was willing to say they are true. "The true is the name of whatever proves itself to be good in the way of belief, and good, too, for definite, assignable reasons."[17]

Thus James' position amounts to something like this: <u>Among the reasons for holding a belief are the positive effects for good that belief has on the believer and the community; if the belief has negative effects these are acceptable reasons for rejecting it.</u>

We do not wish to deny the powerful and sometimes all-pervasive influence a belief may have—certainly James was right here, but there is

---

[16] *Ibid.*, pp. 229–230.
[17] William James, *Pragmatism*, Longmans, Green & Co., New York, 1928, p. 76.

danger in allowing this fact to dominate our thinking too early. It may turn us away too soon from the effort to establish a belief by precise logical methods and the rules of evidence, and thus produce a series of noble sentiments connected only by the radiation of emotion.

It is sometimes said that beliefs in science are more objective than beliefs in philosophy, which by implication are thought to be more subjective. But this distinction, although it can be made more precise, is often kept so vague that it really fails to be of much service. Usually "objective" is regarded as the good word, and "subjective" as the bad word. These terms have been applied to things, such as tables, to qualities, such as blueness, to relations, such as between, to universals, such as beauty, as well as to beliefs. In beliefs, the contrast between believing on the basis of sufficient data and wishful thinking is often taken as marking the difference between being objective and subjective. "Objective" is sometimes applied to method, for example, in the approval of the inductive-experimental procedures of science over methods of introspection. And still another use of these two terms may be discerned in the claim that the objective is that which is independent of thought, and the subjective is that which depends on thought. And at least two more uses may be mentioned. One is that whenever we take the world without reference to human values, some would say we are looking at it objectively, but when we read human values into the world we are falling into subjectivity; this point appears in the following:

As regards human progress, it is clear that subjective criteria cannot and should not be neglected; human values and feelings must be taken into account in deciding on the future aims for advance. But in comparing human with pre-human progress, we must clearly stick to objective standards. I would thus like to make a distinction between biological or evolutionary progress and human progress. The former is a biological term with an objective basis: it includes one aspect of human progress. Human progress, on the other hand, has connotations of value as well as of efficiency, subjective as well as objective criteria.[18]

Finally, there are those who make the distinction between objective and subjective equivalent to the distinction between public and private.

The critical characteristic of the subjective as contrasted with the objective is that the subjective tends to be a private event, whereas the objective is a public event, i.e., an event presumed to be independently observable by many persons.[19]

[18] Julian Huxley, *Evolution, the Modern Synthesis,* Harper & Brothers, New York, 1943, p. 566.
[19] Clark Hull, *Principles of Behavior,* Appleton-Century-Crofts, Inc., New York, 1943, p. 30.

With the various uses of these terms it does not seem illuminating to call science objective and philosophy subjective until one has specified more clearly the way in which the terms are to be taken, for it is quite possible that we shall find subjective features of science and objective aspects of philosophy depending on the meanings adopted.

VI. Beliefs and the Disciplines of Philosophy

Why study philosophy? By now our answer should be clear. We are all believers. We cannot live without trust, that is, accepting some beliefs as true, nor without doubt, that is, rejecting other beliefs as false. But how can we know whether we are right in feeling sure about some beliefs? The best we have done so far is to urge you to be critical, to reflect upon alternative beliefs, and to consider the importance of evidence. For all those who dislike deception and wish to get rid of error, this sounds obvious. But it does not come merely by intending or hoping; we must work at our beliefs until they are as true as they can be made. And if they can be shown to have little or no truth, we must have the courage to modify or abandon them. Santayana put it succinctly when he said, "Believe, certainly; we cannot help believing; but believe rationally, holding what seems certain for certain, what seems probable for probable, what seems desirable for desirable, and what seems false for false."[20]

Now how does one go to work on beliefs? By using tools designed for the problems. These tools are provided in a study called logic, and we shall try to sharpen them for you in Chapter III, but now we want you to notice how logic as a philosophic discipline emerges naturally from a consideration of the problems of belief. For example, many beliefs rest on other beliefs. "Rest" is a metaphorical term referring to some kind of logical connection among beliefs. The question may then easily arise, must there not be some beliefs that do not rest on others but are so fundamental they cannot be proved or disproved? We will have more to say on this a little later, but here we call your attention to the use of axioms in geometry. What evidence would you offer in defense of the belief that "things equal to the same thing are equal to each other?" Once that belief is accepted many others can be established, such as "the sum of the interior angles of a square equal 360 degrees." Too many persons, facing the necessity of justifying beliefs by grounding them upon other, ungrounded beliefs, assume that a dogmatic authority must be found. We

---

[20] George Santayana, *Character and Opinion in the United States*, Constable, London, 1920, p. 87.

are working, as philosophers, on the assumption that though our beliefs are not now as true as they can be made, we can do without an infallible authority and still not fall into complete scepticism and unnerving despair. We can, in short, make a distinction between basic beliefs and derived beliefs.[21] A basic belief is one that is taken for granted, or assumed. It is not argued for, but something argued from. It is a belief so fundamental, that without it we could not establish other beliefs. Philosophers have sometimes called these postulates, or basic propositions, or primitive beliefs. Derived beliefs, on the other hand, are those deduced from basic beliefs. They are the beliefs for which we may be expected and required to state our premises or our evidence. Now, neither science nor religion can escape having both types of belief—each has its basic beliefs or presuppositions. Part of the work of philosophy is to get these basic beliefs out into the open, to bring them to our attention, to ask for their justification, and to keep them as few as possible.

Logic may now be thought of as philosophy's way of identifying and testing those beliefs that are deduced from other beliefs. Whether these beliefs are justified is a matter of logical form. Logic is thus one of the "disciplines" of philosophy because many beliefs are said to be true solely on the basis that they "follow from" other beliefs.

In a similar way, we can show how the other disciplines of philosophy naturally arise from attending to the problems of belief. For example, we claim some of our beliefs to be true because they are based on reports assumed to be correctly stating the case. This is not a matter of logical form or deduction. It is a question of reliability, that is, whether the statement really reports what is the case. If it does, we have knowledge. An examination of the difficulties in this area is called epistemology, or theory of knowledge. It is concerned with the nature, sources, limits, and conditions of knowledge.

Two other types of beliefs lead to what may be called the disciplines of metaphysics and value theory. The former attempts to distinguish between our beliefs about the real and our beliefs about what is only appearance. The source of the latter is the activity of making and justifying choices. Common discourse abounds in expressions of liking and disliking. Some statements, called appraisals of value, or evaluations, state what we believe is good or bad, beautiful or ugly. These make up our beliefs in the subdivisions of value theory, ethics and aesthetics.

Again, there are other beliefs that combine expressions of what is real

[21] Cf. Max Black, *Critical Thinking*, 2nd ed. Prentice-Hall Inc., New York, 1952, p. 251.

and of supreme worth. These beliefs assert that there is something in the nature of things that is favorable to man and the achievement of his goals. They concern man's place in his world and try to express what it is that leads to the fulfillment of human destiny. These beliefs are the concerns of theology and philosophy of religion.

This is sufficient to show how our beliefs lead to the main interests and business of philosophy. There are, of course, many fields to which philosophy may be related—we have philosophy of history, philosophy of education, philosophy of science, philosophy of law, and so on. Perhaps it would not be unjust to say that whenever one is concerned about the philosophy of anything, he is probing deeply for the basic beliefs and the derived structure of the discipline that interests him. We hope this book will introduce you to some of the major problems of philosophy and their connections with other beliefs you may hold. We do not want to suggest that all beliefs are untrustworthy. Rather, we seek to help you find the clearest expression of your beliefs and to help you to defend what you believe true by the most powerful and appropriate methods.

VII. Suggested Methods of Study

The question often arises among beginning students, "Am I really a philosopher, and doing the work of a philosopher?" Teachers also ask this of themselves. How, then, can one tell whether one is really fitted for this kind of study? Plato attempted to guide a young prince into the ideal way of thought and conduct. He had misgivings about Dionysius of Syracuse and in his Seventh Letter he tells how he would test whether the young nobleman was "really all on fire with philosophy."

To such persons one must point out what the subject is as a whole, and what its character, and how many preliminary subjects it entails and how much labour. For on hearing this, if the pupil be truly philosophic, in sympathy with the subject and worthy of it, because divinely gifted, he believes that he has been shown a marvellous pathway and that he must brace himself at once to follow it, and that life will not be worth living if he does otherwise. After this he braces both himself and him who is guiding him on the path, nor does he desist until either he has reached the goal of all his studies, or else has gained such power as to be capable of directing his own steps without the aid of the instructor. It is thus, and in this mind, that such a student lives, occupied indeed in whatever occupations he may find himself, but always beyond all else cleaving fast to philosophy and to that mode of daily life which will best make him apt to learn and of retentive mind and able to reason within himself soberly; but the mode of life which is opposite to this he continually abhors. Those, on the other hand, who are in reality not philosophic, but superficially tinged by opinions,—like men whose bodies are sunburnt on the surface—when they see how many studies are required and how great labour, and how the orderly mode of daily life is that which befits the subject, they deem it difficult or impossible for themselves, and thus they become in fact incapable of pursuing it; while some of them persuade themselves that they have been sufficiently instructed in the whole subject and no longer require any further effort.

Now this test proves the clearest and most infallible in dealing with those who are luxurious and incapable of enduring labour, since it prevents any of them from ever casting the blame on his instructor instead of on himself and his own inability to pursue all the studies which are accessory to his subject.[22]

We need not think that the philosopher is "divinely gifted," but we must agree with Plato that there is an immense amount of labor required if one is to learn to "reason within himself soberly." There is no easy road to philosophic understanding. All men may be said to share some degree of philosophy, to accept some noble sentiments or to be convinced that certain propositions are true. But this is a far cry from real philosophy, which insists that the connections between beliefs be logical and not senti- mental. As there is no easy road through this subject, so there is not only one road. Our suggested ways of study are therefore only aids to the stu- dent. They are designed to help him get started, not guarantees of suc- cess. The interested and serious student will find other means, and from his experience draw other lines of approach leading to a mastery of the material. But the following may be useful for taking the preliminary steps.

A. Define the Problem

Try to grasp clearly the nature of the problem being discussed. It may be that the problem is new, never before having troubled your mind. More frequently, however, the issue will be one to which you have given some, even if only passing, attention in the course of your life. Here is your op- portunity to fix the question, to state it sharply, to see its limitations and its connections with your previous experience. This means that you should begin early to develop the critical attitude; to read and think with ques- tions in mind; to ask for evidence, to distinguish between evidence and conclusions, to search for weaknesses that do not square with your own knowledge or experience. But a warning is necessary. It is sometimes far too easy to criticize without comprehension. Therefore let these first ques- tions be directed toward understanding what is said. Every philosopher has a right to be heard through. He cannot say everything at once. Many of your early perplexities will diminish as you get deeper into the subject,

[22] Reprinted by permission of the publishers from the Loeb Classical Library edition, Translated by R. G. Bury, Plato, *Timaeus, Critias, Cleitophon, Menexenus, Epistles*, Vol. 7, Harvard University Press, Cambridge, Mass., 1929, Seventh Letter, pp. 527–529.

so you must acquire the ability to hold the problem in mind until you comprehend the full position of the author. This is by no means easy. It is characteristic of beginning students to want immediate and final answers to their inquiries, to gain too quickly that inner satisfaction and peace that comes when the restless mind is presented with an acceptable answer. Seek first, therefore, to capture the problem, to make it your personal concern; the courtship of wisdom begins here.

B. Define the Terms

As a second aid in the study of philosophy we advocate the obvious necessity and practice of asking for the meaning of terms. We all know what confusion of thought and action results when we use words with double or triple meanings. It is always an intellectual safeguard to ask at the beginning of any argument or statement of opinion, "What do you mean?" We intend to give you some help in definition in Chapter III, but for the present, it is enough to urge you to acquire the habit of looking for meanings. Philosophy, like the sciences, has a vast technical vocabulary. You must become acquainted with it and be willing to submit yourself to the labor of exact definition. But again a warning is in order. Any fool may stop a freightload of conversation by an interminable and petulant reiteration of the demand for meaning. It should be evident that thought and discussion could not get under way at all unless we assume some common understanding of the words we use. Thoughts must be expressed, propositions stated, often with provisional meanings in mind. Later, thought will turn upon its product and recast or refine the tentative definitions.

Certain contemporary philosophical circles stress that the whole mission of philosophy is to clarify the meaning of terms; that it can make no addition to knowledge. Clarifying meanings is not adding information. Thus, for example, its business is not to find reality, but to make clear what the word "real" means; not to discover truth, but to show in what contexts the term "truth" may be used meaningfully. Such an accent in reflection can perform a distinct service, but we feel it is a much too limited conception of the scope and possibility of philosophy. If all meanings were precise, the human spirit would still be asking questions that philosophy has tried to answer.

C. Discover the Premises

A further help in the pursuit of philosophy is to train yourself to see presuppositions and assumptions. This must be done not only in your estimate of another's point of view but also in judging your own. A kind of intellectual courage is required in the latter case, for few men are able to examine impartially the bases of their own beliefs. It is accomplished by trying to find out what is taken for granted; what is felt to be necessary for a start; what is regarded as so fundamental that without it the position would either collapse or be seriously weakened. Bertrand Russell makes the point in these words:

The first thing to realize, if you wish to become a philosopher, is that most people go through life with a whole world of beliefs that have no sort of rational justification, and that one man's world of beliefs is apt to be incompatible with another man's, so that they cannot both be right. People's opinions are mainly designed to make them feel comfortable; truth, for most people, is a secondary consideration. You, dear readers, have of course no prejudices; but you will admit that in this you are different from most people. I shall suppose that you are a Baptist from Tennessee. It is obvious to you that America is the greatest country in the world, that Tennessee is the most distinguished of the States, and that the Baptists are the sole repositories of theological truth. Let us suppose that I concede all this. What am I to say to a man from another State or another country: How can I persuade a French Canadian Catholic of the truths which are so luminously evident to you? There are still a good many points about which you and he will agree, but how if you have to argue with a Turk or a Hindu or a Confucian? You will find them questioning most of what you have accepted as unquestionable, and if you are to argue profitably with them you will have to find common ground beneath your respective assumptions.[23]

D. Reformulate Ideas in Your Own Words

You will remember Plato's insistence that philosophy demands a considerable amount of labor. There is no escape from this. A part of the work is the practice of restatement or reformulation—especially through writing. We suggest, therefore, that you keep pencil and paper at your side as you read, jotting down significant points of the position and argument. Then, after finishing a section try to restate the material in your own manner. No better test of your comprehension can be found. Along with this should go the trying out in your conversation of the ideas you encounter. There is no reason at all why you should not introduce into your verbal exchanges the discoveries and puzzles you meet in the classroom or text. Philosophy will be an exciting adventure when it is brought into the arena of social intercourse. And the practical uses of this process are by no means minor. We know, for example, that language expression, whether spoken or written, is an aid to thought. Ideas come and grow as we attempt to express them. It is quite true, as William James has said, that,

[23] Bertrand Russell, "How to Become a Philosopher," E. Haldeman-Julius Publications, Girard, Kansas, 1942, p. 5.

Something forever exceeds, escapes from statement, withdraws from definition, must be glimpsed and felt, not told. No one knows this like your genuine professor of philosophy. For what glimmers and twinkles like a bird's wing in the sunshine it is his business to snatch and fix.[24]

And fixing may be partially executed when the passing thought is forged into an intelligible and communicable statement.

E. Relate What You Learn to Your Life

One way to a sense of satisfaction, completeness, and progress in learning is relating new facts and ideas to previous experience or to a more general scheme of thought, or to other areas of interest. All of you will have had some acquaintance, no matter how casual, with many of the problems we discuss, to which you can connect your present work. For example, you must have wondered about yourself, why are you here; what it means to exist; what purposes you may fulfill; what God is like, if there is a God; what is most worthwhile, etc. These momentary periods of contemplation or reflection may have given you some convictions around which you plan your life and center your activity. Here is your opportunity to put these occasional insights to use, to penetrate more deeply into the major concerns of the human spirit, to try your intellectual equipment by bringing order, meaning, and relatedness to detached experiences.

Moreover, your success and advance in philosophy will be greatly increased by the degree to which you relate what is done in this course with other courses. For instance, if you park your psychology outside the door when you enter the philosophy classroom, much of our discussion of mind and thinking will be incomplete and mediocre. Or if you forget your philosophy when you study economics, you will certainly miss the chance to see how the problem of value may be relevant; and if the facts you have presumably mastered in the sciences are blissfully ignored in philosophy, you will get the impression that we spin worlds out of our subjective aims and wishes—a disservice to yourself and a dishonoring of philosophy. Therefore, make it your business to see connections, relationships, interdependencies, and associations among the numerous separate facts and truths out of which your philosophy must be constructed. One last word. You will frequently be impatient both with the text and work in class because so many questions are raised and so few answers are given. But this is not something to be deplored. The beginning work in philosophy is designed to make you aware of a world of living possibilities, not to give you rigor mortis of the intellect.

[24] Quoted by Ralph Barton Perry, *In the Spirit of William James,* Yale University Press, New Haven, Connecticut, 1938, p. 114.

In this chapter we have tried to show the central role of the concept of belief in philosophy. The range of man's belief may, of course, be extended almost without limit. Around each of his major concerns—for example, the world, man, beauty, knowledge, state, God, mind, destiny—there clusters a wide variety of possible beliefs. But philosophy is not a mere catalogue of beliefs, nor a classification of attitudes, nor a genealogy of convictions. It is less interested in the causes of beliefs than it is in the reasons for beliefs. In this book we intend to present and examine some of the great beliefs men have held, to see how they are defended and how they are related to each other. By working at this we hope you may learn how to handle your own beliefs and also discover some areas of possible belief that had not occurred to you before. Moreover, we may expect, if the quest is sincere, the acquiring of a certain habit of mind that may be called creative tolerance. Such a tolerance is not a mere naive hospitality to any belief that beckons or is proposed. It is rather a deliberate adoption of a viewpoint that will permit all sides to be heard through, and an attempt to draw from minor differences, as well as from gigantic opposites, whatever insights they may contain. Something of this aim was expressed by John Locke when he wrote the following:

Since, therefore, it is unavoidable to the greatest part of men, if not all, to have several *opinions*, without certain and indubitable proofs of their truth; and it carries too great an imputation of ignorance, lightness, or folly for men to quit and renounce their former tenets presently upon the offer of an argument which they cannot immediately answer, and show the insufficiency of: it would, methinks, become all men to maintain peace, and the common offices of humanity, and friendship, in the diversity of opinions; since we cannot reasonably expect that any one should readily and obsequiously quit his own opinion, and embrace ours, with a blind resignation to an authority which the understanding of man acknowledges not. For however it may often mistake, it can own no other guide but reason, nor blindly submit to the will and dictates of another. If he you would bring over to your sentiments be one that examines before he assents, you must give him leave at his leisure to go over the account again, and, recalling what is out of his mind, examine all the particulars, to see on which side the advantage lies: and if he will not think our arguments of weight enough to engage him anew in so much pains, it is but what we often do ourselves in the like case; and we should take it amiss if others should prescribe to us what points we should study. And if he be one who takes his opinions upon trust, how can we imagine that he should renounce those tenets which time and custom have so settled in his mind, that he thinks them self-evident, and of an unquestionable certainty; or which he takes to be impressions he has received from God himself, or from men sent by Him? How can we expect, I say, that opinions thus settled should be given up to the arguments or authority of a stranger, or adversary, especially if there be any suspicion of interest or design, as there never fails to be, where men find themselves ill treated? We should do well to commiserate our mutual ignorance, and endeavour to remove it in all the gentle and fair ways of information; and not instantly treat others ill, as obstinate and perverse, because they will not renounce their own, and receive our opinions, or at least those we would force upon them, when it is more than probable that we are no less obstinate in not embracing some of theirs. For where is the man that has incontestable evidence of the truth of all that he holds, or of the falsehood of all he condemns; or can say that he has examined to the bottom all his own, or other men's opinions? The necessity of believing without knowledge, nay often upon very slight grounds, in this fleeting state of action and blindness we are in, should make us more busy and careful to inform ourselves than constrain others. At least, those who have not thoroughly examined to the bottom all their own tenets, must confess they are unfit to prescribe to others; and are unreasonable in imposing that as truth on other men's belief, which they themselves have not searched into, nor weighed the arguments of probability, on which they should receive or reject it. Those who have fairly and truly examined, and are thereby got past doubt in all the doctrines they profess and govern themselves by, would have a juster pretense to require others to follow them: but these are so few in number, and find so little reason to be magisterial in their opinions, that nothing insolent and imperious is to be expected from them: and there is reason to think, that, if men were better instructed themselves, they would be less imposing on others.[25]

PROBLEMS FOR THOUGHT AND DISCUSSION

1. In September 1956 a Bishop of the Roman Catholic Church advised Catholic students not to study philosophy in non-Catholic colleges and universities because it might undermine their faith. Such an attitude has been expressed at times by religious leaders of all faiths. How would you reply to this charge?
2. One often hears of a philosophy of education, a philosophy of religion, a philosophy of science, and even a philosophy of business. What do you think is meant by such uses of the term "philosophy"?
3. What beliefs seem most fundamental in your own life? Can you give reasons why you hold them?
4. Because philosophers are concerned with reasons and arguments it is often thought they seek to prove something. Can you think of various ways of proof? How do they apply to philosophy?
5. In what ways may beliefs be said to be similar or different? For example, consider the terms certain, personal, private, difficult to establish, universal, etc.

PERTINENT READINGS

Ayer, Alfred Jules, et. al., *The Revolution in Philosophy*, Macmillan and Co., Ltd., London, 1956.

[25] John Locke, *An Essay Concerning Human Understanding* (A. C. Fraser, annotator), The Clarendon Press, Oxford, 1894, Vol. II, pp. 371–372.

Clifford, William Kingdon, "The Ethics of Belief," *Lectures and Essays,* Macmillan and Co., Ltd., London, 1886, pp. 177–211.

James, William, "Philosophy and Its Critics," *Some Problems of Philosophy,* Longmans, Green & Co., Inc., New York, 1940, Ch. I.

Peirce, Charles S., "The Fixation of Belief." In: Morris Cohen (ed.), *Chance, Love, and Logic,* Harcourt Brace & Co., New York, 1923, pp. 7–31.

Russell, Bertrand, *The Problems of Philosophy,* Oxford University Press, London, 1948.

Whitehead, Alfred North, "The Organisation of Thought," *The Aims of Education,* Mentor Books, New York, 1949, Ch. 8.

II

Belief and Knowledge in the History of Philosophy

I. A Common Theme in the History of Philosophy

You are now prepared for the thesis that belief and knowledge, together with opinion and faith, are key terms in the history of philosophy. By this we mean that when we understand how a philosopher uses them we are able to unlock much of his thought. Almost all the great philosophers used these concepts and their philosophies depend on the meanings they gave to them. Since we cannot report everything done in philosophy in the past twenty-five hundred years we must select, and the principle of our selection is the examination of the different interpretations given to these key terms by ancient, medieval, modern, and contemporary philosophers. That such a principle is justifiable is suggested in Russell's statement, " . . . on the view we take of belief our philosophical outlook largely depends."[1]

But first let us summarize the alternatives we have discovered so far. One could adopt the view that the distinction between belief and knowledge lies in the objects of our propositions. That is, it is commonly held that what we can sense we can know, but what is beyond sense is in a realm where empirical evidence is necessarily deficient, hence we can only believe. Another possibility is that the difference lies in the feeling we have as a subject, rather than in the object. When we feel certain we make a claim to know, when we do not feel certain we claim only to believe, or if even less certain, to merely hold an opinion. A third possi-

[1] Bertrand Russell, *The Analysis of Mind*, George Allen & Unwin, Ltd., London, 1921, p. 231.

40

bility is that the difference lies not in the character of the object or subject but in the definitions of the terms. That is, when one has a clear conception and can analyze the proposition into distinct elements, then only
should one claim to know what one is talking about, otherwise one should
claim only to believe. If one claims to know that "the sum of the interior
angles of a triangle equal two right angles" one must know that "triangle"
means by definition "a plane closed figure of three sides." But if one could
not define triangle, by this criterion one should claim only to believe the
theorem. A fourth distinction between belief and knowledge hinges upon
the method by which one tests the claim. If a method of checking conclusions by reason and observation is provided, then one may claim to
know. But without a specified method, one should claim only to believe. A
fifth possibility may also be discerned, namely, that in the process of
testing a belief, one shifts from believing to knowing when the hypothesis
is confirmed. Finally, some thinkers stress the active character of belief
and faith, in contrast to opinion which seems too weak to motivate action,
and also to knowledge which seems to involve little or no risk. However,
these are not the only alternatives, as we shall see in this and some of the
following chapters.

Western or European philosophy began in ancient Greece. For Plato
and Aristotle philosophy begins in wonder. This wonder is not a kind of
incoherent and innocent awe before the majesty of nature, rather it is the
seed of inquiry, the desire to know, the dissatisfaction with ignorance,
fable, and mere opinion. An uneasiness, a discontent with traditional answers to perplexities can be discovered in the earliest attempts to philosophize, that is, to have good reasons for believing whatever it is one
does believe. " . . . They philosophized in order to escape from ignorance" said Aristotle about his predecessors.

In each generation following the ancient Greeks, philosophers have tried
to get some so-called knowledge demoted to the level of opinion and to
get other claims recognized as knowledge. The work never is finished.
New insights, new facts, and new methods keep urging men on to seek
new knowledge. But the labor of the past cannot be ignored, for philosophers see more clearly when they stand on the shoulders of their predecessors. In the conviction that truth is at least embryonic in the process
by which fuller knowledge develops, C. S. Peirce wrote that "any philosophical doctrine that should be completely new could hardly fail to prove
completely false."[2]

[2] Justus Buchler (ed.), *Philosophical Writings of Peirce*, Dover Publications, Inc.,
New York, 1955, p. 269.

To fill in our great gap in the previous chapter from Plato to William James, we must show some links between ancient Greek and medieval, between medieval and modern, and between modern and contemporary philosophy. But of course these are not neat blocks of time, so do not expect precise divisions. There are some breaks between pagan and Christian thought, between pre- and postscientific thought that have seemed so momentous to some historians that they call them revolutions in philosophy. There were radical changes when philosophy came to flourish only in conjunction with theology, and then again when philosophy seemed to flourish only in conjunction with natural science. Some today claim that philosophy can flourish only in conjunction with a study of language. What is philosophy? Is it seeking knowledge? Seeking salvation? Reforming methods of the sciences? Or showing how language works? You cannot appreciate these and similar questions without seeing each in some context of history. We know a little about how philosophy began, perhaps more about how it developed. If you too become aware of this past, you are less likely to repeat its mistakes and more likely to appreciate its problems. We can offer you here only a fragmentary account. Nevertheless, we hope it will arouse enough curiosity so you will do some intellectual prospecting on your own.

II. The Ancient Philosophers

A. The Pre-Socratics

Let us begin with a group of thinkers in the fifth and sixth centuries before Christ, known as the pre-Socratics. They are among the first to ask the questions, "What do we know?" and, "What evidence do we have for this knowledge?" They reject the answers and the methods of the poets and mythologists and have begun to rely on their own powers of observation and reflection. Two questions excite these early Greek philosophers: "What is the stuff of the world?" and, "Is change real?" The diversity of nature is as evident to them as it is to us, but they cannot help wondering if underneath all the variety there is not a basic substance common to everything. They refuse to take the obvious as true. But their wonder is not idle gaping. It arises from careful observation (although scientific and metaphysical questions were not strictly distinguished).

The earliest answers to the first question seem insignificant to us now, but there was some evidence for their beliefs. For example, Thales (585 B.C.)[3] believes everything is made of water. Might it not have been its

---

[3] Dates for the pre-Socratics are approximately the time when they were working or approximately the time of birth and death.

transformation from a solid into a liquid and into a vapor that impressed him? Anaximenes (525 B.C.) chooses air for his universal substance. Was it not clear that air is necessary for life and that the planets and stars float in it? Pythagoras (582–495 B.C.) and the Pythagoreans seek for knowledge through reason rather than through use of sight, hearing, taste. More certain than any opinion that honey is sweet is the knowledge that 2 and 2 equals 4. They had found the mathematical relation between the length of a string of a musical instrument and its pitch, as well as other interesting arithmetical and geometrical ratios. Do they not bring harmony? and is there not harmony and order in the cosmos? This suggests that the key to everything is number—not abstract number but numbers as actual, concrete entities. Thus says Aristotle:

And further, discerning in numbers the conditions and reasons of harmonies also; since, moreover, other things seemed to be like numbers in their entire nature, and numbers were the first of every nature, they assumed that the elements of numbers were the elements of all things, and that the whole heavens were harmony and number.[4]

Heraclitus (500 B.C.) is known in western thought as the man struck with the changing character of things. For him everything flows and you "could not step twice in the same river." Still there is some basic substance. He selects fire. Not arbitrarily, because there is some empirical evidence to support him, for example, man's consciousness is associated with warmth, for at death the body becomes cold. Man has in him the fire of the universe. Moreover, fire is always fire, though always changing. Hence, midst all change, the law of change itself is fixed. Here we see the attempt to reconcile two opposed conceptions, permanence and change. Are both features of our universe? To which does knowledge belong? To which opinion? These questions will acquire more significance as we proceed.

A second group of thinkers turn to man's reflective capacities for their clues about the world. Logic requires that the world be one. If it were other than one, it would not be a world. Its oneness, moreover, precludes the reality of change. The great figure here is Parmenides (475 B.C.) whose fundamental principle is that "thought and being are the same thing," that is, everything real can be coherently thought and what cannot be thought without contradiction is not real. Now the question is, can change or motion be consistently thought? Zeno (450 B.C.), a disciple of Parmenides, (not to be confused with Zeno the Stoic) thinks not and has constructed some famous arguments to prove it. One of them is restated here:

[4] Milton Nahm (ed.), *Selections from Early Greek Philosophy*, Appleton-Century-Crofts, New York, 1934, p. 75.

Consider an arrow flying from a bow. At any moment in its flight it is just where it is and not some other place, neither forward nor backward. Therefore, the arrow is at rest. But this is true for all possible positions. Motion is thus a series of rests, which is a contradiction. If motion cannot be made logically intelligible, then motion is not an object of knowledge and must be unreal. In this way the evidence of logic as well as of observation supports the view that there is something unchanging and universal in the world.

There were other philosophers of ancient Greece who felt that the variety of the world could not be reconciled with its supposed oneness, nor its fluent character with a kind of block sameness. They thought the evidence of reason and sense pointed to the existence of parts infinite in number, so small they cannot be seen, and of a void or space in which the parts move. Atoms moving in space; this alone is real and of this alone do we have genuine knowledge. As the atoms move around and shift positions, we experience change. As they cluster and hang together by means of projecting hooks, we observe objects. Here is the beginning of the atomic theory, invented by Democritus (born 460 B.C.) and Leucippus (flourished about 430 B.C.) to explain how it is possible to have permanence and change in the same universe. Atoms are the unchanging substances, their movement is what we experience as change. The rich expression of this theory by Lucretius (96–55 B.C.), a Roman poet, we will meet in Chapter VII.

The beginning of science lies in the speculations of these early Greeks. They revolted against religious myth and the world as a playground for capricious gods. Some took another step, revolting against speculations as well. For example, Hippocrates, the Father of Medicine, shares with the philosophers a habit of mind called looking into the causes of things. But to make medicine a science, the physician need not answer the metaphysical question of the causes of whatever exists. Indeed the progress of science, then as now, is frequently the isolation of particular problems. What Hippocrates carries over from metaphysics is the conviction that disease is no exception to the lawfulness and regularity men had ascertained clearly only in the stars and planets. The relationship of empirical science to rational metaphysics is made by a historian of science: "While the philosophers developed the conception of a rational world, it was the physicians, typified by Hippocrates, who first put the rational conception to the test of experience."[5] Hippocrates deals with disease in unique cases,

[5] Charles Singer, *A Short History of Science to the 19th Century,* The Clarendon Press, Oxford, 1941, p. 28.

but from the careful and repeated attention to patients, he makes judgments about the class of diseases, and on this inductive basis predicts the probable future recovery or death of his patient. This, too, like metaphysics, is reasoning from the known to the unknown, but the unknown is the future course of the disease, which proves or disproves what the physician has predicted.

The pre-Socratic philosophers, then, take the position that men can observe and reason, and on this basis reach views of the world superior to the religious myths retold by the poets. Whether we call these pre-Socratics primitive scientists, poetic metaphysicians, or rational theologians, makes little difference. Rather clearly, they oppose their own formulations to the traditional ones popularly held. More specifically, they demonstrate that there are a number of possible answers to such questions as "What is the ultimate substance?" Whereas a mythologist would prefer one tale of the world's origin to another because it happened to fascinate him, a philosopher proposed a hypothesis because it was arguable. In stating a view that might be supported or confuted by evidence, a philosopher raised the hope that one alternative might be demonstrated to be true, that is, to be knowledge rather than opinion.

A method is being born. To gain knowledge of the world one must go to the world and observe what goes on—the roots of empiricism are here. But in addition one must employ reason to demonstrate how one judgment leads to another. This is the genesis of deduction. The continuous refinement of these early steps is one of the major contributions of philosophy to knowledge.

B. The Sophists

In the middle of the fifth century B.C. a group of wandering teachers promised to instruct Greek youth in the art of persuasive speech. They are known as the Sophists. One writer described them as "itinerant university extension professors without a university base."[6] They are said to be the first to demand and receive fees for instruction in philosophy. They were less concerned with problems about the world of nature than with questions about man. Socrates, Plato, and Aristotle are sharply critical of the Sophists and accuse them of being tricky, shallow popularizers of Greek knowledge. It is not entirely evident that all of this criticism is justified. True, there were some charlatans among the younger Sophists, but others raised important questions about method, about language, and about the epistemological and metaphysical assumptions made by the

[6] Paul Shorey, *What Plato Said*, University of Chicago Press, Chicago, 1933, p. 13.

Greek philosophers. Only one figure of any real stature is worth our consideration in this connection. His name is Protagoras (480–410 B.C.). He reflects on the fundamental problems of knowledge and conduct, and asks what we can make of the differences among those who think they have the right view of the world. What measures can we apply? His conclusion is that there are no objective standards at all, that "man is the measure of all things." Each man's judgment is as true as any other man's. There is no sharp line between the true and the false, the good and the bad. All is personal and social opinion rising out of the circumstances of a particular time and place. Thus our beliefs do not constitute knowledge, they are always only opinions. Everything is relative to the individual and the culture to which he belongs.

The Sophists make an important contribution to our thinking about knowledge and opinion, namely, the role of convention. Opinions of each man are a matter of habit, and opinions of each group are a matter of custom. The opposite of custom is nature. Fire burns in Greece and in Persia. Everywhere the natural has the same force and character and is not dependent upon any people's thinking this or that. But the conventional enactments of Persia and Greece differ, and change from time to time. Of course a man can change his opinions to suit his interest and taste. It is not reason that accounts for the prevailing opinions, it is only the weight of the majority. The way to secure a majority is to talk to people and persuade them to agree with you. But it is always true that if you prefer one opinion, then it is true for you; if you reject it, then it is false for you. This may be extended to groups. If one society approves murder, then it is right for that society. If a society forbids educating women, then educating women is a wrong for that society. Socrates, Plato, and Aristotle demanded a more adequate definition of knowledge and truth, and insisted on the superiority of logic and science over rhetoric and force in settling disputes. But since the Sophists, men have had to take convention and custom into account when considering beliefs.

C. Socrates, Plato, and Aristotle

Socrates. Socrates (469–399 B.C.) is the greatest hero of the courageous intellect. Like heroes of physical battle, his ability to risk death, face enemies, and drink comrades under the table have become legendary. Unlike the Alexanders, Caesars, and Napoleons, his mission was not one of conquest, but of criticism. He heeded an inner voice and created a new mission among men: to ask questions of all phases of human activity. Persistently he sought to get people to say exactly what each important term means. Thus Socrates furthered logic. He demanded that men tell him exactly why they did what they did. Thus Socrates furthered ethics. Although his supreme conviction was religious, he was accused of atheism, for he made innovations in religion.

The highest excellence is of the soul, hence any evil that happens to the body is less to be feared than injury to the soul. Even death is to be feared less than the dishonor of the inner man. He died in prison by poison rather than sacrifice his doctrine that a man ought to remain loyal to his own city-state.

In opposition to the Sophists, Socrates believes that there are objective standards by which we can measure conduct and knowledge. These standards are found when we have located the essence or the quality common to the various objects described by the same term. No philosopher since Socrates has ignored the relation between particulars of a kind and the essence or "universal." For example, consider a beautiful tree, a beautiful house, a beautiful picture, and a beautiful mountain. If we can find the common quality of these four instances of beauty, we will have a definition of beauty and find its standard. But this is never seen. It is only grasped by the mind. Thus the mind knows the universal beauty, and the senses perceive the particular beautiful object. A similar argument is constructed for justice, courage, triangularity, and so on. What the mind grasps in this manner is a standard not dependent on personal idiosyncrasies, or the accidents of particulars, for if we destroy all thinkers, as well as all sensed objects, we do not destroy the common essence any more than we destroy triangularity if we erase all or any particular triangles.

The Socratic method must always be distinguished from the method of the Sophists. The former was the method of dialectic, that is, of criticism; the latter was a method of rhetoric, that is, of persuasion. Socrates showed great scorn for the supposed knowledge of the masses, as well as that of the poets and politicians. Often he would point to the experts of a certain trade or craft for illustrations of genuine knowledge. He seemed to think that somehow knowledge lies within us and all that we need is assistance and encouragement to bring it out. Thus he did not think of himself as a teacher in the manner of the Sophists, but as a midwife who delivered young minds of the knowledge latent within them.

In his conversation with Meno, Socrates admits that "There are not many things which I profess to know, but this is most certainly one of them," namely, that "knowledge differs from true opinion." In addition to having the truth or being right, knowledge consists in seeing the reason why it is true. Practically, "right opinion" is not less useful than knowledge. The man with right opinion "will be just as good a guide if he thinks the truth, as he who knows the truth."[7] The difference is not in the truth of the conclusion, but in the way that the conclusion has been reached or is maintained.

Socrates belongs with the Sophists only in his lack of interest in the natural world and his great concern with human problems. His method emphasizes the process of definition, gathering instances to support his beliefs, and a persistent, canny questioning, by which a chosen position is recast and redefined. The dialectic is a movement towards a solution of a problem not merely an oscillation nor a clever jockeying for position. It involves asking the questions that will lead the argument on, and following the argument wherever it leads.

Plato. Plato (428–348 B.C.), a pupil and disciple of Socrates, is the most famous name in philosophy, although we know almost nothing of his life until his sixtieth year. Except for very unimportant references, there is no mention of himself in his works. But of some things we seem to be quite sure. His early and long friendship with Socrates was undoubtedly the most powerful factor in the molding of his mind. He founded the Academy which has been called one of the most memorable events in Western European science. It was an indirect ancestor of the medieval and modern university and continued its activity for nine hundred years, being finally closed by Justinian in 529 A.D.

No brief account can do justice to the enormous range of Plato's thought, his penetrating insights, or the continuous impact he has made on all succeeding generations of thinkers. A. N. Whitehead (1861–1947) put it succinctly when he wrote, "The safest general characterization of the European philosophical tradition is that it consists of a series of footnotes to Plato."[8] When we reach Plato we need no longer rely on fragments, or stories, or verbal tradition. With the craftmanship of an artist he wrote many volumes, known to us as Dialogues, none of which, so far as we know, has been lost. This is in itself an indication of the value men have found in them. In Plato the full scope of philosophy is exemplified, and the Dialogues may be read for their significant contributions to logic and epistemology, aesthetics and ethics, metaphysics and theology. He speculated about men and society, and every history of psychology, soci-

---

[7] Plato, *Meno* (Benjamin Jowett, tr.), The Liberal Arts Press, New York, 1957, p. 57.

[8] From Alfred North Whitehead, *Process and Reality*, Copyright 1929 by The Macmillan Company, Copyright renewed 1957 by Evelyn Whitehead and used with permission of the Macmillan Company, p. 63.

ology, economics, and political theory acknowledges a debt to Plato and to his student Aristotle.

From his teacher Socrates, and probably from some of the other earlier philosophers, Plato learned the distinction between the universal and the particular. But he extends it far beyond the realm of ethics and aesthetics. There is a universal beauty, a universal goodness, and a universal justice, but also there are universals of motion, rest, and being. Plato calls them *forms* or ideas, though they are not ideas in the sense of being thoughts in our heads. Now why should a philosopher require such objects as forms or universals? What role do they have? What problems do they solve? For Plato the world of the senses is untrustworthy, it is constantly changing or vacillating. But even worse, it is the world of appearance and not of reality. It varies from man to man and from circumstance to circumstance. Thus we can have of this world only opinion and never knowledge. Knowledge must be trustworthy, it must be of the permanent and the real. We do not have knowledge of particular things and their qualities, of this tree and this red and this sweet. But we can have knowledge of "treeness," and "redness" and "goodness." The things of the sense world have reality only by participating in universal forms. Thus any green object gets a portion of its reality by participating in the form of greenness. Any particular just act is just because it participates in the form of justice. These forms, according to Plato, are indispensable for knowledge.

A reason for Plato's scornful rejection of the sociological and humanistic approach of the Sophists is that the forms are unchanging, eternal, spaceless, immaterial, and independent of all particulars and all knowers. There are thus two orders to be distinguished, the intelligible and the sensible. The mind belongs to one, the body to the other. One is most intimately acquainted with this distinction in mathematics and physics, where the number 2 may be regarded as a form, and two chairs (*this* chair and *that* chair) are particulars; or where $s = \frac{1}{2}gt^2$ is the form and a falling object the particular. We obtain real knowledge in conceiving the permanent form rather than in sensing the evanescent particular. It is important to keep this distinction in mind, for much of the history of thought may be interpreted in terms of those who supported and those who denied its validity. Battles were fought among medieval scholastics over the origin and status of universals. Whether they are necessary for knowledge continues to be debated as well as the metaphysical problem of what they really are.

There is for Plato a final knowledge, which is available only to those who have successfully passed through a long and rigorous education. This is the knowledge of "the good." Just what this is Plato never makes entirely clear. In fact, in the light of its enormous importance he has remarkably little to say about it. Of its nature we are given little but hints, and these are poetic metaphors rather than literal definition or description.

> Now, that which imparts truth to the known and the power of knowing to the knower is what I would have you term the idea of good, and this you will deem to be the cause of science, and of truth in so far as the latter becomes the subject of knowledge . . . the good may be said to be not only the author of knowledge of all things known, but of their being and essence, and yet the good is not essence, but far exceeds essence in dignity and power.[9]

It is obvious to Plato that only the man who has knowledge should rule the state. Knowledge is defined as apprehension of the forms. Whoever is able to grasp these is a philosopher. Therefore the philosopher should be king. The guardians, that is, the philosopher-rulers, are those who have survived thirty-five years of rigorous education. All other members of the state have their places according to their ability determined in their educational history. Women are to have the same opportunities as men. This will be a society where everyone has his place, and by occupying it performs the best service to himself and his fellows. Now if justice is defined as the condition of society where each member does what he is fitted to do for that society, it follows that this is the just state.

Both Socrates and Plato take the position that from the conflict of alternative views knowledge may emerge. Such knowledge depends on definition or knowing the essence of a thing. This essence is a universal, shared by particular instances of members of a class. The method of resolving the conflicts has been called *dialectic,* which in the history of thought has a number of developments. It is one answer to the challenge from the scientists to the metaphysicians that the latter produce a method by which results may be checked.

Aristotle. In Aristotle (384–322 B.C.), Plato's pupil, we have a mind of vast dimensions and interests. There was almost no area of the knowledge of his day he had not mastered, and almost all sciences are in his debt. His great love was for the concrete world of facts and their classification. If you go to the world, as he did, what seems most evident? Definite divisions, structure, classes, in which each particular thing belongs. Knowledge comes by classifying, that is, putting particular objects under their proper heads. But it is the individual object that is real, not the classifying system, nor the form, as Plato had taught. Now if the particular

[9] Plato, *The Republic* (Benjamin Jowett, tr.), Random House, New York, 1937, p. 778.

is real, and not the timeless forms, then at the very heart of reality is change. For Plato the real was an eternal unchanging form, while the thing was an appearance that comes into being and passes away. The problem is met by Aristotle with the concept of development. Reality is not static but dynamic, except for the Unmoved Mover whom we shall meet in a moment. A thing can become only what its nature designs it to become by the limitations imposed. Its potentialities unfold and it becomes real. To know what a thing is, one must necessarily know what it is becoming or what its purposes are. For example, we know this is an apple tree because it produces apples. Each class in the universe has its own end or purpose, which particular objects are in the process of realizing.

It is important to learn and remember two terms used by Aristotle in this connection. They are *actuality* and *potentiality,* or act and potency. Their use and meaning can be made clear in the following way. Suppose we consider the stages in the growth of a tree from seed to sapling to tree. When we have only the seed we have indeed an actual seed but only a potential sapling and tree. If the seed develops into an actual sapling then we have also a potential tree and when the sapling becomes the tree its end or *telos* has been reached in the actual tree. Now what has been occurring in this process? In Aristotlelian terms matter has been putting on form. With respect to the tree the sapling is matter. Whatever has any potency in it is to that degree not actual. Therefore what is truly actual, fully realized, must be pure form or pure actuality. But what about the seed? Is it too the form of some preceding potency? Aristotle is quite clear on this point. Actuality is prior to potency both logically and temporally. The potential could not even exist as potential except through its capacity to be actualized. Moreover, as Aristotle says, "For from the potentially existing the actually existing is always produced by an actually existing thing, e.g. man from man, musician by musician; there is always a first mover, and the mover already exists actually."[10]

Let us see how this works with respect to the nature of men. Whereas for Plato, man's soul is one thing and his body is something else in which the soul is imprisoned, for Aristotle, the soul is the living organism in action. Its highest function is rationality, when it is active in thought and moved by ideals. Human life is the serious business of managing one's affairs in the light of man's highest function, that is, being reasonable or

[10] Richard McKeon (ed.), *The Basic Works of Aristotle,* Random House, New York, 1941, p. 829, *Metaphysica,* W. D. Ross (tr.), The Clarendon Press, Oxford, 1928, 1049b, 24–26.

rational. As each particular seems to have its own end to reach, and as most ends are only steps toward some other end, the question arises, is there an ultimate end, a supreme good toward which all of life moves? As man's peculiar function is to be rational, his greatest good is found in the contemplative life. Nevertheless, when it comes to making deliberate moral decisions, reason must consider the alternatives and decide so as to avoid the extremes of defect and excess. Find the mean between these extremes, and it will offer the most reasonable choice.

We have seen that the end or purpose of a thing is part of the explanation as to why that thing exists. How and why anything exists is a problem of *cause*. Explaining the gymnasium, for example, involves the distinction between four types of causes. There is the material cause, that is, the bricks, iron, and glass. These alone will not produce the building, so we must have an efficient cause, that is, the contractor. But we could not have any building without a blueprint or plan, that is, the formal cause. All three would not achieve the observable result unless there was some purpose served by the gymnasium. This is final cause. Whatever is, is accounted for by the operation of these four causes.

In Aristotle's theory of development, the stress is upon final cause. Each object is striving toward completeness—toward something it lacks. It is not hard to conceive movement towards this goal, but Aristotle wants us to conceive of movement begun and continued by this goal. Such a process cannot go on forever either logically or temporally. There must, therefore, be an Unmoved Mover who cannot be involved in the struggle to be something higher; one in whom all possibilities are totally realized. This is God, who moves the world by drawing all things toward himself without compulsion or external force. He has no activity save thinking— thinking about the highest because the highest being engages in the most perfect activity. But the highest is his mind. Therefore God's thinking is continuous thinking about thinking, or God thinks about Himself. Aristotle, like Plato, constructed demonstrations of God's nature. From these spring most of the various "proofs" of God's existence. The point of such demonstration is to take theology out of the realm of opinion and to fit it into the sciences.

D. Stoicism and Epicureanism

In the fourth century B.C. two movements in philosophy began that have not yet ceased to influence moral thought and conduct. These are Stoicism and Epicureanism. Essentially both views offer ways of salvation, and stress the unhappy condition of man and the means by which happiness may be realized.

Stoicism. The Stoics insist that the good life means a stable, imperturbable condition, arrived at through self-control. This is possible because nature, and man as a part of nature, is permeated with reason. Man is his best self when he lives according to nature, that is, as a rational being. Anyone who is subject to passing impulse has no inward security. Because he is at the mercy of any outward force that plays upon him, he is not guided by reason alone and cannot but be bad and unhappy.

The wise or rational man does not have opinions, rather he has knowledge, firm and steady. Ordinary men run into error because they make too hasty assertions. The sage, on the other hand, considers well whether any presentation is true, and he gives his assent only if he is assured that it is so. Cicero wrote that the Stoic Zeno (336–264 B.C.) illustrated the advance in knowledge and assurance by showing his hand with the fingers extended and saying. "Perception is like this"; then after partially closing his fingers he would say, "Assent is like this"; then completely closing his fist he would say, "Comprehension is like this"; finally he brought his other hand over the closed fist and grasped it tightly saying, "This is knowledge and only the wise man is capable of it." It is not always clear how to interpret such metaphors, but at least it suggests that there is a distinction between opinion and knowledge; that there are stages in the advance toward knowledge; and that the attainment of knowledge calls for an exercise of the will as well as the intellect.

Epicureanism. Epicurus (342–270 B.C.) wanted a philosophy that the plain man could understand. He distrusts the study of logic and the special sciences for their own sake and is convinced that the surest way to knowledge is sense-perception. But for him too, the happiness of man is philosophy's most important problem. It is gained when man has pleasure, lost when he is in pain. However, there are two kinds of pleasure and pain, mental and bodily. The latter are intense but relatively short-lived. The former are less intense but greater in duration. The wise man, therefore, will seek that pleasure which is freest from pain, longest lasting, and least violent. This can mean only mental pleasure. He will find his greatest delight in congenial social relationships, especially in discourse with friends. What he seeks primarily is tranquillity, a state in which he fears neither gods nor death.

For Epicurus, knowledge is primarily the result of sense-perception and not of reason. By repeating sensations we somehow attain concepts from which our opinions and knowledge arise. But no knowledge is possible without sensation, and all knowledge must be confirmed or verified by our sense-perceptions. There is here an anticipation of some of the features of empiricism, so prominent in later philosophy.

These are only some of the major beliefs of some of the ancient Greek philosophers. As history moves they will be picked up for further elaboration and usefulness, or discarded as increased knowledge makes them untenable. But our debt to these thinkers is inestimable. No better tribute can be found than Whitehead's:

In the first place, they were unboundedly curious. They probed into everything, questioned everything, and sought to understand everything. This is merely to say that they were speculative to a superlative degree. In the second place, they were rigidly systematic both in their aim at clear definition and at logical consistency. In fact, they invented logic in order to be consistent. Thirdly, they were omnivorous in their interests—natural science, ethics, mathematics, political philosophy, metaphysics, theology, esthetics, and all alike attracted their curiosity. Nor did they keep these subjects rigidly apart. They very deliberately strove to combine them into one coherent system of ideas. Fourthly, they sought truths of the highest generality. Also in seeking these truths, they paid attention to the whole body of their varied interests. Fifthly, they were men with active practical interests.[11]

III. The Medieval Thinkers

Plotinus. In the transition from Greek philosophy to the thought of the Middle Ages, we will direct our attention to only two figures. The first, Plotinus (ca. 205–270 A.D.), was born in Alexandria but went to Rome where he developed his philosophy about the year 250. He was the last of the great line of pagan philosophers. Because he and his disciples interpreted certain features of Plato's thought, and made them central, the movement is called Neo-Platonism.

His philosophy is essentially religious in character, stressing man's consciousness of evil and his felt need for salvation. Evil is associated with body or with matter. Only pure spirit, that is, the soul without any tincture of matter, is good. Such a soul has a high degree of unity, as contrasted with the body which may be broken into parts. The unity of the soul gives us a clue to the nature of reality. Wherever there is a higher unity

---

[11] Alfred North Whitehead, *The Function of Reason,* Princeton University Press, Princeton, New Jersey, 1929, p. 66.

there is a higher reality. Like Plato, Plotinus believes that the most real is that which is uncreated, unchanging, immaterial, and indivisible. There is, then, an ascending order from sheer manyness to the absolute One or God. This reality can be known neither by the senses nor by the intellect —they are able to grasp only the discrete. The pure oneness of God is known by a mystical experience of ecstasy, in which all divisions, separateness, distinctions disappear, and in which man becomes aware of his identity with the Divine. No qualities may be ascribed to the One. It transcends all we can say or think. Nothing that can be said of human personality can be said of God. To ascribe human attributes to God would be to limit God. But God is unlimited or absolute. All positive attributes fail to apply. Only when these distinctions are laid aside and we become fused in the absolute oneness have we reached the final goal.

St. Augustine. It was this spiritual character of Neo-Platonism that attracted the young Augustine (354–430 A.D.). As the method of Socrates was expressed in the literary form of the dialogue, and the method of Aristotle in the treatise, so the method of Augustine was expressed most appropriately in his Confessions, celebrated as the first autobiography.

His self-portrayal makes vivid the connection between the stages of personal development and the various philosophies through which he passed. The vividness springs from the intensity of love. It is how and what a man loves that is at the center of personality. When Augustine is ashamed of the sensuality of his body, which he knows interferes with his scholarly career, then he believes the physical world is evil and that the soul must strive for good by freeing itself from the despised flesh. When he is trying in vain to tear himself from his mistress, he aspires to be a stoic sage. When he fails to live without passion, he falls into scepticism. When he believes that the mind can lead its own pure life in spite of the flesh by thinking of the universal forms independent of the world, then Plato is his guide. The one ancient philosophy that he does not seem to understand is Aristotle's, probably because Aristotle was impersonal and scientific in his approach. Moderation and restraint seem impossible for Augustine. He cannot by his own self-control avoid excess. The middle path between extremes, that is, the golden mean, has become a weak opinion by which, Augustine might argue, no man can live.

Man as man cannot save himself. What man is to be saved from is sin, and the deepest sin is pride, or belief in man's sufficiency. It is not folly or ignorance, as Socrates claimed, not vice, as the Stoics thought, not body or flesh as the Neo-Platonists claimed, but self-satisfaction and trust in one's own powers. The way in which God saves man is called "grace."

Man is saved, though he does not merit it. Why man cannot merit grace is explained in various ways, the most famous being the theological belief that in Adam the human race rebelled and lost its ability not to sin. But in Christ, God and man were reconciled, and a way to salvation opened by sacrifice.

In a second way the salvation of the Christian differed from the salvation of noble pagans. Augustine deals little with the ideal wise man, rather he describes the ideal community. The ideal itself is fulfilled in the heavenly Church, but the Church on earth is striving to reach the ideal, and is in part achieving it. A man is saved by membership in a community that has existed since Abel was chosen to obey God. In unbroken continuity there have been and will be in each age a few noble and sacrificing members who keep covenant with God. Theirs is ultimately the victory, though it is rarely evident. At the Last Judgment all will know who are saved and who are damned. For the time being history is a grand struggle between two Cities—the society of those who love God and strive for justice and peace, and the society of those who strive for the glory of conquest by war and oppression. In spite of the defects of the earthly Church, Augustine as a bishop came to believe that the infallible authority of Scripture gave it authority over philosophy and science, as well as public and private morality.

The Christian philosopher accepts the doctrine that God has revealed his nature and will in the Scriptures, and aids man in comprehending these writings. It may be said that any religion based upon scripture raises the issue of whether what is there written is to be classed with opinion or with knowledge. Why should I believe stories of the Old Testament? Do I know that events took place as there described? A Jew or a Moslem might raise just the questions St. Augustine put. His difficulty is that to know one must have more than words, one must have events. But a scripture does not give us events, rather words only:

I confess . . . that I believe rather than know that the things written in those stories were done at that time as they have been written; and those whom we believe knew the difference between believing and knowing. For the Prophet says: "If ye will not believe, ye shall not understand." Surely he would not have said that, had he not thought that believing and understanding are different. Therefore, what I understand I also believe, but I do not understand everything that I believe; for all which I understand I know, but I do not know all that I believe.[12]

---

[12] St. Aurelius Augustine, *Concerning the Teacher and on the Immortality of the Soul* (George G. Leckie, tr.), Appleton-Century-Crofts, New York, 1938, p. 47.

St. Augustine suggested to St. Anselm the formula *credo ut intelligam,* "I believe in order that I should understand." Believing is deficient in that one holds something true (or false) on the authority of some one else; that someone else may (or may not) have evidence for what he says. That, too, I cannot now know. One would think, then, that belief in scripture should be called "opinion." But to suggest this would, from the position of the religion itself, ignore two features that the religious man stresses. The first is that when one has mere opinion, this is quite compatible with doubting, or not being sure, or wavering. But the religious man tells us he does not doubt. Indeed he states he is quite sure. From the outside one may say that he confuses his subjective certitude with objective certainty. From the inside the religious man stresses yet another feature. If he is St. Augustine, he stresses that his religious belief is called "faith" rather than "opinion." The ancients might well have been surprised by the distinction. Now faith is connected with the ultimate well-being of the person. The word might better be translated as "trust," with a strong element of hope in what is to be the case. There is also an element of fear. If faith is necessary for salvation, then to lack faith is to fail to be moving toward God or heaven or ultimate bliss. We cite St. Augustine's theses:

Faith is needed—faith in God, which will make man good and faithful, enable him to endure the miseries of this life, and finally come to the life of eternal blessedness, when he may live as he will. The philosophers, in their pride, have thrown only a feeble light on this problem. We maintain that future blessedness is eternal, not as a result of human reasoning, but by faith.[13]

St. Augustine was well aware that his conversion demanded a radical readjustment of his philosophic orientation. Had he continued as a Mannichaean, he would not have accepted on faith what no Christian offered to demonstrate rationally. Had he continued as a Sceptic he would have stressed only the cognitive deficiency of faith. Had he continued a Platonist he would have relied upon his own rational powers and not expected genuine knowledge of the changing world in which, according to Christianity, the eternal or divine became united with the temporal or natural and human.

Thus philosophy for a thousand years and more came to be expressed in the dramatic language of the soul's inner history, and the career of mankind was believed subject to the threat of hell but proffered the bliss of heaven. Concern for the inner life and absorption in man's destiny have

[13] Whitney J. Oates (ed.), *Basic Writings of St. Augustine,* Random House, New York, 1948, Vol. II, p. 826.

continued since the Renaissance in no less vivid and vigorous ways. Despite the evident secularization, or statement in languages other than that of the Church, and even without belief in a God who loves men, or in any supernatural deity, the concern with human destiny has not vanished. Hence, Augustine is more than a bridge between pre-Christian and Christian philosophies. His thought is also a bridge between ancient and modern philosophies.

St. Thomas Aquinas. In the Middle Ages philosophy was largely concerned with problems that are primarily theological in character: questions about the existence and nature of God, the relation between reason and faith, the salvation of man, and the adaptation of Aristotelian physics to Christian doctrine. But we come now to a thinker who defended the autonomy of philosophy. Medieval thinkers were competent on nontheological questions also, among them literal and analogical language, pure and applied logic, universals, and metaphysical discourse on being as such.

The philosophy and theology of St. Thomas Aquinas (1225–1274) is the most balanced and complete expression of the learning and faith of the Christian Middle Ages. It is a grand design trying to do justice to each aspect of life within a scheme that seeks to keep things in proportion. Although St. Thomas quotes often from St. Augustine, he calls Aristotle "the philosopher," and he sets out to show that Aristotle's science and philosophy may be interpreted in accord with Christian theology. Philosophy is not to be absorbed into theology, nor theology into philosophy. They mutually supplement each other. The role of faith is necessary because there are men incapable of arriving at beliefs through the work of reason. But salvation must be open to them. Men ought not to go to hell merely because they are not philosophers. Moreover, with respect to those articles of faith for which we do not now have the evidence, all of us, including philosophers, argues St. Thomas, must accept the authority and decision of the Church, which is based on God's revelation. Though beyond reason, these articles can be shown by reason to be not contradictory in themselves, nor contradictory to any other knowledge.

One may easily stand in wonder at the works of St. Thomas. They constitute a cultural monument comparable in vastness and intricacy to a cathedral. A mere casual reading of his system in the Summa Theologica and Summa Contra Gentiles gives an impressionistic survey which seems as inappropriate as a tourist's account of what he saw in Canterbury Cathedral. The architectronic structure takes a master builder to appreciate. Each problem is stated as a question, such as "Whether there is a God?" Arguments follow against the proposition that God exists. Atheists are sometimes delighted to have their position stated forcefully, and here they may find it. St. Thomas then quotes Scripture against atheism. But this is not enough, for reason and fact also assure the believer that he can know demonstratively that God is. St. Thomas would not be happy with mere contrary opinion. He takes the atheistic arguments as serious objections to be answered seriously. So it goes, with each general area divided into questions, each question divided into articles, each article divided into arguments for and against a proposition. It is an astonishing and impressive march of ideas.

The central problem for St. Thomas is to reconcile Christian views with those of Aristotle. St. Thomas does not turn away from the interests and demands of this world to the sole contemplation of another transcendent world. He is too realistic for that. But how are these two worlds related? The answer he gives draws deeply from Aristotle. The universe is a hierarchy of substances from pure potency or matter to pure act or God. The facts of the inorganic world, man, and angels constitute the levels between. We shall later ask whether St. Thomas has indeed demonstrated God's existence. From the fact of God's existence he claims one can also demonstrate His nature, although His full essence can never be known. This much, and it is a great deal, can be shown, namely, that God is not material, therefore he is not compound or made up of parts. Therefore He is His own essence, and this means there is nothing in God not necessary to His own nature. Therefore He is completely actual, and can be said to lack nothing. Therefore He is perfect. Therefore He is supremely good and intelligent. Therefore He not only knows, but cares. Therefore He is the providential creator of all things, as well as First Efficient Cause and Final Cause.

St. Thomas is scrupulous in stating explicitly all the premises from which his conclusions follow. In general, if you grant this man his premises, his conclusions follow. That is, the mind cannot validly agree with the premises and adopt propositions contradictory to the conclusions. The conclusion of one syllogism is the premise of the next, so there is a great chain of propositions. He is also scrupulous in stating explicitly what he cannot demonstrate, because reason may adopt contrary premises. One such problem is whether the universe is eternal, as Aristotle held, or whether the universe had a temporal beginning. Thomas adopts the latter on faith. It is beyond reason, but not contrary to reason, that the world was created by God out of nothing, and that the world will end.

Likewise, in making out man's place within the ordered structure of the universe, some propositions are demonstrated, others cannot be demonstrated. But Thomists call attention to the coherence of the vision. Man fits into the structure as an animal participating in the natural realm. But he is also a rational spirit, participating in the divine or supernatural realm. He cannot be happy as a mere animal. He must also seek his supreme good in knowing God.

To attain such knowledge is to reach the degree of happiness that is possible in natural life. This end, however, cannot be gained by men in their individuality alone, for man is a social animal, able to find his natural good only in company with his fellows. He must, in short, live in communities. Thus, the state is required in order for men to attain their natural ends. Since to attain ends is good, the state is not morally suspect, as with St. Augustine. Although man is created with free will, which is necessary to make sense out of morality, God, through the operation of His providence, will bring some men to eternal salvation and abandon others to their own sin. This idea of the damnation of some men is, strangely enough, required by the goodness of God, for it is His goodness that demands that all possible grades of being be contained in the universe. Being, as being, is a value; and on St. Thomas' metaphysical grounds, whenever some potency has become actual, to that degree there is goodness.

It was in part through St. Thomas that the rudiments of the scientific achievement of Greece came to be adopted by the Christians. But Europeans had to go beyond Aristotle in method, because they went beyond him in knowledge of the world. This brought both St. Thomas and Aristotle into bad repute. Modern philosophy began as a revolt against them. Whether modern philosophy has misunderstood them and not improved them is not answerable in general. Each particular question must be taken up and dealt with in detail. Responsible followers of St. Thomas admit that he made errors in scientific points. But St. Thomas did no less than we can do today, namely, take the best achievements available at the time.

Duns Scotus. We can be more sure that Duns Scotus was a member of the Franciscan Order and a teacher in Oxford and Paris than about his dates (1266?–1308?) or his place of birth. His life will probably remain obscure, but his doctrines may in time become as well known as those of St. Thomas.

Few philosophers have been more cruelly treated in the corruption of their names into a term of contempt. Duns Scotus, Duns the Scot, the Subtle Doctor, had his name corrupted into "dunce." His life remains legendary, his significance debatable, his writings unknown to those who do not read Latin. We dare to explain a few of his points on faith and reason, because there ought to be some contrast to St. Thomas—not every philosopher of the thirteenth century was a Thomist, nor is every Catholic philosopher today.

Duns draws subtle distinctions between belief and knowledge. One of his examples is helpful to us:

Suppose there were a mind not able to understand geometrical propositions, it could nevertheless believe they were true; nevertheless geometry would be in itself a science, because it would be so to an intellect capable of understanding it.[14]

This is a point still worth making: science is knowledge to the scientist who knows the demonstrations and experiments. To the rest of us it is a matter of belief, for to quote scientific words is not to have adequate scientific knowledge. The more knowledge experts claim in many fields, the more faith is required of the nonexpert that the experts really know. Scotus' question is: to what extent do we have knowledge of God, in other words, is theology a science?

Both St. Thomas and Duns work within the tradition that man should believe certain propositions even when he knows that he does not know. Evidence for these beliefs is lacking, that is, the object is not present, or known in itself. Nevertheless some propositions are matters of faith and not opinion, for the mind can be certain. What kind of certainty? Thomas tended to associate faith with argument. Duns tends to stress another side, not the intellectual content of our faith, but the nonintellectual character of our believing. This is called "will." It looks as though Duns were saying this: God is not primarily for us the most perfect being, or something to contemplate; God is primarily for us our supreme happiness, something to love and serve. If natural reason does not tell us how to attain this supernatural happiness, and guarantee sufficient means, God must give this to men if they are to fulfill their destiny.

But accepting propositions about God is quite different from accepting propositions of geometry. For one thing, since God is free, His acts are contingent upon His will. Since they cannot be said to be necessary, they cannot be deduced. Of course Aristotle included propositions about God in his first philosophy, and made such propositions in the context of his physics, or propositions about nature. But theology as a practical science deals with what man ought to love; it is a kind of wisdom found in a good life rather than a kind of "speculation" or theory.

[14] C. R. S. Harris, *Duns Scotus*, The Clarendon Press, Oxford, 1927, Vol. I, pp. 86–87. Freely translated from the Latin quoted by Harris.

Speculative knowledge concerns what must be so, and cannot be otherwise. But practical knowledge concerns what should be so, and may be otherwise.

Yet medievalists warn us not to exaggerate the differences between Duns and St. Thomas. Duns also maintains that although philosophy and theology are each sovereign in their own spheres, truth is one, and faith and reason have one ultimate object. God's existence and nature are demonstrated by Scotus as by St. Thomas.

Theology is not ranked beneath the "theoretical" sciences; that is sciences concerned only with knowing. Quite the reverse, according to Duns. Theology is practical in its imperative role of directing the will to its supreme object. Theology, then, not only argues from the authority of sacred scripture, founded on divine revelation, but it also commands us to love God and shows us those actions by which He is worshipped and served.[15]

The Transition to Modern Philosophy. The philosophies that flourished during the early centuries of the Christian era were dominated by the desire to escape evil and to secure ultimate release from the world. We are tempted, therefore, to call these philosophies religion. By no means was Christianity the only alternative set of doctrines and way of life. But Christians insisted that their way was superior. The most exclusive position was that the wisdom of the Greeks is foolishness (St. Paul) and that man's reason is no asset in the quest for salvation. Were this the only position, we should mention the rise of Christianity only as the subversion of philosophy. But the view that finally triumphed was that philosophy can be useful in the attack by Christianity upon its alternatives. By "philosophy" here is meant chiefly Platonism, or more specifically Neo-Platonism, a religious philosophy remembered for the speculative doctrine that all the diversity of this world emanated from the primal unity of God's Spirit. This doctrine had its practical side, namely, that the human spirit could retrace the path whence it had come and find itself again united with God.

Of course Christianity, in common with Judaism and later Islam, appealed to more than mystical experience. This experience of the union of the soul with God was considered by the Church as in itself too private. One person may feel perfect assurance that does not convince another. Moreover, it lacked what the religious scriptures made eminent, namely, practical morality. But the question arises, for example, in Augustine, what evidence do we have that what scripture asserts is true? The events mentioned are past, and prophecies of the future are even more difficult to

[15] *Ibid.*, pp. 92–93, 94, 95–96, 99, 102–103.

check for veracity. Hence, if scriptures are to be accepted, it must be on "faith"; there must be an attitude of trust. But why trust the testimony of scriptures when one cannot employ sense or reason to guarantee their trustworthiness? This problem remains foremost in philosophy for a thousand years after St. Augustine.

Is faith knowledge? A Christian trained in philosophy could not claim this. And if faith is not knowledge, should it not be classed with opinion? He could not remain a Christian if he drew this conclusion. Hence, appears the doctrine that in addition to our human capacities for knowledge and opinion is another capacity for faith, which is superior even to knowledge because it comes to man as a gift from God, or by grace. St. Thomas admitted faith as a mean between opinion and knowledge, like opinion in that evidence is deficient, but like knowledge in its certainty.

At the close of his fine work on the history of Christian philosophy in the Middle Ages, Gilson has this to say:

Something happened to philosophy during the fourteen centuries which we call the middle ages. The easiest way to see what happened to it is to remember the general view of the world propagated by the last Greek philosophers and to compare it with the interpretation of the world common to the founders of modern philosophy, namely, Descartes, Malebranche, Leibniz, Spinoza and Locke. In the seventeenth century, the commonly received philosophical notions of God, of the origin of the world, of the nature of man and of his destiny are strikingly different from those which the middle ages had inherited from the Greeks. Strict monotheism, an undisputed truth in the minds of all the metaphysicians of the thirteenth century, is only one of the points in case. In its content, the metaphysics of Descartes was much more a continuation of the metaphysics of the scholastics than of the Greeks. He himself was a Christian and it is no wonder that his philosophy continued, in a most original way, the tradition of the Christian theology of the middle ages. True, Descartes called it a philosophy, and it certainly was one, but the upshot of his *Meditations on Prime Philosophy* was to confirm by a new method all the main conclusions already established in metaphysics by Augustine, Anselm, Bonaventure, Thomas Aquinas and Duns Scotus: The existence of one single God, infinite in being and in power, free creator of heaven and earth, conserving the world by his all-powerful will and acting as a Providence for man whose soul can be proved to be spiritual in nature. With Descartes, Malebranche and Leibniz, the point of departure of modern philosophy coincides with the point of arrival of medieval theology. Even Spinoza cannot be fully accounted for without taking into account the speculation of the middle ages. To overlook what happened to philosophy in the thirteenth century is to deprive the history of Western thought of its continuity and, by the same token, its intelligibility.[16]

[16] From *History of Christian Philosophy in the Middle Ages,* by Etienne Gilson. Random House, New York, p. 542 (c) Copyright 1955 by Etienne Gilson.
Reprinted by permission of Random House, Inc. and Sheed & Ward Ltd., London.

There is undoubtedly much that is true in this statement. But it would be fallacious to draw from it the conclusion that modern philosophy is only a kind of echo of certain phases of medieval thought. For in modern philosophy there is revolt against the past based not only on new methods, but on new discoveries about the world. Let us turn now to these developments.

IV. *The Major Themes of Modern Philosophy*

The philosophy of the Renaissance was marked by an exuberant interest in the viewpoint and values of ancient Greece and Rome, by a high optimism for the future, by a declining attachment to the supernaturalism or other-worldliness of the Middle Ages, by the exciting rediscovery of this world, and by an increased enthusiasm for man and his powers which developed into a movement called humanism. Humanism took either the form of admiration of the classics, or planning a future from the applications of science to this world. Some say that this view was neither new nor profound, nevertheless, the spirit and the attitude of Renaissance man brought philosophy out of the theological interests which had dominated it.

Modern philosophers, too, were critically interested in the problems of knowledge, belief, and opinion, and in all that followed upon taking a certain view of these concepts. They not only rejected some beliefs of their predecessors, but also looked for a new and different method in thinking that would enable man to transform his opinions into knowledge. The past, of course, could not be completely excised, nor should we expect it to be. All philosophies have their antecedents without which the present is inexplicable and in part incomprehensible.

Man not only will have knowledge and believe that he can devise ways to attain it, but he will also strive to translate his knowledge into practical human achievement. When ancient answers fail to satisfy present problems, man turns his back on old ways and seeks a new direction for his mind. Thus is born a Novum Organum, a Discourse on Method, a work On the Improvement of the Understanding, and another on The Principles of Human Knowledge, to mention only some of the outstanding expressions of man's desire to bring his beliefs nearer to knowledge and farther from opinion. From what he can claim to know come the central beliefs man holds about himself, his world, and his society. Belief may outrun knowledge but if it gets too far ahead without steady scrutiny and critical testing, then the knowledge itself is drowned in a stream of irrationalism. Modern philosophy is born in the spirit of criticism.

Bacon. Let us begin with Francis Bacon (1561–1626). He complains that philosophy had fallen into disrepute and that it was infested with errors. He revolts against the method of the Scholastics, as the philosophers and theologians of the Middle Ages were called. What is this method against which he rebels? It involved two characteristic features: first, the acceptance of certain truths as revealed, including reliance upon the authority of the Bible and the Church; and second, the deductive and syllogistic procedures of Greek logic. Bacon was convinced that this method was responsible for the miserable status of philosophy and had produced the "distempers of learning," such as beliefs in ghosts, miracles, and magic; a great deal of controversy with little effect; and a kind of dilettantism that brought forth many polished phrases but no real substance or meaning in philosophy.

Above all, he says, philosophy should be practical and secular. The human mind, applying itself to the secrets of nature, gains control over the environment, and this is man's greatest concern. Knowledge is power. A new instrument for acquiring it was designed by Bacon. If one is to get genuine knowledge of the world, to the world one must go, accumulating large numbers of particular facts which are seen to be so. When these are properly classified, the laws of nature and her secret connections will appear. This is the beginning of a deliberate attempt to substitute inductive for deductive logic, and it will be taken up again in the next chapter.

Bacon also draws attention to a number of fallacies with which philosophy is threatened, and insists that they must be eliminated if knowledge is to be achieved. He calls these fallacies "idols" and we must give a brief survey of them. There are first, the idols of the Cave, which are the prejudices peculiar to the individual and which vary from person to person. Many of them arise because of the dominance of a favorite subject or topic, so that the individual is less critical than he ought to be. Second, are the idols of the Tribe. These are the prejudices common to the race of man that interfere with scientific thinking, such as the tendency to believe only what is agreeable, to see purpose in all things, to interpret everything anthropomorphically, and so on. Third, are the idols of the Market Place. These arise in part because of the ambiguity of language and lead us to assume that there exist things corresponding to all the names we use. Thus we tend to make entities out of chance, fortune, witch, and fail to distinguish between literal and metaphorical meanings. Finally, there are the idols of the Theater, by which Bacon means that overconfidence in and loyalty to special systems of thought and philosophy. All of these result in the failure of man's critical powers and turn him away from knowledge.

Kepler and Galileo. Others also were objecting to the methods of the scholastics. Johannes Kepler (1571–1630) and Galileo Galilei (1564–1642) with great ingenuity and resourcefulness of method were making significant discoveries in astronomy. The latter, however, ran into ecclesiastical and academic opposition. In a letter to Kepler he describes his predicament and disgust.

I wish, my dear Kepler, that we could have a good laugh together at the extraordinary stupidity of the mob. What do you think of the foremost philosophers of this University? In spite of my oft-repeated efforts and invitations, they have refused, with the obstinacy of a glutted adder, to look at the planets or the Moon or my glass [telescope]! . . . Why must I wait so long before I can laugh with you? Kindest Kepler, what peals of laughter you would give forth if you heard with what arguments the foremost philosopher of the University opposed me, in the presence of the Grand Duke, at Pisa, labouring with his logic-chopping argumentations as though they were magical incantations wherewith to banish and spirit away the new planets [the satellites of Jupiter] out of the sky.[17]

Galileo's method was an improvement over Bacon's. Four principles in the achievement of knowledge seem to have guided his thinking. First, reduce explanations to the fewest and simplest possible. Second, when going to the world for observations, have some hypothesis in mind that will help to eliminate all that is irrelevant. Third, whenever possible resort to measurement. Fourth, find the variable degrees of the phenomena present under certain circumstances.

With Galileo, experiment began to modify dogmatic argument, and quantitative expression to replace classification and the search for essences. It was an important step leading to science as we know it today. Among the conclusions to which Galileo was led was the distinction between two kinds of qualities of things, namely, those that are basic, absolute, and independent of the observer, and those that are relative to the observer. Thus, color and sound appear only when an observer is present, but figure, magnitude, and motion exist independently of the fact that they are being known. This distinction must be kept in mind in our brief history, for it appears again and again.

Newton. With the aid of more precise instruments and sharply defined procedures, a picture of the physical world was being formed culminating in the grand vista of Newtonian physics. Galileo's method brought him

[17] A. Wolf, *History of Science, Technology, and Philosophy In the 16th & 17th Centuries,* The Macmillan Co., New York, 1935, p. 29.

to the conclusion that motion among bodies is primary, and physical phenomena for the most part must be explained in terms of motion. For Isaac Newton (1642–1727) the world was one vast machine, operating according to mathematically determined laws that apply everywhere. It is composed of matter, which in turn is made up of hard, indestructible atoms moving in "absolute" space and "absolute" time. In man is a soul, locked in the body, somewhere in the brain, getting its knowledge via the nerves, which transmit the images of objects. The entire scheme of the universe in all its magnificence and order has been intelligently planned, and created, and is now governed by a living, powerful, eternal, and infinite being.

Hobbes. Thomas Hobbes (1588–1679) had little sympathy or patience with experimental science. Although he was not himself an experimenter, his method and system is a clear prophecy of a psychology based on knowledge of physiology, and an interpretation of man by the methods called "naturalistic," because there is no break between physical nature and the supposedly "spiritual" aspects of man. His delight in mathematics assured him that this method is needed in philosophy, the proper approach to which is deduction.

Deductive procedures should give us exact definition and lead to what is most important in philosophy, namely, coherence. All reasoning is really a kind of reckoning, illustrated most perfectly in mathematical calculation. In his metaphysics Hobbes is a thoroughgoing materialist, insisting that motion is the one cause of all phenomena and therefore philosophy is really a study of the motion of bodies. The main areas of interest for philosophy and knowledge are body, man, and society. Bodies consist of atoms which have extension and motion. Consciousness too is an atomic phenomenon, that is, associated with the movement of atoms. It arises when the body is disturbed by impact from the atoms outside. When the atoms in the body move tranquilly we are in a pleasurable state and this is good, but when they move violently, we are in pain and this is evil. Thus Hobbes, to this degree, belongs with the ancient Stoics, who made tranquillity the goal of life. Man himself is a naturally selfish, egotistical body, a condition that leads to continual warfare against his neighbors, and in this natural state the life of man is "solitary, poor, nasty, brutish, and short." This intolerable situation gives rise to society and government, in which men agree to respect each other's rights, not from any altruistic motives, but for protection and expediency. Hobbes offered a political system of absolutism in which the ruler is sovereign over practically all of life. His commands define what his subjects must believe and his prohibitions define what they must not believe. Such a policy Hobbes recommends to keep men from fighting their neighbors. It makes for survival.

Descartes. We have already mentioned the great confidence modern philosophers were placing in mathematical thinking and knowledge. In René Descartes (1596–1650) this comes to full fruition. Like Bacon, he too became disgusted with the number of different opinions offered by various philosophers, each claiming his was true. He decided to start afresh and dismiss all the work of the past philosophers and strike out on his own. This, of course, he could not do without a method, and he was so impressed with the clearness and consistency of mathematical demonstration that he sought for a way of reaching similar certainty in philosophy.

In 1637 he published his famous Discourse on Method, in which four steps of a new method are proposed. First, one should doubt systematically everything that is not as "clear and distinct" as the elements of mathematics. Second, one ought to break up a problem into its constituent parts rather than try to solve it all at once. Third, beginning with the most simple parts, that is, the most clear, one should work toward the complex, always extending the area of clarity. And fourth, there should be continuing review of the steps to be sure nothing of importance has been left out and no errors have crept in.

Whether Descartes' philosophy is a result of the close application of this method may be questioned, but at least it stated his aim. His effort to doubt revealed what he regarded as a self-evident principle, namely, that he could not doubt unless he existed. Thus, the famous *cogito ergo sum:* "I think, therefore I am," is introduced into modern philosophy. This gave Descartes his first island of certainty. From it he derived the existence of God and the world by the following steps.

First, as we have seen, we exist as thinking beings. This means we are in possession of ideas. They can be classified in three ways, as *factitious,* that is, those that we have constructed ourselves, such as mermaids, sirens, and hippogryphs; as *adventitious,* that is, those that come to us by the impact of things in the external world upon us; and third, *innate,* that is, those that are grounded in our being so that we would not be the beings we are without them. They are born and produced in us at the moment of our creation. Among the ideas we have is the idea of God, that is, the idea of an infinite being. As a finite being cannot produce the idea of an infinite being, such an idea cannot be factitious. Nor do we ever have experience of the impact of an infinite being, so it cannot be an adventitious idea. Therefore the idea of God is innate, that is, God "put this idea in my nature in much the same way as an artisan imprints his mark on his work."[18]

Now that we have the self and God, we need only to get the world to complete one of the most remarkable "triumphs" over doubt in the history of thought. Briefly the argument is something like this. God exists. He is a perfect being. Therefore, he would not deceive us. Hence we can trust our best-tested sense-judgments which tell us that there is a world.

Finally we must mention those beliefs of Descartes' that lead to a dualistic view of the world. He finds two substances, namely, things that are conscious but unextended—these are minds; there are also things that are extended but unconscious—these are bodies. Thus mind and matter are the ultimate substances of the world.

Here we must leave Descartes. There is much more of great interest, but that is for the student to discover on his own.

Spinoza. So enamoured of the rigor and precision of mathematics were some of the philosophers, that it became the model as well as the aim for much of their work. Benedict Spinoza (1632–1677), for instance, wrote his chief work in the form of a geometry book. It took twelve years of patient labor to get it expressed. Even a casual glance at Spinoza's Ethics: Proved in Geometrical Order, will show that it really does resemble a geometry book. Here are definitions, axioms, propositions, and corollaries. Every sentence following the definitions and axioms refers to a previously proved statement. We cannot possibly present the great richness of his thought in a short sketch, and only a portion of its basic structure can be offered here. We cannot enter into proof, or argument, or dialectic; but we may try to set forth his basic beliefs.

Let us begin with a belief that is at the foundation of his work, namely, the world is one and it is rational. Spinoza is not speaking of a political, or economic, or ethical oneness, but rather of a logical unity. The world has on a vast scale the kind of unity exhibited by a vigorous mathematical proof. Each step is absolutely necessary. It is a rational world because it is completely open to reason. There is no obscure corner of mystery. What is, can be understood, because what is, is a magnificent, interdependent, interconnected system of ideas. And now comes the shock: this rigid, necessary system is what Spinoza calls God. Sometimes he calls it nature, sometimes merely substance. But he prefers to call it God. Thus God is the one real existence, everything else is less real. Such a deity is obviously not a person. It cannot be Father, or Judge, or Creator, yet, says Spinoza,

---

[18] From René Descartes, *Meditations*, New York 1951. Reprinted by permission of the publishers, The Liberal Arts Press, Inc., p. 46.

It is divine and to know It is to be led to a peace the world cannot give or take away. The world is One, the One is God, and God is reality.

To some degree we must resist this idea, for to us there are a multitude of particular objects in the world, this tree, this pain, and this day, which seem to be real. And what of man? Is he too merely a passing ripple on an ocean of being, with no real importance or worth? This leads to the second basic belief in Spinoza's philosophy. Anything, including man, may be viewed from two aspects: from the aspect of its independence of the One and its relation to other temporal things, or from its dependence and its relation to the eternal One. When seen from the first point of view, all things are found to be rigidly necessary, precisely determined. There is no freedom, no liberty. It is a world of irrevocable causal processes, with consequences following antecedents in irresistible constancy. In relation to things man is caused, sustained, and destroyed by them. We are as finite and transient as they are.

But there is another aspect. Man is an incident only with relation to other incidents, but he may be viewed also with relation to the Infinite, and then he is no longer enslaved by circumstance. He may see himself as an essential part of the whole universe, not as a fleeting manifestation, but as real as God himself, and real because he is a necessary part of God. Once he sees this, man is saved. He rids himself of all bondage to sorrow, despair, and terror. Whatever his lot, he feels no bitterness because things are what they are. It is as absurd for a man to complain that he is not an athlete instead of a cripple, or a genius instead of a fool, as it would be for a circle to complain because God had not given it the properties of a sphere.

Thus man fulfills his destiny when he forgets ephemeral goods and turns to the enduring good. When he releases himself from the mighty desires that bind him to things, and views his life *sub specie aeternitatis*, under the aspect of eternity, then and then only does he love God with his whole mind. Then and then only does he find happiness.

There is at the center of Spinoza's philosophy a conviction about knowledge and opinion. The latter is derived from hearsay, vague experience, and the manner in which we use words. Many of our beliefs have these as their sources. But genuine knowledge requires something else—a seeing of the connections of things, and their true essences. This cannot be reached by a process of inference. Here are his own words:

By *hearsay* I know my birthday, and that certain people were my parents, and the like: things of which I have never had any doubt. By vague experience I know that I shall die: and I assert that inasmuch as I have seen my equals undergo death, although they did not all live for the same space of time, nor died of the same illness. Again, by *vague experience* I know also that oil is good for feeding a flame, that water is good for extinguishing it. I know also that a dog is a barking animal, and man a rational animal: and thus I know nearly all things that are useful in life. We conclude one thing from another in the following manner: . . . after I know the nature of vision and that it has such a property that we see a thing smaller when at a great distance than when we look at it close, I can conclude that the sun is larger than it appears, and other similar things. Finally, a thing is said to be perceived *through its essence alone* when from the fact that I know something, I know what it is to know anything. . . ."[19]

Beyond what the senses reveal and what reason can deduce there is, for Spinoza, still a higher form of knowledge. He calls it intuition, but it is difficult to make out his exact meaning. It seems to refer to man's capacity to grasp the wholeness of things; to see the necessary interdependence and relatedness of all things, without becoming lost in the details. At any rate, such knowledge is never the cause of doubt or error. "He who has a true idea, knows at the same time that he has a true idea, nor can he doubt concerning the truth of the thing."

Leibniz. Hobbes, Descartes, and Spinoza have one thing in common— they all stress the mechanical interconnections of nature and its material existence. But we find a modification of this in Gottfried Wilhelm Leibniz (1646–1716). He was a brilliant critic of the materialistic, mechanistic world views of the preceding philosophers.

For him the world is not the monistic block of Spinoza; rather it is made up of an infinite number of psychical units called monads—each a kind of separate and independent soul, the life and behavior of which is strictly fixed. The monad is a simple substance, that is, without parts; it is unextended and indivisible, indissoluble, and imperishable. Monads are the elements of all things. They cannot be changed by any other created thing, but being created, they are subject to change, therefore the change can occur from an inner principle only. The monad is a multiplicity in unity, having a plurality of conditions and relations even though it has no parts. Such a condition is best represented in perception, so monads are small units of perception or consciousness, and they may be arranged in order, from those that are most alert to those that are in a state of perpetual swoon. These are the monads we know as matter.

Leibniz declares that the present state of any monad is a natural consequence of its preceding state, that is, its present is big with its future. Thus when we wake up from a deep sleep or faint, we become conscious,

---

[19] Benedict Spinoza, *Ethics*, E. P. Dutton & Co., Inc., New York, 1938, p. 233.

and therefore we must have had perceptions immediately before, for one perception can come only from another perception. Leibniz's theory of monads is worked out in his famous document called The Monadology. It is a fascinating account, and we recommend it to the student. The end result is a pluralistic world of unextended units of psychical force.

Leibniz also gives attention to various kinds of knowledge that result in various degrees of satisfaction or certainty. When we are able merely to distinguish one thing from another without being able to tell what the differences are or what the characteristics of the things are, we have confused knowledge. If we are able to explain its characteristics our knowledge is called distinct. "Such is the knowledge of an assayer who discerns the true gold from the false by means of certain proofs or marks which make up the definition of gold." But distinct knowledge has degrees, for we are not always clear about the concepts in the definition. When everything that enters into the definition is known distinctly, then we possess adequate knowledge. Finally, there is intuitive knowledge, that is, the mind grasps distinctly and at once all the "primitive ingredients" of a conception. This, says Leibniz, is "extremely rare as most human knowledge is only confused or indeed assumed."[20]

Two fundamental principles guide all reasoning:

. . . First, that of Contradiction, by means of which we decide that to be false which involves contradiction and that to be true which contradicts or is opposed to the false.

And second, the principle of Sufficient Reason, in virtue of which we believe that no fact can be real or existing and no statement true unless it has a sufficient reason why it should be thus and not otherwise. Most frequently, however, these reasons cannot be known by us.[21]

Given these principles, human knowledge ranges from the certainty of experienced sense-qualities to the formal certainty of logic. But in between lies most of our experience, and here we are largely confined to uncertainty and probability. In his New Essays, Leibniz writes of the degrees of knowledge. Although knowledge is contrasted to opinion, not all knowledge is equally certain or true. Nor is all that is classed with faith or opinion equally uncertain or dubious. There is no sharp break between knowledge and opinion. Just as there are degrees of excellence in the universe, from God who is perfect in every way, through the angels, to man, and down to conscious and unconscious things, so in opinion, faith,

---

[20] Gottfried Wilhelm Leibniz, Discourse on Metaphysics, Correspondence with Arnauld and Monadology (George Montgomery, tr.), The Open Court Publishing Co., La Salle, Illinois, 1945, pp. 41, 42.
[21] Ibid., p. 258.

and knowledge, between any two different instances, we may find an intermediate case. This is sometimes called the principle of continuity.

But there is in Leibniz also a vision of a universal calculus that would bring order to all human reflective activities and would resolve all quarrels and distinguish the certain from the uncertain, when the disputants would simply say to each other, "Let us calculate!" He never reached this goal, but his anticipation of the continuity between logic and mathematics came to be realized in the twentieth century.

Leibniz is also known in the history of thought as the author of the belief that this is the best of all possible worlds. By this he means that this world is only one out of an infinite number God could have willed; but God wills to create not just any world, only the best possible. Out of all the combinations, God sees one in which it is possible to achieve the greatest possible good with the least possible evil. He chooses this one. Voltaire, in anger and misunderstanding, wrote the famous Candide, to place Leibniz's theory in contempt.

The mind and attainments of Leibniz are poorly represented in such a brief statement of his beliefs. He had an enormous versatility and mobility of thought and made significant contributions to law, science, mathematics, and other fields. He and Newton discovered independently the differential calculus. It is not an exaggeration to call him one of the great seminal minds of Western civilization.

Locke. One of the most important intellectual forces in seventeenth-century England was John Locke (1632–1704). He was drawn to philosophy by a chance incident, which you may read about in his enormously influential book, An Essay Concerning Human Understanding.

There is in all his works a common theme, namely, the futility of empty words and of mere acquiescence in tradition at the expense of hard, vigorous mental labor, based on real facts. He cannot accept Descartes' belief in innate ideas, and he presents a thoroughgoing criticism of them. In fact, he rejects the approach of the Continental rationalists who accounted for knowledge by finding its origin or source in the mind itself. All knowledge, Locke insists, comes from experience. And experience is simply having ideas that arise from contact with the external world. The ideas may be of two sorts, simple and complex. The former are derived from one sense, for example, color, heat, sound, and so forth; the latter may be derived from two or more senses, for example, space, extension, figure, motion. This suggests the distinction between two kinds of qualities we noted in Galileo, and they also became important to Locke. From now on we shall speak of them as *secondary* and *primary qualities*.

The mind itself has certain capacities of sensation, imagination, memory, judgment, etc., but it will not with these powers generate ideas. There must be an impact of the external world on the body and mind of the knower before knowledge is possible. Locke does not regard the mind as inert; it is capable of activity, and is somehow waiting to be set in motion by experience. But in the sense that it possesses no ideas whatsoever until experience happens, it is a *tabula rasa,* a blank tablet upon which no impressions are made, or perhaps a clean white sheet of paper not yet the bearer of writing or print. The belief that all knowledge is said to originate in experience, usually sense-experience, is termed empiricism.

Locke, of course, had other interests than the question concerning the origin of knowledge. In modern philosophy the problem of the organization of society was also a living issue. Nearly all the great philosophers rounded out their philosophies with well-defended beliefs in this area. As the foundations of medieval society gave way, the necessity for a theoretical and practical solution of the increasingly complex social and political problems became apparent. In most instances these solutions were made consistent with other beliefs held by the philosophers with respect to nature, the self, and human destiny. Locke took a strong position against the divine right of kings and insisted that no people should be governed without their consent. He proposed a constitutional government that would be rejected if and when it opposed or defied the will of the people.

Berkeley. The problems of the self, knowledge, substance, and God received subtle and careful analysis from one of Great Britain's most influential philosophers, George Berkeley (1685–1753). He criticizes the distinction between secondary and primary qualities on the grounds that the latter are never found separate from the former. But the secondary qualities depend for their existence upon a perceiving mind, so, therefore, do the primary qualities. The key phrase in Berkeley's thought is *esse est percipi,* to be is to be perceived. The elaboration of these beliefs leads Berkeley eventually to a view that is strictly antimaterialistic, that is, all things depend upon mind for their existence, either an individual mind or a Supreme Mind. If all we can know are our sensations and ideas, then there is no way of proving the existence of material substance; it is a useless term in philosophy and ought to be discarded. In Berkeley's universe there are only spirits and their ideas.

Common-sense knowledge seems satisfactory and is usually undisturbed, says Berkeley. It is only when we begin to reflect, to reason, to meditate, that scruples and doubts begin to arise. This may be due to our limited capacity to understand the nature of things or to the faulty use we make of our own intellectual powers, or to the nature and abuse of language. But many of our perplexities and errors arise because we have the opinion that we can frame abstract ideas of things. Berkeley tells us what he means: the mind, it is claimed,

. . . by leaving out of the particular colours perceived by sense that which distinguishes them one from another, and retaining that only which is common to all, makes an idea of colour in abstract which is neither red, nor blue, nor white, nor any other determinate colour. And, in like manner, by considering motion abstractedly not only from the body moved, but likewise from the figure it describes, and all particular directions and velocities, the abstract idea of motion is framed; which equally corresponds to all particular motions whatsoever that may be perceived by sense.[22]

In addition it is said that we have abstract ideas about man, animals, body, and so on, which have none of the attributes of men, animals, or bodies. Berkeley doubts that such abstracting can occur and denies that he is able to do it, therefore, he concludes that the abstract ideas do not exist. We have been led to believe in them by the misuses of language. Our knowledge is properly limited to particulars, and these particulars are ideas. Thus the objects of all knowledge are ideas, either of sensation, feelings, or images, but reflection upon these will lead us to belief in spirit, God, and the immortality of the soul. Because we shall meet Berkeley's arguments again in Chapter V we will have to leave him now with these fragmentary suggestions of his philosophy.

Hume. David Hume (1711–1776), another British philosopher of extraordinary influence, insists that all knowledge comes from experience and is limited to the world of phenomena that experience reveals. His name is largely associated with scepticism in knowledge, agnosticism in religion, associationism in psychology, humanism and utilitarianism in morals and politics, and positivism in methodology. He agrees with Locke in rejecting innate ideas—all our ideas must be traceable to sense-impressions (although Hume seems to have made an exception in the case of mathematical ideas).

Among a person's ideas are those of substance, cause, and the self. With respect to the first, Hume finds it impossible to get an "impression;" we get only experienced qualities. Thus we have no real conception of substance, either physical in Descartes' sense, or spiritual in Berkeley's sense. Again, because the idea of cause as a necessary connection between

[22] George Berkeley, *The Principles of Human Knowledge,* The Open Court Publishing Co., La Salle, Illinois, 1904, p. 9.

events cannot be traced to an impression, cause can mean only the conjunction of two events we habitually associate on the basis of previous impressions. That is, because we observe that A follows B constantly, we develop a habit of expectancy that it will continue to do so. And this is all we can mean by cause. With respect to the self, again Hume fails to find one impression. All we get is some impression of color or warmth or feeling, but never an impression of an identity which preserves itself throughout all changes. His famous statement is:

> When I enter most intimately into what I call *myself*, I always stumble on some particular perception or other, of heat or cold, light or shade, love or hatred, pain or pleasure. I never can catch *myself*, at any time without a perception, and never can observe any thing but the perception.[23]

Our beliefs, says Hume, arise from the constant conjunction of things experienced together.

> All belief of matter of fact or real existence is derived merely from some object, present to the memory or senses, and a customary conjunction between that and some other object. Or in other words; having found, in many instances, that any two kinds of objects—flame and heat, snow and cold—have always been conjoined together; if flame or snow be presented anew to the senses, the mind is carried by custom to expect heat or cold, and to *believe* that such quality does exist. . . .[24]

Philosophers had traditionally distinguished between knowledge and belief on the basis of the objects known, for example, knowledge relates to the permanent and unchanging objects, while belief relates to the changing world. But Hume claims we do not know objects, but only impressions, or ideas. How then should we distinguish between fantasy and fact, between poetry and information, or as he puts it, between "fiction and belief." He does not want to fall into this difficulty and so admits that we can know the difference. "We can, in our conception, join the head of a man to the body of a horse; but it is not in our power to believe that such an animal has ever really existed."[25] If the difference between fiction and belief is not in the object of belief, not in the ideas, then, says Hume, it must be found in "some sentiment or feeling." Although Hume cannot define this feeling, we are said to know it. "Belief is the true and proper name of this feeling; and no one is ever at a loss to know the meaning of that term; because every man is every moment conscious of

[23] David Hume, *A Treatise of Human Nature* (L. A. Selby-Bigge, ed.), The Clarendon Press, Oxford, 1896, p. 252.
[24] David Hume, *Enquiries Concerning the Human Understanding* (L. A. Selby-Bigge, ed.), The Clarendon Press, Oxford, 1927, p. 46.
[25] *Ibid.*, p. 48.

the sentiment represented by it."[26] But if belief cannot be defined adequately, it may be described as "a more vivid, lively, forcible, firm, steady conception of an object, than what the imagination alone is ever able to attain."[27]

We often say that one account of an event "feels real" or "feels convincing," but is it not also true that fiction can be more vivid, lively, and forcible than factual accounts? Could we, on Hume's basis distinguish fiction from fact in Tolstoy's War and Peace? And why may not a very personal metaphysical system, say Spinoza's, present a more "firm, steady conception" of the world than a scientific theory? Are logical tests not needed for checking on our beliefs? But if so, how can this be reconciled with Hume's theory that belief is nothing but a sentiment?

Why, asks Hume, do we believe a friend is in the next room when we hear a voice? His answer is that we have associated our friend's look with his sound, and custom is the explanation of the belief-feeling. Thus, in his famous theory of association, *"Resemblance, Contiguity,* and *Causation;* which are the only bonds that unite our thoughts together . . . beget that regular train of reflection or discourse, which, in a greater or less degree, takes place among all mankind."[28] We then associate the sound of the voice as the effect of our friend, who is the cause of the sound.

But suppose that we are accustomed to sounds from phonographs and radios. Sounds may not then give us the belief that our friend is in the next room, but only that his voice comes from a machine. Hume would not regard this as fatal to his position. We simply have presupposed a different "belief of the correlative object." But then how could we settle the issue between Hobbes and Berkeley? Bodies felt real to Hobbes, and spirits unreal. Spirits felt real to Berkeley and bodies unreal. On Hume's grounds we must say they each had different presuppositions, and that men differ in this respect. Faced with this problem Hume makes a last defense. There is "a kind of pre-established harmony between the course of nature and the succession of our ideas . . . ."[29] Other philosophers too had taken this way out. Descartes, for example, thought that God would not deceive us. We find in the history of philosophy a number of instances in which deeply sceptical minds confess that in the end we must rely on faith of some kind.

Kant. Immanuel Kant (1724–1804) was a philosopher of such immense importance that no contemporary thinker can be excused for going around

[26] *Ibid.,* pp. 48–49.
[27] *Ibid.,* p. 49.
[28] *Ibid.,* p. 50.
[29] *Ibid.,* p. 54.

him. He gathered up the beliefs and difficulties of past thought and forged answers that, together with his original contributions, set the program of philosophical thinking for generations to come. It is utterly impossible to give more than a vague sense of the direction his thought took, but his beliefs are so crucial for understanding much of modern philosophy that we must have a look at some of them, beginning with those that appeared in perhaps the most famous work of modern philosophy, The Critique of Pure Reason.

Kant agrees with Locke, Berkeley, and Hume that all our knowledge begins with experience, but from this it does not follow that "it all arises out of experience." What is this knowledge that does not arise out of experience? There are two ways in which a person may have knowledge about his world; he may sense it, or he may think about it. Let us ask the question, what is it without which we could not get sense-knowledge of things; or put another way, given our sensory equipment, what are the conditions necessary for knowing any sensible thing? If we are to have knowledge, these conditions must be universal—that is, apply to all know-ers—and necessary—that is, without them knowledge is impossible. The conditions Kant gives for sensory knowledge are space and time. This means that if these two conditions are absent, no sensible thing can be known. Experience can never give us universal and necessary knowledge. Thus space and time belong to the knower and not to the world. We impose these forms upon the world.

If we think about our world we must also do so in certain universal and necessary ways, which also belong to the knower. These Kant calls *categories of the understanding*, such as quantity, quality, relation, and modality. All knowledge that has this character, that is, which is universal and necessary, Kant calls a priori. But neither the knowledge we have from the senses, nor that from the understanding gives us knowledge of reality—we learn only about a world of appearance, never in this way about the reality of which this world is an appearance. In Kant's words we never have knowledge via the senses or understanding of "things-in-themselves." There is always a curtain of appearances between us and the real.

Space and time and the categories are said to be constitutive of knowledge. In addition, however, we possess ideas of reason, such as the soul, the cosmos, and God. These are simply names for ways in which we organize the data we get from the senses and thought and therefore are not constitutive but, as Kant puts it, regulative. In this case God, for example, is not a being but merely a regulative principle of knowledge. The Critique of Pure Reason thus shows the limitation of knowledge and is sceptical about getting knowledge of God in the ways described.

But Kant had by no means finished his work with the first Critique. He wrote a second, called The Critique of Practical Reason. In this he sought also for a priori knowledge, but for the moral life. He thought he found it in what he calls a *categorical imperative,* which states that in all cases of moral conduct one ought to act on a principle one would be willing to make a universal law. Then in order to make sense out of morality, that is to make it intelligible, one needs three *postulates,* Freedom, Immortality, and God. To say one ought to do something makes no sense unless one can do it, that is, be free to do it; inasmuch as the ought is never completely fulfilled, one must have an infinite time to work at it, thus immortality; and in a just world there must be a relationship between happiness and righteousness, else the nerve of duty is cut, therefore there must be a power great enough to bring about this union the moral individual is unable to achieve. This power is God—a postulate of the moral will.

Kant's beliefs were so rich in suggestions for various approaches to philosophical problems that an enormous literature has grown out of them, and even today philosophers must come to terms with him. His insistence that the self is essential to any knowing situation because it actually contributes to what the known object is, set a problem for philosophers that is still being debated.

Fichte. We have observed, since Descartes, the impressive role the self plays in all knowing. One of the most thoroughgoing philosophies of the self is that of Johann Gottlieb Fichte (1762–1814).

For him the world is a projection of the self, which in turn limits the self. If this is a difficult conception to grasp, think of a dramatist projecting his characters, which limits what he can do with the nature and development of his drama. Why the self posits the nonself has no ultimate answer. One may shed some light on this problem by analyzing moral thought and action. Only by struggle can one become a moral self; only by suffering does one become a mature moral being. Character, in short, must rise by overcoming opposition. Thus the self sets problems for itself in order to reach a higher self.

In his book, The Vocation of Man, Fichte works his way from a state of doubt, through knowledge, to faith. The crucial question is, "What am I and what is my vocation?" I have truth about things but no truth about myself. If I look to nature for an answer I end up in an intolerable condition because everything in nature is determined throughout. As a part of nature I am caught in its causal network and I am in fact the product of its power. Thus I am not free, but in my immediate consciousness I appear to be free. Fichte then rejects the rigid determinism in order to save moral freedom. That is, the freedom to accept or refuse the good, and thus give meaning to responsibility. Then comes the startling suggestion that to be free we must in some way make ourselves free. Therefore, we must already be that which we become in order to become so. In some sense we create ourselves so that in "knowledge and observation of outward things, we at all times recognize and observe ourselves only; and that in all our consciousness we know of nothing whatever but of ourselves and of our own determinate states."[30] But knowledge is not reality, it is only pictures and representations. There is always something lacking, namely, that which corresponds to the representation. "This want cannot be supplied by knowledge; a system of mere knowledge is necessarily a system of mere pictures, wholly without reality, significance or aim."[31] Thus neither my vocation nor myself can be found in nature or knowledge. Then comes the intuition that man is not only a knower but also a doer. "Not for idle contemplation of thyself, not for brooding over devout sensations; —no, for action art thou here; thine action, and thine action alone, determines thy worth."[32] Thus my existence points in one direction alone, namely, to do what I ought to do, to carry out my duty.

In short, there is for me absolutely no such thing as an existence which has no relation to myself, and which I contemplate merely for the sake of contemplating it;—whatever has an existence for me, has it only through its relation to my own being. But there is, in the highest sense, only one relation to me possible, all others are but subordinate forms of this:—my vocation to moral activity. My world is the object and sphere of my duties, and absolutely nothing more . . . .[33]

Such a belief, however, is based on faith not on knowledge. It leads Fichte ultimately to the further belief in an infinite mind which creates the world through the finite minds.

Hegel. Although the philosophy of Georg Hegel (1770–1831) is expressed in a language which is almost completely incomprehensible, it has had extensive influence, or perhaps it would be better to say that what his interpreters said was his philosophy has had widespread influence. It is

[30] Johann G. Fichte, *The Vocation of Man* (William Smith, tr.), The Open Court Publishing Co., La Salle, Illinois, 1940, p. 83.
[31] *Ibid.*, p. 91.
[32] *Ibid.*, p. 94.
[33] *Ibid.*, p. 108.

extremely difficult to read even a few pages of some of Hegel without wondering whether he knew what he was talking about. He is full of monumental obscurities.

It does seem clear, however, that knowledge for Hegel can be set forth only in the form of system; in fact truth can be realized only by systematic development, the achievement of which is the work of philosophy. This system is thoroughly rational, therefore to reason we must look for its character. Reason works in the following way: a certain position is established, or belief accepted, called the thesis. This contains within itself the seeds of its destruction or negation, which grow stronger, eventually becoming the antithesis. The opposition between thesis and antithesis propels thought to a higher stage, which includes elements of both, called the synthesis. What characterizes thought also characterizes reality. Thus the dialectic, as this movement is called, is found in nature and history. The real is, therefore, the rational and the rational the real.

Schopenhauer. A contemporary of Hegel's, Arthur Schopenhauer (1788–1860), finds his clue to reality not in the rational processes of the self, but in those changes and conditions usually associated with the active will. Thus it is in man's desires, passions, drives, not in his intellect, that we find the key to the beliefs he holds. Our consciousness has two sides: one a consciousness of our own selves, which is the will, and the other a consciousness of things, which is knowledge through perception of the external world. As one side comes to dominate, the other withdraws. There is an actual antagonism between the will and knowledge. The more we are conscious of the object, the less we are conscious of the subject, that is, of ourselves. But if consciousness of ourselves occupies our attention, the less perfect is our perceptual knowledge of the external world. It seems possible, then, to have genuine knowledge of the world of objects only when the will does not interfere, but remains perfectly silent. Such a condition, however, cannot be long maintained, the will is too insistent. So also with the intellect and the will. The function of the intellect is to know only the relations of things, but it too is primarily in bondage to the will, and although capable of achieving a "brief hour of rest," it cannot reach a "lasting emancipation."

With this we must leave the major beliefs of modern philosophers, always bearing in mind that we have done nothing more than sketch a few ideas in the complex movement of man's intellectual life, and that the reasons that were given for supporting or holding these beliefs, in short, the arguments, have not been presented. To get the arguments, the student is invited to courses in the history of philosophy where a much more sustained, thorough, and critical study than can be attempted here is made.

V. Contemporary Philosophy

It is impossible, of course, to present all the nuances of the movement of thought in contemporary philosophy, but a brief sketch may help you to appreciate its major lines of development, particularly if we direct your attention to the concepts of opinion, belief, and knowledge.

Every major philosophical tendency of our age is in some sense in revolt against its immediate predecessors. There are indeed traditionalists who adhere to some long-established system or philosopher, but these adherents to authority also tend to be truculent in rejecting contrary systems and in complaining about the neglect of their exalted masters. It is also apparent that the social, biological, and physical sciences have brought enormous contributions of factual and theoretical knowledge to the philosopher. As the sciences have become more specialized, more accurate, more critical, the philosopher's debt to them has increased. The temptation to say more than one really knows, to out-talk the data, has always been one of the hazards of philosophy. As our store of facts from the sciences expands, this particular sin ought to be less frequently committed. Not only has factual knowledge been increased, but also scientific methods have been improved and refined. In the social sciences we no longer rely upon anecdotes, hasty generalizations, and casual observation. Methods of research and the sharpening of statistical tools have aimed at the validation of knowledge and warned against wild or pontifical guesses. In the biological and physical sciences the story is similar—refine the methods, get the data, verify the knowledge. In short, the emphasis in the sciences has been naturalistic, that is, look for the explanation of events in terms of the known facts and laws. It has thus been empirical, that is, if you want to know what the world is like, go to the world to find out.

Peirce. One philosophy that has sought to express this new spirit and bring to completest fruition the results of science is known as pragmatism. You have heard of this view before in connection with James' defense of the "will to believe." He was not the first proponent of pragmatism, which he modestly called a new name for an old way of thinking. He owed much to his contemporary, Charles S. Peirce (1839–1914), a thinker whose neglect in his own age is being justly compensated for by his growing fame in ours.

Peirce's pragmatism is primarily a theory of the way to establish the meaning of certain concepts.

. . . If one can define accurately all the conceivable experimental phenomena which the affirmation or denial of a concept could imply, one will have therein a complete definition of the concept, and *there is absolutely nothing more in it*.[34]

Peirce illustrates his central principle by an example from theology, the doctrine of transubstantiation. Catholics maintain that the wine and bread are literally flesh and blood but sensibly possessing the characteristics of bread and wine. But, says Peirce, our idea of anything is just the idea of its sensible effects. Or consider the concept "hard." On Peirce's principle, if anything is called hard, it can mean only that is will not be scratched by many other substances. Similarly with weight. To say a body has weight is simply to say that in the absence of opposing force it falls.

The most striking feature of pragmatism, says Peirce, is its recognition of an inseparable connection between rational cognition and rational purpose. Thus we meet the pragmatic claim that knowledge is not merely a matter of the intellect but also a matter of will and action. Our beliefs, according to Peirce are habits of mind, while our doubts indicate the absence of habit. A rational person is one who has habits of belief, but who can also exercise control over them. Pragmatism is a forward-looking philosophy, with its eyes on consequences, on what follows, or, in short, the future. Peirce extends this key notion into the realm of meaning.

The rational meaning of every proposition lies in the future. How so? The meaning of a proposition is itself a proposition. Indeed, it is no other than the very proposition of which it is the meaning; it is a translation of it. But of the myriads of forms into which a proposition may be translated, what is that one which is to be called its very meaning? It is, according to the pragmaticist, that form in which the proposition becomes applicable to human conduct, not in these or those special circumstances, nor when one entertains this or that special design, but that form which is most directly applicable to self-control under every situation, and to every purpose. This is why he locates the meaning in future time; for future conduct is the only conduct that is subject to self-control. But in order that that form of the proposition which is to be taken as its meaning should be applicable to every situation and to every purpose upon which the proposition has any bearing, it must be simply the general description of all the experimental phenomena which the assertion of the proposition virtually predicts.[35]

Peirce's knowledge of science and the experimental method, along with his pragmatic principles, leads him to reject metaphysics as a philosophical

[34] Justus Buchler (ed.) *op. cit.*, p. 252.
[35] *Ibid.*, p. 261.

discipline. It is, he says, "meaningless gibberish" and "downright absurd." (However, the student should consider well whether one can reject metaphysics as such except on other metaphysical grounds.) At any rate, the pragmatic claim is in some respects simple and clear: The meaning of a belief is discovered in the difference made in the conduct of the person acting on the belief. If there is no consequent action there is no meaning. If there is no difference between consequent actions among men who use different forms of expression, then the beliefs are really the same. No one who reads the Hegelian literature produced during the late nineteenth century can fail to be grateful for the insistence that beliefs make some difference and that the consequences be made clear.

James. This principle was also defended by William James (1842–1910) as a method for settling philosophical problems. His classic statement is:

> The pragmatic method in such cases [that is, in cases of metaphysical dispute] is to try to interpret each notion by tracing its respective practical consequences. What difference would it practically make to any one if this notion rather than that notion were true? If no practical difference whatever can be traced, then the alternatives mean practically the same thing, and all dispute is idle.[36]

James was a physician and a psychologist. His Principles of Psychology is still worth reading, for he dealt with problems of knowledge and metaphysics, such as our belief or "feeling" that there is a real world. He acquired a reputation for championing the ideas, persons, and causes of many who were considered by scientists to be either misfits or mad. Thus he came to the defense of saints, mystics, and psychic mediums. Why?

Because the beliefs that seem to have the most momentous consequences are religious beliefs. The ordinary moral convictions of decent and respectable people are what society demands of them. But saints who give away all their property rather than invest it at 6 per cent compound interest have a charm James savored. We will have more to say about James and his pragmatism in Chapter IV.

Dewey. Quite in contrast to James is the attitude of John Dewey (1859–1953), although Dewey belongs in the pragmatists' camp. He fosters the extension of scientific method toward the study of society. The reconstruction of philosophy is to be a close partner of the reconstruction of our views of man in society, and this is to reconstruct society itself. James tended to warn off the sociologist, to leave the soul of man a privileged sanctum. But Dewey sees continuity in the development of a person so that we cannot say where the "physical" ceases and the "psychic" begins.

---

[36] William James, *Pragmatism*, Longmans, Green & Co., New York, 1928, p. 45.

Consequently, science has no limit to its realm. All of life falls in the realm of possible science. How can science achieve knowledge of man's values? By methods of inquiry shared by all the sciences. Whereas James comforted the devout by saying that they knew by faith and had "evidence of things unseen," Dewey leaves no doubt that theology in our age is the authoritarian preservation of superstition. Unless false beliefs are attacked and demolished, true beliefs cannot take their place.

In Dewey, then, there comes to prominence the doctrine that knowledge is distinguished from belief or opinion in that knowledge is inseparable from a method. Indeed the one thing worth knowing is how to carry out an experiment. This is "logic" for Dewey, and has very little to do with the syllogisms of Aristotle or the mathematical reckoning of Leibniz and Peirce. Whereas the latter strive for exactitude in the interest of certainty, that is, the kind of certainty found in Euclidean geometry, Dewey considers the very "quest for certainty" an erroneous ideal for a philosopher. So, in contrast to Plato and Aristotle and the great rationalists of the seventeenth century, Dewey would say be satisfied with "warranted" belief. Knowledge is not regarded as contemplation of the eternal, as in Plato, but rather as work upon a changing and fluid situation.

Dewey prefers to call his position instrumentalism, rather than pragmatism. He describes it as "an attempt to constitute a precise logical theory of concepts, of judgments and inferences in their various forms, by considering primarily how thought functions in the experimental determination of future consequences."[37] What a thing does is more important than what it is. How we think and should think rather than the nature of thought, how we behave and ought to behave rather than the nature of man, are the truly significant questions for Dewey.

Moore. Pragmatism was only one of a number of "isms" that appeared and developed around the turn of the twentieth century. There were in addition: idealism, materialism, realism, personalism, naturalism and so on. Some of these "types" of philosophy will be discussed in Chapter VII. The tendency of philosophies to be identified with schools or systems or types often led to the facile pigeonholing of philosophers and to the mistaken view that philosophical problems could be settled by affixing labels. As each system made claims to knowledge and truth and yet each differed in fundamental respects, it became increasingly difficult for some philosophers to accept any one of them. There seemed to be no adequate proof

[37] John Dewey, "The Development of American Pragmatism." In: Dagobert D. Runes (ed.), *Twentieth Century Philosophy*, Philosophical Library, Inc., New York, 1943, pp. 463–464.

86 / Philosophy: The Study of Alternative Beliefs

for any system and no clear statement of agreement even among the proponents of a given position. This situation was responsible, in part, for the repudiation of speculative philosophy or the effort to arrive at a comprehensive, synoptic account of nature and man. Disturbed by the failure of philosophy to solve its ancient and persisting problems, and by the barriers of disagreement among the systems, philosophers began to scrutinize more carefully what was actually asked and meant by the questions they raised. This led to the attempt to settle philosophical problems piecemeal rather than within an overarching system. Perhaps no better illustration of this new direction can be found than in the preface to Principia Ethica, written by George E. Moore (1873–1958) in 1903.

It appears to me that in Ethics, as in all other philosophical studies, the difficulties and disagreements, of which its history is full, are mainly due to a very simple cause: namely, to the attempt to answer questions, without first discovering precisely *what* question it is which you desire to answer. I do not know how far this source of error would be done away, if philosophers would *try* to discover what question they were asking, before they set about to answer it; for the work of analysis and distinction is often very difficult: We may often fail to make the necessary discovery, even though we make a definite attempt to do so. But I am inclined to think that in many cases a resolute attempt would be sufficient to ensure success; so that, if only this attempt were made, many of the most glaring difficulties and disagreements in philosophy would disappear. At all events, philosophers seem, in general, not to make the attempt; and, whether in consequence of this omission or not, they are constantly endeavoring to prove that 'Yes' or 'No' will answer questions, to which *neither* answer is correct, owing to the fact that what they have before their minds is not one question, but several, to some of which the true answer is 'No,' to others 'Yes.'[38]

Around the turn of the century the work of Moore began a movement in philosophy which has been called by some philosophers a revolution—a revolution, of course, in thought, not society. It was a turning away from traditional methods of philosophizing and an effort to devise a new way of looking at the philosopher's job and his problems. In general it was opposed to large-scale philosophizing, that is, to system-making, and sought rather to attack philosophical beliefs by way of "analysis." This is the key term, although it does not mean the same thing for all philosophers interested in the same end. Primarily analysis meant an effort to clarify the language in which philosophical problems were formulated, and by so doing show that the problem itself could be resolved. At least it tried to show that frequently so-called philosophical questions were really problems

[38] George E. Moore, *Principia Ethica*, Cambridge University Press, Cambridge, 1903, p. vii.

of language structure. Moore insisted that philosophical problems could be solved by a better understanding of the meaning of language, not in a purely verbal or literary sense, but in the sense that such a clarification will help one to understand the nature of a certain object or idea. Moore's simplicity and clarity of writing is well known in contemporary philosophy.

Russell. Two men besides Moore should certainly be mentioned for their contributions to the relation between philosophy and language, namely, Bertrand Russell and Ludwig Wittgenstein.

Russell has spent the greater part of his long and creative philosophic life trying to formulate and clarify the problems associated with belief, knowledge, and truth. He writes that his original interest in philosophy rose out of the desire to discover whether philosophy "would provide any defense for anything that could be called religious belief, however vague" on the one hand; and on the other he wanted to persuade himself that "something could be known, in pure mathematics if not elsewhere." Finding no defense for religious beliefs, he thought he could find certainty in mathematics. But in the end this hope too was abandoned, and the fundamental principle that remains for him is that we all "view the world from the point of view of the here and now, not with that large impartiality which theists attribute to the Deity."[39] But we cannot stay longer with Russell here.

Logical Positivism. One of the most distinctive features of contemporary philosophy also shows the profound influence of the achievements of science and mathematics, particularly with respect to their continuous improvement in method and the application of this method in some form to other aspects of human behavior. The position, if it can be called a position, is known as logical positivism. So many variations within the movement can be discerned that it is impossible to catch up with all of them in a brief description. However, it is probably not unfair to say that the positivists agree on at least three points:

First, they belong to and desire to extend the empiricist tradition. By this we mean that the term knowledge is applicable only to those beliefs characteristic of the sciences. All other forms of expression are designed to persuade or command or to evince or evoke emotion. The positivists like to make a distinction between cognitive beliefs and emotive beliefs. Only the former may become knowledge. Secondly, the positivists tend to regard the primary task of philosophy to be the clarification of language, through a process of logical analysis. Such analysis leads them to accept

[39] Bertrand Russell, "My Philosophical Development," *The Hibbert Journal*, Vol. 52, 1958, pp. 2, 8.

another kind of statement as cognitively significant, namely, those called tautological. The truth of these statements is unconditional. It is not established by appealing to empirical evidence, nor to other premises. It depends solely upon the structure of language or some other symbolic system. Thus "A is A" is a tautology. So is "a brown cow is a cow." Thirdly, the positivists consider any questions that cannot be answered by their methods to be meaningless, and therefore they assert that all questions incapable of empirical verification, primarily those of metaphysics, theology, and so on, are meaningless. Such interests reflect an emotional state not a state of affairs. Their proper expression is in poetry, not science.

Wittgenstein. In 1922 Ludwig Wittgenstein published his famous Tractatus Logico-Philosophicus. Its influence on linguistic philosophy has been enormous, and many of the features of this movement were developed from suggestions in the Tractatus.

Wittgenstein does not seek to solve or answer philosophical problems but rather asks in what senses these are problems and questions. He claims that philosophical questions are not genuine questions, they are puzzles, which need to be dissolved rather than solved. The puzzles arise from the forms of statements made in ordinary language, which in turn arise because we are dominated by certain "pictures." For example,

of every noun correlated with some visible or etherial substance; of private thoughts and feelings imprisoned in the body like genii in a bottle. One breaks the spell of such pictures by showing how variously most words are actually used and sometimes by inventing "language games" to suggest other possible uses.[40]

For Wittgenstein, philosophy gives no information about the world. It is a way of clarifying propositions that claim to report facts of the world. Philosophy is thus not a theory, but an activity. Wittgenstein rejects Moore's method. What we are looking for is not hidden, but before our very eyes. We must learn to examine the actual use of words in ordinary language. This is the right place to look, for then we shall gain an understanding of our problems. Thus the new emphasis in philosophy is on meaning. Ryle has summed it up well:

The story of twentieth-century philosophy is very largely the story of this notion of sense or meaning. Meanings (to use a trouble-making plural noun) are what Moore's analyses have been analyses of; meanings are what Russell's logical atoms were atoms of; meanings, in one sense but not in another, were what Russell's 'incomplete symbols' were bereft of; meanings are what logical considerations prohibit to the antinomy-generating forms of words on which

[40] Margaret Macdonald (ed.), *Philosophy and Analysis*, Blackwell, Oxford, 1954, p. 12.

Frege and Russell had tried to found arithmetic; meanings are what the members of the Vienna Circle proffered a general litmus-paper for; meanings are what the *Tractatus*, with certain qualifications, denies to the would-be propositions both of Formal Logic and of philosophy; and yet meanings are just what, in different ways, philosophy and logic are *ex officio* about.[41]

Since the work of Moore, and others with similar beliefs, the literature of philosophy has been enormously enriched by the work of philosophers who have been content to deal intensively with what previous philosophers might have considered mere fragments, or at least as preliminaries to the great tasks. We ought not to bring this brief account of contemporary movements and ideas to a close without some statement concerning the philosophy called existentialism.

Existentialism. It is by no means easy to say in a few lines what this view is all about, but perhaps the most basic beliefs of the existentialists can be set forth. One thing seems clear—existentialism is primarily a philosophy of man, not of nature. This links its present formulation to all the great past philosophers of human nature, such as Socrates, Augustine, and Nietzsche. The existentialists do not find their clues to the nature of man in the statistical summaries of sociologists, nor in the controlled experiments of the psychologists, nor in the microscope slides of the biologists, nor, in fact, in any of the interpretations of the social and natural sciences, rather, it is from the concrete, personal sense of existence that the categories for the description of reality are taken. When the individual man feels himself involved in the crises of life, for example, death, or the need for making moral choices, he is agonizingly aware of his own existence and its finitude. Then he experiences despair and anxiety. In the atheistic branch of this philosophy, represented largely by Jean-Paul Sartre, these experiences teach that there is no reason for existence—life is without purpose or meaning. In the theistic group, these experiences stress the total otherness of God from man. This group stems from the work of the Danish philosopher, S. Kierkegaard (1813–1855), and has among its contemporary representatives Gabriel Marcel and Martin Buber.

This rapid excursion through some of the beliefs of some of the major philosophers in the history of thought is presented with the hope that it will be useful to the student. We have been limited to giving a minimal account of the march of philosophy, and we have left it to you to add more, to criticise the doctrines you discover, and to consider how theories apply.

[41] Gilbert Ryle, *The Revolution in Philosophy*, Macmillan and Co., Ltd., London, 1956, p. 8.

Many men of great stature, and many beliefs of great vitality and significance have been omitted in this survey, but it is hoped that the student has been able to get some degree of appreciative experience of the exciting and perennial themes of philosophy, namely, the nature of knowledge and belief in their historical relationships. Some of the gaps in this account will be filled in later as we move from problem to problem in the attempt to discover the order and nature of beliefs. It will frequently be necessary to ask what has been believed, in order to understand the character of our own beliefs.

PROBLEMS FOR THOUGHT AND DISCUSSION

1. Francis Bacon claimed that truth arises more easily out of error than from ignorance. What positions taken by the philosophers seem to you to be erroneous? Which true? On what grounds do you make your judgment?

2. It is sometimes said that every man is either a Platonist or an Aristotelian. Others have claimed that everyone is a rationalist or an empiricist. Still others that everyone is either a positivist or an existentialist. Does it seem to you that your own way of thinking can be formulated so that it fits into one or another of these patterns? Or some other pattern?

3. It is said that science is possible only as a cooperative enterprise. Do you think a similar claim can be made for philosophy?

4. We have presented the views of many philosophers apart from their times, cultures, and environments; does this seem to you to lead to inevitable distortion and misunderstanding? Is it possible for one to transcend the age in which one lives and not be completely its product? If so, in what ways might this be accomplished?

5. Ernst Cassirer, in *An Essay on Man,* wrote the following about the history of philosophy:

The facts of the philosophical past, the doctrines and systems of the great thinkers, are meaningless without an interpretation. And this process of interpretation never comes to a complete standstill. As soon as we have reached a new center and a new line of vision in our own thoughts we must revise our judgments. No example is perhaps more characteristic and instructive in this respect than the change in our portrait of Socrates. We have the Socrates of Xenophon and Plato; we have a Stoic, a sceptic, a mystic, a rationalistic; and a romantic Socrates. They are entirely dissimilar. Nevertheless they are not untrue; each of them gives us a new aspect, a characteristic perspective of the historical Socrates and his intellectual and moral physiognomy. Plato saw in Socrates the great dialectician and the great ethical teacher; Montaigne saw in him the antidogmatic philosopher who confessed his ignorance; Friedrich Schlegel and the romantic thinkers laid the emphasis upon Socratic irony. And in the case of Plato himself we can trace the same development. We have a mystic Plato, the Plato of neo-Platonism; a Christian Plato, the Plato of Augustine and Marsilio Ficino; a rationalistic Plato, the Plato of Moses Mendelssohn; and a few decades ago we were offered a Kantian Plato. We may smile at all these different interpretations. Yet they have not only a negative but also a positive side. They have all in their measure contributed to an understanding and to a systematic valuation of Plato's work. Each has insisted on a certain aspect which is contained in this work, but which could only be made manifest by a complicated process of thought. . . . The history of philosophy shows us very clearly that the full determination of a concept is very rarely the work of that thinker who first introduced that concept. For a philosophical concept is, generally speaking, rather a problem than the solution of a problem—and the full significance of this problem cannot be understood so long as it is still in its first implicit state. It must become explicit in order to be comprehended in its true meaning, and this transition from an implicit to an explicit state is the work of the future.[42]

Do you agree or disagree with Cassirer's point about the truth value of different interpretations of various philosophers? How does the last point about the determination of a concept relate to philosophy as a cooperative endeavor?

6. Many philosophers who know their predecessors are not concerned about telling the story of philosophy. Rather they are eager to proceed directly to the question of the truth or falsity of the claims. William of Ockham wrote about philosophers of past ages, " . . . I cannot accommodate myself to everybody's opinions when one opinion contradicts another."[43]

Do you see any difference in this approach and that of Cassirer? Which do you prefer?

PERTINENT READINGS

The following anthologies are useful for an introduction to problems and points of view that are characteristic of important philosophers. Some of the selections are too brief but they may be sufficient to arouse your curiosity and lead you to read more extensively whatever author or problem interests you. All of these volumes are published by the New American Library, New York in the Mentor Books series.

Aiken, Henry D., *The Age of Ideology: the 19th Century Philosophers*, 1956.
Berlin, Isaiah, *The Age of Enlightenment: the 18th Century Philosophers*, 1956.
Freemantle, Anne, *The Age of Belief: the Medieval Philosophers*, 1954.
Hampshire, Stuart, *The Age of Reason: the 17th Century Philosophers*, 1956.
Santillana, Giorgio de, *The Age of Adventure: the Renaissance Philosophers*, 1956.
White, Morton, *The Age of Analysis: the 20th Century Philosophers*, 1955.

[42] Ernst Cassirer, *An Essay on Man: An Introduction to a Philosophy of Human Culture*, Yale University Press, New Haven, Connecticut, 1944, pp. 179–180.
[43] William of Ockham, *Philosophical Writings* (Philotheus Boehner, O.F.M., tr.), Thomas Nelson and Sons, Edinburgh, 1957, p. 2.

III

Beliefs Deductively Derived and Inductively Inferred

I. What Is Logic?

It is ordinarily thought a compliment when one is said to be logical, but it is not always clear what it is we approve when this is said. Sometimes it means the opposite of being emotional, that is, when the more or less violent and disruptive states of the organism are subjected to the more or less quiet appraisal of rational judgment. Sometimes it means that one is clever in winning an argument. Or again it may mean that one refuses to accept a statement or a belief until satisfied with the evidence. Or it may have a stricter meaning, which we shall explore in this chapter.

If we were to say now that philosophy has nothing to do with belief or with the analysis of belief, we could be rightly charged with contradiction. We would be denying what we had previously affirmed, which is bad logic unless we could specify reasons for our change. If, on the other hand, we could show what it is for beliefs to be true together and how they support each other, that is, whether they are consistent and coherent, then we should regard this as good logic. Thus for the purposes of this book we define logic as the study of how the truth or falsity of any belief is related to the truth or falsity of any other belief.

Not all philosophers and logicians would accept this, for there is no universal agreement about the nature and purpose of logic. Undoubtedly this was apparent in the brief history in the previous chapter. How very different logic seems when practiced by a Sophist, by Socrates, by Aristotle, by Bacon and

92

Galileo, or by a logician in the tradition of Leibniz. Suppose each of these asked a student, "Does your college teach logic?" He might say yes to each, yet each time mean something different by "logic." If he said yes to the Sophist he could have in mind the teaching of forensic art or debating; if he said yes to Socrates he would mean that in any subject students and teachers make a sustained effort to define what they talk about; if he said yes to Aristotle he could mean that there is an examination of the principles common to all the sciences as well as an investigation into the rules that govern the form of syllogistic arguments. But if he should answer yes to Bacon or Galileo, he would probably mean that one does not bother much any more with syllogisms because they give no new knowledge; rather, logic is stressed as a tool or instrument of discovery to be used in the procedures of the laboratory sciences. Finally, in answering the question put by Leibniz and his successors, e.g., Charles S. Peirce, A. N. Whitehead, or Bertrand Russell, he might reply that the philosophy and mathematics departments share an interest in the kind of truths that give no information such as, "if a proposition is true, then it is true."

When we claim that logic is essential to the analysis of belief, in which of these five senses, or any other, do we use the word "logic"? Certainly not in the sophist sense of an art enabling one to trounce an opponent, for we feel the purpose of reasoning is to achieve knowledge, not to triumph in an argument. Nor do we limit logic to the view ascribed to the followers of Aristotle that deductive reasoning is exhausted by the syllogism. Nor do we agree that all logic is to be identified with the methods of the sciences. And finally we cannot accept the view that the only logic worth knowing is symbolic logic, if this implies that ordinary discourse and philosophic discussion, which differ notably in style from mathematical demonstration, are therefore in every way inferior. We admit that all these views of logic make valuable contributions to our examination of alternative beliefs. Thus we show our indebtedness to the Sophists by including a section on fallacies, that is, misleading or invalid arguments. Nearly every succeeding chapter will deal with the fallacies that may be involved in the topic under discussion. Our debt to Socrates is evident whenever we stress the definition of terms. And we shall follow the Aristotelian analysis of terms, propositions, and arguments, although we shall also present a glimpse of some of the techniques of contemporary symbolic logic. Finally, we acknowledge our debt to Bacon, Mill, Hume, and others when we deal with the problem of establishing the truth of our premises.

Our aim in this chapter is primarily practical, rather than theoretical and critical. We simply want to provide the student with the preliminary tools needed in any examination of beliefs to reveal which beliefs may be true together, that is, are consistent, and which beliefs cannot be true together, but are inconsistent or contradictory. Such a study will enable the student to begin to understand when the truth of one belief guarantees the truth of another, or when an argument is "valid." A practical goal of logic is stated succinctly by Aristotle: ". . . the ability to raise searching difficulties on both sides of a subject will make us detect more easily the truth and error about the several points that arise."[1] In Chapter IV we will consider in detail the meaning of "truth." Now let us look more closely at "validity."

Certainly one of the key terms in logic is "structure" or "form." Our beliefs, when logically ordered, exhibit a kind of form such that the conclusion is adequately supported by the evidence. To achieve this is the aim of thought in almost all of its diverse aspects. When the structure is weak the conclusion is suspect. How to build this structure and how to test it constitutes one of the functions of logic. Validity is a word appropriate only to arguments, not to words or concepts. The validity of an argument depends strictly on its structure or form, and its form is revealed when the descriptive content of the argument is removed and replaced by certain symbols. A number of valid forms will be introduced shortly. There is, however, a connection between truth and validity. Usually this is expressed by saying that if all the premises of a valid argument are true, then its conclusion must be also true. Or to put it another way, it is not possible for the premises of an argument to be true, and the conclusion false in a valid argument. If we have a valid argument and a false conclusion then at least one premise must be false. It is evident that certain alternatives are possible. For instance, an argument may have true premises and a true conclusion and be either valid or invalid. Consider a valid argument:

All planets move in ellipitical orbits.
Mercury is a planet.
Therefore, Mercury moves in an elliptical orbit.

Now, consider an invalid argument in which all the statements are true:

All philosophers are human beings.
All philosophers die before they reach the age of two hundred years.
Therefore, all human beings die before they reach the age of two hundred years.

[1] Richard McKeon (ed.), *The Basic Works of Aristotle*, Random House, New York, 1941, P. 189. *Topica*, W. A. Pickard–Cambridge (tr.), The Clarendon Press, Oxford, 1928, 101a35.

Also, we may have an argument with false premises and a true conclusion which may be valid or invalid. Consider a valid argument:

> Harvard University is a small college.
> All small colleges have large faculties.
> Therefore, Harvard University has a large faculty.

Now, consider an invalid argument in which the premises are false and the conclusion true:

> Harvard is a small college.
> Only small colleges have large endowments.
> Therefore, Harvard has a large endowment.

Finally, we may have an argument with both premises and the conclusion false, which may be either valid or invalid. Consider a valid argument:

> All horses are crows.
> All crows are pink.
> Therefore, all horses are pink.

Now, consider an invalid argument in which premises and conclusion are false:

> All elephants are roosters.
> All egg-layers are roosters.
> Therefore, all elephants are egg-layers.

The point of all this is that the validity of an argument is determined not by the actual truth of its statements, but by something else, which we have called its structure or form. The rules of valid inference are laid down to protect us from arriving at falsehood from a truth, the principle being that what is validly implied by a true proposition is true. But there are other principles that are also fixed basic beliefs. Aristotle regarded principles as necessary in order to avoid an infinite regress of assumptions. Let us now state three celebrated principles, or laws of logic, which are also taken by some philosophers to be laws of being. If we regard them as laws of being, the bases of logic and metaphysics are indistinguishable. As metaphysical principles they may be stated in the following way:

1. Law of Identity: Whatever is, is, or A is A.
2. Law of Contradiction: Nothing can both be and not be, or nothing can be both A and not A.
3. Law of Excluded Middle: Everything must either be or not be, or everything is either A or not A.

As logical principles they may be stated as follows:

1. Law of Identity: If a proposition is true, then it is true.
2. Law of Contradiction: No proposition is both true and false.
3. Law of Excluded Middle: A proposition is either true or false.

The claim of logicians from Aristotle to Bertrand Russell, different as they are, is that we cannot even set out to demonstrate that these logical principles are false without contradicting ourselves. Suppose it is false that "A is A," or that "if a proposition is true, then it is true." In that case the principle should be stated "A is not A" or "if a proposition is true, it must be false." But if the principle holds universally and applies to itself, then if it is true, it is false, and if it is false that A is not A, then A is A. Hence, concludes Aristotle, the principle is undeniable. Russell once stated in a Cartesian way that the principle is "certainly true," by which he meant that it is "impossible to doubt," and that it is known in such a way that experience cannot weaken it for it does not rest upon evidence gained through the senses. Not being a generalization from experience, it is a misconception to expect any fact to be an exception to it.[2]

Attempts have been made to revise the laws of thought to take account of a changing world in which a thing becomes what it was not. The law of contradiction, it is said, could hold only for a world that does not change, and this is not the kind of world we live in. Thus Hegel, and after him Marx, insisted that everything is both itself and its opposite. This is the logical source of the historical doctrine that each movement in history has in it the seeds of its own destruction and is the negation of a negation. We shall examine this view in Chapter VIII on philosophies of history. Aristotle would respond sharply that the principle "A thing both is and is not," if applied to itself means that it is both true and false, hence absurd.

Whether there could be a world without some such principles is a metaphysical question. Whether we can think or reason or communicate our beliefs about a world without these principles is an epistemological question. Certainly there could not be bodies of belief, either of science or systematic philosophy, or legal and moral codes, without the use of principles of the kind we have presented. Whitehead once put it bluntly, "no logic, no science." But he also put the case for logic more positively:

Logic, properly used, does not shackle thought. It gives freedom, and above all, boldness. Illogical thought hesitates to draw conclusions, because it never

[2] Bertrand Russell, *Problems of Philosophy*, Home University Library Edition, Oxford University Press, London, 1912.

knows either what it means, or what it assumes, or how far it trusts its own assumptions, or what will be the effect of any modification of assumptions. Also the mind untrained in that part of constructive logic which is relevant to the subject in hand will be ignorant of the sort of conclusions which follow from various sorts of assumptions, and will be correspondingly dull in divining the inductive laws. The fundamental training in this relevant logic is, undoubtedly, to ponder with an active mind over the known facts of the case, directly observed. But where elaborate deductions are possible, this mental activity requires for its full exercise the direct study of the abstract logical relations. This is applied mathematics.

Neither logic without observation, nor observation without logic, can move one step in the formation of science. We may conceive humanity as engaged in an internecine conflict between youth and age. Youth is not defined by years but by the creative impulse to make something. The aged are those who, before all things, desire not to make a mistake. Logic is the olive branch from the old to the young, the wand which in the hands of youth has the magic property of creating science.[3]

II. Definition of Terms

We sometimes forget that words are given meanings, that is, they have no natural meaning. To assume that they have is to commit an error similar to that of the lady who acknowledged the scientific accomplishment of the astronomers who discovered Pluto; but she thought it even more astonishing that they knew it was Pluto. The strictly human process of giving meanings to words is never ending. New terms constantly appear in a language which need to be made precise by various techniques. For example, we have recently had to clarify such terms as "limited war," "indirect aggression," "welfare state," "taxable income," "recession," and "the beast generation." The process of clarification and of making terms precise, that is, reducing their ambiguity and vagueness, is called definition. The result of such a process is also called a definition. It may seem that we have provided ourselves with all that is necessary for defining words, namely, a dictionary. But this useful book does not take us far enough toward the solution of many of the problems. Often an adequate definition will require more than another word; we may need a paragraph, a page, and perhaps even a whole book to convey as precisely as we can what we mean.

One might expect the subject of definition to be clear and uncomplicated in logic books. But this is often not the case. There is some agreement about some terms but there is also widespread variation and disagreement. No two logicians seem to think exactly alike on this matter, and the result

[3] Alfred North Whitehead, *The Aims of Education and Other Essays*, Mentor Books, New York, 1949, pp. 122–123.

is different names, different types, different classification, as well as different meanings in the discussion of the problems. Often we find each writer preferring a special vocabulary, or inventing a new one. In short, we find the topic considerably confused by the frequent use of stipulation, a kind of definition we shall discuss later. Out of this somewhat disorderly condition we shall try to bring order by selecting a few common issues about which there is more or less agreement, and describing them with a relatively common terminology. We have no intention of offering a theory of definition. Our aim is much lower, namely, to introduce the student to some of the problems, and to show how to attempt to reach satisfactory definitions.

The necessity of definition is felt when we meet a new word, when we find ourselves using a word without clear meaning, when we use a word in different senses, when someone else uses a word we do not recognize, and when we want to make ourselves understood to another person. These are psychological and social contexts, but they are worth noticing, because in different settings the search for a definition varies both as to process and product. In part, defining terms means, according to context:

1. Tell how the term is used.
2. Tell how you intend to use the term.
3. Tell what word may be substituted for this word.
4. Tell the characteristics things of this kind have.
5. Point out an example of what is meant.
6. Tell how, in this discourse or system, the definition fits in with other terms and how they are defined in relation to each other.

It is obvious that the reply to any one of these may not be appropriate for the others. This should make clear the point that different types of definitions serve different purposes.

There are many kinds of definitions, but they may all be said to have the following form: *definiendum = definiens,* where definiendum refers to the term to be defined and definiens is the expression that states the meaning of the definiendum. With one type of definition (ostensive) such a pattern does not seem to fit. But this is a small matter.

Let us begin by stating abruptly that words and not things are defined. An automobile as a thing can be driven, painted, wrecked, or traded; it cannot be defined. On the other hand the word "automobile" cannot be driven, painted, wrecked, or traded; it can be defined. This leads us to make a distinction that is fairly common among philosophers, between verbal and real definitions. It was once thought that verbal definitions were

only about words, but that real definitions were about things. Some logicians even retain this older meaning. But more often now it is not thought
possible to define things, though they may be described. If description is
taken to be a kind of definition, then we would have to admit that in this
way things may be defined.

Verbal definitions, also called nominal definitions, are statements that
the symbols of the definiendum have the same meaning that other symbols, the definiens, have in the given language. A verbal definition is a
kind of declaration of intention, or a recommendation, or proposal to use
the words in a certain way. Thus to offer a synonym for the meaning of an
unknown word is to give a verbal definition. And there are other ways—
any time we say "let us take so and so to mean such and such" we are
also proposing a verbal definition.

One interpretation of real definition is that the definiens analyzes the
concepts, or makes explicit the concepts implicit in the definiendum. Both
the definiendum and the definiens have an independent meaning apart
from the process of definition. The definition may be said to be true if
those meanings are equivalent, that is, if the definiens can be substituted for the definiendum without changing the meaning. If such definitions can be true or false they can serve as premises in an argument.
Verbal definitions, which cannot be said to be true or false, cannot be
premises.

The classic illustrations of the fundamental search for real definitions
are found in the early dialogues of Plato. The problem of the Laches is,
"What is courage?"; of the Charmides, "What is temperance?"; of the
Republic, "What is justice?"; of the Euthyphro, "What is piety?"; of the
Theaetetus, "What is knowledge?" The central figure in the search is
Socrates, who felt deeply the need for definition in the quest for knowledge. Let us recall his dialectical method. Briefly it comes to this. Socrates
asks what *x* is. A provisional definition is offered and tried out. Something is found wrong with it and a new attempt springs from the first
failure. The weaknesses of the initial definition are exposed by a persistent,
canny questioning. From this beginning in Greek thought the processes
and techniques of defining have been refined. Today we have rules, but
they lie embedded in the practice of Socrates, as we shall demonstrate
later. Philosophers are, unfortunately, responsible for producing some of
the most ambiguous terms in the language, for example, absolute, transcendental, *élan vital*, essence, and so on. Nevertheless other philosophers
become critics and accept the responsibility of prosecuting vigorously
offenders among their own kind.

But let us return to verbal and real definition. Having made the distinction we must now blur it a little, for it is not always clear whether a definition is one or the other. Often it depends on interpretation, or on the intention of the definer. For instance, is it clear that the following is a real definition: a triangle is a closed plane figure of three sides. Certainly the definiens seems to make explicit the concepts in the definiendum, that is, closed, plane, figure, and three-sidedness. In this respect it is a real definition. But might one not intend something quite different, namely, to propose or resolve to use the group of words in the definiens to stand for the word "triangle"? And even in many verbal definitions there may be some degree of analysis present. So we must conclude that the distinction between verbal and real definition is useful in some respects but cannot be maintained absolutely.

All philosophers agree that there are different types of definition, but they differ on the classification and the number of types. We have no desire to make innovations in this area, so we select a few of the most common types for a brief discussion. Some of these are more obviously verbal than real and vice versa.

Let us recall the different ways of regarding the demand for a definition. The first one was to tell how the term is used. We would properly respond here with a _lexical_ definition, which reports one of the actual ways in which the term is used within a given language, at a given time, by a given class, in a given society. Such definitions may be found in dictionaries. Thus one of the definitions of knowledge in an English dictionary is, "familiarity gained by actual experience." If this is one of the actual meanings of the term "knowledge" accepted by actual people then the definition may be said to be true. For most of us the problem here is not defining the term, but merely looking up the definition. Though it may often settle disputes, it is often found unsatisfactory for specific issues.

A second way was to tell how you intend to use the term. This calls attention to _stipulative_ definitions, which have the form of declarations, proposals, or announcements. They indicate one's intention to use a word in a certain way. Thus, for example, in mathematics i is defined to mean "the square root of a minus one." Such definitions have their uses in the technical vocabularies of the various fields of knowledge. That is one reason we have an increasing number of specialized dictionaries. We are all free to stipulate as much as we like, but we certainly ought to avoid cluttering up the language with excessive jargon and making cumbersome or unnecessary departures from conventional usages.

A third way was to tell what word may be substituted for this word. This may be merely a request for a synonym and could be called a *synonymous* definition. It is a type of verbal definition. But it does not take us very far. To define "liberty" as "freedom" scarcely gives us an understanding of the term, because no characteristics are separated out of the definiendum.

The fourth way was to tell the characteristics things of this kind have. This may give us a definition by *genus* and *differentia.* A genus is a class that includes one or more subclasses called species. *Class* means no more than a number of members with something in common. That which distinguishes one species from another in the same genus is called the differentia. Thus "man is a rational animal" is a definition by genus and differentia, for the genus is "animal" and the differentia is "rational." If we wished to define automobile in this way we might say an automobile is a self-propelled vehicle, in which case "vehicle" is the genus and "self-propelled" is the differentia. One of the problems associated with this type of definition is to make the definiens correspond as nearly as possible with the definiendum. Would the above definition exclude motor boats and airplanes from the class of automobiles?

The fifth way was to point out an example of what is meant. Such a type of definition has been called *ostensive.* Children learn the meanings of some words when an object is presented and the name of the object is spoken. The request for a meaning may lead one to point to the object. There are some obvious weaknesses in ostensive definitions. For example, some things we cannot point to, sometimes the pointing is vague, and again the process does not direct us to the essential characteristics of the term to be defined. Thus one cannot point to "democracy," although one could say "the United States is a democracy," which is a kind of pointing. But this helps very little in knowing what features of the United States are to be selected for the meaning of the term. However, in learning a foreign language ostensive definition may be quite useful.

Finally, a request for a definition may be regarded as a request to tell how, in this discourse or system, the definition fits in with other terms and how they are defined in relation to each other; the response to this is a systematic or, as it is sometimes called, a theoretical definition. Here attention is being called to the characteristics of the objects to which the term is applied which relate to an organized system or theory. Many terms in the natural sciences may be defined in this way, e.g., "force," "heat," and so on. A housewife's definition of water would not be the same as a chemist's, for the latter needs a definition in terms of, let us say, the molecular theory. Such definitions may change as the theories change. Also in the social sciences one may define "property," "capital," or "income," differently according to one's economic theory.

The "rules" of definition grew from seeing what is satisfactory and unsatisfactory in the process of defining. "Rule" here does not mean something like the statute law defining what is or is not a crime. Rather than legislating a set of statutes, let us again go to Socrates to see how good reasons for these rules emerge out of practice. We turn to Plato's dialogue Euthyphro.[4] Socrates is awaiting trial when Euthyphro finds him. The latter cannot believe that the great Socrates is accused, but then discovers it is for impiety. Ironically, Euthyphro is accusing his father of a variety of the same type of crime. The young man brashly professes to know what he is doing and what it is to be pious. This is the opportunity Socrates has been waiting for, so he questions Euthyphro about the meaning of piety. His first definition is " . . . piety means prosecuting the wrong-doer who has committed murder or sacrilege . . . impiety means not prosecuting him." Here Socrates objects, "I did not ask you to tell me one or two of all the many pious actions there are: I want to know what is the idea of piety which makes all pious actions pious." He is asking for a real definition. Sometimes this is called giving the connotation rather than the denotation, that is, stating just the necessary and sufficient characteristics of the class, rather than citing members of the class.

Euthyphro tries a second time. "What is pleasing to the gods is pious, and what is not pleasing to them is impious." Socrates, however, objects again. "The gods will quarrel over these things." This suggests that what is not clear to gods must be far less clear to men. Here the rule is: A definition should be clear, not obscure.

The third attempt produces the following: "Whatever all the gods hate is impious, and whatever they all love is pious." After Socrates questions this, Euthyphro says that it means that acts are pious because the gods love them, and the gods love them because they are pious. Hence the definition boils down to "piety is piety." This is formally or logically true, but it tells us nothing because it is circular. The rule is that a definition should not use the term defined in the defining phrase; in other words, it should not be circular.

Euthyphro's fourth definition suggests that "all piety must be just." If this means, as Socrates asks, that all justice is piety, then the definition is too broad. When Euthyphro modifies it to read, "that part of justice which

<hr/>

[4] Plato, *Euthyphro, Apology, and Crito* (F. J. Church, tr., Robert D. Cummings, reviser), The Liberal Arts Press, New York, 1948.

has to do with the attention which is due to the gods," that definition is found to be too narrow.

The fifth and final effort brings forth a definition that is objectionable on other grounds and makes plain another rule. " . . . The opposite of what is acceptable to the gods is sacrilegious, and this it is that brings ruin and destruction on all things." This is a negative definition. It defines the pious as not impious, which does not seem to get very far. It can easily be seen that a negative definition tends to be circular. The rule is to define positively wherever possible.

The dialogue ends without ever discovering a satisfactory definition of piety. But the numerous attempts were not fruitless. In the process we have learned much about definition itself. Let us summarize the rules designed to insure good definitions and avoid ambiguity:

1. A good definition should state the essential characteristics of that which is defined. Violation: Man is a two-legged creature.
2. A good definition should not be expressed in obscure or metaphorical language. Violation: Time is the moving image of eternity.
3. A good definition should not be circular, that is, will not contain the subject defined in the defining part. Violation: A sleeping powder is a substance having soporific qualities.
4. A good definition should not be too broad or too narrow. Violations: A fish is an animal that lives in water (too broad). Money is a metal substance (too narrow).
5. Insofar as possible a good definition should be in positive rather than negative terms. Violation: A moral man is one who is not intemperate.

III. Propositions

Ambiguity of terms is primarily a failure to specify and grasp one clear meaning. Ambiguity of propositions is primarily a failure to communicate the meaning of a proposition. Remember that we define proposition to mean the sort of thing that can be true or false. "Some paper is white" is an English sentence that expresses a proposition. To know whether it is true or false requires definitions, but definitions do not make it either true or false. The fact of this paper's white color makes it true or false. To discover the proposition, ask the question, "Is this paper white?" A proposition is what completes the meaning of the form "I (or we, you, or they) believe that. . . . " Grammatically the expression of a proposition is a declarative or indicative sentence. Thus a question, a command, a wish, are not propositions. "Is this paper white?" makes no commitment as to truth or falsity. It is nonsense to ask, "Do you believe that question?" "Make the paper white" is imperative and is not true or false. "Would that the paper were white!" is optative or expressing a wish. That someone expressed such a command or wish may be true or false, but what is commanded or wished is not.

Categorical Propositions.

Traditional logic distinguishes four types of the categorical proposition. "Paper is white," makes sense in common English. Grammatically we would say noun-verb-adjective are the elements of this sentence. Logically we refer to the noun "paper" as the *subject*, the verb "is" as the *copula*, the adjective "white" as the *predicate*. Note that in this analysis we use the timeless or tenseless "is" or "are" rather than the many other possible forms of the verb. The logical term predicate should not be confused with the meaning of that word in grammar. We distinguish four types of subject-copula-predicate (*ScP*) propositions according to two principles, universal-particular, and affirmative-negative. If we mean each and every member of the subject class, the proposition is called *universal*. If we mean less than each and every member, or fewer than all, but at least one, the proposition is called *particular*. This is the difference of quantity. The universal quantifier is "all," the particular quantifier is "some." The difference of quality is indicated in the universal negative proposition by the quantifier "no," in the particular negative by the copula "are not." In affirmative propositions the quality also is indicated by "all" and "some." Each has been given a name—merely a letter of the alphabet. We can put all these features together in a simple table.

Name	Symbol	Quantifier	Subject	Copula	Predicate
Universal	*A*	All	philosophers (Dist)	are	wise (Undist) (Affirmative.)
	E	No	philosophers (Dist)	are	wise (Dist) (Negative.)
Particular	*I*	Some	philosophers (Un)	are	wise (Un) (Affirmative.)
	O	Some	philosophers (Undist)	are not	wise (Dist) (Negative.)

One type of categorical proposition does not quite fit into this scheme. An example is, "Socrates is wise." This form is called a *singular* proposition and is treated in traditional logic as if it were of type *A*, that is, "(All) Socrates is wise." The alert student will wonder about propositions beginning with "five" or "ten" or "51 per cent" or "few" or "many" or "most." These and similar words expressing less than "all" are in this system of logic taken to mean "some," which is said by definition to mean "at least one."

There is more to the analysis of the categorical proposition than is at first apparent. The next important concept to grasp is that of *distribution of terms*. A term is said to be *distributed* if it refers to all the individuals in the class denoted by it, and *undistributed* if it denotes only part of the class. Thus in the *A* proposition the subject term "philosophers" is distributed because all philosophers are said to be wise. But according to this view, nothing is said about all wise people. Therefore the predicate term is undistributed. The *E* distributes both subject and predicate; the *I* neither; the *O* the predicate.

To see the importance of distribution, consider the proposition, "All Englishmen are Europeans." Given the truth of this, may we conclude that "All Europeans are Englishmen"? Certainly not. The class of Englishmen and the class of Europeans are not coincidental. In an affirmative proposition in which only one term is distributed, the terms may not be interchanged unless the quantity of the proposition is changed, that is, we could conclude that "Some Europeans are Englishmen." We will have more to say of this in a moment. Of course, where the two classes are coincidental, one may interchange the terms without falling into error. For example, if it is true that "All equilateral triangles are equiangular," then it is also true that, "All equiangular triangles are equilateral."

Frequently we try to derive from one proposition another proposition having the same subject and predicate, a process known as *immediate inference*. Sometimes this is done validly, sometimes invalidly. There are many forms, only a few of which we can treat here. Suppose a philosopher makes a statement in metaphysics that, "All space-time objects are real." Can we then infer validly that "All real things are space-time objects"? There is a strong temptation to handle propositions in this way. If the philosopher were Descartes, he would reply: "I did not say *only* space-time objects are real. I have said elsewhere that thinking minds are real and this does not contradict the statement that all space-time objects are real." (Remember the proposition about Europeans!) All you are entitled to infer is that "some real things are space-time objects." In other words, the *A* implies the necessary truth of an *I*. This statement will be qualified shortly, when we mention the "existential import" of particular propositions.

Now suppose Hobbes says, "No spiritual things exist." Can we draw the inference that "No existing things are spiritual"? This is valid, because both terms are distributed. By this time, it should be clear that we can derive "some mortals are men" from "some men are mortals," but not "some bright people are not students" from "some students are not bright."

This process of interchanging subject and predicate just described is called *conversion*. When done illegitimately, it results in the fallacy of false conversion. Watch out for it. It is tricky business and you can easily go astray. In Lewis Carroll's Alice in Wonderland, Alice was given a lesson in logic by the March Hare and Mad Hatter.

"I'm glad they've begun asking riddles—I believe I can guess that," she added aloud.

"Do you mean that you think you can find out the answer to it?" said the March Hare.

"Exactly so," said Alice.

"Then you should say what you mean," the March Hare went on.

"I do," Alice hastily replied; "at least—I mean what I say—that's the same thing, you know."

"Not the same thing a bit!" said the Hatter. "Why, you might just as well say that 'I see what I eat' is the same thing as 'I eat what I see!' "

"You might just as well say," added the March Hare, "that 'I like what I get' is the same thing as 'I get what I like!' "

Suppose now we have the following proposition: "All professors are wise," and we wish to know whether another proposition can be derived from this that is universal in quantity but negative in quality. Such a result when validly obtained is called *obversion*. It requires two simple steps. First, change the quality of the proposition (never the quantity), and second negate the predicate term. All four types of categorical propositions will yield an obverse. Thus the obverse of "All professors are wise," is "No professors are nonwise" (or stupid?); of "No dinosaurs are timid," is "All dinosaurs are nontimid" (or courageous?); of "Some students are bright," is "Some students are not nonbright" (or dull?); of "Some poems are not clear," is "Some poems are nonclear" (or obscure?). The obverse of any proposition is equivalent to the original proposition.

Two other types of immediate inference need to be mentioned. They depend upon relations between propositions called respectively *contrariety* and *contradiction*. We sense some vague sort of opposition between the following: "All things are material" and "No things are material." These propositions differ only in quality. Suppose the first is false, is the second necessarily true? Not at all—both may be false. This is the characteristic of all contraries. Contrariety is involved in many types of arguments. Let us imagine an ideological issue. A debater argues that "Communism is not the best political and economic system." From this proposition alone can he draw the conclusion that "Capitalism is the best political and economic system"? Not at all. The point is that both these propositions might be false.

Two propositions are contradictory if the truth of one implies the falsity of the other and the falsity of one implies the truth of the other. Thus, according to our scheme, *A* and *O*, *E* and *I*, are contradictories. Notice the difference in quantity and quality of these contradictories. Consider once again the materialism-idealism controversy: If materialism is the belief that "all things are material," this is the contradictory of "some things are not material." If the first is true, the second is false; if the first is false, the second is true. If the second is false, the first is true; if the second is true, the first is false. Apply this to idealism. If idealism means "all things are spiritual," then the contradictory is "some things are not spiritual." The various relations between the types of categorical propositions can be visually presented by the famous *square of opposition*.

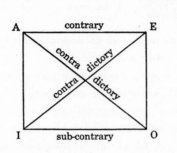

One more point about categorical propositions is necessary—the relationship between an *A* and an *I* and an *E* and an *O*. If we assert that "All things are material" and mean each and every member of the class, we cannot deny that "Some things are material," meaning that at least one is. If "No things are material," then we cannot deny that "Some things are not material." This reasoning goes on the assumption that these forms of universal belief are about existing things. They will not fit propositions about mermaids or unicorns. If someone says, "All mermaids have tails" he does not commit himself to the proposition that there are mermaids. Particular propositions, unlike universal propositions, according to most modern logicians, do carry *existential import*. If this is the case, the proposition "Some mermaids have tails," commits one to the belief that there are mermaids. If attention is paid to the existential interpretation of particular propositions, then an *I* cannot be derived from an *A*, nor an *O* from an *E*.

The reason for this lies in the fact that one may not say more in the conclusion than one does in the premises. As "existence" is not affirmed in the universal propositions, we cannot derive particular propositions from them, because they do assert the existence of what is named by their subjects.

This illustration about mermaids, like many used to illustrate principles of formal logic, should not blind the student to the bearing of existential import on beliefs of great importance. For example, in the ontological argument—the most celebrated attempt to establish a belief in the exist- ence of something on a premise about an idea—St. Anselm begins with the *idea* of something "than which nothing greater can be conceived" and deduces the belief in the existence of God. The distinction should be kept in mind in Chapter X on religious beliefs. However, for purposes of ordi- nary discourse the existential import of propositions may be ignored, for we usually assume when we say "All oranges are sweet" that there really are oranges.

Other Types of Propositions.

Let us look now at other types of propositions. Many statements of be- lief do not take the simple categorical form that unites terms either by way of inclusion or exclusion. Frequently one wishes to relate propositions rather than terms, and a complex or compound proposition results.

In the categorical form its elements are symbolized ScP. Similarly, the propositions that make up the complex proposition are symbolized p and q. The four major types of complex propositions are certainly not un- familiar in common language. In the next section we will examine argu- ments in which these propositions are used.

Hypothetical or Implicative, e.g., "If we feed the hungry peoples of Europe, then we can prevent the spread of Communism." In symbols, $p \supset q$, where $\supset$ is the symbol of implication, and can be read "if . . . then." The symbols p and q are called *antecedent* and *consequent*. This form means that if the antecedent is true, the consequent is true. Implica- tion is a logical relationship and should be distinguished from inference, which refers to an act of inferring. In modern logic the $\supset$ is not always treated as simply as has been suggested here. Part of the reason is the way we may use "if . . . then" propositions—there are a number of ways in which the antecedent may be related to the consequent. Thus in an argument we say that if the premises are such and such, then the con- clusion *logically* follows. Or we may say, if John is a brother then John is a male; here the consequent is related to the antecedent by *definition*. Or again, we may say, if I take an aspirin then my headache will be cured, meaning that there is a *causal* relation between antecedent and consequent. Sometimes we also say something like this: If Senator Jones wins the election I'll eat my hat; in this case antecedent and consequent are related by a *decision*.[5]

Finally, it should be mentioned that some modern symbolic logicians do not interpret the ⊃ at all as "if . . . then," but take it as a purely operational symbol. In our discussion, however, we shall use the "horse-shoe" to symbolize implication, although it is not always clear which relation is meant. This much at least is clear, that no hypothetical can be true if its antecedent is true and its consequent is false.

Disjunctive, e.g., "Not both do we feed the hungry people of Europe and fail to prevent the spread of Communism." The sign of negation is ∼. In symbols, $\sim (p \cdot q)$; p and q are *disjuncts*. This form means that either p or q is true, but not both. It is *logically impossible* for two disjuncts to be true together.

Alternative, e.g., "Either we feed the hungry people of Europe, or we will stop the spread of Communism." In symbols, $p \vee q$. The symbol for alternation is ∨; p and q are *alternants*. This form means that p and q is true, at least one, and possibly both. The relationship in this case is one of *compossibility*.

Conjunctive, e.g., "We will feed the hungry people of Europe and stop the spread of Communism." In symbols, $p \cdot q$. The symbol for conjunction is ·; p and q are *conjuncts*. This form means that both p and q are true. If either p or q is false, the whole proposition is false.

Each of these types has a different use in discourse. Sometimes the situations and problems call for one form rather than another. You may by a little work find out how to convert a categorical into a hypothetical proposition. Thus alternative and disjunctive equivalents of the hypothetical "If anyone is a Communist, then he is brutal," are "Either one is not a Communist, or one is brutal," and "It is not the case that one is a Communist and not brutal." In the next section we will examine some instances of reasoning in which complex or compound propositions are employed.

IV. Validating Forms of Argument

A. Categorical Syllogisms.

We have now seen that given the truth or falsity of a single proposition we may derive the truth or falsity of another proposition. This is called

[5] Irving M. Copi, *Introduction to Logic*, The Macmillan Co., New York, 1954, p. 230.

immediate inference. Also, we have seen that there are various ways of compounding any two propositions, namely, implication, alternation, disjunction, and conjunction. What of two propositions using three terms, one of which is common to both propositions? Then a third proposition may be deduced. For example, if both "Philosophers are critics of belief," and "Critics of belief are students of logic" are true, then another proposition is true, namely, "Philosophers are students of logic." ↑

This is a common pattern of argument known as a *categorical syllogism*. The term "critics of belief" is present in the first two propositions and is said to *mediate* between them as a kind of bridge; we call this inference mediate. The first two propositions are known as *premises*, because they are "sent ahead," up front in the argument, and the third proposition, which "follows from" them, is called the *conclusion*. The conclusion has the familiar subject and predicate form. The predicate term, "students of logic" represents a larger class (consider, mathematicians are also included in it), hence the term is called the *major term*, and the smaller subject class, "philosophers," is the *minor term*. Each of these terms is present in one of the premises. The premise in which the predicate of the conclusion occurs is called the *major premise*. The subject of the conclusion appears in the *minor premise*. The common term in the premises, which does not appear in the conclusion, is called the *middle term*. Thus,

All *critics of beliefs* are students of logic,   MAJOR PREMISE
   (MIDDLE TERM)
Philosophers are *critics of beliefs*,   MINOR PREMISE
             (MIDDLE TERM)
_____
   Philosophers are *students of logic*.   CONCLUSION
   (MINOR TERM)   (MAJOR TERM)

The nature of this form of argument is explained in various ways. Let us consider the most famous paradigm in logic:

All men are mortal.
Socrates is a man.
Socrates is mortal.

Using the symbols S and P for the subject and predicate of the conclusion, and symbolizing the conclusion first, we can get this:

$$P$$
$$\frac{S}{S \, c \, P}$$

Then the term that occurs in each premise, but not in the conclusion, can be named *M* for middle.

M c P	Major Premise
S c M	Minor Premise
S c P	Conclusion

This is a valid form of argument. What makes it valid? We might say that if *P* is predicated of *M*, and *M* is predicated of *S*, then *P* is predicated of *S*. Thus, to use our paradigm, if mortality characterizes men, and manhood characterizes Socrates, then mortality characterizes Socrates. In this case, the relation of predication is said to be *transitive*. We shall discuss this type of relation in the next section.

A second explanation is easier to see. It concerns classes and their members. *Class* means any number of members that have something in common. "All men are mortal," means "each and every member of the class 'men' is a member of the class 'mortal.'" Socrates is a member of the class of "men" and each and every member of this class is included in the class of "mortals"; therefore, Socrates is in the class of "mortals" too. Happily classes can be represented by two-dimensional enclosed spaces. What is included is inside the space, what is excluded is outside. So we draw a circle for Socrates:

That Socrates is a man requires a second circle:

The major premise tells us that the *M* is entirely inside the class *P*, or mortals. Then we may visualize the conclusion with the aid of a third circle:

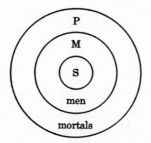

The *M*, however, need not always have the same location in the pattern. But where it is determines what is called the *figure* of the syllogism. There are four, as follows:

I	II	III	IV
M c P	P c M	M c P	P c M
S c M	S c M	M c S	M c S
S c P	S c P	S c P	S c P

If we add to this the names of our propositions, that is, *A, E, I,* and *O,* we have what is called the *mood* of the syllogism. Now, combining mood and figure, there are 256 possible patterns of syllogistic argument, of which only 19 are valid. The rest are eliminated by applying the rules, some of which are based on principles you already know. We shall state the rules and briefly illustrate them.

1. Every syllogism must contain only three terms. If it has more, we have the *fallacy of four terms.* No conclusion can be drawn if there is not one common middle term. Strictly, this holds true of unrelated premises, for example:

   Atomic warfare will destroy civilization.
   Communism will destroy human freedom.

   where there are obviously four terms. But this fallacy also appears in arguments that contain an ambiguous term, for example, it may be argued that since

   We go to college to improve our faculties.
   And our faculties are our instructors.
   Therefore, we go to college to improve our instructors.

2. The middle term must be distributed at least once, that is, in at least one premise. If this is not done, we have the *fallacy of undistributed middle.* The middle term mediates between the premises and conclusion, but it fails in this function if it is not distributed, for then the major and minor terms may be related to only an indefinite part of the middle term, and evidence is lacking that they are related to the same part. For example;

   All professors are wise.
   All students are wise.

   does not yield the conclusion that all students are professors.

3. No term may be distributed in the conclusion if it is not distributed in the premises. Here two fallacies are possible, called *illicit major* and

illicit minor, depending upon which term in the conclusion is illegitimately distributed. This rule is obvious when we remember what distribution means. We cannot say more in the conclusion than we are allowed by the premises. For example,

All citizens are taxpayers.
No alien is a citizen.
No alien is a taxpayer.

This is a fallacy of illicit major.

All voters are over twenty-one.
All voters are citizens.
All citizens are over twenty-one.

This is a fallacy of illicit minor.

4. No conclusion can be drawn from two negative premises. When this rule is violated, the fallacy is known as *negative premises.* Negative propositions exclude. When S and P are excluded from M, there are no grounds that justify a necessary conclusion concerning their relation to each other. For example,

No student failed the test.
No one who failed the test can be promoted.

Can a conclusion be drawn about students?

5. If there is a negative premise, the conclusion must be negative, and there can be no negative conclusion unless one of the premises is negative. A negative premise can yield only a negative conclusion, since with respect to S and P one is said to belong to M and the other not to belong. Thus the only conclusion to be drawn is that S and P have no relation to each other.

6. No conclusion can be drawn from two particular premises, and if one premise is particular, the conclusion must also be particular. If this rule is breeched, the fallacies already mentioned are involved.

The arguments in which these rules are broken are *formally fallacious,* the fault lying in the structure of the argument. The logical fact is that the premises do not imply the conclusion, which may itself be independently true.

It is true that we do not ordinarily talk in syllogisms, but it is not unusual for our reasoning to take this pattern. Sometimes a premise or a conclusion may be suppressed in order to gain psychological effectiveness, but the absent element must be brought out for analysis. This truncated type of syllogism is called an *enthymeme.* But there are further difficulties.

Our written and spoken discourse does not always fall into such crisp and precise patterns. For instance, the following are not clearly in the *AEIO* form and should be put into these forms if we want to use the rules of the syllogism to test validity. The usual translations are supplied.

1. "Few professors are wealthy," in logical form becomes, "Some professors are not wealthy." Few are = some are not.
2. "A few lions are tame," becomes "Some lions are tame." A few = some.
3. "All idealists are not practical," becomes "Some idealists are not practical." All are not = some are not.
4. "Only sophomores are permitted to leave," becomes "All those permitted to leave are sophomores." That is, "Only *A* is *B*" is interpreted to mean "All *B* is *A*."
5. "The only people admitted are Democrats," becomes "All people admitted are Democrats." No interchange of terms is necessary with "the only."
6. "Not all automobiles are expensive," becomes "Some automobiles are not expensive." Not all are = some are not.
7. "All except children are charged two dollars," becomes "All those who are not charged two dollars are children."
8. "None but the brave deserves the fair," becomes "No nonbrave person is one who deserves the fair."

There are other ambiguous quantifiers and expressions in everyday speech that need to be given precise meaning and then put into correct logical form. We cannot here extend the list but will merely say that it is always necessary to examine these ambiguous statements carefully to see what meaning is intended and then put this meaning into one of the standard patterns.

The discussion of the categorical syllogism is concluded with the following suggestions for analyzing an argument of this form.

1. It is always important first to be sure to get the point of the argument, that is, to know what the conclusion is. Once we have the conclusion, we get the terms straight and can separate the conclusion from the premises.
2. Next it would seem useful to clear up all ambiguous or unknown terms, that is, to provide adequate and agreed upon definitions.
3. Many arguments contain irrelevant statements and data. To get at the structure these should be eliminated.
4. Put each proposition in its standard form.

5. Put the propositions in one of the standard forms of the syllogism, that is, with respect to figure and mood.
6. If either a premise or the conclusion is missing, it should be supplied.
7. Finally, test the validity of the syllogism by means of the rules.

Logic provides other tests, but we have not felt it necessary to present them, because a syllogism that is invalid by one test will ordinarily be invalid by others.

This rapid survey of the categorical syllogism must not be regarded as exhaustive. There are several other tests of validity, but we have enough here to begin the critical work of examining our beliefs.

B. Other Types of Syllogisms.

Suppose now, the premise is a compound proposition and it is combined with a categorical proposition. This will yield another familiar pattern of argument about which the question of valid and invalid forms also arises.

Let us consider first that form of argument that begins with a hypothetical or implicative proposition. Leibniz, a seventeenth-century German philosopher, argued somewhat as follows:

> If the mind is an organic whole, then it is false to treat it as made up of parts.
> The mind is an organic whole.
> Therefore, it is false to treat it as made up of parts.

In symbols:

$$p \supset q$$
$$\underline{p}$$
$$q$$

The argument is valid, for the hypothetical proposition means that if the antecedent is accepted as true, then the consequent is true. Suppose the argument takes this form:

> If the mind is an organic whole, then it is false to treat it as made up of parts.
> It is not false to treat it as made up of parts.
> Therefore, the mind is not an organic whole.

In symbols:

$$p \supset q$$
$$\underline{\sim q}$$
$$\sim p$$

This also is valid, for if *q* is not true, then *p* is not true, because if *p* were true, *q* would be true instead of false.

These are the two valid ways of reasoning with this form. The other two possible forms lead to fallacies. Let us look at them.

If the mind is an organic whole, then it is false to treat it as made up of parts.
The mind is not an organic whole.
Therefore, it is not false to treat it as made up of parts.

In symbols:

$$p \supset q$$
$$\sim p$$
$$\overline{\quad\quad}$$
$$\sim q$$

This is called the *fallacy of denying the antecedent*. Notice that the major premise does not say that *p* is the only condition of *q* being true. All it says is that *q* is the case whenever *p* is the case. It may, of course, happen that *q* is the case under other circumstances as well. Similarly, for the second invalid form:

If the mind is an organic whole, then it is false to treat it as made up of parts.
It is false to treat it as made up of parts.
Therefore, the mind is an organic whole.

In symbols:

$$p \supset q$$
$$q$$
$$\overline{\quad\quad}$$
$$p$$

This is called the *fallacy of affirming the consequent*. To accept the consequent does not entitle one to accept the antecedent, for the given antecedent is not the only condition of the given consequent, and therefore there is not a logically necessary relation between them. These two arguments are *deductively* fallacious, but they may have some *inductive* force. That is, the occurrence of the consequent is some evidence for the antecedent but not certain evidence.

Now let us try the alternative proposition with a categorical. Plato believed something like the following, "Either the philosopher is king, or the state declines." Remember that the alternative proposition means at least one of the alternants is true, possibly both.

Either the philosopher is king or the state declines.
The philosopher is not king.
Therefore, the state declines.

[handwritten: p ∨ q at least one is true]

In symbols:

$$p \vee q$$
$$\sim p$$
$$\overline{}$$
$$q$$

That this is valid should be apparent from the meaning of alternation.

Either the philosopher is king, or the state declines.
The state does not decline.
Therefore, the philosopher is king.

In symbols:

$$p \vee q$$
$$\sim q$$
$$\overline{}$$
$$p$$

This, too, is valid. By now the student should know why, and be able to work out the invalid forms also.

Finally, consider the disjunctive proposition combined with a categorical. Remember again that disjunction means that one or the other of the disjuncts is true, but not both. It is easy to work out the valid forms. We leave this to the student.

V. *Relations and Relational Propositions*

One of the aims of logic is to be as general as possible, for in this way it acquires increased power. The traditional subject-copula-predicate analysis of propositions is found to be insufficient for dealing adequately with certain other types of statements, such as, "Mary is older than Elizabeth." If we take this as a premise, and add "Elizabeth is older than Ann" a conclusion obviously follows, namely, "Mary is older than Ann." But if we try to set up this argument in strict syllogistic form we run into difficulties. First, there are four terms, and second, there is no middle term. "Older than Elizabeth" and "Elizabeth" are not the same term. The trouble is that we now have to deal with relations between terms rather than with a copula. But what are relations? We are all well acquainted with them, for example, "father of," "greater than," "east of," "friend of," "teacher of," and so on.

Though relation is hard to define, we can be more successful in classifying relations. Two ways are open. First, according to the number of terms involved, and second, according to the characteristic of the relation itself. Thus consider the relation "equal to." It requires two terms to make sense of a proposition, e.g., "A is equal to B." Similarly with "greater than," "father of," "lover of," and so on. These relations are all _dyadic._ If a relation takes three terms, such as "between," it is _triadic;_ if four, such as, "Paul bought a house from Charles for 10,000 dollars," the relation is _tetradic._

The second way of classifying relations has to do more directly with the nature of the relation. If "Elizabeth is a cousin of Margaret" it is obvious that "Margaret is a cousin of Elizabeth"; "If A is equal to B" then "B is equal to A." All such relations are said to be *symmetrical,* or more formally expressed, if xRy then yRx, where R stands for "relation." But not all relations have this character. For instance, "A is greater than B" will not yield "B is greater than A" nor will "John is the father of Jim" yield "Jim is the father of John." All such relations are said to be *asymmetrical.* That is, if xRy then not possibly yRx.

Once again consider, "Margaret loves Charles"; does this necessarily imply that "Charles loves Margaret"? All unrequited lovers know the logic of this. Happily, however, Charles might love Margaret. From the original statement, we just cannot tell. All relations of this type are *non-symmetrical.* That is, if xRy, then yRx is undetermined.

Another property of relations is exceedingly important for logical analysis. The great philosopher-mathematician Leibniz expressed as Axiom 1 of his "Principles of a Logical Calculus" the following: "A contains B and B contains C, therefore A contains C."[6] If you examine this you will see that the relation between the first and second terms is the same as the relation between the second and third terms. It is then concluded that the relation holds between the first and third terms. All such relations are said to be *transitive,* that is, if xRy and yRz, then xRz. The basis for syllogistic argument may be interpreted as a special case of this relation, that is, when the copulative verb is transitive.

The student should be prepared to move more rapidly now and see that we may have *atransitive* and *non-transitive* relations. Thus "father of" is an atransitive, and "friend of" a non-transitive relation. Or if xRy and yRz, then not possibly xRz, and if xRy and yRz, then xRz undetermined.

The relations we have classified according to symmetry and transitivity overlap. We then have the following possibilities:

[6] Philip P. Wiener (ed.) *Leibniz Selections,* Charles Scribner's Sons, New York, 1951, p. 26.

1. Symmetrical transitive, e.g., "is equal to"
2. Asymmetrical transitive, e.g., "is greater than"
3. Non-symmetrical transitive, e.g., "implies"
4. Symmetrical atransitive, e.g., "spouse of"
5. Asymmetrical atransitive, e.g., "father of"
6. Non-symmetrical atransitive, e.g., "closest friend of"
7. Symmetrical non-transitive, e.g., "different from"
8. Asymmetrical non-transitive, e.g., "benefactor of"
9. Non-symmetrical non-transitive, e.g., "lover of"

Whenever relational arguments are used, their validity depends on the character of the relation. Thus when the premises involve transitive relations, the relation must remain the same in the conclusion. For example, from "A is parallel to B" and "B is parallel to C" we can conclude that "A is parallel to C." If the premises involve atransitive relations, the conclusion must be a proper combination of these two relations. For example, from "John is the father of Henry" and "Henry is the father of Jim" we may conclude that "John is the grandfather of Jim." And when the premises are non-transitive, any conclusion drawn must show the non-transitive character of the relation. Thus, from "Socrates was the teacher of Plato" and "Plato was the teacher of Aristotle" we may conclude only that "Socrates may or may not have been the teacher of Aristotle." In this last we are, of course, talking about the form of the argument, not historical possibilities.

This is as far as we can go with relations in this chapter. But the student should explore independently and attempt to discover the character of spatial, temporal, mathematical, and other kinds of relationships. Such thinking has worked a revolution in contemporary physical knowledge, leading for example, to Einstein's theories of relativity.

VI. Some Modern Developments

Contemporary logic has become a highly specialized and abstract science similar if not identical to pure mathematics. In fact, the great work of Russell and Whitehead, Principia Mathematics, set out to show that mathematics has its basis in certain logical principles. Some mathematicians have disagreed on this point. But there is no need and certainly no space for us to deal with this complex subject. All that we can possibly do is to illustrate a few points and mark out a few directions these newer developments took.

Let us recall the character and definitions of the hypothetical (or implicative), the conjunctive, the disjunctive, and alternative propositions. Each of these is a compound proposition, that is, made out of two categorical propositions. The point to keep in mind here is that the truth-value of the compound proposition is determined only by the truth or falsity of its constituents. Thus $p \supset q$ means that if p is true, q is not false, that is, $p \supset q$ is true when p is true and q is true, when p is false and q is true, when p is false and q is false. But it is never true when p is true and q is false. Again $p \cdot q$ is true only when p is true and q is true. It is false in all other instances. And $p \vee q$ is true when p is true and q is true, when p is false and q is true, when p is true and q is false. The one case excluded is p false and q false.

All of this can be expressed by the use of a matrix device called a truth table. Let us remember that a proposition is either true or false. Truth or falsity constitutes the truth-value of a proposition. Thus if p is a proposition, its truth value is either T or F. If q is a proposition its truth-value is also T or F. Now if p and q are propositions then we have the following possibilities:

p	q
T	T
T	F
F	T
F	F

With this as a reference column, we may now define the compound propositions listed previously.

p	q	$p \supset q$	$p \cdot q$	$p \vee q$
T	T	T	T	T
T	F	F	F	T
F	T	T	F	T
F	F	T	F	F

This table shows the conditions under which the hypothetical, conjunctive, and alternative propositions as a whole are true, given the truth or falsity of their constituents. In short, each column defines, for truth-functional purposes, the symbols $\supset \cdot \vee$.

With the aid of these definitions and tables we can test very complex propositions in order to find their truth or falsity. For example, let us try one of the valid forms previously discussed, namely, if p then q, p therefore q. This may be written $[(p \supset q) \cdot p] \supset q$. Its validity can be shown on a truth table:

p	q	$[(p \supset q) \cdot p] \supset q$
T	T	T
T	F	F
F	T	T
F	F	T

This first step gives us the truth table for $\supset$. But $p \supset q$ is related to p by $\cdot$. So we must have this table too, for $[(p \supset q) \cdot p]$ is itself a conjunctive proposition with one conjunct a hypothetical.

p	q	$[(p \supset q) \cdot p] \supset q$	
T	T	T	T
T	F	F	F
F	T	T	F
F	F	T	F

Finally we need the table for the hypothetical that connects $[(p \supset q) \cdot p]$ with q. We must now refer to the "dot" column and to the reference column for q to give us the table under $\supset$. The result is as follows:

p	q	$[(p \supset q) \cdot p] \supset q$		
T	T	T	T	T
T	F	F	F	T
F	T	T	F	T
F	F	T	F	T

The column of T's under the final $\supset$ shows that the form we were testing is true under all possible variations of the truth or falsity of its constituents.

There are limitations of the truth-table method which are surmounted by other kinds of tests in modern logic. But within limits, this manner of showing the validity of compound propositions is useful.

Contemporary logic has produced a great many *elementary valid argument forms* all of which can be tested by means of the truth tables. Once these are achieved they can be used in further logical analysis, for instance, in what is called *formal proof*, which is "a sequence of statements each of which is either a premise of that argument or follows from preceding statements by an *elementary* valid argument, and such that the last statement in the sequence is the conclusion of the argument whose validity is being proved."[7]

Let us now list a few of the elementary valid argument forms and their names.

1. Modus Ponens (M.P.): $[(p \supset q) \cdot p] \supset q$
2. Hypothetical Syllogism (H.S.): $p \supset q, q \supset r, \supset (p \supset r)$
3. Exportation (Exp.) $[(p \cdot q) \supset r] \equiv [p \supset (q \supset r)]$

We know these are valid because they have been tested by means of the truth tables. These forms may be illustrated as follows:

1. If roses are red then violets are blue; roses are red, therefore violets are blue.
2. If roses are red then violets are blue, and if violets are blue then marigolds are yellow, therefore if roses are red then marigolds are yellow.
3. If roses are red and violets are blue, then marigolds are yellow says the same as, if roses are red, then if violets are blue marigolds are yellow.

The forms are valid for any content, not merely roses, violets, and marigolds. Suppose we have the following argument: "If the demand stays constant and prices are lowered then the volume of business will increase. If the lowering of prices will cause the volume of business to increase, then we can control the market. Demand is bound to stay constant. Thus we can control the market."[8] The problem is to construct a formal proof of the argument's validity. Let us take a letter from one of the important words in each statement and let it be the basis for our notation, thus in this case D, P, B, C. Now we can set it up in this way:

1. $(D \cdot P) \supset B$
2. $(P \supset B) \supset C$
3. D

These are all the premises from which is concluded C. Now we begin the proof:

4. $D \supset (P \supset B)$ by 1 and Exportation.
5. $D \supset C$ by 2, 4, and Hypothetical Syllogism.
6. C by 3, 5, and Modus Ponens.

[7] Irving M. Copi, *Introduction to Logic*, The Macmillan Co., New York, 1954, p. 258.
[8] Irving M. Copi, *Symbolic Logic*, The Macmillan Co., New York, 1954, p. 50.

Notice that no step is taken unless it can be justified by a premise or by an elementary valid form. This is a simple argument and proof, but much more complex ones are possible with the aid of many more valid forms. This is as far as we can go with some of the advances over the traditional logic. Contemporary logic has become increasingly technical and has developed new abstract forms which are not restricted by the demand for content from experience. Along with this development new speculative and theoretical problems have appeared that can be discussed only after a more thoroughgoing experience with the discipline of symbolic logic.

VII. Some Common Fallacies

The problem of bringing consistency and clarity into our beliefs is not only a matter of paying strict attention to their forms and their relations; it is also a matter of avoiding certain pitfalls hidden by linguistic and psychological factors. It is almost impossible to get a universally acceptable classification of the ways in which the thinker may fall into error, but there are a number of common dangers the beginning student should recognize and shun. Many of these errors, called fallacies, are due to failures of language, many to deliberate attempts to confuse or deceive, many to misconceptions of the subject under consideration. No attempt will be made here to list these fallacies in appropriate classifications. We will simply describe and illustrate some of the obstacles that may prevent the communicating, defining, or criticizing of beliefs. Most of our trouble comes when the communication, defense, or criticism is apparently sound or plausible, but in fact is neither.

One of the commonest sources of fallacious thinking is the misuse or abuse of language. Words, we know, seldom have only a single meaning. In the course of an argument, if a word shifts its meaning we cannot tell what is being affirmed or denied. Consider the following: "If anyone obeys a law he yields to a superior being. Nature obeys laws and therefore yields to a superior being." Here we have a change in the meaning of the term "law" from prescription to description. The invalidity of the argument becomes apparent. The student may raise his own questions about "obey" and "superior being." Such errors are frequently called *equivocation*. They can be avoided, first by watching out for them, second by careful definition, third by keeping the terms within an argument as strictly univocal as possible.

Two fallacies, each the converse of the other, also result from the ambiguous use of a word. They are known as *composition* and *division*. The former occurs when we argue from the fact that because individuals have certain properties, therefore the wholes that these individuals constitute also have these properties. It does not follow that a jury is weak because each of its members is weak, or that it is tall because each juryman is over six feet. The fallacy of division directs attention to the opposite error, namely, that what is said truly about the properties of a whole is not necessarily true about the parts. Just because in a democracy we trust the majority to do what is right in the long run, this is no reason for insisting that John Doe, a member of the majority, can be trusted to do what is right in the long run. We all know that persons acquire different attitudes and characters in a group.

If beliefs are based on unqualified generalizations, this can lead to shoddy thought. For example, suppose student *X* would argue that it is his duty to help his fellow student *Y* on an examination because it is an absolute duty to do unto others as one would have them do reciprocally, and if *X* were in trouble, he would appreciate help. The muddle in this argument is, of course, that the unqualified generalization needs qualification—as do most so-called absolutes. This fallacy has been named *a dicto simplicter,* that is, from taking simply or without qualification what has been said; and sometimes it is called the *fallacy of accident.*

In general we should say that any argument concerning our beliefs ought not to move in a circle. That is, if we argue that *p* is true because *q* is true; and *q* is true because *r* is true; and *r* is true because *p* is true, we have come around to our starting point and assumed what is being proved. The most usual names for this type of weak reasoning are *petitio principii* or *begging the question,* or *arguing in a circle.* To argue that the Bible is infallible because every statement in it is true, and every statement in it is true, because the Bible makes no false statements, and this is true because it is infallible, is to be caught by this fallacy.

Another source of confused thinking lies in the failure to distinguish between relevant and irrelevant material—and there may be both with respect to a many-sided argument. It is important to admit all relevant points for any side and omit all irrelevance. There are a number of fallacies that arise from this: for instance, *post hoc ergo propter hoc* (after that, therefore caused by that), *false analogy,* and *hasty generalization.* A brief description of each is all that is necessary. A *post hoc* fallacy consists in arguing that because an event occurred in time before another event, that it was the cause of the succeeding event.

The boll weevil hasn't touched the seven acres set aside here for the Lord. The seven farmers who consecrated an acre each to the church are prospering in everything they have planted. Their flourishing farms present a marked contrast to the areas of devastation in this section.[9]

An analogy is said to be false when it is argued that because x and y are alike in certain respects, they are therefore alike in other respects, although in fact they are different. If one should argue that since government is nothing but national housekeeping, therefore women should have a more important role in political affairs than men, the weakness of the argument becomes evident as soon as the significant differences between running a government and running a household are noted. Analogies, of course, are useful. They may suggest fresh hypotheses and direct attention to easily overlooked data, but they are dangerous if they lure one into certainty or blind one to crucial differences and necessary distinctions.

Hasty generalization is such a common error that it needs only to be mentioned to be recognized. It is the attempt to establish a rule or principle from too few instances and then to use the rule as if it were good evidence. There are no rules to tell us when we have collected too few. The student can easily find his own examples.

There are a great many fallacies that might all be described as *getting away from the point at issue.* Thus one may attack the character of one's opponent, or his family background, or his associates, or his past history. Or one may appeal to sympathy, pity, or prestige to get one's view across. All of these are devices by which the real point is obscured or evaded. They can be met adequately by insisting on paying attention to the real issue.

We have not tried, in this relatively brief survey of the principles of deductive logic, to make a logician out of the reader. Rather we have called attention to the fact that our beliefs may be well or poorly grounded, and how we may achieve the former and avoid the latter. But this is only a beginning, not only because we have not exhausted the subject, but also because there is another way in which we acquire and test our beliefs. This is the problem of the next section.

VIII. *The Logic of Evidence: Induction*

In the preceding sections we have tried to show that some of our beliefs may be held because they follow necessarily from other beliefs. When they do, a logical structure is discernible that gives the argument for the belief validity or invalidity. It is usually good reasoning to hold a belief because it is the result of a valid argument and to reject or question it when the argument is invalid. Such acceptable beliefs are said to be certain in a

[9] Alburey Castell, *A College Logic*, The Macmillan Co., New York, 1935, p. 35.

logical sense, that is, if you accept *p,* then you must accept *q* or, to put it another way, the premises of a valid argument are said to entail the conclusion. It would be self-contradictory to hold the premise as true and the conclusion as false.

The logical force of a valid argument is obviously not a physical compulsion. It is always psychologically possible to refuse to accept the conclusion of a valid argument with true premises. But when this occurs, we should suspect that the refusal comes from either a failure to understand the meanings of the terms in the argument or from a basic rational incompetence in following the steps of an argument.

But it is extremely difficult to get our experiences and our beliefs organized into neat logical patterns, and for some beliefs it may be impossible. Most of us believe a great deal more than we are able to demonstrate as formally valid. How we acquire these beliefs and how we attempt to establish them, or what good reasons we offer for believing them, is the problem of this section. The evidence for these beliefs cannot be obtained from the structure of the argument alone, but requires an examination of a state of affairs or observations of the external world, external, that is, to the argument itself. Such beliefs may be said to be inductively inferred. But first let us look at a number of illustrations of inductive arguments.

1. The milk bottle has been in the sun all morning so the milk is probably sour.
2. These pens don't leak in high altitudes so it will be safe for me to keep one in my pocket when I fly to Paris.
3. In very hot weather, people lose salt through perspiration. Therefore it is good sense to take a salt pill if you are working in the heat.
4. The average income of the farmer in this county is $7000 a year. Probably this is the average for the entire state, too.
5. Ten people at the picnic became ill. They are known to have eaten a salad not shared by others. It is thought that the salad brought on the sickness.

But just a word again on the use of terms. By deduction we shall mean a relation between premises and a conclusion, such that, a conclusion validly deduced from true premises cannot be false. An inductive inference does not give this degree and kind of certainty. The premises could be true and the conclusion false, or the conclusion could be true independently of the particular premises. Inductive conclusions are said to be in some degree *probably* true or false.

Let us turn now to the history of philosophy and science for a remarkable contrast between deduction and induction. This contrast may be a key to the conflict between rationalists and empiricists. Tentatively we may say that a rationalist thinks that some beliefs about the world do not need to be verified by experience; that these beliefs are seen to be true when their meaning is understood; and that using them as premises, together with processes of deduction, we can arrive at knowledge of the world without examining the world. But an empiricist thinks that all beliefs are not only derived from experience but must be verified or are verifiable by experience, where experience usually means some kind of sensory test or observation.

A. Deductively Implied Beliefs and Inductively Inferred Beliefs

To elaborate this contrast we present a case study of a master of mathematical method, René Descartes, and a master of experimental technique, William Harvey. Each called attention to the problem of the motion of the heart and the blood and each approached the problem with different techniques.

Descartes. Descartes was one of the great figures in the exaltation of deduction and the search for certainty in belief. His first step toward certainty he regarded as a necessary truth, that is, one that could not be doubted or denied without self-contradiction. It is succinct, and to many, convincing: "I think, therefore, I am." The point here is, that it is inconsistent to doubt the existence of the self, for doubting (a kind of thinking) presupposes the existence of the doubting (thinking) self. Thus to doubt that I am is to know certainly that I am. I cannot both be and not be. "I think" and "I am not" are not both true together. This is logically equivalent to "I think, therefore, I am."

Descartes not only believed that his proposition about the self was as certain as the truths of arithmetic and geometry, but also that God, the perfect being, can not not be, and that the philosopher can deduce all truths about the world if he has self-evident premises. For example, he thought that the nature of animals could be deduced from certain premises in the following way: All things in space and time are material things in motion. The bodies of animals are in space and time; therefore, they are material things in motion. Now animals owe their life to motion, and motion in a body is heat, and heat is derived from the heart, therefore, "life consists simply in the warmth of the heart."[10] Furthermore, warmth is a case of

---

[10] Norman Kemp Smith, *New Studies in the Philosophy of Descartes*, Macmillan and Co., Ltd., London, 1952, p. 126.

heat; heat is with or without light; there is no light in the heart, therefore, the heart is "one of those fires without light."[11]

Of course Descartes' argument is not purely deductive. He has made several statements about his observations as well. But the argument is chiefly a chain of propositions moving from more general to less general truths and claiming certainty for the conclusions because they follow with logical necessity. Why does the blood circulate? Descartes deduces his answer. Blood expands when heated; it is heated by the heart; when expanded it fills more space and the heart is unable to contain it, hence it must flow out. The deductive process then goes on:

For the rest, so that those who do not appreciate the force of mathematical demonstration and are not accustomed to distinguishing between good and bad reasons should not make the mistake of denying this without examining it, I must warn them that the motion which I have just explained follows necessarily from the mere disposition of the parts of the heart visible to the naked eye, from the heat which one can feel with the fingers, and from the nature of the blood, which one can learn by experiment; just as the motions of a clock follow from the weight, location and configuration of its counterweights and wheels.[12]

Descartes' "mathematical demonstration" does "follow necessarily" from his premise about the fire in the heart, but his proof is a curiosity in the history of science, and the explanation he thought he had refuted is considered correct. The great force of inductive logic on the same problem can be seen in the method of William Harvey in The Motion of the Heart and Blood.

Harvey. Harvey's inductive method does not by any means exclude deduction, but it is inductive in its emphasis on what can be observed. The failure of past explanations he points out, was partly a confusion in terms. For example, there was no precise definition distinguishing "vein" from "artery." But more seriously, it was a failure *to see what lies before their eyes.* Descartes' demonstration moved from a universal view of matter and motion to the nature of animals, then to the nature of the heart. Harvey "multiplied demonstrations" to confirm a general view of the heart and blood. The inductive procedure he employed required a repetition of experiments, because the confirmation of the argument increases with the number of known cases. It is risky to say something about *all* hearts if we only know *some.* It is also risky to predict what *future* hearts will be like, from what *past* hearts were like. The case for inductive logic is

[11] René Descartes, *Discourse on Method* (Laurence J. Lafleur, tr.), The Liberal Arts Press, New York, 1950, p. 30.
[12] *Ibid.,* p. 32.

strengthened because men like Harvey did succeed in this risky business. We may now ask, are there principles that can help us to distinguish more from less reliable induction? Although Harvey's rules cannot be as neatly stated as Descartes', if we reflect on his procedure, the following steps seem to emerge. The question is, what *evidence* is there that is relevant to the motion of the heart and blood. Evidence is acquired, for Harvey, by using the senses to give trustworthy reports. "I profess both to learn and to teach anatomy, not from books but from dissections: not from the positions of philosophers but from the fabric of nature."[13]

From his treatise we can derive the following:

1. *Look for those facts that can be observed rather than those that cannot.* Example: You see the spurting of bright blood from an artery coming from the heart. You cannot see "spirits."
2. *Make general statements about what is common to every observed case.* Example: All examined cases of red-blooded animals have hearts. All examined creatures without red blood are without hearts.
3. *Describe the facts as faithfully as possible. Some analogies may be closer to the facts than others.* Example: Descartes compared the heart to a clock moved by counterweights. Harvey compared it to a pump "as by two clacks of a water bellows to rayse water." Liquid flows through a pump, not through the kind of clock Descartes suggested.
4. *Seek and describe the cause and effect relationships and fit the description into the knowledge of other factors.* Example: Valves in the arteries permit blood to flow from the heart, and prevent flow to the heart. This fits in with binding a limb above a wound and not also below, to stop spurting blood.
5. *Measure whatever can be measured.* Example: How much blood is in the heart? and how much in the body? If two ounces are emptied from the heart 72 times a minute, then in an hour 8,640 ounces, or 540 pounds are thrown into the system. "Where can all this blood come from? Where can it all go to? The answer is that the blood is a stage army which goes off only to come on again. It is the same blood always returning."
6. *Correlate the known facts functionally.* Example: When the heart contracts, the pulse is felt. This was opposed to Descartes' view that the pulse is felt when the heart dilates. Again, when an artery is opened, the blood spurts out. Whenever this happens the veins collapse and are not filled.

[13] William Harvey, *Motion of the Heart and Blood,* Henry Regnery Co., Chicago, 1949, p. 5.

7. *Consider every explanation.* Prefer the one that accounts for all the known facts. Reject the theory that is contrary to fact or that neglects the facts. Analyze each alternative theory to see in what respect it fails to describe, and then try to meet the objections offered to the preferred theory. (To get the full impact of this the student will have to read the document.)

8. *Submit the theory to further observations.* Admit that what is not observed is inferred, and subject to correction by observation. Example: The theory requires capillaries connecting arteries and veins.

The consensus is that although Harvey's reasoning is not deductively certain, as is Descartes', his results are more trustworthy and fruitful. The appeal to observation of instances did secure results and suggested that the formal certainty of deductive reasoning seems to be a snare and delusion for factual problems.

B. The Traditional Problem of Induction

The nature of inductive inference, or for short, induction, is considered by many philosophers to be one of the most important and troublesome questions in philosophy. C. D. Broad once wrote, "May we venture to hope that when Bacon's next centenary is celebrated the great work which he set going will be completed; and that Inductive Reasoning, which has long been the glory of Science, will have ceased to be the scandal of Philosophy?"[14]

But why is induction a problem? Let us remember that a deductively valid argument has a timeless character because of its formal nature, that is, whatever the content, whatever the place, and whatever the time, if the premises are true and the argument is valid, then the conclusion is true. Inductive arguments seem also to go beyond present time and predict what will be the case in the future. But the justification offered for this is not a formal pattern but rather what is known from observations of past and present instances. If we do not know all past instances, as we seldom do, nor even all present ones, what is the justification for affirming something about future cases? In short, there is always the possibility that we will make mistakes in our inferences because we do not view the world as a god might view it. No matter how many times we have observed that an unsupported object falls, we may not conclude certainly that "all unsupported objects fall," because the millionth time it may go up rather than down. Still, we do make successful predictions in

[14] C. D. Broad, *Ethics and the History of Philosophy*, Routledge & Kegan Paul, Ltd., London, 1952, pp. 142–143.

common life as well as in science. And many of our beliefs are generated in this way. But are we justified in accepting them?

If we look for the same justification we have for deduction we are looking for the wrong thing. This does not mean there is *no* justification for inductive inferences. If philosophy is defined as the analysis of belief, the discovery of the grounds and criteria of belief is crucial for philosophizing. Many of our beliefs rest on empirical grounds, that is, experience or the appeal to facts. Hence we may succeed or fail in our philosophizing depending on whether we get clear the meanings of inference, the processes so named in our philosophic tradition, and the inductive logical patterns that we can employ in analyzing our beliefs and their grounds. No one of these three tasks is easy. Each has become so complicated that confusion of the issues is common.

Contemporary philosophers do not always have the same meaning in mind when they speak or write of "induction." It is sometimes thought of as a psychological habit; as the use of analogy; as inferring from a known past to an unknown future; as the process called "generalization" in which one moves from beliefs about "some" to beliefs about "all"; and as a mathematical calculus of probability answering such questions as "what are the odds?" or "what are the chances that *A* is *B*?" The ambiguity of the term, however, should not lead us to conclude that induction is shapeless and haphazard. True, it does not have the clean-cut structure of deduction, but then it is not deduction. There are arguments in philosophy and history and experimental science which, while not deductively valid, are nevertheless sound or correct or reasonable. The critical standards or rules of deduction are simply not appropriate to these arguments, but that is not a sufficient reason to reject their conclusions, for the conclusions are not entailed by the evidence. In short, there are reasons for accepting beliefs other than their demonstrated validity in a deductive argument. We may get a better understanding of induction if we examine more closely some of the traditional patterns and interpretations.

Why philosophers used "induction" in so many ways needs explaining. The palpable reason is a fault in definition, but other reasons appear if we look at history. Aristotle's logic of terms, propositions, and syllogisms became established as "logic" properly so called. But men noticed, beginning with Aristotle himself, that not all successful reasoning fitted this system. In fact, he offered a case that was valid, but not by his rules. He called it *epagogé*, which is reasoning from "perfect enumeration of cases" to a universal proposition, rather than from a universal to a universal. This Greek word was translated "induction," and ever since, whenever anyone spotted a nonsyllogistic kind of reasoning that he considered useful, even indispensable, it was set down as "induction." Since Aristotle had worked out a deductive logic, Bacon and Mill took upon themselves the task of constructing systems of inductive logic. Pascal and Hume also made critical additions to its theory and practice.

Let us consider the contributions made by these five men and the questions they considered essential to a philosophy of belief based on knowledge of facts.

Aristotle: Intuitive Induction. This type has also been called "perfect" because the reasoning is from knowledge of all the instances. Aristotle's *epagogé* meant "leading to." This suggests the use of examples offered as evidence for a general conclusion. It also suggests the activity of leading a pupil from a particular judgment to a universal. It may even call to mind the bringing of witnesses into a law court.[15] The problem is: How can one establish the truth of universal propositions? According to the principles of the syllogism, to deduce a conclusion that is a universal proposition requires two universal propositions as premises. The premise of one syllogism may be the conclusion of another, but we cannot go on with this regress ad infinitum. Hence, syllogistic logic depends on some other way to establish universal propositions, a nonsyllogistic way. And this is *epagogé* or induction, more accurately called "summative induction by complete enumeration." We may illustrate it in the following manner.[16] Suppose the question is raised, "Has there been a Catholic President of the United States?" The answer may take this form, Washington was a Protestant, Adams was a Protestant, Jefferson was a Protestant . . . to Eisenhower is a Protestant. Hence, there has been no Catholic President. Is the conclusion certain? It seems to be demonstrated by this procedure. But has there not been a premise suppressed? Namely, that the list "Washington . . . Eisenhower" contains the names of all the American Presidents? If so, there is a middle term and the argument is deductive.

There are at least three objections to perfect induction. First, the argument may be stated as a valid syllogism if a suppressed premise is stated. In this case the claim that the argument is inductive rather than deductive is mistaken. The second objection is that it has limited use, that is, it is restricted to finite lists, such as days of the week or the number of chairs in a room. The third objection stems from the fact that the laws of nature established by science are not limited to known cases. They

[15] This account is based on William Kneale, *Probability and Induction,* The Clarendon Press, Oxford, 1949, Part II.

[16] Adapted from Morris R. Cohen and Ernest Nagel, *An Introduction to Logic and Scientific Method,* Harcourt, Brace & Co., New York, 1934, p. 275.

are framed to hold for future and hence unknown instances. Bacon pointed out that although perfect induction is logically valid, it is scientifically sterile. If one has examined all the instances, and it is known that these are all the instances, then any conclusion about all the instances simply repeats what is already known.

According to Aristotle, the knowledge of summed-up particulars is sharply different from another kind of knowledge. It is necessary, he affirms, to have first principles or axioms in reasoning. Our syllogistic reasoning, for example, goes back to a firsthand knowledge of universal truths. These are used in the familiar demonstrations of geometry. Axioms are needed to prove theorems, but they are not themselves subject to deductive validation, or to factual verification. Such truths are not innate. They are found by a kind of intuition. Since there cannot be discursive knowledge of the primary premises, it must be intellectual intuition (nous) which grasps them.[17] For example, it is necessary for whatever is colored to be extended. One knows this to be true of all cases because it is necessarily true in any single instance. Thus the conclusion of intuitive induction is not, as in summative induction, restricted to known particular cases.

Some modern philosophers disagree with Aristotle. They grant that we do know that whatever is colored is extended, but they claim this is only knowledge of the way we use language. Aristotle, however, asserts that by intuitive induction we know the structure of the external world. The difficulties of knowledge by intuition are discussed in Chapter V on epistemology and truth.

Bacon: Ampliative Induction and Induction by Elimination. Bacon pointed out that by induction we mean more than a summing up of old knowledge. We gain also new knowledge, particularly of the relationships between cause and effect. Although Aristotle did not provide a logic of causal relationships between particular events, certainly many instances of common thinking are of this type. For example, we often say it will rain when we see dark thunder clouds. The need for predictive knowledge in the routine demands of ordinary living, as well as in the stricter requirements of science, is one source of our search for the laws of nature. Aristotle's failure to supply this logic led Bacon to provide a new guide for scientific practice. This is the Novum Organum, the "new instrument." "As the present sciences are useless for the discovery of effects, so the present system of logic is useless for the discovery of science."[18] Bacon rejects

[17] Richard, McKeon, (ed.) *The Basic Works of Aristotle,* Random House, New York, 1941, p. 186. *Posterior Analytics,* The Clarendon Press, Oxford 100b.
[18] William Kneale, *op. cit.,* pp. 48–49.

Aristotle's intuitive induction. He asserts there are only two ways of investigating truth.

'There are and can exist,' he says, 'but two ways of investigating truth. The one hurries on rapidly from the particulars of sense to the most general principles and from them as premisses (supposed to be of indisputable truth) derives the lesser laws. This is the way now in use. The other constructs its generalizations from the particulars of sense by ascending continually and gradually till it finally arrives at the most general principles, which is the true but unattempted way.'[19]

But Bacon also challenges Aristotle's summative induction, or induction from "simple enumeration."

'We must invent a different form of induction from that hitherto in use. . . . The induction which proceeds by simple enumeration is puerile, leads to uncertain conclusions and is exposed to danger from one contradictory instance. . . . A really useful induction should separate nature by proper rejections and exclusions. . . . Now this has not been done, except perhaps by Plato, who certainly uses this form of induction in some measure to sift definitions and ideas.'[20]

Ampliative induction and induction by elimination are so intimately connected that we present them conjointly, as in fact Bacon did. His celebrated case deals with both knowledge of cause and effect and the use of negative instances to rule out absence of connection.

Can we generalize, for instance, about the relationship between motion and heat? We suspect some causal connection, let us say, between the heat and the motion of a wheel. The test of negative instances is useful here. Thus we may ask, "Do you ever turn wheels without having them increase in warmth?" "I wouldn't believe this if you could show me one wheel that wasn't hotter in motion than at rest." One negative case might disprove or eliminate this hypothesis that conjoins these two properties. Bacon asks, does motion "generate" heat? He thinks this can be proved. What generates is "cause," what is generated is "effect." He made tables to symbolize the relationship between these two. The table that shows that wherever there is motion (C), there is also heat (E), Bacon called the *Table of Presence*. Since both motion and heat vary in degree it may be true that the faster the motion the greater the heat, and the slower the motion the less heat. Thus we get another table, e.g.,

Less C . . . Less E
More C . . . More E

[19] *Ibid.*, p. 49.
[20] *Ibid.*, p. 49.

called a *Table of Degrees*. This is also called *Co-variance,* in contrast to *Co-presence* and *Co-absence.*

Bacon's views were seriously criticized on two grounds. The first attack showed that working scientists did not get results in the way he prescribed. This we can see in the actual scientific practice of Pascal, who did not use tables of multiplied instances, rather, following Galileo's practice, and Bacon's sage advice, he performed "crucial experiments." It was Galileo, not Bacon, who urged quantitative rather than qualitative procedures. Both Aristotle and Bacon *described* the world. The method lacked what Galileo insisted on, *measure* the world.

The second ground upon which Bacon is open to attack is that his notion of cause is far from clear. He defined cause in the following way; "a form as a generating nature distinct from the generated nature of which it is the form."[21] This seemed to the philosopher Hume as unclear as Aristotle's four causes, and he attacked Bacon on this score.

Pascal: Induction by Crucial Experiment and the Calculus of Chances. Pascal's logic of experiment is so clear that one cannot do better than quote him. It illustrates the method of crucial experiment.

And so, on the subject of a vacuum, they were right in saying that nature does not tolerate a vacuum, because all their experiments had always led them to see that she abhors and does not tolerate it. But if the new experiments had been known to them, perhaps they would then have had grounds for affirming what they had cause to deny when a vacuum had not yet made its appearance; since to make a generalization it would not be enough to have seen nature constant on a hundred occasions, nor a thousand, nor any other number, however great it might be. For if a single case remained to be examined, it alone would suffice to prevent general definition, and if a single case were in disagreement, it alone . . . [two lines missing]. For in all matters where proof consists in experiments and not in [reasoned] demonstrations, we can make a general assertion only by the general enumeration of all parts and of all different cases. And so when we say that the diamond is the hardest of all bodies, we mean of all the bodies that we know, and we cannot, nor should we say that gold is the heaviest of all bodies; it would be temerity if we included in this general proposition those which we do not yet know, although there may be some in nature. Similarly, when the ancients asserted that nature tolerates no vacuum, they meant that she tolerated none in all the experiments they had seen, and without temerity they could not have included those of which they had no knowledge. For if these had existed, the ancients would doubtless have drawn the same conclusions as we, and by their approbation they would have invested them with the authority of this very antiquity which people wish to set up today as the sole principle of science.

And so, without contradicting them, we may assert the contrary of what

[21] *Ibid.,* p. 52.

they said, and no matter what influence this antiquity had, the truth must always prevail, even though it be newly discovered. For the truth is always older than all the opinions which men have held of it and we should be ignoring the nature of truth, if we imagined that truth began at the time when it began to be known. . . .

Certainly, after this experiment, there was cause for being persuaded that it is not abhorrence of a vacuum, as we thought, which causes the suspension of quicksilver in the ordinary experiment, but rather the weight and the pressure of the air, which counterbalance the weight of the quicksilver. But because all the results of this last experiment with the two tubes—which are explained so naturally by the pressure and weight of the air alone—may still be explained plausibly enough by a horror of a vacuum, I am adhering to that ancient maxim. Nevertheless I am resolved to seek full enlightenment of this difficulty by a decisive experiment. I have imagined one which may alone suffice to give us the light we are seeking, if it is properly carried out. This is to perform the ordinary experiment of the vacuum several times in the same day, in the same tube, with the same quicksilver, now at the foot and now at the summit of a mountain, at least five or six hundred fathoms high, to determine whether the height of the quicksilver suspended in the tube will be found the same or different in these two locations. You will doubtless see that this experiment is decisive for the question, and that if the height of the quicksilver should be less at the summit than at the foot of the mountain (as I have many reasons to believe, although all those who have meditated on this matter are opposed to this belief), it will necessarily follow that the weight and the pressure of the air are the sole cause for this suspension of the quicksilver, and that it is not the horror of a vacuum. For it is quite certain that much more air bears down upon the foot of the mountain than upon its summit, whereas one could not say that nature abhors a vacuum more at the foot of the mountain than at its summit.[22]

Pascal claimed that his experimental results were as conclusive as any Descartes had expected from deduction. These results were also more than mere lists of associated instances. Unlike Bacon, Pascal planned his experiments carefully and controlled the conditions. This Bacon tried to do and encourage others to do; but his advice was better than his practice.

Pascal's further advance on Bacon had to do with what we may call the calculus of chances. He devised techniques for answering such questions as, what is the "probability of getting at least one double-six in twenty-four throws of a pair of dice."[23]

Hume: Induction by Association and Habit. David Hume denied that any argument from experience can be deductive and affirmed that all arguments from experience have the form of causal inferences. His work on in-

[22] Emile Cailliet and John C. Blankenagel, *Great Shorter Works of Pascal,* The Westminster Press, Philadelphia, 1948, pp. 55, 57–58.
[23] William Kneale, *op. cit.,* p. 123.

duction is said to be "one of the most important advances in the whole history of thought."[24]

Here are his own words:

'Tis therefore by experience only, that we can infer the existence of one object from that of another. The nature of experience is this. We remember to have had frequent instances of the existence of one species of objects; and also remember, that the individuals of another species of objects have always attended them, and have existed in a regular order of contiguity and succession with regard to them. Thus we remember to have seen that species of object we call *flame,* and to have felt that species of sensation we call *heat.* We likewise call to mind their constant conjunction in all past instances. Without any farther ceremony, we call the one *cause* and the other *effect,* and infer the existence of the one from that of the other. In all those instances, from which we learn the conjunction of particular causes and effects, both the causes and effects have been perceived by the senses, and are remember'd: But in all cases, wherein we reason concerning them, there is only one perceiv'd or remember'd, and the other is supply'd in conformity to our past experience.[25]

To guide his thinking in this area Hume fixed what he called "general rules" which should help in distinguishing cause and effect. Let him speak for himself.

(a) The cause and effect must be contiguous in space and time.
(b) The cause must be prior to the effect.
(c) There must be a constant union betwixt the cause and effect. 'Tis chiefly this quality, that constitutes the relation.
(d) The same cause always produces the same effect, and the same effect never arises but from the same cause. [Today we would say that a cause must be sufficient and necessary to produce the effect.]
(e) . . . Where several different objects produce the same effect, it must be by means of some quality, which we discover to be common amongst them. For as like effects imply like causes, we must always ascribe the causation to the circumstance, wherein we discover the resemblance.
(f) The difference in the effects of two resembling objects must proceed from that particular, in which they differ. [This means that if an effect arises from A and not from B, then A and B differ and the difference is the cause of the effect.]
(g) When any object increases or diminishes with the increase or diminution of its cause, 'tis to be regarded as a compounded effect, deriv'd from the union of the several different effects, which rise from the several different parts of the cause. The absence or presence of one part of the cause is

---

[24] H. H. Price, "The Permanent Significance of Hume's Philosophy," *Philosophy,* Vol. 15, No. 57, 1940, p. 7.
[25] David Hume, *A Treatise of Human Nature* (L. A. Selby-Bigge, ed.), The Clarendon Press, Oxford, 1951, p. 87.

here suppos'd to be always attended with the absence or presence of a proportionable part of the effect. This constant conjunction sufficiently proves, that the one part is the cause of the other. [Here Hume is saying that if A (the effect) increases or diminishes while corresponding changes occur in B (the cause), then the absence or presence of a part of the cause must be accompanied by the absence or presence of a proportionate part of the effect.]

(h) . . . An object, which exists for any time in its full perfection without any effect, is not the sole cause of that effect, but requires to be assisted by some other principle, which may forward its influence and operation. [That is, if A exists for a period of time without B following, it cannot be the whole cause of B.][26]

This is a heterogeneous collection of rules which is reminiscent of and is undoubtedly influenced by Bacon's theory, and which also anticipates, as will shortly be seen, Mill's "canons of induction." Having stated them, Hume confidently says, "Here is all the logic I think proper to employ in my reasoning," although he confesses that it is easier to invent rules than it is to apply them. For Hume, then, inference from effect to cause is not certain and necessary, but a matter of the association of ideas, a constant conjunction of events, and a habit or feeling of expectancy that is present when we have experienced frequently the association of these events. On Hume's grounds therefore, induction can be nothing more than the association of ideas without rational justification. It was Mill who tried to give a more rational basis for induction. Let us turn to him.

Mill's Methods of Experimental Inquiry. In 1843 John Stuart Mill published A System of Logic, Ratiocinative and Inductive, Being a Connected View of the Principles of Evidence and the Methods of Scientific Investigations. He recognized that the method of simple enumeration is delusive and insufficient. It gives us no new truth at best, and at worst, erroneous impressions because we neglect negative instances.[27]

Moreover, Mill did not accept what Aristotle called intuitive induction.

The truths known by intuition are the original premises from which all others are inferred. Our assent to the conclusion being grounded on the truth of the premises, we could never arrive at any knowledge by reasoning unless something could be known antecedently to all reasoning.[28]

What is known immediately is not universal truth but "bodily sensations and mental feelings." These are clearly particulars.

[26] *Ibid.*, pp. 173f.
[27] John Stuart Mill, *Philosophy of Scientific Method* (Ernest Nagel, ed.), Hafner Publishing Co., New York, 1950, pp. 230, 290–291.
[28] *Ibid.*, p. 8.

Mill attempted to state more precisely what Bacon, Hume, and Pascal had suggested. His exposition resembles Bacon's use of "tables." To probability in the mathematical sense, he gave scant, and at first, grudging attention. He thought mathematical calculation was too abstract to be the real foundation of knowledge and insisted that knowing the odds, that is, having grounds "for acting on one supposition rather than on another," seemed to look through probability to "causation."[29] Hume had questioned our ability to know cause and effect relationships. Pascal doubted our need to know them. Mill, however, was not troubled by either kind of doubt. He set out to provide rules for the discovery of causes and effects, although he stated them in a language certainly more cumbersome than Descartes'. Symbolic representation may make them clearer. They are called *canons*.

1. Method of Agreement:

First Canon. If two or more instances of the phenomenon under investigation have only one circumstance in common, the circumstance in which alone all the instances agree is the cause (or effect) of the given phenomenon.

In symbols:

First instance	*ABCD*, consequently *pqrs*
Second instance	*AEFG*, consequently *ptuv*
Third instance	*AHIJ*, consequently *pwxy*

A is the only event present in all antecedent instances, and *p* the only event present in all the consequents. Thus *A* is said to be the cause of *p*.

2. Method of Difference:

Second Canon. If an instance in which the phenomenon under investigation occurs and an instance in which it does not occur have every circumstance in common save one, that one occurring only in the former, the circumstance in which alone the two instances differ is the effect, or the cause, or an indispensable part of the cause, of the phenomenon.

In symbols:

First instance	*ABCD*, consequently *pqrs*
Second instance	*BCD*, consequently *qrs*

Each instance has everything in common, except that in the second, *A* is absent and so is *p*. Hence *A* is said to be a cause, or an indispensable part of the cause, of *p*.

[29] *Ibid.*, pp. 279–286.

3. Joint Method of Agreement and Difference:

Third Canon. If two or more instances in which the phenomenon occurs have only one circumstance in common, while two or more instances in which it does not occur have nothing in common save the absence of that circumstance, the circumstance in which alone the two sets of instances differ is the effect, or the cause, or an indispensable part of the cause, of the phenomenon.

In symbols:

Positive instances	$ABCD$,	consequently $pqrs$
	$AEFG$,	consequently $ptuv$
	$AHIJ$,	consequently $pwxy$
Negative instances	BCK,	consequently qro
	EFL,	consequently tun
	HIM,	consequently wxy

Again, says Mill, we conclude that A is causally related to p.

4. *Fourth Canon.* Subduct from any phenomenon such part as is known by previous inductions to be the effect of certain antecedents, and the residue of the phenomenon is the effect of the remaining antecedents.

In symbols:

$$ABCD, \text{ consequently } wxyz$$

In this case wxy are known from earlier inductions to have followed from ABC. Thus z is a consequent of D.

5. Method of Concomitant Variations:

Fifth Canon. Whatever phenomenon varies in any manner whenever another phenomenon varies in some particular manner is either a cause or an effect of that phenomenon, or is connected with it through some fact of causation.[30]

In symbols:

$ABCD_1$,	consequently $pqrs_1$
$ABCD_2$,	consequently $pqrs_2$
$ABCD_3$,	consequently $pqrs_3$

It is clear that when D increases, so does s.

$ABCD_{-1}$,	consequently $pqrs_{-1}$
$ABCD_{-2}$,	consequently $pqrs_{-2}$
$ABCD_{-3}$,	consequently $pqrs_{-3}$

When D decreases so does s.

Hence, D is causally related to s.

[30] *Ibid.,* pp. 214, 215–16, 221, 223, 227.

It is generally agreed that Mill's canons do not do what he had hoped, that is, they are neither entirely reliable methods for *proving* causal connections, nor are they sufficiently penetrating for the *discovery* of causal connections. Investigations that might require something like these canons need to begin with hypotheses about possible causes, hypotheses that enable one to select relevant circumstances based on one's previous knowledge. These hypotheses are not provided by the canons and must be supplied by the knowledge, imagination, and intelligence of the investigators. Nevertheless, the canons do have some value in the formulation of our beliefs, although such value is largely negative. That is, they may help in eliminating irrelevancies and proposed causes, or as Cohen and Nagel put it with respect to the method of agreement, "Nothing can be the cause of a phenomenon which is not a common circumstance in all the instances of the phenomenon."[31] And with respect to the method of difference, "Nothing can be the cause of a phenomenon if the phenomenon does not take place when the supposed cause does."[32] And similarly for the method of concomitant variations, "For nothing will be regarded as the cause of a phenomenon if when the phenomenon varies that thing does not, or when the phenomenon does not, that thing does."[33]

IX. *The Use of Analogy*

We cannot leave the subject of inductively inferred beliefs without some comment on the frequent use of analogy. It belongs to this discussion because along with the inductive patterns, analogies do not give certainty to their conclusions, but only probability. Of course, analogies may be used in nonargumentative ways, for example, in description or explanation, but our interest is now only with their argumentative use to establish beliefs.

Arguments by analogy may be said to be cogent rather than valid. These arguments draw inferences from the resemblances between instances rather than from the number of instances. A strong and commonly used analogy is that between a map and a country, where the *relationships* are similar. Models, as in science, are also analogically useful.

Perhaps the most important thing to say here is that the resemblances must be significant and relevant, two characteristics that are not always easy to define, though they may be illustrated in comparatively simple cases. If, for example, you have been buying Ford cars over a period of

[31] Morris R. Cohen and Ernest Nagel, *op. cit.*, p. 255.
[32] *Ibid.*, p. 259.
[33] *Ibid.*, p. 264.

years, your reasons for buying again this year could be based on analogy, that is, the past purchased cars have been mechanically very satisfactory, so you infer this new car will be too. If the dealer changed his location, or married, or if wages were raised in the Ford plant, or if an extra pocket were put in the door, you would hardly regard these as significant or relevant to the smooth performance of the automobile. But other changes might be highly relevant and cause you to buy a different type of automobile.

In general the simplest form of the analogy is,

> X has a and b
> Y has a
> therefore Y has (probably) b.

Or this form may be used,

> a,b,c,d all have the properties M and N
> a,b,c also have the property P
> therefore d (probably) has the property P.

If carefully used, analogies may be extremely suggestive, if not powerful forms of argument. But some caution must be exercised to avoid the fallacy of false analogy. One must be certain, for example, that the number of entities between which the analogy is said to hold is adequate, to avoid jumping too quickly to the conclusion. Furthermore, it is extremely important to notice the significance and the number of differences between the instances. Finally, the relationships and the qualities said to be similar must be relevant.

Analogies do support some of our beliefs. A good analogy may be a good reason for holding a belief. But they must be used critically and cautiously, for they do not provide a belief with certainty.

X. Concluding Remarks

It is now quite clear that many of our beliefs, from the lowest level of common sense, to the highest level of experimental science, are obtained by nondeductive procedures. Our knowledge of nature and ourselves is largely acquired by making observations, gathering instances, relating causes and effects, measuring and calculating chances when possible, and then affirming that there are sound reasons for accepting conclusions, even though exact proof is lacking. In the widest ranges of human experience, neither exactness nor absolute certainty is required. Induction gives neither. But it is a mistake to regard inductive beliefs as an inferior form of deductive beliefs. Induction is not deduction. They may be wedded, but not welded. Nevertheless, beliefs based on induction may be just as firmly grounded, or, to put it another way, there are sound reasons for holding inductively grounded beliefs, just as there are reasons for the validity or invalidity of a deductively based belief.

Our study of inductive methods has at least taught us the following:

Although induction does not have the formal strictness of deduction, it is not utterly without formal characteristics. If inductive reasoning is defined as "reasoning from one non-necessary statement (or conjunction of statements) to another, in which the first does not entail the second,"[34] then its various features may be brought together under the universal form,

$$p \text{ so probably } q$$

remembering that "probably" may be expressed in many ways to determine a degree of precision all the way from slightly probable, probable, quite probable, highly probably to an expression in mathematical ratio. Thus it always makes sense in inductive reasoning to ask for the "support" of the conclusion. It is the evidence that is the support and it can be said to be good, bad, weak, strong, conclusive, slender, better, worse, reasonable, unreasonable, correct, incorrect, but never valid or certain.

Secondly, we may not expect to achieve formal validity or logical certainty by induction. However, such ends are seldom needed in science or common life. This does not leave the door open to wild, irresponsible guessing, for there are still rules to obey.

In the third place we should have learned that the utility, correctness, and power of our inductive generalizations are related to our general body of knowledge. The more we experience our world, the more we may remember our experiences; the more we correlate these experiences, the sounder are our beliefs about the world. An ignorant man may construct a valid argument. It is absurd to think that he could come to an acceptable generalization about something of which he is ignorant.

He [Russell] asks us quite simply, "What reason is there to suppose that if a number of observed A's are all B, all A's are therefore B?" And the answer, so far as I can see, is that *in general* there is no reason. It all depends upon the A's, the B's, and what we already know about them. If the A's are specimens of a new strain of corn, selected according to a well-tested sampling procedure, there may be excellent reasons for expecting the generalization to hold. But if

[34] P. F. Strawson, *Introduction to Logical Theory*, John Wiley & Sons, Inc., New York, 1952, p. 237.

the A's are objects of which all we know is that they resemble one another in respect of being instances of B, a reasonable man will refuse to draw any conclusion. To insist that there must be a conclusion would be like saying that because a good chess player knows what move to make in a game of chess, he ought to be able to know what move to make when presented with a chessboard containing only a single piece. But this is not a problem of chess and there is nothing the chess player could do to solve it. The problem of what to infer when we know *only* that some A's are B is not a genuine inductive problem; and there is no way to solve it except by recognizing that it would be improper to try.

But we are never in this situation of almost total ignorance if we are in a position to raise "the problem of induction." We really do know a good deal about the sun, and anybody who can intelligently ask a question about its rising tomorrow also knows a good deal about empirical regularities. For the very young child or the very ignorant savage, there really may be a question whether there is any material body to be called *"the* sun"—since perhaps all that he sees is a celestial radiance that appears and disappears at irregular intervals. But at least he knows all kinds of things about other material bodies. If my questioner already knows *some* empirical generalizations (e.g., that there is a material body called "the sun") I can teach him about other matters of fact in perfectly familiar ways. But a man who averred that *no* matters of fact had already been established would be somebody with whom rational discourse would be impossible. The ordinary words that I would want to use (words like "man," "sun," and "tomorrow") would seem to him to involve presuppositions that begged *his* question. For to use a word like "sun" is to presuppose the regularities that give point and purpose to the use of that word. And the paradigms that we use in teaching a young child the meanings of "good evidence," "reasonable estimate," and the other terms needed for prediction and the appraisal of evidence about matters of fact, would likewise be unacceptable to our skeptic. I could no more argue with such a man than I could with a foreigner ignorant of my language.[35]

In the fourth place, it is clear that it is impossible to pursue the interests of philosophy, science, and practical affairs without employing in various degrees the processes of inductive logic. We are a part of, and belong to, this world. The way we relate ourselves to it will determine our knowledge of its structure and activity. Such knowledge-revealing relationships are those established by inductive procedures which may be said to be reliable but not infallible. If we do not trust the tested methods of induction, we may not survive long enough to formulate and enjoy the certainty of deduction.

Finally, we should see now that the strength of induction is related to the completeness and coherence of the general body of knowledge pos-

[35] Max Black, *Problems of Analysis*, Cornell University Press, Ithaca, New York, 1954, pp. 188–189.

sessed by mankind. The more we know of any subject the easier it is to know more, and the more confident we become in what we do or do not know. Inductive procedures demand the cooperation of all knowers—even the international community of knowers.

The beginning student should be prepared by what we have said about induction not to expect "proof" in philosophy, where proof is taken to mean deductive validity. Many, if not most, of the great beliefs that arise in the diverse philosophical disciplines are not susceptible to the rigorous proof of deduction. But that is no reason for abandoning them. Where we have certainty and validity we may also have abstraction and triviality; where we have good and sound reasons for belief, we may have concreteness and significance at the expense of absolute precision and deductive proof.

PROBLEMS FOR THOUGHT AND DISCUSSION

1. Is a dictionary definition always sufficient? If not, under what conditions do you employ other types of definition?
2. Charles S. Peirce said "The very first lesson that we have a right to demand that logic shall teach us is, how to make our ideas clear." Can you think of unclear ideas that need to be clarified? Can logic help to bring clarity to our social, political, economic, religious beliefs?
3. It is sometimes said of discourse in some specific area that logic does not apply. For example you may have noticed in reading Macbeth that although Macduff says of Macbeth "He has no children," his Lady says

    > . . . . I have given suck, and know
    > How tender 'tis to love the babe that milks me.
    > I would, while it was smiling in my face,
    > Have pluck'd my nipple from his boneless gums
    > And dash'd the brains out, had I so sworn as you
    > Have done to this.

    Goethe claimed "that the poet always lets his characters say what is in some particular place fitting, effective, and good, without worrying a great deal, or anxiously calculating, whether these words might not perhaps offer an apparent contradiction to another passage."[36]
    If you believe you know other such examples, state why formal logic, syllogistic or symbolic, is inapplicable. If you believe that formal logic applies to discourse of every area, defend this position.
4. It is said by Russell that philosophers who employ logical demonstration of a belief have probably ceased to believe. Is anxiety to demonstrate evidence of disbelief? Do you look for logical grounds for a belief only when you are at least wavering in attitude?
5. The syllogism is frequently said to be useless for discovery. For if the conclusion of a syllogism stated something other than what is already in the

[36] Walter Kaufmann, *Critique of Religion and Philosophy*, Harper & Brothers, New York, 1958, p. 267.

premises, then it is an invalid deduction. But if the syllogism is valid, the truth of the conclusion is already present in the premises. But discovery is of some *new* truth. Hence the syllogism is useless for discovery. Do you agree with this demonstration?

6. A. N. Whitehead wrote, "There is a tradition of opposition between adherents of induction and of deduction. In my view, it would be just as sensible for the two ends of a worm to quarrel. Both observation and deduction are necessary for any knowledge worth having." Discuss this point with respect to some subjects you know.

7. Hume claimed that of matters of fact our knowledge is probable only, and certain truth is impossible. What do you think could be meant by the contrast between "probable" and "certain"?

8. The logical copula "is" (or "are") is used because of the notion that every affirmation or negation can be stated as a subject-copula-predicate proposition. Set down twenty ordinary sentences employing "is" (or "are"). Do you discover in these cases one basic common meaning of the verb "to be"? If you do not, state how many basic types there are.

9. Draw up a truth table for the proposition "If Hitler had been killed in the Munich Putsch of 1923, then World War II might never have been fought." What does your attempt show about this kind of proposition and about truth tables?

10. We remarked that ⊃ is not to be read "if . . . then" as this implicative relation is understood in ordinary discourse. A logician and historian of symbolic logic, C. I. Lewis, made the following comment:

> Mr. Russell for example, bases *his* logic on an implication relation such that if twenty sentences be cut from a newspaper and put in a hat, and then two of these be drawn at random, one of them will certainly imply the other, and it is an even bet that the implication will be mutual. Yet upon a foundation so remote from ordinary modes of inference the whole structure of *Principia Mathematica* is built. This logic—and there are others even more strange—is utterly consistent and the results of it entirely valid.[37]

Examine common uses of beliefs taking the if . . . then form. What more is meant than the truth functional implication ⊃ ?

11. In some philosophies "dialectic" is contrasted to "logic." Consider Socratic dialectic and Aristotelian logic. How do they differ? May they be used together? What are the advantages of each within some area of discourse?

PERTINENT READINGS

Campbell, Norman, *What Is Science?*, Dover Publications, Inc., New York, 1952.
Northrop, F. S. C., *The Logic of the Sciences and the Humanities*, The Macmillan Co., New York, 1948.
Robinson, Richard, *Definition*, Clarendon Press, Oxford, 1950.

[37] Clarence Irving Lewis, "A Pragmatic Conception of the *a Priori*." In: H. Feigl and W. Sellars (eds.), *Readings in Philosophical Analysis*, Appleton-Century-Crofts, Inc., New York, 1949, p. 287.

Russell, Bertrand, "Logic as the Essence of Philosophy," *Our Knowledge of the External World as a Field for Scientific Method in Philosophy*, George Allen & Unwin, Ltd., London, 1949, pp. 42–69.

Santayana, George, "Some Meanings of the Word 'Is,'" *Obiter Scripta*, Charles Scribner's Sons, New York, 1936, pp. 189–212.

Thouless, Robert N., *Straight and Crooked Thinking*, Hodder & Stoughton, London, 1930.

Toulmin, Stephen, *The Uses of Argument*, Cambridge University Press, London, 1958.

IV

Belief and Truth

I. Preliminary Questions

When we say that a belief is true or false, what do we mean? The classical tradition of philosophy draws a distinction between the acts of believing, disbelieving, doubting—and what is affirmed, denied, questioned. The latter is the content of belief which we learned in logic to call the proposition. The former, as psychological acts, may have causes; the latter as content may be said to have reasons. When we give reasons for our beliefs we are aiming at truth; when we specify causes we are trying to understand the motives for holding a belief. If this distinction is slurred, truth and falsehood will be relative to the desires, wishes, and hopes of persons and to their situations. It is true, of course, that most philosophers are concerned about practical consequences in social relations— they are not cynics. But for the most part when philosophers demand reasons for a belief, they are not interested in the causes or consequences of an act, but rather in the cognitive grounds, logical or empirical, formal or factual, for declaring a proposition true or false.

The philosopher's aim is not directly to ennoble society, nor is his method the citation of lofty sentiments. He knows that men praise truth, that some fight for it, others wrestle with it, and some die for it even when they would find it difficult to say what this truth is they suffer, fight, and die for. But a philosopher must be wary of noble texts, such as "The truth shall make you free," for he knows how these vague words can be twisted in the attempt to persuade some-

148

one to share a particular religious, political, or economic perspective. The philosophic job is primarily of a second order, more general and speculative. That is, not whether, for example, a man is guilty or innocent of a crime, but what is meant by saying that he has been truly or falsely condemned. If we say "The true verdict is that he is guilty," we mean two things. One is factual. We mean that this man did what he is said to have done. The other is logical. If this man performed this act, and this act is defined as a crime, then he committed a crime. In logic we learned to call the first the truth of the premise and the second the validity of the conclusion.

This introduces another important distinction, namely that between *truths of fact* and *truths of reason*. When an attorney asks the witness questions of the form, "Where were you?" or "What did you see?" etc., he expects to get in reply material evidence, that is, reports of fact. This is the kind of truth that empiricists stress in epistemology. It involves the use of the senses in gaining knowledge. But mathematics and the principles of logic are hardly true in this way—they are the truths of reason defended by the rationalists. A jury listening to evidence must watch for contradictions, thus implicitly accepting the so-called laws of thought.

When we talk about knowing the truth we are posing epistemological questions, such as, "How can we know the truth?" and "How can we avoid error?" The empiricists' answer is to use the senses to the maximum; the rationalists' is to use reason to the maximum. Insofar as theories of truth are recommendations of certain criteria, they are epistemological. But is it not possible that something is true even though we do not know it to be true? Logic commonly takes as its starting point that a proposition is either true or false; true even if no one believes it or false even if everyone believes it. If truth, as distinguished from knowledge of the truth, can exist without the agency of a knowing mind, then the problem of truth is not only epistemological, but also metaphysical. Truth, according to one great metaphysical tradition, is eternal and absolute, that is, neither subject to changes of time nor relative to knowing minds. There are versions of this view that inspire speculative philosophers as much as they puzzle analytic philosophers. But the point needs to be made that a theory of truth is inseparable from a consideration of the world to which beliefs are true. Thus the philosophic problem of truth will lead us to the metaphysical question of Chapter VI, namely, "What is there?"

To see how certain problems and theories of truth arise, consider a common situation. A mother suspects her son of lying. Here surely we have all had one of our earliest bouts with truth, as did the mother and son in Menotti's opera Amahl and the Night Visitors.

Amahl: . . . Mother, come with me. I want to be sure that you see what I see.
The Mother: What is the matter with you now?
Amahl: Mother . . . outside the door there is . . . there is a King with a crown.
The Mother: What shall I do with this boy, what shall I do? If you don't learn to tell the truth I'll have to spank you! Go back and see who it is and ask them what they want.
Amahl: Mother, Mother . . . Mother, come with me. I want to be sure that you see what I see.
The Mother: What is the matter with you now, what is all this fuss about?
Amahl: Mother . . . I didn't tell the truth before.
The Mother: That's a good boy.
Amahl: There is not a King outside.
The Mother: I should say not!
Amahl: There are two Kings!
The Mother: What shall I do with this boy, what shall I do? Hurry back and see who it is, and don't you dare make up tales! (*Amahl returns with the protest:*) If I tell you the truth I know you won't believe me.
The Mother: Try it for a change!
Amahl: But you won't believe me.
The Mother: I'll believe you if you tell the truth.

(*When the incredible statement is made that there are three Kings, "and one of them is black," the Mother rises.*)

The Mother: I'm going to the door myself. . . .

(*After the Kings have greeted his mother, Amahl has the satisfaction of saying, "What did I tell you?"*)[1]

Of course we have all been advised to "tell the truth" and threatened with punishment if we lie. Truth-telling and lying are characteristics of persons, and one is generally called a virtue, the other a vice. Whether it is always right to tell the truth, and always wrong to deceive, are moral questions. We shall set them aside until we come to ethical beliefs.

Having set aside the moral question of veracity, let us suggest three analyses of the meaning of truth in this charming dialogue.

The first is that Amahl's belief that the men at the door were kings is true because they were in fact kings. Had the Mother asked what

[1] Gian Carlo Menotti, *Amahl and the Night Visitors*, copyright 1951, 1952, by G. Schirmer, Inc. Reprinted by permission.

"true" means the boy might have said, "It's when, if you ask me whether something I said is so, it is so." Observe the two terms and a relation. One term is _belief_, the other is ~~fact~~, and the relation between them is commonly called _correspondence_. The belief corresponds to the fact. Amahl reports what is the case. His sentences refer to a state of affairs, or are in agreement with fact.

The second analysis shows that Amahl's judgments are coherent. There is no contradiction between "There is a King" and "There is also a second and a third King." His judgments are at first partial, incomplete, not as true as his final account. Of course Amahl interprets what he senses. Only thus does a jagged yellow sense-datum get reported as "crown." And crown is interpreted as a royal sign. To the poor widow it is incredible that kings should come to call. Because a king had not come before, she draws the fallacious conclusion that no king will ever come. Once freed of this presupposition her judgments agree with Amahl's and every report and act of the kings fit together as part of one interrelated whole. Hence on this second analysis, there are not only beliefs referring to facts, but judgments about reality. It is the whole that is true, wholly true, and every part is to the degree that it is partial, false.

The third analysis is concerned with the situation in which a problem gets solved. Amahl is excited about a star. Something unexplained puzzles him. Hence he goes outside to observe. That three kings come with treasures is only more puzzling. He watches closely and begins to ask questions. There is a problem here and in the course of the story it gets solved. A belief is what guides action, and Amahl's conduct leads to a solution. Truth-seeking is a process that creates hypotheses, and what is true is a successful consequence in which the problem no longer exists. If the problem remains, this failure defines falsehood.

In this brief way we have set forth tentatively three perspectives in which "true" and "false" are given an interpretation. According to the first, the _correspondence_ theory, "false" means, not to refer to what is, or to fail to report how things are. According to the second, the _coherence_ theory, "false" means partial agreement of judgment with judgment. According to the third, the _pragmatic_ theory, "false" means failure of a hypothesis to solve some problem, or failure to remove whatever gave rise to the course of inquiry.

Let us now consider these alternative uses of "truth" at greater length, and then investigate _self-evident_ truth, the _verificationist_ theory of truth, and a _semantic_ conception of truth.

II. The Correspondence Theory of Truth

Both its defendants and opponents agree that some version of the correspondence theory is implicit in nearly all of common life; that it has been made explicit by nearly every major philosopher of the ancient and medieval worlds; and that only in our own times has it been confronted with serious alternatives.

Moore says that a belief is true if and only if it corresponds to fact. He does not claim that his theory holds for all uses of "true," but recommends it because

. . . it does take account of and does not conflict with many millions of the most obvious facts. One such obvious fact is that my friend's belief that I have gone away for the holidays certainly will be true, in one common sense of the word, *if* and only if I actually have gone away.[2]

In his Metaphysics Aristotle wrote, "To say of what is that it is not, or of what is not that it is, is false, while to say of what is that it is, or of what is not that it is not, is true." This statement seems to have something in common with Moore's and each makes more precise what the boy answered—"Truth is when, if you ask me whether something I said is so, it is so." Notice that the boy calls attention to two terms—what is said, and what is so. Aristotle calls attention to the structure of propositions, affirmative or negative, and to the structure of what is the case, that is, either a substance has or has not a given attribute. Moore calls attention to the state of affairs, whether anyone knows it, believes it, or states it.

But all philosophers are not satisfied with the boy's account nor with Aristotle's and Moore's. One can believe a proposition, yet not express it in a sentence, whether spoken or written. And could a proposition not be true even if no mind believed it? Webster's Dictionary says that a conception, a judgment, or an idea is true if "in strict accordance with what is, has been, or will be." The problem is to unpack what is meant in the boy's powerful little word "so." Of course we say of a false empirical belief that it is contrary to fact, or of a prediction that the facts belie the expectation. Sometimes we mean by "fact" simply an existent thing or an event of which we can say when and where it is. But we also talk of the "fact" that Germany lost two wars in the twentieth century. The wars can be dated and given geographical specification, but the question,

[2] George E. Moore, *Some Main Problems of Philosophy*, The Macmillan Co., New York, 1953, p. 281.

"When and where is the fact that Germany lost a war?" seems nonsense. "Fact" used in this sense of being the case, or having been the case, or even to be the case, resembles "true" and "false," and is in many cases independent of time and space. Examine general statements such as, "It's a fact that mother whales suckle their young," or "It's true that whales are mammals." Here "fact" does not mean single event with a date and a place. In any proposed correspondence theory it would be useful if the theory made clear exactly what the two terms are and what the relation is.

There is one kind of correspondence relation that is commonly understood, namely, *copying* or *mirroring*. When shown a photograph of a friend, we may say, "That is a true likeness." We can compare a present perception or memory image of the friend with the image of the photograph. The friend is the object to be true to, the photograph is a kind of claim that it represents his likeness truly.

But this analysis breaks down. The picture really claims nothing. Nor does our mental image. They are neither true nor false in themselves. However, if we should say of a picture of Jefferson that it is of George Washington, that would be false. For it is a proposition that may be said to be properly true or false. But how can a proposition copy a fact? This seems to count strongly against the theory.

And yet the copy theory does help by calling attention to some significant points about truth. For example, it stresses the fact that a belief, or judgment, or proposition, depends in some way on the thing, event, or state of affairs. Unless there were facts there could not be true or false propositions. The theory, according to Aristotle, means that the relation between a true statement and the fact that it states may be put as follows:

If a man is, the proposition in which we allege that he is, is true; and conversely, if the proposition wherein we allege that he is, is true, then he is. But the true proposition is in no way the cause of the being of the man, whereas, the fact of the man's being does seem to be the cause of the truth of the proposition. . . .[3]

In a second way the analogy of copying helps us to understand truth. There is a similarity of structure in the picture and the object, that is, between the subject and the portrait. The metaphor becomes strained, however, if we expect the *propositions* that state the similarity to mirror the event or object. More helpful in this respect is the analogy of the relation

[3] Mortimer J. Adler (ed.), *The Great Ideas: A Syntopicon of Great Books of the Western World*, Encylopaedia Britannica, Chicago, 1952, Vol. II, p. 916.

between a diagram, a chart, or a map, and what is charted or mapped. Here there is no question of private mental images. The map is designed to convey correctly the relations of land to water, house to roads, and so on. A map can be said to picture its object. But once again we must ask whether this can be said intelligibly of a proposition? We must remember that there are different kinds of propositions, for example, not only categorical but also hypothetical, not only positive but also negative. Since all these are said to be true or false it would be misleading to discuss only certain elementary types such as "The cat is on the mat," for when we read these words we may have a visual image such as we do not have with many other propositions.

The concept of correspondence between one complex and another complex has been made more precise by Bertrand Russell. Every proposition, he says, can be analyzed into at least one element and one relation. Now if every *fact* can also be analyzed into at least one element and one relation, then we should be in position to say precisely why one proposition is true, and another false, namely, when the elements and relations of the proposition correspond to the elements and relations of the facts.

Consider Russell's celebrated examples: "Charles I died on the scaffold"; "Othello believes *falsely* that Desdemona loves Cassio," and "York is between London and Edinburgh."[4] Here we have terms united by relations. If the terms and relations of the *beliefs* are the terms and relations of the *facts* then the belief is true, if not, the belief is false. This theory of truth requires also a judging mind. Russell does not accept the view that propositions can always be analyzed simply into a subject term and a predicate term. When Othello believes that Desdemona loves Cassio, his mind knits together three things, Desdemona, Cassio, and the relation loving. It is, of course, essential that these three be in the right order. Whether this relation does or does not hold in fact marks the difference between judging truly and judging falsely. Thus, concludes Russell:

Although truth and falsehood are properties of beliefs, yet they are in a sense extrinsic properties, for the condition of the truth of a belief is something not involving beliefs, or (in general) any mind at all, but only the *objects* of the belief. A mind, which believes, believes truly when there is a *corresponding* complex not involving the mind, but only its objects. This correspondence ensures truth, and its absence entails falsehood. Hence we account simultaneously for the two facts that beliefs (a) depend on minds for their *existence*, (b) do not depend on minds for their *truth*.[5]

  [4] Bertrand Russell, *The Problem of Philosophy*, Home University Library, Oxford University Press, London, 1959, pp. 124, 128.
  [5] *Ibid.*, p. 129.

Proponents of the correspondence theory of truth, in any of its versions, admit it has difficulties. Although some critics have considered the difficulties to be thoroughly destructive, those who favor it have been most ingenious in restating it. It is not possible to give here a full account of the attacks, nor assess all the merits of the theory. The following points, however, need to be made in summary fashion:

1. Russell and others who defend the correspondence theory do not mean by correspondence the relation of copying. Hence the supposed refutation of the copy theory does not touch the theory outlined above.
2. Russell and his colleagues have not suggested that correspondence is the only criterion of truth. Hence the objections based upon this supposition miss their mark. Russell does not suppose that because one employs coherence to test the truth of historical beliefs that one must admit any deficiency in one's theory of the nature of truth.
3. Russell and others who have attempted an analysis of true beliefs have managed to state a definition without major explicit metaphysical commitments beyond the belief that there is an external world. Were all relations internal and truth and reality ultimately one, the theory should be abandoned. But the meaning of this idealistic doctrine is a greater difficulty than our common belief that some things would be as they are even if not known. The question "Is all reality mind-dependent?" will have to be considered in Chapter VII on metaphysics.
4. Russell admits that this theory does not provide an answer to the pragmatic question, "Why should one prefer true to false beliefs?" This is a matter of the causal efficacy of beliefs and the appropriateness of responses. It has to do with purposes, not with a theory of truth.[6]
5. No claim is made that the correspondence theory explicates the principles of logic and mathematics. Russell is not blurring the distinction between truths of fact and truths of reason.

The correspondence theory does insist upon an existing external world of objects and a mind that reflects upon, experiences, and judges that world. The authors do not see how it is possible to avoid accepting this theory for all judgments to which it is appropriate. It is true that the relation of correspondence itself is not altogether clear, but if we mean by it the relation that holds between a proposition and its object when the object actually is of the nature the proposition asserts, then the theory has a wide and useful application in human experience.

[6] Bertrand Russell, *The Analysis of Mind*, George Allen & Unwin, Ltd., London, 1921, p. 278.

Later, another approach to this theory from the semantic point of view will be examined.

III. The Coherence Theory of Truth

This theory also predicates truth of propositions; not, however, of any single proposition, but of all propositions tied to each other in one all-embracing system. A particular judgment or proposition is true when it can be shown to be in harmony with, that is, logically connected to, all other propositions. When knowledge becomes fully coherent every judgment implies the complete system of all judgments. This, of course, is an ideal not yet attained, but is none the less present in thought. Taken singly and apart from the totality of judgments, we find them in opposition, conflicting, incompatible, and contradictory. But when the separate judgments are brought into relation to each other and to the whole, these contradictions are resolved and the incompatibilities vanish. Truth, then, is not primarily a relation between a proposition and a fact, rather it is a matter of attaining the completest network of relationships among propositions. This totality has been called the Absolute. It alone is true. It is the standard of all lesser truths. This theory of truth is so closely tied to idealism that its full force may not be appreciated until one looks at the world as idealists do. This will be attempted in Chapter VII.

It is evident that the coherence theory involves a view concerning the relation of thought to reality. Thought represents or reflects the real, not accidentally, but necessarily; otherwise knowledge would be no more than a lucky guess. Or worse, if thought were not necessarily related to reality, then we would seem to be forced to scepticism for we could never be sure that what we think has any relevance or relation to the real world. Spinoza gave the most succinct statement of this belief: "The order and connection of ideas is the same as the order and connection of things." Thus for the proponents of the coherence theory all knowledge is systematic, that is, coherent, and it reflects the nature of things that form an intelligible, and fully ordered system. Of course, our knowledge is partial, but reality is a completely integrated whole. Blanshard said it well, if somewhat metaphorically when he wrote:

Truth is the approximation of thought to reality. It is thought on its way home. Its measure is the distance thought has travelled, under the guidance of its inner compass, toward that intelligible system which unites its ultimate object with its ultimate end. Hence at any given time the degree of truth in our experience as a whole is the degree of system it has achieved. The degree of truth of a particular proposition is to be judged in the first instance by its coherence with experience as a whole, ultimately by its coherence with that further whole, all-comprehensive and fully articulated, in which thought can come to rest.[7]

A characteristic of this theory is that it requires a kind of logic that will admit the notion of degrees of truth. Only the all-inclusive system of propositions is true, but since no proposition is entirely outside the system, there is no perfectly false assertion. Again from Blanshard:

> Between these untouched limits of perfect truth and perfect falsity thought moves in a middle region where all its insights, however varying in acuteness and sweep, can be called true in degree only. A given judgment is true in the *degree* to which its content could maintain itself in the light of a completed system of knowledge, false in the degree to which its appearance there would require its transformation.[8]

The argument for degrees of truth consists in first pointing out that whenever we think of any object we think of it in its relations; every object stands in some relation to all other objects. Some of these relations are so significant for the nature of the object and what we understand the object to be, that if they were cut away it could not be that object nor could we know it as such. Thus an adequate grasp of the object would be unattainable until we had comprehended all these relations. Anything less than this is an inadequate, though not necessarily a contradictory, conception of the object. There is a degree of adequacy present, and therefore a degree of truth. Partial, incomplete, fragmentary truths, are the only truths attainable by human thought, but they are still truths, and some, depending upon the extent of their relatedness to other truths, are more true than others. If any of us were to speak the whole truth about anything, we could not shut our mouths until we had exhausted the universe.

A number of criticisms have been offered against this theory, but its defenders have not been slow to answer. A frequent objection to it is that it leads to scepticism. Because we find it impossible to relate all propositions, we always have less than the truth. So far as we can see, however, this is not denied by the proponents of the theory. They admit that we cannot know the Absolute, but they insist that we can know and discover the relations within our present knowledge, which will then point to a system of greater inclusiveness and coherency.

A further criticism of this theory asks whether it does not suggest that what was true once may now be false, and that what is true now may be-

[7] Brand Blanshard, *The Nature of Thought,* George Allen & Unwin, Ltd., London, 1948, Vol. II, p. 264.
[8] *Ibid.,* p. 284.

come false as knowledge grows. The critic's assumption is that a truth, once true, ought always to be true. Here the defender replies that a truth does not become false though it may become less true, nor does a falsehood become true, rather a lesser truth reaches a higher level and fullness of truth by virtue of its increased integration with other known truths.

Again, the critics of this theory wonder if there may not be systems of great unity and inclusiveness which are, however, false. Certainly, it is said, other systems are possible and any system must try to incorporate all the known facts. Let us suppose a system X opposed to system Y. Then system Y is not a fact included in system X, and vice versa. Therefore the two systems do not include all known facts. Each, in a sense, is a rival hypothesis of the other, and when this occurs a suspension of judgment is necessary until some significant fact or crucial experiment appears to justify the acceptance of one and the rejection of the other. An answer to this objection is clearly given by one of the defenders of the view.

The notion of two systems, each all-inclusive, is meaningless; and . . . when two systems less than all-inclusive come in conflict with each other, as they do when dream conflicts with reality, or vagary with science, or one world-view with another, the issue always tends to be settled by acceptance of the view that, in the sense defined, is more coherent.[9]

This reply, however, does not fully satisfy some of the logical difficulties of the coherence theory. Suppose we conceive of a set of perfectly coherent propositions. Call it S. Now any proposition in this set has a contradictory, call it not-P, which is excluded from S. Thus there is another whole set of propositions, call it M, which consists of the contradictories of the propositions of S. In this case, of course, no coherent set of propositions can contain all propositions. Furthermore, suppose P and Q to be any two propositions of the set S, and that P implies Q. There will then be in M two contradictory propositions, one of which implies the other, namely, not-P and not-Q. Therefore the set M will be as coherent as the set S. Now if the coherence theory is true, then the propositions of M are as true as those of S. But this is impossible by the law of contradiction, for the propositions of each set are the contradictions of the propositions of the other set. It does not appear then that coherence can alone be the nature, test, and criterion of truth.[10]

[9] *Ibid.*, p. 284. Our debt to Prof. Blanshard throughout this discussion is gratefully acknowledged.
[10] This argument we owe to Prof. C. J. Ducasse, "Propositions, Truth, and the Ultimate Criterion of Truth," *Philosophy and Phenomenological Research*, Vol. 4, 1943–44, p. 325.

Blanshard seems to admit this when he writes that the

. . . theory does not hold that any and every system is true no matter how abstract and limited; it holds that one system only is true, namely the system in which everything real and possible is coherently included. How one can find in this the notion that a system would still give truth if, like some arbitrary geometry, it disregarded experience completely, it is not easy to see.

But it does seem easy to see that here Blanshard is making an appeal to experience to decide what is real and possible in a system, and this requires him to go to something other than coherence.

Another objection to this theory must be considered. There seem to be many possible examples of coherence where the question of truth is unimportant and even irrelevant. For instance, there may be a high degree of coherence to dreams, or to a novel. There may even be logical systems or geometries that are tight in their internal coherence but that are in conflict with each other to the point of contradiction. When there are incompatible coherent systems, coherence, as shown above, fails as a theory of truth. The answer often given to this objection lies in making a distinction between coherence and consistency. It is not mere formal noncontradiction that is meant by coherence, but a kind of organic relatedness of the known facts and principles that constitute human knowledge. When such knowledge is fully coherent, every fact and judgment will be seen to be not only compatible with, but necessary to, every other fact and judgment. This systematization of knowledge is truth, truth proportional to the degree of systematization. And it can be achieved only by a mind able to see unity in diversity. A description of such a mind by Newman is worth quoting in full.

That only is true enlargement of mind which is the power of viewing many things at once as one whole, of referring them severally to their true place in the universal system, of understanding their respective values, and determining their mutual dependence. Thus is that form of Universal Knowledge, of which I have on a former occasion spoken, set up in the individual intellect, and constitutes its perfection. Possessed of this real illumination, the mind never views any part of the extended subject-matter of knowledge without recollecting that it is but a part, or without the associations which spring from this recollection. It makes everything in some sort lead to everything else; it would communicate the image of the whole to every separate portion, till that whole becomes in imagination like a spirit, everywhere pervading and penetrating its component parts, and giving them one definite meaning. Just as our bodily organs, when mentioned, recall their function in the body, as the word "creation" suggests the Creator, and "subjects" a sovereign, so, in the mind of the Philosopher, as we are abstractedly conceiving of him, the elements of the physical and moral world, sciences, arts, pursuits, ranks, offices, events, opinions, individualities, are all viewed as one, with correlative functions, and as gradually by successive combinations converging, one and all, to the true center.

To have even a portion of their illuminative reason and true philosophy is the highest state to which nature can aspire, in the way of intellect; it puts the mind above the influences of chance and necessity, above anxiety, suspense, tumult, and superstition, which are the portion of the many. Men, whose minds are possessed with some one object, take exaggerated views of its importance, are feverish in the pursuit of it, make it the measure of things which are utterly foreign to it, and are startled and despond if it happens to fail them. They are ever in alarm or in transport. Those on the other hand who have no object or principle whatever to hold by, lose their way, every step they take. They are thrown out, and do not know what to think or say, at every fresh juncture; they have no view of persons, or occurrences, or facts, which come suddenly upon them, and they hang upon the opinion of others, for want of internal resources. But the intellect, which has been disciplined to the perfection of its powers, which knows, and thinks while it knows, which has learned to leaven the dense mass of facts and events with the elastic force of reason, such an intellect cannot be partial, cannot be exclusive, cannot be impetuous, cannot be at a loss, cannot but be patient, collected, and majestically calm, because it discerns the end in every beginning, the origin in every end, the law in every interruption, the limit in each delay; because it ever knows where it stands, and how its path lies from one point to another.[11]

When truth is identified with the coherent whole, it is obvious that the identity of truth and reality is affirmed. They are not separate realms but one, and when we have knowledge of the truth we also have knowledge of the real. An interesting result of the affirmation of degrees of truth and its identity with reality is the fact that no proposition can be entirely false, there is always some portion of truth in it; that is, some aspect of reality is described no matter how erroneous the judgment is. This leads to the startling consequence that other theories of truth, in opposition to the coherence theory, are true, and they are, admit the defenders of the view, but they are only partially true, as they are partially false. Only the one, coherent whole, is ultimate truth. Within the great surety and sweep of its embrace all minor claims are welcome to compete for momentary attention, but they owe their partial truth to an indissoluble tie with the Absolute.

The weaknesses of the coherence theory suggest that it cannot stand alone as an adequate definition or criterion of truth. There is no proof that beliefs form the kind of systematic unity demanded by this theory. Partial systems do exist in the formal sciences where, it is true, one of the tests of the truth of a system is coherence, but this is far removed from a systematization of all propositions into one absolute truth.

[11] John Henry Cardinal Newman, *On the Scope and Nature of University Education*, E. P. Dutton & Co., New York, 1915, pp. 129–130.

Furthermore, it is not clear what coherence should mean. If it means non-contradiction, then the theory presupposes the truths of the laws of logic, which in turn cannot be tested by the coherence theory. This suggests that there may be some truths that we must accept because they are self-evident. But this is another theory. Let us examine it.

IV. Truth as the Self-evident

The most celebrated use of the notion of *self-evident truth* is found in the Declaration of Independence. A nice discrimination between opinions, facts, and self-evident truths is made by the author or authors of this historical document. Opinions are what men had when they considered the causes that impelled the dissolving of the political bonds; facts are what are referred to by the statements describing the actions of the King. Opinions may be changed, and indeed the document is designed to influence opinion. Facts could once have been different, and indeed the King would not have been blamed if he had used, rather than abused his powers. Past facts cannot be undone. But the argument of the authors rested upon what we commonly call "principle." Without a principle no conclusion can follow from any fact. In the Declaration of Independence the principles appear at the beginning: "We hold these truths to be self-evident. . . . " To establish the truth of the proposition that "the King is a tryrant" the document cites twenty-eight factual propositions, but the truth of the principles rests upon no factual argument.

The principles are said to be self-evident truths. What might this mean? One answer is that they simply seemed obvious to Thomas Jefferson. A self-evident truth, then, is one to which you say, "Of course." Still, is this enough? We might say that because there were fifty-five signers, these general statements represent common agreement. In this case "self-evident" means that which men agree to take for granted. But if this is all that is meant, why should these propositions be called truths? Since the contrary view, namely, that government rests upon the will of the stronger, seems obvious to others, it cannot be common consent or agreement that makes these propositions true.

Let us go back to possible sources. We know that the authors of the Declaration of Independence had studied the philosophy of John Locke. They were probably then acquainted with Locke's example of a truth of reason: "That it is impossible for the same thing to be, and not to be!" This he calls a general, abstract truth. How do we know it? Locke says that our reason comes to know it without proof.

In this the mind is at no pains of proving or examining, but perceives the truth, as the eye doth light, only by being directed towards it. Thus the mind perceives that white is not black, that a circle is not a triangle, that three are more than two, and equal to one and two. . . . It is on this intuition that depends all the certainty and evidence of all our knowledge.[12]

It is probable that this is in the background of the self-evident truths that were affirmed by the authors of the Declaration of Independence. A man by his nature ought to claim liberty, and a man without rights is an absurdity. Likewise a government by its nature exists to protect this claim of liberty, and a government that denies liberty is an absurdity.

But now the idea of self-evident truth has been introduced, let us look more closely at the alternatives.

Do we have propositions that we call true, although we do not know to what they correspond? And do we have propositions we are willing to call true not because they cohere with other propositions but serve themselves as norms of coherence? If we do, then the proposition makes its truth evident. Its truth may be seen, or taken, or granted, in isolation from other propositions and facts. Hence such truths are called self-evident. They are not relatively true, but true absolutely, or as is sometimes said, they are necessarily true, or indubitably true. Such a claim has been made for a variety of truths. Blanshard has given us a possible list.

Among these are propositions about conduct, such as, 'it is my duty to produce the greater good rather than the less'; propositions about existence, such as 'I am'; propositions about quantity, such as 'things equal to the same thing are equal to each other'; spatial propositions, such as 'two straight lines cannot enclose a space'; temporal propositions, such as, 'what is before A is before all that is contemporary with A'; laws of logic, such as 'x must be either A or not-A'.[13]

In Descartes we may find one of the most thorough attempts to defend self-evident, necessary, or indubitable truths. The success of his whole philosophic enterprise depended upon the discovery of at least one necessary and certain truth. Remember, he thought he found it in *cogito ergo sum*. Bertrand Russell puts the Cartesian question: "Is there any knowledge in the world which is so certain that no reasonable man could doubt it?"

It seems clear that mathematics could not be a demonstrative science, nor could logic demonstrate that a conclusion must follow when certain premises are affirmed, unless there were axioms. It is not assuming too

[12] John Locke, *An Essay Concerning Human Understanding*, (A. S. Pringle-Pattison, ed.) The Clarendon Press, Oxford, 1947, p. 261.
[13] Brand Blanshard, *op. cit.*, Vol. II, p. 238.

much to say that a reasonable person would grant that if a proposition is true, then it is true; that the same proposition cannot be both true and false; and that any proposition must be either true or false. These are the familiar laws of thought, which once granted, enable us to demonstrate many other truths. Without them we would find it impossible to order our beliefs in a rational way. These may be called self-evident truths in logic, although there may also be others which are independent of experience in the sense that experience cannot prove them. Just because these are "obvious" does not mean they are trivial or unimportant. The vast achievement of mathematics is based upon the clear statement of what is so obviously the case that one cannot entertain the contrary. St. Thomas Aquinas employed a mathematical example when he introduced the concept of self-evident truth. He could have said axiomatic truth.

> Those propositions are said to be self-evident that are known immediately upon the knowledge of their terms. Thus, as soon as you know the nature of a *whole* and the nature of a *part*, you know immediately that every whole is greater than its part.[14]

The word "immediate" is a technical logical term meaning that no middle term is employed in proof. Indeed an axiom has the peculiar status of being indemonstrable, but yet necessary for demonstration.

There are many attempts to account for the origin of these self-evident truths. Some philosophers such as Aquinas and Descartes ascribe them to principles implanted in us by God. Others, such as Spinoza, find them in the very nature of everything that is. Still others, for example, Aristotle, claim that man has a special faculty of insight or intuition that enables him to grasp these truths. Mill tried to show how they could be derived from experience, and some contemporary philosophers think they are a matter of rules of grammar. But it is difficult to see how the last two suggestions can account for the universality and necessity of these truths. Both our experiences and languages are various in content, quality, and extent. Yet there appears to be more uniformity, convergence, and agreement than experience and language could ever account for.

But how shall we tell which truths are self-evident? The situation is bewildering because mathematicians, for example, have constructed different geometries by selecting different axioms. A. N. Whitehead cautioned teachers of mathematics against either trying to teach without axioms, or teaching that any set, say Euclid's, is the only set. For purposes of demonstration we may choose, but then; "They are *our* axioms of geometry, not

---

[14] St. Thomas Aquinas, *Summa Contra Gentiles*, Book I, *God* (Anton G. Pegis, tr.), Image Books, Doubleday & Co., Inc., Garden City, New York, 1955, p. 79.

the axioms of geometry; and from them, by the most rigid reasoning, justifying every step as we go along, the remainder of the schedule should be proved."[15]

But what justifies a geometrical truth? It is "its own justification." Sometimes Whitehead appeals, as a mathematician must, to direct insight. If one said, "It seems to me that the whole is no greater than any of its parts," he could only say, "Work out your system."

Another direction may be taken. Suppose we ask why a whole is greater than any of its parts? One common answer is that the predicate is contained in the subject. For instance, consider "A triangle is a plane closed figure with three angles." The predicate makes explicit the concept triangle, which is the subject of the proposition. Related to this is the following: The contrary of the above proposition is, "A triangle is a plane closed figure with more or less than three angles." A four-sided triangle! A two-sided triangle! These are absurdities, self-contradictories. Hence, we might say a self-evident truth is one of which all the opposites are self-contradictory or logically absurd.

It is doubtful whether we can do without some form of a self-evidence theory applied to some truths. Without this we cannot account for the truth of axioms of logic or mathematics. To base their truth on experience, or to deny that they are true leads to difficulties. It seems best to supplement a correspondence and a coherence theory with some version of self-evidence. Self-evidence is too limited a theory to cover all the instances. Nevertheless, it certainly has a negative role to play. We do discard a great quantity of nonsense because it is so patently nonsense. But this ought not to be done with too much abandon. Sometimes what seems self-evidently nonsense, turns out upon closer scrutiny to be true.

V. *Pragmatist and Verificationist Theories of Truth*

Another approach to a theory of truth is revealed when we ask concerning a proposition not only whether it refers to a state of affairs, or what relations it has to other propositions, but what job does it do? Many contemporary philosophers have not been satisfied that the meaning of "true" and "false" has been adequately explicated in realistic empiricism with its notion of correspondence, or in idealistic rationalism with its notion of coherence. Elements of both correspondence theories and coherence theories suggested that the truth or falsity of a proposition are discovered

---

[15] Alfred North Whitehead, *Essays in Science and Philosophy*, Rider & Co., London, 1948, p. 138.

in a process sometimes called "inquiry." In this case we are not interested in the noun "truth," which suggests an entity or substance, nor in "corresponding to" or "coherent with," which are relations of a logical character, but with a verb, such as "verify," which suggests doing something. Literally, according to its Latin roots, verify means "to make true." Pragmatists, especially William James, sometimes stressed this meaning. Others, especially positivists, stressed the question, how do we go about finding out whether a proposition is true or false? To this view we give the name *verificationism*. John Dewey, for example, said, " . . . the true means the verified and means nothing else." And from a leader of positivism, Hans Reichenbach, "When we speak of truth in ordinary language we actually mean verifiability, i.e., the possibility of verification."[16]

The capacity of truth to "work," that is, to resolve a perplexity, to predict an effect, to satisfy an inquirer, to reach an agreement, all of which may be verified, is the core of the pragmatic meaning. John Dewey has given an excellent description of this position:

If ideas, meanings, conceptions, notions, theories, systems are instrumental to an active reorganization of the given environment, to a removal of some specific trouble and perplexity, then the test of their validity and value lies in accomplishing this work. If they succeed in their office, they are reliable, sound, valid, good, true. If they fail to clear up confusion, to eliminate defects, if they increase confusion, uncertainty and evil when they are acted upon, then they are false. Confirmation, corroboration, verification lie in works, consequences. Handsome is that handsome does. By their fruits ye shall know them. That which guides us truly is true—demonstrated capacity for such guidance is precisely what is meant by truth. The adverb "truly" is more fundamental than either the adjective, true, or the noun, truth. An adverb expresses a way, a mode of acting. Now an idea or conception is a claim or injunction or plan to *act* in a certain way as the way to arrive at the clearing up of a specific situation. When the claim or pretension or plan is acted upon *it guides us* truly or falsely; it leads us to our end or away from it. Its active, dynamic function is the all-important thing about it, and in the quality of activity induced by it lies all its truth and falsity. The hypothesis that works is the *true* one; and truth is an abstract noun applied to the collection of cases, actual, forseen and desired, that receive confirmation in their works and consequences.[17]

It is a characteristic of contemporary philosophy to couple the question "Is the belief true?" with the question "Is the belief meaningful?" We are all indebted to pragmatists and positivists for the point that the latter is

[16] Paul A. Schilpp (ed.) *The Philosophy of Bertrand Russell*, Tudor Publishing Co., New York, 1951, pp. 42–43.

[17] John Dewey, *Reconstruction in Philosophy*, Beacon Press, Boston, 1948, reprinted by arrangement in Mentor Books, The New American Library, New York, 1950, pp. 128–129.

the more general question. If a belief is meaningful, it is either true or false. What is not meaningful cannot be either true or false; it is meaningless.

To demonstrate to a pragmatist or a positivist that a proposition makes sense, one is asked to show what consequences follow from affirming or denying it. Pragmatists stress consequences of disbelieving or believing. James and Dewey, following Peirce, asked of a belief, "What difference does it make?" Positivists profess to get no meaning in "true" and "false" unless it can be clearly stated how one should go about testing the belief. Both pragmatists and positivists appeal to common life and to scientific practice. In practical concerns we face problems to be solved; in science we formulate hypotheses. Whether we solve our problem or confirm our hypothesis, time is required. We are in a process. Because this process is one of developing knowledge, the question "What is truth?" is badly formulated. Rather we should ask, "Under what conditions are we prepared to call one solution true rather than false, or one hypothesis confirmed rather than disconfirmed?"

If these positions claimed no more than to recommend criteria of truth there would be no deep quarrel between verificationists and proponents of correspondence or of coherence. The trouble develops when pragmatists or positivists claim that their account answers all questions about "true" and "false."

Let us first make sense of verification. We all make predictions and live by the predictions others make, for example, "rain tomorrow." Is the prediction meaningful? Surely the pragmatist would say yes. If we believe the prediction we may call off the picnic and stay at home. If it rains tomorrow the prediction has come true, if it is hot and dry the prediction is made false. It seems meaningless to ask about the truth of a prediction as though it were something timeless. Rather, is it not plain that truth in this context is relative to time and circumstance, and also to our interests? If the prediction has kept us from being drenched far from shelter then it has been successful, that is, true, relative to a specific problem. Before going on to a positivist account, let us introduce William James' best formulated expression.

Truth . . . is a property of certain of your ideas. It means their agreement, as falsity means their disagreement, with reality. Pragmatists and intellectualists both accept this definition as a matter of course.

Where our ideas [do] not copy definitely their object, what does agreement with that object mean? . . . Pragmatism asks its usual question. 'Grant an idea to be true,' it says, 'what concrete difference will its being true make in any one's actual life? What experiences [may] be different from those which would obtain if the belief were false? How will the truth be realized? What, in short, is the truth's cash-value in experiential terms?' The moment pragmatism asks this question, it sees the answer: *True ideas are those that we can assimilate, validate, corroborate, and verify. False ideas are those that we cannot.* That is the practical difference it makes to us to have true ideas; that therefore is the meaning of truth, for it is all that truth is known as.

The truth of an idea is not a stagnant property inherent in it. Truth *happens* to an idea. It *becomes* true, is *made* true by events. Its verity is in fact an event, a process, the process namely of verifying itself, its *verification.*

To agree in the widest sense with a reality can only mean to be guided either straight up to it or into its surroundings, or to be put into such working touch with it as to handle either it or something connected with it better than if we disagreed. Better either intellectually or practically. . . . Any idea that helps us to deal, whether practically or intellectually, with either the reality or its belongings, that doesn't entangle our progress in frustrations, that *fits*, in fact, and adopts our life to the reality's whole setting, will agree sufficiently to meet the requirement. It will be true of that reality.

The true to put it very briefly, *is only the expedient in the way of our thinking, just as the right is only the expedient in the way of our behaving*. Expedient in almost any fashion, and expedient in the long run and on the whole, of course; for what meets expediently all the experience in sight won't necessarily meet all farther experiences equally satisfactorily. Experience, as we know, has ways of *boiling over* and making us correct our present formulas.[18]

When the critics of James' theory restated his position, he complained that he had been misunderstood and that the critics were attacking a parody of pragmatism. The interchanges between Russell and James are of particular value for those new to philosophic controversy. In the flush of enthusiasm we are all apt to preach a new gospel as James did so very well. Then we find the debate begins and our epigrams are examined meticulously. Take, for example, "A truth is anything which it pays to believe." Russell wants to know when we cease tracing consequences, and whether they are good or bad. His point is that there may be "plain questions of fact" far more simple to verify. Furthermore, does it follow from the proposition that a certain belief is useful that the belief is true? Russell cites Rousseau's myth of a social contract, altogether useful for political revolutionaries, but still a myth, not a truth. James professed not to know the difference between a useful belief and a true belief. But Russell insisted that there are useful falsehoods and useless truths.

Again Russell attacks James with these questions: If it makes for happiness to believe that other people exist, and such a consequence makes the

[18] William James, *The Meaning of Truth*, Longmans, Green & Co., Inc., New York, 1909, pp. v–vii.

belief pragmatically true, does it follow from this that other people in fact do exist? Or if the hypothesis that God exists "works satisfactorily" does this make the belief true? Russell, quite a defender of orthodoxy in this respect, protested: "what religion desires is the conclusion that God exists, which pragmatism never even approaches." His point is that propositions are not more or less true merely because beliefs are more or less strong. James confused what we called certitude with certainty. Scientists are not concerned when testing beliefs in the beneficial results of believing; rather, they try to get indirect inductive evidence for the truth of what is not obviously true.[19]

Russell's criticisms of James' pragmatic theory prepares us for a positivist view of truth as verification or verifiability. Not all positivists agree with Reichenbach that "true" means "verifiable." But nearly all have at one time defended the doctrine that unless a proposition is verifiable it cannot be meaningful, that is, either true or false. Let us take as our representative of this view a contemporary British philosopher, Alfred Jules Ayer. Ayer does not propose a theory of truth in the sense of answering the question "What is truth?" Rather, he proposes to show how the words "true" and "false" function. In themselves the terms "connote nothing." "True" functions to assert a sentence. Nothing is added to the meaning of a proposition by saying that it is true or false. Hence speculation as to what truth might be is vain. There are no genuine concepts truth or falsehood.

Suppose we say, "It's true that Cortez captured Mexico City." All we should do if someone asks for the nature of its truth is to restate the proposition in an equivalent proposition that does not contain the word true. Thus we would simply affirm, "Cortez captured Mexico City." Or, if the proposition were "It is false that the Aztecs held Mexico against Cortez," we would simply deny the sentence, "The Aztecs held Mexico against Cortez." In this way we show how we use the symbols "true" and "false." Thus the question "What is truth?" only means, "How can we translate sentences containing the word true, into equivalent sentences without this word?" Ayer thus denies that the question "What is truth?" is legitimate. There is no real quality or real relation for which the word truth stands. The important question then is, "What makes a proposition true or false?" which put more strictly, means, "With regard to any proposition p, what are the conditions in which p (is true) and what are the conditions in

---

[19] Bertrand Russell, *Philosophical Essays*, Longmans, Green & Co., London, 1910, pp. 134, 135.

which not-*p*."[20] This is simply the question of describing the criteria by which the validity of various kinds of propositions are determined.

There are two classes of propositions, the a priori or analytic, and the a posteriori or synthetic. The former constitute for the most part the principles of logic and mathematics in which the test of truth is purely formal. But this will not do for synthetic or empirical propositions. Here we must have not a formal criterion but a material criterion. Some philosophers have said that certain propositions are directly recorded from immediate experience, and have called them *protocol sentences*. But Ayer objects that language never merely points to an object without describing it. When we say something about the object, we are classifying it in some way or other, and this means going beyond what is immediately given. Thus, there are no

. . . absolutely certain empirical propositions. . . . Empirical propositions are one and all hypotheses, which may be confirmed or discredited in actual sense-experience. And the propositions in which we record the observations that verify these hypotheses are themselves hypotheses which are subject to the test of further sense-experience. Thus there are no final propositions. When we set about verifying a hypothesis we may make an observation which satisfies us at the time. But the very next moment we may doubt whether the observation really did take place, and require a fresh process of verification in order to be reassured. And, logically, there is no reason why this procedure should not continue indefinitely, each act of verification supplying us with a new hypothesis, which in turn leads to a further series of acts of verification. In practice we assume that certain types of observation are trustworthy, and admit the hypothesis that they have occurred without bothering to embark on a process of verification. But we do this, not from obedience to any logical necessity, but from a purely pragmatic motive. . . .[21]

It is evident from this account that there are possibilities of agreement between James and Ayer. James often called attention to the loose connections between facts and beliefs, and Ayer said that the facts of experience "can never compel us to abandon a hypothesis." Both agree that necessary connections belong in logic and mathematics and should be kept there. This, as we have seen, is in strict opposition to the coherence theory which tends to identify the connections of propositions with the connections of facts.

The practical motive, so central to James' thinking is also present in Ayer's. We formulate hypotheses and construct systems out of them in

[20] Alfred J. Ayer, *Language, Truth and Logic,* Dover Publications, Inc., New York, n.d., p. 90. Reprinted by permission of Victor Gollancz, Ltd., London.
[21] *Ibid.,* pp. 91, 93–94.

order to anticipate the course of our sensations. They serve as warnings about future experience as well as enabling us to make accurate predictions.

The hypotheses may therefore be described as rules which govern our expectations of future experience. There is no need to say why we require such rules. It is plain that on our ability to make successful predictions depends the satisfaction of even our simplest desires, including the desire to survive.[22]

Thus, for both James and Ayer one set of beliefs is truer than another if it is more workable, useful, or successful.

We come, then, to the original question: By what criterion do we test the validity of an empirical proposition? Here is Ayer's reply:

The answer is that we test the validity of an empirical hypothesis by seeing whether it actually fulfils the function which it is designed to fulfil. And we have seen that the function of an empirical hypothesis is to enable us to anticipate experience. Accordingly, if an observation to which a given proposition is relevant conforms to our expectations, the truth of that proposition is confirmed.[23]

It is true, of course, that Ayer does not use the emotionally rich terms so common in James' work, such as "faith" and "will to believe" and "working," but he does use the term "confidence," that is, when a hypothesis has been confirmed, our confidence in it is increased in the sense that we are willing to rely on it in practice to forecast sensations. In short, it becomes a guide for future behavior.

This sort of theory encounters a number of objections. Consider first, in its Jamesian form, the obvious question, "What does workability mean?" It does seem reasonable to think that if a proposition is true it will work, but can this situation be described without requiring some feature of the coherence theory? That is, a proposition may be regarded as working when its truth is found to be compatible with other known truths, or if it fits in with our experience. Thus a pragmatic theory seems to lean on a form of the coherence theory, and on a form of the correspondence theory. Moreover, are not the pragmatists in danger of committing a logical error, called false conversion? That is, from "All propositions work," which seems acceptable, one may not infer, "All propositions that work are true."

There are also some difficulties with Ayer's more extreme position. The simplest objection to any verificationist definition of truth is that it tends to be circular. As Ayer presented his views there is no obvious circle, for

[22] *Ibid.*, p. 97.
[23] *Ibid.*, p. 99.

he denied that "truth" either stands for anything or connotes anything. He denied, you remember, that there is any concept such as truth; there are only uses of the sign of assertion, "true," and the sign of denial, "false." Thus he gives no definition of truth and in this sense may escape the charge of circularity. Yet "true" and "false" apply to verifiable and falsifiable hypotheses, so we must ask what verifiable means. For Ayer it means that the hypothetical proposition agrees with experience. Yet, as Russell pointed out, verificationists do not give us an account of what it means to agree.[24] Within the verificationist position, to agree could be defined only as a prediction that some hypothesis is verifiable. Ayer does just this, "for every synthetic proposition may be regarded as asserting that certain sensations would occur in a given set of circumstances."

There is a further difficulty with the word "verifiable." Does it refer to logical or practical possibilities? The possibility of a proposition being true in a logical sense simply means that it is non-contradictory. It is not absurd that there are plants on the moon, unless "moon" is defined as a satellite without plants. But to settle the issue regarding the presence or absence of plants on the moon, we might conceivably make observations. The question then becomes practical. Can we get there to observe? At the present time at least this cannot be done, so the proposition is not practically verifiable. In Ayer's sense then, "There are plants on the moon" is neither true nor false.

If the verificationist insists that we must identify "true" with "verifiable" this leads to another bit of trouble. Suppose we say p (some proposition) is verifiable is to say that the proposition is true. But to say this within the verificationist scheme, we are allowed to mean only "that p is verifiable is verifiable." But are we ever to say that it is true "that p is verifiable is verifiable"? No, we may only say "that p is verifiable is verifiable, is verifiable." This is an infinite regress and nothing is ever simply true or false. Ayer, of course, wants to say that all empirical propositions are always subject to further testing. They are only probably true or false. But is the proposition "All synthetic or empirical propositions are always subject to further testing" itself only probably true? If at some point in an inquiry we are satisfied that we know a proposition to be true in the light of past or present experience and ask for no further testing, then with G. E. Moore we would have to reject Ayer's position.

Although there is always the possibility that further evidence may change our knowledge of the truth of our beliefs, this is not the same

[24] Bertrand Russell, *Inquiry into Meaning and Truth*, W. W. Norton & Co., Inc., New York, 1940, p. 395.

thing as saying that the truth of our beliefs means no more than our knowledge. Russell insists that we understand the proposition "It snowed on Manhattan Island on the first of January in the year 1 A.D.," and that the proposition may be true or false although we cannot practically verify it in our experience.[25] On a verificationist theory the historical claims we make about past facts are all hypotheses about future experience. Ayer admits this.[26] Anatol Rapoport put it this way:

> Even statements about the past, if they are verifiable, implicitly contain predictions. The statement, 'Napoleon entered Moscow in 1812,' is verified by looking at records. To say that it is true is to say in effect, 'Look at such and such records and you will find such and such accounts of Napoleon's sojourn in Moscow.'[27]

The objection to this is that the meaning of a historical reference is to report a past fact. Because such statements may be true or false, we do endeavor to verify or falsify them. But we should not confuse the truth of a proposition with our knowledge of it, for a proposition may be true when we lack knowledge. If one holds that it is meaningful to say "Brutus did have breakfast on the morning of the assassination," even if this proposition cannot be verified, then one cannot accept the verificationist theory.[28]

VI. A Semantic Conception of Truth

Alfred Tarski, a contemporary logician and philosopher has made an interesting attempt to define "true" semantically. A number of points need to be brought out first. Somewhat loosely defined, semantics here means a discipline that "deals with certain relations between expressions of a language and the objects (or 'states of affairs') 'referred to' by those expressions."[29] Semantics is, says Tarski,

> . . . a sober and modest discipline which has not pretensions of being a universal patent-medicine for all the ills and diseases of mankind, whether imaginary or real. You will not find in semantics any remedy for decayed teeth or illusions of grandeur or class conflict. Nor is semantics a device for establishing that everyone except the speaker and his friends is speaking nonsense.[30]

---

[25] *Ibid.*, p. 347.
[26] A. J. Ayer, *op. cit.*, p. 102.
[27] Anatol Rapoport, *Operational Philosophy*, Harper & Brothers, New York, 1953, p. 33.
[28] Cf. Brand Blanshard, *op. cit.*, Vol. I, p. 365.
[29] Leonard Linsky (ed.), *Semantics and the Philosophy of Language*, University of Illinois Press, Urbana, 1952, p. 17.
[30] *Ibid.*, p. 17.

Second, we must make the distinction between the *use* and *mention* of a linguistic expression. Whenever we wish to say something about anything, that is, to mention that thing, we must use a name for it. The thing mentioned is a *referent;* the name used to refer is a *sign.* Leonard Linsky, whose account is followed closely here, puts the matter neatly in these words:

Consider, for example, the sentence: (1) John is tall. This sentence mentions the person John, but what appears in the sentence is not John but John's name. The sentence mentions John but does not use him; it uses John's name but does not mention it. Now we might attempt to use John himself in this sentence instead of using his name. We might attempt to do this by placing John himself on this page in approximately the same position now occupied by his name. The result would be a physical object consisting of John followed by the words "is tall." But nobody, I believe, would be inclined to call this a sentence of any language.[31]

When put this way it does not seem possible for anyone to confuse a thing with its name. Few of us have any difficulty in distinguishing the names of our children from the actual sweet and reasonable creatures they are. Still confusion does arise, particularly when the subject to be mentioned is language itself. If, instead of (1) "John is tall," we write (2) "John consists of four letters," we would all understand this sentence to be about John's name and not about John himself. But there is no name for John's name and confusion could result. If we should argue that because "Mary is a girl. Girl ends with an *L*. Therefore Mary ends with an *L*," we should be violating the principle that requires us to distinguish between the use and the mention of a linguistic expression. The absurdity of the argument is the result of *using* the word "girl" in the first sentence, and *mentioning* it in the second.[32] This distinction can be easily maintained by the use of quotation marks. Thus any expression that is a name may be so designated by placing it within quotation marks. Sentence (2) then becomes correctly expressed as: " 'John' consists of four letters." This does not mention John, but rather his name.

The third distinction to be kept in mind is that between *object-language* and *meta-language*. This means that there is a difference between the language we use to talk about objects, e.g. tables, dogs, trees, mountains and the language we use to talk about language. Tarski seeks to construct a definition of truth that applies to sentences in the object-language. This definition will, however, be in terms of the meta-language.

[31] *Ibid.*, p. 4.
[32] See Max Black, *Critical Thinking*, 2nd ed., Prentice-Hall, Inc., Englewood Cliffs, New Jersey, 1952, p. 188.

The definition, Tarski insists, will be materially adequate, that is, it will correspond to what we usually have in mind when we use the term "truth." But it must also be formally correct which is a matter of specifying the words or concepts to be used in the definition and also stating the formal rules to which the definition must conform. In general, "we must describe the formal structure of the language in which the definition will be given." Tarski then points out the ambiguity of the term "true." It may serve as a predicate applied to psychological phenomena, for example, to beliefs; to physical objects including linguistic expressions (physical in the sense of sounds or words); and so on. He proposes to apply it to some linguistic expressions, specifically to sentences. As a sentence must be related to a specific language, so truth must be related to a specific language for "it is obvious that the same expression which is true in one language can be false or meaningless in another." Thus, let us say, "John is tall" is true in the object-language, but meaningless in the meta-language.

We are now ready to state the criterion for the adequacy and formal correctness of this theory of truth. Consider the sentence "Snow is white." If we ask under what conditions this is true or false we would ordinarily say it is true if snow is white and false if snow is not white. This could be expressed as, "The sentence 'snow is white' is true if, and only if, snow is white."[33] Notice that on the left "snow is white" is in quotation marks, but not on the right, because on the left it is the name for a sentence and not the sentence itself. It is a fundamental convention of language that in any statement about an object we must use the name of the object and not the object itself.

We may now generalize. Let p stand for any sentence and X for the name of this sentence. If now we ask what the logical relation is between "x is true" and "p," we discover the following equivalence: "X is true if, and only if, p." This Tarski calls an equivalence of the form (T). It is not itself a definition of truth. "We can only say that every equivalence of the form (T) obtained by replacing 'p' by a particular sentence, and 'X' by a name of this sentence, may be considered a partial definition of truth, which explains wherein the truth of this one individual sentence consists."[34]

Tarski does not suggest that this is the only right way to define "true," if "right" has any meaning at all in this connection. It is merely an attempt to make clear one of the concepts, out of several denoted by the term. He thinks it helps to solve certain paradoxes of language and that it can be adapted to most of the ordinary meanings of "truth." Other philosophers

[33] Leonard Linsky, op. cit., p. 15.
[34] Ibid., p. 16.

do not fully agree with him on this last point, and it is certainly difficult to see how, for example, the method could fit the pragmatic uses of "true."

It is questionable whether Tarski has made any contribution to our understanding of truth. There is a growing critical literature dealing with his theory, but as yet few philosophers outside the ranks of linguistic analysts have studied it. Several of these conclude that Tarski's work, however valuable as a technical exercise, is not of great philosophic relevance. It is not possible to present here the kind of criticism offered, for it requires considerable preparation in technical linguistic analyses. Only a few points will be mentioned, but we will refer to certain articles that require closer attention and more minute treatment than can be offered in an introduction.

P. F. Strawson, a contemporary Oxford analyst thinks that this view may throw some light on artificial languages, but is not relevant to the use of actual or ordinary language. That is, the phrase " . . . is true" is ordinarily used not to talk about sentences, but to talk about states of affairs or subject matters. Although it is true that to say that a sentence is true is not to add anything else to the meaning of the sentence, this is nevertheless misleading and inadequate. Thus, "Moths fly by night" makes the same assertion as "It is true that moths fly by night." But the latter is not making an assertion about an English sentence, but about moths.[35]

Max Black has written one of the few extended criticisms of Tarski's view, but it is much too technical to discuss here.[36] We can say only that Black thinks Tarski has given no analysis of the concept truth, but only a paraphrase of a true sentence, e.g., "Snow is white." When the meaning of truth is spelled out in Tarski's theory, it would have to contain every name in a language. Hence, "the definition would become obsolete whenever new names were introduced into the language." Black thinks the neutrality of Tarski's theory with respect to various theories of truth is evidence of its lack of philosophic relevance. When Tarski says that " 'Snow is white' if and only if snow is white," this is not what is wanted by philosophers concerned with the problem of truth. Rather, they want to know what the "general property of the designata of true object-sentences" is. This the semantic definition does not supply. The situation is something like the following: If I say by "tall" I mean any man over six feet, three inches, my definition fits in very well with conventional usage of "tall" when it is applied to men. But it would not fit when applied to buildings or mountains. It has, in short, a limited range of application, although it does not tell us what the general meaning of "tall" is. So with Tarski. His theory applies to a limited range, say, true sentences in an artificial language, but it does not explain what is meant by truth in general.

VII. Concluding Remarks

The student may have noticed during this brief survey of the theories of truth that some of them were devised to supplement rather than to contradict the others. William James intends to make his pragmatic theory a more precise and efficacious criterion of correspondence. Likewise Tarski professes to accept Aristotle's definition of truth, a classic formulation of correspondence, and to articulate precisely the semantic relation. Hence at least three of the above are versions of the same type of theory. It was noted also that although the defender of the coherence theory claims that coherence is the one and only nature of truth, as well as its criterion, he cannot completely avoid thinking that a belief is true because it conforms to some fact. And although rationalists of the seventeenth century, Descartes, Spinoza, and Leibniz, made much of self-evident and necessary truths, we cannot limit ourselves in all areas of knowledge to calling only axioms and what is deduced from them true. Descartes really claims self-evidence for very few truths, and considers statements of fact to be true because they correspond to what is observed. Spinoza and Leibniz do consider necessary truths to be of a superior sort, but neither tries to deduce history from axioms. If we were God, says Leibniz, we could see that all that Adam ever did, and all that ever happened to him are predicates contained in his substance. But we are not gods, we are children of Adam.

If proponents of all these theories employ the criterion of correspondence, may we also say that proponents of all these theories also employ criteria of coherence, self-evidence, and verification as a criterion, and are not closed to a semantic interpretation? Bertrand Russell, to name one philosopher, has explicitly accepted all these criteria. That is, there is some instance to which each criterion is appropriate. Clearly, there are also instances to which certain criteria do not apply. When laws of logic were discussed, Russell denied that they could be verified or said to correspond to anything, but that they are self-evident and the very ground of coherent human discourse. Most empiricists now concede this.

What, then, is there left to quarrel about? One issue is whether there is a nature of truth as well as a set of criteria. Russell's version of correspondence and Blanshard's version of coherence are theories of the nature of truth and not merely proposed ways to test truth. Some extreme pragmatists, verificationists, and some semanticists assert that there is no nature or essence of truth and they accuse traditional philosophers of trying to solve a pseudo-problem. Of course, if the truth is identical with the real, then it does make sense to talk about its nature. This brings us to another problem, namely, whether there is an irreducible difference between what is thought and what is. Realists deny that thought and things, or reason and reality are ultimately one. Idealists who defend coherence do so in order to deny ultimate duality. Thus theories of truth introduce us to metaphysical systems. For the realist, "true" and "false" are meaningless terms if the world is a unity such as idealists claim. For idealists these terms have meaning only if there is an identity between thought and the real. The beginning student may well be baffled by these conflicting claims, but when we come to the study of systems, he will see that both views point to something that is very difficult to deny.

Although we have not been able to reduce all uses of the words "true" and "false" to one essential truth and falsehood, we have at least been able to sort out various different uses. The distinction between truth of fact and truth of reason is still worth making. We know that we can apply a correspondence theory to problems where we depend on sense-observation. The adjustment of equipment, the observation and recording of results, frequently call forth a judgment of the kind, "The temperature of the water is now 100° Centigrade," or "The residue weighs 2 ounces," or "The rate of the heart beat has slowed." In every such case we regard these judgments as true if the water is 100° Centigrade, the residue does weigh 2 ounces, and the heart beat has actually slowed. Whether we can ever make clear what the relation of correspondence is, it seems impossible to express ourselves adequately without assuming it. It may be that correspondence is indefinable. Some terms must be primitive, and it is likely that this is one. At least it is impossible to talk about what we observe and believe about these observations without assuming that our statements report more or less accurately what we observe.

Similarly, the coherence theory fits the task of systematizing our beliefs. With its aid one stage in science may be related to another, or a particular science may be shown to be related to another. In short, we are not content to leave knowledge as unrelated bits. As our factual knowledge of the world increases, we are not satisfied to have it pile up in heaps. A newly purported fact is fitted in with what we already know, and if it cannot be related in any way, doubt is cast on the fact. Many such obstreperous facts would throw doubt on the system, and a new way of connecting data would be sought. The coherence theory is appropriate to all those occasions of order and harmony achieved in human life.

The pragmatic theory of truth is commonly accepted for many, if not most, of our judgments in the ordinary pressures of daily experience. We often try out an action or a belief, without sufficient knowledge, willing to put it to the test of workability. If it works, that is, if the consequences are fruitful, beneficial, or successful (whatever these may mean) then we are also eager to assert the truth of our previously tentatively held judgments. But there are dangers. It has been shown that William James was saying in a rather folksy way what Ayer puts more technically. We are all aware of the fact that the phrase "it's true if it works" can be abused in corrupt politics and dishonest advertising, as Ayer's doctrine cannot be.

You will often hear that poetry and religion are true in some different way, or even in a "higher" way. On the whole philosophers are not scornful of such claims. It may be that some insights are conveyed in a language that does .not fit standard textbook paradigms of propositions and arguments. We may get nowhere with a poem by asking whether its truth is correspondence, coherence, verifiability, self-evident, or capable of semantic analysis. It is a difficult task for philosophers to discover just what is meant when artists and critics talk of artistic truth. We have not closed the door by saying that "true" and "false" may never be used in a way not canonized by contemporary logical theory. But this does not excuse the artist or critic from trying to make clear what is being said. Similarly, if a religious person talks of false gods, he is required to help us understand what he means.

Finally, can we meaningfully ask which of these theories of truth is the "true" one? If such a question is raised do we not have to appeal to a criterion not supplied by any theory itself? Is the answer that each theory must lean on some other for its test? This may not be disastrous. But it will be if we are led to designate a proposition true in one theory but false in another. That would imply that the same proposition can be both true and false.

Most of these theories involve basic metaphysical assumptions about the nature of reality. This problem will be discussed in Chapters VI and VII.

PROBLEMS FOR THOUGHT AND DISCUSSION

1. In court of law as witnesses we swear to tell the truth, the whole truth, and nothing but the truth. What would human discourse be like if we held to this pledge in all circumstances?
2. A. N. Whitehead once said that it is "more important that a proposition be

interesting than that it be true." What could he mean by "interesting"? Consider your beliefs. Do you hold them simply because they are true?

3. Men commonly believe that no true proposition can possibly contradict another true proposition. If you cannot find evidence to prove this belief, do you hold it to be self-evident?

4. Justice William Douglas, dissenting from the condemnation of a book for obscenity, said, "I have the same confidence in the ability of our people to reject noxious literature as I have in their capacity to sort out the true from the false in theology, economics, politics or any other field."[37] How capable do you think people really are to make these distinctions? Do you think it is a natural or acquired capacity?

5. Make a list of statements in which the word "truth" is used significantly. Can you restate these sentences using the adjective "true" without loss of meaning? Now try it by substituting the adverb "truly"; for example, consider: "He spoke the truth," "What he said is true," "He spoke truly." How do these expressions relate to theories of truth?

6. In discussing the Old and New Testament, Austin Farrer writes:

The relation of the one to the other finds expression in a special and strange use of the word 'true.' The Church is the 'true' Israel, Jesus is the 'true' Anointed King, his death is the 'true' sacrifice. The opposite of 'true' in this way of speaking is not (as we might expect) 'false' but 'literal and prefigurative.' The Israel of King David was a literal Israel, prefiguring the true; David himself was a literally Anointed King, prefiguring the true Christ; and so on. You might suppose that, once possessed of the 'true' things, we could afford to forget the literal prefigurations of them. But this is not so. If you do not know what the love of a literal father is like, it will be useless to talk about the true paternal love of God, and if you cannot discover what literal sacrifices were once thought to be, you will gain no light on the death of Christ from hearing it called 'the true sacrifice.'[38]

What do you think of the opposition between the "literal" and the "true"? Suppose you have a problem of religious truth; which theory of truth would you consider appropriate to apply? Of aesthetic truth? Of ethical truth? Do you think the word truth is applicable in any of these areas? What are some of the difficulties involved?

7. Contrast the above quotation with the following from Santayana:

Goethe is reported to have said that he conceived the character of his Gretchen entirely without observation of originals. And, indeed, he would probably not have found any. His creation rather is the original to which we may occasionally think we see some likeness in real maidens. It is the fiction here that is the standard of naturalness. And on this, as on so many occasions, we may repeat the saying that poetry is truer than history.[39]

In what sense or senses can poetry be said to be truer than history?

[37] Justice William Douglas quoted in "The Supreme Court on Sex and Obscenity" *Time*, Vol. 70, July 8, 1957, p. 11.
[38] Austin Farrer, *The Core of the Bible*, Harper & Brothers, New York, 1957, pp. 10–11.
[39] George Santayana, *The Sense of Beauty*, Dover Publications, Inc., New York, 1955, p. 179.

PERTINENT READINGS

Ayer, A. J., *Language, Truth and Logic*, Dover Publications, Inc., New York, pp. 87–102.

Bradley, F. H., *Essays on Truth and Reality*, The Clarendon Press, Oxford, 1914, reprinted 1944, Chs. IV, V, VII, XI.

Ewing, A. C., *Idealism: A Critical Survey*, Methuen & Co., Ltd., London, 1934, Ch. V.

Hospers, John, *Meaning and Truth in the Arts*, University of North Carolina Press, Chapel Hill, 1946.

Moore, George E., "True and False Beliefs," *Some Main Problems of Philosophy*, George Allen & Unwin, Ltd., London, 1953, pp. 270–287.

Royce, Josiah, "Error and Truth." In: James Hastings (ed.), *Encyclopaedia of Religion and Ethics*, T. & T. Clark, Edinburgh, 1912, Vol. V, pp. 366–373.

Russell, Bertrand, *An Inquiry into Meaning and Truth*, W. W. Norton & Co., Inc., New York, 1940, especially pp. 283–294, 295–308, 362–383.

Santayana, George, *The Realm of Truth*. In: *The Realms of Being*, Charles Scribner's Sons, New York, 1942, pp. 401–546.

Whitehead, Alfred North, "Truth," *Adventures of Ideas*, Mentor Books, The New American Library, New York, 1955, pp. 240–251.

V

From Belief to Knowledge

I. Scepticism

We have tried to show that much of the history of philosophy could be written using the concepts knowledge, belief, and faith, as a theme common to many diverse patterns of thought. Some thinkers say that all claims to know are mere opinion. In short, they have not all been convinced that a cognitive claim can be justified. These are the sceptics. They call to our attention that every proposition can be doubted, and that at least verbally we may deny every claim to truth. But is it possible to doubt seriously that knowledge is attainable? This is, in part, to deny that the term knowledge has any significant job to do in our language. We must examine the sceptical view more closely.

Let us first select three historically famous sceptical positions for illustrations. The first is that of a Sophist of ancient Greece by the name of Gorgias. He is reputed to have denied three things:

1. That anything exists.
2. That if anything did exist it could be known.
3. That even if anything were known, what is known about it could be communicated.

Now this radical view was defended by argument, that is, by moving from certain premises to a conclusion. His reasons will not be stated now, for soon a comprehensive summary of such reasons will be given, but is it not strange to argue that knowledge is impossible? Does not logical discourse involve

181

knowledge that can be communicated, even if logic itself makes no existential claims?

In the first century B.C. a Greek philosopher named Aenesidemus taught at Alexandria and revived the doctrines of another earlier Greek philosopher whose name was Pyrrho (365–270 B.C.). Pyrrhonism has become a synonym for scepticism. Aenesidemus states the main reasons for his scepticism as follows:

1. There are different ways of perceiving among animals.
2. Differences of like kind are found among men.
3. Sense-data are often contradictory even for the same individual.
4. Sense-data vary from time to time with physical changes and with respect to logical relations.
5. Objects are known only indirectly through a medium of air and moisture and are perpetually changing in color, temperature, size and motion.
6. All perceptions are relative and interact one upon another.
7. By repetition and custom impressions become less deep.
8. All men are brought up with different beliefs, under different laws and social conditions.[1]

These considerations, he argues, make it impossible for there to be any knowledge. Notice, however, that the evidence is not drawn from logical concerns but from the character of our observations of the external world, including human society, and the conditions of perceiving. Again we are faced with the peculiar statement that nothing can be known, based on definite claims that the world and our experience of it is such and such, and that we know it to be this way. It is difficult to make sense out of a scepticism of the possibility of knowledge which itself requires knowledge.

In Descartes we have a philosopher who takes only an initial stance of doubt. Scepticism can be, as was suggested earlier, a useful attitude toward many beliefs, most of which are suspected of being false. Descartes' question is, can any one of these be true and known to be true?

He begins by admitting that since his youth he has accepted many opinions as true and that this led him to conclusions that were highly doubtful and uncertain. If any knowledge is to be attained it will require a radical adjustment of thought, namely, "to set aside all the opinions which I had previously accepted among my beliefs and start again from

---

[1] "Aenesidemus," *Encyclopaedia Britannica*, 11th Edition, University Press, Cambridge, England, and New York, 1910, Vol. 1, p. 257.

the very beginning."[2] He now finds himself in circumstances favorable for this experiment so he promises to "make a serious and unimpeded effort to destroy generally all my former opinions." This will be accomplished not by attacking particular beliefs, but rather the principles upon which opinion and belief are founded, "since the destruction of the foundation necessarily involves the collapse of all the rest of the edifice."

The natural way to begin is to examine the knowledge we think we have of things, that is the knowledge that comes to us through the senses. But can we trust their reports?

Everything which I have thus far accepted as entirely true [and assured] has been acquired from the senses or by means of the senses. But I have learned by experience that these senses sometimes mislead me, and it is prudent never to trust wholly those things which have once deceived us.

Still would it not be sheer lunacy to affirm the complete unworthiness of the senses? Are there not some of them that we cannot reasonably doubt, such as

. . . that I am here, seated by the fire, wearing a [winter] dressing gown, holding this paper in my hands, and other things of this nature. And how could I deny that these hands and this body are mine, unless I am to compare myself with certain lunatics whose brain is so troubled and befogged by the black vapors or the bile that they continually affirm that they are kings while they are paupers, that they are clothed in [gold and] purple while they are naked; or imagine [that their head is made of clay, or] that they are gourds, or that their body is glass? [But this is ridiculous]; such men are fools, and I would be no less insane than they if I followed their example.

But now another possibility occurs to him: May we not be in a perpetual sleep and merely dreaming that the world is as our senses report? We must quote in full the famous passage.

Nevertheless, I must remember that I am a man, and that consequently I am accustomed to sleep and in my dreams to imagine the same things that lunatics imagine when awake, or sometimes things which are even less plausible. How many times has it occurred that [the quiet of] the night made me dream [of my usual habits;] that I was here, clothed [in a dressing gown], and sitting by the fire, although I was in fact lying undressed in bed! It seems apparent to me now, that I am not looking at this paper with my eyes closed, that this head that I shake is not drugged with sleep, that it is with design and deliberate intent that I stretch out this hand and perceive it. What happens in sleep seems not at all as clear and as distinct as all this. But I am speaking as though I

[2] René Descartes, *Meditations* (L. J. Lafleur, tr.). Reprinted by permission of the publishers, The Liberal Arts Press, Inc., New York, 1951. All quotations are to be found in the First Meditation.

never recall having been misled, while asleep, by similar illusions! When I consider these matters carefully, I realize so clearly that there are no conclusive indications by which waking life can be distinguished from sleep that I am quite astonished, and my bewilderment is such that it is almost able to convince me that I am sleeping.

So let us suppose now that we are asleep and that all these details, such as opening the eyes, shaking the head, extending the hands, and similar things, are merely illusions; and let us think that perhaps our hands and our whole body are not such as we see them. Nevertheless, we must at least admit that these things which appear to us in sleep are like [painted] scenes [and portraits] which can only be formed in imitation of something [real and] true, and so, at the very least, these types of things—namely, eyes, head, hands, and the whole body—are not imaginary entities, but real and existent. For in truth painters, even when they use the greatest ingenuity in attempting to portray sirens and satyrs in [bizarre and] extraordinary ways, nevertheless cannot give them wholly new shapes and natures, but only invent some particular mixture composed of parts of various animals; or even if perhaps [their imagination is sufficiently extravagant that] they invent something so new that nothing like it has ever been seen, and so their work represents something purely imaginary and [absolutely] false, certainly at the very least the colors of which they are composed must be real.

And for the same reason, even if these types of things—namely, [a body,] eyes, head, hands, and other similar things—could be imaginary, nevertheless, we are bound to confess that there are some other still more simple and universal concepts which are true [and existent], from the mixture of which, neither more nor less than in the case of the mixture of real colors, all these images of things are formed in our minds, whether they are true [and real] or imaginary [and fantastic].

Of this class of entities is corporeal nature in general and its extension, including the shape of extended things, their quantity, or size and number, and also the place where they are, the time that measures their duration, and so forth. That is why we will perhaps not be reasoning badly if we conclude that physics, astronomy, medicine, and all the other sciences which follow from the consideration of composite entities are very dubious [and uncertain]; whereas arithmetic, geometry, and the other sciences of this nature, which treat only of very simple and general things without concerning themselves as to whether they occur in nature or not, contain some element of certainty and sureness. For whether I am awake or whether I am asleep, two and three together will always make the number five, and the square will never have more than four sides; and it does not seem possible that truths [(so clear and)] so apparent can ever be suspected of any falsity [or uncertainty].

Notice how Descartes strives to preserve those beliefs that are so clear and evident that they can be doubted, if at all, only with the severest strain on our intelligence. Notice also that these beliefs are found primarily in mathematics and not in the sciences that assert something about the world of nature. But the end is not yet in sight. For now another troublesome thought occurs to him: May it not be the case that there is a God who is really an evil spirit, a demon, bent on deceiving him?

I will therefore suppose that, not [a true] God, [who is very good and] who is the supreme source of truth, but a certain evil spirit, not less clever and deceitful than powerful, has bent all his efforts to deceiving me. I will suppose that the sky, the air, the earth, colors, shapes, sounds, and all other objective things [that we see] are nothing but illusions and dreams that he has used to trick my credulity. I will consider myself as having no hands, no eyes, no flesh, no blood, nor any senses, yet falsely believing that I have all these things. I will remain absolutely attached to this hypothesis; and if I cannot attain the knowledge of any truth by this method, at any rate [it is in my power to suspend my judgment. That is why] I shall take great care not to accept any falsity among my beliefs and shall prepare my mind so well for all the ruses of this great deceiver that, however powerful and artful he may be, he will never be able to mislead me in anything.

So Descartes sets himself in opposition to this supposed demon. He will not be taken in, not be misled. But, of course, to prepare himself for such a contest will require the acceptance of many knowledge-claims that cannot be doubted.

Remember that Descartes moves rapidly from his clear and distinct principle *cogito, ergo sum,* to the existence of a trustworthy God and then to a belief in an external world. Although the argument must be left now, at least this much has been learned, namely, how difficult it is to take up, without qualification, the position of complete scepticism. There may be grounds for doubting that any knowledge at all is possible, but to say there are such grounds would seem to be again a self-refuting position. Whatever grounds for total scepticism there are they would not appear to be logical; the consequences of complete scepticism could hardly then be consistent.

Another argument against scepticism rests on the premise that action is impossible without knowledge. The sceptic says he acts without knowledge; but if he acts, he must know. The anti-sceptic often believes he triumphs easily over any position of total doubt. But of course the sceptic meets the argument by denying that knowledge is necessary for action. Indeed, does not all action carry us into the future? And since the future is not yet, and knowledge, if there is any, is of what is and is present, the sceptic will not allow that his conduct belies his philosophic position. But can the sceptic act by blind faith alone? We may have only probable rather than demonstrable knowledge in some matters. For example, sceptics and their opponents commonly make their exit from third-floor rooms not by the windows, but by the doors, etc. The sceptic often claims that he acts on animal faith. Is it therefore obvious, as often claimed, that scepticism is a biological, or sociological, or psychological impossibility?

More common than either dogmatic scepticism, or Pyrrhonism, or methodological scepticism, or Cartesian doubt, is agnosticism, namely that some particular assertion is in doubt. This is probably the most common meaning of "being sceptical." We may doubt that we know things, or other minds, or universals, or what space and time and causality are; we may question whether we can know ultimate reality or whether or not there is a God; or we may doubt that we know beauty or the good, or the past or the future. We may share the troubled spirit of Walt Whitman when he writes in Leaves of Grass

Of the terrible doubt of appearances
Of the uncertainty after all that we may be deluded . . .
May-be the things I perceive, the animals, plants, men, hills, shining and flowing waters,
The skies of day and night colors, densities, forms—may-be these are (as doubtless they are) only apparitions, and the real something has yet to be known,

. . . .

But the possibility of particular doubts ought not to be equated with total scepticism, rather it may be the condition of inquiry. Santayana once put the point this way: " . . . Scepticism is an exercise, not a life; it is a discipline fit to purify the mind of prejudice and render it all the more apt, when the time comes, to believe and to act wisely."[3]

The fact that we are able to doubt so many cognitive claims leads us to ask whether there are times when we do not doubt, and the simple answer is, when we know. Knowledge precludes doubt. When we know we do not doubt. When we doubt we would not ordinarily say that we know. But what is knowledge? And if it is obtainable, under what circumstances? This is the beginning of a group of questions that are the proper concern of the philosophical discipline called epistemology. It is a very complex study in which logical, linguistic, psychological, physiological, and even sociological matters may be conjoined. It is not possible here to present or work through all the intricacies of this subject, but the short introduction following will help the student feel some of the difficulties, and thus perhaps in his own way he may make contributions to their solution.

[3] George Santayana, *Scepticism and Animal Faith*, Charles Scribner's Sons, New York, 1929, p. 69.

II. *The Ideal of Knowledge*

Let us begin with a problem of meaning or use of terms. It is quite evident that we find different uses for the terms "belief" and "knowledge." There are situations in which we would prefer to say "I believe such and such," rather than "I know such and such," or vice versa. But why is this the case? What does the term "know" do that "believe" does not do? Or to put it another way: What do we demand of knowledge that we do not demand of belief?

From Descartes there is one answer, namely, that all knowledge must have the kind of certainty that is possible in mathematics; that is, it must be such that it is logically necessary, and psychologically impossible to doubt by anyone who understands what is going on. The question is, however, whether such an ideal is required for knowledge of the good, of the past, of the future, of other minds, and so on. May it not be that Descartes, and all the rationalists, have set not only an unattainable ideal but an inappropriate one? If we hold out for this ideal in all knowledge, scepticism may be inevitable. Thus one way to avoid scepticism would be to deny that the ideal of mathematical certainty should be acceptable in other areas of human concern. It is not that we merely fall short in these other fields, which suggests that if we had more facts, more time, more brains, that we could then make our knowledge of the past, of other minds, etc., as certain as mathematics; rather, if this ideal is not appropriate to all kinds of knowledge, then no increase in facts or brain power or time will make the knowledge identical with the kind of knowledge we have in mathematics.

A second approach to knowledge, as was shown earlier in Platonism, is to define it as grasp of forms, independent of times, places, and circumstances. Must knowledge, then, be independent of acts of knowing? Must knowledge also be independent of the sensuous embodiments of the forms? Only in this way could knowledge be eternal and absolute, unconditioned. This demand, as the Cartesian identification of knowledge with certainty, also seems to be unattainable. The failure here seems to be the imposition upon all claims to know of one criterion that ignores the varieties of knowledge-claims, each conditioned by what there is to know and the means available at specific times. The knowing situations under which we claim to know seem to be various. Examine how such propositions come to be made: "Water boils at 100° Centigrade," "Napoleon was defeated at Waterloo," "I have a toothache," "He is angry." If the kind of knowledge varies with what there is and our access to it, then it would seem that we must examine in each type or instance the specific criteria pertinent to the claim.

When specific knowledge-claims are investigated more thoroughly this problem will come into better focus. But at present it may be said that the transition from belief to knowledge is not necessarily the transition from a lack of logical certainty to the achievement of logical certainty, although it is a transition from a condition of possible doubt to one of inadmissible doubt.

A third demand usually made of knowledge is for its grounds. Whenever we say "I know," we may justly be asked for the grounds of our knowledge, the question frequently taking the form, "How do you know?" When this is requested, we are expected to give the reasons that would justify the claim. The answer might take various forms, for example, "I saw (or heard) it"; "I worked it out"; "He told me"; "I learned it in mathematics, (or physics, or biology, etc.)"; "I read it"; and so on. We may be wrong, of course, in judging these grounds to be sufficient, but it would certainly seem reasonable to demand that, if we say we know, we can give the grounds of the knowledge. It is true that there may be instances in which we are not able to supply the grounds, or at least not adequate grounds, and when this occurs we would probably prefer to say "I believe." But the distinction is not absolute, for it is quite reasonable to ask for the grounds of belief too, although in this case we may be let off with a less stringent requirement. This calls attention to the fact that belief and knowledge are not separated by a logical or psychological gulf, but are on a continuum. Or to put it another way, a belief sentence is a candidate for the status of a knowledge claim.

It also is true that there are some uses of "I know" for which we do not normally demand grounds. Suppose one should say, "I don't know how I know it, I just know it." This need not be a confession of incompetence or failure to supply grounds, it may be that in this case the demand for grounds is simply unsuitable. This would be so if there is such a thing as intuitive knowledge, for which some claims have been made. Frequently it is maintained that the knowledge derived through intuition is of a higher, more certain, and truer kind than that gained through the intellect or the senses. Thus, for example, the mystic's vision of God or The One, and his experience of union with the divine is neither the product of thought nor of senses, but of something like intuition. Henri Bergson developed a view that contrasted intuitive ways of knowing with the analytical methods of science. He described intuition as a kind of intellectual sympathy by which we seize an object from within. All other ways involve analysis, which operates with symbols. In such cases knowledge is only of symbolic representation and not of reality.

Of course, the question whether intuition is possible is the crucial point. This depends on what is meant by intuition and what is meant by knowledge. There is one use of the term which is linguistically common but philosophically useless. For example, we often hear of "hunches," "feelings in the bones," etc., which lead one to say "I just know such and such to be the case." Sometimes these hunches work out and what was felt sure of turned out as expected. But these instances are philosophically uninteresting. They are incapable of being checked and therefore open the way to intellectual irresponsibility.

Another use of the term is more important for philosophers. It involves the claim that there is a way of knowing that is direct and immediate and requires no grounds for its justification. Sometimes this knowledge is said to be of facts of the external world, sometimes of values, sometimes of axioms, and sometimes of supernatural beings, such as gods. With respect to knowledge of facts, intuition is highly suspect. It does not seem to be an improvement on other ways of knowing which are public and open to accepted methods of checking. With respect to values it is also highly dubitable because it permits a wide range of diverse claims. A Hitler and a Ghandi may defend their contradictory points of view on intuitive grounds. Some philosophers would admit the dangers of intuition in regard to social and political values, but support a form of intuitionism in relation to aesthetic values. For example, F. S. C. Northrop writes,

> This aesthetic component or any part of it has one other characteristic. It must be immediately experienced to be known. Unlike that factor in the nature of things which is designated by theory, the aesthetic component cannot be conveyed syntactically and deductively by the postulational, formalized technique of a Newton or a St. Thomas Aquinas. This is the reason why no amount of verbal description will enable one to convey the sensed color blue to a person born blind.[4]

When intuition is used in this way to mean a kind of apprehension of the ineffable, a grasp of wholes or Gestalts, it is not the kind of knowledge for which grounds are sought.

These remarks suggest that with respect to knowledge-claims there comes a time when the ceaseless demand for "grounds" becomes ridiculous. If, in response to your question, "How do you know the temperature is 80°?", I reply, "Because I looked at the thermometer," and finding this

[4] F. S. C. Northrop, *The Meeting of East and West,* The Macmillan Co., New York, 1947, p. 304.

unsatisfactory you persist with "How do you know the thermometer is accurate?", or "How do you know your eyesight is trustworthy," we will find no way of ending this game and therefore no significant use for the term knowledge at all, since nothing will count now in its favor. Somewhere along the line a decision has to be made, an agreement arrived at, with respect to the criteria of knowledge, such that doubt would be inappropriate. But the criteria are not invariant for all kinds of knowledge.

Another distinction may help at this point. It is part of our everyday speech to say sometimes, "He knows how," and at other times, "He knows that." The first expression undoubtedly refers to the possession of a skill or competence or ability to perform an act or to fulfill a function. We do not ordinarily ask for the grounds of a skill or ability. But we might ask how successful over a period of time a person has been who claims to "know how." Thus if a surgeon says he knows how to do a particular operation we might ask what success he has had in the past with this operation, or similar ones; or if a man says he knows how to read Sanskrit we do not ask for the grounds of his statement, but we could give him a passage to translate. On the other hand, the claim to "know that" does seem usually (with the exceptions noted above) to require the offering of grounds if one is pressed. Showing that we know ordinarily takes the character of a statement, not of a performance. Here we may legitimately be asked for grounds and if we are unable to supply them we are open to the charge that we really did not know. Thus if I say, "I know that the president vetoed the bill," and am asked how I know this, any number of different replies might serve as grounds, e.g., "I read it in the paper," "Congressman Jones told me," "It was announced in a special radio broadcast to which I was listening," etc. Here I do not exhibit a skill, I offer a warrant for my claim; if you accept my warrant you will admit my knowledge. In general, "I know how" may be met with the response, "Show me," while "I know that" may call forth, "How do you know that?" or "What reasons do you give for claiming to know that?"

Although this distinction is useful it is not absolute. Some philosophers think there are cases of "knowing how" in which performances are not involved, for example, "I know how you felt when you lost the race"; and also cases of "knowing that" which do not refer to knowing facts, for example, "Richard knows that he ought to vote." Attempts have also been made to reduce all "knowing that" statements to "knowing how" statements. We cannot pursue all these possibilities, but we have learned that there are instances of knowledge-claims that do not require proffering of grounds. Again we see how extraordinarily difficult it is to find any common quality to all instances of knowledge, except perhaps the absence of doubt.

The problem of defining knowledge may be illustrated by taking an example from C. I. Lewis, a contemporary philosopher whose work in this field is widely recognized. This definition is a set of criteria designed to aid us in distinguishing the conditions that permit us to say truly, "I know." It will be useful to have these before us, but the student should also notice very carefully the difficulties the author himself sees in this analysis.

1. Knowledge must be apprehension of or belief in what is true or is fact, as against what is false or is not fact. An apprehension which is in error is properly called a cognition; but only cognitions which are true or correct should be classed as knowledge.
2. Cognition generally, or the content of it, must have meaning in the sense that something is signified, believed in, or asserted which lies beyond or outside of the cognitive experience itself. When such cognition is veridical or is knowledge, it must correspond to, accord with, or be true of what is thus meant or affirmed.
3. Knowledge must have a ground or reason. An ignorant person may assert what happens to be the case by hazarding a guess or irrationally committing himself. Or a fanatic may believe something which is true but believe it solely from emotional compulsion and in the absence of supporting evidence. Or a mentally flabby person may assert what, as it happens, is so, merely because he wishes it to be so. But such holding of belief in the absence of any warrant or justifying consideration is not to be classed as knowledge even when it happens to accord with the facts.

It is questionable whether we should not add another requirement also:

4. Knowledge, or at least knowledge in the best and quite strict sense, must be certain. If what is believed is no better than probable, then the belief may be justified, or justified in some degree; but in that case our knowledge is not—it may be said—of the fact believed, but of the different fact that this believed-in state of affairs has genuine probability.

However, the attempt to impose all these requirements at once, in the delimitation of what is properly to be called knowledge, would be certain to result in difficulties of the first order. Each by itself is plausible; but the combination of them would threaten to eliminate every kind of apprehension of which humans are capable. To mention only difficulties which lie close at hand; it is doubtful if (2), which calls for something believed in but not contained within the cognitive experience itself, can be combined with (4), which calls for certainty, and still find any cognitive phenomenon meeting the requirements. The doubt increases when (3) is added, which demands that such certainty of something beyond the cognitive experience itself should have a sufficient ground.[5]

[5] Clarence Irving Lewis, *An Analysis of Knowledge and Valuation*, The Open Court Publishing Co., La Salle, Illinois, 1946, pp. 27–28.

It is apparent that neither philosophers nor laymen are willing to get along with the term "believe"; each expects and tries to "know" as well. But knowledge and belief are confronted with the possibility of doubt and also with the very great difficulty of definition. For we have seen that we cannot attain absolute certainty in knowledge (excluding mathematics and logic), nor can we say that there is any one characteristic alone which when present turns belief into knowledge. This leads us to accept a kind of scepticism, not as a way of life, but as a raised eyebrow or a serious inquiry, to keep us from dogmatic assertion, that is, from the unwillingness to offer any evidence for the knowledge-claims we make. Whatever else is needed in defining knowledge it would seem to require at least these three things: First the "acceptance," "acknowledgment," "affirmation," etc. of a statement that something is the case, second that one has "adequate," "good," "sufficient," etc. evidence that something is the case; and third that what is "affirmed," etc. actually is the case.

The terms are vague. "Acceptance," "adequate evidence," and "actually is the case" all need more precise definition. But is there any assurance that defining them more accurately would make "knowledge" any clearer to us? In short, if it is required to have a precise definition of "knowledge" we will never get to examine specific knowledge claims, and it may be that with a somewhat vague concept of knowledge we can still pursue with profit an inquiry into these claims. Everything cannot be said at once, and philosophical problems are interrelated. Thus the third point above shows that "truth" is indeed an epistemological concept, although some would say it is also metaphysical. A. J. Ayer has suggested the following criteria for knowledge; you should compare them with those we have given above, and also with those of C. I. Lewis.

I conclude then that the necessary and sufficient conditions for knowing that something is the case are first that what one is said to know be true, secondly that one be sure of it, and thirdly that one should have the right to be sure. This right may be earned in various ways; but even if one could give a complete description of them it would be a mistake to try to build it into the definition of knowledge, just as it would be a mistake to try to incorporate our actual standards of goodness into a definition of good. And this being so, it turns out that the questions which philosophers raise about the possibility of knowledge are not all to be settled by discovering what knowledge is. For many of them reappear as questions about the legitimacy of the title to be sure. They need to be severally examined; and this is the main concern of what is called the theory of knowledge.[6]

[6] A. J. Ayer, *The Problem of Knowledge*, Macmillan and Co., Ltd., London, 1956, p. 34. Reprinted by permission of the author, St. Martin's Press, Inc. and Macmillan & Co. Ltd.

Let us proceed then, in spite of the difficulties of definition, to an examination of more specific knowledge-claims—an examination of the problems and some of the alternative answers.

III. Knowledge of Physical Things

In a prephilosophic condition no one doubts the existence of an external world. It is only when one has been introduced to the critical questions philosophy raises that it seems quite intelligent to wonder whether the things we take to be in a material world may really not be. In short, what seems so certain, namely, that there are things that possess qualities, and to which we must adjust, such as tables, trees, mountains, moons, cows, and continents, becomes less certain when attention is called to some facts that might have escaped notice. What are these conditions that make possible a scepticism about knowledge of material things?

There are first the experiences of illusion. People sometimes see mirages and reflections and double images and so on. Ordinarily these are taken to be appearances rather than real objects, although we admit some condition in the external world as a cause of the appearance. But if illusions are possible may not all perceptions be illusory? How can those that are be distinguished from those that are not?

Second, people sometimes "hear" voices when there are no voices, or "see" daggers when there are none. These are hallucinations in which there are appearances but no objects.

Third, there are variations in what the senses tell about the world, for example, lemonade tastes sweet before one eats chocolate cake, but if the cake is eaten first the lemonade is tart. And there is the well-known experiment in which one hand is in hot water, the other in cold, and both are then placed in luke-warm water; the result is a reversal of the sensations of heat and cold in the hands.

Fourth, there are the puzzles that occur when a person acquires some new information about the world that makes him reconsider earlier beliefs. For example, we now know the speed of light and that it takes eight minutes to travel from the sun to the earth. This seems to force us to say that we never see the present sun but only the sun as it was eight minutes ago. That vast, glowing disc we see on the horizon is not the sun, but a visual echo of the real thing, which disappeared eight minutes ago. For all we know it could have blown up five minutes ago and we would be ignorant of this for another three minutes. Thus some judgments we would make about the sun on the basis of perceiving it would certainly be false. When this is extended to interstellar space, the imagination can scarcely take it in. For we must now be seeing effects of physical occurrences that happened millions and millions of years ago. But now think of this puzzle in another direction; what about my perceptual knowledge of this paper in front of me? Does the same principle not hold, that is, for the light to travel from the paper to my eye takes time, and so also for the nerve current from the eye to the visual centers in the brain. The time is, of course, too small to measure, but still given the finite velocity of light it is a fact of the perceptual situation. This would seem to mean that all perceptual knowledge is about the past, about what has happened, and never about what is just now the case.

But there is another reason for the sceptic's lament that we can never know physical objects by way of perception. Let us approach it through the position of John Locke. Recall the following points of his philosophy: before experience the mind is a *tabula rasa,* blank tablet; when perceptual experiences occur ideas are, so to speak, imprinted on the mind. Ideas are of two kinds, simple and complex.

Simple ideas are those obtained from one sense only such as colors, sounds, tastes, heat and cold, and the ideas that arise from reflection— that is, those of which we are aware when we observe our own mental processes, namely ideas of perceiving, thinking, doubting, willing, and so on; and also ideas of both sensation and reflection such as pain, pleasure, existence, unity, power, and succession.

Complex ideas are those that arise through the mind's capacity to compare, name, and abstract. In this way arise ideas of beauty, gratitude, man, universe, etc. There are three sorts of complex ideas: First, *modes,* which are not existences in themselves, but depend on a substance, for example, ideas of triangle, gratitude, and murder; this means that triangles exist only as triangular things, gratitude exists only in grateful persons, and murder only when there are murderers. Second, *substance* is also a complex idea of a collection of qualities existing together or inhering in an object. Finally, there are *relations,* which are gained by comparing ideas.

The question "How does experience happen?" brings us to a consideration of the object. Here is mind with its capacities, e.g., sensation, imagination, memory, etc. Will a mind with its powers generate ideas? Not at all. There must be an impact from the external world of which one has a sensation or perception. The mind is not purely passive—it is ready to be set in motion by an object, and in the object is a power to produce the idea. This power is called a quality of the object. Locke accepts and defends the distinction between two kinds of qualities, primary and secondary. The former are independent of the observer, such as bulk, figure, number, motion; the latter are dependent upon the observer and thus not in the bodies themselves. The connection between primary and secondary qualities is undiscoverable, says Locke.

According to this theory of knowledge we do not perceive objects in the external world directly. They come to us only by the interposition of ideas, the data of sense-experience. But these data, for Locke, represent the real external world. Secondary qualities, of course, are not in the objects; they are in us as tastes, sounds, and colors, but in the objects as powers to produce sensations in us. Primary qualities constitute the objects, which are represented by ideas.

Now let us see what this theory leads to. It effectively places between the knower and the object an idea or impression. Thus what is immediately given in sense-perception is not the external object itself, but something caused by the object and which represents it. But does this not make scepticism possible? For on Locke's grounds how can we ever know that the representative really represents the object? We cannot compare the representative with the original, because according to the theory we are never aware of the original in perception. And certainly the representative does not carry a title or sign guaranteeing that it is a representative of something else. Furthermore, when Locke tells us that the immediate data are sometimes like the qualities they represent and sometimes not, how are we to know this? Are we not cut off from the original for comparison?

Any account of perceptual knowledge that leaves a gap between the perceiver and the object, or that tries to bridge the gap with a representative or a sense-datum or an appearance is open to the sceptic's challenge, namely, to justify claims to knowledge of physical things on the basis of knowing only how they appear. How, he asks, can we ever cross the gulf between things as they seem to be and things as they are? A number of attempts have been made to answer the sceptics, all of which are modifications of two extreme positions. There is not the space here to examine all the alternatives, but much can be learned by considering the extremes.

Let us begin with a view called naive realism. It meets the sceptic's challenge by flatly denying that physical objects are inferred from sense-data; rather, it insists, our knowledge of things is direct. We do not need substitutes or vehicles or representatives to close the gap between ourselves and physical objects, for they can be known directly. Thus things are as they are perceived to be. Such a view seems highly favorable to common sense and is probably the position most widely accepted by uncritical minds. Most of us probably once believed that not only do physical objects continue to exist when they are not perceived, but that they exist when not perceived in precisely the same way as they would normally when perceived. For naive realism, we know the world just as it is, and in knowing it we do not change it, we merely take it in. But if we adopt the naive realists' view we have no way of meeting the puzzles that were mentioned earlier, namely, of illusion, hallucination, and so on. In short, this position oversimplifies the epistemological problem. By failing to recognize the gap between what things are and what they seem to be, the naive realists do not provide an answer to questions that can legitimately be asked, and are in fact asked.

The polar opposite to naive realism is a view called phenomenalism. Very generally this meets the sceptic's query by saying that things are the way they seem to be, for things are only logical constructions out of their appearances. More specifically, the phenomenalist says that anything we know about physical objects can be expressed in statements referring solely to sense-data.

The phenomenalist contends that, if we ask ourselves just what it is we are believing when we think we perceive something to have a certain characteristic, we will find that our beliefs really pertain only to the *appearances* of the thing we think we are perceiving. He then infers that our ordinary statements about physical things—such statements as "That is a tree" and "This thing is red"— logically *entail* many statements referring solely to appearances. And he concludes that, if only we were to list the appearance statements entailed by any thing statement, we would have for that thing statement the type of translation the phenomenalistic thesis requires: we would have a set of appearance statements expressing everything that the thing statement is ordinarily used to express.[7]

For the phenomenalist it is nonsense to regard a physical object as a kind of unobservable entity hiding behind a curtain of sense-data. There is no veil or curtain of appearances that needs to be penetrated to get to real physical objects, because to talk of physical objects is just to talk about sense-data. But anti-phenomenalists do not agree that the reduction of physical-object statements to sense-data statements can be successfully carried out. A. J. Ayer, for example, offers the following objections:

First, according to the phenomenalist, describing a physical object is a matter of saying what sense-data do appear or would appear if certain conditions were fulfilled. But, says Ayer, it will not do merely to make vague claims that what is meant by saying, for example, that there is a table

[7] Roderick M. Chisholm, *Perceiving: A Philosophical Study*, Cornell University Press, Ithaca, New York, 1957, p. 190.

in the next room, is that if one were in that room one would perceive the table.

For his being there is a matter of a physical body's being in a certain spatial relationship to other physical objects, and, on the assumption that to talk about physical objects is always to talk about sense-data, this situation must itself be described in purely sensory terms. But it is not at all easy to see how this could be done.[8]

The point is that if an observer is present there is the possibility that his presence will affect the situation and thus "falsify the analysis."

In the second place, any philosophical description must describe the place and setting in which sense-data occur and the description must also be in purely sense-data statements. But Ayer thinks it would not be possible to get a set of sensory descriptions that would sufficiently distinguish one place from another. The difficulty is particularly evident with respect to times:

Suppose, for example, that the problem were to give a phenomenalist translation of such a statement as that Julius Caesar crossed the Rubicon in 49 B.C. How would one set about rendering "49 B.C." in purely sensory terms? To this the phenomenalist may reply that we do in fact succeed in identifying places and times by making observations; we note features of the landscape, look at watches and calendars, and so forth; and these performances in the end consist in our sensing sense-data. It does not follow, however, that any description of these sense-data would be sufficient to identify the place or time uniquely; and so long as no such description is found the phenomenalist's reduction has not been carried out.[9]

Third, Ayer next points out that if the phenomenalist is right, the existence of a physical object is sufficient, under appropriate conditions to produce sense-data; that is, there is a deductive step from descriptions of objects to descriptions of actual or possible sense-data. And the converse is also true, namely, that any occurrence of sense-data is a sufficient condition for the existence of the physical object; that is, another deductive step is made from descriptions of actual or possible appearances to descriptions of physical objects or reality. "The decisive objection to phenomenalism is that neither of these requirements can be satisfied." It is sometimes denied that physical-object statements are deducible from sense-data statements because no statement about a physical object can be conclusively verified; that is, the possibility of illusion is never completely eliminated. Thus any statement about a physical object may be false. But Ayer rejects this:

[8] A. J. Ayer, *op. cit.*, p. 137.
[9] *Ibid.*, p. 138.

Can there be any doubt at all of the present existence of the table at which I am seated, the pen with which I am writing, the hand which is holding the pen? Surely I know for certain that these physical objects exist? And if I do know this for certain, I know it on the basis of my sense-experiences. Admittedly, my present experiences, taken by themselves, are not sufficient for the purpose: the mere fact that I now seem to see and feel a pen in my right hand does not prove conclusively that either of these objects exists. But when my present experiences are taken in conjunction with all my past experiences, then, it may plausibly be held, the evidence is sufficient; I am entitled to regard the existence of these and many other physical objects which I can now perceive as conclusively established.[10]

It is true that one may never get to the point where doubt is *logically* impossible, but Ayer thinks that one's experiences are such that the phenomenalist's hypothesis ceases to become serious, that is, it is a hypothesis, "which, whatever the further evidence, no sensible person would adopt." One should notice what Ayer accepts as "sufficient evidence" for our knowledge of things. Certainly it is not the kind of evidence one would desire, say, in a mathematical proof. But then that is not the kind of knowledge available with respect to physical objects. Nevertheless, one might well ask whether sense-experiences, each in itself open to doubt, become less doubtful when brought together and used as the basis of an assertion about something other than appearance.

There are a number of intermediate positions between naive realism and phenomenalism, each trying to bridge the gap the sceptic persists in calling to our attention. They cannot be presented here, but the student should now be aware of a nice problem and curious enough to investigate it on his own. At least we have learned that the sceptic cannot be answered by showing him that we have *logically* certain knowledge of physical things. This kind of knowledge is not available to sense-perception, simply because sensing is not a logical process. But this does not mean that the evidence we do have for the existence of physical objects is so inadequate that we must refrain from asserting their existence.

The authors would like to point out that every instance of perceptual knowing is a product of stimulation external to the perceiver, and also of his internal psychological and physiological condition or state. A change in either may very likely produce a change in what is perceived. But it is false to assume that if the properties a thing has when appearing are caused by outside factors or by the condition of the observer, that therefore, these properties do not really belong to the thing. John Locke wrote long ago that if our hearing were more acute and if we had microscopes for eyes

[10] *Ibid.*, p. 139.

then we would experience a totally different world from the one now common to normal observers. If we accept this, and it seems inescapable, then all perceptual knowledge is gained from a certain aspect or perspective. We must then say that the real is such that under certain conditions it has certain qualities. Change the conditions, within the perceiver or outside the perceiver, and reality appears different. Sometimes, as in illusion and hallucination, the perspectives are not shared, but in normal perception we may say we share a common aspect or perspective of reality. This leaves us with a metaphysical problem, namely, what is reality like when it is not perceived or known? Obviously, from the standpoint of human beings, this reality is not a possible object of perceptual knowledge.

IV. *Knowledge of Other Minds*

A lament often heard is that each of us lives alone, that we can never get outside of ourselves and inside someone else so that we can be sure what that person is thinking or feeling. Joseph Conrad put it this way:

No, it is impossible; it is impossible to convey the life-sensation of any given epoch of one's existence—that which makes its truth, its meaning—its subtle and penetrating essence. It is impossible. We live, as we dream—alone. . . .[11]

And Matthew Arnold expressed a similar sentiment in the following lines:

Yes! in the sea of life enisled,
With echoing straits between us thrown,
Dotting the shoreless watery wild,
We mortal millions live *alone*.

If Conrad and Arnold are right, then the sceptic is right when he points to another chasm between knowledge-claims and the justification of them, for certainly we do often say that we know how another person thinks or feels, but if we really cannot know, the claim is unjustified. The problem is not that we do not believe in other minds, for we believe long before we even recognize a problem. The difficulty is in trying to produce a justification or to give good reasons for holding such a belief. It is a fact that sometimes we do not know what another person thinks or feels. His thoughts, feelings, dreams, imaginings, sensations, and memories are said to be utterly private and never public and never transferable although they may be communicable if expressed in verbal or non-verbal ways. This fact makes us wonder whether we ever do have knowledge of other

[11] Joseph Conrad, *Heart of Darkness*, Signet Books, New American Library, New York, 1950, p. 84. Reprinted by permission of J. M. Dent & Sons Ltd., London.

people's minds, and from here the next step is to the sceptic's statement that we never can have such knowledge.

Philosophers have offered a number of alternative accounts to meet the sceptic's challenge. Let us examine some of them with a view toward helping the student think his way through the problem and perhaps come to some decision.

The most frequent justification for knowledge of other minds is the argument from analogy. John Stuart Mill has given a classic statement of it, so let us present it in full. First he asks the question and then proceeds to answer it.

By what evidence do I know, or by what considerations am I led to believe, that there exist other sentient creatures; that the walking and speaking figures which I see and hear, have sensations and thoughts, or in other words, possess Minds? The most strenuous Intuitionist does not include this among the things that I know by direct intuition. I conclude it from certain things, which my experience of my own states of feeling proves to me to be marks of it. These marks are of two kinds, antecedent and subsequent; the previous conditions requisite for feeling, and the effects or consequences of it. I conclude that other human beings have feelings like me, because, first, they have bodies like me, which I know, in my own case, to be the antecedent condition of feelings; and because, secondly, they exhibit the acts, and other outward signs, which in my own case I know by experience to be caused by feelings. I am conscious in myself of a series of facts connected by an uniform sequence, of which the beginning is modifications of my body, the middle is feelings, the end is outward demeanour. In the case of other human beings I have the evidence of my senses for the first and last links of the series, but not for the intermediate link. I find, however, that the sequence between the first and last is as regular and constant in those other cases as it is in mine. In my own case I know that the first link produces the last through the intermediate link, and could not produce it without. Experience, therefore, obliges me to conclude that there must be an intermediate link; which must either be the same in others as in myself, or a different one: I must either believe them to be alive, or to be automatons: and by believing them to be alive, that is, by supposing the link to be of the same nature as in the case of which I have experience, and which is in all other respects similar, I bring other human beings, as phaenomena, under the same generalizations which I know by experience to be the true theory of my own existence.[12]

The argument in a nutshell comes down to this: Whenever I behave in a certain way I feel anger, or joy, or grief; therefore, when I observe another human being behaving in this way he too probably feels anger, or joy, or grief. Obviously the argument allows only probability, no certainty,

---

[12] John Stuart Mill, *An Examination of Sir William Hamilton's Philosophy*, 2nd ed., Longmans, Green & Co., London, 1865, p. 208.

for one can "put on an act," thus manifesting the appropriate behavior without having the correlative feeling. But if the argument is sound, we have at least met the sceptic part way, that is, it is very probable that one can have knowledge of other minds, but it is not certain. Should we be satisfied with this? Philosophers are not in agreement. Those who refuse to give credit to the analogy say that it is a form of inductive inference based on the observation of a single instance and all such inferences are very weak. Moreover, it is objected that no direct check on the conclusion is possible. But those who give some weight to the analogy say that probable conclusions are reached in science, too, where no direct check is possible, for example, in determining the chemical constitutions of the surface of a star.

Another objection to the analogy may be made. Suppose one starts with a general principle that similarity of inner experiences is accompanied by similarity of physical behavior. Then if I observe *A*'s behavior I can infer that he has the same inner experience. But what are the grounds for the general principle? If I know only my own thoughts and feelings I have no way of judging whether the resemblances between *A*'s physical behavior and mine are sufficient reasons for saying that he has the same thought and feelings. If the analogy is to have any weight in a given case, one must know independently that similarity of behavior and similarity of experience go together at least in some instances. But if one knows this, the analogy is not needed.[13]

Josiah Royce was also unhappy with the argument from analogy, first of all on psychological or empirical grounds. He thought we have a vague belief in the existence of other persons before we have any definite formation of our own consciousness. Thus a reversal of the argument is possible, namely, that it is truer to say we first learn about ourselves from the existence of other persons. Furthermore, we know others to be real because they are

. . . the endless treasury of more ideas. . . . They answer our questions; they tell us news; they make comments; they pass judgments; they express novel combinations of feelings; they relate to us stories; they argue with us, and take counsel with us. . . . *Our fellows furnish us the constantly needed supplement to our own fragmentary meanings.* That is, they help us to find out what our own true meaning is.[14]

Further elaboration of Royce's position would take us too far into his metaphysics but it is interesting to see that for him the question "How do

[13] Cf. A. E. Taylor, *Elements of Metaphysics,* Methuen & Co., London, 1903, p. 205.
[14] Josiah Royce, *The World and the Individual,* The Macmillan Co., New York, 1913, Vol. II, pp. 171–172.

I know that other persons exist?" comes round to the question "How do I know my own thoughts and feelings, or my own meaning or existence?" And his answer is "I cannot know this fully unless I know others."

Professor Norman Malcolm finds almost no worth in the analogical argument. He points out that the sentence "That human figure has thoughts and feelings" cannot mean anything to Mill, who asserted it, because he has no criteria for determining whether a walking and speaking figure has or does not have thoughts and feelings.

> If he had a criterion he could apply it, establishing with certainty that this or that human figure does or does not have feelings (for the only plausible criterion would lie in behavior and circumstances that are open to view), and there would be no call to resort to tenuous analogical reasoning that yields at best a probability. If Mill has no criterion for the existence of feelings other than his own then in that sense he does not understand the sentence 'That human figure has feelings' and therefore does not understand the sentence 'It is *probable* that human figure has feelings.'[15]

Thus Malcolm denies that Mill can go from his own case to the case of others. The analogy fails to bridge the gap.

Philosophers who criticize the argument from analogy often do so because it does not provide a direct experience of another's mind or feelings. But it is not clear just what direct experience of this sort could be. It cannot mean identification with another, for there are two persons (at least) involved and they remain two even when one says one knows what another is thinking or feeling. Moreover, it is undoubtedly a good thing that I do not feel your toothache in the way in which you feel it. Are there left, then, these alternatives: either to accept the analogy or to say another's mind is directly experienced? Other attempts have been made to justify this knowledge. Let us look briefly at some of them.

Samuel Alexander has argued that knowledge of other minds is not acquired by analogy but by direct experience, which is not a kind of identification but is rather based on a social or gregarious instinct. We learn of other minds not by arguing for their existence but by having to take account of them in our social responses. It is in our tendernesses or our dislikes that we are aware of other minds as like ourselves. The feeling of sociality is essentially reciprocal.

> We do not merely feel ourselves performing certain actions towards another but we want him, and in turn we find him playing his part in the joint experience in which we are both concerned. . . . Our social feeling towards him

[15] Norman Malcolm, "Knowledge of Other Minds," *The Journal of Philosophy*, Vol. 55, No. 23, 1958, p. 970.

is the divination that he is like ourselves; his reciprocation confirms it and makes it assurance.[16]

Thus rivalry, anger, jealousy, hate, love imply the existence of other persons from whom we expect an appropriate answer. It is interesting to see here that Alexander argues for the existence or the thatness of other minds, not for their nature or whatness. The latter he admits must be gained by analogy. Notice also that in neither case do we have certainty, rather we have assurance.

Thus I am not aware of B's mind as I am aware of his body, so that I should be able to inspect it and say what it is. Yet experience assures me that he has a mind. What sort of a mind it is, how the other mind feels in a given situation, I am left to divine sympathetically on the basis largely of analogy with my own. But that a mind is there, is assurance. It is not invented by inference or analogy, but is an act of faith forced on us by a peculiar sort of experience.[17]

The argument from instinct is certainly as unsatisfactory as the argument from analogy; "instinct" is itself a vague and ill-defined word, and as used by Alexander records only the fact that we do act as if we knew other minds, but it does not serve as adequate justification for claims to know other minds. To say that we know by instinct would permit a wide range of claims others might well rule out also on instinct.

Another argument for belief in other minds is closely related to the previous one. A. H. B. Allen finds his grounds for such a belief in the fact that men desire that other persons exist. There is in men a deeply felt longing for companionship as well as privacy. But privacy can have no meaning except in a world of other-selves. Thus there is a need for others either as in opposition to or in cooperation with ourselves.

It is impossible not to believe that this impulse must be original and fundamental in human nature and presumably in the nature of all living beings, not only those which we call gregarious animals. It cannot be something that originated as an accidental variation, and was developed by natural selection as favourable to survival. Now no impulse, need or longing can be entirely blind. It must include some idea however indefinite of that which would satisfy it.[18]

As it stands this is simply another version of the instinct theory, although Allen prefers the term impulse. However, he further complicates the problem by saying that "belief in other minds can only be called *a priori*." This

[16] Samuel Alexander, *Space, Time and Deity*, Macmillan and Co. Ltd., London, 1920, Vol. II, pp. 33–34.
[17] *Ibid.*, p. 37.
[18] A. H. B. Allen, "Other Minds," *Mind*, Vol. 41, No. 243, 1952, p. 346.

seems to mean that we are so made that we cannot help but believe in the existence of other minds; doubt would then be impossible.

But there is doubt, and Allen ought not to brush aside so easily the torments of those who feel so utterly alone. Moreover, is it not possible to desire that which does not and cannot exist?

It is sometimes said that the only way we can know directly another person's mind is by telepathy. It is not part of our problem to discuss whether telepathic communication actually occurs, but rather, supposing it possible, would this surmount the difficulty of knowing each other's minds? Evidently not; for telepathic experiences would themselves be private, they would be experiences of one's own and thus logically independent of the experiences of others. One could have one's own experience and still have it denied without contradiction that the other person's experience existed.

All these arguments to justify knowledge of other minds are seen to have weaknesses, that is, they do not permit us to meet the sceptic's challenge with an unassailable stand. But again we must ask, is the sceptic not asking the impossible in knowledge when he demands an unassailable argument? Let us admit that we do not have deductively certain knowledge of other minds. But is this required? We do have the only kind of knowledge that is possible without destroying the difference between one person and another. Solipsism, the view that only the self and its thoughts or feelings exist, is not a necessary consequence of our failure to be another person in order to know what he thinks or feels. Our knowledge of other minds is justified, therefore, in the only way in which such knowledge could be justified, namely, in the whole range of practical, social, linguistic, and emotional concern. Of course other people may lie to us, or deceive us, or fool us; and we may not be able to tell in any given instance whether we are being fooled or not. But it is difficult to see how lying, or deceiving, or fooling, can make sense unless there actually are other persons who do behave in these ways. If we cannot be sure we are deceived, the only recourse is to more experience.

V. A Priori and A Posteriori Knowledge

It has been shown possible to doubt knowledge of physical objects and of other minds. At least, we have had to agree that such knowledge lacks the kind of certainty characteristic of mathematical and logical truths. The sceptic cannot and ought not to be dismissed from our company when we are discoursing about things and persons. But suppose we are talking about mathematical and logical truths, then are we at last out of his range? Or are we in a position where he cannot effectively attack us? What if there is some knowledge even he must have in order to be a sceptic? Will we not then silence him? And further, suppose that this knowledge tells us not only about knowers but also about the world. Then will we be able to bridge the gaps he is always warning us about? These questions lead us into a discussion that requires an understanding of the following technical terms: a priori knowledge, a posteriori knowledge, analytic proposition, synthetic proposition, and a priori synthetic proposition.

The momentous choice between the chief types of modern philosophy hinges upon distinctions among kinds of propositions. Examine for a moment,

1. $A = A$.
2. Business is business.
3. All bachelors are unmarried men.
4. $2 + 2 = 4$.

$A = A$ is one of the principles of logic, and the student will remember that in addition to the law of identity, there is also the law of contradiction, $-(A \cdot -A)$ and the law of excluded middle, $A \lor -A$. It was claimed their truth could be known, but not from observation. Practically no philosopher claims that these formal statements are made more probably true by knowing examples of concrete cases. Generalizations, by contrast, depend upon empirical evidence. And since an example may always turn up contrary to all hitherto known cases, a generalization is always hypothetical. But such a formal truth as the law of contradiction has a status superior to that of any law of nature in that it is a certain, even a necessary, truth. At least so rationalists like Leibniz claimed, adding that it is true of all possible worlds. But Newton's law of gravity is true, so far as we know, only of this world. An American pragmatist characterizes a law of logic as true no matter what. "That is *a priori* which is true, no matter what."[19]

"Business is business" is what logicians call a substitution instance of $A = A$. "Business" is a value that is substituted for the blank A, which is called a variable. We assume that "business" has the same meaning each time it is used. Leibniz claimed that we can deduce only a few true propositions and must therefore appeal to experience, but that all truths are

[19] Clarence Irving Lewis, "A Pragmatic Conception of the *a Priori*." In: Herbert Feigl and Wilfrid Sellars (eds.), *Readings in Philosophical Analysis*, Appleton-Century-Crofts, 1949, p. 286.

known self-evidently to God. Rationalists held out the hope that they could extend *a priori* knowledge to include more than such obvious identities. Indeed, much of rationalist metaphysics claims to explain the world by the use of a priori argument. Leibniz did not assert that he knew a priori whether Alexander the Great died a natural death or died by poison, but this limitation shows that we do not have a perfect concept of Alexander.[20] Empiricists called such a proposition as "business is business" a "trifling proposition." Locke for example, pointed out that such propositions "bring no increase to our knowledge." He agreed that identical propositions are self-evident, certainly true, but they are "barely verbal" and not "real knowledge."

What is this more than trifling with words? It is but like a monkey shifting his oyster from one hand to the other; and had he had but words, might no doubt have said, 'Oyster in right hand is subject, and oyster in left hand is predicate'; and so might have made a self-evident proposition of oyster, i.e., 'Oyster is oyster.'[21]

A later name for "trifling proposition," made common in our day by Wittgenstein, is *tautology*.

"All bachelors are unmarried men" involves more than $A = A$ and oysters are oysters. The difference is that if we would defend our knowledge of the truth of such a proposition, we need a definition. Leibniz, along with his fellow rationalists, considered a definition to be the explication of the attributes of a subject. Since the real definition is not merely a stipulated meaning of "bachelor," we must know what a bachelor is. If we know that a bachelor is a man and unmarried, then "All bachelors are unmarried men" says that the predicates are contained in the subject.[22] Locke, along with his fellow empiricists, considered a definition to be of words. Earlier we referred to such a statement of what a word means as a nominal definition. It follows that to say that "Lead is a metal" conveys no information to one who knows that "metal" is a complex idea, the genus, to which the less comprehensive, even simple, idea "lead" belongs. An empiricist values certainty less than information, hence, unlike the rationalists, Locke recommends that we seek knowledge such as, that a man "would be cast into sleep by opium." This is instructive or real knowledge, and not merely verbal. Rather than "A triangle hath three sides" one should say something

[20] Gottfried Wilhelm Leibniz, *Discourse on Metaphysics*, (George R. Montgomery, tr.), The Open Court Publishing Co., La Salle, Illinois, 1902, p. 14.
[21] John Locke, *An Essay Concerning Human Understanding* (A. S. Pringle-Pattison, ed.), The Clarendon Press, Oxford, 1947, pp. 306–307.
[22] Gottfried Wilhelm Leibniz, *op. cit.*, p. 13.

that is necessarily true, but that also gives information, "The external angle of all triangles is bigger than either of the opposite internal angles."[23]

Now it becomes necessary to introduce a new distinction. We have called $A = A$, business is business, all bachelors are unmarried men a priori truths, that is, what can be known independently of observation. "A priori" has borne successively the following meanings: First, that which is derived deductively from a principle; in scholastic and rationalist philosophies, a rational principle is also a causal ground, and a priori argument is from cause to effect. And second, Leibniz considered truths of reason as purely logical; hence a priori lost the meaning prior in time, and became purely prior in the atemporal logical order. But now exactly how do we know such a priori truths as (1), (2), and (3)? Most clearly in (3) we analyzed the term "bachelor," or in contemporary idiom, we unpacked its meaning. Hence we have been taught to call (3) an analytic truth. Whichever doctrine of definition we adopt, we can then say that all analytic truths are known a priori, that is, from their meanings. It does not follow logically that all a priori truths are analytic. To reason in this way would be to commit the fallacy of simple conversion.

The opposite of analytic is synthetic. Locke predicated of opium the property "casting into sleep." The logical form is not "A is A" but "A is B." Locke argues that we can know a priori propositions of the A is B type. "The external angle of all triangles is bigger than either of the opposite internal angles." Thus there can be a synthetic judgment a priori.

We have now reached the point where we can understand what is at stake in the choice between philosophy in the tradition of Hume and philosophy in the tradition of Kant. Hume denied that there can be synthetic a priori knowledge. Nearly all empiricists hold that all a priori truths are analytic. Nearly all Kantians, and those in the post-Kantian idealist tradition, claim there can be and is some a priori knowledge that is synthetic. Hume's own vocabulary did not actually include the terms "analytic" and "synthetic," rather his contrast is between "relations of ideas" and "matters of fact."

Of the first kind are the sciences of Geometry, Algebra, and Arithmetic; and in short, every affirmation which is either intuitively or demonstratively certain. *That the square of the hypotenuse is equal to the square of the two sides,* is a proposition which expresses a relation between these figures. *That three times five is equal to the half of thirty,* expresses a relation between these numbers. Propositions of this kind are discoverable by the mere operation of thought, without dependence on what is anywhere existent in the universe. Though there

[23] John Locke, *op. cit.,* pp. 307–308.

never were a circle or triangle in nature, the truths demonstrated by Euclid would forever retain their certainty and evidence.

Matters of fact, which are the second objects of human reason, are not ascertained in the same manner; nor is our evidence of their truth, however great, of a like nature with the foregoing. The contrary of every matter of fact is still possible; because it can never imply a contradiction, and is conceived by the mind with the same facility and distinctness, as if ever so conformable to reality. *That the sun will not rise to-morrow* is no less intelligible a proposition, and implies no more contradiction than the affirmation, *that it will rise*. We should in vain, therefore, attempt to demonstrate its falsehood. Were it demonstratively false, it would imply a contradiction, and could never be distinctly conceived by the mind.[24]

Leibniz had assured us that truths of fact are known a priori by God. He also said that man's definitions, based on knowledge of what is, give us knowledge of necessary connections between facts. Thus, systematic knowledge is based upon continuity. But Hume leaves the distinction between facts and relations of ideas as an ultimate difference. He used this distinction in his celebrated condemnation of metaphysics, and the more extreme positivists of our day couple the dicta: All a priori propositions are tautologous, conveying no information; and, necessary propositions cannot be verified.

If we take in our hand any volume; of divinity or school metaphysics, for instance; let us ask, *Does it contain any abstract reasoning concerning quantity or number?* No. *Does it contain any experimental reasoning concerning matter of fact and existence?* No. Commit it then to the flames: for it can contain nothing but sophistry and illusion.[25]

Kant's defense of metaphysics hinges on the possibility of synthetic a priori knowledge. His defense takes this interesting form: Mathematical knowledge is not merely analytic, though it is a priori, hence an attack on the synthetic a priori is an attack not only on metaphysics, but on science itself. Put positively, he argues that neither mathematical nor metaphysical propositions can be verified empirically. Kant's a priori is defined as "that which, as representation, can be antecedent to any and every act of thinking anything."[26]

The second definition is that of "synthetic." Kant grants that $4 = 4$ and "every effect has a cause" are analytic, because the predicate term adds

---

[24] David Hume, *Enquiries Concerning the Human Understanding*, etc., (L. A. Selby-Bigge, ed.), 2nd ed. The Clarendon Press, Oxford, 1902, pp. 25–26.

[25] *Ibid.*, p. 165.

[26] Immanuel Kant, *Critique of Pure Reason* (Norman Kemp Smith, tr.), Macmillan and Co. Ltd., London, 1933, p. 87.

nothing to the subject or states a bare equivalence, but $2 + 2 = 4$ and "every event has a cause" are ampliative, in that the predicate adds to the subject.

It might at first be thought that the proposition $7 + 5 = 12$ is a mere analytical judgment, following from the concept of the sum of seven and five, according to the law of contradiction. But on closer examination it appears that the concept of the sum of $7 + 5$ contains merely their union in a single number, without its being at all thought what the particular number is that unites them. The concept of twelve is by no means thought by merely thinking of the combination of seven and five; and analyze this possible sum as we may, we shall not discover twelve in the concept. We must go beyond these concepts, by calling to our aid some concrete image (Anschauung), i.e., either our five fingers, or five points . . . and we must add successively the units of the five, given in some concrete image (Anschauung), to the concept of seven. Hence our concept is really amplified by the proposition $7 + 5 = 12$, and we add to the first a second, not thought in it. Arithmetical judgments are therefore synthetical, and the more plainly according as we take larger numbers; for in such cases it is clear that, however closely we analyse our concepts without calling visual images (Anschauung) to our aid, we can never find the sum by such mere dissection.[27]

For the general answer to the question "How are synthetic judgments a priori possible?" you may look back to the pages on Kant for the strategy; for the detailed arguments nothing but a reading of the Critique of Pure Reason itself will do.

Bertrand Russell, writing in 1912, was strongly sympathetic to the above argument about $7 + 5 = 12$. But he was dissatisfied with the explanation that the a priori is what mind contributes to raw sensation. This will not do in explaining why $7 + 5 = 12$ is a necessary and universal truth, for mind itself is "as much a fact of the existing world as anything, and there can be no certainty that it will remain constant." The possible change of our nature, such that two and two become five, never occurred to Kant.[28]

Russell's alternative is that a priori knowledge is not the mental forms applied to the non-mental, but what is applicable to mental and non-mental.

The fact seems to be that all our a priori knowledge is concerned with entities which do not, properly speaking, *exist*, either in the mental or in the physical world. These entities are such as can be named by parts of speech which are

[27] Immanuel Kant, *Prolegomena to Any Future Metaphysics*, The Open Court Publishing Co., La Salle, Illinois, 1926, p. 17. *Anschauung* means literally "looking at," and is often translated "intuition."

[28] Bertrand Russell, *The Problems of Philosophy*, Home University Library, Oxford University Press, London, 1957, p. 87.

not substantives; they are such entities as qualities and relations. Suppose, for instance, that I am in my room. I exist, and my room exists; but does 'in' exist? Yet obviously the word 'in' has a meaning; it denotes a relation which holds between me and my room. This relation is something. . . . [29]

This solution is not acceptable to those who do not believe that there are universals, and it is more sharply criticized on the ground that Russell's and Whitehead's Principia Mathematica had demonstrated that $7 + 5 = 12$, along with all mathematics, can be derived from logic alone. Hence it would follow that the equation is analytic and tautologous.[30]

Because the mental is subject to change, Russell rejected Kant's solution to the a priori. But this fact recommended it to an American pragmatist, C. I. Lewis. Russell was happy with the concept of the world of universals, "an independent world which thought apprehends but does not create."[31] C. I. Lewis claims, in contrast, that the a priori "anticipates . . . our attitude toward (the given): it concerns the uncompelled initiative of mind or, as Josiah Royce would say, our categorical ways of acting."

Lewis agrees that the laws of logic are a priori. It is instructive to compare this statement with Russell's, which was quoted in Chapter III on logic. These laws are freely made by the mind, our stipulations, and not forced upon us.

They are principles of procedure, the parliamentary rules of intelligent thought and speech. Such laws are independent of experience because they impose no limitations whatever upon it. They are legislative because they are addressed to ourselves—because definition, classification, and inference represent no operations of the objective world, but only our own categorical attitudes of mind. And further, the ultimate criteria of the laws of logic are pragmatic. . . . The fact is that there are several logics, markedly different, each self-consistent in its own terms and such that whoever, using it, avoids false premises, will never reach a false conclusion.[32]

Lewis' defense of the a priori is so liberal that he grants that even Russell's logic built on the principle that any true proposition implies any other true proposition (truth functional logic with no necessary consequence) may be adopted if it serves any purpose.

If we were jelly-fish in a liquid world, we should probably not add at all, because the useful purposes served by such conceptions would be so slight. Still

[29] Ibid., pp. 89–90.
[30] Morton White, Toward Reunion in Philosophy, Harvard University Press, Cambridge, Massachusetts, 1956, pp. 113–132.
[31] Bertrand Russell, op. cit., p. 98.
[32] Clarence Irving Lewis, op. cit., pp. 286–287.

if some super-jelly-fish should invent arithmetic by a *jeu d'esprit* . . . he would find nothing in any possible experience to controvert it, and he might with some profit apply it to his own distinct ideas.[33]

Lewis is true to Kant in one important doctrine, namely in rejecting Hume's negative answer to the question "Are there any necessary connections in experience?" All knowledge depends on anticipation of future experience. And not any consequent event allows us to understand a sequence in experience. It must be orderly to be interpreted. And what is it that is orderly to the degree of being called a ncessary connection?

Truth which is a priori anticipates the character of the *real;* otherwise, it would possess no significance whatever. The real, however, is not the given as such, but the given categorically interpreted. In determining its own interpretations—and only so—the mind legislates for reality, no matter what future experience may bring.[34]

Kant's intention to save metaphysics from scepticism has been thus followed out, albeit without the synthetic judgment a priori, and with a latitude for alternative systems of order that would have shocked him. Lewis, after all, takes into account non-Aristotelian logics, non-Euclidian geometries, and non-Newtonian physics.

Many contemporary philosophers claim to be followers of Hume, and ascribe to Hume the doctrine that "no *a priori* propositions are synthetic, all synthetic propositions empirical."[35] A. J. Ayer, whose Language, Truth and Logic was quoted in Chapter IV on truth devotes much attention to the a priori. An empiricist avoids metaphysics "on the ground that every factual proposition must refer to sense-experience." This follows from "purely logical considerations."

. . . A proposition is analytic when its validity depends solely on the definitions of the symbols it contains, and synthetic when its validity is determined by the facts of experience. Thus, the proposition 'There are ants which have established a system of slavery' is a synthetic proposition. For we cannot tell whether it is true or false merely by considering the definitions of the symbols which constitute it. We have to resort to actual observation of the behaviour of ants. On the other hand, the proposition 'Either some ants are parasitic or none are' is an analytic proposition. For one need not resort to observation to discover that there either are or are not ants which are parasitic. If one knows what is the function of the words 'either,' 'or,' and 'not,' then one can see that any proposition of the

---

[33] Clarence Irving Lewis, *Mind and the World-Order*, Charles Scribner's Sons, New York, 1929, p. 252.

[34] *Ibid.*, p. 197.

[35] D. G. C. MacNabb, *David Hume: His Theory of Knowledge and Morality*, Hutchinson's University Library, London, 1951, p. 46.

212 / Philosophy: The Study of Alternative Beliefs

form 'Either p is true or p is not true' is valid, independently of experience. Accordingly, all such propositions are analytic.[36]

The student should not fail to notice the definition of analyticity in terms of the usage of words. Words are the units that replace the "ideas" of Hume. But words as such, just as with ideas, are devoid of factual content.

The linguistic theory of the a priori has been met by several arguments defending synthetic judgments a priori.

The proposition that there are no synthetic *a priori* propositions, since it cannot be established by empirical observations, would be, if justified, itself a synthetic *a priori* proposition, and we cannot affirm it as a synthetic *a priori* proposition that there are no synthetic *a priori* propositions.[37]

The usual reply of linguistic analysts is that it is invalid to apply a criterion to itself. Ewing's argument can be stated in this form: The conclusion that synthetic judgments a priori are impossible follows merely from definitions of the terms. But if definitions are arbitrary or conventional, then the conclusion is arbitrary or conventional. So much for the negative half of the argument. The positive half is that scientific observation of the present is used to predict future events that are not now observable. To do this requires a principle to justify induction.

Therefore some *a priori* principle about the world is required if induction is to be justified. The principle must be of such a nature as to justify us in supposing that what has happened in observed cases is likely to recur in unobserved. . . . [38]

If this principle is neither merely formal nor merely empirical, then is it a metaphysical first principle.

The problem of the a priori and the a posteriori and of the analytic and the synthetic remains. No philosopher seems happy with the various solutions we have sketched. The present status is critical. On one hand, the analysts are dissatisfied with the terms in which the problem is stated. No criteria of analytic and synthetic seem to maintain the sharp dualism.[39] Secondly, in saying that "All bachelors are unmarried men" is analytic, the problem is raised: what does it mean to say that "unmarried man" is a

[36] A. J. Ayer, *Language, Truth and Logic,* Dover Publications, Inc., New York, n.d., pp. 78–79.
[37] A. C. Ewing, *The Fundamental Questions of Philosophy,* Routledge & Kegan Paul, London, 1951, p. 33.
[38] *Ibid.,* p. 47.
[39] Morton White, "The Analytic and the Synthetic: an Untenable Dualism." In: Sidney Hook (ed.), *John Dewey: Philosopher of Science and Freedom,* The Dial Press, New York, 1950, pp. 316–330.

synonym for "bachelor?"[40] Thirdly, other analysts find no definition of "necessary" that is clear.[41]

In spite of these lexical matters, most philosophers would agree that a study of the problem can help us to spot fallacies. An Oxford don supplies two charming examples of argument from definition.

Some time ago the governing body of an Oxford College was debating whether or not to insure its pictures, many of which were old masters. The philosophy tutor, who for one reason or another was against the proposal, produced the following argument: 'Insurance is an arrangement for the replacement of the articles insured in case of loss; these pictures are irreplacable, therefore they cannot be insured.' No one could answer this, and the pictures were not insured. . . . The argument does nothing to decide whether the proposed contract would be advantageous to the College or not.[42]

The same author adds a political argument which even more explicitly employs a relation between ideas as though it settled a matter of fact: M. Maurice Thorez argued in 1949

First, the Soviet Union, the fatherland of Socialism, cannot, by definition, practice a policy of aggression and war, which is the characteristic of imperialist powers. Secondly, the Communist position is based on facts, not on hypothesis. . . .

The appropriate conclusion is to submit a list of propositions claimed to be synthetic a priori. The student may learn more of this troubled area of epistemology by trying to decide whether these are necessary truths—in some sense of "necessary"—known independent of experience—in some sense of "independent." It may be interesting to consider the following sentences, claimed to express a priori synthetic propositions. Do you agree that these are genuine examples?

1. No event can precede itself.
2. Whatever has shape has size, and vice versa.
3. A surface cannot be simultaneously red and green.[43]
4. Every tune has a determinate pitch.[44]
5. Nothing is to the right of itself, or above itself, and so on.[45]
6. One thing cannot be both to the right and to the left of another.[46]

[40] Willard Van Orman Quine, *From a Logical Point of View*, Harvard University Press, Cambridge, Massachusetts, 1953, p. 23.
[41] Arthur Pap, *Semantics and Necessary Truth*, Yale University Press, New Haven, Connecticut, 1958.
[42] D. G. C. MacNabb, *op. cit.*, pp. 46–47.
[43] Herbert Feigl and Wilfrid Sellars, *op. cit.*, p. 281.
[44] *Ibid.*, p. 281.
[45] Bertrand Russell, *Logic and Knowledge, Essays 1901–1950*, (Robert Charles Marsh, ed.), George Allen & Unwin, Ltd., London, 1956, p. 115.
[46] *Ibid.*, p. 117.

VI. Knowledge of Universals

Some philosophers claim that the chief objects of knowledge are universals. The student will recall that Socrates insists upon a definition of the essence of justice and other moral qualities. If we arrive at no definition of what is common to all just acts or just men or just states, then we have only examples. These are particulars in contrast to the universals. They are called particulars because of the Platonic suggestion that they share in the common essence.

Plato calls these common essences *ideas*, Aristotle's name for them is *forms*. Both attempt to explain knowledge by saying that the mind grasps in every object what the object shares with other objects of the same class. We often ask "What sort of thing is it?" The thesis of Platonism and Aristotelianism may be said to be this: If we do not know what sorts of things there are in the world, we do not know the world; opinions we may have, and sense impressions, but not genuine knowledge.

Since science develops theories, laws, formulae that are universal propositions, we may feel immediately grateful to these ancient philosophers for creating a philosophic climate in which the sciences could thrive. Plato considered mathematics the prime example, even the exemplar, of all knowledge. Thus his influence guided the founders of modern physics to think of the world as geometrical and arithmetical. Aristotle furthered biological sciences in stressing classification; the definition of each species; in the tracing of the form which becomes more explicit as each living thing goes through its life cycle from egg to maturity. Why then, it can be asked, should there have developed at various periods a vigorous denunciation of both the Platonic and Aristotelian doctrines of universals, and even vigorous disagreement between Platonists and Aristotelians?

Plato claims that universals have being, and are indeed more real than particulars. Universals, then, explain how it is that one man resembles another, or shares the common quality of humanity. Both men are copies of the universal. Aristotle himself protested that he could understand literally how an artist wrote a drama about a man, using a man as his model, but that to extend this to the universe was to speak in poetic metaphor. Every quality will have to be a copy of a model. There is, according to The Republic, a perfect bed. Where is it? The answer is indeed poetic. "Laid up in heaven." But are there, asks Parmenides, also Ideas of "hair, mud, and dirt?"

Plato apparently had no answer, and we can see why. Platonic universals do another job. That is, not only do they attempt to explain knowledge of the constant, rather than of the changing world we experience, and not only what is eternal in the universe rather than transient exemplifications, but also universals are the perfect standards or models by which we judge. Without understanding this aspect of the doctrine the student will not grasp the issues involved either in the multiplicity of metaphysical systems, or in the alternatives to Plato's political and social ideals.

Aristotelians claim to have a sensible answer to the question "Where are universals?" Since the Aristotelian quality is a property of a substance, the quality is where the substance is. But what is it for a quality to be common to a number of instances? It is easy to say that a white pigeon and a white egg have white in common. We know what we mean when we say that the pigeon and the egg share in the nest. But the nest is another particular. Hence this way of speaking fails to explain why it is a universal or common form makes intelligible the sharing in whiteness by the pigeon and by the egg. If it is qualitatively the identical whiteness found in both the pigeon and the egg, then we may well grant that we know our world by naming the properties that belong together in a class, in this case, white things.

The theory may be criticized from the position of our knowledge of things. Is the whiteness in the pigeon and in the egg? Not under all conditions do they appear of identical quality. The Platonist could reply that nothing that we see and call white is perfectly white. Hence the Platonist can allow that by the standard whiteness one white is whiter than the other, which may be said to belong to the class, let us call it, "off-white."

It is often protested that biological classifications are not so neat that everything is either a plant or an animal. You may recall that this is Leibniz' great concept of continuity: between any two instances in a series, there can always be found a third. Another criticism is that the way we classify is controlled by the purposes we have in mind. For economic or culinary purposes, it is quite all right to classify clams and lobsters as well as cod as "fish." They all come from the sea, and none are red meat. Of course, it is Aristotelian to assume that the biological classification is the proper and only right classification. But is this not a prejudice? If someone should say that seafoods do not all share the same properties, and have merely a family resemblance, we could reply that mammals likewise are very different in some respects. Bats fly and whales live their whole lives in the sea and the mammary glands of one curious mammal do not have nipples.

The point of these criticisms is to put the student on guard. The doctrine that is closest to common sense, and that seems to triumph so swiftly over Platonism, is not by any means in a more easily defended citadel of certainty.

It is not necessary to choose—either a Platonic realm of universals, known because the soul was once acquainted with ideas—or Aristotelian forms that the mind somehow abstracts from things to discover to which class they belong. The psychological doctrines of both reminiscence and abstraction are difficult to render intelligible, and it is to the credit of medieval philosophers that in their debates they discovered that Platonism and Aristotelianism are not contradictories, but contraries. That is, both theories may be false, and there may be a third theory more precise and adequate in explaining the role of universals in human knowledge.

We have not yet defined "universal," although we have used examples that suggest definitions. One definition is that all objects of perception are particulars, but all objects of conception are universals. This sharp dualism fits neatly into the Platonic picture, for what we grasp by sense must be at some time and some place, but what we conceive has no temporal or spatial locus. Sometimes universals are called concepts, in contrast to percepts, but these terms suggest the view that universals are things of the mind. And indeed this is what some Aristotelians wish to maintain. If there were no reflection upon what is common to perceptual objects, we should not know universals at all. If a philosopher is an empiricist, he claims that there is nothing in the mind unless it was previously in the senses. If this is true, universals are not ultimate and irreducible objects, as Platonists and most rationalists, Leibniz chief among them, claim them to be. But suppose that I say that I do not see how from this white pigeon, this white egg, this white shirt, etc., the mind ever gets to whiteness as such. Then clearly there must be a third view.

A Platonic view of universals became known as *realism* among the Schoolmen because of the point disputed by Aristotelians, that universals exist apart from particulars. An Aristotelian view of universals became known as *conceptualism*, because according to this view there are no universals as such; a mind is required to grasp the common forms shared by particulars. The third view became known as *nominalism* because the common term is found in the name. It can easily be seen that whenever philosophy identifies itself with analysis of language, the nominalistic view fits its methods.

In answer to the question "Do universals exist?" the Platonist and Aristotelian answer, "Yes." The medieval Platonist said they exist *ante res*, before things. The medieval Aristotelian said *in rebus*, in things. But the nominalist replied, "No," universals are only *post res,* after things, that is, only in our use of words. Ayer puts the question "What is a universal?" His answer is, " . . . this question is not, as it has traditionally been regarded, a request about the character of certain real objects, but a request for a definition of a certain term."[47] The error Ayer so often attacks is to mistake a verbal question for a factual question.

Although most positivists and analysts look upon Hume as their philosophic ancestor, this type of position was well formulated by William of Ockham (1290?–1349.) In phenomenalism the student has already seen an application of his famous principle, *entia non sunt multiplicanda praeter necessitatem,* that is, freely translated, do not use two things where one will do. If sense-data can be constructed into all that is meant by "chair," one may forget about the chair in itself. This is also called the *principle of parsimony,* and *Ockham's Razor.* It is now recognized by everyone that it was the triumph of Newton to reduce the falling of bodies to the earth and the circling of planets around the sun to one principle, where all his predecessors had required two. We mention this because Newton protested against "occult forces."

Ockham's point is, we do not need universals of which things are copies (Plato), nor forms of which our concepts are copies (Aristotle). We need only signs. "A sign is anything that, as apprehended, presents something else to cognition." Just as a sigh is a natural sign of pain, so the term "man" signifies men. "Man" is unlike a sigh in that a sigh is a natural signification, but "man" is artificial and signifies only "by voluntary agreement."[48] The student will see here the strategy of Tarski's semantic theory of truth and the policy of stipulating meanings, which we called nominal definition.

What is this sign? Ockham takes the simplest view. It is not a fictitious likeness of the object, nor a quality distinct from the act of the mind, but the act of mind itself, called an *intention.* Ockham distinguishes between intentions immediately signifying an individual object (say Socrates) or a class (say animals), and intentions signifying a mental intention (say individual and species). This is close to the distinction between the use and mention of a term. Philosophers think it important to distinguish "Father is a male parent" from " 'Father' is a noun of six letters."

Just as in contemporary analysis it is common to distinguish between levels of language, so among Schoolmen the distinction was made between

[47] Alfred Jules Ayer, *op. cit.,* p. 58.
[48] William of Ockham, *Studies and Selections* (Stephen Chak Tornay, ed.), The Open Court Publishing Co., La Salle, Illinois, 1938, pp. 7–8.

signs of the properties of concrete things, called *first intentions*, and signs of the properties or relations between these first intentions. These latter are called *second intentions*.

Since the distinction between particular and universal arises among second intentions, the realm of logic and language, a term is universal only because it is used with universal intention.

Every universal is one singular thing and is universal only by signification of many things. The universal is one and is a single intention of the soul meant to be predicated of many things; in so far, however, as it is a single form subsisting really in the intellect, it is called singular.[49]

The next question is how the mind gets from the experience of individual objects to referring to a group of objects in one representative act. Ockham's answer is that no abstraction is involved, it happens as fire causes heat.[50] More precisely, stimuli create in us "a certain habit." He recognizes, perhaps more clearly than did Hume, that the logical universal must be distinguished from the psychological act. The mind produces logical entities, which are not essences in things, nor are they mere sense-impressions. One logical entity is the word every. Others of the same sort, called syncategorematic, are none, some, whole, besides, only, etc. "When added . . . to 'stone,' it makes the term 'stone' stand for all stones; and when added to 'whiteness,' it makes it stand for all occurrences of whiteness."[51] The conclusion is " . . . we know only propositions, and any science, real or rational, deals exclusively with propositions as such."[52]

How can propositions be true? Our universal terms are likenesses of external things, but not similar as copies. The similarity is in the experiences, and from them the mind molds exemplars. "Every science starts from individuals. From sensation, which gives only singular things, arises memory, from memory experimentation, and through experimentation we get a universal which is the basis of art and science."[53]

Thus Ockham neatly avoids any ontological commitment beyond that of Locke, Berkeley, and Hume that "only particulars exist." And like his successors in the great line of British empiricism, his interpretation of knowledge involves the association of a word, for example, "stone" with "the image of the stone."[54]

[49] *Ibid.*, pp. 10–11.
[50] *Ibid.*, p. 11.
[51] William of Ockham, *Philosophical Writings* (Philotheus Boehner, O.F.M., tr.), Thomas Nelson and Sons, Edinburgh, 1957, pp. 51–52.
[52] William of Ockham, *Studies and Selections* (Stephen Chak Tornay, ed.), The Open Court Publishing Co., La Salle, Illinois, 1938, p. 13.
[53] *Ibid.*, p. 18.
[54] *Ibid.*, p. 18.

Since we have dealt with Ockham's successors in Chapter II, we may abbreviate history in the epigram "all British philosophy is a series of footnotes to Ockham."[55] Empiricism is almost as much American as British, and philosophic literature in our language, particularly at the present time, is rich in argument for and against nominalism.

George Berkeley launched his attack upon substance as a sense-less abstract idea of something existing apart from being perceived. Berkeley's grounds are, in part, psychological. He found himself able to abstract one object from another, but not the object from sensation, for they "are the same thing."[56]

Thus qualities are inseparably united, and not even in thought can qualities of the object (primary) be abstracted from qualities experienced (secondary). "In short, extension, figure, and motion, abstracted from all other qualities, are inconceivable."[57] All this confusion is attributed to "the strange doctrine of abstract ideas." "Abstract ideas" is the name for universals in Locke and Hume as well as in Berkeley. The latter considered not only qualities but relations, for example, great and small, swift and slow, to be nowhere but in the mind, "changing as the frame or position of the organs of sense varies."[58]

Since number is relative, it is also "entirely the creature of the mind," and can have no absolute existence. Here we see an earlier exemplification of Hume's doctrine of the a priori; arithmetic studies only relations of ideas. A Platonist tends to argue, with mathematics in mind, that universals exist, because a number is a universal and a mathematician is talking about something real when he says "there is a number evenly divisible by 2, 3, and 4." Berkeley therefore attacks this interpretation of mathematics itself as a citadel of philosophic error.

Berkeley's positive position as well as his attack upon geometry can be examined in the following pregnant passage. A geometer might claim that

. . . all knowledge and demonstration are about universal notions, to which I fully agree: but then it doth not appear to me that those notions are formed by abstraction in the manner premised—*universality*, so far as I can comprehend, not consisting in the absolute, positive nature or conception of anything, but in the relation it bears to the particulars signified or represented by it; by virtue whereof it is that things, names, or notions, being in their own nature *particular*, are rendered *universal*. Thus, when I demonstrate any proposition concerning

[55] Cf. George Santayana, "Occam's Razor," *Soliloquies in England and Later Soliloquies,* Charles Scribner's Sons, New York, 1922, pp. 194–197.
[56] George Berkeley, *A Treatise Concerning the Principles of Human Knowledge,* The Open Court Publishing Co., La Salle, Illinois, 1904, p. 32.
[57] *Ibid.,* p. 35.
[58] *Ibid.,* p. 35.

triangles, it is to be supposed that I have in view the universal idea of a triangle; which ought not to be understood as if I could frame an idea of a triangle which was neither equilateral, nor scalenon, nor equicrural; but only that the particular triangle I consider, whether of this or that sort it matters not, doth equally stand for and represent all rectilinear triangles whatsoever, and is in that sense *universal*.[59]

Berkeley thinks this "very plain," and indeed it is a very plain use of Ockham's theory.

But how can one image of one particular triangle serve for the demonstration of a truth about all triangles? Here is seen the tie between the problem of universals and the problem of universal propositions. The difficulty is that

. . . because a property may be demonstrated to agree to some one particular triangle, it will not thence follow that it equally belongs to any other triangle, which in all respects is not the same with it. For example, having demonstrated that the three angles of an isosceles rectangular triangle are equal to two right ones, I cannot therefore conclude this affection agrees to all other triangles which have neither a right angle nor two equal sides. It seems therefore that, to be certain this proposition is universally true, we must either make a particular demonstration for every particular triangle, which is impossible, or once and for all demonstrate it of the abstract idea of the triangle, in which all the particulars do indifferently partake and by which they are all equally represented.[60]

Berkeley is thus almost led by logic back into the view of Platonism, which he erroneously attributed to the schoolmen. What can save nominalism from turning into its opposite?

. . . Though the idea I have in view whilst I make the demonstration be, for instance, that of an isosceles rectangular triangle whose sides are of a determinate length, I may nevertheless be certain it extends to all other rectilinear triangles, of what sort or bigness soever. And that because neither the right angle, nor the equality, nor determinate length of the sides are at all concerned in the demonstration. . . . It is not said the three angles are equal to two right ones, because one of them is a right angle, or because the sides comprehending it are of the same length. Which sufficiently shows that the right angle might have been oblique, and the sides unequal, and for all that the demonstration have held good.

This demonstration needed an added comment. Berkeley feels that abstraction in the sense of attending to what is not particular is not framing "an abstract, general, inconsistent idea of a triangle."[61]

One might ask whether this is not a distinction without a difference. Or

[59] *Ibid.*, p. 17.
[60] *Ibid.*, pp. 17–18.
[61] *Ibid.*, p. 19.

is it merely a failure to explain how one knows what is particular without a conception of what is universal or common to all triangles? Or is it a failure to define "triangle"? Ockham told us that general words are acquired by habit, arising as effects of sensing things. This is less plausible when applied to geometrical knowledge of triangles than it is when applied to chairs and tables.

Before considering a restatement of Platonism in the present age, a passage from Locke that has met with the approval of nearly all philosophers should be quoted. In An Essay Concerning Human Understanding, Book III is titled *Of Words*. Writing "Of General Terms" Locke argues:

> *The greatest part of words general.*—All things that exist being particulars, it may perhaps be thought reasonable that words, which ought to be conformed to things, should be so too. I mean in their signification; but yet we find quite the contrary. The far greatest part of words, that make all languages, are general terms: which has not been the effect of neglect or chance, but of reason and necessity.
>
> *For every particular thing to have a name is impossible.*—. . . For the signification and use of words depending on that connexion which the mind makes between its ideas and the sounds it uses as signs of them, it is necessary, in the application of names to things, that the mind should have distinct ideas of the things, and retain also the particular name that belongs to every one, with its peculiar appropriation to that idea. But it is beyond the power of human capacity to frame and retain distinct ideas of all the particular things we meet with: every bird and beast men saw, every tree and plant that affected the senses, could not find a place in the most capacious understanding. If it be looked on as an instance of a prodigious memory, that some generals have been able to call every soldier in their army by his proper name: we may easily find a reason why men have never attempted to give names to each sheep in their flock, or crow that flies over their heads; much less to call every leaf of plants or grain of sand that came in their way by a peculiar name.[62]

Observe that Locke treats at length the psychological question of memory. Much of the effort of empiricism in our age is spent to stress the logical point that with an infinite number of names we could not make a single sentence. Consider an extreme example from Walt Whitman's "I Sing the Body Electric" in Leaves of Grass:

Head, neck, hair, ears, drop and tympan of the ears,
Eyes, eye-fringe, iris of the eye, eyebrows, and the waking or sleeping of the
  lids,
Mouth, tongue, lips, teeth, roof of the mouth, jaws, and the jaw-hinges,
Nose, nostrils of the nose, and the partition,
Cheeks, temples, forehead, chin, throat, back of the neck, neck-slue, etc.

[62] John Locke, *An Essay Concerning Human Understanding* (A. S. Pringle-Pattison, ed.), The Clarendon Press, Oxford, 1947, pp. 226–227.

Nothing is predicated, hence nothing is said. The appropriate reply to a bare list of names is "So what?" or "What about them?" Whitman typically concludes a list by saying something in a proposition, as in this case, that the names refer to not only parts of the body, but also to the soul.

Bertrand Russell took a great step when he reflected upon the parts of speech that make description possible.

> When we examine common words, we find that, broadly speaking, proper names stand for particulars, while other substantives, adjectives, prepositions, and verbs stand for universals. Pronouns stand for particulars, but are ambiguous: it is only by the context or circumstance that we know what particulars they stand for. The word 'now' stands for a particular, namely the present moment; but like pronouns, it stands for an ambiguous particular, because the present is always changing.
> It will be seen that no sentence can be made up without at least one word which denotes a universal. The nearest approach would be some such statement as 'I like this'. But even here the word 'like' denotes a universal, for I may like other things, and other people may like things. Thus all truths involve universals, and all knowledge of truths involves acquaintance with universals.[63]

Most people, argues Russell, have not asked what the words of a dictionary stand for. And if philosophers alone ask whether we know whiteness, they have, nevertheless, concentrated chiefly on adjectival universals. Russell's argument is that subject-predicate logic is too narrow. The effect of neglecting relational logic has been an artificial narrowing of metaphysics.

> Speaking generally, adjectives and common nouns express qualities or properties of single things, whereas prepositions and verbs tend to express relations between two or more things. Thus the neglect of prepositions and verbs led to the belief that every proposition can be regarded as attributing a property to a single thing, rather than as expressing a relation between two or more things. Hence it was supposed that, ultimately, there can be no such entities as relations between things. Hence either there can be only one thing in the universe, or, if there are many things, they cannot possibly interact in any way, since any interaction would be relation, and relations are impossible.[64]

Russell's concentration on relations as the chief type of universals, rather than predicates, is an effort to avoid either the monism of Spinoza or the monadism of Leibniz. Both Ockham and Berkeley had regarded relations as mental, made by mind and not having any reality other than logical or psychological. The great claim of Russell is "we can prove that there

---

[63] Bertrand Russell, *The Problems of Philosophy*, Home University Library, Oxford University Press, London, 1948, p. 93.
[64] *Ibid.*, pp. 94–95.

must be *relations*, i.e., the sort of universals generally represented by verbs and prepositions."[65]

Russell's proof that universals are real takes the following steps. He agrees with Berkeley that we reason from one triangle, making sure that we reason only from characteristics shared with all other triangles. But to do this we must know that a shape is a triangle. And this we do by comparing another shape to the one we took as our triangle. Similarly when dealing with white things, we ask have they "the right sort of resemblance"?

But then the resemblance required will have to be a universal. Since there are many white things, the resemblance must hold between many pairs of particular white things; and this is the characteristic of a universal. It will be useless to say that there is a different resemblance for each pair, for then we shall have to say that these resemblances resemble each other, and thus at last we shall be forced to admit resemblance as a universal. The relation of resemblance, therefore, must be a true universal. And having been forced to admit this universal, we find it is no longer worthwhile to invent difficult and unplausible theories to avoid the admission of such universals as whiteness and triangularity.[66]

Are we then acquainted with universals, and if so, what are we acquainted with? Russell's simplest answer is, from a passage used earlier:

Suppose . . . that I am in my room. I exist, and my room exists; but does 'in' exist? Yet obviously the word 'in' has a meaning; it denotes a relation which holds between me and my room. This relation is something, although we cannot say that it exists *in the same sense* in which I and my room exist. The relation 'in' is something which we can think about and understand, for, if we could not understand it, we could not understand the sentence 'I am in my room.'[67]

Since "in" holds between physical objects, but is not a physical object, and holds between mental objects, but is not a mental object, it follows that "in" and other relations, "must be placed in a world which is neither mental nor physical."[68] A relation "subsists independently of our knowledge of it." When we come to know that Edinburgh is north of London we apprehend a relation that is "a constituent part of the fact." A "subsisting" being cannot be said to "exist" in the sense of being at a particular time and place. A "subsisting" being can be thought, but cannot be said to be sensed, for all sensed objects are at particular times and places. If one

[65] *Ibid.*, p. 95.
[66] *Ibid.*, pp. 96–97.
[67] *Ibid.*, p. 90.
[68] *Ibid.*, p. 90.

questions that "this world of being is unchangeable, rigid, exact," ask only what mathematicians, logicians, and builders of metaphysical systems are talking about.[69]

Thus Russell believes he has not only solved our last problem of a priori knowledge, but introduced our next problem, do we know relations? Three great problems of knowledge are solved at once when we recognize that we know immediately that an event cannot precede itself, that a thing cannot be to the right of itself, and perhaps that everything is caused.[70]

Any dualism, such as Russell's distinction between universal and particular, is always open to being reduced to unity by the ingenuity of fellow philosophers. One alternative here is to deny that there are particulars. This is a tendency of absolute idealism—there is only one concrete entity, the Absolute, and all other things are aspects of this one. The other tendency, a radical pluralism, is far more common—there are no universals, only particulars or individuals.

The most common reasons for rejecting Russell's Platonic doctrine are these:

1. "Timeless entity" makes no sense, and cannot be understood.[71]
2. Even if timeless entities can be understood, a system can be constructed without assuming the reality of universals.[72]
3. A universal is not a name for an object, and Russell fell into error by thinking that since Edinburgh names something, therefore "north of" also names something.[73]
4. Similarity is not an unambiguous universal; there are various acts of noticing similarities and of deciding that similarities are sufficient to group particulars of the same kind.[74]

It is not possible here to go into the details of recent positions because they emerge in the context of the philosophy of mathematics. However, one brilliant recent essay by an eminent logician assures us that the old

[69] *Ibid.*, p. 100.
[70] *Ibid.*, Ch. X.
[71] A. D. Woozley, *Theory of Knowledge*, Hutchinson's University Library, London, 1949, p. 77.
[72] Nelson Goodman, *The Structure of Appearance*, Harvard University Press, Cambridge, Massachusetts, 1951, pp. 31–41.
With I. M. Bochenski and Alonzo Church, *The Problem of Universals*, University of Notre Dame Press, Notre Dame, Indiana, 1956, pp. 13–31.
[73] M. Lazerowitz, "The Existence of Universals," *Mind*, Vol. 55, 1946, pp. 1ff.
[74] A. D. Woozley, *op. cit.*, p. 100.
Antony Flew & (ed.), *Logic and Language*, 2nd series, Blackwell, Oxford, 1953, p. 62.

medieval distinctions between realist, conceptualist, and nominalist re-emerge under new names.[75]

The most appealing conclusion is to consider the role of universals in the development of each of us and their role in our behavior as members of society.

What is the greatest discovery each person has made? Ernst Cassirer, who defended brilliantly and exhaustively the doctrine that symbolism distinguishes man from other animals, calls attention to symbols of universal applicability in every area of human life, and to the remarkable step taken by every human child when it learns to apply the same word to numerically different things. Cassirer was also a historian and documents his claim from Helen Keller's Story of My Life. Laura Bridgman's task was to teach a deaf-mute child of seven to speak. What had to be communicated was that "everything has a name" and that tapping letters onto the child's hand can be "the key to everything she wants to know.[76]

This morning, while she was washing, she wanted to know the name for 'water.' When she wants to know the name of anything, she points to it and pats my hand. I spelled 'w-a-t-e-r' and thought no more about it until after breakfast. . . . [Later on] we went out to the pump house, and I made Helen hold her mug under the spout while I pumped. As the cold water gushed forth, filling the mug, I spelled 'w-a-t-e-r' in Helen's free hand. The word coming so close upon the sensation of cold water rushing over her hand seemed to startle her. She dropped the mug and stood as one transfixed. A new light came into her face. She spelled 'water' several times. Then she dropped to the ground and asked for its name and pointed to the pump and the trellis and suddenly turning around she asked for my name. I spelled 'teacher.' All the way back to the house she was highly excited, and learned the name of every object she touched, so that in a few hours she had added thirty new words to her vocabulary. The next morning she got up like a radiant fairy. She has flitted from object to object, asking the name of everything and kissing me for very gladness. . . . Everything must have a name now. . . . She is anxious for her friends to spell, and eager to teach the letters to everyone she meets. She drops the signs and pantomime she used before, as soon as she has words to supply their place, and the acquirement of a new word affords her the liveliest pleasure.[77]

Cassirer agrees with Ockham that we establish a fixed association between the word and sensation. But he denies that learning meanings are

[75] Willard Van Orman Quine, "On What There Is," *From a Logical Point of View,* Harvard University Press, Cambridge, Massachusetts, 1953, pp. 14–15.
[76] Ernst Cassirer, *An Essay on Man: An Introduction to a Philosophy of Human Culture,* Yale University Press, New Haven, Connecticut, 1944, Doubleday & Co., Garden City, New York, 1953, p. 53.
[77] *Ibid.,* pp. 53–54, quoted from Helen Keller, *The Story of My Life,* Doubleday, Page & Co., New York, 1902, 1903, "Supplementary Account of Helen Keller's Life and Education," pp. 315ff.

merely receiving images of sense. These are "signals"; we also employ "designators." A dog can respond to a bell, but only man is known to employ abstract names to relate the "same individual in a new relationship."[78] The uniqueness of man's communication is the expression of relations to show that he understands things in patterns and configurations. Thus Cassirer would urge us on to our concluding section of epistemology and a study of metaphysical systems. For only by language can man formulate his objective and theoretical attitude toward the order of things in which all of us seem to believe.[79]

Not only are universals the key to individual man as at least Ernst Cassirer understands man, but also to any society, as at least F. S. C. Northrop understands human life in groups. The dominant characteristic of Western man—European and colonial offshoots—is to develop a conceptual interpretation of the world. Newton was dissatisfied with space and time as these are sensed. One may enjoy apparent space and time, as artists do, but to predict and control nature requires "absolute, true, and mathematical" space and time. Man introduces a third term, so that the world is not merely observed qualities, but also "theoretically known factors."[80] Although Eastern cultures, according to Northrop employ "blue" as the directly known or intuited quality, Western culture postulates the wave-length.

Each society is governed in its judgments of value by concepts which are not usually formulated into law, but are presupposed in the making of laws. A philosopher's task today is not merely like Plato's, to make explicit the universal justice for Athenian society, it is to comprehend the universals of every society: capitalist and Marxist, individualist and collectivist. No study is as great an asset in comprehending world history and international relations as epistemology, which seeks the discovery of the universals that most men take for granted.

VII. Knowledge of Relations

Nothing can be or be known except as it stands in relationship to something else. Relations are the necessary if not the sufficient conditions for the existence of any object—this could be called a "relation predicament." An unrelated object is an actual and logical impossibility. It could not be known, recognized, compared, felt, contrasted, combined, or in any other way enter into human experience, for all of these imply a network of re-

[78] Ernst Cassirer, *op. cit.*, p. 51, p. 58.
[79] *Ibid.*, pp. 169–171.
[80] F. S. C. Northrop, *op. cit.*, p. 440.

lations. This principle applies irrespective of one's metaphysics, epistemology, ethics, and so on. A materialist must have his matter (whatever he conceives it to be like) in relations, else he can have no order, law, or levels in his universe. Similarly, the idealist without relations can have no system of mind or minds. And so it is in ethics, for hedonist, stoic, utilitarian, and self-realizationalist all owe the theoretical structure of their convictions to the role of relations. The world in all its aspects, physical, psychological, social, and biological is held together and kept apart by its relations. To step out of all relations is to step out of being. Change may be regarded as a modification or shift in relations—at least nothing can be said to have changed if its relations have not changed. But, of course, any given thing does not dwell in all relations, that is, by the very fact of being in certain relational contexts, other relations are excluded. A man, for example, may stand in the relationship of father, brother, or uncle to another person, and by virtue of these relationships he is excluded from being mother, sister, or aunt, to anyone. Such relations are fixed and cannot be modified. On the other hand, a man may establish a friendly relation with one man today and supplant it with a hostile one tomorrow. Perhaps it is even possible, as claimed in some modern psychologies, to have the friendly and hostile relationship between the same men at the same time.

The importance of relations and knowledge of them is revealed when we remember that without the relation "before" and "after" there could be no history; without relations between citizens and states we cannot conceive of political order; nor can we discuss religions without considering relations between God and the world and between God and man. Beliefs in aesthetics often concern relations between elements of a drama or a sculpture or a symphony. And many men believe that ethics is best discussed as the relation between present acts and future consequences, or between an act and a principle, or an act and a motive. Moreover, we must not forget the ubiquity of logical relations. Implication, negation, conversion, alternation, conjunction have been shown to hold between propositions, and we have classified and defined symmetrical and transitive relations. In contrast to logical relations, without which we cannot think, are relations without which things could not be. Can we know things apart from their spatial relations of "up" or "down" or "behind" or "to the left of"; or apart from their temporal relations, for example, "before" or "after," and neither before nor after, that is "at the same time as" or "simultaneous."

In considering the coherence theory of truth, we saw that those who hold it affirm that every judgment is true only conjointly with other judgments.

On this view nothing is knowable apart from the other things with which it is related. Lotze, a pluralistic idealist held that:

The course of things and their connexion is only thinkable by the assumption of a plurality of existences, the reality of which (as distinguished from our knowledge of them) can be conceived only as a multitude of relations. This quality of standing in relation to other things is that which gives to a thing its reality.[81]

But just as the sceptic questions knowledge of things and selves and universals, so he does again of relations, for not all philosophers share Lotze's confidence in the reality of relations. Certainly we meet relations wherever we turn. There are spatial, temporal, causal, logical, social relations to name a few. But are these relations real or apparent? If they are only apparent, then it cannot properly be said that we have knowledge if we claim to know them.

A. Reality of Relations

Let us turn to one of the classic attacks on the reality of relations by the British philosopher F. H. Bradley. Reality, for Bradley, is the coherent; appearance is the incoherent. Relations are infected with incoherence and therefore cannot be the truth about reality. What is the nature of this incoherence? Bradley first argues that if there are relations there must also be qualities between which relations hold. Then comes the major argument:

But how the relation can stand to the qualities is, on the other side, unintelligible. If it is nothing to the qualities, then they are not related at all; and, if so, as we saw, they have ceased to be qualities, and their relation is a nonentity. But if it is to be something to them, then clearly we now shall require a *new* connecting relation. For the relation hardly can be the mere adjective of one or both of its terms; or, at least, as such it seems indefensible. And, being something itself, if it does not itself bear a relation to the terms, in what intelligible way will it succeed in being anything to them? But here again we are hurried off into the eddy of a hopeless process, since we are forced to go on finding new relations without end. The links are united by a link, and this bond of union is a link which also has two ends; and these require each a fresh link to connect them with the old.[82]

Suppose we have two terms, say, a "dog" and a "flea" and a relation between them, say, "biter of." Each is one distinct thing in itself, but

[81] "Rudolf Hermann Lotze," *Encyclopaedia Britannica*, 11th ed., University Press, Cambridge, England, and New York, 1911, Vol. 17, p. 25.
[82] F. H. Bradley, *Appearance and Reality*, George Allen & Unwin Ltd., London, 1925, pp. 32–33.

different to some degree when it stands in this relation. The flea has the relation "biter of" to the dog; and the dog has the converse relation "bitten by" to the flea. But now we have two new terms, namely, "dog in relation (of being bitten by) to flea" and "flea in relation (of biter of) to dog" and these two terms must be related. Thus the problem breaks out again and the process can never end. Such an infinity of relations is, thinks Bradley, incoherent, leading to the destruction of all relations, hence contradictory and false.

Many philosophers have been dissatisfied with Bradley's argument. Russell, for example, points out that Bradley thinks a relation is something "as substantial as its terms and not radically different in kind." He regards the analogy of the chain as false, since, if the argument is valid, it proves that chains are impossible, but chains do in fact exist. Bradley is misled, says Russell, by the fact that

. . . the *word* for a relation is as substantial as the *words* for its terms. Suppose A and B are two events, and A precedes B. In the proposition 'A precedes B', the word 'precedes' is just as substantial as the words 'A' and 'B'. The relation of the *two* events A and B is represented, in language, by the time or space order of the *three* words 'A', 'precedes', and 'B'. But this order is an actual relation, not a word for a relation. The first step in Bradley's regress does actually have to be taken in giving verbal expression to a relation, and the word for a relation does have to be related to the words for its terms. But this is a linguistic, not a metaphysical, fact, and the regress does not have to go any further.[83]

Another philosopher shows the fallacy in Bradley's thinking with this argument:

The presupposition of this fallacy is that if two somethings are different from one another they must stand to one another in a relation which is different from either, not identical with nor included in the separate nature of either. In other words, r is not identical with A or B nor a part of what is already understood in A or B. So far from being always true, this presupposition can be shown to be never true where A and B are in fact properly described as related.[84]

A further argument against Bradley is sometimes raised, namely, that his own reasoning involves logical relations which he must employ in order to show that there are no relations, and this is self-defeating.

But now that we have heard a sceptical view of the reality and knowledge of relations, let us look at the position of one who exuberantly grants both their reality and our knowledge of them. We turn to William James.

[83] Bertrand Russell, *An Outline of Philosophy*, George Allen & Unwin Ltd., London, 1948, p. 264.
[84] John Cook Wilson, *Statement and Inference*, The Clarendon Press, Oxford, 1926, Vol. II, quoted in A. C. Ewing (ed.), *The Idealist Tradition*, The Free Press, Glencoe, Illinois, pp. 285–286.

James and Bradley have something in common. Each derives his conclusions about relations from a generalized view of reality, which philosophers often call metaphysics. Bradley's metaphysics usually is called absolute idealism or sometimes just absolutism. James created a new label for his view which he called radical empiricism.

The Absolute alone is real, argues Bradley, and it can contain nothing irrational or contradictory; relations are contradictory and therefore they are not part of the real, but only of appearance.

This to James was sheer nonsense. That which enters into experience is real, and everything that Bradley ousted from reality James reinstates. But why a "radical" empiricism? This is where relations come in. Parts, terms, individuals, are experienced, as traditional empiricism asserted, but so are relations, says James, and this is the radical element. It is time now to let him speak for himself.

To be radical, an empiricism must neither admit into its constructions any element that is not directly experienced, nor exclude from them any element that is directly experienced. For such a philosophy, *the relations that connect experiences must themselves be experienced relations, and any kind of relation experienced must be accounted as 'real' as anything else in the system.* Elements may indeed be redistributed, the original placing of things getting corrected, but a real place must be found for every kind of thing experienced, whether term or relation, in the final philosophic arrangement.[85]

So, according to James, the enormous range of the conjunctions and disjunctions of space, time, causes, and effects, as well as quantities and qualities, are to be considered as real as the terms they connect, because they enter just as intimately and sharply into our experience as do the terms. It is to be noted that here James parts with the traditional empiricism of David Hume, who thought of the world in terms of entirely loose and separate events. Although it is true that one event follows another, we can never observe any tie between them. They are conjoined but not connected. Such a view led Hume, as the student will recall from Chapter II, to deny the reality of causal relations if they are regarded as necessary connections.

But is James right? Do we observe relations as we observe terms? Is Hume not right when he says that we do not literally see necessary connections between things? And do we see "to the right of," or "before," or "uncle of"? Does it not seem correct to think of space and time as relational but not as observable? That is, we observe things but think how they

[85] William James, *Essays In Radical Empiricism,* Longmans, Green & Co., Inc., New York, 1922, p. 42.

are related to each other. The words "space" and "time" are observable but is the space and time to which the words refer observable? If there is some doubt about this, then we ought not to be too easily annexed by James' view that relations are experienced as are terms. For at least some relations, James' position seems sound, that is, when we see two boxes of different size we seem to see that one is "bigger than" the other, and conversely that one is "smaller than" the other. But consider two men: is the relation "uncle of" and "nephew of" given in experience? This bit of trouble suggests that each and every relation, or perhaps class of relations, should be examined to discover whether it can be said that they all enter into our experience in the same way. Some might be observed, others defined, others inferred.

B. Time and Space Relations

The importance of relations for science and philosophy can be seen if we examine briefly three central concepts, space, time, and causality. What are some of the alternative beliefs about each of these?

One of the earliest and most desperate attempts to understand time is found in the eleventh book of Augustine's Confessions. The problem was such an "entangled enigma" for him that it brought him to an intellectual agony nearly equal to his moral conflict.

Perhaps a good place to begin is with the challenge made by unbelievers who scornfully asked Augustine what God was doing before he made heaven and earth. Now there was a facetious answer to this question, namely, that "He was preparing Hell for those who pry into such mysteries," but Augustine refuses to treat the problem so lightly. Rather, he tries to offer a view that makes the question itself absurd. But it is not going to be easy to hammer out. Augustine expresses the elusiveness of time by saying, "What then is time? If no one ask of me, I know; if I wish to explain to him who asks, I know not."

Of one thing he seems sure: time is itself created by God, therefore there is no sense in talking about anything *before* time, for *before* is a temporal relation. Time and the world are created together, so there could not be a time before the world. Furthermore, the only way we know time is when things pass away or come to be. Any present time comes into being because it passes into past time. But there are other puzzles. Consider any span of time, a decade, year, month, week, day, hour, minute, second: each can be divided into minuter periods, and if we reach a point where no further division is possible, this is the present, which flies so rapidly from future to past that it cannot delay or be extended. But then how can we say that time is long or short when it has not yet come to be or has passed away? For that which is not cannot be said to be long or short. We can say only it will be long or it will be short, or it has been long, or it has been short.

Moreover, if there is a past and a future where are they? Wherever they are, they are not there as past, or as future, for if they are there as future they are not yet there, and if they are past they are no longer there. Yet whatever and wherever they are, they are always present. The problem now is how to make sense out of all this. Is there anything in our experience to provide a clue? If we look to the external world the puzzle cannot be solved, but if we look within the mind, we may soften the mystery. For the three times, past, present, and future, are together there. That is, in mind we find, "a present of things past, a present of things present, and a present of things future." The present of things past is memory, the present of things present is attention, the present of things future is expectation. Therefore, neither the future nor the past, properly understood *is*, all is an everlasting *now*. Time is subjective, that is, in the mind, which remembers, considers, and expects.

Augustine was not able to solve all the problems he raised about time. It continued to be a tormenting perplexity to him. But he concludes that because God is eternal, that is, timeless and unchanging, that He cannot precede time for that would mean He was in time, for "precede" is a temporal word, God is, therefore, totally outside the time which He creates. The question "Why was the world not created at an earlier time?" is thus meaningless. Time was created when the world was created, and therefore there could be no "earlier." Creation could not occur *in* time because time itself is created. Nor could the creation of the world take time, for time did not precede creation. Thus God created all things "at once," though not necessarily in their present state. Creation is the coming to be of changeable things, and as time is relative to changing things, the beginning of the world was not itself in time.

What are the difficulties here? In part, at least, it may be the temptation to think of time (and space) as entities, or things, which is the result of taking the noun "time" as if it were the name of something in the same sense as "chair" is the name of an object. Let us hear a contemporary philosopher on these perplexities.

'Time flows' we say—a natural and innocent expression, and yet one pregnant with danger. It flows 'equably', in Newton's phrase, at an even rate. What can this mean? When something moves, it moves with a definite speed (and speed means: rate of change in time). To ask with what speed time moves, i.e. to ask how quickly time changes in time, is to ask the unaskable. It also flows, again in Newton's phrase, 'without relation to anything external'. How are we to figure that? Does time flow on irrespective of what happens in the world? Would it flow on even if everything in heaven and on earth came to a sudden standstill as Schopenhauer believed? For if this were not so, he said, time would have to stop with the stopping of the clock and move with the clock's movement. How odd: time flows at the same rate and yet without speed; and perhaps even without anything to occur in it? The expression is puzzling in another way: 'I can never catch myself being in the past or in the future', someone might say; 'Whenever I think or perceive or breathe the word "now", I am in the present; therefore I am *always* in the present.' In saying this, he may think of the present moment as a bridge as it were from which he is looking down at the 'river of time'. Time is gliding along underneath the bridge, but the 'now' does not take part in the motion. What was future passes into the present (is just below the bridge) and then into the past, while the onlooker, the 'self' or the 'I', is always in the present. 'Time flows *through* the "now"', he may feel to be a quite expressive metaphor. Yes, it sounds all right—until he suddenly comes to his senses and, with a start, realizes, 'But surely the moment flies?' (Query: How to succeed in wasting time? Answer: In this way, for instance—by trying, with eyes closed or staring vacantly in front of oneself, to catch the present moment as it is flitting by.) He may come now to look at matters in a different way. He sees himself advancing through time towards the future, and with this goes a suggestion of being active, just as at other times he may see himself floating down the stream whether he likes it or not. 'What exactly is it that is moving—the events in time or the present moment?', he may wonder. In the first case, it looks to him as if time were moving while he stands still; in the second case as if he were moving through time. 'How exactly is it', he may say in a dubious voice, 'am I always in the present? Is the present always eluding me?' Both ring true in a way; but they contradict each other? Again, does it make sense to ask, 'At what time is the present moment?' Yes, no doubt; but how *can* it, if the 'now' is but the fixed point from which the dating of any event ultimately receives its sense?

So he is pulled to and fro; 'I am always in the present, yet it slips through my fingers; I am going forward in time—no, I am carried down the stream.' He is using different pictures, each in its way quite appropriate to the occasion; yet when he tries to apply them jointly they clash. 'What a queer thing time must be', he may say to himself with a puzzled look on his face, 'what after all *is* time?'—expecting, half-expecting perhaps, that the answer will reveal to him time's hidden essence. Ranged beyond the intellectual are deeper levels of uneasiness—terror of the inevitability of time's passage, with all the reflections upon life that this forces upon us. Now all these anxious doubts release themselves in the question, 'What is time?' (*En passant* this is a hint that *one* answer will never do—will never remove all these doubts that break out afresh on different levels and yet are expressed in the same form of words.)

As we all know what time is and yet cannot say what it is it feels mystifying; and precisely because of its elusiveness it catches our imagination. The more we look at it the more we are puzzled; it seems charged with paradoxes. 'What is time? What is this being made up of movement only without anything that is moving?' (Schopenhauer). How funny to have it bottled up! 'I've got here in my hand the most potent, the most enigmatic, the most fleeting of all essences —Time.' (Logan Pearsall Smith of an hour-glass.) For Shelley it is an 'unfathomable sea! whose waves are years', a 'shoreless flood', for Proust—well, why not leave something to the reader?

But isn't the answer to this that what mystifies us lies in the *noun* form 'the time'? Having a notion embodied in the form of a noun almost irresistibly makes us turn round to look for what it is 'the name of'. We are trying to catch the shadows cast by the opacities of speech.[86]

Similar puzzles have been found in our conception of space. Russell, for example, has put it neatly in the following:

The notion of a "place" is also quite vague. Is London a "place"? But the earth is rotating. Is the earth a "place"? But it is going round the sun. Is the sun a "place"? But it is moving relatively to the stars. At best you could talk of a place at a given time; but then it is ambiguous what is a given time, unless you confine yourself to one place. So the notion of "place" evaporates.[87]

Contemporary philosophical and scientific theories of space and time have rejected the notion that space or time can intelligibly be regarded as entities or as absolute in the Newtonian sense. Newton assumed the existence of an absolute space and an absolute time in which all bodies move. There are, he thought, in remote places of the universe "immovable places" which provide fixed points from which all motion can be measured. Similarly, he thought there was a universal time flowing "equably and without regard to anything external" throughout the universe. Both of these concepts have been shown to be untenable by the later theory of relativity, which has introduced the complex idea of space–time, conceived as the structure of the relationships among world events. No simple statement can deal adequately with this notion, but it can be said that it requires the abandonment of a fixed place in the universe, and also of a state of the universe at a fixed time. In some contemporary philosophy this also leads to a reality of events rather than of objects or bodies—a series of events may make up the duration of what we call a body.

If space and time are not entities, but relations, then it can be said that we know some relations, for our claims to knowledge of space and time are as secure as any other knowledge-claim since we have abandoned the requirement of absolute certainty for knowledge.

[86] Friedrich Waismann, "How I See Philosophy," *Contemporary British Philosophy,* Third Series, H. D. Lewis (ed.), copyright 1956, George Allen & Unwin, Ltd., London, and The Macmillan Company, New York. Quoted in *Contemporary Philosophic Problems,* Yervant H. Krikorian and Abraham Edel (eds.). The Macmillan Co., New York, 1959, pp. 61–63.

[87] Bertrand Russell, *An Outline of Philosophy, op. cit.,* p. 115.

C. Causal Relations

Let us turn now to another kind of relation just as ubiquitous in common-sense judgments as space and time relations. This is the causal relation; and again we find some philosophers doubting not only that there are causal relations, but that they can be known. Aristotle's doctrine of four causes could be interpreted as saying that to answer fully why a thing happens we must give four kinds of information, namely, what he called the material, formal, final, and efficient causes. But which of these stands in what we would call a causal connection to the effect? Not the material, formal, or final causes for these constitute the effect, or are identical with it. It is, says Aristotle, the efficient cause alone, the shoemaker, for example, who is the maker of the shoe. But what is this "making"? Can we isolate the relation, scrutinize it, analyze it, and make sense out of it? Nothing seems more useful or frequent in everyday life than to say of one event A, that it causes another event B. The range of possibilities is enormous: heat—boiling water, aspirin—headache cured, overeating—obesity, bullet—death, drunk—accident, slums—juvenile delinquency, tobacco—lung cancer, and so on and on. It is easy to say there are causal relations, but as we shall see it is not quite so easy to know what we are saying, or how to analyze what we are saying.

There are at least three positions about causal relations, namely, the regularity theory, the entailment theory, and the activity theory. Let us look at these alternatives.

Regularity Theory.

David Hume is the classic representative of the regularity theory. Beginning with his fundamental assumption that all knowledge of matters of fact comes from sense-impressions, he asks what impression we have of any causal relation in the sense of necessary connection between A and B? Since we can get no impression of necessary connection, but only of the fact that B follows regularly after the presence of A, all we are permitted to say is just the expression of this fact, namely, B follows regularly after A. But this is a far different statement from, B must follow from A, which implies a necessary relation, and this cannot be known from our sense-experience. In other words, the relation cannot be verified in the only way Hume will permit. Moritz Schlick, a recent philosopher and a follower of Hume in this respect, puts it this way:

If C is *regularly* followed by E, then C is the cause of E; if E only "happens" to follow C now and then, the sequence is called a mere chance. And since (as we just saw) the observation of the regularity was, in this case, the *only* thing that was done, it was necessarily the *only* reason for speaking of cause and effect, it was the *sufficient* reason. The word cause, as used in everyday life, implies *nothing but* regularity of sequence, because *nothing else* is used to verify the propositions in which it occurs.[88]

Before accepting the regularity view of causation, the following objections, which Blanshard and Ewing set up against the theory must be met.[89]

1. Any unique event, such as a biological sport, would have to be regarded as uncaused.
2. No human action could ever spring from a self or a motive because there could be no intrinsic connection between a volition and consequent behavior.
3. Even in the regularity theory such words as "require" and "produce" are used which are inconsistent with the theory.
4. Memory of experiences would be impossible because the past event leads to the recall or at least conditions the recall.
5. The view is sharply opposed to common sense and science.
6. It fails to supply an intelligible statement about the causes of complex events, such as wars and economic depressions.
7. There are instances of constant conjunction or regular sequence that nobody would accept as causation, for example: "The sounding of a hooter at 8 A.M. in London is regularly followed not only by men going to work at that factory in London but by men going to work at a factory in Manchester which also opens at 8 A.M. Yet everybody would say that, while the arrivals at the factory in London were caused by the hooter in that factory, the arrivals at Manchester were not."
8. Certain psychological experiences are inexplicable on the regular sequence view; for example, "When I believe something for a reason, surely my mental state is really determined by the apprehension of the reason and is not merely one of a class of mental states which usually follow the apprehension of similar reasons."

The student should not pass over these objections too swiftly. He should think them through to see if they cannot be met, wholly or in part, by the proponents of the regularity theory.

Entailment Theory.

We shall deal very briefly with Ewing's alternative. The entailment theory declares that the causal relation is analogous to the relation that

[88] Yervant H. Krikorian and Abraham Edel, *op. cit.*, pp. 351–352.
[89] Brand Blanshard, *The Nature of Thought,* George Allen & Unwin Ltd., London, 1948, Vol. II, pp. 509–510.
A. C. Ewing, *The Fundamental Questions of Philosophy,* Routledge & Kegan Paul Ltd., London, 1953, pp. 161–162.

holds between the premises and conclusion of a valid argument, that is, it is a relation of logical necessity. One objection to this view is that the two relations are quite unlike. Most logicians say a logical relation is formal and timeless, while a causal relation is concrete and temporal. Some interpretations of necessary inference claim that validity rests in the identity of the conclusion to the premises. But we can scarcely think of effects as unpacked from causes. Ewing, who defends a form of the entailment theory, agrees that the cause cannot be said to contain the effect, else causation would be simultaneous, but still he feels that in the psychological realm we have some insight into the necessary relation between cause and effect. Here are his words.

It seems to me that we can see and to some extent really understand why an insult should give rise to anger, why love should lead to grief if the object of one's love die or prove thoroughly unworthy, why a success should give pleasure. . . . What we perceive if we perceive anything is not that love *must* lead to grief or that an insult *must* give rise to anger, but that there is a causal tendency for it to do so which will operate unless prevented by other circumstances, but which *may* be counteracted. If A loves B, there is a tendency at least for him to feel grief at B's death. Nor do I suppose that men perceived this general principle to be true in advance of experience; as with all general principles, we first apprehend it in particular instances in our experience, and then by abstraction reach the general principle. I do not hold that such a principle is self-evident in the sense in which a logical principle may be so, but I should insist that we must admit different degrees of self-evidence. In this case our insight is lacking in certainty and clearness, but it is present for all that.[90]

Although Ewing believes there is some kind of real connection between cause and effect such that the former logically involves the latter, he is nevertheless willing to admit that he does not understand how this can be so.

That causality is analogous to a logical connexion is confirmed by the fact that we can argue from the cause to the effect, which, as I have contended, seems to imply that in some manner and sense the one logically involves the other. We do not see any logical connexion; we do not understand why they should be so connected, but I cannot possibly be entitled to argue from A to B unless I assume a connexion by which A really implies B, though I cannot see how it does so.[91]

Activity Theory.

A third view of causality looks to the experience of volition for its key. This, called the activity view, states that in the exercise of what we call

---

[90] A. C. Ewing, "A Defense of Causality" in *Proceedings of the Aristotelian Society,* N.S. Vol. 33, 1933, pp. 124–125.
[91] *Ibid.,* p. 121.

our wills, we are intimately acquainted with causation. Some forms of this theory do not require that volition be conscious, that is, there can be a kind of unconscious causality found in the activity of not only animate, but also inanimate being. The activity view certainly appeals to common sense, for nothing seems more certain that than when I will to raise my arm, the raised arm is felt to be an effect of the willing. But here we must remember that the effect does not follow as directly as it seems. There are many intervening links in the nervous system, and not all of these are clearly known. Moritz Schlick, in denying that the relation of causality is a mysterious "tie" or "glue" between events, cannot find in volition any evidence of this tie.

Even in our times there are some philosophers who say that we directly experience causation, e.g., in the act of volition, or even in the feeling of muscular effort. But whatever such feelings of willing or effort may be, they are certainly events in the world; they can be glued to other events, but they cannot be the glue.[92]

Summary

Hume's regularity theory of causation is no truer than the sense-datum theory of perception. What cannot be traced back to impressions is inexplicable on this theory of experience. Hume did not deny that there are real connections between cause and effect, but his epistemology made a mystery of it. He affirmed, therefore, "secret" causes and "secret connections," although experiences teach us only "how one event constantly follows another."

Although defenders of the constant-conjunction (regularity) theory try to make it appear that those who differ are unnecessarily complicating our interpretation, those who defend the voluntaristic (activity) theory claim two things. First, that they are appealing to what is just as evident in experience as passive reception of impressions, namely, active production of effects; secondly, that Hume's own account of perception rests upon an active relation, and that purely passive experiencing is a self-contradictory notion. The most celebrated expression of this is from Whitehead, in his Symbolism, Its Meaning and Effects.

The irony of this situation is familiar in philosophy: the simpler theory is ultimately more mysterious, and the immediately obscure theory is more adequate to a fuller consideration of experience. Philosophers now commonly present an issue for decision: Do you choose a theory because it is primarily simple or primarily adequate?

[92] Yervant H. Krikorian and Abraham Edel, op. cit., p. 358.

It is doubtful if any acceptable solution to the problems of space, time, and causality can be had apart from a larger context of theory that could be called a metaphysics. Already we have begun to discuss perspectives, which is the subject of the next chapters. Perhaps the best we have done is to affirm that though we have knowledge of spatial, temporal, and causal relations, it is extremely difficult to know how to analyze these relations.

VIII. Concluding Remarks

Our long considerations of some of the problems of knowledge must be closed with most of the questions still unanswered. At least we have seen some of the issues drawn, some of the problems formulated, and some of the alternative attempts to resolve the difficulties. We have heard the sceptic's lament, but have not joined him at the wailing wall. If rejecting the criteria that knowledge, to be knowledge, must be absolutely certain, means that we are compelled to accept a relativistic theory of knowledge, then let us agree to this and take the consequences. But let us at least suggest the ways in which knowledge may be said to be relative.

1. All knowledge is human knowledge, that is, relative to the fact that we are human beings. The questions we ask, and the answers we desire, spring from the kind of creatures we are and the kind of problems we face.

2. Our knowledge is subject to the limitations of our facilities and abilities. By inference we may bridge the gaps between perceived facts, but we do this by means of symbols, which we create in order to grasp relations.

3. The resultant human knowledge is limited by our selection of questions and answers, and the means at our disposal.

4. All our perceiving is done from some specifiable place in relation to the objects. There is no perception totally apart from some point of view.

5. All interpretation of what we perceive is done consciously or unconsciously within some frame of reference. Of course, we vary enormously in our ability and freedom to look at things differently by changing our perceptual points of view or the frame of reference for our judgments.

6. The knower's content of knowledge is conditioned by his experience beyond the time limits during which he observes objects. Some philosophers stress past experience as a preparation. Then all knowledge is in part or wholly remembering. Others stress the purposes of knowl-

edge. Belief is not fulfilled until acted upon. Then knowledge depends on the anticipation of fulfillment, which when fulfilled is relatively genuine.

7. The knower's content of knowledge is more or less organized. Some philosophers, liking immediacy, keep their observations close to the way they come, and if higgledy-piggledly, then experience is, as Hume said, a "shower of atoms." Others, e.g., Kant, mold their experiences according to certain universal patterns present in all knowers.

8. The knower's questions and answers, involving assumptions from the past and anticipations of the future, are more or less qualified by the stage of inquiry. Some believe that nothing new will be discovered to disrupt their systems. Others believe themselves the innovators, with no fixed system, but they feel confident that truth is emerging for the first time. There are, of course, views that combine these two attitudes.

9. Some knowers are conspicuously typical of a special community. They seem to know nothing, see nothing, believe nothing except what is commonly accepted by the community, its traditions, leaders, symbols, and agreed-upon ways of doing and judging things. We sometimes say, "There's a typical American for you. He fits our stereotype." Thus all knowledge-claims are related by sociologists of belief, or sociologists of knowledge, to the existential matrix, the given customs, economic, social, political, religious, and artistic. But other knowers do not seem to follow accepted norms. Because of their genius, or by deliberate revolt, or under other pressures, they become revolutionary, deviants, heretics. They set up very different criteria of knowledge. It is problematic, argue sociologists, how valid either set of criteria can be. They are qualified and conditioned by status in society.

10. Most, if not all, of human knowledge depends on human language, and there are many, many languages with noticeable differences in grammar, for example, some have no past or future tenses; and some insist on relating noun to adjective. The question is: to what extent is our knowledge qualified by our looking for things with properties? Another language might lack this sentence structure. It might stress verb and adverb. If we shift from "What he says is true" to "He speaks truly," we may need a wholly different theory of truth.

11. It is impossible to talk of things without relating terms, and this suggests that many if not all terms are relational themselves. We talk of "motherhood," for example, but there is no such thing except as a female parent stands related in a specifiable way to an offspring. There

is furthermore, no offspring apart from the condition of having been conceived and born. Along these lines some philosophers have reasoned that reality is nothing but a system of relations. This certainly implies that all knowledge can be only of relations.

12. The denial of independent objects may mean only that there is no object absolutely independent of some other obejct. There can always be a degree of exclusiveness, such as, "this cat is not that dog"; but there is also a degree of inclusiveness, for example, both share the characteristics of mammals. This again suggests that whatever is, is in relationship to something else.

13. Not only does knowledge vary considerably from person to person, from group to group, from age to age, but the criteria of knowledge vary and change. Some say there is an eternal, absolute, and necessary truth, but the relativists claim that simple inspection of what men mean by truth will dispel this myth. If there is an absolute truth, which might be described as knowing something from all points of view, it is enjoyed exclusively by an infinite God. Finite men, however, must accept what they can grasp within the limits of their perception and conception.

This array of meanings for the term "relative" is impressive, particularly when we remember that each directs our attention to actual situations. Whatever position in epistemology philosophers adopt, it must take account of these facts. Thus there seems to be great initial advantage to a kind of objective relativism. Yet there are also weaknesses and defects that epistemologies never seem to escape no matter how carefully worked out. Let us examine briefly five advantages and their corresponding defects.

First, the great appeal of a relativist epistemology lies in its flexibility. "Relation" is so general a concept that it cannot be adequately defined. It is impossible to conceive of a world without believing that things stand in various relations to each other. But if we place all our stress on the relations may we not miss the "thing?" This is what troubled Lovejoy. To reason relatively requires, he said, "some element . . . initially taken as *not* relative to a percipient."[93]

That statements are true within a frame of reference does not satisfy this requirement. "If a thing has such and such a character from a given standpoint and in a particular perspective, then it has that character from that standpoint and in that perspective. This tautological proposition is

[93] A. O. Lovejoy, *The Revolt against Dualism*, The Open Court Publishing Co., La Salle, Illinois, 1930, p. 120.

beyond dispute and wholly irrelevant."[94] Therefore, it is charged that relativistic epistemology endangers a stable concept and criterion of truth.

Secondly, the claim to justify a priori or self-evident truths on a doctrine of meaning is met by the accusation that meaning criteria are arbitrary rules applied to arbitrary languages. A relativist epistemology has a distinct advantage in its doctrine of meaning. A sentence is meaningful when its words refer to aspects of our sense-experience and when its logic states necessary relations between concepts. Thus it is insisted that grasping meaning is not merely our arbitrary decision to define a word as we please, but necessitates a relation to experience. Our logic represents world order. This avoids any need for a psychological process in addition to sensation, perception, and conception, and seems to allow for the achievement of objective knowledge.

That the verbal *expression* "All squares are rectangles" conveys a logically necessary fact, could not be determined in entire independence of what the constituent *expressions* "square" and "rectangle" convey, but the fact of the relation *expressed by* "All squares are rectangles" has no dependence upon our conventions of expression or even on the existence of language. No manner of devising a system of language could affect it, and no decision of ours could make it otherwise than it is.[95]

Thirdly, when the objective relativist lays stress on the unity and organization of all knowledge, because of its relational character, he encounters the objection that this doctrine implies one cannot know anything without knowing everything, or one cannot open one's mouth to say one sentence without keeping it open until one has explicated the universe. But knowing is ordinarily of something in particular, not of everything in general; therefore, epistemology must mark out some sharp boundaries and real differences.

Fourthly, the merit of an exact logic of relations is met by the charge that logic then ceases to be logic. It includes mathematics, spatial, temporal, and causal relations, and by its own relational logic, logic takes in every other subject. It is certainly true that relations are capable of great theoretical elaboration. The notion of "dependent on" can be divided into "necessary conditions" and "sufficient conditions." But, again, if "everything correlates," what are the real distinctions?

Finally, the merit of making knowledge a problem of communication is met by the charge that this is a distraction, a lure away from reference to the real world. One protest has called this the fallacy of "dropping the

---

[94] *Ibid.*, pp. 126–127.
[95] Clarence Irving Lewis, *An Analysis of Knowledge and Valuation*, The Open Court Publishing Co., La Salle, Illinois, 1946, p. 153.

object," so that philosophy seems to be only about words and not about what words refer to. Thus, paradoxically, some philosophers who make a specialty of communication become unable to communicate even to other philosophers.

It has not been possible to present all the questions pertinent to a theory of knowledge. But perhaps, it will be easier after this discussion to see that a real problem confronts us. That we have knowledge in some degree very few of us doubt. But so far no one has produced a universally accepted theory that will show us how such knowledge is possible. This study should certainly have the result of making us more cautious, less dogmatic, increasingly critical of our knowledge-claims and cherished beliefs. We must face the fact that there is a certain risk in all knowledge because of its fragmentary or partial character. We are not able to get all perspectives at once, nor grasp all data simultaneously. Recognition of this means welcoming the growth of knowledge as experiences are widened and deepened. The fundamental assumption here is that though knowledge is incomplete, it is also veridical, that is, true to reality. If this is a type of faith it is, nevertheless, the best we have and is a far cry from mere credulity. Knowledge at the human level is a kind of critical or logical faith.

Epistemology is a broad field, and some of the related subjects are discussed in separate chapters. Thus the problems of method and logic and truth are essentially epistemological, but they have been given separate space.

Although it is philosophically inadequate to ignore the epistemological questions that arise in every philosophical discipline, an introduction cannot be philosophically adequate. The student is therefore urged to pursue this subject on his own.

PROBLEMS FOR THOUGHT AND DISCUSSION

1. Some people commonly use the phrases "I know" and "I am certain" as though they were synonymous. Hence, the person who admits he is not certain seems to disclaim that he knows. Is it true that a person who does not hope ever to be certain is necessarily therefore a sceptic—one who claims that we can hold only opinions?
2. In many theories of knowledge the objects known are those seen, heard, touched, etc. For short, the person seeing, etc., is called a spectator. Is it only as spectators that we know the world? If the world is not merely out there to be gazed upon, what follows about a theory of knowledge solely from a spectator's point of view?
3. Consider the following definitions of knowledge by John Dewey: ". . . knowledge is the completed resolution of the inherently indeterminate

or doubtful." And, ". . . knowledge is the fruit of the undertakings that transform a problematic situation into a resolved one."[96] In what ways do they suggest that knowledge is better understood as a "doing" than a "contemplating"?

4. Bertrand Russell has observed that empiricism as a theory of knowledge is self-refuting. "For however it may be formulated, it must involve *some* general proposition about the dependence of knowledge upon experience; and any such proposition, if true, must have as a consequence that itself cannot be known. While, therefore, empiricism may be true, it cannot, if true, be known to be so."[97] What do you think of this argument? Does it mean we must reject empirical knowledge? or only a theory about knowledge?

5. It is often thought that we have knowledge of something when we can offer proof. Does "proof" always have the same meaning? For example, consider the following:

a. Prove to me that you exist.
b. Prove to me that you love me. 5) Prove to me that you are in pain.
c. Prove that 2 plus 2 equals 4.
d. Prove that you were not in that vicinity when the accident occurred.
e. Prove that the square on the hypotenuse of a right triangle is equivalent to the sum of the squares on the other two sides.

Does "proof" mean something different in each case? Is there something common to all instances? What is accomplished when anything is proved?

6. There are many frightfully abstract terms that sometimes are names for a clear epistemological doctrine. You will sometimes be asked whether you are a "realist" or an "idealist," a "rationalist" or an "empiricist," a "monist" or a "dualist," a "pragmatist" or a "solipsist," a "positivist," a "sceptic," a "phenomenalist." Imagine these questions put to you. Practice giving each term a clear definition, and then answering whether it applies to you or not, and stating why you accept or reject the concept of knowledge of the given "-ism." If you find any of these ambiguous, practice stating two definitions and stating whether both or neither applies to your position, or one and not the other. You might try asking such questions of your teachers, but if you do, they are likely to ask, "What do you mean by that term?"

7. D. H. Lawrence tried to persuade Bertrand Russell to give up thinking, lecturing, and writing. Lawrence had epistemological grounds.

There is another seat of consciousness than the brain—and nerves. There is a blood-consciousness which exists in us independently of the ordinary mental consciousness. One lives, knows and has one's being in the blood, without any reference to nerves and brain. This is one half of life belonging to the darkness. When I take a woman, then the blood-percept is supreme. My blood-knowing is overwhelming. We should realize that we have a blood-being, a blood-consciousness, a blood-soul complete and apart from a mental and nerve consciousness.[98]

[96] John Dewey, *The Quest For Certainty*, George Allen & Unwin, Ltd., London, 1930, pp. 217, 231.
[97] Bertrand Russell, *An Inquiry into Meaning and Truth*, George Allen & Unwin, Ltd., London, 1948, p. 165.
[98] Bertrand Russell, *Portraits from Memory*, George Allen & Unwin, Ltd., London, 1956, pp. 106–107.

For a time Russell thought Lawrence had an insight denied to him, and that he was not fit to live. But then he rejected Lawrence's doctrine as the sort of rubbish popularized later by Fascists. What do you think of the way of knowing illustrated by Lawrence in his novels?

8. The epistemological assumptions of a science are sometimes made explicit in what is called scientific method. Perhaps you have heard more of the scientific method from teachers of other subjects known for their anxiety to be recognized as scientific by physicists, chemists, and biologists. Can we achieve, or have we achieved, knowledge of man in psychology, sociology, political science, that you would regard as scientific in the sense in which physics, chemistry, and biology are knowledge? What would you expect history or theology to be like if they were sciences?

PERTINENT READINGS

Aaron, R. I., *The Theory of Universals,* Oxford University Press, London, 1952.

Ayer, Alfred J., *The Problem of Knowledge,* Macmillan and Co., Ltd., London, 1956.

Blanshard, Brand, *The Nature of Thought,* George Allen & Unwin, Ltd., London, 1939.

Lewis, Clarence Irving, *Mind and the World Order,* Charles Scribner's Sons, New York, 1929.

Plato, *Theaetetus,* In *Plato's Theory of Knowledge,* (Francis M. Cornford, tr.). The Liberal Arts Press, Inc., New York, 1957.

Russell, Bertrand, *Human Knowledge: Its Scope and Limits,* Simon and Schuster, Inc., New York, 1948.

Sinclair, William Angus, *The Conditions of Knowing,* Routledge & Kegan Paul, Ltd., London, 1951.

VI

Metaphysics: Beliefs about Reality

I. Definitions of Metaphysics

The term *metaphysics* is one of the vaguest in all philosophy, and its lack of a relatively fixed meaning has led to absurdities among non-philosophers. A visit to a secondhand book store will often confirm this—one may find catalogued under "metaphysics" a hodgepodge of drivel all the way from the sexual aberrations of the natives of Bongo-Bongo to studies in the occultism of the Far East. And I once found Stephen Leacock's book Moonbeams from the Larger Lunacy in a college library placed on the shelves under "metaphysics." Maybe the cataloguer had a sense of humor, or maybe she thought she knew what she was doing.

The origin of the term reveals absolutely nothing about its various uses. Aristotle's work on first philosophy was placed after (*meta*) his books on physics. Hence, metaphysics. Undoubtedly the best way to see what some philosophers have meant by this term is to look at their own statements. Let us begin with one of the earliest, Aristotle.

Aristotle. Metaphysics is "a science which investigates being as being and the attributes which belong to this in virtue of its own nature." Then, in order to distinguish this from other areas of human knowledge he says, "Now this is not the same as any of the so-called special sciences; for none of these others deals generally with being as being. They cut off a part of being and investigate the attributes of this part."[1] The study of being as such is also often called ontology.

---

[1] Aristotle, *Metaphysics*. In: (W. D. Ross, tr. and ed.) *Aristotle Selections,* Charles Scribner's Sons, New York, 1927, p. 53.

What is this search for being as being? Can we make sense out of it? Can we understand what we are after if we engage in it? Certainly it would seem to require an enormous effort of abstraction. Take, for example, the statement "Here is a table." If asked to describe it, one would presumably give it various qualities—it is hard, brown, and rectangular. But *is* the table its qualities? Suppose one thinks the qualities away—after all it does not have to be hard, or brown, or rectangular. Then what is left? Suppose one thinks away all characteristics of everything, what is left? Well, perhaps this is what Aristotle means by being as being—that is, neither tall being nor sour being nor animal being nor vegetable being, and so on, but being in itself, pure isness, being without any qualifications whatsoever. This may seem a bit dizzying, or even fishy. Or it may come out relatively clear and strong. Philosophers are lined up on both sides, and we shall have to return to the problem.

Bradley. Now let us jump to modern philosophy. F. H. Bradley wrote that metaphysics is "an attempt to know reality as against mere appearance, or the study of first principles or ultimate truths, or again the effort to comprehend the universe, not simply piecemeal or by fragments, but somehow as a whole."[2] Here a number of important contrasts are discernible, appearance–reality, provisional–ultimate, part–whole. Metaphysics, according to Bradley is always aiming at the second member of these pairs. This suggests that what most often impresses itself on our lives is unreal, for it is fleeting and vague and tentative and fragmentary, and that beyond this blurred and restless world of appearances is the delightful world of exactness, completeness, and finality. To reach this world has been the goal of many metaphysicians. Others have denied that there is any such reality, or that we could ever know it even if it did exist.

What about this search for first principles? What does it involve? Perhaps a simple example can give a clue. Suppose a teacher of mathematics informs his class before the final examination that only those who bring to the examination a round-square will receive a passing grade. His students protest that they have never seen a round-square. But, he replies, that is no proof that they cannot produce one. Then if they say that there just cannot be round-squares, they have made a statement that is something like a first principle. They have committed themselves on what the world cannot contain. And how could such a claim be justified? Empirical facts would not suffice. According to the logic of induction, they may conclude only that up to now they have never found a round-square, and even if

---

[2] F. H. Bradley, *Appearance and Reality*, George Allen & Unwin, Ltd., London, 1925, p. 1.

no one has ever reported the discovery of one, its possible existence is left quite open. Therefore it is necessary to reason as some metaphysicians have done: Either a plane figure has all points of its circumference equidistant from the center, or it does not. If it is round it does, if square it does not. The same figure at the same time, seen from the same position, cannot both have all points of its circumference equidistant and not equidistant from the center. This would be absurd. Thus the principle of non-contradiction seems to be emerging as a first principle.

Whitehead and Bergson. In contrast to a world of fixity and certainty is another possibility, namely, one of change and novelty. Philosophers who defend this view would not say that metaphysics is about a reality that is rigid, exact, and final, but rather about becoming, a world that is ever-changing, fluid, and anything but exact. Alfred North Whitehead puts it this way: "By 'metaphysics' I mean the science which seeks to discover the general ideas which are indispensably relevant to the analysis of everything that happens."[3] Or consider Bergson's definition, "Metaphysics, then, is the science which claims to dispense with symbols."[4] Why dispense with symbols? Because they are static and unable to hold a vital, flowing reality. Language and all other symbolic representation is not the net by which we can capture the movement of the real. Neither Whitehead nor Bergson regards change as imperfection, or unreal; rather in changing things one discovers the relevance of anything to the actuality of anything else.

Notice how often metaphysicians call their pursuit a science. By this they do not mean that their truths come out of laboratories, but they do mean to say that their efforts really do add to the knowledge we have of ourselves and our world. It is against this claim that much contemporary opposition to metaphysics arises. We shall return to the problem.

Montague. Another attempt to state the business of metaphysics is found in the work of W. P. Montague. He says that its function is to bind or unify all the separate knowledge we have in the sciences, physical, biological, and sociological.[5] Thus the metaphysician is a kind of super-scientist, not in the sense that he knows more science, or makes actual contributions to the special sciences, but that his real work begins where the separate sciences leave off.

[3] Alfred North Whitehead, *Religion in the Making,* The Macmillan Co., New York, 1926, p. 84, footnote.
[4] Henri Bergson, *An Introduction to Metaphysics,* G. P. Putnam's Sons, New York, 1912, p. 9.
[5] W. P. Montague, *The Ways of Knowing,* Prentice-Hall, Inc., Englewood Cliffs, New Jersey, 1940, p. 10.

It is certainly true that most metaphysicians are acutely distressed by unbridgeable areas of belief, and many non-metaphysicians are aware of the contrast between brute fact for which there seems no reason, and the rational solution to a problem that seems useless and impractical. Many of us are also aware of the contrast between actual injustice and ideal justice, of existent evil and possible good. The motivation of the metaphysician is to remove the gaps and achieve for knowledge a high degree of order and relatedness. The ultimate justification for this is the conviction that reality itself is ordered and related rather than chaotic.

Blanshard. This stress upon the unity of knowledge and the belief that reality itself is coherently related leads many metaphysicians to emphasize the role of system in philosophy. In fact, metaphysics is sometimes called systematic philosophy. Brand Blanshard brings out the point nicely in the following:

. . . Reality is a system, completely ordered and fully intelligible, with which thought in its advance is more and more identifying itself. We may look at the growth of knowledge, individual or social, either as an attempt by our own minds to return to union with things as they are in their ordered wholeness, or the affirmation through our minds of the ordered whole itself. And if we take this view, our notion of truth is marked out for us. Truth is the approximation of thought to reality. It is thought on its way home. Its measure is the distance thought has travelled, under guidance of its inner compass, toward that intelligible system which unites its ultimate object with its ultimate end. Hence at any given time the degree of truth in our experience as a whole is the degree of system it has achieved.[6]

But again we must face alternatives, for not all metaphysicians would agree that reality possesses the kind of rational coherence Blanshard finds so attractive and necessary. Contemporary existentialists, for example, see in the real an irrational element not only not subject to systematic thought, but in opposition to it. And Nietzsche protested against systems, declaring that "they are descended from registrars and office secretaries whose whole business is to label things and put them in pigeon holes." Other philosophers have suggested that all systems are human inventions and do not reflect the nature of reality. To this problem we will return when considering some of the attacks on metaphysics.

The Linguistic Approach. Among many contemporary philosophers there is a conviction that metaphysics is largely a matter of linguistic trouble; that the questions raised by metaphysicians are only symptoms of a mental cramp resulting from certain peculiar uses of language. Thus meta-

[6] Brand Blanshard, *The Nature of Thought,* George Allen & Unwin, Ltd., London, 1955, Vol. II, p. 264.

physics is something that calls for a cure, a therapy, so that we can be rid of the persistent irritations or puzzles that have tormented our minds. The questions of metaphysics, says one philosopher, are not like questions of science that seem to permit one to aim at a direct answer. Rather they are paradoxes that need to be resolved, or they are a kind of illuminating falsehood; they suggest a different way of looking at things with the hint that this will give us a truer, perhaps deeper understanding of the way things are. Thus metaphysical statements are not meaningless, they have their own sort of sense or use. Consider, for example, "No one really knows the past."

This couldn't but be true in its paradoxical rôle. For in that rôle either it refers to the peculiarities of knowledge of the past which make it knowledge of the past or it's a deduction from the wider paradox that no one really knows anything as to what is gone or what's to come, only what is so. And this paradox couldn't but be true; for either it refers to the peculiarities of knowledge of what was and what will be so or it's a deduction from the wider paradox that no one really knows anything as to what was so, will be so or is so, only what seems. And this paradox couldn't but be true; for either it refers to the peculiarities of knowledge of what was, is, or will be so as opposed to knowledge of what seems or it's a deduction from the wider paradox that knowledge is impossible, since a claim that goes beyond what seems goes too far and one that doesn't go beyond what seems doesn't go far enough.[7]

It is evident that when this direction is taken in metaphysics, all thought of a universal system is abandoned—nor is there any effort to search for first principles, or for the unity of knowledge. The function of metaphysics is rather to examine what is peculiar about certain kinds of questions, about certain kinds of discussions, and about certain claims to knowledge.

The Theological Approach. We conclude this section by saying that some people take metaphysics as a kind of theology. They want to find and adopt a wide context in which to consider and understand human life. Thus some metaphysical views would be disclaimed because they are religiously unsatisfying, while others are found to be more compatible with religious experience. That metaphysics and theology are historically close is doubtless true; that some religious questions are metaphysical in character is also true; but still they are not identical, for a religion that is metaphysically absurd would have a hard go of it, except for the lunatic fringe.

Concluding Remarks. We have not exhausted the possibilities. Other definitions, other views may be described. But this is sufficient for our purposes and enough to get us under way. In this and the following chap-

---

[7] John Wisdom, *Other Minds,* Blackwell, Oxford, 1952, p. 258.

ter we will not try to develop a single deductive system, nor to present a single metaphysical view all nicely wrapped and parcelled ready for delivery. Rather, we will continue our usual procedure, namely, to set out alternatives that are open to belief. And we will give some of the critical objections to the whole enterprise from those who hold contrary beliefs and who would rid themselves of all metaphysical commitments. Once more we remind the student of Aristotle's good counsel—the goal is "to raise searching difficulties on both sides of a subject which will make us detect more easily the truth and error about the several points that arise."

If the student is beginning to have the melancholy feeling that there is something murky about metaphysics, even at the start, that is, in definition, he joins many contemporary philosophers. Perhaps he will find satisfaction in Bradley's quip that "metaphysics is the finding of bad reasons for what we believe upon instinct, but to find these reasons is no less an instinct."[8] On the other hand, he will find it very difficult after reading philosophy to keep from calling some men materialists, others idealists, and still others dualists. Study, for example, the great Leviathan of Thomas Hobbes. You will soon reach the metaphysical bedrock that whatever is real occupies space and is in motion. A body can meet and cause effects in another body, but a mind independent of a body is as unreal as a ghost. All through his epistemology, psychology, sociology, and politics, Hobbes scorned ghosts as nothing a reasonable man could believe. Or, again, look into Berkeley's Three Dialogues, to see a contrary view and how difficult it is to define "body" or "matter," let alone to conceive or know it. At the very least, it takes a kind of courage to diverge so radically from conventional beliefs that there are both bodies and minds, or physical and mental activity. And yet if this kind of thinking is ridiculed, or denied its proper role, then are we not prevented from asking and trying to answer the most general metaphysical or philosophical question, namely, what is the perspective that makes the most sense out of the whole range of our experiences?

Metaphysical distinctions are tedious to learn, and one often suspects they are pettifogging, because the terms may be used as roughly equivalent in everyday language. Who bothers in everyday speech to distinguish "exist" and "subsist"? Who bothers to distinguish "a being" from "being," which are nouns, from "being" as a participle? Who bothers about the meaning of "is" involved in "essence" from the meaning of "is" involved in "existence"? In reading a serious ontologist, however, these are the distinctions, above all others, to get clear. And this has been the case since the

---

[8] F. H. Bradley, *op. cit.*, p. xiv.

first elaborate text, and in many ways still the best text to examine carefully, the Metaphysics of Aristotle.

The refrain that lingers from the Metaphysics, and which leads directly into the way in which contemporary as well as medieval ontology is done is " 'being' has many senses."

There are several senses in which a thing may be said to 'be' . . . for in one sense the 'being' meant is 'what a thing is' or a 'this', and in another sense it means a quality or quantity or one of the other things that are predicated as these are. While 'being' has all these senses, obviously that which 'is' primarily is the 'what', which indicates the substance of the thing. For when we say of what quality a thing is, we say that it is good or bad, not that it is three cubits long or that it is a man; but when we say *what* it is, we do not say 'white' or 'hot' or 'three cubits long', but 'a man' or 'a god'. And all other things are said to be because they are, some of them quantities of that which *is* in this primary sense, others qualities of it, others affections of it, and others some other determination of it. And so one might even raise the question whether the words 'to walk', 'to be healthy', 'to sit' imply that each of these things is existent, and similarly in any other case of this sort; for none of them is either self-subsistent or capable of being separated from substance, but rather, if anything, it is that which walks or sits or is healthy that is an existent thing. Now these are seen to be more real because there is something definite which underlies them (i.e. the substance or individual), which is implied in such a predicate; for we never use the word 'good' or 'sitting' without implying this. Clearly then it is in virtue of this category that each of the others also *is*. Therefore that which is primary, i.e. not in a qualified sense but without qualification, must be substance.[9]

Modern philosophers agree that at least part of the confusion and difficulty of metaphysics springs from the ambiguity of the little word "is." George Santayana saw this some years ago and set about to separate its various meanings. It greatly needed to be done and now we may profit from his analysis.

1. "Is" may mean *identity*. We say with assurance that "a thing is what it is." But we are not thereby describing an object or asserting its existence. Of course if a thing is not what it is, we could not think about it, describe it, deny or affirm its existence. Without this meaning of "is" philosophy would be a wild-goose chase.
2. "Is" may mean *equivalence*. This use of the word does not assert identity of terms, rather it shows that the same thing is signified in many different ways, for example, we can say *"Mensch"* is "man."

[9] Richard McKeon (ed.), *The Basic Works of Aristotle*, Random House, New York, 1941, p. 783; Aristotle, *Metaphysica*, W. D. Ross (tr.) The Clarendon Press, Oxford, 1028a 10–30.

3. "Is" may be used in *definition*. This is the "is" that tells one what an object is, for instance, man is a rational animal, and so on. This use of "is" does not mean that a thing *is* its definition any more than a man is his name. "Definitions are complex names and they have the same function as names."

4. "Is" may be used in *predication*. This is the "is" that marks off some property of a thing that also has other properties. A is B does not assert an identity, else it would be self-contradictory.

5. "Is" may be used to assert *existence*. Here the "is" asserts that a thing may be spatially and temporally encountered. It is not the "is" of pure being. Some languages, Santayana notes, have at least three different verbs for "to be" which cannot be used interchangeably. "Is" when used to refer to existence designates the external relations in which an object stands.

6. "Is" may be used to affirm *actuality*. Here "is" refers to those aspects of life with which we are familiar but which do not stand in external relations as do physical objects:

> *Is*, applied to spirit or to any of its modes, accordingly means is actual; in other words, exists not by virtue of inclusion in the dynamic, incessant, and infinitely divisible flux of nature, but by its intrinsic incandescence, which brings essences to light and creates the world of appearances.

7. "Is" may assert *derivation*. We employ this use when we say one thing is derived from another. The "is" is synonymous in this case with "comes from," as in, "This spark is a firefly and not a star." Thus the "is" serves for attributing sources and connecting things genetically. Such a use is often found among those who are fond of saying that something is "nothing but."

> Thus we hear that a word is nothing but a *flatus vocis*, that a house is nothing but bricks and mortar, that a mind is nothing but a bundle of perceptions, that God is nothing but a tendency not ourselves that makes for righteousness, or that matter is nothing but a permanent possibility of sensation.[10]

What about the "is" of being, as in Parmenides' "Being is"? None of the above distinctions seems to fit. Indeed, are we not at the limits of language here? Is "being" so basic a category that upon it everything else must depend? If we make the distinction between being and existence, then is it intelligible to say of something that it has being but does not exist? Some theologians (and some philosophers) are not averse to such

[10] George Santayana, *Obiter Scripta*, Charles Scribner's Sons, New York, 1936, pp. 189–213.

statements. Here, for example, is one from Paul Tillich, a highly regarded contemporary thinker:

Thus the question of the existence of God can be neither asked nor answered. If asked, it is a question about that which by its very nature is above existence, and therefore the answer—whether negative or affirmative—implicitly denies the nature of God. It is as atheistic to affirm the existence of God as it is to deny it. God is being-itself, not *a* being.[11]

There is another use of "is" that does not seem to fall under any of the usages we have just mentioned. We can call it the "is of subsistence." We shall get at it in an indirect way by presenting a now historic contribution of Bertrand Russell's to logic and philosophy. He accused metaphysicians of the last two thousand years of being muddle-headed about "existence" and thought it was time to clear up the difficulties. To achieve this he produced a "theory of descriptions." We must try to get his point.

First it is necessary to see that there is a distinction between a name and a description. Thus "Scott" is a name, but "the author of *Waverley*" is a description; "Socrates" is a name, but "the gadfly of Athens" is a description. Descriptions have given philosophers a lot of trouble, because, says Russell, they had not noticed that although a name cannot occur significantly in a proposition unless there is something that it names, a description can. Russell found that the German philosopher Meinong failed to see this, and thus was led to asserting the existence of very strange entities.

He pointed out that one can make statements in which the logical subject is "the golden mountain" although no golden mountain exists. He argued, if you say that the golden mountain does not exist, it is obvious that there is something that you are saying does not exist—namely, the golden mountain; therefore the golden mountain must subsist in some shadowy Platonic world of being, for otherwise your statement that the golden mountain does not exist would have no meaning.[12]

Russell was once convinced that Meinong was right and he accepted a realm of subsistent entities, until he hit upon his theory of descriptions. Then he was able to reject this use of "is" and give up the subsisting objects. This meant that he had found a way to eliminate descriptions from significant propositions and thus to eliminate the tendency to seek for

[11] Paul Tillich, "The Actuality of God." In: Yervant H. Krikorian and Abraham Edel (eds.), *Contemporary Philosophic Problems*, The Macmillan Co., New York, 1959, p. 451.

[12] Bertrand Russell, *My Philosophical Development*, George Allen & Unwin, Ltd., London, 1959, p. 84.

their referents in some kind of existence. This can be done in the following way, says Russell:

> The proposition "The golden mountain does not exist" becomes "The propositional function '*x* is golden and a mountain' is false for all values of *x*." The statement "Scott is the author of *Waverley*" becomes "for all values of *x*, '*x* wrote *Waverley*' is equivalent to '*x* is Scott.'" Here, the phrase "the author of *Waverley*" no longer occurs.[13]

And so it would be with respect to unicorns, "the horse-like animal with one horn," and mermaids, "the girl with a fish tail," and so on. We need not be misled by grammar, which seems to give them a status in existence when we say, for example, "Unicorns do not exist." Put precisely, this means "The propositional function '*x* is a unicorn' is false for all values of *x*," and thus we have eliminated the puzzle about non-existing existing unicorns.

Russell claims that his theory makes explicit the meaning of the definite article in all sentences of the type "the so-and-so." Consider for example, "The author of *Waverley* was Scotch." This implies, says Russell, the following three propositions, or put another way, the following three propositions define precisely what is meant by "The author of *Waverley* was Scotch": (1) At least one person wrote *Waverley*, (2) At most one person wrote *Waverley*, and (3) Whoever wrote *Waverley* was Scotch.[14] This theory, Russell claims, shows that while a phrase may contribute to the meaning of a sentence in which it appears, it may nevertheless have no meaning in isolation, that is, outside of a sentence. For this he thinks there is a decisive proof:

> If "the author of *Waverley*" meant anything other than "Scott," "Scott is the author of *Waverley*" would be false, which it is not. If "the author of *Waverley*" meant "Scott," "Scott is the author of *Waverley*" would be a tautology, which it is not. Therefore, "the author of *Waverley*" means neither "Scott" nor anything else—i.e. "the author of *Waverley*" means nothing, Q.E.D."[15]

Russell's confidence that he has cleared up a number of problems about existence with this theory has not been shaken. And many philosophers agree with him. But still there are dissenters—those who feel, as perhaps the student may, that there is something perverse about the whole business; that we often do use a referring phrase meaningfully in a sentence without feeling it necessary to say that every time it is so used there must

---

[13] *Ibid.*, p. 84.
[14] Bertrand Russell, *Introduction to Mathematical Philosophy*, George Allen & Unwin, Ltd., London, Reprinted 1950, p. 177.
[15] Bertrand Russell, *My Philosophical Development*, *op. cit.*, p. 85.

exist something to which it refers. To follow these objections through would take us too far afield and into areas requiring more technical competence in logic than we can expect from beginning students in philosophy. However, those who would like to see more of the argument will find much help in P. F. Strawson's book, Introduction to Logical Theory (John Wiley and Sons, New York, 1952).

Against the whole metaphysical search for an ultimate reality, a first principle, an all-encompassing system, or for being as such, there has developed in modern thought a widespread hostility. It is said that metaphysics is neither logically nor cognitively possible; that it may offer a kind of emotional satisfaction to certain minds, but it cannot tell anything about the way things are, because its claims cannot be verified even if they could be made conceptually clear. We must set out these arguments as honestly as we can. On the other hand, not all philosophers have surrendered—many refuse to retreat from what they regard as the mainland of all philosophy. We shall want to hear their claims and mark their defenses. But now let us plunge into the controversy.

II. Attacks on Metaphysics

A. Is Metaphysics Pseudo-Knowledge?

Hume and Kant

Contemporary opposition to metaphysics has its roots in the philosophies of David Hume and Immanuel Kant. Hume, you will remember, insisted that all knowledge must come from experience and that any knowledge-claim we make must be traceable to an impression. All propositions are to be divided into those that state matters of fact and those that state relations of ideas. The latter alone are necessarily true, and the former are contingently true, that is, they are dependent upon particulars learned through sense-experience. It is on this basis that Hume rests his scepticism concerning anything beyond or transcending experience. Thus,

when we run over libraries, persuaded of these principles, what havoc must we make? If we take in our hand any volume, of divinity or school metaphysics, for instance; let us ask, *Does it contain any abstract reasoning concerning quantity or number?* No. *Does it contain any experimental reasoning concerning matter of fact and existence?* No. Commit it then to the flames; for it can contain nothing but sophistry and illusion.[16]

---

[16] David Hume, *The Philosophical Work of Hume, An Inquiry Concerning the Human Understanding,* Little, Brown & Co., Boston, 1854, Vol. IV, pp. 187–188.

Kant wrote in 1781 that metaphysics, while once known as the Queen of the sciences was now held in scorn. She is, he said, "a matron outcast and forsaken." Toward any metaphysical system we may adopt four possible attitudes, he wrote. We may affirm a system without inquiring, as he put it, into the lineage of the supposed Queen. But this is dogmatism, and opens us to the charge of "groundless pretensions." Or we may attempt to trace all knowledge to "common experience" in the senses, and like Hume, cast doubt upon the claims of reason itself to grasp the structure of reality. But this is scepticism, and the danger of it is that it destroys also the basis of scientific thought. Again, we may weary of the alternative claims to truth that are characteristic of metaphysics, and out of weariness fall into indifference. Then we say, at least by implication, that the questions of metaphysics are not worth asking because we are not sure of any set of answers. Kant doubts that we can sincerely take this way, particularly if we pursue a science, for thereby we adopt a set of more general answers while solving particular problems. His own answer is neither dogmatic, nor sceptical, nor indifferent, but is called critical, because it seeks to restate metaphysical principles as principles of reason. Reason can be known, and he proves it perhaps more deeply than any other philosopher. If we cannot know what transcends reason, at least we can know the nature of reason itself, although we may not judge that what belongs to reason also belongs to a reality beyond reason.

It is true, thinks Kant, that man has a kind of natural propensity to search for something beyond all the facts of experience that would account for existence. But, nevertheless, it is a mistake to do so, because all our categories of explanation apply only to the facts within experience. Thus we cannot say anything meaningful about a reality behind or beyond experience. The categories lose all sense when we try to extend them outside of the context of experience.

The forms of language itself show what this context is, and they are what they are because of it. Underneath all the particular grammars of particular languages, there is a deeper grammar which reflects the universal features of human experience, that is, the position of persons as observers in space and time of a succession of events. For instance, we have to think of our experience as an experience of things, existing in space and persisting as the same things through time with changing qualities. This is part of the unavoidable grammar of our thought, equally part of the unavoidable nature of experience. We cannot think it away. But at the same time we are aware of this limitation on our thought and experience as a limitation; and this is why we are tempted, hopelessly, into metaphysical speculation, trying to break the bonds, as it were, where the bonds are the necessary forms of experience as we know it. All we can do, as philosophers, is to penetrate to this deeper grammar, which reflects the presuppositions of all our thought and experience; and then we shall realize why it is that our knowledge can never be complete, and why we can never have unconditional explanations of the nature of things, as they are in themselves, apart from the conditions of our experience of them.[17]

A. J. Ayer

With the powerful artillery of Hume and Kant in support, modern criticisms of metaphysics could not fail to make considerable advance. Perhaps the most straightforward and vigorous critic is A. J. Ayer. His views, and those of men who think as he does, are usually labelled *positivism* although *logical empiricism* seems to be a better name. Let us turn to their major objections against metaphysics.

Metaphysical beliefs are defined by Ayer as those purporting to "describe the nature or even to assert the existence of something beyond the reach of empirical observation." This defines the old metaphysics that Kant judged impossible: It concerns "reality underlying or transcending the phenomena which the special sciences are content to study." If any question about a reality underlying phenomena is a bogus question, any answer will be worthless as knowledge, and any statement of belief will take the form of a pseudo-proposition. Propositions are capable of being true or false, and if meaningful is defined as capable of being verified or falsified, then all metaphysical beliefs are meaningless. So Ayer summarizes his logical empiricist predecessors in a celebrated article "Demonstration of the Impossibility of Metaphysics."[18]

It has been commonplace for those philosophers who derive all knowledge from sense-experience to suspend judgment on issues that cannot be matters of experimental testing. On this basis Hume entertained strong suspicions about the meanings of God, the human self, and cause (except in the restricted sense that one kind of event is observed to occur constantly before another sort of event, and in proximity to it). Kant called attention to the self-contradictions into which reason falls when reason is unaided by the senses, as in discourse about ultimate reality. But he could not on this agnostic basis deny that a being of less limited reason might know. Metaphysical problems remained, he claimed, genuine, partly because the theoretical sciences also employ propositions that are both synthetic and a priori.

---

[17] D. F. Pears (ed.), *The Nature of Metaphysics,* Macmillan and Co. Ltd., London, 1957, p. 25.

[18] A. J. Ayer, "The Elimination of Metaphysics," *Mind,* Vol. 43, No. 171, 1934. Reprinted in Paul Edwards and Arthur Pap, *A Modern Introduction to Philosophy,* etc., The Free Press, Glencoe, Illinois, 1958, pp. 555–556.

Nor is it any novelty for men to claim that when the positive or factual sciences are developed, the sciences will give genuine answers to problems of traditional speculation, as superior to metaphysical answers as these were in their day to the older theological answers. It is sometimes cogently argued that the standard way to found a science is to begin with issues formulated by philosophers, but to engage in seeking data experimentally. Studies as widely different as physics and psychology are historically children of speculation about matter and mind.

Logical empiricism is best known for its criterion of meaning. Ayer's formulation is a new turn in the attack on metaphysics:

. . . To give the meaning of a proposition is to give the conditions under which it would be true and those under which it would be false. I understand a proposition if I know what observations I must make in order to establish its truth or falsity. . . . I understand a proposition when I know what facts would verify it. To indicate the situation which verifies a proposition is to indicate what the proposition means.[19]

If a speaker cannot specify the situation that verifies the statement, he is not uttering a proposition. He may be expressing feelings, but "he does not thereby make any assertion about the world." Even if the utterance seems to be in conventional grammatical form, as "The moon is the square root of 3," we do not what is asserted.

Some logical empiricists have examined the statements of metaphysicians, as Carnap analyzed a famous essay of Heidegger's called "What is Metaphysics?" Other analysts have painfully considered statements about God, substance, matter, mind, etc. But these are unnecessary, says Ayer, if "the aim of metaphysics is to describe a reality lying beyond experience." For, by definition, any proposition that can be verified is not metaphysical. Consequently, although it seems to be an assertion to say "There is a super-phenomenal reality," this fundamental postulate of metaphysics is senseless and meaningless. Ayer illustrates his point by postulating an idealist who says that a painting of Goya's is a collection of ideas (his own or God's). A realist claims that its colors are objectively real. Since by the criterion of meaning, neither metaphysician can indicate empirical means of settling the question, the problem is not genuine. One can tell whether it is raining, but one cannot tell whether rain is real or ideal. Some unverified propositions are meaningful, for example, although we cannot now verify hypotheses about the other side of the moon (Ayer wrote before October 1959), we know the circumstances under which they could be verified. But metaphysical beliefs are not relevant to any factual situation. Consequently, they are not hypotheses and they are not explanations.

If a philosopher objects that metaphysicians do not intend nonsense, Ayer agrees, and explains that they have been misled by language. Men do talk about "imaginary illness," and it seems profound to ask about the nature of this object, "imaginary illness." The whole problem of real and apparent things is infected. But there is a simple cure: namely, rather than saying "His illness is imaginary," say "He is not ill although he thinks he is."[20]

But why have men been misled by language? Ayer is typical of positivists in his answer: Men "desire to express their feelings about the world." Literature and the arts afford the most satisfactory medium for such expression. "Metaphysics results when men attempt to extrapolate their emotions: they wish to present them not as feelings of their own, but somehow objectively as facts; therefore they express them in the form of argument and theory." Man desires also to unify his knowledge. But metaphysicians have the impulse of science without the training; consequently, they postulate a new and superior kind of knowledge.[21] Thus, metaphysicians are poets who have chosen "an unsuitable medium of expression."

Ayer grants that Wittgenstein, to whom he ascribes his inspiration, had a way of using metaphysical propositions that avoided this sort of condemnation. At the end of Tractatus Logico-Philosophicus, Wittgenstein asserted that the propositions contained in it are nonsensical, but they are means for enabling us to "see the world rightly." Or if we used as our criterion of significance the influencing of action, then metaphysical propositions could be meaningful. But Ayer warns against a more liberal criterion. It might allow as meaningful "jealousy pronouns live" or "siffle hip brim."[22]

Later statements of Ayer's are readily available. "The Elimination of Metaphysics" (Chapter I of Language, Truth and Logic, first published in 1935, Dover Publications, Inc., New York, n.d.) modifies the above position by denying to metaphysics, not meaning in general, but "literal meaning," and granting to metaphysicians "genuine mystical feeling." More important is the distinction between "weak" and "strong" verification. The admission of degrees weakens the absolute contrast between science and metaphysics. Most important is the regret expressed in the introduction

[20] Ibid., p. 561.
[21] Ibid., p. 562.
[22] Ibid., p. 564.

to the second edition (1946) that the meaning criterion is not more precise. A widespread concern among logical empiricists is that the criterion is so narrow that it excludes scientific theories.

A Psychoanalytic Theory

One of the most curious attempts to show that metaphysics is impossible has recently been offered by Morris Lazerowitz. Its problems, he says, are intrinsically insoluble, that is, no new fact will establish one answer as true and another as false, the reason being that we do not understand the words we use to express and argue for the theories. But there is a deeper reason for our failure to understand our own linguistic products, namely, that metaphysics is actually a creation of the unconscious mind.

A metaphysical theory, I shall try to show, is a verbal dream, the linguistic substructure of which has to be uncovered before we can see what it comes to and how it produces its effect. The main problem will be to expose to clear view the linguistic machinery which is used to create the illusion that metaphysics gives us views about pervasive and fundamental phenomena and that the arguments for or against these views are demonstrations of their truth or falsity.[23]

Metaphysical statements, says Lazerowitz, express unconsciously held beliefs whose purpose it is to

. . . satisfy a repressed longing or to ward off a repressed fear. . . . Thus, the philosophical sentence "Nothing really changes" constitutes a fantasied, holiday rejection of the word "change"; which because it is not made consciously, creates the illusion of being a startling pronouncement about things—and in doing this it perhaps indulges our wish to be able to do magical things with words, our wish, as one of Freud's patients phrased it, for "omnipotence of thought." But more specifically than this, the make-believe rejection of the word "change" indicates that the word has become charged with special meaning. The rejection must play an important and serious role in the drama of our unconscious life.[24]

Thus if a metaphysician says that "change is unreal," he is not reporting anything he knows about the actual state of affairs, rather he is giving expression to an unconscious wish that things and conditions should remain as they are. He fears change and the unconscious fear gets expressed in a metaphysical statement against the reality of change. So "change" really means "dreaded change." There is a hidden sense to the denial of change, namely, "No changes which would create anxiety in me are real."

[23] Morris Lazerowitz, *The Structure of Metaphysics*, The Humanities Press, New York, 1955, p. 26.
[24] *Ibid.*, p. 68.

If a metaphysician happens to assert the opposite, that "change is real," he too expresses an unconscious wish, namely, to overcome his fear of change, to show that after all change is really harmless. Lazerowitz does not carry his analysis to the next possible stage and show what could be the case if a metaphysician asserted that change is both real and unreal. Presumably the logical problem should not trouble him, for this is a psychological explanation. And it is true that some philosophers have described a world in which some things change and others are permanent.

There is much that is intriguing in Lazerowitz's account, and probably a good deal of truth in it. But it is rather difficult to think that all the great attempts at metaphysics, Plato, Aristotle, Spinoza, and Whitehead, have been motivated by nothing more than unconscious wishes. If Lazerowitz will allow no other reason for metaphysics, how can he be answered? Nothing that can be said will count as evidence, for he can always reply, "You have just given linguistic expression to a repressed fear or an unconscious wish." And there seems to be a kind of genetic fallacy involved in this position, that is, because we can show the origin or the motivation of a statement, therefore, the question of the truth or falsity of the statement cannot arise, or does not make sense.

A further difficulty in any psychoanalytic attack upon metaphysics is that it raises the question of the motivation of the anti-metaphysician. Why should we not wonder whether the anti-metaphysician is expressing his Oedipus complex? Perhaps the earliest metaphysics he acquired was belief in God as some fatherly image. To attack metaphysics would then be a symbolic way of destroying his father, which Freud assures us, is essential in the subconscious motives of every male. Any argument that leaves one so open to counterattack and whose truth value is undeterminable is rather fruitless.

B. Fallacies in Metaphysical Argument

When twentieth-century philosophers read metaphysical arguments they examine carefully the terms, the statements of propositions, and the deductive steps of argument. For it has been gravely charged that many terms are abused in metaphysics, and are used fallaciously, in the sense of equivocally (a term introduced in logic). And many of the propositions, it is charged, are empty or tautological statements masquerading as some fact about the world, or claiming to deduce a fact from a definition. With such equivocal terms and ambiguous propositions, we should not expect that the arguments could amount to more than sophistry.

The student might wonder, since fallacies in general have already been introduced, why specific attention needs to be called to fallacies in meta-physics. One reason is that metaphysical positions are often unfortunately presented with rhetorical flourishes that mark the "grand" style, and one can be so awed by the message of salvation that it seems ignoble to de-mand precise meanings, clear statements and logically permissible transi-tions from premises to conclusion. Criticism of the grand style is gen-erally voiced by those whom Berkeley called "minute" philosophers, who have themselves no total vision and fervor to elevate mankind. Surely, in spite of whatever justification there may be for a literary grandeur that might at first impress us with the wisdom of philosophy, the spell under which one is cast is a cheap delusion if obscurity, when analyzed, turns out to be the mask for careless thought.

The first three fallacies will be drawn from authors who talk as though all metaphysicians commit these fallacies, and that this spells inevitable ruin to the enterprise. In other words, to avoid fallacy, one must abandon metaphysics. We shall then discuss further fallacies that metaphysicians themselves have pointed out, sometimes it must be noted, in a form of argument like the ontological argument, which some metaphysicians re-ject as fallacious in other metaphysicians' systems.

1. Extending terms of discourse analogically from the known to the un-known.
2. Failure to distinguish predicational from existential propositions.
3. Arguing from essence to existence, or ontologizing.
4. The fallacy of misplaced concreteness.
5. Propositions of unrestricted generality; the fallacies of self-referential propositions.
6. The circularity of metaphysical systems; the fallacy of being viciously circular, that is, grounded only in themselves, hence inevitably dog-matic and claiming something called special privilege.

We shall state each of the first three charges boldly, because the student must keep them in mind so as to judge arguments in this and succeeding chapters. Ask of every metaphysical position whether it is bad in its exten-sion of meanings, in its use of equivocal propositions, in its unwarranted step from mere conception to matter of fact.

1. *Extending terms of discourse analogically from the known to the un-known.*

Terms in everyday language seem clear enough, when used in everyday speech. A metaphysician may begin with an illustration of a man's hand moving a stick; then he says the moving hand is the cause of the stick's moving. So St. Thomas argues, and soon he extends the meaning of "cause" to God's causing the world's motion, and even to bringing the whole finite creation into being. St. Thomas has a theory that his term "cause" is not indeed univocal, but not equivocal either. It is analogical, that is, there is a proportional relation between the hand's motion and the stick's motion and God's creating and the world's existence and motion. Lest the student think this is merely a peculiarity of Thomism or theism, let us cite the general case for four other kinds of systems considered viable for twentieth-century Americans. Each of these, claims S. C. Pepper in World Hypotheses (University of California Press, Berkeley and Los Angeles, 1948), is based on a root metaphor.

The happiest example is that of the materialist Hobbes, who extends the notion of a machine from such a common example as a lever to the whole human person, who is nothing but a complex machine, thence to society as nothing but an even more complex machine, and finally the whole world as nothing but the most complex machine. But is it legitimate to extend the use of a term from common life to the whole of reality or to ultimate reality? We might argue that the sciences have taken over the old Greek term for tool, "organ," and that now without fallacious equivocation we can talk of the organ of sight, hearing, etc.

The example from science of analogical extension of meaning shows that the term is controlled empirically in the extended use by the fact to which it is applied. But metaphysical theories, according to one critic, are wholly subject to verbal usage. The meaning is drawn entirely from the meaning of the ordinary usage. The old Greek word for lumber gets extended from what is literally the wood of a house to the clay of a pot or the bronze of a sword. But then a component of the world is called prime lumber, or prime matter, which quite unlike literal lumber is unknowable in itself and indescribable. It has no characteristics at all. But one still thinks one knows what "lumber" means, even prime lumber, which is not like real lumber at all. On this basis Margaret Macdonald charges that metaphysical theories

. . . do not extend the use of these words but generally only misuse them. It is for this reason that such philosophical propositions have been called senseless. They try to operate with ordinary words when they have deprived them of their ordinary functions. They recombine known words in an unfamiliar way while trading on their familiar meanings. But these analogies lead to hopeless difficulties and so it seems that philosophical problems are never solved at all.[25]

---

[25] Margaret Macdonald, "The Philosopher's Use of Analogy." In: Antony Flew (ed.), *Essays on Logic and Language*, First Series, Blackwell, Oxford, 1951, p. 82.

The application of this analysis to the ancient distinction between matter and form leads to doubt about the meaning of materialism and idealism.

Materialists have asserted and idealists have denied the existence of matter or material substances. Both have assumed that the world must be made of *something*. For Thales the world was made of water; for Russell events are the "real stuff" of the world.

The problem begins with wondering what a thing is after all its properties are ignored, or every quality changed. Why have metaphysicians supposed a thing is anything without its properties by which we know it? Because this something is called the "foundation" or "base," the "substratum" or "substance." If the whole question is about a category of speech, then to assume the question is about the existent world is fallacious.[26]

If any metaphysical theory that employs "matter" and "form," or even "substance" in these general ways, is fallacious because of its equivocal terms, then practically the whole tradition of Western metaphysics and nearly all of the alternatives should be abandoned.

2. *Failure to distinguish predicational from existential propositions.*

Propositions in everyday language are not dangerously ambiguous even when they say two different things. For example "Dogs are faithful" says both that dogs have the property of being faithful, and that there are dogs. The first meaning is predicational, the second existential. But just as with terms, beginning with ordinary meanings, we may extend meanings until we do not know what we are talking about; so on the model of "Dogs are faithful" we say "Unicorns are fictitious." The two sentences are grammatically similar and therefore we suppose they are of the same logical type, that is, one might also say, however fancifully, "Unicorns are friendly" and however falsely, "Dogs are fictitious."

What is the fallacy? Some metaphysicians have argued in the following way:

Dogs must exist in order to have the property of being faithful, and so it is held that unless unicorns in some way existed they could not have the property of being fictitious. But, as it is plainly self-contradictory to say that fictitious objects exist, the device is adopted of saying that they are real in some non-empirical sense—that they have a mode of real being which is different from the mode of being of existent things.[27]

---

[26] *Ibid.*, pp. 85–88.
[27] Alfred Jules Ayer, *Language, Truth and Logic*, Dover Publications, Inc., New York, n.d., p. 43. By permission of the author, Dover Publications, and Victor Gollancz, Ltd., London.

Apart from being unverifiable, which makes it nonsense according to the verifiability criterion, "being fictitious" is no more an attribute than being non-fictitious, or existent. Here the student should recall Russell's theory of descriptions.

Analytic philosophers rebuke the superstition of metaphysicians that leads them to believe that every grammatical subject names a real entity. Not only is the belief in real universals a consequence, so is the popular existentialist belief "that 'Nothing' is a name which is used to denote something peculiarly mysterious. . . ."[28] Can "nothing" function as a name?

Gilbert Ryle's famous essay, "Systematically Misleading Expressions," goes one step further.

> Until fairly recently it was not noticed that if in 'God exists,' 'exists' is not a predicate (save in grammar), then in the same statement 'God' cannot be (save in grammar) the subject of predication. The realization of this came from ex-amining negative existential propositions like 'Satan does not exist' or 'unicorns are non-existent'. If there is no Satan, then the statement 'Satan does not exist' cannot be about Satan in the way 'I am sleepy' is about me. Despite appear-ances the word 'Satan' cannot be signifying a subject of attributes.[29]

How, then, should one express disbelief in unicorns? By saying: "Noth-ing is *both* a quadruped *and* herbivorous *and* the wearer of one horn." That is, if these are the marks of being a unicorn. And how should one express belief in God? By saying: "Something, and one thing only, is omniscient, omnipotent, and infinitely good." That is, if those are the marks of God and the only God. What Ryle recommends is that one should never say of anything that "It exists," or "It is an entity," or "It has being," etc.[30]

3. *Arguing from essence to existence, or ontologizing.*

Arguments for the reality or existence of something are not in ordinary discourse marred by fallacy. Some entities in science are indeed hypo-thetical, i.e., assumed in order to account for a particular phenomenon.

But metaphysicians, at least some of the strongly rationalistic ones of the seventeenth and nineteenth centuries, construct arguments that begin with the essences of things, or what can be conceived and defined, and from this alone attempt to draw the conclusion that the things must there-

---

[28] *Ibid.*, p. 44. In the next section we present the argument from Heidegger here at-tacked by Ayer.

[29] Gilbert Ryle, "Systematically Misleading Expressions." In: Antony Flew, *op. cit.*, p. 15.

[30] *Ibid.*, pp. 16–17.

Cf. "Final Discussion." In: D. F. Pears, *op. cit.*, pp. 142–164.

fore exist. In Chapter X on religious beliefs, we shall discuss the particular kind of ontologizing called the Ontological Argument, which purports to establish the existence of God. But ontologizing has also been used more generally, for example, by Spinoza. He begins his Ethics: "By cause of itself I understand that whose essence involves existence, or that whose nature cannot be conceived unless existing."[31]

Kant protests that existence is not a quality or a predicate. By this is meant that between a thing with a given quality and a thing without this quality there is a conceptual difference. An illustration would be Alexander drunk and Alexander sober. But, as Kant might argue, the difference between Alexander existent and Alexander non-existent is not a difference in the concept of Alexander at all. As far as essence is concerned, the merely possible and the actual Alexander are the same. Actuality or existence, then, is not what we conceive as an essence. If this is so, then there is no quality of existence that could entail existence. Therefore existence is not a quality included in our concept of Alexander. Further, the judgment positing the existence of something is synthetic, whereas the unpacking of a predicate from a subject is merely analytic.[32]

Most generally interpreted, ontologizing is involved when a metaphysician, from the basis of definitions alone, comes to conclusions about what is or is not in fact the case. Often scientists protest that philosophers are prone to make factual claims "from an armchair." This is a picturesque condemnation of anyone who spins out factual claims from his own private musings. It is indeed to be condemned generally as a method, even if the thinker in question cannot be pinned down to anything as precise as an ontological argument.

Francis Bacon wrote gracefully that

The men of experiment are like the ant: they only collect and use; the reasoners resemble spiders who make cobwebs out of their own substance. But the bee takes a middle course; it gathers its material from the flowers of the garden and of the field, but transforms and digests it by a power of its own.

It may seem incredible that apparently sober metaphysicians have tried to excogitate the universe—that is, without appeal to observable fact, and depending entirely upon the inner world of ideas, have claimed that things are thus and so. Little wonder that metaphysicians of this sort are suspected of being arbitrary and irresponsible, and even worse, ludicrously lacking

[31] Benedict de Spinoza, "Part One, of God," *Ethics, Preceded by On the Improvement of the Understanding.* Hafner Publishing Co., New York, 1949, Df. 1, p. 41.
[32] Immanuel Kant, *Critique of Pure Reason* (Norman Kemp Smith, tr.), Macmillan and Co., Ltd., London, 1933, pp. 504–505.

in the humor that forces most of us to distinguish the inner world of wish and fantasy from the outer world of hard and resisting "reality."

But is all metaphysics a flight of fancy, or less charitably, are all metaphysicians madmen? At least one point distinguishes them from most madmen and quite a few poets. This is that when metaphysicians postulate the nature of the unobservable whole or ultimate reality they do try to guide their speculation by logical principles. Certainly the deductive rationalists, who follow Parmenides who began with "Being is, and nonbeing is not," are trying to be rigorous, and do subject themselves to canons that most thinking men share. But this is not all, nor would it be sufficient. For the other side of the coin is that most metaphysicians have a strong respect for given matter of fact, although they call attention to our varied interpretations of "fact." Since man can by thinking come to understand unobservable connections among facts, and since, as Whitehead argues, there could be no science without logic, most philosophers intend to be bees rather than spiders. Some claim only to collect facts, but can anyone gather facts without having in mind a problem to which the facts are relevant, or better a hypothesis the facts tend to support or confute?

Hence we conclude our presentation of these three charges of fallacy against metaphysics with a qualification. Some metaphysicians grant all these charges as needed warnings, but persist in their faith that speculation can avoid sheer equivocation and the fallacies noted above. Whether this faith is justified is for the student to judge.

Now let us proceed to the second triad of fallacies that metaphysicians themselves have spotted in the terms, propositions, and arguments of their discipline. The first of these is often mentioned among general fallacies as *reification* or *hypostatization*, that is, taking a quality or relation or anything abstract as if it were something concrete and actual and substantial. Whitehead applied this brilliantly in metaphysics, to systems other than his own, and he called it the fallacy of misplaced concreteness.[33]

4. *The fallacy of misplaced concreteness.*

Many people do undoubtedly use abstract terms as if they were the names of concrete things. Instead of saying that some historians say so-and-so, they may say "History says so-and-so." It seems uncivil to reply to such a remark that history never said anything and never could, it is only a general name for the whole process and product of giving a reasoned

[33] Alfred North Whitehead, *Science and the Modern World*, Copyright 1925 by The Macmillan Company, copyright renewed 1953 by Evelyn Whitehead, and used with permission of The Macmillan Company and the Cambridge University Press, Chapter III.

account of the past. But such an uncivil attack is called for in metaphysics when, to such abstractions as "being" and "nothingness," are attributed the functions and processes of concrete space–time entities. It is not necessary to read far in metaphysics to find such use of terms, for example, in the claim that "nothingness embraces being," "nothingness challenges being," etc.

Whitehead's observation was not altogether original. The student will recall Aristotle's reason for parting company from Plato was that Plato regarded the forms or entities as real in themselves, more real than individuals like Socrates, which led him to argue that Socrates was an imitation of humanity. Whitehead's application to the alternative systems of the modern world is arresting and instructive. In company with many other philosophers, he interprets the sciences as more abstract than philosophy. The usual way of putting this is that each science takes account of certain aspects of what there is. Physics and chemistry leave life out of account, and all the sciences taking physics as their model, claims Whitehead, leave feeling and value out of account. Abstraction as a limitation of interest is good and necessary; otherwise we should be distracted from the simple regularities of law. But philosophies based on modern science have been nourished on scientific abstractions, rather than upon a far richer reality that requires also, according to Whitehead, the arts, religion, and history to reveal those aspects closed to experimental and theoretical science.

The enormous success of the scientific abstractions, yielding on the one hand *matter* with its *simple location* in space and time, on the other hand *mind*, perceiving, suffering, reasoning, but not interfering, has foisted onto philosophy the task of accepting them as the most concrete rendering of fact.

Thereby, modern philosophy has been ruined. It has oscillated in a complex manner between three extremes. There are the dualists, who accept matter and mind as on equal basis, and the two varieties of monists, those who put mind inside matter, and those who put matter inside mind. But this juggling with abstractions can never overcome the inherent confusion introduced by the ascription of *Misplaced Concreteness* to the scientific scheme of the seventeenth century.[34]

Descartes considered matter defined by one property, spatial extension, and this has proved inadequate in physics, yet some metaphysicians have thought they could get along with a borrowed conception of matter once useful in physics. The attempts to generate everything from matter, or the opposite—to generate everything from mind—are vitiated. And, claims Whitehead, even the two abstractions cannot be combined to yield the

[34] *Ibid.,* pp. 81–82.

concrete; "whenever a vicious dualism appears, it is by reason of mistaking an abstraction for a final concrete fact."[35]

It will be up to the student shortly to examine the materialistic conception of matter and the idealistic conception of mind to see whether they are indeed reifications, and further to see whether Whitehead has a non-fallacious alternative.

5. *Propositions of unrestricted generality; the fallacies of self-referential propositions.*

Metaphysical propositions are remarkable in their use of the universal quantifier. They are unlike generalizations such as biological statements about all bats. They are not restricted to all the instances of a certain sort, but characteristically are about all things. If it is true that everything is what it is, then the statement of this truth is what it is, and therefore there is only one truth, namely $A = A$, and the only thing to be true to is itself, otherwise there must be something else. Hence the world is unreal, or as metaphysicians say, mere appearance, and all difference and change are illusion. But there always seems to be something other than identity, if no more than this: the denial that there is anything else.

Hence the question, do all self-referential propositions lead to paradox? To put this another way, are all propositions of unrestricted generality bound to lead to the irresolvable situation that when they are true they are false, and when they are false they are true? Some logicians take pains to avoid propositions of the ancient model "The Cretan says all Cretans are liars." If logicians in their systems strive to avoid absurdity, why should metaphysicians do less?

Yet although the Darwinian theory is about species of organisms, the Newtonian theory about particles of matter and their relations, Whitehead's theory is about all theories, hence about itself. Plato's philosophy, you will recall, is among other things, about philosophy—that is the philosopher, his methods, his way of life.

This is a fruitful and important point to bear in mind. Many a metaphysic has seemed fallacious because it is like the sceptic's proposition that nothing can be known. Since this is familiar from the last chapter, consider the metaphysical scepticism of the proposition that nothing can exist. Just as, if nothing can be known, how can it be known that nothing can be known, we ask, if nothing can exist, what is thinking that nothing can exist? Systematic scepticism is self-refuting in that it quickly gives rise to its dogmatic opposite.

[35] Alfred North Whitehead, *Adventures of Ideas,* The Macmillan Co., New York, 1956, p. 245.

If metaphysicians urge us to have nothing to do with sceptical sophistry and incoherent solipsism, are their propositions really in a better way? One metaphysician, suspecting fallacy, urges us to ask of any first principle whether

. . . the fact of its truth would be compatible with the fact of its being *known* to be true. This is the appeal to educated and critical common sense which is meant by metaphysics: anything called by that name which turns out to be an appeal to anything else is only bad metaphysics.[36]

The student must examine metaphysical statements in the light of the paradoxes of self-reference that arise from propositions of unrestricted generality. We have oversimplified a logical issue on which some logicians claim to have refuted any metaphysical position. Yet other logicians formulate systems just for use by metaphysicians.[37] Briefly the point resembles Aristotle's. What is wrong with a philosopher's holding that he cannot reason about anything without the principles of identity, contradiction, and excluded middle, hence presupposing them even while he proposes them? Whether there is any vicious circularity in thinking in conformity with one's own principles leads us to the final point.

6. *The circularity of metaphysical systems; the fallacy of being viciously circular, that is, grounded only in themselves, hence inevitably dogmatic and claiming something called special privilege.*

We cannot, without 'begging the question', prove any proposition to be a true principle by the use of methods which themselves depend for their validity on assuming the proposition at stake. And yet we must have some test by which we can judge whether an assumed principle is itself true or not.[38]

Whitehead tells us that good metaphysics states its factual ground and demonstrates the coherence of its claims. But much metaphysics is called bad because it begs the question, having, that is, no ground but itself.

Descartes calls one argument that moves in a circle, "vicious" because it appears to demonstrate the existence of God, but merely restates the assumption.

Although it is absolutely true that we must believe that there is a God, because we are so taught in Holy Scriptures, and, on the other hand, that we must believe in Holy Scriptures because they come from God (the reason of this, that, faith being a gift of God, He who gives the grace to cause us to be-

[36] A. E. Taylor, *Does God Exist?*, Macmillan and Co. Ltd., London, 1948, p. 18.
[37] F. B. Fitch, *Symbolic Logic: An Introduction*, The Ronald Press Co., New York, 1952; we are deeply indebted to Appendix C, "Self-Reference in Philosophy," an article in *Mind*, Vol. 55, n.s., 1946, pp. 64–73.
[38] A. E. Taylor, *op. cit.*, p. 18.

lieve other things can likewise give it to cause us to believe that He exists), we nevertheless could not place this argument before infidels, who might accuse us of reasoning in a circle.[39]

But how can there be a metaphysical argument, especially one that sets out to include everything, without circularity?

Writing of his first book, Reality, Paul Weiss presents systematically the essential features of knowledge and nature. In trying to rely only on the world as portrayed in the system, and in trying to avoid assuming anything outside the system, the author confesses gladly to the circularity of the system. "It maintained that knowledge and nature presupposed one another, making the philosophic enterprise a circle, but one large enough to encompass all forms of thought and reality."[40]

Whitehead's alternative to Weiss was to claim that his own system was but one of many possible interpretations, and would be superseded. Weiss is truer to the traditional claims of a closed or absolute system.

It is a common mistake to suppose that there is something invalid in a circular argument. Logically viewed it is unimpeachable. A conclusion which repeats the premise, conforms neatly to the requirements of the most stringent logic. What is wrong with a circular argument is that it is often uninformative, coming back to its beginning too quickly. But if its circle is all-inclusive, if it encompasses all there is, it does all that a philosophic system demands.

Weiss goes on to consider non-circular methods. One of these is the linear deduction from one or a few truths. But this would require getting first principles directly, and therefore needs the assumption of an intuitive grasp of principles apart from everything to which they apply. Another is simply to describe what one finds. But this empirical method can never inductively arrive at "tests, limits, or principle of order." It may merely assume systematic background, or disallow justification. And surely this is failure in metaphysics. The way to test a theory of knowledge is to examine whether the world can be known within the theoretical framework.

An adequate theory of knowledge presupposes a grasp of what is the case, and an adequate account of reality presupposes an understanding of what is reasonable, certifiable, and certified, and what is not. An epistemology presupposes an ontology, and conversely. Many coherent systems are possible, however. Circular systematic philosophies in which an epistemology grounds an ontology and conversely, must be tested by their capacity to ground an ade-

[39] René Descartes, The Philosophical Works (Elizabeth Haldane and G. R. T. Ross, trs.), Dover Publications, Inc., New York, Vol. I, p. 133.
[40] Paul Weiss, Modes of Being, Southern Illinois Press, Carbondale, Illinois, 1958, p. 8.

quate theoretical and practical ethics, politics, history, art, and good common sense. The test of a philosophy is the understanding and wisdom it sustains and clarifies.[41]

In our presentation of the last three alleged fallacies we have followed metaphysicians who are keenly anxious to avoid fallacy in their use of terms, propositions, and arguments. But we have not exhausted the subject of the alleged fallaciousness of metaphysics.[42]

III. Defense of Metaphysics

1. *That anti-metaphysicians are themselves metaphysicians.*

Arguments in defense of metaphysics seem at first more complex and diverse than the arguments against metaphysics. Indeed the most common argument is that the supposed anti-metaphysician is himself also a metaphysician. This is complex, since the defender takes it upon himself to state what he thinks are the ontological commitments of his opponent's conceptual scheme. The argument often takes the form of "you're another," called by logicians *tu quoque*. The clearest and most common example takes Hume's philosophy as an implicit ontology and a speculative system. If the argument could persuade any Humean, he should then draw the conclusion that his own position also is but "sophistry and illusion." The student may recall that Hume attacked as useless, indemonstrable, and gratuitous the belief in substances beyond our sense-impressions. But, goes the metaphysician's argument, Hume's world is made up of individual sense-impressions, and the attack upon the reality of an unperceived thing rests on the assumption of the reality of ideas. Then runs the defense, if a Platonist seems to overcomplicate the world by the principle that sensed things are copies of the forms, a Humean would oversimplify it by the principle that sensed things are all there is, according to the familiar phenomenalist doctrine that material objects are nothing but collections of sense-impressions. Both Plato and Hume are answering the same quandary about the material world, and the alternative answers are

---

[41] *Ibid.*, pp. 84–85.
[42] An instructive set of fallacies found in the anti-metaphysical arguments can be found in Everett W. Hall, "Metaphysics." In Dagobert D. Runes (ed.), *Twentieth Century Philosophy*, Philosophical Library, Inc., New York, 1943, especially pp. 175–183.

An odd lot of fallacies, mostly in metaphysical positions the author dislikes, is found indexed in James K. Feibleman, *Ontology*, Johns Hopkins Press, Baltimore, 1951.

You may profitably turn back to Chapter III, Section IV, on some common fallacies, and to later sections on fallacies of historical belief, fallacies of political belief, the section on the ontological argument in the chapter on religious beliefs, fallacies in our beliefs about aesthetic values, and fallacies in our beliefs about ethical values.

not simply metaphysical and anti-metaphysical. If one is metaphysical, so is the other.[43]

2. *That attacks are periodic and on various illusory answers.*

Another defense is quite common. It runs thus: Attacks upon metaphysics are periodic in the history of philosophy. The anti-metaphysician supposes that after his refutation, metaphysics will at last be finally abandoned.

The sceptics of the later Classical period abolished it. It revived in the form of Neoplatonism and of Christian metaphysical theology. In the 18th century Hume abolished it, and Kant imposed the most drastic restrictions upon it. But not for long. It arose again, more vigorous than ever, in the great speculative systems of the Romantic period. The Positivists and Agnostics of the later 19th century abolished it once more; and once more it revived in the speculative systems of Bergson, Alexander, and Whitehead.[44]

What is the moral? Some, with Price, say that men have the need for a general scheme of things mapping more kinds of facts than any scientific scheme. Another way of putting the point is that numerous answers to metaphysical questions are indeed illusory, but repeated failure cannot condemn the quest itself. The failures can only discredit certain answers to the question, but not the question itself. This way of answering is very common among Thomists who share with positivists a dislike of idealists because they attempt to deduce existence from essence. But the Thomist believes that he can replace false metaphysics with true.

3. *That the questions of metaphysics are genuine and not merely verbal.*

We may tie together these two first defenses by saying that the metaphysical quest has not been ended by citing failures, and that those who intend to abolish false conclusions based on inadequate data or fallacious arguments may be rejecting error so that truth may prevail. The anti-metaphysician would not protest so vigorously against deception if he were not deeply concerned to find out what there is, and to know it. Thus one might take one further step; anti-metaphysics is evidence that the metaphysical quest is inevitable and cannot be cut short without satisfying answers.

Observe that metaphysicians persist in regarding their statements as meaningful, and therefore capable of being true or false. The arguments spring from a decision as to whether there are genuine metaphysical questions. For all his attack upon illusory answers, Kant could not decide other than affirmatively. Basically the problem is one that can be stated only

[43] D. F. Pears (ed.), *op. cit.*, pp. 10, 18–19.
[44] H. H. Price, "Clarity Is Not Enough," *Proceedings of the Aristotelian Society*, Supplementary Vol. 19, 1945.

personally. The anti-metaphysician is saying: "Admit that your questions spring from puzzles about words." The metaphysician replies: "I deny that my questions are only about words." The metaphysician at this point can only retort *ad hominem* "Admit that you must ask what is real over against what is not real." The common reply of many anti-metaphysicians seems to be "This is no task a philosopher should accept." And to this metaphysicians reply "Not to consider reality is to fail in the distinctive and historic role of philosophy."

4. *That metaphysics can be useful because speculation in the past proved useful.*

What of the argument that metaphysical schemes are useless? One attack upon metaphysics on pragmatic grounds comes from the religious reformer of India, Gautama Buddha. His interest was solely in reducing misery, not in trying to answer whether or not the world is eternal. We often meet people who cannot see that speculation will make men better. But generally now the critic takes scientific theories as his norm of profitable thought. The defender may therefore argue that some particular past metaphysics proved a stimulus to science.

The metaphysical view of nature put forward by Descartes—that the physical world is a system of extended material bodies, mechanically interacting and endowed only with measurable qualities—at once stimulated and established the terms of reference of seventeenth-century physics. And it might be argued that the metaphysics of Hegel had a comparable influence on historical studies in the nineteenth century.[45]

In an interesting article Philip Merlan has suggested that it can be shown historically that metaphysical speculation has had an important and useful role in the growth of the sciences. Thus against those scientists who reject metaphysics, the metaphysician assets the right to say:

I precede you in that I anticipate what later will be a scientific theory, and I precede you in that I provide you with a frame of reference which will make it possible for you to understand what you are doing, although I formed my concepts before you were doing it. My realm is the realm of possibilities, preceding your actualities. I do not deny the right of my more modest colleague to clean up after you. May I, however, claim the privilege of lighting up a multiplicity of paths in front of you, on any of which you may find yourself walking one day? If you ask me what the source of my light is, perhaps it wouldn't be immodest to reply: Never mind, just assume it is illegitimate contraband—but, legitimate or not, it does give light.[46]

[45] Anthony Quinton, *The Nature of Metaphysics,* D. F. Pears (ed.), Macmillan and Co. Ltd., London, 1957.
[46] Philip Merlan, "Metaphysics and Science—Some Remarks," *The Journal of Philosophy,* Vol. 56, No. 14, 1959, p. 618.

Of course the defense needs to assume that our own age is not unlike the specified former period, and that such stimulation could come only from metaphysics. The debate has made philosophers aware that it is not easy to distinguish between a metaphysical first principle and an assumption of science.

5. *That the verifiability test reveals that science and metaphysics are interrelated and overlap.*

What of the argument that metaphysical statements are meaningless? The meaning criterion was intended to draw the distinction between scientific statements and metaphysical statements. The problem is how to distinguish between them so that no sentence will possibly be on both sides of the line. Does the verifiability test remove all doubt? Clearly not in the case of axioms. If "meaningful" means belonging to empirical science, then the statement that metaphysical statements are not meaningful is trivial, because metaphysics is defined by positivists and many others as something not attainable by sense-observation. A philosopher close to the Vienna Circle—logical empiricists who developed the ideas we quoted earlier from Ayer—expressed his alarm about the damage of the verifiability test to science:

. . . In their anxiety to annihilate metaphysics [logical empiricists] annihilate natural science along with it. For scientific laws, too, cannot be logically reduced to elementary statements of experience.[47]

I am inclined to think that scientific discovery is impossible without faith in ideas which are of a purely speculative kind, and sometimes even quite hazy; a faith which is completely unwarranted from the point of view of science. . . .[48]

6. *That there are meaningful beliefs that are not empirically verifiable.*

A succinct summary of the great to-do about the meaninglessness of metaphysics from a defender of metaphysics follows: "The alleged distinction between meaningful and meaningless statements shows itself, when scrutinized, to contain a real distinction between statements that mean in one way, and statements which do not mean in that way."[49] Another way of making the same point is to take such a common belief as, for example, that other persons are conscious. If one is sure that it is meaningful to ask whether other persons are conscious or not, then one cannot accept the verifiability criterion of meaning. So runs the argument:

[47] Karl Popper, *The Logic of Scientific Discovery*, Basic Books, Inc., New York, 1959, p. 36. (Translation of *Logik der Forschung*, Vienna, 1935.)
[48] *Ibid.*, p. 38.
[49] Winston H. E. Barnes, *The Philosophical Predicament*, Beacon Press, Inc., Boston, 1950, p. 166.

The existence of other minds is . . . meaningful. I cannot verify your consciousness, and therefore, on the verificational view, my statement that you are
conscious is without meaning. But "consciousness" is a concept which has application in experience. I experience *my own* consciousness. Therefore it has
meaning to attribute this same experiencible [sic] character of myself to
you. The fact that it is impossible for me to experience your particular consciousness is . . . irrelevant. . . .[50]

The author adds that the question of the similarity of one's sensations and
another's is meaningful, even "though the answer to it may be impossible
to discover." The further step is for the student to discover just what is his
criterion of meaning. This is more difficult, and should be clarified as he
develops his metaphysical beliefs, if he is convinced that he holds any, and
if he is convinced that they are worth making explicit.

We have now given six defenses of metaphysics:

1. That anti-metaphysicians are themselves metaphysicians.
2. That attacks are periodic and on various illusory answers.
3. That the questions of metaphysics are genuine and not merely verbal.
4. That metaphysics can be useful because speculation in the past proved
   useful.
5. That the verifiability test reveals that science and metaphysics are interrelated and overlap.
6. That there are meaningful beliefs that are not empirically verifiable.

A metaphysician might adopt all six of these above defenses coherently. But there are other defenses that exclude one another. Put another
way, one might claim either, but not both, of the following:

7. That metaphysics is indeed, as positivists have claimed, utterly different from science, and like poetry, but that you chose to do metaphysics
   in this way.
8. That metaphysics can be stated as hypotheses which can be attested
   by experience.

After explaining the diversity between these two ways of doing metaphysics, we shall proceed to sketch briefly other alternatives that our contemporaries find to be live options. These are:

9. A descriptive account of beliefs is safe from attack on the ground of
   fallacy.

[50] W. T. Stace, "Metaphysics and Meaning," *Mind*, Vol. 44, No. 176, 1935. Reprinted
in Paul Edwards and Arthur Pap, *op. cit.*, p. 574.

10. A simple ontology can be stated in a logically faultless way.
11. Metaphysics is the historical science of uncovering the absolute presuppositions that underlie the factual sciences.
12. Metaphysics is a matter of fundamental rules called metaphysical directives, such as guide a scientist's search for laws of nature or probabilities.

7. *That metaphysics is indeed, as positivists have claimed, utterly different from science, and like poetry, but that you chose to do metaphysics in this way.*

One of the ways of meeting this attack is to say that metaphysics is like poetry, and to proceed to do metaphysics in this manner.

Heidegger, in "What is Metaphysics?" characterizes science as dealing in a specific manner with what is, and allowing "the object itself the first and last word." But because science limits itself to what is, "science wishes to know nothing of Nothing."[51] Such a defense of metaphysics seems to run counter to the logical rule that one should avoid the contradiction involved in postulating nothing as something.

How can nothing be known? Everything we know is something, but nothing can be "revealed" to us or we can "encounter" nothing. Heidegger states his case:

This may and actually does occur, albeit rather seldom and for moments only, in the key mood of dread (Angst). . . . And although dread is always "dread of", it is not dread of this or that. "Dread of" is always a dreadful feeling "about"—but not about this or that. The indefiniteness of *what* we dread is not just lack of definition: it represents the essential impossibility of defining the "what". . . . Dread reveals Nothing.[52]

How should one read such a "revelation"? Heidegger answers: not as science, but as poetry. Hence the eloquent conclusion:

Out of long-guarded speechlessness and the careful clarification of the field thus cleared, comes the utterance of the thinker. Of like origin is the naming of the poet. But since like is only like insofar as difference allows, and since poetry and thinking are most purely alike in their care of the word, the two things are at the same time at opposite poles in their essence. The thinker utters Being. The poet names what is holy.

We may know something about the relations between philosophy and poetry, but we know nothing of the dialogue between poet and thinker, who "dwell near to one another on mountains farthest apart".

One of the essential theatres of speechlessness is dread in the sense of the

---

[51] Martin Heidegger, *Existence and Being*, Henry Regnery Co., Chicago, Illinois, 1949, p. 357, p. 359.
[52] *Ibid.*, pp. 362, 365–366.

terror into which the abyss of Nothing plunges us. Nothing, conceived as the pure "Other" than what-is, is the veil of Being. In Being all that comes to pass in what-is is perfected from everlasting.[53]

8. *That metaphysics can be stated as hypotheses, which can be attested by experience.*

Some philosophers could not consistently do metaphysics as poetry, that is, on the basis of revelation, without claiming that what they believe is true to fact. An excellent statement comes from Ernest Nagel. He likes to call his view *naturalism,* but says that the label itself is of no importance.

I prefer not to accept in philosophic debate what I do not believe when I am not arguing; and naturalism as I construe it merely formulates what centuries of human experience have repeatedly confirmed. At any rate, naturalism seems to me a sound generalized account of the world encountered in practice and in critical reflection, and a just perspective upon the human scene.[54]

This philosopher asserts two theses about nature: first, that events depend on the organization of bodies in space and time; and second, that there are many things in contingent rather than logically necessary relations. These statements may be taken as hypotheses and tested in experience. They are not physical theories as exact as Newton's axioms of motion, or competitors of any scientific theory, or underpinnings of science known in special ways. If one can admit these hypotheses as the "best tested conclusions of experience," then the problem of the usefulness, the cognitive and logical possibility, and the systematic nature of metaphysics is solved. We will have fuller exposition of this aspect of Nagel's philosophy in the next chapter.

Another part of this position is the claim that every man lives "within the framework of certain comprehensive if not always explicit assumptions about the world" he inhabits. If the linguistic analyst refuses to make the assumptions of his analysis explicit, and if it is philosophy that makes tacit beliefs explicit, then the analyst is evading his philosophical duty.[55]

Quite different from the revelation of being (Heidegger) or the confirmation of hypotheses about events (Nagel) are two linguistic methods of doing metaphysics. One is from a representative of those British phi-

[53] *Ibid.,* pp. 391–392.
[54] Ernest Nagel, "Naturalism Reconsidered." In Yervant H. Krikorian and Abraham Edel (eds.), *Contemporary Philosophic Problems,* The Macmillan Co., New York, 1959, p. 339.
[55] *Ibid.*

losophers who analyze ordinary use of language. The other is from a philosopher who develops systems of mathematical logic.

9. *A descriptive account of beliefs is safe from attack on the ground of fallacy.*

An analysis of ordinary beliefs shows that we accord bodies and persons the central position among particulars. In Chapter V we discussed our knowledge of material objects and our knowledge of other minds. These are the things in space and time about which people make statements. A philosopher of ordinary language promises no new truth about the world, only a rational account of "beliefs, and stubbornly held ones, of many people, at a primitive level of reflection, and of some philosophers at a more sophisticated level of reflection. . . ." What of the arguments against the dualistic scheme of things and persons?

It is difficult to see how such beliefs could be argued for except by showing their consonance with the conceptual scheme in which we operate, by showing how they reflect the structure of that scheme. So if metaphysics is the finding of reasons, good, bad or indifferent, for what we believe on instinct, then this has been metaphysics.[56]

A descriptive account of beliefs is quite safe from attack on the ground of fallacy. Where there is no argument, there cannot be a misleading argument. Strawson denies nothing, comparable to the naturalist's denial of immaterial mind and God. He brings no new revelation; only a way of getting clear what people believe, and this is a task of metaphysics.

10. *A simple ontology can be stated in a logically faultless way.*

We hope the student will recall from Chapter IV the contribution of Tarski to the understanding of the use of the word "true." Another symbolic logician, Willard Quine, undertakes the clarification of such phrases as "there is" or "there are." Tarski had said that to make a true sentence about John, as in "John is tall," we need a name for John. Otherwise we could not mention the thing or object that John is. But are all names to be included in the object-language? That is, are all names references to objects? Of course we have little or no trouble with tables, dogs, trees, mountains, and so on—they all refer to what there is. But the noun "truth" is not in the object-language according to Tarski. If we should believe that every noun, however abstract, refers to some real object we would be lining up with the Platonists. Thus we could put Plato's view in this way: in the sentence "John is tall" we are saying that John participates in tallness, and this is true because there are two objects, "John" and "tallness."

[56] P. F. Strawson, *Individuals*, Methuen & Co., Ltd., London, 1959, p. 247.

There is also a contradictory position, which has already been discussed, called nominalism (as distinct from the above realism). This view claims that some nouns at least do not mention objects, and that only particulars exist, hence, "John is tall" mentions only John. Unhappily Tarski's theory sheds no light on the things designated by true object-sentences. This criticism calls attention to the fact that his semantics raises metaphysical questions, although it does not investigate alternative solutions. Hence the importance of Quine's work, which asks whether certain nouns are nouns in our object-language, for example, Pegasus, round-squares, possible fat men, and possible bald men. These certainly are unusual, for we cannot perceive any of them, or ascribe to them any physical properties.

Much credit for the logical work on these problems also goes to Bertrand Russell, who puzzles about the meaning of the sentence, "the present King of France is bald." We would ordinarily understand "the King of France" to be a descriptive phrase doing the job of a name, that is, functioning as a demonstrative symbol. But this cannot really be the case, because there is no present King of France to be named. So Russell comes to suspect the realistic assumptions that there are subsistent entities, and also any metaphysics that seems to rest on the naive assumption that all descriptive phrases and names are references to entities. For even to say "Round-squares cannot exist" seems to say of these very odd things that they *are* nonexistent and impossible. If metaphysics, and its presuppositions of this kind, is the way into a mare's nest, then perhaps linguistic analysis is the way out. Ayer suggests that a translation from "The round-square cannot exist" to "No one thing can be both square and round," illustrates "the way in which any definite descriptive phrase which occurs as the subject of a negative existential sentence can be eliminated."[57]

It may seem fantastic to say, as Russell and Quine do, that all names are eliminable. The habit of naming objects and believing that the world is made up of these named objects is indeed strong.

We are prone to talk and think of objects. Physical objects are the obvious illustrations when the illustrative mood is on us, but there are also all the abstract objects, or so there purport to be: the states and qualities, numbers, attributes, classes. We persist in breaking reality down, somehow, into a multiplicity of identifiable and discriminable objects, to be referred to by singular and general terms. We talk so inveterately of objects that to say we do so seems almost to say nothing at all; for how else is there to talk?[58]

[57] Alfred Jules Ayer, *Language, Truth and Logic*, Dover Publications, Inc., New York, p. 61. By permission of the author, Dover Publications, and Victor Gollancz, Ltd., London.
[58] W. V. Quine, "Speaking of Objects," *Proceedings and Addresses of the American Philosophical Association, 1957–1958*, Vol. 31, 1958, p. 5.

Just as Tarski showed us that since we can say "The sentence 'John is tall' is true" and have no need of the noun "truth" so we can now say that the name Bertrand Russell can be eliminated by saying, "the author of 'the theory of description,'" and W. Quine can be eliminated in favor of "the author of 'On What There Is.'" Although this seems to complicate our language, it also prevents us from being committed by language to belief in objects that are not in space and time. The noun "nothing" even when we say "what is not," seems to commit us to belief in the being of nothing.

This is the old Platonic riddle of non-being. Non-being must in some sense be, otherwise what is it that there is not? This tangled doctrine might be nick-named Plato's beard; historically it has proved tough, frequently dulling the edge of Occam's razor.[59]

The belief that every name refers to an object results in a "bloated" or "overpopulated universe."

It offends the aesthetic sense of us who have a taste for desert landscapes, but this is not the worst of it. [The] slum of possibles is a breeding ground for disorderly elements. Take, for instance, the possible fat man in that doorway; and, again, the possible bald man in that doorway. Are they the same possible man, or two possible men? How do we decide? How many possible men are there in that doorway? Are there more possible thin ones than fat ones? How many of them are alike? Or would their being alike make them one? Are no *two* possible things alike? Is this the same as saying that it is impossible for two things to be alike? Or, finally, is the concept of identity simply inapplicable to unactualized possibles? But what sense can be found in talking of entities which cannot meaningfully be said to be identical with themselves and distinct from one another.[60]

We cannot go further here with Quine's analysis. Rather more equipment in logic is required to understand and appreciate his further contributions. But at least we can say that with his logical tools he tries to cut away from metaphysics all commitment to a reality that he thinks merely clutters up our world of beliefs. His method is primarily to scrutinize those remarks one uses to *say* that something exists. If these cannot stand up under the assault of logic then we must revise our statements and presumably also our beliefs. It is quite clear that Quine himself would prefer a metaphysical view as simple and compelling as a logical scheme—a world in which there are no nonsense objects, such as round-squares, indistinguishable possible objects, such as possible fat or bald

[59] W. V. Quine, "On What There Is," *Review of Metaphysics*, Vol. 2, 1948, p. 21.
[60] *Ibid.*, pp. 23–24.

men, or mythological objects, such as Pegasus, or Platonic objects, such as universal beauty and justice.

Thus it would seem that a metaphysics or ontology that asserts the existence of physical objects and minds would be sufficient. Other metaphysicians might think that Quine's ontological picture of the world is too thin, flat, and monotonous, that he ignores the richness of possibilities and squeezes out the vital drama of events and existence by the pressure of his logical devices. But there must always be champions of clarity and enemies of obscurantism in philosophy. If at times Quine's clarity is not quite clear, we at least know which side he is on.

Two other ways of doing metaphysics have been proposed by contemporary philosophers which, in their opinion, avoid the usual complaints and charges. Let us examine them briefly.

11. *Metaphysics is the historical science of uncovering the absolute presuppositions that underlie the factual sciences.*

One of the most interesting reconsiderations of metaphysics comes from R. G. Collingwood, who, as we shall see in Chapter VIII, is noted for an equal interest in history. He begins by disarming the opponents of metaphysics, that is, he too would deny that there can be a science of being as such. Aristotle, says Collingwood, tried to reach the furthest abstraction, namely, pure being. But if we could get to this, Collingwood declares, it could not be distinguished from nothing. Pure being as the absence of all characteristics is just nothing; since nothing cannot be described there can be no knowledge, much less organized knowledge of this abstract being. He has as much fun with his jibes at metaphysics as does a positivist. The following is not his ideal of a valid argument, nor his final view:

Metaphysics is the name given to the non-existent science of a non-existent subject matter. Now I will not deny that a book professing to be a metaphysical treatise may contain valuable truths; but so far as what it contains is true it is not metaphysics, and so far as it is metaphysics it is not true; therefore everything in the book is either irrelevant or untrue, so nothing in it is worth reading.[61]

What is there, then, for a metaphysician to investigate? Collingwood finds that in the process of asking and answering questions there are certain presuppositions, that is, beliefs without which we could not ask the questions we do ask nor set about answering them. To disclose these presuppositions is the task of metaphysics.

[61] R. G. Collingwood, *An Essay on Metaphysics*, The Clarendon Press, Oxford, 1957, p. 19.

I write these words sitting on the deck of a ship. I lift my eyes and see a piece of string—a line, I must call it at sea—stretched more or less horizontally above me. I find myself thinking 'that is a clothesline', meaning that it was put there to hang washing on. When I decide that it was put there for that purpose I am presupposing that it was put there for some purpose. Only if that presupposition is made does the question arise, what purpose? If that presupposition were not made . . . that question would not have arisen.[62]

As a matter of fact, men in different ages have had various sets of presuppositions. It is not the duty of a metaphysician to determine which of these three sentences is true: Some events have causes. All events have causes. No events have causes. "Each is important, and fundamentally important, to the science that makes it, because it determines the entire structure of that science by determining the questions that arise in it, and therefore determining the possible answers." But the question of being true or being thought true is not raised by these presuppositions. They need only to be supposed. To inquire into the truth of a presupposition is to assume that it is not an absolute presupposition, but a relative presupposition. Any question of right to presuppose is a nonsense question. Nor is it the business of a metaphysician to propound a presupposition, nor a scientist's business to verify one. The scientist presupposes, and the metaphysician "propounds the proposition that this or that one of them is presupposed."[63]

12. *Metaphysics is a matter of fundamental rules called metaphysical directives, such as guide a scientist's search for laws of nature or probabilities.*

Our last alternative way of doing metaphysics, in such a way as to meet the contemporary attacks, is to conceive metaphysical principles as rules that give direction in our search for knowledge. Körner's conception regards positivistic anti-metaphysics as one set of beliefs among many alternatives open to us. In other words, as was said at the beginning of this section on defense of metaphysics, there is no genuine choice of whether to hold basic beliefs. There is only the choice of which basic beliefs to hold.

In developing his position Körner appeals to the common distinction between what we observe and how we interpret the world. "A soldier in the field will be careful to distinguish clearly between what appears to be a moving branch and his interpretation of it as an actual moving branch."[64]

[62] *Ibid.*, pp. 21–22.
[63] *Ibid.*, p. 33.
[64] S. Körner, "Some Types of Philosophical Thinking." In: C. A. Mace (ed.), *British Philosophy at Mid-Century*, George Allen & Unwin, Ltd., London, 1957, p. 116.

We should begin our metaphysical research with actual cases of such dis-crimination and not with "those cross-roads whose uninformative sign-posts are inscribed 'materialism,' 'realism,' 'idealism' (absolute and sub-jective), 'pragmatism' or something-or-other-ism."[65] Then what can we establish? Körner thinks that philosophers of opposed schools largely agree about the world as observed. Therefore what philosophers disagree about is interpretation. It is in interpretation that we simplify man, for example, as a selling and buying animal, into economic man motivated, some theories assume, by self-interest alone.

Now the crucial questions: Is the analysis of philosophers who claimed, as we saw, to hold no metaphysical beliefs, wholly observational? Is sci-ence itself wholly observational? To the first question, on philosophical analysis, Körner answers no. An analytical philosopher begins with a way of speaking—"Unicorns do not exist," for example—that he judges defec-tive, and ends with a way of speaking that he thinks is proper. Körner's point is that the analyst has criteria by which to judge defectiveness. In the light of these criteria he suggests proper statements to replace mislead-ing ones. And if the analyst were pressed to justify his criteria, he would no longer be analyzing language. He would be giving philosophical argu-ments for some metaphysical beliefs.

The second question, whether science is without metaphysical direction, is answered also with a no. Evidence for this is found in a letter from one physicist to another, namely in Einstein's comment on Born's Natural Phi-losophy of Cause and Chance:

You believe in the dice-playing god, and I in the perfect rule of law in a world of something objectively existing which I try to catch in a widely specu-lative way. . . . The great initial success of quantum theory cannot convert me to believe in that fundamental game of dice . . . I am absolutely convinced that one will eventually arrive at a theory in which the objects connected by laws are not probabilities, but conceived facts, as one took for granted only a short time ago. However, I cannot provide logical arguments for my convic-tions. . . .

If Einstein is making explicit the relation between metaphysics and science, then we should conclude that "metaphysical beliefs . . . give di-rection to his whole theoretical endeavour."[66]

Collingwood would go this far in his science of absolute presupposi-tions, but Körner would have the metaphysician go further.

[65] *Ibid.*, p. 117.
[66] *Ibid.*, pp. 123–124.

Once the metaphysical directives which are implicitly accepted by a group of thinkers, usually a very large group, are made explicit, a new kind of philosophical problem arises. It may be that the system of these directives is inconsistent, vague, incomplete or that it is adequate to some non-philosophical theories only. In short, when the critical task is fulfilled and the implicitly accepted directives are made explicit there often arises the new task of reconstructing the system of these directives.[67]

Why must metaphysics be systematic, revisionary, as well as descriptive? Here our author goes beyond the last five alternatives. Our categories in scientific inquiries are often inconsistent with the categories applied in moral thinking.

This real or apparent clash can be made quite clear, if we imagine a judge, who happens to be also a scientist concerned with developing a scientific theory of human behaviour. . . . In the morning he will assume that the persons whom he sends to prison for having committed a crime were free to do otherwise and are therefore responsible for their actions. In the afternoon, in the laboratory, he will try to explain the behaviour of his subjects, and indeed all human behaviour, on the assumption that anybody who performs any action is not free to do otherwise and in this sense not responsible.

Such a difficulty calls for the harmonization of metaphysical problems. One might deny moral responsibility by asserting the scientific cause. But why? Is it because mechanistic directives are successful instruments of prediction? If so, then the principle of verification is implicitly one metaphysical scheme rather than another.[68]

If this analysis is true, then it follows that the positivist antimetaphysician is guilty of all the fallacies with which he has taxed metaphysics. He has argued circularly, assuming implicitly in the meaning-criterion a view of causality. He has taken the abstractions of science to be the concrete world. He has argued from the essence of meaning to what there can and cannot be in the world. He has extended the scientific scheme to areas to which it may not apply. He has constructed a system that would make unintelligible the choice of the meaning-criterion itself.

IV. Criteria of Reality

The distinction between appearance and reality is common enough. Many words in the English language suggest it, for example, mirage, illusion, and apparition. An appearance is sometimes regarded in different ways. First, it may be transient, shifting, changing. One cannot rely upon

[67] *Ibid.*, p. 125.
[68] *Ibid.*, pp. 125–126.

it either for judgment or action because the next moment or the next day it will have passed away or have been so modified as not to be the same appearance. This, however, does not take us very far, for there are many philosophies that stress the changing world as the real world.

Secondly, it is sometimes thought that appearances are of less value than the real. That is why we welcome a "real" friend and are hurt when he turns out to be only a friend in appearance. So the desert wanderer gives way to anguish when the appearing stream is found to be just more sand. But the fact that we do not accord value to something does not mean that it lacks a kind of reality.

Thirdly, it may be said that an appearance is unreal because it has no causal efficacy, that is, it is not an agent or power in its own right. But we do know that whether there are ghosts or not, some people are frightened by them and others are tormented by "voices" when there are no real voices.

Finally, an appearance is often regarded as something wholly dependent. It has no existence in itself. It depends for its seeming existence upon something else and it cannot come to be or continue to be without the presence and operation of "something" of which it is the appearance, or someone to whom it is appearing. But again there are many things we take as real even though they depend upon something else for their reality. In our world children must have had parents.

This brief analysis should show that it is just as difficult to say what appearance is as to say what reality is. Nevertheless, it is usually reality that the metaphysician is after. Let us examine some of the major alternative beliefs about this elusive goal.

Before discussing some proposed criteria of reality, perhaps a word of caution about the term "reality" would not be out of place. Some philosophers, distressed with its ambiguity, have strongly recommended that we cease using the term. Still, if philosophers abandoned all ambiguous and vague terms, philosophy itself might have to be abandoned. It is better to proceed carefully, recognizing the need of some undefined terms, but using the instrument of definition wherever possible to clear the way. One philosopher, understanding how tricky "reality" is, wrote the following:

The term "reality" . . . is intellectually agile. It tends to play tricks with one's prejudices and to lead desire on a merry chase. For to denominate anything real is usually to import a distinction, and to consign, thereby, something else to the region of appearance. Could we keep the region of appearance from becoming populated, it might remain nothing more than the natural negative implication of a region of positive interest. But reality, once a king, makes many exiles who crave and seek citizenship in the land from which they have been banished. The term "reality," therefore, should inspire caution instead of confidence in metaphysics—a lesson which history has abundantly illustrated, but which man is slow to learn. Contrast those imposing products of human fancy which we call materialism and idealism, each relegating the other to the region of appearance, and what are they at bottom but an exalted prejudice for matter and an exalted prejudice for mind?

And had not their conflict been spectacular, as armies with banners, what a pitiable spectacle it would have presented, since a child's first thought destroys the one, and every smallest grain of sand the other? No; everything is somehow real; and to make distinctions within that realm demands caution and hesitation.[69]

Now if it is true that what is taken as real is a kind of "exalted prejudice" and that "x is real" means "I prefer x to y," then some philosophers would object. Whatever reality is, they would say, it must be the same for everyone. If there is anything at all, it may appear different to different people at different times, but it nevertheless is what it is, and thus is not a result of prejudice, no matter how exalted.

There is, of course, a peculiarity about any term that applies to everything as when we say "Everything is somehow real," or "Everything is a thing," or "Everything is an event," or "Everything has being." If everything is, must we say with Plato that even non-being is? Moreover how could we define this term that applies to everything? For to define is to state a difference. Hence it is often said that "thing," "entity," "being," "reality," and "existence" are indefinable. Nevertheless metaphysicians have undertaken to say what the real is. Let us look at a few ancient and modern attempts.

A. Aristotle

There have always been contrasts among reflective men when they seek to answer the question "What is real?" The ancient Greeks sought out the causes or principles of reality, and by the time of Aristotle, as we recounted earlier, there were well-defined cleavages of belief. The thread of all these arguments, he tells us, is to discover substance underlying change, or essence that allows alteration in accident.

Of the first philosophers, then, most thought the principles which were of the nature of matter were the only principles of all things. That of which all things that are consist, the first from which they come to be, the last into which they are resolved (the substance remaining, but changing in its modifications), this they say is the element and this the principle of things, and therefore they think nothing is either generated or destroyed, since this sort of entity is always conserved, as we say Socrates neither comes to be absolutely when he comes to be beautiful or musical, nor ceases to be when he loses these characteristics, because the substratum, Socrates himself, remains. . . . Yet they do not all agree as to the number and nature of these principles.[70]

The metaphysical substance is symbolized by the noun "Socrates," and the metaphysical attribute is symbolized by the adjective, "beautiful," and the proposition "Socrates is beautiful," corresponds, if it is true, to the complete fact. It seems common sense to say that Socrates can be, without being beautiful (and indeed he was judged ugly), but beautiful cannot be unless something is beautiful. The point about independent and dependent reality was made by Alice in Lewis Caroll's Wonderland. When the cat "vanished quite slowly, beginning with the end of the tail, and ending with the grin, which remained sometime after the rest of it had gone," she thinks "Well, I've often seen a cat without a grin . . . but a grin without a cat! It's the most curious thing I ever saw in all my life!"

Aristotle's judgment concerning early metaphysical effort is that it tried to find one principle or many of the same kind. We have already run through the guesses, none too happy, that the one principle is material: water, air, fire, and earth. More fruitful was the suggestion that there are material atoms that, by rearrangement, form different kinds of things. Others agreed that there was just one principle, only it is not material, but rather "that from which comes the beginning of the movement."[71] Anaxagoras, for example, claimed that coming to be is not all "spontaneity and chance," rather "that reason was present—as in animals, so throughout nature—as the cause of order and all arrangement. . . . " Anaxagoras seemed to Aristotle as a sober man among the drunk.[72]

Variations on the Democritean theme are so common that they are called, for the sake of brevity, materialistic and mechanistic. Likewise, and for the same reason, we characterize variations on the theme of Anaxagoras idealistic and teleological. Any attempt to say that both views are right in what they assert, but wrong in what they deny, is called dualism.

Just as earlier we saw Aristotle trying to grant the partial truth of both materialist and idealist in the doctrine of four causes, including material and final, so throughout his categorial scheme the guiding motive is to make a place for every fact. Matter without form is non-being; form without matter is non-being. Or more simply, every real substance is com-

[70] Richard McKeon (ed.), *op. cit.*, pp. 693–694; Aristotle, *op. cit.*, 983b, 7–20.
[71] Richard McKeon *op. cit.*, p. 675.
[72] *Ibid.*, pp. 695–696.

posite, for it is both a particular existence and an essence of a kind with other things. What cannot be in and of itself may nevertheless be thought abstractly.

Substance is composite, and although the absolutely real thing is substance, substance is always qualified by the subcategories: quantity, quality, relation, place, time, position, state, action, and affection. Whatsoever is in this sense are things in development acting and reacting. But as we shall see in proofs of the existence of God, as formulated by Thomas Aquinas more or less true to Aristotle's system, the whole process is relative to a first cause and dependent upon this super-substance, whose being is without matter, wholly actual, immutable, and active, and exempt from generation and decay.

Aristotle's supreme criterion of the real is independence. The doctrine of substance underlying change, the composite from which matter and form can be abstracted, is but one application of the criterion. The God who thinks about thought is divine independence, and the noble man who is indebted to no man is human self-sufficiency. Another application is a logic that regards all predication as indicating that predicates belong to subjects. Yet another is the doctrine that all truth is the conformity of subject-predicate propositions to substances qualified by attributes. Thus an Aristotelian deals with many real beings, and the criterion of independence applies to each.

B. Plato

Plato too seeks for genuine criteria of reality. In Chapter II we discussed his allegiance to a world of universals, or unchanging forms. Perhaps it would be useful to recall the main points: the forms are the immutable standards of all things; they are essential for valid knowledge; they are grasped only by intelligence but they exist whether we know them or not; they are spaceless, timeless, and immaterial; particulars are said to "participate" in them; and they also have great inspirational and emotional appeal.

But Plato has more to say about this tricky problem of reality. In the Republic he makes a distinction between being, becoming, and non-being. Of the first we have knowledge, of the second opinion, and of the third ignorance. In a later dialogue he considers each of these with respect to its place in reality. Thus in the Sophist there is the statement that at least some philosophers would accept "power" as the mark of reality.

I suggest that anything has real being, that is so constituted as to possess any sort of power either to affect anything else or to be affected, in however small a degree, by the most insignificant agent, though it be only once. I am proposing as a mark to distinguish real things, that they are nothing but power.

This notion is certainly deeply rooted in common sense, but Plato does not elaborate it, rather he looks to the forms as the unchanging reality, although not denying that the world of change, that is, of becoming, also has some reality. It is best to turn to the dialogue. The two participants are the Stranger and Theaetetus.

Stranger: Let us turn, then, to the opposite party, the friends of Forms. Once more you shall act as their spokesman.

Theaetetus: I will.

Stranger: We understand that you make a distinction between 'Becoming' and 'Real being' and speak of them as separate. Is that so?

Theaetetus: Yes.

Stranger: And you say that we have intercourse with Becoming by means of the body through sense, whereas we have intercourse with Real being by means of the soul through reflection. And Real being, you say, is always in the same unchanging state, whereas Becoming is variable.

Theaetetus: We do.

Stranger: Admirable. But now what are we to take you as meaning by this expression 'intercourse' which you apply to both? Don't you mean what we described a moment ago?

Theaetetus: What was that?

Stranger: The experiencing an effect or the production of one, arising, as the result of some power, from things that encounter one another. Perhaps, Theaetetus, you may not be able to catch their answer to this, but I, who am familiar with them, may be more successful.

Theaetetus: What have they to say, then?

Stranger: They do not agree to the proposition we put just now to the earth-born Giants about reality.

Theaetetus: You mean—?

Stranger: We proposed as a sufficient mark of real things the presence in a thing of the power of being acted upon or of acting in relation to however insignificant a thing.

Theaetetus: Yes.

Stranger: Well, to that they reply that a power of acting and being acted upon belongs to Becoming, but neither of these powers is compatible with Real being.

Theaetetus: And there is something in that answer?

Stranger: Something to which we must reply by a request for more enlightenment. Do they acknowledge further that the soul knows and Real being is known?

Theaetetus: Certainly they agree to that.

Stranger: Well, do you agree that knowing or being known is an action, or is it experiencing an effect, or both? Or is one of them experiencing an effect, the other an action? Or does neither of them come under either of these heads at all?

Theaetetus: Evidently neither; otherwise our friends would be contradicting what they said earlier.

Stranger: I see what you mean. They would have to say this: If knowing is to be acting on something, it follows that what is known must be acted upon by it; and so, on this showing, Reality when it is being known by the act of knowledge must, in so far as it is known, be changed owing to being so acted upon; and that, we say, cannot happen to the changeless.

Theaetetus: Exactly.

Stranger: But tell me, in heaven's name: are we really to be so easily convinced that change, life, soul, understanding have no place in that which is perfectly real—that it has neither life nor thought, but stands immutable in solemn aloofness, devoid of intelligence?

The conclusion that follows this conversation is that Reality must contain both changing and unchanging things if intelligence is to be given its place in real existence.

But now what of non-being? To say non-being is, is at the very least an odd way of speaking even in these days when we have similar statements coming from some of the existentialists. Can we give sense to such a phrase, or are we simply entangled in a contradiction? Let us hear Plato argue the point.

Stranger: May we not say that the *existence* of the not-Beautiful is constituted by its being marked off from a single definite Kind among existing things and again set in contrast with something that exists?

Theaetetus: Yes.

Stranger: So that it appears that the not-Beautiful is an instance of something that exists being set in contrast to something that exists.

Theaetetus: Perfectly.

Stranger: What then? On this showing has the not-Beautiful any less claim than the Beautiful to be a thing that exists?

Theaetetus: None whatever.

Stranger: And so the not-Tall must be said to exist just as much as the Tall itself.

Theaetetus: Just as much.

Stranger: And we must also put the not-Just on the same footing as the Just with respect to the fact that the one exists no less than the other.[73]

Here we see Plato giving a meaning to "non-being is." He is calling attention to the fact of "difference" or "otherness" in our world. What is

[73] F. M. Cornford, *Plato's Theory of Knowledge*, Routledge & Kegan Paul, Ltd., London, 1949, pp. 239–241, 291–292.

other than beautiful is the non-beautiful, which however is also a part of the real. In this sense non-being can be said to be.

Modern philosophies too are troubled by the notions of reality, being, existence, and so on. We cannot work through the whole range of alternatives. It must be enough now to point out that Descartes' assurance of the reality of the self and its experiences had enormous influence.

C. William James

William James and the phenomenologists turned their attention to perception as the key to reality. Let us hear from James first on the question "What is real within experience?" In an essay entitled, "The Perception of Reality," he puts the problem in this way, "Under what circumstances do we think things real?" This question has its psychological as well as its philosophical aspects. It is with the latter that we are primarily concerned. And here James took the sense of our own reality as the place to begin. Psychologically, whatever excites and stimulates our interest we take as real,

. . . whenever an object so appeals to us that we turn to it, accept it, fill our mind with it, or practically take account of it, so far it is real for us, and we believe it. Whenever, on the contrary, we ignore it, fail to consider it or act upon it, despise it, reject it, forget it, so far it is unreal for us and disbelieved.[74]

It is this psychological account that leads James to the conclusion that "our own reality, that sense of our own life which we at every moment possess is the ultimate of ultimates for our belief." This is, of course, the same truth Descartes had taken as the foundation for his entire system; it is the position Platonists and Aristotelians would label and reject as subjectivism.

The world of living realities as contrasted with unrealities is thus anchored in the Ego, considered as an active and emotional term. That is the hook from which the rest dangles, the absolute support. And as from a painted hook it has been said that one can only hang a painted chain, so conversely, from a real hook only a real chain can properly be hung. *Whatever things have intimate and continuous connection with my life are things of whose reality I cannot doubt.* Whatever things fail to establish this connection are things which are practically no better for me than if they existed not at all.[75]

Thus it is that James stresses emotion and will and interests as a clue to the real, in contrast to formal logic or other rational processes, such as

[74] William James, *The Principles of Psychology,* Dover Publications, Inc., New York, 1950, Vol. II, p. 295.
[75] *Ibid.,* pp. 297–298.

dialectic. For him the Parmenidean attempt to elaborate a purely rational way to the real could only end in failure. Consider the following judgment: Being is. Followers of Parmenides would have to say this is self-evident or an analytically true judgment. But when men say that something exists or is real, and it is conceivable that it does not exist, or is not real, then the judgment is not analytic. Hence logic alone cannot establish the truth of such a judgment. James thinks that most men believe the things of sense are "the absolutely real world's nucleus," that means that the ordinary man trusts his senses a good deal more than his reason. But it is a nice point whether the things men sense are real, or whether they take them as real solely because they sense them. Is there a factor of judgment in all our perceptions of reality? Certainly some philosophers insist that this is the case. If the mind had only one sensation, then there would be no alternative to believing it real. But the moment we begin to fit our sensations together into clues to the outer world in which we act, then clearly some sensations, real enough in a mental way, are not trustworthy as aids to action. From this follows an important conclusion about the meaning of existence.

The syllable *ex* in the word Existence, *da* in the word *Dasein*, express it. 'The candle exists' is equivalent to 'The candle is over there.' And the 'over there' means real space, space related to other reals. The proposition amounts to saying: 'The candle is in the same space with other reals.' It affirms of the candle a very concrete predicate—namely, this relation to other particular concrete things. *Their* real existence . . . resolves itself into their peculiar relation to *ourselves*. Existence is thus no substantive quality when we predicate it of any object; it is a relation, ultimately terminating in ourselves, and at the moment when it terminates, becoming a *practical* relation.[76]

Just because an object appears is not sufficient for it to constitute a reality in the practical sense James is talking about. It must not only appear, it must also be a reality for ourselves, it must have "practical reality." Thus in addition to appearing, it must appear *interesting* and *important*. If it lacks either of these features we reject it as unreal. At different times we find interesting and important the world of sense, the world of science, the world of ideal relations, the world of prejudices common to the race, the various supernatural worlds, the various worlds of individual opinion, and the worlds of sheer madness. "Each world *whilst it is attended to* is real after its own fashion; only the reality lapses with the attention."[77]

Although James can claim that each subworld is "a consistent system," it is only a savage or a child who is not concerned by the lack of relation

[76] *Ibid.*, p. 290, footnote.
[77] *Ibid.*, pp. 292–293.

between Neptune's trident and the Christian heaven. Therefore a reflective man elects *"from among the various worlds some one to be for him the world of the ultimate realities."*[78] Because "discrepancies and contradictions are felt and must be settled in some stable way," in addition to factors of interest and attention, James admits the criteria of congruity and independence. That is, "Congruity with certain favorite forms of contemplation—unity, simplicity, permanence, and the like"; and "Independence of other causes, and its own causal importance."[79]

Although system is demanded to order our various beliefs, a speculative theory of the real world is not wholly settled by logic and fact.

The conceived system, to pass for true, must at least include the reality of the sensible objects in it, by explaining them as effects on us, if nothing more. The system which includes the most of them, and definitely explains or pretends to explain the most of them, will, ceteris paribus, prevail.

There are alternatives in philosophy; but also in the sciences.

Which theory is then to be believed? *That theory will be most generally believed which, besides offering us objects able to account satisfactorily for our sensible experience, also offers those which are most interesting, those which appeal most urgently to our aesthetic, emotional, and active needs.*[80]

Men are torn between various alternatives. This may answer why we actually prefer some system, but James may have failed to answer whether we should allow emotion to tip the scales.

The fight is still under way. Our minds are yet chaotic; and at best we make a mixture and a compromise, as we yield to the claim of this interest or that, and follow first one and then another principle in turn. It is undeniably true that materialistic, or so-called 'scientific', conceptions of the universe have so far gratified the purely intellectual interests more than the mere sentimental conceptions have. But, on the other hand . . . they leave the emotional and active interests cold. *The perfect object of belief would be a God or 'Soul of the World,' represented both optimistically and moralistically (if such a combination could be), and withal so definitely conceived as to show us why our phenomenal experiences should be sent to us by Him in just the very way in which they come.* All Science and all History would thus be accounted for in the deepest and simplest fashion.[81]

This is perhaps the most suggestive answer to the question of why metaphysicians continue to deal more or less intensively with the concept of deity.

[78] *Ibid.*, p. 293.
[79] *Ibid.*, p. 300.
[80] *Ibid.*, pp. 311–312.
[81] *Ibid.*, pp. 316–317.

Here again the student will have to weigh carefully the philosopher's arguments and ask himself whether the position is acceptable. Is James allowing too much to be real when he offers as criteria whatever is interesting and important? Are these not highly personal matters thus making possible a universe of fantastic proportions which must be hospitable alike to the savage's totems, the madman's delusions, the scientist's laws, and the theologian's gods? Moreover, may we not talk sensibly about real things that are not related to us, that is, related in James' practical sense? Does James' position not suggest that our world of reals come into and pass out of being with incredible ease, depending on whether they pass successfully the tests of interest and importance? It may, of course, be pointed out that he does also recognize the necessity of coherence, but he does not seem to be as thorough about this as other philosophers might demand. The issue can be put more strongly. Is coherence or systematic relatedness also a matter of will, emotion, feeling or interest? If so, there seems to be no basis for ruling out the savage's preferences as against the scientist's. On the other hand, if coherence is something other than feeling or will, then James has admitted a test that seems not merely to supplement these criteria but eventually to force them to submission.

D. Phenomenology

We shall introduce the problem before us with a statement from Bertrand Russell.

Are our objects of perception real . . . ? Let us begin with the word "real." There certainly are objects of perception, and therefore, if the question whether these objects are real is to be a substantial question, there must be in the world two sorts of objects, namely, the real and the unreal, and yet the unreal is supposed to be essentially what there is not. . . . The question . . . is . . . what can be meant by assigning "reality" to some but not all of the entities that make up the world. Two elements, I think, make up what is felt rather than thought when the word "reality" is used in this sense. A thing is real if it persists at times when it is not perceived; or again, a thing is real when it is correlated with other things in a way which experience has led us to expect. It will be seen that reality in either of these senses is by no means necessary to a thing, and that in fact there might be a whole world in which nothing was real in either of these senses. It might turn out that the objects of perception failed of reality in one or both of these respects, without its being in any way deductible that they are not parts of the external world with which physics deals.[82]

[82] Bertrand Russell, *Mysticism and Logic*, 2nd ed., George Allen & Unwin, Ltd., London, 1950, pp. 121–122.

Although Russell is not to be classified as a phenomenologist, nevertheless this statement may prepare us for appreciating the contributions of this movement in philosophy. The founder is Edmund Husserl, a German philosopher who was born in 1859 and died in 1938. For this particular problem we shall refer to an article by a contemporary philosopher who contributed to a series of papers published in memory of Edmund Husserl.[83] The issue before us is to determine which phenomena are really real and which are merely supposedly real. The difficulty of getting at reality itself without its being related to us has induced many philosophers to despair of ever saying that a belief is true because it corresponds to fact. The phenomenological position is that we have *"reality-phenomena* which in their very structure . . . refer to something beyond themselves."

The term "phenomena" as used in this connection means everything given to us directly; the term "reality" means the "standing-on-its-own-account," (in and of itself) of any object; as such it is independent of any observer and of his observations. Genuine reality-phenomena are defined as those that actually imply reality. "The central region of reality that is claimed to be accessible to our cognition consists of the immediately perceived objects, i.e., of the perceptual phenomenon." Now, of course, reality cannot be compared directly with its phenomenon as it (reality) is apart from its presentation. In short, reality is always given to us by some phenomenon, never as it is in itself. We must distinguish, however, between "mere" phenomena and "reality-phenomena." The former do not claim any reality, the latter are phenomena that also claim to be real. Thus the critical question arises, to what extent does the reality-phenomenon tell us anything about "real" reality? This question, important as it is, is not satisfactorily answered by Spiegelberg's analysis. It is suggested that the structure of the phenomenon refers to a reality beyond itself, but this tells us almost nothing of the nature of the reality. At times, however, we are told that the reality-phenomenon is not a contradiction (as might seem to be the case) and that there is no real separation between the world of phenomena and reality. Thus "reality and phenomenality do not exclude each other either in concept or in structure." So, at least in some cases, the directly given world is the real world not only as it displays itself, but as it actually is. "Real things, therefore, may, as far as their structure is concerned, remain exactly what they are, if they enter into relations

---

[83] Herbert Spiegelberg, "The 'Reality-Phenomenon' and Reality." In: Marvin Farber (ed.), *Philosophical Essays In Memory of Edmund Husserl,* Harvard University Press, Cambridge, Massachusetts, 1940, pp. 84–85.

with us and are presented to us. This occurrence means only that they adopt the additional character of phenomenality." Still, according to Spiegelberg, we must not think that reality coincides with reality-phenomena. "It only implies that there is *some* reality in or behind the phenomena."

Furthermore, we cannot accept all reality-phenomena as equally revelatory of the real. Those experienced in dreams or half-waking states, as well as those which appear in states of excitement or prejudice need to be subjected to cool self-criticism. Thus James' criteria of interest and importance would be as unsatisfactory as are also the Cartesian criterion of distinctness and the Humean criterion of vividness;

Not only because phenomena even when we are fully awake may remain indistinct and blurred: dream-phenomena can, at least in part, adopt a tormenting over-distinctness and vividness often leading to actual awakening, quite apart from the fact that we do not obtain consciousness of these criteria until later.

With this emphasis upon what is directly given in experience, certain criteria for reality are offered. Spiegelberg makes no claim to completeness but the student should compare his suggestions with others we have presented. Those Spiegelberg feels are important enough to mention are the following:

1. Readiness: This refers to the characteristic of being distinct rather than vague or blurred. The real is in our perceptual field whenever our glance turns toward things, and it is there as ready-made objects. This is in contrast to the phenomena in the periphery of our perceptual field where things are vague and blurred.
2. Persistence: This refers to the characteristic that things have of remaining unaltered when our glance turns away from them. The real does not seem to perish as we cease to attend to it.
3. Perceptual periphery or horizon: The field of objects extends beyond the blurred periphery of our phenomena. This calls attention to the fact that the real does not abruptly end where distinctness reaches its zero point, but rather the world continues beyond our direct evidence. "Thus the transition character of the periphery of our phenomenal field points at an *extra*phenomenal one with which it stands in uninterrupted connection."
4. Boundaries in concrete objects: The structure of that which is not given directly to us is indicated in the structure of what is given. "Thus a ball, as distinguished from a disk, makes it clearly understood that behind the outlines of its front side there is an area not actually presented."

5. Independence: The points of light we call stars cannot be thought away as can our interpretation of them as constellations. The real does not require of us that we support our belief by assumptions. Indeed, we can deny them all, and yet the reality-phenomena endure.

6. Resistance: Everything real offers resistance to our own reality. The real perseveres against every attack of testing, probing, sounding. To experience the real is "an act which somehow shakes, jolts, or challenges."

7. Agreement: Reality-phenomena agree with each other and confirm each other. They refer forward and backward to each other, one promising another beyond our actual data, and another bearing testimony to something real that has passed.

Here then we have another account of this elusive goal of thought, reality. But is it really an account of reality? Do we learn anything about reality from such an approach? We are told what cues we use when we *take* something for real, but do we know what the real is? Is there a kind of metaphysical reluctance in the phenomenologist's analysis to characterize positively the real? Or does the phenomenologist want us to accept as real whatever appears in experience, after sufficient tests have been applied?

It is possible, of course, to find other statements about reality but we have said enough to convey the idea that if sharper and more complete criteria are to be given for this term, they may have to be achieved within a metaphysical system. It is evident that metaphysics has two major emphases in contemporary philosophic thought—it may be regarded either as the analysis of certain kinds of propositions or beliefs, for example, "motion is impossible," "change is unreal," "everything is material," "everything is mental," "time is unreal," "universals exist," or as the denial of these and similar propositions. But there is another goal of some metaphysicians, namely, to find reality in a system so tight, so all-embracing that there is little or no chance of having it slip away, leaving them clutching at appearances. Sometimes this is called speculative philosophy. Can the attempt succeed? We have presented some of the obstacles and hazards and also some of the reasons for trying. Now let us go to some system-makers themselves and examine their alternative structures.

PROBLEMS FOR THOUGHT AND DISCUSSION

1. C. I. Lewis wrote: "The main business of a sound metaphysics is, thus, with the problem of the categories; the formulation of the criteria of reality in its

various types."[84] Can you suggest ways in which one gets to categories of reality? What would you select as the most basic? How did you come to those you selected?

2. Although Immanuel Kant was severely critical of certain metaphysical claims, he nevertheless thought that metaphysics itself was a "natural disposition" in man. "Thus in all men, as soon as their reason has become ripe for speculation, there has always existed and will continue to exist some kind of metaphysics." Do you think Kant is right about man's natural metaphysical curiosity? Or do you think the language-analysis philosophers are more nearly correct when they find the source of our metaphysical perplexities in linguistic confusions?

3. A. O. Lovejoy has said that the history of ideas shows that men are susceptible to diverse kinds of "metaphysical pathos," that is, they are taken in by the mood or tone of the descriptions and words used by philosophers.

For many people—for most of the laity, I suspect—the reading of a philosophical book is usually nothing but a form of aesthetic experience, even in the case of writings which seem destitute of all outward aesthetic charms; voluminous emotional reverberation, of one or another sort, are aroused in the reader without the intervention of any definite imagery. Now of metaphysical pathos there are a good many kinds; and people differ in their degree of susceptibility to any one kind. There is, in the first place, the pathos of sheer obscurity, the loveliness of the incomprehensible, which has, I fear, stood many a philosopher in good stead with his public, even though he was innocent of intending any such effect. . . . The reader doesn't know exactly what they mean, but they have all the more on that account an air of sublimity; an agreeable feeling at once of awe and of exaltation comes over him as he contemplates thoughts of so immeasurable a profundity—their profundity being convincingly evidenced to him by the fact that he can see no bottom to them. Akin to this is the pathos of the esoteric. How exciting and how welcome is the sense of initiation into hidden mysteries.[85]

Can you add to Professor Lovejoy's examples of "metaphysical pathos"? Is the lure of the obscure present only in philosophy? How about poetry? Or science? Or religion?

4. Henri Bergson said that science involves analysis; that analysis operates with symbols; that therefore science cannot get at reality, but only at its symbolic representation. On the other hand "metaphysics, then, is the science which claims to dispense with symbols." The method of metaphysics is intuitive, which Bergson thinks is a true empiricism.

But a true empiricism is that which proposes to get as near to the original itself as possible, to search deeply into its life, and so, by a kind of *intellectual auscultation*, to feel the throbbings of its soul; and this true empiricism is the true metaphysics.[86]

Is Bergson writing sense or nonsense? poetry or philosophy? science or metaphysics? What role, if any, can the intellectual act of listening play in science or philosophy? Do you think Bergson is speaking metaphorically?

[84] Clarence Irving Lewis, *Mind and the World Order*, Charles Scribner's Sons, New York, 1929, p. 14.

[85] A. O. Lovejoy, *The Great Chain of Being*, Harvard University Press, Cambridge, Massachusetts, 1936, p. 11.

[86] Henri Bergson, *An Introduction to Metaphysics*, G. P. Putnam's Sons, New York, 1912, p. 36.

5. P. F. Strawson, a contemporary British philosopher, distinguishes between descriptive and revisionary metaphysics. "Descriptive metaphysics is content to describe the actual structure of our thought about the world, revisionary metaphysics is concerned to produce a better structure." With respect to descriptive metaphysics he has the following comment:

Metaphysics has a long and distinguished history, and it is consequently unlikely that there are any new truths to be discovered in descriptive metaphysics. But this does not mean that the task of descriptive metaphysics has been, or can be, done once for all. It has constantly to be done over again. If there are no new truths to be discovered, there are old truths to be rediscovered. For though the central subject-matter of descriptive metaphysics does not change, the critical and analytical idiom of philosophy changes constantly. Permanent relationships are described in an impermanent idiom, which reflects both the age's climate of thought and the individual philosopher's personal style of thinking. No philosopher understands his predecessors until he has re-thought their thought in his own contemporary terms; and it is characteristic of the very greatest philosophers, like Kant and Aristotle, that they, more than any others, repay this effort of rethinking.[87]

Each sentence in this paragraph contains an idea worth discussing. Do you agree with the points expressed? Does this statement from a philosopher closely associated with the modern linguistic philosophers suggest that under certain conditions metaphysics as a philosophic discipline might receive new encouragement?

6. Examine a protest against the notion that there is a study of being as being:

Being is certainly indefinable, as is existence, when not coextensive with actuality: not merely because, like redness, being is ultimate; but because it is a contentless abstraction. Pure or indeterminate being is not distinguishable, by any assignable character, from nonentity. In order to be, or even to be conceived, an entity must be this and not that.[88]

Metaphysical propositions have sometimes been said to be about being as such. But if all such propositions are about nothing, what sort of propositions should a metaphysician make? If being is indefinable does this mean that we can say nothing about it? How would you distinguish between being and existence?

7. Through Dionysian art, the art of the excitement of the god of wine, Nietzsche says that a man can be identified with "the world building power." "We are for a brief moment, Primordial Being itself, feeling its raging desire for existence and joy in existence." Young men often feel liberated from convention by slight acquaintance with Nietzsche. Just how well would such oracles stand up against Lovejoy's attack?

PERTINENT READINGS

Bergson, Henri, *Introduction to Metaphysics* (T. E. Hulme, tr.), The Liberal Arts Press, Inc., New York, 1950.

Berkeley, George, *A Treatise Concerning the Principles of Human Knowledge*, The Open Court Publishing Co., La Salle, Illinois, 1904. (There are many other editions.)

[87] P. F. Strawson, *Individuals*, Methuen & Co., Ltd., London, 1959, pp. 10–11.
[88] F. R. Tennant, *Philosophical Theology*, Cambridge University Press, Cambridge, 1935, Vol. I, p. 374.

Burtt, Edwin Arthur, *The Metaphysical Foundation of Modern Physical Science*, Harcourt, Brace, & Co., New York, 1925.

Edwards, Paul and Arthur Pap, "Meaning, Verification, and Metaphysics," *A Modern Introduction to Philosophy*, The Free Press, Glencoe, Illinois, pp. 544–618.

Emmet, Dorothy M., *The Nature of Metaphysical Thinking*, Macmillan and Co., Ltd., London, 1957.

Hook, Sidney, "Metaphysics and Theory of Knowledge," *American Philosophers at Work*, Criterion Books, Inc., New York, 1956, pp. 183–331.

Kneale, W., "The Notion of Substance," *Proceedings of the Aristotelian Society*, Vol. 40, 1940, pp. 103–134.

May, Rollo, "The Existential Approach." In: Silvano Arieti (ed.), *American Handbook of Psychiatry*, Basic Books, Inc., New York, 1959, pp. 1348–1361.

Pears, D. F. (ed.), *The Nature of Metaphysics*, Macmillan and Co. Ltd., London, 1957.

VII

Systems of Metaphysical Belief

I. Introduction

A. Systems, Scientific and Philosophic

Metaphysics, we have established, is characterized by propositions of unlimited scope. In this regard it is sharply distinguished from the sciences. Yet systems of philosophy claim the universal acceptance that is accorded to the sciences. Indeed, some philosophies claim to be the final and never-to-be-outdated solution to the most general problems of the universe—how it can be known and for what purpose it is. Yet, whereas the sciences are generally accepted, subject always to the modifications that for a time produce alternative theories, there are a number of different philosophical systems. When many alternative total views claim to be final and universal, and yet no one of them has more than sectarian acceptance, it is well to inquire into what is meant by a philosophic system in contrast to a scientific system.

Our knowledge of astronomy is systematic knowledge, since such principles as Newton's laws apply to all planetary motions. But there is also objectively the solar system, the planets themselves in their relations to the sun and to each other. We can say generally that scientific systems allow us to predict, and if not to control future events, at least to order our actions in relation to them. Since there is for us a time to sow and a time to reap and we order our lives by the succession of the seasons, we may claim that our social order is based upon the natural order.

It is sometimes claimed that the very concept of a natural order is philosophic. Followers of Kant commonly insist that philosophy comprehends how the mind's categories yield us the order of nature from phenomena, and also deal with the orders found in art, morality, and religion. Hence to a Kantian the order of things is not "out there," objective, waiting to be discovered. Rather the order of science is also part of the human ordering. Cassirer, for example, writes: "Science gives us order in thoughts; morality gives us order in actions; art gives us order in the apprehension of visible, tangible, and audible appearances."[1]

Whether our order of thought and conduct is founded upon an objective order of things, or our concept of the natural order is part of the product of the ordering intellect of man, many men take satisfaction in the central theme of system.

We seek system for a variety of reasons. Some of us are satisfied with having everything in its place, and dissatisfied with disarray. And even apart from the serenity of knowing that the universe satisfies our need, there is the usefulness of knowledge. Knowledge of what has been may be fragmentary, but if enough of it can be reduced to regular pattern, it can be extended to predict what is to occur. Only systematic knowledge is predictive, hence we may tend to think that all knowledge should become systematic, and the more systematic the better. But however systematic a philosophy may be, it is characteristically interpretative rather than experimental, speculative rather than predictive.

Some systems of philosophy are like Newton's physics, based on axioms, but whereas Newton's system offers to explain anything in space and time, in a state of motion or rest, philosophic systems, other than mechanistic materialism, characteristically claim that the physical universe is only one aspect of the whole. But how is the whole to be conceived? One claim is that the physical universe is a mechanical assemblage or collection of things externally related. Others insist that the concrete totality of things is an organic whole, that is, to employ root metaphors, not like a machine but like a work of art. A work of art, it is said, is more profoundly ordered than a machine. In the latter we may remove a worn part and replace it with a new part. But in a work of art, it is said, each aspect is part of a living organic whole. No aspect can be different without changing and spoiling the total beauty, which is more than the mathematical sum of individual atomic excellences. Hence it is sometimes claimed that all relations are internal to the universe.

[1] Ernst Cassirer, *An Essay on Man*, An Introduction to a Philosophy of Human Culture, Yale University Press, New Haven, Connecticut, 1953, p. 168.

Of course these two are not the only alternative pictures that generate philosophical systems. Another is the Platonic claim that the real universe is the eternal realm of forms. Just as a mathematician ignores the chance colors and shapes to gain the essential triangles that have necessary properties, so on Plato's view the metaphysician grasps the essential order of things; the changing world is then but an image of the eternal world and events are mere shadows of the forms.

Yet another root notion of a philosophic system is that all events are in necessary and inevitable historical sequence. That is, if we really grasp the becoming of the universe, we know that no event could have occurred except as the consequence of prior events, and nothing could be taking place now except as it issues from the matrix of the past. But some philosophers keep the history, without insisting on a wholly predetermined plan, and allow contingency.

Four great ideas of system: a universal machine, a universal work of art, a universal scheme and pattern, a universal history.

Yet how curious are philosophers who develop systems! Each claims he is telling us "the Truth," the complete and final and objective truth, the world as it really is. But each of these four is a definable perspective or point of view. So that it seems more complete to include alternative views of the universal whole. And it seems more objective to say that this is the way one sect of philosophers says the world really is, from their point of view. So the claim to finality is tricky, for the dialectic of systems continues. One philosopher ends his system with all problems solved—to his satisfaction. And his most loyal follower qualifies the claim by saying that the master's reasoning is incomplete, that here is a *non sequitur,* or that the master is too hasty in ignoring an alternative solution, or that the master is blind to a problem, or that there is some inconsistency in his principles.

But what good are systems of philosophy? We have conceded that they do not give us predictive knowledge of events, and they give us no power of control over events. Philosophic systems are then not useful like systems of medicine that enable us to deal with disease. They are not even useful like systems of sanitation that enable households to get rid of waste. But could they be useful in another sense? Just as we are in need of organized beliefs that help us to interpret problems and solve contradictions, so philosophic systems offer us order in our mental life. For some men to hold beliefs that do not agree is as distressing as an illness. Philosophers offer to cure us of perplexities of the most gnawing sort, such as that of men who cannot square their scientific with their religious beliefs. And if we can rid our mental houses of the clutter of prejudice and illusion, should we not conclude that philosophic systems are a means to personal tidiness and vigor?

Systems of philosophy are not accumulations of facts so much as sets of very general relations. How, then, do they claim to be more than purely formal? All philosophers claim that we cannot order our facts without categories, and that hypotheses of an empirical sort are formulated by using conceptual patterns.

All of us adopt some conceptual order, but a system implicitly held cannot be criticized by contrast to opposite conceptual orders. The student may not think he now subscribes to a conceptual order. It is the authors' aim here to convince him that he does, and to try to show that he holds implicitly two conceptual orders and does not know how to accommodate coherently one to the other. The point here is that the strife of systems is not something that took place in ancient Greece between Heraclitus and Parmenides, or between Plato and Aristotle, or among nineteenth-century Germans such as Hegel and Marx, but that the strife of opposite perspectives is within everyone. If the student comes to feel vividly the necessity of choosing a coherent system, and the impossibility of a system adequate to all areas of experience, then the authors will have achieved the interest that will motivate him to examine materialism and idealism, dualism and process philosophy, with the keenness of a man who must find out which is true, or at least whether one is more adequate than the others.

B. Two Conceptual Orders, the Categories of Nature and the Categories of Mind

In making sense of the world-order philosophies try to say not only what there is, but also how it is related. Indeed what we mean by order can best be made clear by considering the kinds of relation there are. For example, all of us believe that things are related in a spatial order, that is, if we assume a position from which to judge, one thing can be said to stand to another on the same horizontal level, or above, or below; in the same vertical plane, or to the right or to the left, or related in depth as before or behind. It is difficult to see how we can avoid space as a category, and the conclusion that all physical things are spatially related to each other. Moreover, all of us believe that events are related to each other in a temporal order, that is, if we assume a position from which to judge, one event stands to another event as either contemporary, or predecessor, or successor. It is then difficult to see how we can avoid taking time as a category, that is, we conclude that all things are temporally related to each other. Again all of us probably believe that occurrences are causally determined and causally determining. In Chapter V, the seeming ubiquity of the causal relation was described. Can we avoid taking cause as a category and concluding that nothing can arise out of nothing, or fail to have some effect?

It would doubtless appeal to our desire for a tidy world if we could now close our inventory of the kinds of relations in which things are ordered. That is, if we had a complete ordering of our world by answering only the questions where? when? how? If only these questions can arise, we might well say that the most satisfactory body of beliefs about the order of things is found in the sciences. And some philosophers, the *naturalists,* make claims of this sort.

But now suppose that we say that there are also questions about intensive degrees, such as, how deep a red, or how high a note? We are then asking a question about qualities and their degrees of intensity. Answers to questions where? when? and how? do not seem to account for qualities and their degrees, hence we ask another fundamental question: of what sort? to what degree? If a scientific scheme should claim to reduce all questions of quality to questions of quantity, we might legitimately protest that quality itself is an irreducible category. And if we are struck by the relation of one occurrence to another as means to ends, we may ask for the purpose of anything, or its function in achieving another state, or what conditions are needed for the fulfillment of a certain goal. Clearly we are not asking merely how something happens, but what should happen. In short, our question is, why? or, for what purpose? Can purpose be ignored as a category? Can we claim that all things serve some end, either their own or another's?

Now let us say that we order qualities according to our preferences and that we consider one qualitative degree more desirable than another, and therefore call it better. Again a question arises, can value be ignored as a category? Have all things a value simply because they exist or are organized into finite wholes? Is there an order of what ought to be? Many men believe there is and that we must order our personal lives according to it or fail to make intelligible human activities and accomplishments.

It looks as if we are faced with two orders, that of things and events in spatial and temporal and causal relations, and that of qualities, purposes, and values. Are these really two orders, or only one? If they are two how are they related? If there is one order how can we account for the apparent differences?

One familiar way to reduce the two orders to one is to say that both can be stated in propositions, which themselves can be logically related. We could then say that whenever we grasp the coherence of different sorts of true propositions, we have grasped the integral ordering of reality. Spinoza said something like this. Man's good is secured by his knowing the natural order. Hence insofar as he answers correctly where? when? and how? he is fulfilling his need for knowledge. Since man's goal is the greatest degree of intellectual coherence, this is attained when all truths are seen to be necessarily related to each other. This applies to the truths about things extended in space and time, things caused, and also to truths about things thought in the order of qualitative degrees, ends, and preferences. It is this vast interrelationship of the truths of nature and man that Spinoza calls God.

But now let us consider another familiar way to reduce the two orders to one order. Let us say that the first order, or space, time, and external cause is the order of the perceptual world, known by the senses, but that the second order of quality, end, and preference is the order of intellectual judgment. And let us assume that the perceptual order exists for the sake of the intellectual order, the lower for the higher. Then the problem is to account for the existence of the natural world in terms of the intellectual world. We would have to begin with whatever makes such a preferential hierarchy, namely, mind or spirit. And then the world as a whole could make sense if there is a cosmic mind that produces nature, and nature can make sense only if it stands to the goals of spirit as means to end. This is a way to interpret beliefs that are called idealistic, and it is a way to interpret the watchword of the Platonic and Hegelian traditions, namely, that spirit expresses itself in nature.

It would seem that the first alternative has the advantage of claiming that the order of things in nature is discovered, and is found to be one, whereas the order of values is invented by men, and is as various as cultures and times and men's ideals.

But it would also seem that the second alternative has the advantage of adequacy and scope, since in our experience we discriminate qualitative differences and pay attention to where? when? how? only because knowing these aspects of things helps us to answer why? and to secure what we value, or to achieve the good. Thus it is argued that the order and system we attain in the arts, in ethics, in history, and in religion give us as significant knowledge of reality as do the natural sciences. Most idealists have said more significant, since scientific thinking is only one type and the universe is so rich that without the other types our system fails of completeness and adequacy.

Many persons think it is relatively simple to give a reasoned account of things and events within the categories of science and that we can extend the natural categories to all of man's knowledge. As Sir Julian Huxley argues, the animal evolves in a natural environment and so does man, conditioned in the same way, yet with the advantage of more adaptable hands, and a larger brain which makes possible civilization and symbolic communication, moral goals and gods. But why should one animal, supposedly different in degree only, develop contrasts that seem to amount to differences in kind? Man strives to use his hands to make a social environment in which he may love his fellow men and live with them in justice and in peace. Why? Some philosophers think that naturalism cannot give an intelligible answer.

On the other hand, some persons think it is possible to give a reasoned account of man and his world with the categories of the arts, the moral and social order, and religion. One begins with the idea of man responding to degrees of value which awaken within him a desire for excellence and the fulfillment of their promise. He is ashamed to achieve less than his greatest capacity. But now we must ask these idealistic Platonists and Kantians: why, then, the whole mechanical order in space and time? Could not souls in contemplation of the good find their bliss without the downward drag into sensations of the flesh? Some philosophers think that idealisms are romantic and the product of wishful thinking.

Any naturalism is faced with the challenge to do more than rationalize human striving by reducing it to the urges that man shares with animals that do not create arts, or social philosophies, or religions. Any idealism is likewise faced with the challenge to do more than rationalize the natural order by reducing it to a set of tools that a world-engineer might invent so that curiously embodied souls might break through the prison of matter.

Of course we could abandon the effort to account for the world with man in it. We could attempt the desperate expedient of explaining both nature and man's ideals as projections of his divided imagination. If it were merely a psychological urge to feel that life is meaningful, we have ample evidence that a myth can satisfy the needs of many men. If it were merely a psychological urge to place everything in a temporal context, history will do; or if it were a psychological urge to locate everything in space, then geography or astronomy will satisfy. But systems of philosophy as schemes of the most general interpretation arise out of a need for more ultimate explanation. What is that scheme within which we can make sense of man's arts and their insights, man's religions and their visions, man's societies and their moral goals and ideals, man's sciences and their quest for knowledge? In short, how can we reach a perspective that explains the various aspects that enter into human life and make it possible for us to know the way things are?

Can this hope be fulfilled through a naturalism with its primary emphasis on material things in space and time, related as causes and effects? Can it be fulfilled through idealism with its primary emphasis on minds with their qualitative experiences? Or can it be fulfilled by a view that rejects both the reliance on matter and the stress on mind but sees each as abstract characterizations of events in process? To have even tentative answers to these questions it is necessary to look more closely at some of the systems. But first a statement from Whitehead. It is perhaps one of the best accounts of the motivation and aim of all systems of philosophy.

Speculative Philosophy is the endeavour to frame a coherent, logical, necessary system of general ideas in terms of which every element of our experience can be interpreted. By this notion of 'interpretation' I mean that everything of which we are conscious, as enjoyed, perceived, willed or thought, shall have the character of a particular instance of the general scheme. Thus the philosophical scheme should be coherent, logical, and, in respect to its interpretation, applicable and adequate. Here 'applicable' means that some items of experience are thus interpretable, and 'adequate' means that there are no items incapable of such interpretation.

'Coherence,' as here employed, means that the fundamental ideas, in terms of which the scheme is developed, presuppose each other so that in isolation they are meaningless. This requirement does not mean that they are definable in terms of each other; it means that what is indefinable in one such notion cannot be abstracted from its relevance to the other notions. It is the ideal of speculative philosophy that its fundamental notions shall not seem capable of abstraction from each other. In other words, it is presupposed that no entity can be conceived in complete abstraction from the system of the universe, and that it is the business of speculative philosophy to exhibit this truth. This character is its coherence.

The term 'logical' has its ordinary meaning, including 'logical' consistency, or lack of contradiction, the definition of constructs in logical terms, the exemplification of general logical notions in specific instances, and the principles of inference. It will be observed that logical notions must themselves find their places in the scheme of philosophic notions.[2]

[2] Alfred North Whitehead, *Process and Reality*, Copyright 1929 by The Macmillan Company, copyright renewed 1957 by Evelyn Whitehead and used with permission of The Macmillan Company, pp. 4–5.

C. Methods of Metaphysics

Whitehead's program for speculative philosophy cannot be explicated without taking it in the context of his system, which will be sketched later. But now a few problems raised by his goals will be discussed. How can men's beliefs about everything be coherent? How can a logically deductive system have content? If a system is inductive is it not one hypothesis among many? How can a hypothesis be necessary? How are systems generated? To what standards are they subject when we prefer one to another? These are the questions that must be sharpened before expounding dualism, materialism, idealism, and process philosophy.

Metaphysicians do indeed, as Whitehead says, seek coherence of all their beliefs. It is notorious that men's beliefs about God and about man are incoherent. Traditional theology ascribes to God omnipotence and omniscience, and also justice in judging men. But if men are to be rewarded for their virtue and punished for their vice, these paths of righteousness and sin must be of their own choosing. But can men be free without limiting God's power? God cannot, then, be omnipotent in the sense of directing every event. One may think that coherence can be achieved simply by applying scientific method to human nature, but an able sociologist points out that the basic assumptions of present-day research are incoherent:

A paradox rends the social sciences today. Two contradictory views of the nature of man are asserted simultaneously. On the one hand, we are told that it is possible to know and understand more and more about the nature of man and society, for man to use this increasing body of knowledge and theory to improve his condition, to reduce unhappiness and poverty, and to increase the joy and fullness of life. On the other hand, modern social science teaches us to regard man as a creature of his drives, habits, and social roles, in whose behavior reason and choice play no decisive part. Accordingly, man's efforts to acquire knowledge about himself and society, and to use such knowledge, are beset with insuperable obstacles; men are regarded as unable to achieve objective knowledge or to be guided by it.[3]

This is a fine example of how to study beliefs systematically: Discover the most basic assumptions, and state them together. More basic even than beliefs about man are the approaches to man both from the naturalistic and the idealistic viewpoints. The beliefs about man become incoherent because they spring from two world views, or sets of categories, each with its peculiar criteria of evidence.

[3] Reinhard Bendix, "The Image of Man in the Social Sciences," *Commentary*, Vol. II, No. 2, 1951, p. 187.

But if beliefs about man are difficult to bring into coherence, how much more difficult are beliefs about everything!

The builders of a metaphysical system must, as Whitehead says, employ logic. Indeed it is a necessary, though not a sufficient, criterion of a metaphysical system that it be a logical system of general ideas. But can a metaphysical system be purely logical? Our clearest example of a "necessary" system is one deduced from principles to which we have no rational alternative. Self-evident truths and the basic principles of identity, contradiction, and excluded middle have already been discussed. Can a metaphysical system be necessary because deduced solely from these? Some of the great rationalists, especially Leibniz, attempted to deduce the universe from logical principles. But then we may see a paradox: if a system is necessary, as Whitehead says speculative philosophy attempts to be, it could scarcely appeal to experience, especially to matters of fact. For what we observe merely happens to be and is seen from our point of view, hence doubly contingent. Yet without experience how can a system be other than merely formal, without content, and therefore empty? How can there be a necessary account of matters of fact? The very notion of speculative philosophy, as Whitehead describes it, seems incoherent.

What is the escape from the dilemma that a metaphysical system, if necessary and purely rational, is without content, and if empirical, is indeed applied, but without necessity?

Several alternatives have already been introduced. It was not claimed that the logic of metaphysical systems has to be either purely inductive or purely deductive. Hypotheses are formulated on the basis of experience, yet from them deductions are made to be tested by experience. Perhaps this is what Whitehead meant to stress by logic "in its ordinary meaning."

Stephen Pepper claims that speculative systems, or world-hypotheses, are subject to contrary criteria. One standard is clarity, the other is adequacy. To think animistically that everything is moved by a soul is not clear, for if we do not even know what the human soul is, how much less do we know what souls dwell in plants, clouds or mountains? And how inapplicable is the body-soul hypothesis in explaining germination, meteorology, and volcanoes! Yet, claims Pepper, there are other metaphors that do seem to suggest precise and adequate hypotheses, such as a mechanistic scheme that handles everything as though it were made up of parts, one part moving another part. The merit of so regarding alternative systems is methodological.

The method in principle seems to be this: a man desiring to understand the world looks about for a clue to its comprehension. He pitches upon some area of common-sense fact and tries if he cannot understand other areas in terms of this one. This original area becomes then his basic analogy or root-metaphor. He describes as best he can the characteristics of this area, or, if you will, discriminates its structure.[4]

Yet can this method give us a necessary system? It cannot, because in addition to mechanism, Pepper finds three other relatively adequate world-hypotheses, those like Plato's called *formism;* those like absolute idealism that take as their root metaphor the organic life or interrelated wholes, called *organicism;* those like pragmatism, that take as their root metaphor the historical event, called *contextualism.* And each of these develops a distinctive theory of truth. Indeed, Chapter IV developed the correspondence theory to which formists subscribe, self-evidence which others employ, verification which fits contextualism, the coherence theory, which is appropriate to organicism. And who can arbitrate between positions with different doctrines of the nature of truth? Hence in place of the neat doctrine of one ultimately true metaphysics, we now have a doctrine of four alternative, but equally ultimate systems.

Can a philosopher be neutral between alternative views? A contemporary Polish logician argues that we should be neutral in interpreting other's systems, but not in assessing their claims. Neutrality

. . . is untrue if it is taken to mean that philosophical systems should be dealt with as though they were all equally tenable, irrespective of their truth value. If we make such an assumption we are denying to philosophers the respect which is due them; because if systems contradict each other—as they do—but all have the same value, then all of them are false, and can only claim to be appreciated as works of art. This would constitute the greatest perversion of the thought of philosophers worthy of the name, for they are all servants of the one truth and should be treated as such.[5]

Yet Whitehead's doctrine of adequacy may have an answer to this situation. What forbids us from attempting to combine these doctrines of truth, using each at its appropriate level: self-evidence for axioms, correspondence for matters of fact, verification for hypotheses, and coherence for the total final system? And why should we not sometimes analyze into the simplest atomic units; sometimes organize our data as relevant to problems; sometimes study abstract patterns as such; and sometimes study

[4] Stephen Pepper, *World Hypotheses,* University of California Press, Berkeley and Los Angeles, 1948, p. 91.
[5] I. M. Bochenski, *Contemporary European Philosophy* (Donald Nicholl and Karl Aschenbrenner, trs.), University of California Press, Berkeley and Los Angeles, 1956, p. vi.

concrete things as changing and developing? If a system employs all these methods, is it necessarily eclectic and incoherent?

If metaphysics studies the grounds basic to various logics, why should a system not employ both subject-predicate and relational logic? Neither seems ultimate, in the sense that all we have to say can be said equally well in either language.

In the end we may have to sacrifice the clarity of one method only to the demands of adequacy. And if adequacy is our test, we have three methods of guaranteeing relative applicability to various areas of human experience.

The first we learn best from Aristotle. It is to study our predecessors. Taken together, the one-sided character of their opposite points of view becomes evident, and they tend to soften each other, even if they do not cancel out. Democritus demands that we take matter seriously. Plato demands that we take forms seriously. Our task therefore becomes the adjusting of one claim to the other.

The second method is to take various disciplines together. Whitehead, and also Leibniz, made contributions to fields as different as mathematics and history. Metaphysicians like these respect the autonomy of different disciplines but seek a wider perspective. A metaphysics adequate to both of these opposites, mathematics and history, is rare. A metaphysics that exalts mathematics, like Descartes', is as inadequate in one way as a metaphysics like Hegel's, which exalts history, is inadequate in the other.

The third way is to see how terms as basic as "being," "true," "same," apply to all ranges of human discourse, yet with proportion to the subject matter. The exclusive attention to clarity might lead us to reject metaphysical talk as ambiguous. Certainly we cannot claim strict unity or univocity of meaning throughout all discourse. Hence St. Thomas Aquinas made much of the analogical meaning of all basic metaphysical terms. We are not working within one species, but between species. A set of basic categories must therefore be framed to do justice to differences of the meaning of "true" in mathematics, history, biology, art.

There are many systems of metaphysics. Some of them obviously spring, as William James said, from temperamental differences. Some of them obviously spring, as Karl Marx claimed, from difference of economic interests. Yet these personal and social blemishes should not blind us to the effort to see our beliefs in the widest perspective available. Metaphysics has a self-corrective nature. Its inner dialectic leads it to produce now a Hobbes, and now a Berkeley; and their successors will not altogether ignore what they affirmed, even when deploring what they denied. But before studying materialism and idealism, let us inquire into the dualism of body and spirit.

II. Dualism of Matter and Mind

Can we rear a coherent system on the twin convictions that there are things and there are minds? The introduction to system-building has set this problem. There seems to be nothing stranger about these beliefs than about the beliefs that there are men and there are women, or there is sea and there is land. But we can give a reasonable account of how men and women, sea and land are related. But can we think systematically of the conjunction of things and minds? Later it will be shown that metaphysicians attempt systematically to give an account of what it is to be a thing and what it is to be a mind. Indeed some philosophers attempt to account for everything that can be on the basis of either material substance or mental substance. But why has Western philosophy, which traditionally was dualistic in affirming both matter and mind, produced monistic revisions that would reduce one to the other? To understand this, we must inquire whether matter-mind dualism is radically incoherent. Certainly common sense seems untroubled by the beliefs that we are both body and mind, and we seem to know that we need both physical and mental education.

The term *dualism* was invented to characterize not this belief that each human being is a body with a mind, but the dramatic conflict between the principles of light and darkness, good and evil in which the Persian prophet Zoroaster summoned men to serve Ahura-Mazda against Ahriman. And for convenience the name dualism is sometimes applied to the Platonistic view of a world of eternal forms over against a world of temporal becoming. It is sometimes also applied to the Aristotelian view that every substance is composite, and for it to exist it must be stuff in a determined shape. Obviously since Aristotle denied that the forms can exist independently of particular things, if we use dualism with reference to Plato and Aristotle, we should add that the former is extreme and the latter is moderate. But the ancients also contrasted God to the world, and, more elaborately, in such a theistic position as that of St. Thomas Aquinas, it is denied that one can be reduced to the other. Emphatically St. Thomas' system was devised to show why the heresy of pantheism, such as Spinoza later elaborated so brilliantly, should and could be avoided.

Further to complicate the picture, Descartes based his system upon two distinct sorts of substance, matter that is extended but cannot think, and mind that thinks but cannot be extended. The typical modern philosopher could either accept the Cartesian dualism or deny it. If he denied it, as Whitehead put it, he would then have to say that there are only things extended in space with quantitative attributes and in push-pull relations of causal efficacy with other things, or there are only minds with their qualitative ideas in intentional relations with other minds. At least these seemed the only alternatives open to Hobbes and to Berkeley. Since the materialism and idealism that regard Hobbes and Berkeley as their most vivid protagonists, will shortly be introduced, which dualism are we to investigate here? Obviously the Cartesian sort is most appropriate.

Perhaps the most vivid expression of Cartesian dualism comes from Blaise Pascal:

We are composed of two opposite natures, different in kind, soul and body. For it is impossible that our rational part should be other than spiritual; and if any one maintain that we are simply corporeal, this would far more exclude us from the knowledge of things, there being nothing so inconceivable as to say that matter knows itself. It is impossible to imagine how it should know itself.[6]

Is man a body? Pascal argues:

He needs a place wherein to abide, time through which to live, motion in order to live, elements to compose him, warmth and food to nourish him, air to breathe. He sees light; he feels bodies; in short, he is in a dependent alliance with everything. To know man, then, it is necessary to know how it happens that he needs air to live, and, to know the air, we must know how it is thus related to the life of man, etc. Flame cannot exist without air; therefore to understand the one, we must understand the other.

Is man mind (or soul or spirit)? This too seems to Pascal undeniable.

If we are simply material, we can know nothing at all; and if we are composed of mind and matter, we cannot know perfectly things which are simple, whether spiritual or corporeal.

What are the difficulties that emerge from what seems self-evident? Already Pascal is bothered because Descartes had postulated body by itself as that which is extended in space, and mind by itself as that which perceives, reasons, wills, etc. But how can we know body and mind in their simplicity? All that we know, according to Pascal, is colored and stamped by our own complexity.

Hence it comes that almost all philosophers have confused ideas of things, and speak of material things in spiritual terms, and of spiritual things in material terms. For they say boldly that bodies have a tendency to fall, that they seek

[6] Blaise Pascal, *Thoughts*, Henry Regnery Co., Chicago, Illinois, 1949, pp. 7–8. The succeeding quotations are from the same pages.

after their centre, that they fly from destruction, that they fear the void, that they have inclinations, sympathies, antipathies, all of which attributes pertain only to mind. And in speaking of minds, they consider them as in a place, and attribute to them movement from one place to another; and these are qualities which belong only to bodies.

What if these absurdities are avoided by establishing physics as natural philosophy, as science was called until recently, to explain the world quantitatively as a pure mechanism, and leaving to moral philosophy the mind with its qualities? Thence arise the difficulties, examined earlier, of how a thing can have its own geometrical shape as a primary attribute, but borrow its color from a perceiving mind as a secondary attribute. Is the color of a thing, unlike its shape, in the eye of the beholder only? What does he see? Is the shape of the thing impressed by the thing upon the senses? How can the mind think a physical shape or a mere shape suggest a similar quality to different minds?

In short, if Cartesian dualism of simple mind and simple body were true, man could not know it to be true. And if it were true, it is difficult to see how man knows anything.

The crisis of modern dualism occurred in the seventeenth century. Why then, it may well be asked, did it survive to be mocked as an absurdity in the twentieth century? Whitehead, as quoted earlier, essayed the answer that it was a formula that left physical science absolutely free to ignore human values in the realm of extension. And it left philosophy and other studies absolutely free in their realm to ignore nature.

Although Kant attempted valiantly to show that a priori and a posteriori elements are both involved in knowledge, his dualism of noumena and phenomena was quite as extreme in its way as that of mind and body. For, according to Kant, the mind knows only its concepts and sensations and is cut off from things-in-themselves. Although Kant made efforts through aesthetic experience to bridge the gap, the nature that science knows is pure mechanism, and the realm of freedom belongs only to moral wills.

What of this division of the universal field into physical nature for physics and the other sciences to study, and minds for philosophy, theology, and the humanities to study? Apart from the technical philosophic difficulty of accounting for the mind's knowledge of things, the problem that may be more pertinent is how to account for human conduct, which seems to allow both that our minds control our bodies and our bodies more or less affect our minds? At least we often say "She knew what she was doing, walking that way," or "She was knocked silly and couldn't remember how she got there."

The insistence of dualism on the reality of mind requires a fuller statement about the nature of mind. The topic is much too difficult for extensive treatment here, but the following will serve as an introduction to a few of the problems.

Charles Morris has said that views of mind have passed through three periods: First, mind and matter are vaguely conceived and only vaguely differentiated; second, mind and matter are regarded as different in kind, separate and opposed to each other; finally, there is an attempt made to restore the intimate connection of mind and matter.[7]

The primitive tendency to identify mind and nature will not be discussed, for at that stage the philosophical problems are not consciously formulated. But stages two and three must concern us.

Our language, and the way we frame questions, to a great degree determine the character of the problems. We have so many names for things that we find it difficult to think of having names without things of which they are names. "Stone" refers to stones and there are stones; "tree" refers to trees and there are trees; "kangaroo" refers to kangaroos and there are kangaroos. It is easy to go from this to "mind" refers to mind and there are minds. But is there not considerable difference between "there are stones" and "there are minds?" That is, are minds "there" in the same sense that stones are? Again, the difficulty can be brought out when we see that the question "What is a tree?" has the same form as "What is a mind?" The former leads us to believe that there is an actual entity called a tree; the latter also suggests that there is an actual entity called a mind. And yet we know that they are not entities in the same sense. The one can be seen, touched, smelled, and so on, but not the other.

This way of putting the question involves, therefore, the assertion that mind and body are two different substances, one a physical, the other an immaterial substance. What this may mean is well said by Morris: According to this view, "a mind is an immaterial 'that,' capable of continued and independent existence, and analyzable into qualities and a substratum which has relations and supports these qualities, without itself being a relation or quality or sum of qualities."[8] This view of mind, or one approximating it, is found in all those philosophies related to the Platonic-Aristotelian tradition, and in more recent thought to the Cartesian tradition.

There are, of course, very great perplexities associated with these beliefs about mind. First, there is the most general problem of substance

[7] Charles Morris, *Six Theories of Mind*, University of Chicago Press, Chicago, 1932, p. 1.
[8] *Ibid.*, p. 8.

itself. Can we get a clear idea of it? Usually it is thought to be distinct from attributes or qualities it is said to possess. But what can this something, not a quality, be? And even more troublesome is the question how can it be known since all of our sense-knowledge seems to be of qualities? If substance in general is a vague and ambiguous term, then certainly immaterial substance is doubly so. Mind as a substance distinct from its experiences is as difficult to grasp as matter distinct from its qualities. Should sensing, perceiving, thinking, imagining, willing, etc., be taken as attributes of the immaterial substance? Then what is the mind apart from these attributes? We seem to be forced to say that a physical substance is an aggregation or collection of attributes and an immaterial substance must be a union of imagining, willing, thinking, etc. But this belief runs counter to some other beliefs men frequently hold. Mind seems to have a degree of independence and permanence above the passing thought or image or sensation. It seems to have an identity and character quite different from not only its attributes but also from physical substance and its attributes. Our knowledge presupposes our self-identity; our thought implies a thinker distinct from the thought; and our memory supports our judgment that we are the same person who had the original experience and is now remembering it. Is this not evidence that the mind is something that relates our separate experiences into a kind of unity and is therefore distinct from these experiences?

But if we accept this belief then other obstacles appear. For instance, how can two entirely different substances ever enter into a knowing relation? That is, can we ever understand how an inner immaterial "mind" can know an outer material "stuff"? In fact it is extraordinarily difficult to see how any relation can hold between these two substances. Such questions are brought together in philosophy under the name *mind-body problem*, and it is quite safe to say that when formulated in this way, no adequate solution has been found, although names have been given to historic efforts. There is *interactionism*, the view that mind and body, though different, mutually affect each other. This accords with a casual reading of daily experience, but gets us into all sorts of trouble upon more critical analysis. Again, it is sometimes said that mind and body, each opposed to the other and each having its own history, nevertheless move along in parallel ways so that when a physical event occurs a mental event also occurs although no causal relation holds between them. They are, so to speak, "timed" such that the occurrence of one event corresponds to the occurrence of the other. The name for this view is *psycho-physical parallelism*. There are a number of variations and modifications, but none has worked out satisfactorily. It is undoubtedly true that the problem is aggravated by, if not actually the result of, assuming that mind and body are two distinct and totally different substances. Such difficulties have led philosophers to other beliefs about mind in which attempts are made to avoid a substance view. However, it is doubtful that any of these efforts has been successful, for in each case there may be found a lingering trace of the substance-attribute theory. The alternatives are to think of mind as an active process, a relation, and a function. For the most part idealists consider mind as some form of activity, realists commonly accept a relational view, and pragmatists generally regard mind in functional terms. This is, however, a rough classification and must be taken as only a provisional step. As it stands, it obscures the differences and fails to make the nice distinctions required by the variations in beliefs.

But when idealists talk of mind as process or activity and also try to describe the activity, they have a hard time avoiding a substance-attribute language. It is not easy to talk about activity apart from something that is active. And when mind is regarded as a relation between contents, the specific type of relation that constitutes mentality is not made clear. This view, moreover, does not offer a perspicuous account of the higher mental processes. In fact, its description of mind is much too thin. As Morris says,

> One looks in vain for a detailed treatment of the reflective process, dreams, the "constructive" imagination, the "ideal objects" of the scientific and mathematical disciplines, the role of hypothetical judgments, the significance of the *a priori* in reflection, the mental processes of the artist, or the relation of mental processes to the control of behavior. In short, one looks in vain for an appreciation of the insurgent and impudent way in which a mental scaffolding is erected around the actual world, making it more amenable to human purposes and desires.[9]

It is doubtful if any clarity is gained by regarding mind as a relation rather than as a substance, particularly since "relation" is as difficult a term to manage as "substance," and the problem is aggravated if the type of relation required is not specified.

The interpretation of mind as function raises the question about the meaning of this term. Morris points out its ambiguity in the following words:

> The term "function" is often used to denote the normal mode of performance of some thing or organ, as when an engine or a heart is spoken of as functioning well. Closely related to this use is the employment of the term "function"

[9] *Ibid.*, pp. 145–146.

to indicate the purpose which something fulfills, as when we speak of the function of the heart as the distribution of blood. A third use of the term indicates that a thing plays a certain role, as when it is said that a particular actor is Hamlet. Then there is a fourth meaning of the term, in which one variable is a function of another if, when a value is assigned to one, the second variable receives a specific value. Of these four uses, the second and third—purpose and role—bear specifically upon the topic of mind.[10]

Philosophers who adopt this view generally regard mind as an instrument to serve the ends of the organism, for example, making it easier for man to get about in a complex world.

It is one of the discouraging aspects of philosophy that an adequate theory of mind has not yet been achieved. We shall shortly seek from the materialists an adequate theory of matter. However materialism raises several questions:

First, is the mind identical with the brain or with brain states? If we could observe our own brains by some ingenious device, while enjoying, let us say, a musical composition being performed on the piano, would we not be aware of *two* things, not one, that is, the changes in the brain *and* the enjoyment? Moreover, can we get from the one to the other except by inductive inference?

Secondly, are there distinguishable events, namely thinking, perceiving, imaging, believing, etc., which we call mental?

Thirdly, are these events distinct from their physiological correlates, that is, is not mental activity other than bodily behavior? It was the weakness of at least the early forms of behaviorism to fail to see these distinctions. A mental act does not seem identical with a bodily act, for sometimes bodily behavior occurs without a mental experience, and sometimes a mental experience or act occurs with no observable bodily behavior, and sometimes two different mental experiences occur when no two distinguishable bodily acts occur. In short, when we say we are thinking about a mathematical problem, or that we suffer from a toothache, or that we are planning a journey, or that we imagine a fire-eating dragon, we do not find any statement about our overt bodily behavior that is equivalent to these. Dualism, then, leaves us with the conviction that what we mean by mind is conveyed by such terms as interpreting, perceiving, attending, and so forth, none of which is to be identified with any observable physiological correlate. That there are these correlates is not denied, but it is a failure of analysis to identify them with the peculiar and recognizable quality of "mental" experiences. Thus we cannot expect answers

[10] *Ibid.*, pp. 275–276.

from the physical and biological sciences to this problem. There is a science, physics, from which we may expect answers to questions about matter. There is a science, biology, from which we may expect answers about life. But there is no parallel to be drawn between some science and questions about mind. Psychology, of course, suggests itself, but in its physiological and experimental dimensions it gives us information about the body and its acitvity. Perhaps theoretical psychology comes nearer to the parallel, but then, being more speculative, it moves away from being a strict science.

What has just been said can be put another way. The mind is not subject to denotation; it may be connoted but not denoted, that is, it is not a possible or actual ostensible object. There is even some doubt whether the mind is an object of introspection. Do we really directly experience a mind when we "look within"? Some philosophers have denied this and prefer to say that "mind" refers to experiences that are "lived through" or "enjoyed." If mind is not revealed as a datum for observation, then it is unlikely that there can be any science of mind, for it is unquestionably a prerequisite of all science (excepting, perhaps, mathematics) that its objects be denotable. It is, therefore, futile to apply to mind descriptive terms appropriate only to observable entities. The brain, for example, is a denotable object; the mind is not. One philosopher has suggested that the mind can be discerned, but not indicated. It is discerned in dialectics or reflection, that is, in the processes or movements of thought.[11] This seems a sensible way of putting it, but why not extend the point and say the mind is discerned in any and all of its activities, not merely the logical processes called dialectics?

Finally, it does not seem correct to identify consciousness with mind. Researches into unconscious and subconscious activity demonstrate that what would be regarded as mental activity, that is, inference and various forms of creativity, goes on without awareness. Blanshard asked this question: "Is there any characteristic which is always present, and which *alone* is always present, where mind is recognized?" In answering his question he said, "Yes; wherever mind is present, there the pursuit of ends is present. Wherever that pursuit is wholly absent, mind is absent. And when mind is present, it is present precisely in the degree to which ends are in control."[12] We may tentatively accept this, although it requires a

[11] J. Loewenberg, "The Discernment of Mind," *University of California Publications in Philosophy*, Vol. 19, *The Nature of Mind*, 1936.

[12] Brand Blanshard, "The Nature of Mind," *Journal of Philosophy*, Vol. 38, 1941, pp. 208–209.

very broad definition of purpose. At least we can say that the processes that constitute mind are unified by the "purposing" of mind. This means that mind, in its cognitive (knowing), or conative (desiring), or affective (feeling) dimensions is characterized by a means-end relationship that somehow unifies its power and direction, although consciousness may not accompany the relationship. Furthermore, this suggests that there are mental processes below the human level, a point we seem forced to admit from the evidence of both comparative psychology and biology, and as an implication from our premise. It may also suggest that there are potentialities of mind beyond the present human attainment, even if it is not yet clear what mind may become.

The reader should observe that talk about mind is considerably more intelligible when we use verbs rather than nouns. In this way, we at least avoid the temptation to reify our concepts.

If mind is not a denotable entity, nor describable in the way that is appropriate to such entities, then it cannot be an object to which the known laws of the natural world either in its physical or biological determinations can apply. Are there, then, laws to fit this realm, and if so, what are they? This is a topic much too immense for consideration in an introductory account. But it may be said that it is also a topic upon which philosophers have notoriously disagreed, and perhaps it may even be called a scandal, as so little insight has been gained.

Beyond these convictions, which materialism may shake, dualism is not well considered in contemporary philosophy. Whitehead, for example, regards a basic bifurcation of reality as metaphysical failure. Pragmatists like Dewey attack every dualism, not only matter-mind, but deductive-inductive, analytic-synthetic, and God-world. Linguistic philosophers mock the Cartesian view as the doctrine of the ghost in the machine. Particularly Gilbert Ryle, in The Concept of Mind, reduced the error to what he called a category-mistake. That is, because bodies are things, we regard minds also as things, but different in that they are essentially thinking things. Why is this misleading? Because we are led to think of minds as rather like bodily mechanisms, and also as extra centers of causal process.[13]

Because of these criticisms, and many others, it is not uncommon to regard modern philosophy, insofar as it is dualistic, as obsolete.[14]

[13] Gilbert Ryle, *The Concept of Mind*, Hutchinson's University Library, London, 1949.
[14] I. M. Bochenski, *op. cit.*, pp. 1–10, 36–37.

III. *Materialism and Naturalism*

One of the bewildering aspects of systematic philosophy is that the general names, materialism, idealism, and so on, cover a variety of points of view. One would expect that materialists and idealists would agree pretty thoroughly with others who share the same label, but alas such is not the case. We have a number of diverse materialisms and at least a dozen kinds of idealism, thirteen pragmatisms, and a variety of realisms. And, of course, even within the systems we find irreconcilabilities, paradoxes, and contradictions. Perhaps of all types, if it really is a type, there is more universal agreement among the claims of the mystics than there is in any other group.

One must not expect, therefore, to find one consistent type of materialism. There is agreement on some general presuppositions, but beyond that there are major divergences as well as shades of difference. It will not be possible to deal with the differences between materialists. All that can be done is to set forth some general characteristics of the various points of view, but without much confidence that all materialists would accept even these statements of their claims. In fact, it will shortly be apparent that even in definition some divergences appear.

The term materialism has so frequently been used as a pejorative word that it is difficult for some students to think soberly and fairly about any view called materialistic. The materialist has been accused as one who can have no high ethical aims, no regard for human fellowship and love, and no attachment to or belief in anything except the "kickable stuff" of the world. Most of these judgments are premature and based on emotional reaction rather than reflective analysis. When one remembers the extent to which we rely on, enjoy, and need the physical aspects of life, it is perplexing to see the violence with which some people protest against a materialistic view of man and the universe. The clue to the nature of this reaction is to be found, of course, in the *total* claim of the philosophers. It is necessary to regard not only what they affirm but also what they deny. Many thinkers are willing to grant half the truth of materialism, but its denials they cannot agree to. The popular, or perhaps unpopular, conception which regards the materialist as one who measures all values in quantitative terms will not be discussed. The deeper, more thoroughgoing and thoughtful view of philosophical naturalism shall occupy our attention. But first a more careful look at the term *materialism*.

The variety of the meanings of materialism makes it very difficult to speak with any assurance about its systematic character. Following are some of the ways in which the term has been used and understood in modern philosophy.

A. Modern Materialistic Viewpoints

1. Materialism sometimes refers to the view that the primordial existent or existents of the universe are matter and its physical properties. But it is never quite clear what this means. Does it mean that only matter exists or is real? It would not be easy to find a respected philosopher who would accept this. Those who defend the fundamental reality of matter usually also claim that motion, space, and time are also real, and these cannot intelligently be said to be matter. Moreover some of the most persistent defenders of materialism argue for the reality of the "laws" of nature, and these too cannot be matter. The ambiguities are compounded when we try to get a clear idea of what is meant by matter. C. D. Broad once stated what he thought the plain man had in mind when he used the expression "bit of matter." It may be called the common-sense view:

i. It is literally extended. This means it is spread out but bounded by a surface and presents an outside or front.

ii. It is pervaded inside and out with extensible qualities, such as, colors, temperature, smoothness or roughness, and so on.

iii. It is a center from which emanate sensible "atmospheres" which are like surrounding fields, for example, the sound of a bell, the fragrance of a flower, the cold of an iceberg.

iv. Some of the qualities mentioned in 2 and 3 are revealed by different senses, and one may be sensibly aware of some of these while ignoring others. Also it may have some qualities that none of our senses can reveal.

v. It has causal or dispositional properties, such as inertial mass, impenetrability, greater or less elasticity, and so on.

vi. On different occasions the same person can perceive the same bit of matter with the same senses or different senses.

vii. On the same occasion different persons are able to perceive the same or different parts of the same bit of matter by the same or different senses.

viii. A material body can exist, can change or not change, can be acted upon or can act upon other material bodies when no perceiver is present. And none of the extensible qualities is altered or abolished or reinstated by the occurrence or non-occurrence of perception.[15]

[15] C. D. Broad, "Berkeley's Denial of Material Substance," *The Philosophical Review*, 1954, Vol. 63, No. 366, 155ff.

It is interesting to compare this common-sense view of matter with that of modern physics. Here we shall present Russell's statement, which is in non-technical language, and therefore undoubtedly subject to many weaknesses a strictly scientific statement could avoid. Nevertheless, it can be useful in directing our attention to the radically opposed views of matter in ordinary experience and matter as conceived by recent science.

What do we mean by a "piece of matter" in this statement? We do not mean something that preserves a simple identity throughout its history, nor do we mean something hard and solid, nor even a hypothetical thing-in-itself known only through its effects. We mean the "effects" themselves, only that we no longer invoke an unknowable cause for them. We find that energy in various forms spreads outwards from various centres; we find also that such centres have a certain degree of persistence, though this persistence is not absolute— the modern physicist faces cheerfully the possibility that an electron and a proton may mutually annihilate each other, and even suggests that this may be the main source of the radiant energy of the stars, because when it happens it makes an explosion. What is asserted may be put as follows: when energy radiates from a centre, we can describe the laws of its radiation conveniently by imagining something in the centre, which we will call an electron or proton according to circumstances, and for certain purposes it is convenient to regard this centre as persisting, i.e. as not a single point in space-time but a series of such points, separated from each other by time-like intervals. All this, however, is only a convenient way of describing what happens elsewhere, namely the radiation of energy away from the centre. As to what goes on in the centre it-self, if anything, physics is silent. . . .
"Matter" is a convenient formula for describing what happens where it isn't. . . . Materialism as a philosophy becomes hardly tenable in view of this evaporation of matter.[16]

2. Materialism is also used to refer to a view that mental events or processes are caused only by material events or processes, and that mental events themselves have no causal efficacy with respect to other bodily or mental events. This view is sometimes called *epiphenomenalism*. It seems to contradict our common experience that our "mental" states or our thoughts do influence or modify both our bodily reactions and the state of the external world. This view is related to, but distinct from a third possibility, which follows.

3. Mind is derivative, that is, originated from matter, but has causal efficacy after it has emerged. Such a position requires us to believe that from something totally unlike mind, mind will eventually appear. It will be shown later that the idealists find this claim unbelievable.

[16] Bertrand Russell, *An Outline of Philosophy*, George Allen & Unwin Ltd., London, 1948, p. 165.

4. The term may be used to refer to a view about values, that is, that bodily satisfaction and anything that contributes to this condition is the most important end for man to achieve. One could be materialist in this sense without being a metaphysical materialist. Moreover, a metaphysical materialism does not necessarily imply a life devoted to caviar and champagne.

5. "Materialism" is sometimes used as equivalent to "mechanism," that is, the universe and its constituents operate as a machine, and all explanatory principles must take the form of propositions that fit a mechanical explanation. This view may be nothing more than a kind of metaphor or analogy, useful for helping us to gain an image of the universe and its elementary motions, or it may be a complete ontology in which the categories necessary to explain the existence and operation of a machine are directly applicable to the universe. Stephen Pepper has suggested and developed six of these categories:

i. Field of location, which involves the concepts of space and time.
ii. Primary qualities, that is, the measurable or quantitative aspects of the machine.
iii. Laws, which relate the primary qualities.
iv. Secondary qualities, that is, those qualities not directly relevant to the action of a machine, but which are nevertheless present, for example, colors, textures, feelings, etc.
v. The principle, which connects the secondary qualities to the parts of the machine.
vi. Laws, if there are any, which hold among secondary qualities.

Given these categories, derived from the metaphor of a machine, materialism emerges as a full-blown metaphysics.

6. Materialism may also have a historical, social, and political connotation, which indicates that all human interests rest ultimately upon economic concerns. One version of this theory is called *dialectical materialism*. It will be discussed more thoroughly in Chapter VIII, but here it should be pointed out that this view is not necessarily committed to ontological materialism. It does not claim that matter alone is real. Ideas are also real, and particularly ideas as they develop dialectically into an ideology.

7. Finally, although this does not exhaust the possibilities, the term is used to stress the reality of nature and natural processes. This is philosophic *naturalism*, a position that will soon be discussed more extensively.

B. The Ancient Materialism

Now let us present the relatively clear and simple claims of an older and abandoned view. Its beginnings are found in ancient Greece. The names to remember are Leucippus and Democritus, whose ideas received their superb expression in the work of a later poet, Lucretius. In seventeenth-century Europe Thomas Hobbes is the best representative of this view; in eighteenth-century Europe it is Baron d'Holbach.

A fragment of Democritus reads, "By convention there is sweet; by convention, bitter . . . but in truth there exists atoms and the void." And in Hobbes' Leviathan we find the words:

The World, (I mean not the Earth only, that denominates the Lovers of it Worldly men, but the Universe, that is, the whole masse of all things that are) is Corporeall, that is to say, Body; and hath the dimensions of Magnitude, namely, Length, Breadth, and Depth: also every part of Body is likewise Body, and hath the like dimensions; and consequently every part of the Universe, is Body; and that which is not Body is no part of the Universe: And because the Universe is All, that which is no part of it, is Nothing; and consequently no where.[17]

And from d'Holbach's arguments against any form of supernaturalism we read:

Is it not more natural and intelligible to draw universal existence from the bosom of matter, whose existence is demonstrated by all the senses, and whose effects we experience every moment, which we see act, move, communicate motion, and incessantly generate, than to attribute the formation of things to an unknown power, to a spiritual being, who cannot derive from his nature what he has not himself, and who, by his spiritual essence, can create neither matter nor motion?[18]

One of the great classics of Roman literature, which presents an astonishingly thorough attempt to interpret the world in all its aspects, is Lucretius' De Rerum Natura, or On the Nature of Things. Let us begin with this. Lucretius was not himself an original philosopher, but his magnificent poem brings together the views of the early Greek atomists, Leucippus, Democritus, and Epicurus. He was not their contemporary, for he lived during the first half of the first century B.C. Yet it is not quite fair to say he was not an original philosopher and there drop the matter. A mind able to unite in poetic form the reasonings and observations leading

[17] Thomas Hobbes, Leviathan, The Clarendon Press, Oxford, 1929, p. 524.
[18] Paul Henri (Baron) d'Holbach, "An Examination of Supernaturalism." In: J. H. Randall, Jr., Justus Buchler, and Evelyn U. Shirk (eds.), Readings in Philosophy, Barnes & Noble, Inc., New York, 1946, p. 280.

to a comprehensive theory of natural phenomena is a mind of considerable stature and power and sensitivity. This he certainly possessed. By modern standards, of course, he was not a metaphysician. Yet his work is a great achievement and shows the critical and creative intellect attacking false beliefs and seeking to establish true beliefs.

Two principles seem to be fundamental for his views, namely, that nothing can come from nothing, and that nothing can be destroyed to nothing. There is also a practical motive to be found in his work. He hopes to release men from bondage to that superstition and fear which is largely the result of false religious beliefs. This freedom is reached by carefully observing the world of nature and by carefully reasoning from the evidence obtained. Armed with eye and brain, there seems to be no limit to what men may know of natural phenomena.

> For I shall sing of heaven's high laws,
> Of ways of gods, and of those primal elements
> Wherefrom doth nature all things generate,
> And bring them growth and increase, and whereto
> Once more she doth resolve them at their death.[19]

And again,

> So then we needs must render well our tale
> Of things on high, the paths of sun and moon,
> And how they came to be; and what the power
> That ruleth all the earth. Above all else,
> With reasoning keen, our task will be to scan
> Whence is the soul, the nature of the mind,
> And what may be those visions strange that come
> To affright us in our waking hours, or when
> We toss with fever, or in slumber drown,
> That so we seem to see and hear once more
> The dead, whose bones are wrapt in earth's embrace.[20]

We may begin with the idea that the world of nature has a fixity about it. This makes knowledge of it possible. It is fixed both in the sense that there are immortal elements, and also in the sense that laws are present that determine behavior.

> Again, since for each thing in its own kind
> There hath been fixt an end of growth and life,
> And since what each by nature's laws can do,
> And what it cannot do, doth stand ordained

[19] Lucretius, *On the Nature of Things* (Charles E. Bennett, tr.), Classics Club, Walter J. Black, Inc., Roslyn, New York, 1946, p. 5.
[20] *Ibid.*, p. 9.

Nor doth aught suffer change, each several thing
So standing fast that even the various birds,
Each in his order, on their bodies show
The markings of their kind, so must their seed
With frame of changeless nature be endowed.[21]

The unchanging elements are seeds or atoms or particles which are very small, differing only in shape and size. They are solid, single, indivisible, and therefore indestructible. They possess none of the qualities called by later philosophers "secondary," that is, they have neither color, nor heat, nor cold, etc. And they are in incessant motion. It is the motion upon which depends the life and behavior of men, for men and things are atoms in a compounded state. How do they get together to form objects? Here Lucretius presents the hypothesis of the *swerve*. In an uncompounded state all the atoms fall as rain in a parallel motion. In order to get "things," a swerve, or deviation by some atoms in their downward movement is introduced, which produces a bumping and jostling of the other atoms. This continuous collision makes it possible for harmonious atoms to combine and form material substances. No evidence is offered for the swerve. It is required as necessary to explain the facts.

But Lucretius does offer evidence for the seed theory, drawn from the observation of ordinary experiences. For example, from the wind he concludes that unseen forces exist; from scents that minute particles reach our nostrils; from moisture dropping in caves he infers that the stone is porous enough to let through particles of water; and as the ring and plowshare and pavement wear away, though the worn-away substance is never seen, we have evidence of unseen particles. Furthermore, we see growing things but never the minute bits added to the growing plant or animal. Out of these "seeds" are all things formed. They cluster and are held together by the various hooks and prongs the different shapes provide.

Next in importance for the theory is the existence of the void or space, for if there were no void there could be no motion. With these three fundamentals, atoms, motion, and space, Lucretius constructs his entire theory of nature. He rejects all teleological notions and thinks that nature shows too many faults to be the product of a divine will. For him the universe is boundless and one cannot get to an edge to shoot an arrow out of space. In this limitless universe there is an infinite number of worlds which are born and pass away.

With this atomic theory Lucretius thinks he can explain all natural phenomena. And indeed he tries to account in this poem for such diverse

[21] *Ibid.*, pp. 29–30.

features as optical illusions, tastes, hunger, sexual needs, formation of the world, origins of animal and vegetable life, the beginnings of civilization, thunder and lightning, waterspouts, clouds, rainbows, earthquakes, volcanoes, disease and so on. Even soul and mind can be explained on the particle hypothesis. They are also corporeal in nature, but are made up of exceedingly fine and smooth seeds. The mind, which is the reasoning power, is located "midway within the region of the breast" and the soul is dispersed throughout the body. Lucretius is not always clear in the distinction, but soul probably refers to the vital and conscious processes, while mind means more narrowly the intellectual functions.

Death, of course, is merely the break-up of the collection of particles and their wide dispersal. It need not be feared because as the body crumbles all feeling goes too. The first book ends with these fine words of confidence that if we proceed properly we can know the truth.

> Thus shalt thou come, by labor slight and fond,
> These truths to know; for each shall catch a gleam
> From that which went before. Dark night no more
> Shall steal away thy path, but thou shalt see
> Deep into nature's inmost mysteries.
> So things will light the lamp for other things.[22]

Although Lucretius' beliefs about nature can scarcely be called scientific by contemporary standards, and many are simply naive, yet it is astonishing that his views, based on observation, are so close to later conceptions based on experimentation. Certainly we will find that the terms used to describe nature, such as cause, motion, substance, particle, change, space, and so on, are kept when scientific views are developed, although the meanings are not precisely the same.

This, then, is the ancient materialism, progenitor of all succeeding attempts to account for what is, or our world, primarily with the terms used to describe the physical "stuff" of our world that is—matter, space, and motion. The later views of Hobbes, d'Holbach, and others are fundamentally akin to those of Lucretius, although some made verbal commitments to another kind of being called God, which is extremely awkward to fit into the systems given their basic assumptions. Materialism, at this level, shows its tendency to simplicity, that is, to explain all things with as few principles as possible. And therein lies its major weakness—its simplicity was not the simplicity of elegance but of naivete and ignorance. Its categories were too vague and ill-defined. Nor could it maintain itself before the enormous growth in knowledge of our world in its physical,

[22] *Ibid.,* p. 54.

physiological, and psychological dimensions. Thus it had to undergo drastic revision to such an extent that it seemed unwise to keep even its name, although it is true there are some modern philosophers who are proud to belong to the ancient tradition and unwilling to disassociate themselves from it by changing names.

C. Naturalism

The new name is *naturalism*. Let us regard its claims carefully. First allow the naturalists, or new materialists, to speak for themselves, not expecting to find complete unanimity, but rather a common attitude and a series of affirmations that may be said to belong to the same family of beliefs.

Let us begin with George Santayana, who prefers the old-fashioned term "materialism." He writes: "The dominance of matter in every existing being, even when that being is spiritual is the great axiom of materialism. . . ."[23]

And again,

Events have then given birth, in a living organism, to experience of events. My whole description of the spiritual life is thus an extension of my materialism and a consequence of it. . . . I ask myself only what are the fundamental presuppositions that I cannot live without making. And I find that they are summed up in the word materialism. This word denotes and confesses in the first place that I find myself carried along by a great automatic engine moving out of the past into the future, not giving me any reason for its being, nor any reason why I should be. Existence is groundless, essentially groundless; for if I thought I saw a ground for it, I should have to look for a ground for that ground, *ad infinitum*. I must halt at the *quia*, at the brute fact.[24]

The following statement from a contemporary work also used the term "materialism" but calls it "modern."

Modern materialism . . . asserts the following: The inorganic pattern of matter is prior to living, minded and purposive organisms, which arise gradually and only as a result of a complex evolutionary development. With the advent of organic life, new, biological laws begin to operate. The principles of physics and chemistry necessarily apply, but are not by themselves sufficient to the biological level. Thus mechanism or the theory that physico-chemical explanation is adequate to all levels, is emphatically rejected. If a thing can be explained by

[23] Reprinted with the permission of Constable & Company, Ltd. and Charles Scribner's Sons from *Realms of Being* by George Santayana, copyright 1942 Charles Scribner's Sons, New York, p. 292.
[24] *The Philosophy of George Santayana*, (Paul Schilpp, ed.), The Library of Living Philosophers, Northwestern University, Evanston and Chicago, 1940, pp. 504–505.

physics and chemistry, however, it must be so explained, and there is no justification for adverting to any other level of the organization of matter. The inorganic and organic constitute distinctive levels, which can be referred to as
lower and higher, in the sense that organic material systems are more highly
organized and more complex, exhibiting new behavior traits. There are also
many subsidiary levels, gradients, and resonances within the inorganic and organic. Within the organic, for example, we have cell, tissue, organ, organ systems, organism, and population. Each level except the first contains all lower
levels within it. For example, the tissue contains cells, which in turn have
chemical components. The cell within a tissue, however, does not behave just as
it does outside the tissue. Chemistry within the cell, too, is altered by the en-
velope which contains it. The one-floor plan of the classical biological mechanism
is thus superseded by a modern structure displaying many diverse stories. The
top stories, however, are always supported by the lower floors; and all floors
must rest upon the ground floor studied by physics and chemistry. The diverse
stories, the modern materialist insists, can be easily confirmed by scientific methods. Organized matter reveals integrative levels of organization characterized
by distinctive laws.[25]

The next definition from a contemporary philosopher is briefer, but
stresses in its last sentence a central feature of what he calls indiscriminately, naturalism, physical realism, or materialism.

Physical realism, or materialism, is in brief the doctrine that the whole of
what exists is constituted of matter and its local motions, not Aristotelian 'prime
matter' but physical matter, and is hence 'physical' in the literal sense that all
its constituents are among the subject matter of physics. Every entity—stone or
man, idea or essence—is on this principle a vulnerable and effective denizen of
the one continuum of action, and in the entire universe, including the knowing
mind itself, there is nothing which could not be destroyed (or repaired) by a
spatio-temporal redisposition of its components.[26]

In 1944 fifteen American "naturalists" were able to agree sufficiently
on attitude, on basic beliefs, and on method to produce a cooperative volume which is certainly one of the most significant expressions of this philosophy ever written. In trying to summarize the results of the various
essays, John Herman Randall, Jr. had this to say:

Now naturalism, in the sense in which it is maintained in this volume, can
be defined negatively as the refusal to take "nature" or "the natural" as a term
of distinction. As Mr. Lamprecht well points out, it is opposed to all dualisms
between Nature and another realm of being—to the Greek opposition between
Nature and Art, to the medieval contrast of the Natural and the Supernatural,

[25] Roy Wood Sellars, V. J. McGill, and Marvin Farber (eds.), *Philosophy for the
Future*, The Macmillan Co., New York, 1949, p. vi.
[26] D. C. Williams, "Naturalism and the Nature of Things," *Philosophical Review*,
1944, vol. 53, No. 5, No. 317, p. 418.

to the empiricist antithesis of Nature and Experience, to the idealist distinction between Natural and Transcendental, to the fundamental dualism pervading modern thought between Nature and Man. For present-day naturalists "Nature" serves rather as the all-inclusive category, corresponding to the role played by "Being" in Greek thought, or by "Reality" for the idealists. In this sense, as Mr. Dennes recognizes, naturalism, in becoming all-inclusive, ceases to be a distinctive "ism." It regards as "natural" whatever man encounters in whatever way. . . . Naturalism thus merges in the generic activity of philosophy as critical interpretation—the examination of the status of all these varieties of "stuff" in Nature—or in Being, or in Reality—and the discovery of their various relations to each other and their respective functions in man's experience. Positively, naturalism can be defined as the continuity of analysis—as the application of what all the contributors call "scientific methods" to the critical interpretation and analysis of every field.[27]

In a recent address to the American Philosophical Association, Ernest Nagel reconsidered and redefined naturalism. Because of its completeness as a description of the position, a substantial quotation from that address is presented.

Two theses seem to me central to naturalism as I conceive it. The first is the existential and causal primacy of organized matter in the executive order of nature. This is the assumption that the occurrence of events, qualities and processes, and the characteristic behaviors of various individuals, are contingent on the organization of spatio-temporally located bodies, whose internal structures and external relations determine and limit the appearance and disappearance of everything that happens. That this is so, is one of the best-tested conclusions of experience. We are frequently ignorant of the special conditions under which things come into being or pass away; but we have also found repeatedly that when we look closely, we eventually ascertain at least the approximate and gross conditions under which events occur, and we discover that those conditions invariably consist of some more or less complex organization of material substances. Naturalism does not maintain that only what is material exists, since many things noted in experience, for example, modes of action, relations of meaning, dreams, joys, plans, aspirations, are not as such material bodies or organizations of material bodies. What naturalism does assert as a truth about nature is that though *forms* of behavior or *functions* of material systems are indefeasibly parts of nature, forms and functions are not themselves agents in their own realization or in the realization of anything else. In the conception of nature's processes which naturalism affirms, there is no place for the operation of disembodied forces, no place for an immaterial spirit directing the course of events, no place for the survival of personality after the corruption of the body which exhibits it.

The second major contention of naturalism is that the manifest plurality and variety of things, of their qualities and their functions are an irreducible feature

[27] Y. Krikorian (ed.), *Naturalism and the Human Spirit,* Columbia University Press, New York, 1944, p. 357.

of the cosmos, not a deceptive appearance cloaking some more homogeneous "ultimate reality" or transempirical substance, and that the sequential orders in which events occur or the manifold relations of dependence in which things exist are *contingent* connections, not the embodiments of a fixed and unified pattern of logically necessary links. The existential primacy of organized matter does not make illusory either the relatively permanent or the comparatively transient characters and forms which special configurations of bodies may possess. In particular, although the continued existence of the human scene is precarious and is dependent on a balance of forces that doubtless will not endure indefinitely, and even though its distinctive traits are not pervasive throughout space, it is nonetheless as much a part of the "ultimate" furniture of the world, and is as genuine a sample of what "really" exists, as are atoms and stars. There undoubtedly occur integrated systems of bodies, such as biological organisms, which have the capacity because of their material organization to maintain themselves and the direction of their characteristic activities. But there is no positive evidence, and much negative evidence, for the supposition that all existential structures are teleological systems in this sense, or for the view that whatever occurs is a phase in a unitary, teleologically organized, and all-inclusive process or system. Modern physical cosmology does indeed supply some evidence for definite patterns of evolutionary development of stars, galactic systems, and even of the entire physical universe; and it is quite possible that the stage of cosmic evolution reached at any given time causally limits the types of things which can occur during that period. On the other hand, the patterns of change investigated in physical cosmogony are not patterns that are exhaustive of everything that happens; and nothing in these current physical speculations requires the conclusion that changes in one star or galaxy are related by inherent necessity to every action of biological organisms in some remote planet. Even admittedly teleological systems contain parts and processes which are causally irrelevant to some of the activities maintained by those systems; and the causal dependencies known to hold between the parts of any system, teleological or not, have never been successfully established as forms of logically necessary relations. In brief, if naturalism is true, irreducible variety and logical contingency are fundamental traits of the world we actually inhabit. The orders and connections of things are all accessible to rational inquiry; but these orders and connections are not all derivable by deductive methods from any set of premises that deductive reason can certify.[28]

We have given the naturalists the chance to speak for themselves—interrupting them at one place and cutting them off too soon at another which, of course, is not playing quite fair. Still we cannot reproduce the whole of any one naturalist nor present the range of divergence among those who choose this name for their basic beliefs. It would seem possible to gain from these definitions and descriptions not only the spirit or attitudes of the naturalists but also their major claims. Let us try to bring

[28] Quoted by permission of Ernest Nagel, "Naturalism Reconsidered," *Proceedings and Addresses of The American Philosophical Association*, Vol. 28, 1954–55, pp. 8–10.

them into focus, recognizing that not all naturalists would agree even on these points.

1. *The Universe Self-Existent.*

There is a universe which is the totality of objects, relations, and events in space-time. It is self-existent, self-explanatory, self-operating, and self-directing. One need not look beyond it for causes or explanations of its being and activity. Beneath all the variety and multiplicity of the world of nature and men is the same "physical" stuff and all the diverse activity within this world is explicable by the same laws. The realm of the physical is the matrix of all becoming. Naturalists are not wedded to any one doctrine of the nature of the stuff of the world except that it be physical, that is, any concrete entity in all its aspects is in a space-time system; but the basic stuff may be interpreted as minute, spherical atoms, or as electric charges, or electromagnetic waves. Its precise nature is for the chemist and physicist to discover. In any case it is non-spiritual and determined by discoverable laws. Whatever else there is has emerged from it.

2. *The Reductionistic View.*

The astonishing variety within nature is the result of different levels of organization of the same original material. What is molten lava at one level, or the twitch of a frog's leg at another, may be the prophet's indignation or the martyr's sacrifice, or the philosopher's reflection at still another. Contemporary naturalists accept a form of the ancient conception of a hierarchical universe, but in its modern version a higher level differs from a lower not in kind but in complexity of organization. But it is clear that naturalists are not themselves clear on this point. Some disclaim with contempt any kind of reductionistic view, that is, that what is found at higher levels can be "reduced" to the lower levels and finally to the original stuff. Thus,

> To show how a hero's aspiration, for example, is composed of the same sort of elements as a piece of slate, does not in any sense involve 'reducing' the heroic aspiration to pieces of slate. It does involve 'reducing', in an important and intelligible sense, both the aspiration and the slate to components which *ipso facto* are simpler than they, and in a sense 'inferior' to them.[29]

3. *Man's Fate: An Accidental Collocation of Atoms?*

In this physical matrix, then, consciousness, selfhood, personality, and so on, are to be regarded as complex functions of highly organized physico-chemical systems. There is no evidence, it is said, for a resident or disembodied soul. Man's intelligence is determined and conditioned by,

[29] D. C. Williams, *op. cit.* p. 424.

among other things, the development of his nervous system. He is a natural product in a natural world with a natural end. The idea that he has a supernatural origin and destiny or immortality is simply wishful thinking and a failure to examine the evidence. One does not read the naturalists very long before seeing how eager and vigorous they are in their denials. All forms of immaterial entities, cosmic purposes, gods, disembodied souls, intuitions, revealed dogmas are to them anathema and to be driven from philosophy and science by the whip of a method. The affirmations of religion, if they mean belief in supernatural entities, are in error. Religious experience, when genuine, is an emotional response, largely of aesthetic appreciation or of loyalty and courage in the face of the threatening tragedies of existence. Bertrand Russell, though not clearly a naturalist, once gave a resolute expression of this view or attitude when he wrote the following:

That Man is the product of causes which had no prevision of the end they were achieving; that his origin, his growth, his hopes and fears, his loves and his beliefs, are but the outcome of accidental collocations of atoms; that no fire, no heroism, no intensity of thought and feeling, can preserve an individual life beyond the grave; that all the labours of the ages, all the devotion, all the inspiration, all the noonday brightness of human genius, are destined to extinction in the vast death of the solar system, and that the whole temple of Man's achievement must inevitably be buried beneath the debris of a universe in ruins —all these things, if not quite beyond dispute, are yet so nearly certain, that no philosophy which rejects them can hope to stand. Only within the scaffolding of these truths, only on the firm foundation of unyielding despair, can the soul's habitation henceforth be safely built.[30]

4. *Salvation Through a New God.*

Though repulsed both by the claims and the language of theology when it is making cognitive statements, some naturalists nevertheless do use the term "God," not to mean an "omnipotent personal power who guides the destinies of the world he has created" but rather to mean "a principle of order in the universe, the totality of all things, the possibility of good in the world, or the object of human allegiance."[31] Thus man's values and ideals are also natural facts in a natural world. His goals ought to be this-worldly, for there is no other world. His salvation, if one wishes to use theological language, is to be found in the elimination of disease, poverty, war, and in the widest distribution of the conditions and possibilities of

[30] Bertrand Russell, *Mysticism and Logic*, George Allen & Unwin, Ltd., London, 1949, pp. 47–48.
[31] Sidney Hook, "Naturalism and First Principles," *American Philosophers at Work*, Criterion Books, Inc., New York, 1956, p. 253.

growth toward intelligent behavior and mutual comfort. Man must work out his destiny in cooperation with others, each understanding the limitations and potentialities of human nature. There is nothing so warped that human intelligence cannot straighten it without the assistance of supernatural agencies.

5. *Origin of Mental Events.*

All mental events, too, are explicable within the system of levels. Here the naturalist frequently resorts to an argument by analogy. Just as the properties of water are contingent upon the presence and interrelationship of certain elements, so "mental" events occur as distinctive modes of behavior when certain physical conditions are properly related and organized. Here is a statement agreed upon by three contemporary naturalists, John Dewey, Sidney Hook, and Ernest Nagel:

Like the chemist in reference to the properties of water, he (the naturalist) maintains that the states and events called mental exist only when certain organizations of physical things also occur. And also like the chemist, he holds that the qualities and behaviors displayed by physical things when they are properly organized—the qualities and behaviors called mental or spiritual—are not exhibited by those things unless they are so organized. But these qualities and behaviors of organized wholes are not additional things which are *substantially* distinct from the properties and behaviors of spatio-temporal objects in their organized unity. Accordingly, naturalists most emphatically acknowledge that men are capable of thought, feeling, and emotion, and that in consequence of these powers (whose existence is contingent upon the organization of human bodies) men can engage in actions that bodies not so organized are unable to perform.[32]

6. *Naturalists, Science, and a Poetic Lament.*

Most naturalists claim to be close allies of science, not only in spirit, but more importantly in method. This is one of the sturdiest affirmations upon which contemporary naturalists unite. The laws of logic, the canons of evidence and relevance, they insist, are the same in science and philosophy. On this point again let us quote from the work of Sidney Hook.

If the foregoing is sound then I think it constitutes some reason for believing that there is only one reliable method of reaching the truth about the nature of things anywhere and at any time, that this reliable method comes to full fruition in the methods of science, and that a man's normal behavior in adapting means to ends belies his words whenever he denies it. Naturalism as a philosophy not only accepts this method but also the broad generalizations which are established by the use of it; *viz.,* that the occurrence of all qualities or events depends upon

[32] John Dewey, Sidney Hook, and Ernest Nagel, "Are Naturalists Materialists?" *The Journal of Philosophy,* Vol. 42, 1945, p. 521.

the organization of a material system in space-time, and that their emergence, development and disappearance are determined by changes in such organization.[33]

It is with the methods of science that naturalists think they can eliminate mystery from human life. And yet we must remember Santayana who could find no way beyond the mystery of all mysteries, namely, existence itself. Probably other naturalists would regard Santayana's words nearer to a poetic lament than a pronouncement concerning the limitations of science. It is easy to see that not only the beliefs of naturalists but also their denials are the consequences of their method. Thus minds as "mental" substances, gods, universals, and so on, are denied because they are not possible objects of scientific knowledge, that is, there is no empirical evidence that will justify belief in these objects. Furthermore, the naturalist doubts that any other method could be valid, and therefore the claims of another method with respect to these objects are always suspect. Nature is all there is. There is no unbridgeable chasm between nature and man, thus man can know nature by the proper methods. When he does, nature is seen to be lawful, and to know the laws is to know the truth— but not the Absolute Truth. Naturalists ordinarily make no claim to this, rather they aim for reasonableness, reliability, and adequacy.

7. *Concluding Remarks.*

It is difficult not to be a naturalist of some sort. The position seems so clear, so simple, so well-argued. The range of human experiences it is able to account for is enormous. In spite of divergences among the naturalists on some matters of detail, there is a generous amount of agreement on basic principles, and they exhibit a contagious sense of confidence in man and his competence to solve problems. Naturalists have few doubts about themselves or their methods. They are not sceptics, but exuberant believers when belief is justified by their rigorous tests.

And yet the position is not without its difficulties. Its absolute reliance upon scientific methods as the only acceptable way to reliable knowledge, does seem to many non-naturalists to exclude somewhat arbitrarily other possible ways of knowing, e.g., intuition, revelation, introspection, metaphor, the a priori, and so forth. On the other hand, these ways have offered very little in the way of concrete results that can stand up under naturalistic criticisms. Again, naturalism tends to give the impression that science presents one vast block of total acquiescence, but this does not represent the actual state of modern science. On some basic points alternative positions are possible and defended, as we have seen in this brief account. If

[33] Sidney Hook, "Naturalism and First Principles," *op. cit.,* p. 248.

the naturalists take science and its methods as the paradigm of knowledge, what shall be done with the divergent views of the scientists, some of whom have a view not compatible with a thoroughgoing naturalism? Of course, the naturalist may reply that being a scientist does not make one also a critical philosopher, and that the non-naturalistic scientists are simply not philosophic though they may be sound scientists.

Moreover, it is not clear how the naturalistic categories are sufficient to account for life, memory, reason, comparison, purpose, and so on. They really put us in the peculiar position of never being able to object with any force, because it is easy for them to admit the presence of these phenomena and to say they are merely the consequences of prior physical conditions and an extraordinarily complex organization of the basic elements. Of course, this may be true, but it certainly has not been demonstrated to be true by any method acceptable to the naturalists themselves.

In describing the views of Alfred North Whitehead, I. M. Bochenski brings together a number of weaknesses Whitehead had found in materialism, and which he thought must lead to its rejection as an acceptable metaphysics.

Materialism inevitably leads one to deny the existence of secondary qualities, a clear contradiction of all experience; it leads just as inevitably to the equally false denial of human responsibility. Ultimately it destroys its own premise, that is, induction, because if matter simply consists of isolated fragments linked together through spatio-temporal relations alone, then there is no justification for inferring what will happen to one entity from what has happened to another. At the present day, materialism can no longer look to the natural sciences for support; the undulatory theory of light, the idea of atomicity (since its transference to biological fields), the doctrines of the conservation of energy and of evolution have all brought forth facts which point to the inadequacy of scientific materialism. Finally, the quantum theory has proved this philosophy to be quite untenable by demanding that "matter" itself should be conceived as organic. Nevertheless the chief argument against materialism remains philosophical—one can easily demonstrate that in its essence this doctrine attributes reality to a convenient and very fertile abstraction. Body, as Galileo and Descartes understood the term, does not rust; it is but an abstraction—the concept of body is a typical instance of the fallacy of misplaced concreteness.[34]

But some of these objections do not apply to some modern materialists or naturalists. Not all deny the existence of secondary qualities—both Santayana and Nagel come to mind—unless this means the "ultimate" reality of secondary qualities. And certainly contemporary naturalists have no intention of denying the proper place for human responsibility. They

[34] I. M. Bochenski, op. cit., p. 230.

may be honorable men without being inconsistent with their metaphysical beliefs.

One cannot take any naturalist as typical. Any one always has beliefs not shared by other naturalists and rejects some beliefs they hold. This is why it is so difficult to speak of modern materialism or naturalism as a system. All contemporary naturalists have abandoned the older materialism, which tended to reduce everything to "billiard balls in motion." The newer reduction strives to give the most ultimate explanation of reality in terms of the laws of physics and chemistry. Certainly at this stage in our history such an accomplishment has not been fulfilled. But this is not to suggest that, given time, the goal will be reached. The non-naturalist claims that it is impossible to reach this end, not merely technically but logically. The differences between a neural event and an idea, between a wavelength and a visible red color, between glandular activity and the love of one person for another, between a printed or spoken word and its meaning, between terms and their relations, are irreducible differences, says the non-naturalist, so that waiting for more delicate instruments and smarter men to solve the problem is hopeless. But when the non-naturalist protests in this way, he forgets that some naturalists do not reduce qualities to anything else. For example, Dennes denies that qualities "are (or can be reduced to) bodies in motion; events in relation, or anything else but just themselves."[35]

Nevertheless, it is probable that all naturalists think that whatever is, has a "physical" base although "physical" may be a highly ambiguous and vague conception. It would not be unfair to say that naturalists find it difficult to get together on a theory of reality, but are united on a theory of method, namely the one so successfully employed in the sciences.

IV. Idealism

1. Introduction.

There are many varieties of this view (the Dictionary of Philosophy mentions twelve), but it will not be necessary on a first acquaintance to explore all of its detailed subtypes. At appropriate points variations that assume importance because they try to answer specific difficulties will be indicated. Very generally stated, idealism is a philosophic position that affirms the sole reality of mind or spirit, and denies the ultimately real nature of matter. In this sense it goes contrary to common sense, which ascribes reality to the physical phenomena of experience.

[35] Y. Krikorian, *op. cit.*, p. 284.

But even this statement is unsatisfactory because it would be difficult to find any idealist who would accept it as it stands. Perhaps it would be better to say that the idealists think that matter is unintelligible apart from a logically prior spirit or mind. One American philosopher has tried to sum it up this way:

Idealism is that philosophical doctrine which undertakes to show that, in order to think matter or the spatio-temporal order of events in its ultimate nature, we are logically compelled to think mind or spirit along with it as in some sense foundational to it.[36]

For the idealist, the apparently real is distinct from the ultimately real, and the latter is mental or spiritual in character; it is known through thought, and is of the nature of thought. The knowing mind is prior to the object known, and the being of the object itself is dependent on its being known by some mind, finite or infinite. Idealists tend to believe that a rightly reasoned philosophy is a true philosophy, because the world is rational, and the more perfect our reason the nearer we come to truth.

The guiding principle of right reason, which they take as basic, is the principle of non-contradiction. What is contradictory to rational thought cannot be. Thought has needs that are satisfied only by what is self-consistent, harmonious, self-complete and all-inclusive. Moreover, many idealists stress the importance of consciousness, because what is in our consciousness we can be certain of. Finally, it should be pointed out that idealists tend to think that human values, particularly moral ones, are trustworthy indices to the nature of reality. Thus philosophic idealism must be distinguished from the more or less popular conception of the idealist as one who affirms the existence of transcendent ideals or who gives himself to ends and causes that expect more from man than he is ordinarily able to achieve.

Like materialism, or naturalism, idealism is a vast system, seeking to account for all the phenomena of nature and experience on the basis of one principle. Both views are, therefore, often called monistic. However, there is a form of idealism that stresses the reality of many minds, rather than one mind, which may be called pluralistic idealism.

It is unfair to classify a thinker as an idealist without showing where and how he differs from other idealists; nevertheless, the student should know the names of a few of those who belong somewhere in this great

[36] G. W. Cunningham, *The Idealistic Argument in Recent British and American Philosophy*, The Century Co., New York, 1933, p. 339.

tradition, such as Plato, Plotinus, Leibniz, Berkeley, Kant, Hegel, and Royce. Idealism is also basic to much of the ancient and modern Hindu philosophies.

The diversity and variety of idealistic systems is so confusing that Ewing has tried to reduce the difficulties by suggesting the following classifications:

(1) There is the type which argues that physical objects involve mind, and since they are independent of *human* minds, therefore imply a divine mind, or that a divine mind is required to think the moral law or other universal laws which we cannot help recognizing as objective. (2) There are the "absolute idealists" who view the whole of reality as a *single experience* or mind, although they may differ in ascribing or not ascribing personality to this mind. (3) There is the idealism which makes reality consist of a *society* of spirits who are either very highly developed already, although they may not appear so now, time being unreal, or if time is real, will at least become so eventually. On this view, no single spirit holds the supreme position of God. (4) There is the "pan-psychic" form of idealism according to which physical objects are the appearance of non-human but low grade minds or, rather, psychical entities. Just as animal minds are inferior to human, so these sub-minds are conceived as inferior to animal. This view may or may not be combined with theism. (5) There is the view according to which physical objects are just abstractions from human experience.[37]

2. *Monistic vs. Pluralistic Idealism.*

In setting forth the major claims of idealism we will keep the distinction between its monistic and pluralistic forms. As a monistic philosophy it affirms the following:

First, mind alone is ultimately real, and it is directly given in human experience as well as deductively arrived at from certain premises. It is the rational aspect of the mental life, not the movements of feeling and will, that is stressed. In other words, the approach to mind is through logic and epistemology, and not through psychology.

Second, reality includes all individuals, not as drops of water in an ocean, but as cells in an organism. The universe is one, vast, organic whole, in which the parts or fragments are abstractions and the *totality* alone real. Thus it denies the absolute separation of things, and the apparent manyness of the world is just that—apparent.

Third, the interdependence of things is so thorough and absolute that a difference anywhere would make a difference everywhere. There is no irrational looseness in the nature of things, no chance operations, no caprice;

[37] A. C. Ewing, *The Idealist Tradition,* The Free Press, Glencoe, Illinois, 1957, p. 24.

all is rationally determined, and freedom is to be interpreted as rational behavior. One representative of the position defends this point by the following argument:

Suppose I climb the hill behind my farm house in Vermont and look across at Mount Washington. I am wearing a felt hat at the time. Is it sensible or quite sane to argue that if I had worn a straw hat instead, that fact would have made a difference to Mount Washington?

I not only believe it would, but that the argument for this conclusion is strong almost to demonstration. In outline it is as follows: my putting on this particular hat had causes, which lay in part in the workings of my brain; these workings also had causes, which lay in part in the workings of other bodily organs; these in turn depended upon countless physical factors in the way of food, air, light, and temperature, every one of which had its own conditions. It is plain that before we took many steps in this retreat, we should find ourselves involved in millions of conditions, and that if we were able *per impossible* to traverse all the diverging branches, there would probably be no region of the universe that would remain unpenetrated. Now if we reject, as I suppose we must, the plurality of causes, and hold that the causal relation is reciprocating, then a denial of the causal consequent will require a denial of its antecedent. A different event, then, from that on which these various lines converge would require differences throughout the range of the countless conditions themselves. Very well; let us assume such a different event to have occurred— my wearing a straw hat instead of a felt one—and having ascended the causal lines, let us now descend them. If the antecedents of the present event were scattered throughout the universe, and we suppose them altered throughout, is there any reason whatever to suppose that the present state of the world would be as we find it? The answer is obvious. The world would not only be different, but so extensively different that we could point neither to Mount Washington nor to anything else and say that it would be exempt from change.[38]

Fourth, monistic idealists tend to regard their system as a synthesis of all views. Opposing philosophies are therefore not so much in error, they are merely incomplete, and idealism gathers them up in its all-embracing totality. Another representative of this position puts it this way:

We hold that our conclusion is certain, and that to doubt it logically is impossible. There is no other view, there is no other idea beyond the view here put forward. It is impossible rationally even to entertain the question of another possibility. Outside our main result there is nothing except the wholly unmeaning, or else something which on scrutiny is seen really not to fall outside. Thus the supposed Other will, in short, turn out to be actually the same; or it will contain elements included within our view of the Absolute, but elements dislocated and so distorted into erroneous appearance. And the dislocation itself will find a place within the limits of our system.

[38] Brand Blanshard, *The Nature of Thought,* George Allen & Unwin Ltd., 1939, 1948, 1955, Vol. II, pp. 293–294.

Our result, in brief, cannot be doubted, since it contains all possibilities. Show us an idea, we can proclaim, which seems hostile to our scheme, and we will show you an element which really is contained within it. And we will demonstrate your idea to be a self-contradictory piece of our system, an internal fragment which only through sheer blindness can fancy itself outside. We will prove that its independence and isolation are nothing in the world but a failure to perceive more than one aspect of its own nature.[39]

And last, idealists claim that their position is not only a philosophy of being, but also of value. It is animated by a search for the good and for better ways of living. These goods and ways are to be found in the realm of spirit and mind, rather than in what is called matter. Thus idealism is thought to be compatible with, and indeed to promote, the highest affirmation and intimation of the religious attitude toward human existence.

The claims of pluralistic idealism involve a denial of some of the major features of the monistic type. In general we can say that the pluralists are unwilling to accept the "block universe," as William James called it, of the monists. They see in such a system the loss of individual minds, which alone to them are real. Reality is a kind of community of selves, superintended by a great Self who is the author of their being. The finite self is known directly in, for example, our experience of memory, desire, and pain. Manyness is a fundamental category for the pluralistic idealist; not a manyness of matter, but of minds, persons, or selves. This view allows therefore, for some indeterminateness, looseness, or finiteness in the world. It usually has led to a religious conception of the world called theism.

It is possible, however, to construct a pluralistic idealism without finding it necessary to arrive at the existence of a supreme Self or Spirit or God. The British philosopher McTaggart tried to do this. His claim is that reality is a society of spirits fundamentally related by love; that the world of our perceptions is unreal; but that there will be an eventual immortality in which we become conscious of our true nature. Such a condition will be one of utter goodness and bliss. It does not require a God for its attainment.

It will not be possible in this brief account to present the whole range of argument and evidence for idealism. In its long history many ingenious and subtle ways of demonstrating the sole reality of mind have been worked out, for it is not easy to shake one's belief in the reality of solid, non-conscious stuff called matter, or to convince another that hot suns and cold moons are really thoughts or colonies of selves. But with some of the argument and evidence we must be acquainted. Fools may be idealists

[39] F. H. Bradley, *Appearance and Reality*, George Allen & Unwin, Ltd., London, 1925, pp. 518–519.

but idealists are not foolish. They have made rigorous demands upon themselves for logical rigor and manifested great intellectual courage to "follow the argument wherever it leads."

3. *The Epistemological Argument: Berkeley and Royce.*

We will first consider what may be called the epistemological argument for idealism as it appeared in the work of two first-rank philosophers, George Berkeley and Josiah Royce. To follow Berkeley's argument we need to recall a distinction, familiar since the work of Galileo, between the secondary qualities and primary qualities of any thing. The former are relative to the observer; that is, they owe their existence to the fact that they are being perceived. Thus consider this orange. Its color and taste depend on my seeing and tasting; different perceivers in different conditions may not register the same color or taste. But each sees one, spherical, measurable, motionless, or perhaps moving object; number, shape, size, and motion are examples of primary qualities. Now, the argument runs, as secondary qualities are never found separate from primary, that is, we never see just red, but always a red thing, nor taste sweetness but always something sweet, therefore, the primary qualities too must be dependent for their being on the perceiver and his act of perception. But our perceptions are forms of ideas—mental occurrences. Thus all known things are ideas and nothing but ideas. Matter itself is known only as idea. Berkeley's famous conclusion in his own words is worth quoting:

Some truths there are so near and obvious to the mind that a man need only open his eyes to see them. Such I take this important one to be, viz., that all the choir of heaven and furniture of the earth, in a word all those bodies which compose the mighty frame of the world, have not any subsistence without a mind, that their *being* is to be perceived or known; that consequently so long as they are not actually perceived by me, or do not exist in my mind or that of any other created spirit, they must either have no existence at all, or else subsist in the mind of some Eternal Spirit—it being perfectly unintelligible, and involving all the absurdity of abstraction, to attribute to any single part of them an existence independent of a spirit. To be convinced of which, the reader need only reflect, and try to separate in his own thoughts the *being* of a sensible thing from its *being perceived.*[40]

Royce, America's most powerful defender of idealism, once put his argument in the form of a dilemma.

Either, as you see, your real world yonder is through and through a world of ideas, an outer mind that you are more or less comprehending through your experience, *or else,* in so far as it is real and outer it is unknowable, an inscrut-

[40] George Berkeley, *The Principles of Human Knowledge,* The Open Court Publishing Co., La Salle, Illinois, 1950, p. 32.

able *x*, an absolute mystery. The dilemma is perfect. There is no third alternative. Either a mind yonder, or else the unknowable; that is your choice.[41]

The argument depends on the fact that the only thing we do know or can know is an idea. What is not an idea is therefore not only unknown but unknowable, and nothing can be said about it.

4. *The Ego-Centric Predicament: Perry.*

The strength of these arguments has been thought to be considerably weakened by the discovery of what is called the *ego-centric predicament.* The fact that one cannot mention, report, know, anything except an idea is a predicament of the cognitive situation but does not prove that such a relationship is necessary for the being of the known thing, or that it can have no existence outside of this relationship.

The argument, more technically stated, was first worked out by Ralph Barton Perry in 1910.[42] Let us accept the following symbols, $E = $ Ego; $T = $ everything, anything, "unlimited denotation"; and $R^c = $ any form of consciousness that relates to an object, for studying, comparing, and so on. Now, says Perry, ontological idealism is a name for this proposition: $(E) R^c (T)$ defines T; that is, T necessarily stands in the relation, R^c to an E, or $R^c (E)$ is indispensable to T. But the attempt to prove this reveals the predicament. Whenever one tries to discover the precise nature of the modification of T by $R^c (E)$, one finds that $R^c (E)$ cannot be eliminated. All cases of "I study," "I eliminate," "I think," "I observe," etc. are cases of $R^c (E)$. $R^c (E)$ is "peculiarly ubiquitous." This is the fact. But what does it prove? Nothing, says Perry. It is a methodological predicament and shows only the impossibility of using this method to solve a problem.

In order to discover if possible exactly how a T is modified by the relationship R^c (E), I look for instances of T *out* of this relationship, in order that I may compare them with instances of T *in* this relationship. But I can find no such instances, because "finding" is a variety of the very relationship that I am trying to eliminate. Hence, I cannot make the comparison, nor get an answer to my original question by this means. But I cannot conclude that there are no such instances; indeed, I now know that *I should not be able to discover them if there were.*

In thus eliminating all knowledge I do not experimentally eliminate the thing known, but only the possibility of knowing whether that thing is eliminated or not.[43]

[41] Josiah Royce, *The Spirit of Modern Philosophy*, Houghton Mifflin & Co., The Riverside Press, Cambridge, Massachusetts, 1892, p. 364.

[42] Ralph Barton Perry, "The Ego-Centric Predicament," *The Journal of Philosophy*, Vol. 7, No. 1, 1910, pp. 5–14.

[43] *Ibid.*, p. 8.

The idealists, however, were not dismayed by Perry's argument. They felt he misconceived the nature of idealism by taking as its central feature the idea that the being of anything depends on its being in the mind of some thinker. They insisted that the major problem, namely, the nature of the objective world or reality, was their real concern, and that the ego-centric predicament did not refute their claims about this reality.

Idealists insist that it is impossible to get mind from non-mind, and many have taken this as the first premise of their argument. If, it is said, we begin with unconscious, physical stuff, and that is all there is, we can never produce conscious, mental beings, which seem obviously to be present in the world. This argument, however, does not show the unreality of matter, but at most is a proposal to grant mind a place no less original than matter. Moreover, why may one not point to the difficulty of getting matter, which also seems obviously present, if mind is the sole reality?

5. *The Theories of Internal and External Relations.*

Idealists also argue from the interdependence of things and the nature of relations. It is quite true that all of our experience is involved in a network of relations. In many ways we are interdependent beings. Science has taught us the universality of gravitation and the social sciences stress the fact that man is a social being, that is, not an independent individual. Idealists have usually insisted on making a distinction between internal and external relations and then denying that the latter have any reality. Perhaps the clearest statement of the theory of external relations was given by Spaulding. He said

(1) that, if two terms are related, neither term influences the other, (2) that the absence of either term would be *without effect* on the other, (3) that either term may come into being and into relation with the other term without affecting it, (4) that, accordingly, no term is *complex* by virtue of being related, and (5) that no third term, *u,* underlying *aRb* . . . is necessary. . . . Briefly, the theory of external relations is that *relatedness and independence are quite compatible.*[44]

This view should be contrasted with the explicitly formulated theory of internal relations presented by Blanshard. He says

(1) that every term, i.e. every possible object of thought, is what it is in virtue of relations to what is other than itself; (2) that its nature is affected thus not by some of its relations only, but in differing degrees by all of them, no matter how external they may seem; (3) that in consequence of (2) and of the

[44] E. G. Spaulding, *The New Rationalism,* Henry Holt & Co., New York, 1918, p. 177.

further obvious fact that everything is related in *some* way to everything else, no knowledge will reveal completely the nature of any term until it has exhausted that term's relations to everything else.[45]

Idealists have argued that this vast system of mutual relationships implies the reality of mind because relations have no meaning apart from mind. This principle is taken almost as self-evident by the idealists. If there can be no relatedness apart from mind, and no space apart from relatedness, and no matter apart from space, it follows that apart from mind there can be no matter.

Two examples from British philosophers show how the argument from relations is used to prove the unthinkability of physical things apart from mind. Consider first the statement from T. H. Green.

Relation is to us such a familiar fact that we are apt to forget that it involves all the mystery, if it be a mystery, of the existence of many in one. Whether we say that a related thing is one in itself, manifold in respect of its relations, or that there is one relation between manifold things, e.g., the relation of mutual attraction between bodies—and one expression or the other we must employ in stating the simplest facts—we are equally affirming the unity of the manifold. Abstract the many relations from the one thing, and there is nothing. They, being many, determine or constitute its definite unity. It is not the case that it first exists in its unity, and then is brought into various relations. Without the relations it would not exist at all. In like manner the one relation is a unity of the many things. They, in their manifold being, make the one relation. If these relations really exist, there is a real unity of the manifold, a real multiplicity of that which is one. But a plurality of things cannot of themselves unite in one relation, nor can a single thing of itself bring itself into a multitude of relations. It is true, as we have said, that the single things are nothing except as determined by relations which are the negation of their singleness, but they do not therefore cease to be single things. Their common being is not something into which their several existences disappear. On the contrary, if they did not survive in their singleness, there could be no relation between them—nothing but a blank featureless identity. There must, then, be something other than the manifold things themselves, which combines them without effacing their severalty.[46]

The argument here is that if A and B are related they are separate and together at the same time. This is possible only if there is an intelligence that holds the things together in thought, e.g., when we think A and B we keep them distinct, but they fall within the same unity of consciousness and therefore are together.

[45] B. Blanshard, *The Nature of Thought*, George Allen & Unwin, Ltd., London, 1955, Vol. II, p. 452.
[46] T. H. Green, *Prolegomena to Ethics*, 3rd ed., The Clarendon Press, Oxford, 1890, p. 31.

Rashdall has a similar argument, based not on relation in general, but specifically on space relations which cannot be meaningful apart from mind.

Relatedness only has a meaning when thought of in connection with a mind which is capable of grasping or holding together both terms of the relation. The relation between point A and point B is not *in* point A or *in* point B taken by themselves. It is all in the 'between': 'betweenness' from its very nature cannot exist in any one point of space or in several isolated points of space or things in space; it must exist only in some one existent which holds together and connects those points. And nothing, as far as we can understand, can do that except a mind. Apart from mind there can be no relatedness: apart from relatedness no space: apart from space, no matter. It follows that apart from mind there can be no matter.[47]

These arguments depend on the fact that relations imply mind, which is usually taken by idealists as self-evident rather than demonstrated. But the puzzles about relations themselves, e.g., whether they are *in* terms or *between* them, are difficult enough and not settled. It does seem rather unsure ground, therefore, to base an argument for idealism on a tangle of puzzles. The motive back of this argument is the longing for unity, totality, and wholeness, which is considered to be not only real but also good. The idealist has no patience with disorder, frivolity, irresponsibility, waste, caprice, and so on. But is it not a fact that these enter into human experience with compelling force? True, they may change their character when we change our point of view, but their presence is still too vivid and bitter to permit us to dismiss them as unreal or appearance. Moreover, things are certainly related externally in some degree or sense, for not all the relations in which a thing stands are equally necessary for its character or being.

Idealists have generally striven to demonstrate the existence of moral values and ideals, which, it is claimed, would have no significance or reality apart from minds to which they are present. This is another way of showing the importance of spiritual ends in human experience. Such an attitude is at least friendly toward religious affirmations, as materialism is not. The argument is, of course, a far cry from sufficient evidence for idealism. It does not establish the unreality of matter or the sole reality if mind. At the most it emphasizes that something more than physical stuff may be required to make the world of experience and behavior intelligible.

[47] H. Rashdall, *Philosophy and Religion*, Charles Scribner's Sons, New York, 1916, p. 11.

6. *Concluding Remarks.*

There has been no attempt to present the wide range and variation of the idealistic position and argument. But enough has been said to show the student that the aim of this philosophy, as with all great philosophies, is to give an account of the total character of nature and man. It can never be satisfied with local, particular, provincial points of view. One vast system constitutes reality; a system that is rational, intelligible, and spiritual, capable of being apprehended by mind. As a practical creed, idealism has frequently displayed its strength. Idealists are said to be known for their ability to stand above the minor irritations, as well as the overwhelming tragedies of existence, and to face life with a serenity and assurance that makes many others look like fussy little worriers. No generalization must be made here, however, for some naturalists too have achieved that high level of unconcern about their personal existence. The logical justification for idealism is a different matter. Its genuine appeal to the mind is marred by its failure to explain errors, mistakes, delusions, separateness, and distinctions, the persistence of evil, human freedom, and the difference between the "ought" and the "is." In short, there are irrationalities that we encounter daily that do not seem to fit the idealistic framework, but with which any philosophy must contend.

V. *Substance: Materialism and Idealism*

A. Introduction to the Problem of Substance

Nothing seems of more importance towards erecting a firm system of sound and real knowledge . . . than to lay the beginning in a distinct explication of what is meant by *thing, reality, existence;* for in vain shall we dispute concerning the real existence of things, or pretend to any knowledge thereof, so long as we have not fixed the meaning of those words.[48]

Because materialists and idealists disagree on whether things, reality, and existence are basically physical substance or mental substance, we must examine the meaning of "substance" before we can decide whether the issue is clearly stated. Since "reality," "existence," and "being" turned out to be dangerously ambiguous, the student may have suspected the same of "substance." The previous chapter has already quoted from philosophers who reject both materialism and idealism. If it could be established that any view of substance is untenable, then we could spare ourselves the trouble of examining the lengthy arguments between various

[48] George Berkeley, *The Principles of Human Knowledge,* The Open Court Publishing Co., La Salle, Illinois, 1950, pp. 81–82.

positions called "materialism" and "idealism." Indeed the attacks upon the concept of substance have been so strong that considerably fewer philosophers now take either of these alternatives seriously. The value of the attacks may be to stimulate increasing care in using the word "substance," just as Berkeley's question about the meaning of material substances has forced men to think of what "matter" could mean.

One attack goes as follows. When we designate a substance we normally use a name, or what is commonly called a noun. By false conversion many have therefore concluded that every noun is the name of some object, and by unwarranted generalization some have even thought any kind of word refers to something. "Not" is quite meaningful without naming an object, and what could it refer to? Hence the objection made famous by Bertrand Russell, that to speak of the world as substances qualified by attributes is naively to transfer to things the grammar of nouns and adjectives. Since the familiar grammar of "Snow is white" is shared by other Indo-European languages, the possibility that the world may be described otherwise comes only with the discovery or inventions of languages with a different principle of order.

The haunting possibility is that our whole philosophic tradition is prejudiced in favor of a view of reality that seems plausible only because it employs familiar arrangements of words. We need not learn Chinese to find an alternative; our philosophic age has proliferated artifical languages. Such logics may be based on the unconventional principle illustrated above that anything may be represented by a bare x, whether it exists or not, whether it has any predicated attribute or not; thus to exist means to be a class of at least one member, or anything quantified. The proposals of some metaphysical schemes, such as Whitehead's, depend on discrediting the exclusive claim of subject-predicate logic as the only right way to reason about things. At least there is no ontological significance in saying of the relational proposition "John is taller than Mary," that of the subject "John" we predicate "being taller than Mary." For we could just as well say "Mary is not as tall as John." The relational form allows us to think one term refers to as full a reality as the other.

A second objection to the concept of substance is that substance is unknowable. Indeed Locke confessed that substance is "something I know not what." The Kantian point was that reality is the thing-in-itself and all we know is the thing in relation to us. Now if we begin with the empiricist epistemology that only qualities and relations are known, of what use is the notion of substance in the sense of substratum? For qualities can just as easily be interpreted as belonging to each other as belonging to something else. Worse than useless, the use of a name for a substance-in-itself is misleading. A man, say Jones, is known only as Jones doing something, say, walking. Just as Aristotle argues that the attribute, walking, cannot be without something, the substance Jones, that walks, so Russell argues that Jones cannot be without doing something. Hence, he concludes that walking is not unsubstantial. Then anything may stand in the subject place of a proposition. But if any term can be a subject we are then not distinguishing one kind of object from any other kind. Hence the concept of substance is metaphysically useless.[49]

Without extending the anti-substance case, consider what defense of the concept there might be. Obviously the first attack does not prove that men believe in substance because our language takes the substance-at-tribute form. We might as well say that our logic mirrors our metaphysics as our metaphysics mirrors our logic. We might as well say that our grammar mirrors our logic as our logic mirrors our grammar. In other words, the assumption of priority of logic and language may be an idol of the analytic tribe. One may say cogently that language takes this form because of an antecedent belief about things. This is Santayana's point that belief in substance cannot be eliminated. The student will soon notice also that to the second objection, Santayana would reply that he does not claim to *know* substances, only to have *faith* in them.

The stoutest defense of belief in substance comes from George Santayana.

That . . . external things exist, that I exist myself, and live more or less prosperously in the midst of them is a faith not founded on reason but precipitated in action, and in that intent, which is virtual action, involved in perception. This faith, which it would be dishonest not to confess that I share, does no violence to a sceptical analysis of experience; on the contrary, it takes advantage of that analysis to interpret this volatile experience as all animals do and must, as a set of symbols for existences that cannot enter experience, and which, since they are not elements in knowledge, no analysis of knowledge can touch—they are in another realm of being.[50]

What does Santayana mean by "substance"? He does not restrict the meaning to that of which we predicate accidents or properties. Nor does he mean something self-subsistent in the sense of independent or unrelated to anything else. Nor does he mean that which is indivisible, nor that in which qualities inhere. These four meanings had been attacked,

[49] Bertrand Russell, "Words and Meaning," *Selected Papers of Bertrand Russell,* Modern Library, New York, 1927, esp. pp. 352–357.
[50] George Santayana, *Scepticism and Animal Faith,* Charles Scribner's Sons, New York, 1923, p. 106.

particularly by Berkeley—who disposed of material substance, leaving only minds, notions, and impressions—and Hume, who left only impressions. Go as far with your analysis as you please, says Santayana, until phenomena are the only objects left in which to believe, and the only objects left to know. Then these are the substances of your system.

From the point of view of knowledge, every event, even if wholly psychological or phenomenal, is a substance. It is a self-existing fact, open to description from the point of view of other events, if in the bosom of these other events there is such plasticity and intent as are requisite for perception, prophecy, or memory. . . .

My whole past lies waiting for memory to review it . . . ; and the whole future of the world in the same manner is spread out for prophecy . . . . Yet the future and the past are not ordinarily called substances; probably because the same material substance is assumed to run through both.[51]

On the basis of animal faith, Santayana develops his materialistic doctrine of substance. But there is no reason why one might not use the same basis for idealism or dualism. To make sure that the impression is avoided that materialists have a superior claim to the category, or are its only defenders, let us follow several non-materialist defenses of substance.

One is the claim that what each of us knows best is his own self, not as a substance separable from his activities, but as an on-going process. F. R. Tennant claims that "we are being active," and only this "immanent causation within a numerically singular entity" can explain the connection of events recognized as "mine." This denies Hume's doctrine that the self is but a collection of states or a class of members. If this is so, we have no ground for ascribing to any group of impressions more than logical unity. But they belong to me as a substance, something with power to will and to do.[52]

Perhaps the basic analogy of the idealists is that every substance is like a self or a soul. One may be reminded of Berkeley's insistence on the self as active. Why then is Tennant, who also uses the self as his basic analogy or root metaphor, not an idealist? Because he extends it to things of the world.

It is knowledge of self, and of other selves, that encourage the venture in believing things to continue a life history when not being 'perceived.' Thus to conceive of things, is to personify, to assimilate to the self, to interpret scattered data in terms of self, and so to 'understand'. 'A substance' does not then mean

[51] *Ibid.*, p. 182.
[52] F. R. Tennant, *Philosophical Theology*, Cambridge University Press, Cambridge, 1935, Vol. I, pp. 19, 179.

a *collection* of discretes; it refers rather to their *connexion*. Quite another purpose than that for which this concept was fashioned, is served . . . by such objects of higher order as collection or series, by which the Humean psychologist or the logistician may seek to replace substance or continuant, and so construct 'psychology without a soul'. They ignore the fact-element which evokes this particular category, and invoke another that is inadequate and irrelevant. Substance . . . indicates a ground or sufficient reason, such as reasonableness cannot dispense with, but which logical rationality, aloof from full-orbed fact, can superciliously ignore.[53]

Here Tennant, however involved the argument, is simply saying that Russell's view is unacceptable.

You will notice that Santayana refers to "such plasticity and intent as are requisite for perception, prophecy, or memory" and Tennant to the connections of things that "continue a life history." These may not be the cleverest phrases devised in defense of substance. How much time is required for a life history? Everett Nelson by contrast, in his defense of substance, asks us to reflect upon the meaning of statements such as: that gold is fusible, that sugar is soluble, that arsenic is poisonous. These sentences employ attributes called "dispositional properties." We refer to them in hypothetical arguments.

When I say that this lump of sugar is soluble in coffee, I do not mean that it ever was put into coffee and dissolved or ever will be put into coffee and dissolve. Nor do I mean simply that if it was put into coffee, it did dissolve, or that if it shall be put into coffee, it will dissolve. I mean also that if it *had been* put into coffee, it *would have* dissolved. Similarly, when we say that arsenic is poisonous, an essential part of our meaning is that if certain conditions *had been* satisfied, it *would have* poisoned someone.[54]

What is the importance of such a commonplace hypothetical contrary-to-fact as "This sugar might have dissolved in coffee"?

That the sugar has a *nature* which does not necessitate its being in just this state or in just these relations to these other things at this time, and that it would have been the same thing even if it had not been in these states or in these relations in which it now is. The lump of sugar is then a *substance*, and its specific nature as such is constituted at least in part, by certain of its dispositional properties.[55]

Nelson has stressed temporal duration, as we express it through the use of tensed verbs. Some logics exclude our saying that "if this vase had been

[53] *Ibid.*, pp. 177–178.
[54] Everett J. Nelson, "The Category of Substance." In: Roy Wood Sellars, V. J. McGill, and Marvin Farber, *op. cit.*, p. 107.
[55] *Ibid.*, p. 108.

hit a sharp blow, it would have shattered." So much the worse, he argues, for such logics. For this is an empirical inference, and logic should not exceed its proper task by begging the substantive metaphysical issue. Specifically, then, substances are what have "power" or power to act in a certain way.[56] Power is not always active, it may be potential.

It is a common point to argue that the Humean who says that a substance is nothing more than the sum of "its" qualities, owes us an explanation of the mysterious "it" that can possess qualities. It does seem to be a fuller account of a thing to say that we refer to its nature by dispositional properties. But which powers so expressed are essential, and which are accidental? To say that the "something" is what has "capacity to synthesize conditions or to act in a certain way" seems forever elusive. Yet Nelson's basis seems sound. We cannot help talking as though there were substances. And a dynamic version of the doctrine is an attempt to do justice to Plato's elusive insight that being is power.

B. Santayana's Material Substance

It is a mistake to think, argues Santayana, that materialists claim that matter is the only reality. Rather, their first principle is that "matter is the only *substance, power,* or *agency* in the universe. . . ."[57] There have indeed been materialists who claimed that only material things or bodies could be. Hobbes made such a claim, but since the belief itself is not something extended, having dimensions of magnitude, length, breadth, and depth, can we say that a belief is material? The position seems self-contradictory.[58] The old Democritean position postulates atoms and a void, hence something other than atoms is real. Santayana, like many critical defenders of materialism, would not wish to defend silly denials that characterize traditional materialism. Among these are denials that something thinks and that what is thought may be true or false, and that there are characteristics other than those of extension, weight, mass, and density. Hence the axiom of materialism, according to Santayana, is "the dominance of matter in every existing being. . . ."[59]

The point of the dominance of matter is that mind is passive, a mere result and never a cause, and essences and truths are merely there to be

---

[56] *Ibid.*, p. 115.

[57] George Santayana, "Apologia Pro Mente Sua." In *The Philosophy of George Santayana, op. cit.*, p. 509.

[58] *Ibid.*

[59] Reprinted with the permission of Charles Scribner's Sons from *Realms of Being* by George Santayana, copyright 1942 Charles Scribner's Sons, p. 292. Used by Permission of Charles Scribner's Sons and Constable and Company, Ltd.

known. But if knowing is an activity, then we deal basically with a power or an agency, which we commonly call a body. Only matter exists, but matter is only one realm of being. So desirous is this materialist of an adequate metaphysics that he admits not only a realm of essence, which Plato considered most real, and a realm of truth, which Russell has stressed, but also a realm of spirit, which idealists such as Berkeley stressed. Even a supernatural realm can be regarded as a phase in this materialism. Heaven and hell, (even if *incredible*), are conceivable, which is a sufficient test of being or reality, though not of existing thinghood or substance.[60]

The realm of matter is what any animal must take account of as it acts. Santayana sees no alternative open to us but "to believe in things," and without this propensity we cannot believe in our ideas as if they described things.[61] Matter is characterized as "the principle of existence: it is all things in their potentiality, and therefore the condition of all their excellence or possible perfection." Therefore it is a mistake to regard matter as morally evil. It is also a mistake to regard matter as superfluous, because we cannot know it directly in its very essence, and because all our definitions of matter are from particular perspectives.[62]

Men have many concepts of matter; already we have referred to matter as that which enables things to be individual, that which is characterized by spatial extension, that which is made up of ever smaller units down to atoms, or whatever ultimate least parts we can measure, etc. It is to be expected of any basic belief, claims Santayana, that it should be expressed in unlimited ways.

Thus to a stone-cutter extension and impenetrability may well seem the essence of matter; the builder, intent on strains and dangers of position, will add degrees of cohesion and weight to his definition. At this stage metaphysicians and moralists will look down on matter as something gross and dead, and will imagine that motion and organization must be imposed on matter from without: not seeing that this external force, if it governed and moved matter, would be the soul of matter, and much nearer to its proper essence than the aesthetic aspects which its aggregates may wear to the human eye. Yet what could be more obviously material than thunder and lightning, sunshine and rain, from which the father of the gods borrowed his poetic substance? Weight and figure are not more characteristic of matter than are explosiveness, swiftness, fertility, and radiation. Planters and breeders of animals, or poets watching the passing generations of mankind, will feel that the heart and mystery of matter lie in the seeds of things, *semina rerum*, and in the customary cycles of their transforma-

---

[60] *The Philosophy of George Santayana, op. cit.,* p. 509.
[61] George Santayana, *Realms of Being, op. cit.,* p. 196.
[62] *Ibid.,* p. 183.

tion. It is by its motion and energy, by its fidelity to measure and law, that matter has become the substance of our world, and the principle of life and of death in it.[63]

Although most materialists have been officially atheists, Santayana argues that most men mean by God or the gods this ultimate power which they confront in action. And so long as expectation and action are not misled by the symbol, men may as well call matter "the devil." Santayana also would end the bickering among materialists as to whether matter is to be characterized in static or dynamic terms by saying that matter is both. Attacks, then, upon any materialistic metaphysic as an attempted reduction of the complexity of life to the simplicity of dead atoms is an attack merely on one inadequate notion of matter, not at all on a materialism that allows for levels of complexity. Nor does Santayana allow that materialism limits man's desires to possession of things, as though they are all he could care for.

The realm of matter . . . from the point of view of our discovery of it, is the field of action: it is essentially dynamic. . . . Moreover, our action is interpolated in a world already in existence. Our existence and purposes are things of yesterday; they were evidently drawn from that very world on which they react. . . . The realm of matter is the matrix and the source of everything. . . .[64]

A frequent question put to a materialist is whether all causal process is mechanistic, that is, whether the scheme excludes purpose, or direction of conduct to preferred ends.

A spiritual mind might well look over the head of nature to a First Cause, and beyond the vicissitudes of life to a supreme good: therein would be a genuine aversion from the realm of matter, and absorption in essences which, at best, existence can illustrate or suggest for a moment to the mind, as it does beauty or the laws of number. But, though, not prized for itself, the realm of matter, would remain standing; otherwise those divine essences would never have been illustrated or suggested at all.[65]

The "spiritual mind" would not be content with the position that without matter, the forms would not be in a concrete and perceptible state, for he demands also that the First Cause explain the existence of matter. Whereas the theist believes that without God matter could not exist, the materialist claims that without matter, nothing could exist. The usual be-

[63] *Ibid.*, p. 187.
[64] *Ibid.*, p. 189.
[65] *Ibid.*, p. 190.

lief in God is that there is a ground of existence; for all materialists, matter neither admits nor requires explanation or justification.

Faith in an existing world is a basic assumption, "which indeed can never be justified." But the task of natural philosophy is to enlighten and guide the faith involved in action. To show that all belief is animal faith about nature, Santayana outlines the indispensable properties of substance.

A World in Which Action Is to Occur Must Be External, Spatial, and Temporal, Possessing Variety and Unity.

1. Since substance is posited, and not given in intuition, as essences may be given, *substance is external to the thought which posits it.*
2. Since it is posited in action, or in readiness for action, the substance posited is external not merely to the positing thought (as a different thought would be) but is external to the physical agent which is the organ of that action, as well as of that thought. In other words, *Substance has parts and constitutes a physical space.* Conversely, the substantial agent in action and thought is external to the surrounding portions of substance with which it can interact. *All the parts of substance are external to one another.*
3. Since substance is engaged in action, and action involves change, *substance is in flux and constitutes a physical time.* Changes are perpetually occurring in the relations of its parts, if not also in their intrinsic characters.
4. Since the agents in action and reaction are distinct in position and variable in character, and since they induce changes in one another, *substance is unequally distributed.* It diversifies the field of action, or physical time and space.
5. Since there is no occasion for positing any substance save as an agent in the field of action, all recognizable substance must lie in the same field in which the organism of the observer occupies a relative centre. Therefore, wherever it works and solicits recognition, *substance composes a relative cosmos.*[66]

Other properties of substance are assumed in practice and may be assumed in natural philosophy:

6. *Substance,* in diversifying the field of nature, *sometimes takes the form of animals in whom there are feelings, images, and thoughts. These mental facts are immaterial.* They offer no butt for action and exercise no physical influence on one another.

Action, when Rational, Presupposes That the Transformations of Substance are Continuous, Quantitatively Constant, and Regular in Method; and That the Spirit, without Being a Part of That Material World, Is the Consciousness Proper to One of the Agents There.

7. The same *mental facts are manifestations of substance;* in their occurrence they are parts of a total natural event which, on its substantial side, belongs

[66] *Ibid.,* pp. 202–203.

to the plane of action. They are therefore significant and relevant to action as signs, being created and controlled by the flux of substance beneath.

8. Beneath the intermittence of phenomena, *the phases or modes through which substance flows are continuous.*

9. As far as action and calculation can extend, *the quantity of substance remains equivalent* throughout.

10. *Each phase or mode of substance, although not contained in its antecedents, is predetermined by them in its place and quality, and proportionate to them in extent and intensity.* An event will be repeated if ever the constellation of events which bred it should recur. This regularity in the genesis of modes or phases of substance is constantly verified in action on a small scale. To expect it in substance is the soul of science and art; but to expect it in phenomena is superstition.[67]

The conclusion of Santayana's materialistic thesis is that all events are determined by underlying material substance. Indeed he identifies his determinism with the Hindu doctrine of Karma, which states that each thing is the result of its prior deeds. Earlier it was shown that naturalism, at least in Nagel's version, rested on the postulate that things lie in contingent rather than necessary relations. The student may prefer to consider, as will be discussed in Chapter XII on moral beliefs, that human choice may be efficacious in directing an act. If it is, then materialism of Santayana's type is false. The student should also examine the assumption that all future facts lie open to inspection as do some past facts. If there is a genuine difference between past and future, then also a materialism of Santayana's type is false. That is, if it is true that the future is the indeterminate realm open to alternatives between which our choice is efficacious, it is false that future events are eternally fated to be thus and not other.

C. McTaggart's Spiritual Substance

Just as vigorously as Santayana the materialist affirms the belief that "matter is the only substance . . . in the universe," McTaggart the idealist affirms that "it is reasonable to believe, and unreasonable to disbelieve that all substances are spiritual."

Berkeley's epistemology has been frequently mentioned to the student as an idealism that leaves us with a world of active human selves, with impressions created and sustained by God. The term "idealism" has also been applied to the coherence theory of truth which states that all judgments individually are erroneous but are collectively the absolute truth. In the next chapter Hegel's doctrine of history—namely that human develop-

[67] *Ibid.,* pp. 233–234.

ment is the expression of Spirit unfolding itself rationally in temporal stages—will also be termed "idealism." Just as we do not expect all Smiths or Joneses to be alike because they bear a common name, so we should not expect all beliefs to be alike because—they are "idealistic," but there is a family resemblance among most of the examples of idealism one meets.

McTaggart stresses what seems to be the basis of this resemblance: "Ontologically I am an Idealist, since I believe that all that exists is spiritual."[68] Epistemologically McTaggart is a realist, in the sense that knowledge is true belief, and "a belief [is] true when, and only when, it stands in a relation of correspondence to a fact." Herein this system differs from nearly all the others previously called idealism. Few philosophers have dealt with the metaphysical problem of substance as rigorously as did the Cambridge philosopher, John McTaggart Ellis McTaggart. His work deserves a reputation like that enjoyed by his contemporary fellows of Trinity College, G. E. Moore, Bertrand Russell, Alfred North Whitehead, and Ludwig Wittgenstein. C. D. Broad recommends McTaggart to us because his view on spirit as the only substance "is definite where other forms of it are discretely vague."[69]

There appear to be substances of two very different kinds: matter and spirit. The method, of which McTaggart is a brilliant exponent, deliberately begins with what is commonly accepted in perceptual judgment. Appearance must be examined to discover whether it is misperception or perception of reality. The rational principle is that if appearance is contradictory it cannot be real. Can it be that anything real possesses the characteristic of being in time? Time would not be time without a past, a present, and a future. Yet how can anything be past and present and future? Unless a thing is all three, it is not in time. But these three are incompatible determinations. McTaggart refuses to remove the contradiction by saying that what *was* future *is now* present and *will* be past; for this starts an infinite regress which is vicious. Hence he denies what appears to be the case, that everything is in time. And since time implies change, he denies what appears, that change is a real characteristic of the existent.

McTaggart rejects the relational and perspectival approach favored by much of contemporary philosophy (this book included) for a good reason.

[68] J. Ellis McTaggart, "An Ontological Idealism." In: J. H. Muirhead (ed.), *Contemporary British Philosophy*, First Series, George Allen & Unwin, Ltd., London, 1953, p. 251.
[69] C. D. Broad, *Examination of McTaggart's Philosophy*, Cambridge University Press, Cambridge, 1938, Vol. II, Part I, p. 148.

With Hegel and Bradley, earlier absolute idealists, McTaggart identifies the truth with an absolute and eternal vision of the way things really are. But if there is only a moment ever new with its own perspective ever transcended and never completed, we have an infinite regress. Such a series, without finality, repels the absolutists' concept of reason. Like Spinoza's substance, their reality is things *sub specie aeternitatis,* under the aspect of eternity. With the axiom that reality is rational and eternal, the logical conclusion is that time and change are only apparent.

Yet McTaggart does not deny that under the aspect of eternity, in reality and truth, one state of a thing is earlier than another state. This relation is stable, and does not change, as being future changes into being present and being present changes into being past. And not only does the relation of x before y, and y after x, abide while time changes, the earlier-later relation is reality which appears as past-present-future. Although we *perceive* events as present, remember them as past, anticipate them as future, as St. Augustine said when he insisted this is essentially what time is, McTaggart wants to know how time can be conceived without contradiction.

Yet the earlier-later relation is itself not ultimate. Temporal series are merely forms of what we called asymmetrical transitive relations. Hence, typical of idealism, the temporal is accounted for by the atemporal and logical. Thus he concludes that there is no real time-series; there is, however, a real series misconceived. Another way of putting this is that the terms of the real series are not events, but, as we shall see, spirits and their experiences. But how account for this series? Again, typical of idealism, McTaggart claims that spirit or self is presupposed, which alone can perceive. There are qualitative degrees of perception. At least we can say meaningfully that compared with seeing the same object through a fog, we see more of it through a mist.[70]

McTaggart also calls our attention to "what happens as we slowly wake after sleep. . . ." for then we come to realize that we *had* observed imperfectly and erroneously. However, no analogy adequately gives us the notion of perceiving with greater and greater adequacy, for the notion does not involve increase in the number of parts of the object perceived.

Although much of the elaboration of the system, interpreting one series as a misperception of another, is unique, McTaggart is similar to many other absolute idealists in two ways. First, he argues dialectically from

[70] S. V. Keeling, "McTaggart's Metaphysics" In: G. Lowes Dickinson, *J. McT. E. McTaggart,* Cambridge University Press, Cambridge, 1931, p. 149.

our awareness of misperception or error to our knowledge of perception or truth. Since we know "what happens as we slowly wake after sleep" we can come to realize that what we had observed imperfectly and erroneously we now observe more adequately. However, this is a mere analogy of the movement of mind to the eternal vision, which is qualitatively complete and not a mere increase in the number of parts of the object.[71] Second, he tries to tell us what reality is that is misperceived. McTaggart gets back to an ultimate that includes all that exists. Thus metaphysics deals with existence as a whole. But this whole is a society, rather than a unity without distinction of members.

Because the whole, existence itself, is a series that is infinite, we have gained a criterion of genuine substance. Substance is an "infinite series of sets of parts, and the number of members in each set increases as we pass from precedent to sequent sets."[72] Therefore we should ask of anything proposed as substance whether there is a one-to-one correspondence with an infinite series of sets of parts. Propositions fail to be substances because, although complex, they are made up of simple parts—characteristics or universals—which cannot be analyzed further.

But what, then, are substances? McTaggart considers the materialists' candidate, material things and physical events; the Humean or phenomenalists' candidate, sensa; and the idealists' candidate, minds and their experiences. He applies his criterion of an infinite series or endless divisibility to material things. The answer is very elaborate, but in brief, McTaggart takes matter to mean what has dimensions in space and in time and "size, shape, and position." He adds "impenetrability, colour, hardness, sound, smell, and so on," in approximating to what he thinks is our ordinary view. Since these are qualities and therefore cannot be divided into parts of parts, it follows that matter is not substance.[73] Are sensa substances?

If sensa did exist, they must have parts within parts to infinity. If so, sufficient descriptions of such parts must be determined by determining correspondence. And it seems to me that this is impossible, for much the same reasons that led to a similar conclusion in the case of matter.[74]

If no other candidates for substance are conceivable other than propositions, material things, sensa, and spirits, and the first three are not sub-

---

[71] *Ibid.*, p. 245.
[72] John McTaggart Ellis McTaggart, *The Nature of Existence*, Cambridge University Press, Cambridge, 1927, Vol. I, p. 208.
[73] *Ibid.*, Vol. II, p. 34.
[74] *Ibid.*, p. 57.

stance, then only Spirit can conceivably exist. Spirit does satisfy the criterion of an infinite series or endless divisibility—that is, not only are the experiences of any self unlimited, but the self knows it is experiencing, and there is no known terminus to experience of any self. Death itself does not, according to McTaggart, end the career of a self, however it may deprive a spirit of an apparent, finite, material body.

Spirituality is defined as

. . . the quality of having content, all of which is the content of one or more selves. Nothing can have this quality except substances, and so nothing but substances are spiritual. Selves, of course, will answer to this definition, and so will parts of selves, and groups of selves . . . and groups whose members are selves and parts of selves. The content of any such substance will be called spirit.

How is self known?

I should say that the quality of being a self is a simple quality which is known to me because I perceive—in the strict sense of the word—one substance as possessing this quality. This substance is myself. And I believe that every self-conscious being—that is, every self who knows that he is a self—directly perceives himself in this manner.[75]

The consciousness of the "I" is a case of intuitive knowledge, which Russell and James called knowledge by acquaintance. McTaggart denies that he or any other self is a mere group of states, or what Hume called "a bundle." For any two states together, says McTaggart, form a group, and Hume does not suppose, for example, that an emotion of James II and a volition of William III belong to the same self.

Moreover the relations between mental states cannot be temporal or spatial. Most explicit is McTaggart's denial that states of mind belong to the same self because, as on a materialistic view, they are caused by the same brain. This will not do, because persons who have never heard the doctrine that mental states are caused by bodily states, still know that two states belong to the same self. Moreover, how could one "observe his own brain, and . . . observe it in two states which he could identify as the causes of the emotion and the judgment respectively?"[76]

Hence, if the "I" is to be known, it must be by acquaintance. And without knowing the "I", a person cannot know the meaning of "I was envious yesterday." But self-conscious selves do know the meaning of such an expression.

[75] *Ibid.*, p. 62.
[76] *Ibid.*, p. 74.

Apart from the argument, which depends upon the characterization of existence as an infinite series of parts, what is McTaggart's vision? It bears, argues Broad, more resemblance to the mentalism or spiritualism of Leibniz than to the idealism of Berkeley. The selves of McTaggart are more like the monads of Leibniz than the entities of any other system included among our key beliefs in the history of philosophy. But there is no hierarchy among the selves and there is no chief self, corresponding to the God of Leibniz, who postulated a divine pre-established harmony. Nothing, as we shall shortly see, can stand outside the series of selves. McTaggart's idealism differs from the absolutism of Hegel or Royce in that they were never reluctant to rationalize God as a prephilosophical doctrine of the absolute. Yet the strangeness of saying that existence is a community of selves comes from our lingering belief that there are real material things producing changes in a space-time continuum. At least Leibniz made a serious effort to account for such beliefs as produced by our seeing the world in physical perspective. But just as McTaggart condemns past-present-future to illusory appearance, so he reasons that spatial properties also are irrational, infected with logical contradiction. His argument is that it makes no sense at all to say that a substance, that is a self, can be, for example, globular![77]

Although the personal convictions of the metaphysician do not appear as part of the system, they were evident to McTaggart's friends and students. McTaggart's most fervent beliefs were in the immortality of each spirit and in the relation of love between spirits. Broad writes of him

> In January, 1925, McTaggart and his wife were taking a holiday in London. He was seeing many of his old friends, and was to all appearance in the best of health and spirits, when he was suddenly stricken down. After a short but painful illness, borne with admirable courage and patience, he died . . . in London at the age of fifty-eight; passing, as he firmly believed, to the next stage in the long but finite journey from the illusion of time to the reality of eternal life.[78]

His body, as ample as Thomas Aquinas' in bulk, was cremated and the service consisted of a passage from Spinoza, and his ashes rest in the chapel of Trinity College, Cambridge, but without Christian symbol.

McTaggart is an interpreter of Hegel, but he never regards institutions as ends in themselves. He is an individualist, not a collectivist, in his social theory. Yet he loved his school, his college, and England; the devotion of a spirit to his fellow spirits is, along with the conviction that they are im-

[77] C. D. Broad, *Examination of McTaggart's Philosophy*, Vol. II, Pt. I, Cambridge University Press, 1938, pp. 255–256.
[78] C. D. Broad, "John McTaggart Ellis McTaggart," in *Ethics and the History of Philosophy*, Routledge & Kegan Paul, Ltd., London, 1952, pp. 70–71.

mortal, of profound metaphysical significance. The "love of one man for another is of infinite value. . . ."[79]

Love, according to McTaggart, is the fundamental emotion; and by 'love' he means, not philanthropy or benevolence, but that passionate personal affection which none of us in this life can feel towards more than a very few persons. No philosopher but Plato has treated love so seriously, has analysed it so carefully, or has written about it so eloquently as McTaggart. Yet there is a profound difference between the two philosophers on this point. For Plato the love of a man for his friend is only a stepping-stone by which the soul rises to the contemplation and love of the Idea of the Good. For McTaggart it is the one supremely valuable thing in the universe; it cannot be a step toward something higher, for there is nothing above it.[80]

Such beliefs are often held neither on rational ground, nor as part of a system of metaphysical truths. What makes any philosopher interesting is how he argues his beliefs. McTaggart is, according to Broad, not so much a prophet of the Absolute, as was Hegel, or its knight, as was Bradley, as its "extremely devoted and extremely astute family solicitor."[81]

Then how, finally, can we grasp the points of this philosopher's brief? Happily, his literary executor, C. D. Broad, drew up the position into ten propositions.

1. "It can be truly and significantly said of any self that it 'has experiences.' This cannot be significantly said of anything but a self."
2. "Every experience which a self has is a part of that self." Are the experiences which a self has parts of it? ". . . The only fact that might seem to cast doubt on an immediate affirmative answer is that [experience] involves a relation between the [experiencing] self and the [experienced] particular."
3. ". . . Every self has a *set of parts* . . . *each of which* is an experience of that self. This is quite compatible with the self having parts which are not experiences." We feel, when we contemplate our cogitations, volitions, and emotions, that, taken together, they do in some sense exhaust the self, so that it is completely comprised in them.
4. ". . . There can be no unowned experiences; every experience must belong to some self." This, he claims, is self-evident, for it states the meaning of "being an experience."
5. "No particular can be part of more than one self . . . no experience can be owned by more than one self. . . . The peculiar unity which a

[79] *Ibid.*, p. 73.
[80] *Ibid.*, p. 85.
[81] *Ibid.*, p. 73.

self has puts it into a relation with its parts which is such that two selves cannot have it to the same part. If we combine this with Proposition 4 above, we get the following principle. It is self-evidently impossible that anything which *ever is* a part of any self . . . should *ever be not* a part of *that self.*"

6. "One self cannot be part of another self. . . . Obviously, if two selves cannot have any part in common and all selves have parts, it follows immediately that one self cannot be part of another. For if [one self] were a part of [another self], every part of [the first] would be also a part of [the second]."

7. "The characteristic of being a self does not, by itself, convey the property of being aware of something or other at every moment." It is logically possible to be a self when not cogitating at all. But as a matter of fact every self is aware of something or other at every moment of its existence.

8. "It is possible for there to be selves which are not self-conscious." Although it is inappropriate to call something a self which is "never aware of itself, even though such a being were at times aware of other things," one can be aware of other things without grasping oneself. However much of our attention is engrossed by other things, we could, if we chose, attend to ourselves. "It is difficult, if not impossible, for us to form any clear conception of a being which is capable of [grasping] other things but is incapable of being aware of itself and its own experiences."

9. "Every human self does in fact from time to time [grasp] itself as a self." This grasping of a self as a self is more, as we shall see next, than being self-conscious. For "the particular which is one's self is more elusive than . . . other . . . realities we are aware of. . . ." It is therefore easy to grasp the parts, and as in hearing we notice select noises but not the auditory field, so we miss the faint dull background of continuous selfhood. A further point lies in the reciprocal relation of a self to itself. There is no a priori impossibility in a particular experiencing itself. "Terms can stand in relation to themselves; e.g., a man can be his own cousin or his own trustee." Yet when at a moment I grasp myself as a whole, I do not grasp any part of myself which falls outside the temporal limits of my specious present. Therefore I grasp "a different thin temporal slice of the history of myself." Yet the perception is not merely of one strand, as of a rope, but has the "breadth" or "thickness" of all the components. I therefore grasp myself through its whole temporal "thickness."

10. "The characteristic of being a self, i.e., selfhood, is simple and unanalysable. Each of us has an idea of it simply because each of us has
[grasped] a certain particular, viz., himself, as having it. In this respect it is like redness or temporal succession. . . . We can perceive
no parts or elements of which it is composed, any more than we can
with the quality of redness. Like redness it is simple and indefinable."

This is not to say that every self is a simple particular, since no
particulars are simple. And indeed selves are complex particulars and
their experiences are parts of them. This view is neither the bundle
theory, that makes the self a group of experiences, nor a Pure Ego
theory that makes the simple particular self a constituent of all its
experiences.[82]

The student's reaction to McTaggart's belief that it is reasonable to believe, and unreasonable to disbelieve that all substances are spiritual, may
be to affirm with Santayana that matter is the only substance. Or, he
may feel that somehow both selfhood and material thinghood are two
different specifications of substance.

Santayana and McTaggart provide us with ample materials for further
reflection. The former has concentrated on what things are, the latter on
what selves are. Are the relations of things to thought different from the
relations of experiences to selves? Is there some point to the issue over
external and internal relations? How are things related to each other? Experiences to each other? Is there some point in the issue of the primacy of
spatial to temporal relations and the ultimacy of non-temporal and non-
spatial relations? How does each system allow for manyness and unity?
Is it clear that each system gives some account of the diversity of entities
and the unity of an entity? Does either system give an adequate account
of experience and what is experienced? Which account of something continuous and abiding in the flux of events or experiences is preferable?
Which is ultimate, material substance or simple and unanalyzable selfhood?

Neither idealism nor materialism can do without the concept of substance. But, as we have seen, it is an extremely difficult concept to fix.
Somewhere in its complexity there persists the idea of permanence, of
the unchanging, of that to which qualities and relations are applicable but
which is not itself either a quality or a relation. The authors have tried to
show some of the obscurities that attend this view.

Suppose now that we accept another category as basic which allows us

---

[82] C. D. Broad, *op. cit.*, Vol. II, Pt. I, pp. 141–169.

to introduce novelty, process, growth, and creativity into the world. Let us call it the category of event. Will this lead to a metaphysics as thoroughgoing and as powerful as any of those we have looked at? It will indeed. As we have seen there are systems of metaphysics that stress Being. But there are others that stress Becoming. To one of these we now turn.

VI. Becoming: Philosophies of Process

A. Introduction

Søren Kierkegaard, as shrewd a critic of metaphysical systems as any, points out that metaphysicians are guilty of transferring the categories of one area to another. In the mathematical realm we have deductive demonstrations of what must be the case. And such a metaphysician as Hegel, dealing with historical events, attempts to demonstrate that they likewise must be as they are. This would also be a drastic criticism of McTaggart. This is "systematic legerdemain," according to Kierkegaard, for "the one thing that it is impossible to become, is to become necessary." His ground is that "contingency is precisely one factor in all becoming."[83] In the more than a hundred years since the Concluding Unscientific Postscript, we have seen many metaphysical attempts based on the belief that full actuality is found only in events or the realm of change, and that being is an abstraction from becoming. That is, a characteristic of process philosophies is to turn Plato on his head. Whereas Plato regarded particulars as lacking perfection, philosophers such as Whitehead say that universals lack actuality. An actuality is superior to a form or idea in that it decides, within limits set by other actualities, what it becomes.

It follows from this that philosophies of becoming cannot coherently claim finality. For philosophies are themselves events, and philosophizing is ever in process. They would not properly then be called "systems" according to Kierkegaard's usage. "System and finality are pretty much one and the same, so much so that if the system is not finished, there is no system." Kierkegaard's protest is that the metaphysician, with Hegel in mind, is also a man, subject to limitations, but pretending that in his system these limitations have been overcome.

Yet philosophies of process are deeply indebted to Hegel. For he attempted to introduce movement everywhere. Ironically, Hegel's effort "in introducing movement . . . in logic" is the least influential side of his work (at least outside the Soviet Union). In the next chapter the logic of

[83] *Kierkegaard's Concluding Unscientific Postscript*, (D. F. Swenson and Walter Lowrie, trs.), Princeton University Press, Princeton, New Jersey, 1944, p. 90.

perpetual movement from thesis to antithesis to synthesis will be illustrated. The point here is that defenders of process philosophy in the twentieth century consider logic to be confused by Hegelian dialectic.

It follows from the notion that each actuality moves into its own future with freedom to make itself, that both Kierkegaard's existentialism and process philosophy must be pluralistic. For these actualities are existent, and existence means to be an individual among other individuals. As Kierkegaard puts it: "Existence separates, and holds the various moments of existence discretely apart. . . . "[84] Monistic or closed systems attempt to reason to the identity of subject and object. "Existence, on the other hand, is their separation."[85] The student has doubtless encountered the belief popularized by existentialism that a man's act of faith or radical choice is ultimate and groundless. The basis of this lies in a revolt against the systems that are called "closed." They are closed to novelty because whatever a man does, according to essentialism, merely unpacks his nature or essence. The denial of this is that man has no nature apart from what he chooses to become. This is one application of an "open" system.

It is commonly said of closed systems, such as materialism and idealism, that they failed to take time seriously. Whereas philosophies of substance needed to explain how things could change or why we perceive them changing, philosophies of process need to explain how events can be relatively permanent or why we sometimes seem to perceive stable things. If we begin with entities as substances that are essentially so-and-so, then our problem is created by our assumption that the passage of time is accidental rather than essential to their being. But if we begin with events that are ever changing, then our problem is created by our assumption that what a thing is is how it becomes, in other words, the passage of time is essential to becoming. On the substance view, does a tadpole change into a frog at one moment of time? If not, then during the same period of time it is both, and this seems to violate the logical principle of non-contradiction. On the process view, the problem is the opposite, a frog is always changing, so why is it that it has any nature at all? And ever to change seems to violate the logical principle of identity.

The great issue is between a conception of reality as being and a conception of reality as becoming. According to the first, any man "can only act according to nature, his being or essence." Thus action is derived from being, and substance is supposed to explain change. Defenders of the second conception claim that we cannot derive action from being. "A man's

[84] *Ibid.*, p. 107.
[85] *Ibid.*, p. 112.

'nature' is a cross-section of his acting and not something with prior status. It is an explanation after the fact, an abstract of the concrete reality which is process, and never mere being or essence." Hartshorne and Reese then coherently deny that even God could make a man what he is: "He made it possible (but not inevitable) for us to make ourselves. . . . "[86]

Before presenting a reasoned case for this very common declaration that the world is a process, that it is not made up of things but events, that existence is prior to essence, that becoming is prior to being, let us hear a voice in praise of change. It is a commonplace that the Darwinian doctrine of the origin of species introduced development into a realm that had been considered static. Nietzsche is a philosopher of becoming because he prefers change to permanence:

Evil I call it and hostile unto human beings, all that teaching of the one thing, the full, the unmoved, the satisfied, the imperishable!
All that is imperishable—is only a simile! And the poets lie too much.
But for a simile the best images shall speak of time and becoming; a praise they shall be and a justification of all perishableness![87]

However, a philosophy of becoming would surely be bad metaphysics if there were no basis other than a love of novelty.

Moritz Schlick, the great center of the Vienna Circle, considers a world of becoming presupposed in contemporary physics.

The world does not consist of substance, but of a system of ordered events or occurrences. The interval between two neighbouring occurrences or events in the four-dimensional representation . . . is characteristic of the objective or absolute order of the world. Thus, the velocity of light is essential for spatio-temporal order; it makes possible the uniform relations of the world so that all causal order is based on it.[88]

If your metaphysics of existence is not framed in accordance with what scientists of a period assume about nature, perhaps the appeal to experience carries more conviction. Pure experience is prior to the logical distinctions that require abstraction and aid demonstration. William James stated his case beautifully:

Experience in its immediacy seems perfectly fluent. The active sense of living which we all enjoy, before reflection shatters our instinctive world for us, is

[86] Charles Hartshorne and William L. Reese, *Philosophers Speak of God,* University of Chicago Press, Chicago, 1953, p. 444.
[87] Friedrich Nietzsche, *Thus Spake Zarathustra,* The Macmillan Co., New York, 1896, p. 117.
[88] Moritz Schlick, *Philosophy of Nature* (Amethe von Zeppelin, tr.), Philosophical Library, Inc., New York, 1949, p. 54.

self-luminous and suggests no paradoxes. Its difficulties are disappointments and uncertainties. They are not intellectual contradictions.

'Pure experience' . . . is of *a that* which is not yet any definite *what* . . . full both of oneness and of manyness, but in respects that don't appear; changing throughout, yet so confusedly that its phases interpenetrate and no points, either of distinction or identity, can be caught. Pure experience in this state is but another name for feeling or sensation. But the flux of it no sooner comes than it tends to fill itself with emphases, and these salient parts become identified and fixed and abstracted; so that experience now flows as if shot through with adjectives and nouns and prepositions and conjunctions.[89]

B. Broad's Linguistic Defense of Process

C. D. Broad makes a very clear case that the world is "things" and "states" and "events" and "facts." Of these let us deal with the distinction between "things" and "events." Most of us believe one cannot be reduced to the other. Broad's ready evidence is that this distinction is deeply rooted in our language. If it is a mistake, then a substance philosophy should not merely dismiss it as a vulgar prejudice, but show it to be an error. Some names are conjoined with predicate phrases that answer questions about what is happening, going on or taking place. "There is a noise going on" or "a movement taking place." We do not say of things that "There is a chair going on in my bedroom." Broad says, "A noise or a movement seems a clear instance of a process, and a chair or a self seems a clear instance of a thing."[90]

A substance metaphysics, Broad continues, masks this fundamental distinction. McTaggart claims to have restated the traditional definition. If we accept the definition that a substance is what is existent, which has qualities and is related, but is not itself a quality or a relation, then among substances we should include sneezes and flashes of lightning, which some of us would call occurrences. Among substances we should include facts such as the fact that McTaggart visited New Zealand. And substances would include, as McTaggart agreed, a bridge party, or a group of redheaded archdeacons. If one believes that a chair or a person is essentially different from a noise or a sneeze, from facts, and from meetings and groups of people, then one should develop a metaphysical view other than either materialism or idealism, insofar as these would commit one to a view that the existing world is made up of either material things or mental things exclusively. Not that a process philosophy must involve the denial that there are both material and mental things. A process philosophy, such

[89] William James, *A Pluralistic Universe*, Longmans, Green, & Co., Inc., New York, 1909, pp. 347, 348.
[90] C. D. Broad, *op. cit.*, Vol. I, p. 142.

as Broad's, allows us to say that there are minds and physical objects, like chairs or books. In this respect, this view being developed would say that both materialism and idealism are right in what they affirm, but mistaken in the ontological interpretation of a continuant as a substance.

Why affirm that anything else is real and existent? Because, if the definition of an existent is what has characteristics, then surely

. . . processes have characteristics. A noise may be loud, continuous, "buzzy", and so on. A movement may be slow, jerky, rectilinear, and so on. Processes can have temporal relations to each other; e.g., a certain buzzing may partially overlap in time a certain hissing, and one buzzing may be louder than another, and so on.[91]

We may distinguish things from processes by the kind of temporal phrases we properly attach to names of things and names of processes. In the most general terms, according to Broad, we talk of processes as "going on *for*" longer or shorter periods of time, but we talk of things as enduring or "persisting *through*" a period of time. Likewise we can properly speak of processes as having successive temporal parts, but the parts of things are like the dome of St. Paul's, a part that is not a temporal phase.

We talk of processes "starting", "going on", and "stopping". I have made the applicability of such predicates the distinguishing mark of processes. But do we never apply them in the same sense to things? We say: "A buzzing started, went on for some time, and then stopped". Now I can, of course, quite properly say of a train that it started, went on, and stopped. But here I plainly mean that a *movement* of the train started, that it went on for some time, and that it then stopped and was succeeded by a resting of the train which went on for some time. It is plain that here "starting", "going on", and "stopping", as applied to a thing, are derived from these notions as applied to a certain kind of process, viz., a movement.[92]

Of composite things, we may also say that they started to exist, when their construction was complete. And as compounds are made of elements that existed prior to construction, so the elements continue after they cease to be interrelated. A noise that I heard some time ago is now nowhere, but there may be now another noise that I hear. It is to things that we ascribe dispositional adjectives, such as "poisonous," "fusible," "massive," etc. It is to processes that we ascribe temporal continuance, as in "The history of this is long and is getting longer."

Can either Things or Processes be dispensed with? . . . Suppose it were found that sentences which contain thing-names could all be replaced, without loss or gain of meaning, by sentences which contain process-names and do not

[91] *Ibid.*, p. 143.
[92] *Ibid.*, pp. 143–144.

contain thing-names. Then we can say that Things can be dispensed with in favour of Processes.[93]

Traditionally the opposite has been proposed as self-evident, "that any process, whether of change or of quiescence, must be a state of or a process in a thing. If so, it would seem clear that things cannot be dispensed with in favour of processes." How is this defended? Consider the statement "There is a noise going on." We ordinarily ask further *"What is making the noise?"* We expect to be told that a physical object, such as a bee, is producing the buzzy noise by rapid movement of its wings. But we may be concerned with the *subject* of this buzzing, that is the "auditory process which is buzzy. . . . " Broad's point is that to such a question as "What is *noising?"* he has not the faintest idea of an answer.

One way to see the puzzle is to see the contrast between movement and noise. When something ceases to move, and is at rest, we can see that thing. But when a noise ceases, what is there to hear?

If we have no idea what might be the subjects of this sort of process, we should not think that every process is a state of a thing. Therefore we should be prepared to admit the possibility of "Absolute Processes."

If processes cannot be dispensed with in favor of things and facts about things, then what of the opposite question: Can Things be dispensed with in favor of Processes?

Broad argues that some processes, such as noises, seem to be absolute, and not to have any thing for their subject. But there are "certain predicates, such as changing in respect of a certain characteristic and remaining identical through change that can properly be applied to processes, such as noises, even though these should be absolute." An example of the latter is a noise remaining constant in loudness. But the most difficult problem faces a projected translation of statements about the movement of things, such as a golf ball. If "This is a golf ball" is a macroscopic statement of what physicists regard microscopically, then we might conclude that we are dealing with a transmission of states. Broad argues that movement is like "a track in some thing, e.g., in a pool of water. Each particle of water in this track is being translated to and fro about a fixed mean position in a certain characteristic period." The microscopic processes and macroscopic processes are transmissions of microscopic processes.[94]

Much philosophy of the twentieth century has concluded that the notion of process is more ultimate than the notion of thing, but few accounts rest, as Broad's, upon linguistic analysis. It is perhaps the best example that after revolting against old metaphysics, analysis produces new metaphysics.

[93] *Ibid.*, p. 151.
[94] *Ibid.*, pp. 151–163 *passim.*

But few people have the patience to follow a labored and detailed argument of this sort. Nor is the premise of Broad's whole argument certain or even highly probable: namely, that language unequivocally supports process philosophy rather than substance philosophy. More prominent is the massive vision of Whitehead, culminating in Process and Reality.

C. Whitehead's Speculative Defense of Process

Newtonian or traditional physics attempted to account for the transition of material particles within a framework of absolute time and absolute space. The physicist is supposed to express in precise mathematical terms the spatial positions of particles of matter at one durationless instant of time. The metaphysical doctrine of the ultimacy of material substance was held by Hobbes prior to Newton's physics. Whitehead's point is that the world should not be described as "a distribution of material throughout all space at a durationless instant of time" because it leaves no room for "velocity, acceleration, momentum, and kinetic energy, which certainly are essential physical quantities."[95] How can there be any state of change at a mere point of time? This is self-contradictory. The ultimate facts must be conceived as including change and time in the fundamental sense of passage from their past into a future—which is called "duration." Whitehead's alternative is that "a thing itself is what it does," or is an event; nor are events independently actual as particles of matter.

Whitehead acknowledges his debt to James, whose method, as we have seen, was to begin with concrete experience from which we abstract and formulate categories.

. . . The immediate fact for awareness is the whole occurrence of nature. It is nature as an event present for sense-awareness, and essentially passing. There is no holding nature still and looking at it. . . . Thus the ultimate fact for sense-awareness is an event. This whole event is discriminated by us into partial events. We are aware of an event which is our bodily life, of an event which is the course of nature within this room, and of a vaguely perceived aggregate of other partial events. This is the discrimination in sense-awareness of fact into parts.[96]

Is Whitehead saying that there is nothing but events in the world? He thinks not, because in spite of the interrelation of events, there are also distinctions between them. The student may recall that the ancient philosophers raised the question of how things can be many, one thing other than another thing. Whitehead cannot conceive of manyness without dis-

[95] Alfred North Whitehead, *An Enquiry Concerning the Principles of Natural Knowledge*, Cambridge University Press, Cambridge, 1955, p. 2.
[96] Alfred North Whitehead, *The Concept of Nature*, Cambridge University Press, Cambridge, 1955, pp. 14–15.

tinguishing forms. These forms of definiteness are called "objects," and the most obvious objects, in this system, are colors and shapes. "For example, sky-blue is found in nature as situated in a certain event."[97]

Why are not space and time absolute and ultimate? Whitehead's answer is that spatial and temporal extension is derivative from process.

Objects are of course essential for process, as appears clearly enough in the course of any analysis of process. . . . Particular times cannot result from the mere relations between objects which are at all times; and analogously for space. Accordingly space and time must result from something in process which transcends objects.

But natural objects require space and time, so that space and time belong to their relational essence without which they cannot be themselves.[98]

Both the physics and philosophy of our century have abandoned the classic view of the absoluteness of space and time. Not only are time and space viewed relationally in a space-time continuum, but also the conclusion from these points is that events are in process and complex in essence, by being interrelated with other events. Yet each event is a unity. "The event is the unit of things real."[99] This concept of a complete fact is expressed problematically by calling events "processes of unifying." How can events be coherently conceived? Whitehead identifies his question with Plato's and Aristotle's. "The final problem is to conceive a complete . . . fact. We can only form such a conception in terms of fundamental notions concerning the nature of reality. We are thrown back upon philosophy.[100]

Why search for the "complete" fact? Because some metaphysical schemes, as Plato's, had exalted the forms to the status of the really real. " . . . The general Aristotelian principle is maintained that, apart from things that are actual, there is nothing—nothing either in fact or in efficacy."[101] Whitehead calls this "the ontological principle." Actual entities are the only existents, but as with Leibniz's monads and McTaggart's spirits, they constitute a society. Somewhat as the latter has experiences as parts of spirits, Whitehead has "eternal objects" as ingredient in actual entities.

Earlier we posed the problem of how a thing can change into something new, and how a thing can remain what it is through change. Whitehead's

---

[97] *Ibid.*, p. 15.
[98] Alfred North Whitehead, *An Enquiry Concerning the Principles of Natural Knowledge, op. cit.*, p. 202.
[99] Alfred North Whitehead, *Science and the Modern World*, Copyright 1925 by The Macmillan Company, copyright renewed 1953 by Evelyn Whitehead, p. 219. Used by permission of The Macmillan Company and Cambridge University Press.
[100] Alfred North Whitehead, *Adventures of Ideas*, The Macmillan Co., New York, 1956, p. 203.
[101] Alfred North Whitehead, *Process and Reality, op. cit.*, p. 64.

answer is ingenious. The eternal objects are forms of definiteness given to and always available to actualities, much as the multiplication table's 12×12 is available to us. They are not existent by themselves, nor is there activity purely as such. For actual entities must be definite in form. Yet Whitehead often sounds Platonic.

In such a philosophy the actualities constituting the process of the world are conceived as exemplifying the ingression (or participation) of other things which constitute the potentialities of definiteness for any actual existence. The things which are temporal arise by their participation in the things which are eternal.[102]

But this is Platonism with a great difference. The forms are not existent apart from actual entities. Since there cannot then be a heaven of forms, whence are they derived? They come from past actualities. That is, things realized enable other things to be realized. As far as a present event is concerned the forms are "pure potential" for its developing definiteness.

The notion of potentiality is fundamental for the understanding of existence, as soon as the notion of process is admitted. If the universe be interpreted in terms of static actuality, then potentiality vanishes. Everything is just what it is. Succession is mere appearance, rising from the limitation of perception. But if we start with process as fundamental, then the actualities of the present are deriving their characters from the process, and are bestowing their characters upon the future. Immediacy is the realization of the potentialities of the past, and is the storehouse of the potentialities of the future.[103]

How, then, can an entity both remain in continuity with what it was, and change, ever becoming something new? Continuity is made possible by the inheritance of a form from its past actuality. Novelty is possible because there is a succession of unit becomings. The epochal units of becoming exclude a continuous process of becoming. Actual entities perish perpetually, and inheritance of their forms by new entities excludes material substance as the ultimate entity. Therefore Whitehead can say that "actual entities perish, but do not change; they are what they are."[104]

How can there be novelty if all forms of definiteness derive from past actualities? Each actual entity creates itself. Becoming or creativity is nothing in itself, it is only the generic characteristic of all actualities. Yet creativity is the ultimate category. We are familiar in other metaphysical schemes with ultimates that are more real than the many things of the world; in much theological and philosophical language "Ultimate Reality" is a metaphysical name for the traditional God, Creator of heaven

[102] *Ibid.*, p. 63.
[103] Alfred North Whitehead, *Modes of Thought*, The Macmillan Co., New York, 1956, p. 136.
[104] Alfred North Whitehead, *Process and Reality, op. cit.*, p. 52.

and earth. This notion is, according to Whitehead, an example of misplaced concreteness, an abstraction invested with full existence and definiteness.

'Creativity' is another rendering of the Aristotelian 'matter,' and of the modern 'neutral stuff.' But it is divested of the notion of passive receptivity, either of 'form,' or of external relations; it is the pure notion of the activity conditioned by the objective immortality of the actual world—a world which is never the same twice, though always with the stable element of divine ordering. Creativity is without a character of its own in exactly the same sense in which the Aristotelian 'matter' is without a character of its own. It is that notion of the highest generality at the base of actuality. It cannot be characterized, because all characters are more special than itself. But creativity is always found under conditions, and described as conditioned.[105]

Only one important aspect of the system remains to be discussed. What is this "divine ordering of the world?" What is this "objective immortality of the actual world?"

If forms were merely derived from past actualities, the question about the origin of forms would lead to infinite regress. Therefore the system requires, for rationality, a non-temporal actual entity. This is God. Whitehead does not introduce God as a religious belief. Aristotle "found it necessary to complete his metaphysics by the introduction of a Prime Mover . . . he would have no motive, except to follow his metaphysical train of thought withersoever [sic.] it led him." Similarly, Whitehead seeks a "Principle of Concretion," or a ground "of the course of actual occasions,—that is to say, of the process of realization."[106]

We conceive actuality as in essential relation to an unfathomable possibility. Eternal objects inform actual occasions with hierarchic patterns, included and excluded in every variety of discrimination. Another view of the same truth is that every actual occasion is a limitation imposed on possibility, and that by virtue of this limitation the particular value of that shaped togetherness of things emerges. In this way we express how a single occasion is to be viewed in terms of possibility, and how possibility is to be viewed in terms of a single actual occasion. But there are no single occasions, in the sense of isolated occasions. Actuality is through and through togetherness—togetherness of otherwise isolated eternal objects, and togetherness of all actual occasions.[107]

Earlier, in considering the category relation, it was said that to be is to be related. Whitehead's doctrine is an argument for this position that involves a definition of past, present, and future which, the student will recall, in McTaggart's system condemned the apparent world to irrationality. Whitehead's system is based upon temporality in order to defend "un-

[105] *Ibid.*, pp. 46–47.
[106] Alfred North Whitehead, *Science and the Modern World*, op. cit., pp. 249–250.
[107] *Ibid.*, p. 251.

bounded freedom," which both materialism and idealism have tended to deny.

Every actual occasion exhibits itself as a process: it is a becomingness. In so disclosing itself, it places itself as one among a multiplicity of other occasions, without which it could not be itself. It also defines itself as a particular individual achievement, focussing in its limited way an unbounded realm of eternal objects.

Any one occasion α issues from other occasions which collectively form its *past*. It displays for itself other occasions which collectively form its *present*. It is in respect to its associated hierarchy, as displayed in this immediate present, that an occasion finds its own originality. It is that display which is its own contribution to the output of actuality. It may be conditioned, and even completely determined by the past from which it issues. But its display in the present under those conditions is what directly emerges from its prehensive activity. The occasion α also holds within itself an indetermination in the form of a future, which has partial determination by reason of its inclusion in α and also has determinate spatio-temporal relatedness to α and to actual occasions of the past from α and of the present for α.

This future is a synthesis in α of eternal objects as not-being and as requiring the passage from α to other individualisations . . . in which not-being becomes being.[108]

The last point is explained by the doctrine that the actual includes what it is not. Spinoza had defended the doctrine that all limitation is negation; that is, to be something definite is to exclude alternatives. Whitehead holds that without non-being a metaphysic could not explain error, truth, art, ethics, and religion.

Restriction is the price of value. There cannot be value without antecedent standards of value, to discriminate the acceptance or rejection of what is before the envisaging mode of activity. Thus there is an antecedent limitation among values, introducing contraries, grades, and oppositions.

According to this argument the fact that there is a process of actual occasions, and the fact that the occasions are the emergence of values which require such limitation, both require that the course of events should have developed amid an antecedent limitation composed of conditions, particularisation, and standards of value.[109]

Therefore we must find a principle of limitation.

Some particular *how* is necessary, and some particularisation in the *what* of matter of fact is necessary. The only alternative to this admission, is to deny the reality of actual occasions. Their apparent irrational limitation must be taken as a proof of illusion and we must look for reality behind the scene. If we reject this alternative behind the scene, we must provide a ground for limitation which stands among the attributes of the substantial activity. This attribute provides the

[108] *Ibid.*, pp. 253–254.
[109] *Ibid.*, p. 256.

limitation for which no reason can be given: for all reason flows from it. God is the ultimate limitation, and His existence is the ultimate irrationality. For no reason can be given for just that limitation which it stands in His nature to impose. God is not concrete, but He is the ground for concrete actuality. No reason can be given for the nature of God, because that nature is the ground of rationality.[110]

There can be no metaphysical reason for any further determination of God. Abstract reason knows only a principle.

What further can be known about God must be sought in the region of particular experiences, and therefore rests on an empirical basis. In respect to the interpretation of these experiences, mankind have differed profoundly. He has been named respectively, Jehovah, Allah, Brahma, Father in Heaven, Order of Heaven, First Cause, Supreme Being, Chance. Each name corresponds to a system of thought derived from the experiences of those who have used it.

Among medieval and modern philosophers, anxious to establish the religious significance of God, an unfortunate habit has prevailed of paying to Him metaphysical compliments. He has been conceived as the foundation of the metaphysical situation with its ultimate activity. If this conception be adhered to, there can be no alternative except to discern in Him the origin of all evil as well as all good. He is then the supreme author of the play, and to Him must therefore be ascribed its shortcomings as well as its success. If He be conceived as the supreme ground for limitation it stands in His very nature to divide the Good from the Evil, and to establish Reason 'within her dominions supreme.'[111]

The authors cannot pretend to present Whiteheadian metaphysics in its fulness. Some philosophers make it a life task to unravel the arguments that carried Whitehead from symbolic logic through physical theory and cosmology to a theory of science and metaphysics. Is this a view that can do justice to every facet of experience? Leaving this question for the student to answer himself, we proceed to the problematic issue with which this chapter began, what is a metaphysical system?

VII. Philosophic Systems as Perspectives

It was easy for Immanuel Kant to assume that Aristotle was the author of one true system of logical truths, that Euclid was the author of one true system of geometrical truths, and that Newton was the author of one true system of physical truths. Such a scientist-philosopher as Whitehead admits, as he formulates his system, that it is but one of many, an attempt to be superseded, because necessarily limited by the author's insight, knowledge, and logical skill.

[110] *Ibid.*, pp. 256–257.
[111] *Iibid.*, pp. 257–258.

. . . The true method of philosophical construction is to frame a scheme of ideas, the best that one can, and unflinchingly to explore the interpretation of experience in terms of that scheme.

There remains the final reflection, how shallow, puny, and imperfect are efforts to sound the depths in the nature of things. In philosophical discussion, the merest hint of dogmatic certainty as to finality of statement is an exhibition of folly.[112]

Whitehead admired in metaphysicians knowledge of particular sciences. His list of four men, who make important contributions to philosophic system, is Plato, Aristotle, Leibniz, and William James. All assembled particular knowledge. Leibniz was profoundly learned in mathematics, physics, politics, and theology. James "knew the world in which he lived, by travel, by personal relations to its leading men, by the variety of his own studies. He systematized; but above all he assembled." Whitehead admires in Plato the many-sided suggestiveness more than his grasp of mathematical system, and Plato more than Aristotle because Aristotle inherited from Plato and because in "systematizing as he assembled," he "imposed" metaphysical structure.[113]

And why, according to Whitehead, are other men second-rate?

We must grasp the topic in the rough, before we smooth it out and shape it. For example, the mentality of John Stuart Mill was limited by his peculiar education which gave him system before any enjoyment of the relevant experience. Thus his systems were closed. We must be systematic; but we should keep our systems open. In other words, we should be sensitive to their limitations. There is always a vague 'beyond', waiting for penetration in respect to its detail.[114]

Many contemporary metaphysicians would agree that the thoughts of Plato, Bacon, and Leibniz "never crystallized into final systems." A. E. Taylor regards Aristotle and Descartes as great system-makers. Taylor remarks of Whitehead:

Probably no man living understands better why Plato is always careful to warn us that all his conclusions need to be 'reconsidered another time;' none probably, is further removed from the temper of Kant, who ends the *Critique of Practical Reason* with the suggestion that Newton and himself between them have finally settled for all time the principles of natural and moral philosophy, so that nothing is left to their successors but to build higher on the foundations they have laid.[115]

[112] Alfred North Whitehead, *Process and Reality, op. cit.*, p. x.
[113] Alfred North Whitehead, *Modes of Thought, op. cit.*, pp. 3–4.
[114] *Ibid.*, p. 8.
[115] A. E. Taylor, "Dr. Whitehead's Philosophy of Religion," *Dublin Review*, Vol. 181, 1927, pp. 17–18.

If this contrast is true, it follows that no comment about philosophic systems can be taken simply to apply to all of them equally. There is little doubt that most of the objections to system-building are objections to building closed or final systems. These strictures may be ever so legitimate and warranted and have not the slightest bearing on open systems.

This is exactly the point about metaphysical system from a leader of analytic philosophy in Oxford. When Kant criticized metaphysics as a mistaken search beyond experience for something which would explain experience, he was rebuking transcendental and deductive metaphysics; that is, the search for unconditional explanation, or propositions of the form, "so-and-so must exist, therefore so-and-so must follow."[116]

This ideal of system-building, whether deductive or critical or dialectical, extrapolates from our limited knowledge to the top of the scale, knowledge without limitation. The crucial step is this: since we know what it is for knowledge to be less limited by our perspective, therefore we know what it is for knowledge to be from no perspective at all. The rational argument, according to S. N. Hampshire goes like this:

We distinguish different levels of comprehensiveness and objectivity in our actual knowledge. Knowledge becomes more genuinely knowledge the more comprehensive it is and the less it reflects the viewpoint of the knowing subject. Therefore, at the top of the scale, perfect knowledge would be absolutely comprehensive and it would not reflect the viewpoint of the knowing subject even to the smallest degree; indeed the knowing subject would have no particular viewpoint; he would know things as they are in their own true, objective order.[117]

There is a story by Anatole France of a condemned monk who lies sleeping in his prison cell. In his dreams he sees a magnificent rose window similar to those in some of the great cathedrals. But this is a weird window, for its structure is composed of living figures, human, non-human, and mythological. All peoples, classes, ranks, and offices are represented, each different from all the rest in hue and form and each bearing a scroll stating a different view of life and existence. In all this variety and multiplicity there is one thing in common, each scroll concludes with the same words, "Such is Truth." This brings dismay and anguish to the monk, for how, he asks, can truth be so contradictory? He cries out for the real truth. In answer the great window begins to spin, faster and faster, until all the separate, brilliant colors merge into the one, white, dazzling truth.

[116] S. N. Hampshire, "Metaphysical Systems," In: D. F. Pears (ed.), *The Nature of Metaphysics*, Macmillan and Co. Ltd., London, 1957, p. 24.
[117] *Ibid.*, pp. 32–33.

This story suggests the view that might be taken toward philosophic systems, each claiming to be true. They may be regarded as perspectives. That such an interpretation is not novel in philosophy may be demonstrated by presenting statements from a number of first-rate philosophers. The view, though not novel, has seldom been developed as thoroughly as it deserves. After casually bowing to it, or admitting it by way of introduction, most writers have then proceeded to state their own views as if they were the only legitimate ones.

First some statements about perspectives. Morris Cohen puts the point this way:

Metaphysical propositions are perspectives. They determine the point of view from which all human experience or all our sciences and anticipations can be coordinated.[118]

And Hodges:

All differences between one type of inquiry and another, or between rival views in the same field of inquiry, are due to the taking up of different standpoints. A sociological analysis and a moral judgment may bear upon the same complex of actions, but because they approach it from different standpoints they discover different things about it. Within the one field of ethics, again, there is a difference of standpoint between the utilitarian and the Kantian. Every philosophical or religious system, every intellectual or aesthetic tradition, every civilization or culture, may similarly be seen as the embodiment of a distinctive standpoint.[119]

J. B. Baillie says:

Philosophy as an attitude of mind towards the world, and a philosophical system as the expression of such an attitude, occupy a region midway between poetry on the one hand and the science on the other. It is an activity of that imagination which is "reason in her most exalted mood," and an attempt to articulate this in the form of a connected scheme of thought. It always implies an individual point of view and a perspective of the world, which are central and final for the individual, but are different in each case. There is thus no final philosophical theory for all men any more than there is one poetic vision for all.[120]

Josiah Royce put it this way:

Thus everything in philosophy is properly subject to re-interpretation from new individual points of view. No sincere individual point of view is absolutely

[118] Morris Cohen, *A Preface to Logic*, Henry Holt & Co., New York, 1944, pp. 62–63.
[119] H. A. Hodges, *Language, Standpoints, and Attitudes*, Oxford University Press, London, 1953, p. 16.
[120] G. W. F. Hegel, *The Phenomenology of Mind*, 2nd rev. ed. (J. B. Baillie, tr.), George Allen & Unwin Ltd., London; New York, The Macmillan Co., 1949, Translator's Preface, p. 51.

erroneous, for every such interpretation is a portion of the interpretation which the universe gives to itself through the variety of individuals. On the other hand, every finite individual's account of the world is subject to re-interpretation, and in the progress of thinking will doubtless become, so to speak, absorbed in higher syntheses. At any point in time the returns, so far as truth is concerned, are not all in. For countless individual interpretations have not yet been made, or are not now in synthesis. Hence philosophy is peculiarly subject to the reproach of being unfinished and unstable.[121]

And Santayana has written:

As the senses open to us only partial perspectives, taken from one point of view, and report the facts in symbols which, far from being adequate to the full nature of what surrounds us, resemble the coloured signals of danger or of free way which a railway engine-driver peers at in the night, so our speculation which is a sort of panoramic sense, approaches things peripherally and expresses them humanly.[122]

Finally we may quote George H. Mead:

. . . it is only in so far as the individual acts not only in his own perspective but also in the perspective of others, especially in the common perspective of a group, that a society arises and its affairs become the object of scientific inquiry. The limitation of social organization is found in the inability of individuals to place themselves in the perspectives of others, to take their points of view. I do not wish to belabor the point, which is commonplace enough, but to suggest that we find here an actual organization of perspectives, and that the principle of it is fairly evident. This principle is that the individual enters into the perspectives of others, in so far as he is able to take their attitudes, or occupy their points of view.[123]

This conception of philosophic systems as perspectives may be made clearer by a simple analogy. Like many analogies it has its weaknesses, but it will be useful. Let us suppose four persons come into a college chapel: an architect, a clergyman, an artist, and the janitor. The architect is aware of an interior with a certain style, of the proportions relating nave and choir, of the distribution of mass, and the character of the vaulting. The clergyman sees a place of worship where the voice of man seeks to become the word of God. The artist is conscious of the interplay of light and darkness, of color and shadow, of the innumerable

[121] Josiah Royce, *Lectures on Modern Idealism*, Yale University Press, New Haven, Connecticut, 1919, p. 244.

[122] George Santayana, *Character and Opinion in the United States*, Constable and Company, Ltd., London, 1920, p. 32.

[123] George Mead, *The Philosophy of the Present*, The Open Court Publishing Co., La Salle, Illinois, 1932, p. 165.

abstract forms. The janitor sees the dust and sighs with the anticipation of future labor. Each is in the midst of one reality—yet each has a different perspective on it. Which is truer? Are they not all equally real discriminations of what is before them? Some may be more limited, more restricted views than others, but nonetheless a perspective of the real. This is the way it could be with our systems. We all stand in the midst of one reality. Each with our own perspective. How absurd it is to deny that those about us see the real, because they see less or more or something different. It is impossible for any human being to have all perspectives.

What the authors are doing here is simply calling attention to what must be acknowledged, namely, that anything that is known, seen, or experienced in any way is grasped by capacities and within limitations that are strictly human. This is our standpoint, our perspective, and it seems utterly unavoidable.

Now there are some general remarks that can be made about perspectives.[124] For example, our perspectives are represented in our judgments or statements of beliefs. No single judgment, however, adequately represents the total perspective, any more than a single proposition makes a science, or a philosophy, or a religion. As the judgments become connected the perspectives become clearer and the structure of a point of view begins to emerge. It seems perfectly sure that at least some perspectives are shareable (although not all are), else we would find it difficult to communicate with each other. Furthermore, it is also evident that perspectives may sometimes be fixed or solidified so that to change the perspective requires a radical readjustment of thought, which is not often done with ease or assurance. Political legislation, for example, and moral codes, and ecclesiastical doctrine, and perhaps scientific theory, are ways of fixing perspectives. But the finality so obtained is an imposed one, it does not belong to the perspective itself. The fixing of perspective is the characteristic of all orthodoxies. Irrationality may be defined as the unwillingness to discover, or share, or participate in other perspectives. A fanatic is one who refuses to allow for alternative perspectives. He is, perhaps, seen at his best, or worst, in contemporary totalitarian states.

But it is also true that perspectives may overlap, or comprehend other perspectives, as for instance my perspective as a citizen of the United States comprehends and overlaps my perspective as a citizen of my local community. In fact, unless perspectives do in some degree overlap, it is difficult to understand real conflict, which is not merely collision, or mis-

[124] Justus Buchler, *Toward a General Theory of Judgment*, Columbia University Press, New York, 1951, Ch. V.

386 / Philosophy: The Study of Alternative Beliefs

understanding, but opposition arising out of different ways of viewing something held in common.

Perspectives, moreover, have no precise boundaries, although the boundaries are clearer in narrow and formal perspectives, for example, in certain aspects of logic and mathematics. It is this feature of perspectives that makes it possible for them to overlap. There must always be something in common among perspectives or else there is ground for neither disagreement nor agreement.

This seems to have important consequences for a theory of truth. If philosophy is a search for perspective, must it not give up its ancient goal of absolute truth, and be content with particular truths relative to the chosen perspective? The answer could be put this way: We may try to achieve the completest perspective possible although we know in advance that it will never be final. This is merely an admission of our finiteness. Because man is fallible and finite, whatever view he has will be an approximation. This means that any philosophy, no matter how internally consistent, or adequate in scope, is always unfinished, and with this man must learn to live. But to be unfinished, incomplete, and partial, is not the same thing as to be false. Philosophies may always be made truer, but never true. Truth in philosophy has the status of an ideal, and like all ideals it is never fully actualized in any life. What we must seek for is a greater articulation of the truth as it is revealed in our particular perspectives. When this is done we achieve mastery of the content of the perspective, and we are able to call attention to something ignored or missed in the perspective of another. On such a basis, science, philosophy, art, religion, and politics may each have a perspective on truth, and by a sharing of these perspectives contribute to the establishment of a rational community.

The beginning student will have to think his way among idealists, materialists, pragmatists, pessimists, optimists, theists, atheists, communists, capitalists, scientists, and poets, each trying to annex him, or capture his loyalty. He ought not to be an easy prospect. He ought not to be tempted by any pretenses and claims to possess the full and only reality. Each system is partial, each in its own way a perspective distilled into beliefs, and each may be suffering from the delusion that it is the exclusive guardian of truth.

PROBLEMS FOR THOUGHT AND DISCUSSION

1. Our age is marked by redefinition of what the old controversy between materialists, idealists, and dualists is about.

Ontological questions, concerning mind and matter, substance, universals, and the rest, are questions about the categories of being and existence, about the fundamental kinds of things or features that must be recognized as parts of the make-up of our world. Are there bodies? Are there minds? In at least one sense in which these questions can be construed, they can be easily answered by all of us, and in the affirmative. Of course there are. But this is not the sense in which these questions are asked and disputed about in metaphysics. The ontological questions about bodies and minds are not at all like the question whether there are drug stores in Iowa City, Iowa. One important clue to this is that no ontological question is ever settled by experimental or experiential evidence in the direct, tidy way in which questions like that about the drug stores can sometimes be settled. Following the suggestion in this clue one sees that philosophers disputing about ontological questions are not in some mad way contending over whether they are all disembodied spirits, or bodies like stones with no mental characteristics whatever. They are disputing over whether, in a basic inventory of the kinds of things that are the constituents of the world, both these kinds of things must be included (dualism), whether perhaps one of them is sufficient for such an inventory and the other can be regarded as a form of it (materialism or idealism), or whether perhaps neither need be included in such an inventory, since both of them can be conceived as forms of a third something else (neutral monism). The questions about how these things can be conceived, about whether they have to be conceived separately or whether they can perhaps be conceived in terms of each other, naturally translate into questions about how these things can be defined.[125]

> Can you say everything you have to say about man and the universe in any one of the systems you have studied? If not, wherein does each fail? If you can devise a less one-sided language, using "event" as the basic constant, show its superiority.

2. McTaggart argues that religious beliefs are essentially metaphysical, and a metaphysical justification is the only right we can have to decisions on whether a God exists, whether our will is free, whether we survive bodily death. Therefore, since these are the most important issues, metaphysics only seems impractical. But the results of metaphysics cannot be enjoyed without our own investigation.

I can eat bread, although I have never learned to plough or bake. I can be cured of an illness, though I have never learnt medicine. But if—and this is the case at present—I have no right to rely on any metaphysical result which I have not myself investigated, then the study of metaphysics will be for many people the most momentous of all studies. . . . One great reason why so few people have reached metaphysical conclusions for themselves, is to be found in the fact that so few people have tried to reach them.[126]

> Can you, on the basis of the techniques of this chapter, reach one metaphysical conclusion on your own?

3. After hearing William James lecture, W. E. Hocking commented

Are not all systems arrogant simplifications? What is materialism but a simplification, resolved to do justice to our natural ties at all costs? What is idealism but a simplification? What is monism? A simplification at the expense of the abundance and surprise of life. What is pluralism? It, too, is a simplification which values the richness and drama of living too deeply to fill in the connectives. All the structural red-ink and lettering in which the architectural engineer delights are for the architectural artist an abomination: they burden and spoil his picture. The philosophical synthesizer must be a strong

[125] Frederick L. Will, Review of Gustav Bergmann, *The Metaphysics of Logical Positivism, The Journal of Philosophy,* Vol. 53, 1956, p. 471.
[126] Quoted by S. V. Keeling in G. Lowes Dickinson *op. cit.,* p. 136.

man; whoever writes a plausible philosophical thesis must be a strong man. These are the tyrants of truth. . . .[127]

To what extent is it fair to attribute to systems such traits of character as arrogance, tyranny, or strength? Is anti-systematic protest, then, by parity of reasoning, a weakness of will, perhaps subservience or meekness? Is it an intellectual crime to simplify? What is the alternative?

4. Does the danger of system-building lure you to the safety of piecemeal analysis?

It is easy for a profound philosopher to commit a mistake in his subtle reasonings; and one mistake is the necessary parent of another, while he pushes on his consequences, and is not deterred from embracing any conclusion, by its unusual appearance, or its contradiction to popular opinion. But a philosopher, who purposes only to represent the common sense of mankind in more beautiful and more engaging colours, if by accident he falls into error, goes no farther; but renewing his appeal to common sense, and the natural sentiments of the mind, returns into the right path, and secures himself from any dangerous illusion. The fame of Cicero flourishes at present; but that of Aristotle is utterly decayed.[128]

Can Hume argue at all without presupposing principles? Is Hume himself merely beautifying common sense? Is common sense without system? Can Hume fail to damage scientific thought by his exaltation of piecemeal beliefs?

5. Oliver Wendell Holmes compared a system of thought to a carriage. Because it is called "The Deacon's Masterpiece," the "one-hoss shay" has usually been taken as a reference to Calvinism. But the point about this system may apply to any thought-structure.

> Have you heard of the wonderful one-hoss shay,
> That was built in such a logical way
> It ran a hundred years to a day,
> And then, of a sudden, it—ah, but stay,
> I'll tell you what happened without delay,
> Scaring the parson into fits,
> Frightening people out of their wits,—
> Have you ever heard of that, I say?
> . . .
> Now in building of chaises, I tell you what,
> There is always *somewhere* a weakest spot . . .
> And that's the reason, beyond a doubt,
> That a chaise *breaks down*, but doesn't *wear out*.
> . . .
> You see, of course, if you're not a dunce
> How it went to pieces all at once,—
> All at once, and nothing first,—
> Just as bubbles do when they burst.
> End of the wonderful one-hoss shay.
> Logic is logic. That's all I say.

[127] W. E. Hocking, "Some Second Principles." In: George P. Adams and William Pepperell Montague (eds.), *Contemporary American Philosophy*, George Allen & Unwin, Ltd., London, 1930, p. 390.

[128] David Hume, *Enquiries, An Enquiry Concerning Human Understanding*, 2nd ed. (L. A. Selby-Bigge, ed.), The Clarendon Press, Oxford, 1927, p. 7.

This is a witty analogy that infuriated New England clergymen a century ago. The analogy suggests that systems of thought have a life cycle. That is, at some point of time, their weakest place can no longer be fixed, and they are doomed. If you have taken over a system, and are trying to make it run, you might consider the loss and gain in abandoning the old system against the loss and gain in adopting some new system.

Would Holmes' analogy apply to an open as well as to a closed system? Consider what would be left of McTaggart's system without the infinite divisibility of substance. What is left of Descartes' or Spinoza's system without the ontological argument? In short, does every system have a weakest spot?

6. Often in literature we meet with characters who act out metaphysical systems. For example, Arthur Koestler's Age of Longing has a Russian commissar who claims everything is mechanical.

"There is no mystery, only reflexes, as in this radio machine. . . . You turn a knob, there is a reaction. You hit it, there is damage; you repair it, it is all right again. It talks, it screams, it makes music—all very useful and amusing; but there is no mystery. . . ."
[An American girl, Hydie, responds to Fedya]: "You talk exactly like grandad. . . . He was a president of a railway company. In between buying up other companies, he spent his spare time reading pamphlets about 'the survival of the fittest' and 'man, a machine?' You talk just like him. . . ." [Fedya tells about Pavlov's experiments with dogs] "So, you see . . . after a while when the bell rings the dog drops his spittle although there is no meat. . . . And that explains what we are: conditions and reflexes, and the rest is stupid superstition." He was now standing at the couch, bending over her, and her heart was pumping away violently. "Oh, rot," she said breathlessly, waiting to be taken.[129]

From the mechanist's view, the girl is a machine to be manipulated, like a radio or a dog. But from her point of view this approach is degrading, and she kills the mechanist. Is mechanism an insult to our humanity as we know it inwardly? Can you think of how a novelist might similarly ridicule a dualist, an idealist, or a process philosopher? Can any such parable be re-stated as an argument?

7. "There is thinking; consequently there is that which thinks—this is what Descartes' argument comes to. Yet this means positing our faith in the concept of *substance* as a priori true".[130] Have the various defenses of process philosophy shaken your confidence in substantial entities?

8. Simone de Beauvoir writes of reading the Hegelian system. To read such a theory is to put oneself

. . . on the plane of the universal, thus, of the infinite. That is why reading it is so comforting. I remember having experienced a great feeling of calm on reading Hegel in the impersonal framework of the Bibliotheque Nationale in August 1940. But once I got into the street again, into my life, out of the system, beneath a real sky, the system was no longer of any use to me: what it had offered me, under a show of the in-finite, was the consolation of death; and I again wanted to live in the midst of living men. I think that, inversely, existentialism does not offer to the reader the consola-

---

[129] Arthur Koestler, *Age of Longing*, The Macmillan Company, New York, 1953.
[130] Walter Kaufmann, *The Portable Nietzsche*, Viking Press, New York, 1954, p. 455.

tions of an abstract evasion: existentialism proposes no evasion. On the contrary, its ethics is experienced in the truth of life, and it then appears as the only proposition of salvation which one can address to men.[131]

In the light of testimony from Koestler and Holmes, are men devoid of metaphysical systems? Are the systems of mechanism and Calvinism abstract, and only existentialism concrete? Is all abstract thinking evasion of the issues of ethics and salvation? (You should recall that Mme. de Beauvoir was writing of an experience in the darkest period of the World War II, and that some existentialists were deeply involved in resisting the Nazis through the underground. You may profitably reconsider the question whether all metaphysical schemes are irrelevant to periods of despair when we consider philosophies of history in the next chapter.)

PERTINENT READINGS

Broad, C. D., "Critical and Speculative Philosophy." In H. J. Muirhead (ed.), *Contemporary British Philosophy*, First Series, George Allen & Unwin, Ltd., London, 1924, pp. 77–100.

Calkins, Mary Whiton (ed.), *The Metaphysical System of Hobbes*, 2nd ed., The Open Court Publishing Co., La Salle, Illinois, 1948.

Hall, Everett W., "Metaphysics." In: Dagobert D. Runes, *Twentieth Century Philosophy*, Philosophical Library, Inc., New York, 1943, pp. 147–194.

Lee, Otis, *Existence and Inquiry*, University of Chicago Press, Chicago, 1949.

McKeon, Richard, "Philosophy and Method," *Journal of Philosophy*, Vol. 48, No. 22, 1951, pp. 653–682.

McTaggart, J. Ellis, "Personality." In: James Hastings (ed.), *Encyclopaedia of Religion and Ethics*, T. & T. Clark, Edinburgh, 1917, Vol. IX, pp. 773–781.

Pepper, Stephen C., *World Hypotheses: A Study in Evidence*, University of California Press, Berkeley and Los Angeles, 1948.

Russell, Bertrand, *A Critical Exposition of the Philosophy of Leibniz, with an Appendix of Leading Passages*, 2nd ed., George Allen & Unwin, Ltd., London, 1951.

Urban, Wilbur Marshall, *The Intelligible World: Metaphysics and Value*, George Allen & Unwin, Ltd., London, 1929.

Whitehead, Alfred North, *Modes of Thought*, The Macmillan Co., New York, 1956.

[131] Simone de Beauvoir, *Ethics of Ambiguity* (Bernard Frechtman, tr.), Philosophical Library, Inc., New York, 1948, pp. 158–159.

VIII

Historical Beliefs and Beliefs about History

I. Introduction

Philosophy of history has often been thought of as an attempt to deal with a single question to which a variety of alternative answers is possible. But it is no longer adequate to conceive of the subject in such a relatively simple way, rather we are now aware that philosophy of history is an extremely complex subject around which clusters a whole family of different, but related beliefs. First, some questions about history are raised by our beliefs about the past, where we have been; about the present, how we got where we are; and about the future, where we are going. Second, other questions are epistemological, raised by claims to know past events rather than merely to believe, for often we distinguish between "fact" and "interpretation"; we need definition of terms and principles used in testing the validity of historical argument. Third, other questions are raised by various metaphysical orientations of our historical beliefs, such as idealism and realism. And finally, we shall also see that contemporary philosophers are beginning to look sharply at the linguistic problem; that is, the language in which historical beliefs are expressed. Let us make a few preliminary remarks about these problems before dealing with them separately and more extensively.

One of our most common beliefs is that something happened. Since events "in the past" are not now present to our senses, we look for support to memory. Although it supports some beliefs with unshakable conviction, most beliefs about past events are too remote for any man's memory. These are commonly called "historical beliefs," and are said to rest upon evidence. Without this assumption historical research could not begin, and without the skills of historians in recognizing what evidence adequately supports belief, we cannot hope to attain knowledge.

Although historical beliefs answer questions about what happened, such questions are not asked out of pure curiosity, nor are historical beliefs entertained out of pure interest in their truth. As some personal memories are treasured by every man, so groups of men build traditions. As poets, such as Homer, hand down stories, so historians of literate societies, Herodotus, for example, preserve what they desire posterity to remember. Historians assume at least this about the future: someone will care to know. The opening sentence of Herodotus is in the present and future tenses, as well as in the past tense:

Herodotus of Halicarnassus presents the results of his researches . . . with the twofold object of saving the past of mankind from oblivion and ensuring that the extraordinary achievements of the Hellenic and the Oriental worlds shall enjoy their just renown—particularly the transactions which brought them into conflict with one another.[1]

So human concern with the past is coupled with concern for the future. We ask what will happen. Even if we cannot imagine, we anticipate something. The bare minimum of certainty is that something will happen as surely as something has happened. But what will happen? Will it be something glorious or something terrible? It is rarely claimed that beliefs about future events have absolute certainty. Events "in the future" are possible rather than actual as events "in the past" were. But lack of reliable methods in predicting human events does not diminish what is called concern with "destiny." Indeed, the more uncertain the future, the more intense our hopes and fears.

It is not uncommon to try to show that actual and possible events are necessary. "Destiny" carries a suggestion that there is some agency beyond mankind foreseeing and controlling the human story. We have used it to refer to this kind of question: "Can I accept whatever will happen?" or "Can I or humankind cope with situations successfully?" or "Can the race survive?"

"Man looks before and after, and pines for what is not." These correlative extensions of time from an ever-shifting now are subjects of bodies of belief. Shall we accept prophecy as being as credible in its way as history

[1] Arnold J. Toynbee, *Greek Historical Thought*, New American Library, Inc., New York, 1952, p. 29.

is in its? It is not only the Hebrews of the eighth and seventh centuries before Christ who were plagued with the problem of whether to believe their prophets, Amos and Isaiah and Jeremiah. We of the twentieth century after Christ have historian-prophets with their revelations too. It is, for example, very difficult to know what to say of Spengler's doctrine of the decline of the West, or Toynbee's hope that a great world religion will redeem the failure of secular civilization. The problem is: Does knowledge of the human past provide clues to more or less precise knowledge of the future?

The basic fact in the fortunes of men is change. This mutability neither the prophets of Israel nor the historians of Greece allow us to forget. Great powers can be brought low and small powers can be exalted. There is at least this minimum agreement about the future drawn from the past: Do not expect you can maintain your present condition. The ancient wise men found this folly in individuals and in societies. "Call no man happy till he dies," says Herodotus. The great philosophic doctrine of Hebrew prophecy and Greek history is that change is not sheer chance. That is, the changes are not all accidental, but can be understood; but how?

Although Yahweh, God of Israel, was somewhat bad-tempered in his dealings with men, his anger with the children of the "third and the fourth generations" was provoked by the "sins of the fathers." The prophets found history as intelligible as their God. Not all the Hebrews, of course, believed this. But even today it is the assumption of our Thanksgiving proclamations that a nation enjoying peace, plenty, and prosperity has found favor with the Deity and is being rewarded. Thucydides discerned a plot or pattern in the course of Athenian events. The defeat of Athens at the hands of Sparta was not an event disconnected with what the Athenians had done, and he pondered upon their doings to find some tragic fault. It was, he believed, the overweaning pride of his countrymen that led them to think that they had power to carry out their conquest. At least pride can blind men to possible failure, and those who misuse their power can expect disaster. Thucydides assured his readers that however the situations might differ—a wholly new cast of actors, and a seemingly new play—some future dramas would repeat the old plot.

If we discover changes, can we also discover what endures through the changes? Can we perhaps find anything permanent throughout human history? For instance, ancient cultures produced at least two strong faiths that human communities could persist. Hebrew faith in God is sometimes indistinguishable from the faith that Israel would never be destroyed but would continue and multiply to the end of time, indeed not until then be perfected. Roman historians elaborated a similar doctrine that Rome was eternal. The faith was still strong in Dante, nine hundred years after the celebrated "fall" of Rome.

Our traditional beliefs about history were created by men who wondered about the survival of the Jews without a land throughout centuries. The phenomenon cried out for explanation. It was deeply stirring for the Roman Augustine to consider the persistence of Jews and Christians as one continuous succession from the Old Testament prophets. It is conceivable that Christians had learned from the stubborn hopes of the Hebrews and had come to share in some knowledge that the Romans had missed. Why should a minor people survive, however obscurely and in seeming failure, when great empires rise to power only to crumble into ruins for some future Caesar to build upon?

It is possible that we will have to go beyond human events to find permanence. Some men, for example, Socrates, concluded that the rational soul of man is something unchanging, evidenced by its capacity to "survey all time and all eternity." Behind this is a traditional doctrine that all changing things are imperfect and even evil, while only unchanging things are perfect and good. One can face all disasters, like death of the body, if they are only the release of the eternal from the temporal. But all this makes puzzles of why there should be change, how to live as a full human being, and as a member of a society, and, more practically, why one should bother to cope with situations of the temporal order.

It is clear that some men have thought that an unchanging principle beyond human history explains our shifting fortunes. The simplest expressions are that God and his plan are unchanging. Shakespeare wrote: "There's a divinity that shapes our ends, Rough-hew them how we will." It has also been said that nature's patterns are eternal. Ecclesiastes has it: "What has been is what shall be, what has gone on is what shall go on, and there is nothing new under the sun." These doctrines can, of course, be attacked as a refuge of ignorance, as a failure even to attempt an understanding of men as they actually live on earth. But they have been powerful beliefs in human experience.

The consideration of human events in time involves many more questions than are customarily thought within the scope of historical knowledge. It would be simple if we could say that historical knowledge reports only "the facts," or gives us a series of propositions picturing the human past "as it actually occurred." We might then set "the facts" over against "interpretations" and say that apart from knowledge, all else is "speculation." We could then relegate to the latter field questions about the plan of God, questions about the laws that are said to hold in the historical process, and questions about the end or purpose of the process, such as human progress. Some philosophers have indeed regarded all statements that answer such questions as neither true nor false, but as meaningless, since factual evidence does not seem either to confirm or to refute them. One extreme position bases all beliefs about history upon faith alone. "Faith" here means that a belief is incapable of being supported by argument or evidence.[2]

This sharp division between factual history and interpretation of history, between historical beliefs and beliefs about history, fails to do justice to historical knowledge. We shall endeavor to show that historians themselves introduce interpretations into their narratives. Indeed, if this is inevitable, the sharp antithesis between facts and faith is a mistake.

The most convincing evidence that no historian can work without some implicit philosophical commitment is that every historian must say what his history is about. Is the individual man an aspect of a social movement, or is the expression "social movement" mere shorthand for describing the relations between individual men? Another way of stating the question is, which is the real or concrete entity, which is the abstraction?

Another aspect of the same problem is the selection of terms and relations. The units of discourse may be as wide as the whole of man's past or as narrow as Cleopatra's nose. The relations claimed to hold between historical units are nearly always in some sense temporal. But are events conceived correctly as mere points of time? Often we learn history as a series of dates, and we reason that if A happened before B, then B happened after A. It would be simple if all the relations of history fell into such a pattern, called transitive-asymmetrical. But historical events, for example, like the American Revolution, constitute a series of events over a span of time. The dates we learn, 1775–1783 for example, are very abstract boundaries. A part of the reign of George III, also falls within these dates. Hence the durations of events in history overlap, and are called "contemporaneous." The reign of George III (1760–1820) is said to be in temporally symmetrical relation to the American Revolution. But part of that reign was before and part after the Revolution. Hence the two events are not exactly contemporaneous. But from what point of view shall we judge?

Nor is the transitivity of historical durations exclusively temporal. Dates are assigned to explain why and how the reign of George III influenced the

[2] Karl Löwith, *The Meaning in History*, University of Chicago Press, Chicago, 1949.

writing of the Declaration of Independence. We may say that the first term is a set of conditions and the second term is a set of results. Yet the Declaration is itself a set of conditions and the actions of George III after July 4, 1776 are a set of results. Hence we may well be puzzled by the problem of locating any simple cause and effect. It is a problem whether any history can fail to commit itself to a doctrine of causation. Later Edmund Burke will be quoted; he insisted that historical understanding is inadequate if it fails to grasp economic, religious, and legal factors in the situation.

Some historical methods assume that the result of any cause had to happen, other methods assert that the outcome was foreseen or planned, yet others that the effect cannot be fully accounted for or that the conjunctions of factors are by "chance" or unpredictable. These issues are of the highest philosophic importance. They would face us in examining our beliefs about history even if we had no theological tradition from the Greeks and Hebrews, or no attempts from modern philosophers to show that all history happened as it did because it is a rational system the major premise of which they claim to know.

Philosophers who write now about history are mindful of the swift and often destructive pace of events. The confidence that prevailed before World War I, expressed as faith in the "inevitable" or steady progress of mankind, has not withstood the evidence drawn from World War II. There is unquestioned groping for new hope to replace the one that seems to have failed in its prediction of an irreversible trend toward Utopia. One understandable reaction is self-pity, which may be expressed in talk of "lost generations," "the age of anxiety," or "the age of crisis," as though there had never been such victims as we are. This belief marks the audience eager for prophecy of an "end of the world" by atom bombs, new-style, with or without avenging angels. Another reaction is that of various aggressive political movements. They often claim to be based on a doctrine that one race or one class, whatever these might mean, should triumph. Thus pressure is generated, tempting men to philosophize for other than philosophic results. Philosophers are on the whole most reluctant to forge arguments as weapons in any "war for the minds of men." Although talk about "destiny" enlists emotional support, it dulls the capacity for critical thought. Hence, in spite of the charge of irrelevance against them, most philosophers try to produce something more honest than ideology.

It is certainly true that, "the philosophy of history customarily includes multiple problems which are as difficult to separate completely as to treat simultaneously."[3] A convenient way to see one aspect at a time is to begin by trying to define history. Although there are many definitions and no one essential meaning, the alternatives rest on various diverse epistemological and metaphysical assumptions. Similarly there are various meanings given to the name "philosophy of history."

Historical beliefs are not adequately analyzed without considering both the form of the arguments used and the factual evidence considered relevant to belief. Perhaps the most useful approach to historical reasoning is to be awakened by a historian to the fallacies he seeks to avoid. On this logical basis we can advance to various theories of how we achieve historical knowledge. An obvious name for this discipline is "critical philosophy of history" or "epistemology of history." But statements of how we know, assume answers to questions about what there is to know. This has to do with the metaphysical problem, and there are many alternative "speculative philosophies of history."

Beliefs about history are not exhaustively considered from only logical, epistemological, and metaphysical perspectives; for questions about human evil and the possibilities of good also excite historians, theologians, and philosophers. Furthermore, we have not done justice to the field unless we add a word on why philosophies of history often become moral philosophies, or applications of ethical systems.

The appearance of order may be deceptive in so confused an area. At best this division into sections may help us see how many different kinds of questions men ask, each reflecting a possible belief. If we do no more than to see the complexity of issues in a less dim light, it will be contribution enough in an introduction.

II. Definitions of History

The word "history" is notoriously ambiguous. Although the Greeks once used it to refer to knowledge of some sort, it has come to refer to events themselves. Hence we play upon the double meaning in such quips as "history teaches that history teaches nothing." This may be translated: "historical knowledge provides evidence that the course of events does not make men wiser."

It is not correct to think that "history" had only one meaning among the ancient Greeks. The word before Herodotus meant "knowledge in the

[3] "The Philosophy of History." In: Marvin Farber (ed.), *Philosophical Thought in France and the United States,* University of Buffalo Publications, Buffalo, New York, 1950, p. 301.

widest sense."[4] When Herodotus and his successor Thucydides narrowed the meaning toward knowledge expressed in narrative style, this might have caught the attention of Socrates and Plato. Although Socrates sought certainty in knowledge and Plato stressed its achievement in mathematics, he did not write a dialogue on the meanings of "history." This very lack of interest is accounted for by the fact that history is the knowledge of changing things; hence, for Plato, falling in the realm of mere opinion, and not genuine knowledge at all. If knowledge rests upon a grasp of essences, then Aristotle made a correct judgment when he said, "poetry is more philosophic and of graver import than history," that is, if we are right in judging that poetry grasps the essential or universal, and historical opinion is about the mere particulars of non-recurrent events. Whether we are to follow classical or modern epistemologists who also rank history lower than the sciences is an issue that will be discussed shortly.

As a minimal initial definition we may say that history is knowledge of particular events related in order of their occurrence. This has the merit of unpacking the meaning of "narrative" and avoiding the suggestion that a historian is as indifferent to issues of truth and falsity as a novelist may be. What kind of truth historical knowledge may achieve in contrast to artistic and scientific knowledge is yet to be determined and specified.

But this definition of history is too broad. First, do we intend to use the word "history" to cover knowledge of all particular events, or only of some? Second, do we intend to include all temporally organized knowledge or only some?

The first question is about the content of history: the second about its form. In order not to include knowledge of geological changes, men have been led to say "knowledge of *human events*." And in order to distinguish "chronicle" from "history" men have been led to say "*explanatory* narrative." A chronicle, such as one of our sources for a history of medieval Europe, fails to satisfy what we expect of a history, namely, to establish not only dates but causal relations between events.

If we accommodate our definition, in Socratic fashion, we have: History is the knowledge of particular human events related in their order of occurrence and explaining these events causally.

This definition is exceedingly vague in two respects. First, any way we try to make more precise the notion of "human events" we encounter difficulty. Second, any way we try to make more precise the notion of cause,

---

[4] J. P. Peters, "History," *Encyclopaedia Britannica*, 11th ed. Cambridge University Press, Cambridge, England, and New York, 1910, Vol. 13 p. 527.

we encounter difficulty. "Difficulty" here means that our definition can be shown to be too narrow, that is, excluding something from the historical realm we should wish to include. Let us illustrate these points. If we substitute for "human events" the notion of "human actions," then one might say that the subject matter of history is whatever men have done. But in fact historians do take into account non-human circumstances, such as the storm that helped disperse the Spanish Armada in 1588. We might say that this storm happened to men, and seen from a human point of view, it is a "human event." But not by any plausible stretch can it be called a "human action." Or suppose we stress "human thought." This can, at least according to idealists, be made more precise than "human event." But then we neglect the circumstances under which men make plans, and the consequences of trying to carry plans into effect. Again, our definition would be too narrow and thus do violence to historians. It seems better, then, to recognize that the phrase "human events" is, although vague, perhaps as precise as the subject matter allows.

The sense in which historical narrative is causal explanation is also difficult to grasp. If we define cause as constant conjunction of event A with another event B, that is, every case of A implies B, we have a precise formulation. But although a historian may sketch the background of Athenian life that makes the ethics of Plato and Aristotle intelligible, he may not care to argue that the funeral oration of Pericles implies the philosophic doctrine of four cardinal virtues. Historians may be wise in admitting explanatory relations far looser than a chemist's judgment that all cases of burning are cases of oxidation. It would be more precise if we could say that all historical explanations discover some one specific set of factors that always underlie all other factors. A familiar example is the doctrine of economic determinism. This may take a psychological or sociological form. That is, the economic interests of each individual or the economic system of each society may be called the "cause," and politics, art, religion, science, philosophy the "effects." This precision, too, comes at the price of denying a priori that political measures may control or regulate economic behavior. But this may be what we want to know, and historians may be in position to tell us whether it can occur.

Human events are said to be non-recurrent. For example, the Napoleon who led his army into the Russia of Czar Alexander lived only once. In its concrete aspects each event is called unique. Yet in reporting such events, perhaps even in observing them, we use universal names, common nouns such as "war," and predicates that describe this whole class of singular events such as "disastrous." If we concentrate on questions of why events happened, rather than on what happened, our language becomes increasingly general. And it is difficult to see that explanation can be achieved without assuming some general principles of human behavior.

Historians do compare the French Revolution of 1789 to the Russian Revolution of 1917, and in reversion to traditional political order, with appeal to national sentiment, they find an analogy between Napoleon and Stalin. Do all revolutionary movements with an international doctrine revert to the old nationalistic pattern? This would be a general law, and indeed, what in principle sociologists and other social scientists seek.

The extent to which historians may generalize, or fit particular series of events into a schematism of concepts and laws can be examined in Toynbee's Study of History. On the basis of a definition such as the one given here, many historians refuse Toynbee's study the title "history." He seems to write narratives of particular series of events only to show the application of some law, such as "challenge and response."

It is certainly true that history on the whole has been less general than sociology. But is past practice to legislate against further development? Are definitions based on past practice to hold the study static? From the perspective of the year 4000, Toynbee may some day appear as the modern Herodotus, and the work done prior to him may then seem as Homeric legends appeared to the original Greek Father of History.

But we are not only unable to get a definition that marks a clear line between history and the social sciences. Suppose that we consider the definition philosophically. Would philosophers of all epistemological and metaphysical positions accept the general sense of our definition? Let us repeat the definition: History is knowledge of particular human events related in their order of occurrence and explaining these events causally. To answer the question is to enter upon an area of sharp disagreement among philosophers. At least three groups of philosophers would find the definition unsatisfactory, each specifying a way in which it is subject to attack. We shall call these the idealistic attack, the positivistic attack, and for want of a better name, the relativistic attack.[5]

The definition is realistic or dualistic in that events and knowledge of events are distinguished. Any idealist who says that being and knowledge are one would find our definition quite unacceptable. The definition assumes that there are distinct and different ways of knowing and quite diverse sorts of beliefs worthy of the name knowledge. Any positivist, or others of similar persuasion, who says that certain "scientific" methods

[5] Maurice Mandelbaum, *The Problem of Historical Knowledge*, Liveright Publishing Corp., New York, 1938, pp. 1–174.

alone guarantee that the product is knowledge, would find our definition also unacceptable. The definition assumes that temporal and causal principles or organization are sufficient to distinguish the knowledge of human events called history. But many historians and philosophers of history insist that interest or preference or taste is essential to the existence of historical beliefs. Our definition has ignored this factor, and the relativists say it destroys any claim to knowledge. There is, insist the relativists, no route from subject-matter to historical beliefs except through knowers who color the product with various valuational dyes.

To spell out these positions a discussion of the reflective enterprise called philosophy of history will be presented. Certain issues of deductive logical relations are discussed in Section IV. Epistemological and metaphysical alternatives are discussed in Sections V and VI, and the evaluational factor is assessed in Section VII. As the student takes a position in each of these areas, a wise procedure would be to reformulate a definition of his own to fit his basic conceptions or beliefs.

III. What Is Philosophy of History?

There are many definitions of philosophy of history. Perhaps most of them are verbally similar to that of Karl Löwith, who writes in Meaning in History that philosophy of history is "a systematic interpretation of universal history in accordance with a principle by which historical events and successions are unified and directed toward an ultimate meaning."[6] Nearly all contemporary writers in the field talk of "meaning," and feel distressed that most of the events and accounts of the events give them a sense of futility. They find such a diversity of movements that they cannot tell where the evidence points. Nor does the human scene seem to illustrate one law or principle. Moreover, it includes so much evil that they feel uncertain whether any constructive good could issue from such violence and waste. Karl Löwith asserts that these impressions are true. Ultimate meaning cannot, he argues, be attained by reason or be based on historical evidence. Only by revelation can God disclose to man what his salvation, or ultimate meaning is, and only by faith can man appropriate it. Salvation can never be discovered in the course of human effort. Man's will is blind and perverse. Only in another age or world will man fulfill the end to which God destines him.

Is a philosophy of history basically a confession of a theological faith and an expression of religious hope? It was against this position that Voltaire inveighed in the eighteenth century. He was the first to use the

[6] Karl Löwith, *op. cit.*, p. 1.

term philosophy of history. He insisted that if man trusts in his reason, he can design for himself an ultimate meaning, and supply such means to fulfill it that the "age of reason" will so outshine the darkness of the "age of faith" that the church's teachings will be known by all to be unintelligible in principle and wicked in practice.

The contemporary Löwith and the celebrated Voltaire share a common ground: the philosophy of history in either case deals with the problem of what man should do to be saved. Whether by reason or by faith, whether in this world or in another world, the problem is, what is man's aim or end or goal. Pertinent to answering the question is the whole course of events, including future as well as past human actions and thoughts. With such a purpose, and with so vast an array of materials, the statements about history take the form of laws or patterns of utmost generality. If this is what philosophy of history is, then mere history that deals with one nation, or with a single aspect such as naval warfare, seems impossibly petty and narrow. Philosophy of history is based on universal or synoptic history, the grasp of the whole macroscopically rather than microscopically. Further, the philosopher of history is a prophet of the future rather than a mere annalist of the past. The relationship between philosophy of history and history is that the latter supplies the materials, while the former generalizes them. "Historical facts are regarded as ephemeral instances of the unchanging truths which philosophy of history propounds."[7]

Although the two preceding sections were in part a defense of philosophy of history, we may now ask whether we ought to follow the way defined by Löwith or by Voltaire in our philosophy of history? Are we to limit philosophy of history to the defense of divine revelation, or its supplementation by reason? Or to put it another way, is philosophy of history an extension of biblical prophecy that God will save whom He will save; or does it develop the idea that man is his own savior? In the first two sections we attempted to show the range of questions and answers that gave rise to a philosophy of history; even if one finds no "principle by which historical events and successions are unified and directed toward an ultimate meaning," still there are many humbler questions that anyone reflecting upon historical beliefs and beliefs about history should not fail to answer for oneself.

Indeed the range of questions about history is so wide, that the traditional conception of a pronouncement upon man's "nature and destiny" is

[7] Michael Oakeshott, *Experience and Its Modes*, Cambridge University Press, Cambridge, 1933, p. 154. Note: This is not the author's own belief; quite the contrary, it is a view he rejects.

too narrow. At least it seems hasty to overlook, in the interest of "salvation," the humbler questions of how one is to survey universal history, how one is to conceive historical knowledge, how one is to discover a norm by which to judge whether man does progress in time. In this section the reasons philosophy of history may be pluralistic rather than monistic, that is, why it may deal with many civilizations rather than with one human drama, will be discussed. Also, philosophy of history may be critical rather than speculative, that is, dealing with how one knows anything about the human past rather than with how one conceives of the whole human past and future. Thirdly, philosophy of history may be concerned with a standard for evaluating human history rather than with giving assurance that man will do his best or his worst in the future. The argument is that metaphysics of history in the twentieth century has discovered the pluralistic alternative; that epistemology of history is no longer limited to the a priori methods of divine revelation, or of rationalism, but that it can deal with problems of verifying empirical beliefs, even the humble though momentous issues of the language of historical explanations; and finally that the moral issue of norms needs to be made explicit, and should no longer be restricted to classical theological or metaphysical formulations.

These distinctions within philosophy of history will for the sake of clarity be called the pluralistic philosophy of history, the epistemology of history, and the ethical or moral philosophy of history. We are hardly now in position to say that any one is a subordinate or inferior variation of the others, but this division is helpful for seeing what answers may be entertained and how these answers may be elaborated to enrich the field in ways unsuspected either by St. Augustine, or by Hegel, or by Marx.

The Pluralistic Philosophy of History. In contrast to searching for one "law of history" that explains "the ultimate direction of historical change," why should we not consider universal history as made up of "self-enclosed civilizations"? It will be shown later that Hegel and Marx in the nineteenth century followed Augustine in the fifth century in finding a place for each civilization within the totality of human development. But has not historical research revealed many civilizations not known to have been produced or even much influenced from the outside? If it is a "law" of human development, such as classical monistic metaphysics spurs us to seek, why not seek it in each particular civilization?

This assumes that the philosopher of history is not so much putting together the particular histories into one whole as generalizing from the features of all the particular civilizations he knows about. The work of

Spengler, Toynbee, Sorokin, and Northrop in the twentieth century points to a comparative study of civilizations. These are too various to be simply lumped together. But what is sought by all these inquirers is a theory of types of culture and a theory of their succession. Such work is still highly intuitive and carried out in personal and even in idiosyncratic ways. But that this method is capable of harmonizing with the work of historians will be shown at the end of the section on the metaphysics of history.

The Epistemology of History. It is certain that there are epistemological problems connected with historical knowledge even if we do not ask, as did traditional metaphysicians, about the ultimate meaning of history. This is the basic claim of those who redefine philosophy of history as an inquiry into the nature of historical knowledge. Just as philosophy of science analyses the logical and linguistic problems encountered in the sciences, so analogous problems receive systematic treatment in philosophy of history. But to avoid ambiguity, philosophers have suggested that these analyses be called epistemology of history rather than metaphysics of history, or sometimes formal rather than material philosophy of history.[8]

Many of those who work on epistemology of history claim that metaphysics of history is a mistake. This often means that the philosopher cannot assign any clear meaning to the object referred to as "the ultimate direction of historical change." Sometimes it means that the philosopher does not care for synoptic history, either because it is an attempt to do what historians could do better, if they attempted it, or because it is a presumptuous effort that should not be made at all.[9] It is not necessary to address oneself to these polemic charges against metaphysical or speculative philosophy of history if one takes epistemological or critical philosophy of history seriously.

Epistemology of history is, by one definition,

> . . . a critical enquiry into the character of historical thinking, an analysis of some of the procedures of the historian and a comparison of them with those followed in other disciplines, the natural sciences in particular. Thus understood, philosophy of history forms part of the branch of philosophy known as theory of knowledge or epistemology.[10]

Another Oxford philosopher, whose linguistic analysis will be examined later, pictures the relationship between the philosopher and the historian in this way:

[8] W. H. Walsh, *An Introduction to the Philosophy of History*, Hutchinson's University Library, London, 1953.
Maurice Mandelbaum, "Some Neglected Philosophic Problems Regarding History," *Journal of Philosophy*, Vol. 49, 1952, p. 317.
[9] Michael Oakeshott, *loc. cit.*
[10] W. H. Walsh, *op. cit.*, p. 119.

[The latter seeks to answer the question] was there a connection between the Protestant Reformation of the sixteenth and seventeenth centuries and the emergence of a capitalist economy? . . . [The philosopher, however, is] very interested in the kind of evidence an historian might bring forward to substantiate his claim, in the criteria he uses for deciding whether or not a connexion existed.[11]

When philosophy of history is regarded in this way it seeks to answer certain questions, such as:

'Is history a science?', 'How can we know historical facts?', 'Is there any such thing as an objective historical account?', 'What is the nature of historical "theories" and interpretations—the Marxian, for example?', 'Are there historical laws?'. These are questions which genuinely give rise to puzzlement and it is difficult to see who, other than the philosopher, is in a position to attempt their answer.[12]

The Ethical Philosophy of History. Although an epistemologist of history scorns problems created by man's anxiety about the future, there is still the problem of preparing one's self for the future "before it actually occurs." Often this is connected with questions about "the meaning or purpose of the historical process, the nature of human destiny, the course of human history, and the future of mankind."[13] These questions have often been answered by the great metaphysical systems. But the grasp of the "meaning of the process" may be the real issue, and the analyses of change, cause, and law merely groundwork. So Morris Cohen's work has been interpreted.[14] He said himself that his task was to develop "a conception or picture of the whole course of human events as a continuous unitary play in which successive generations or eras play distinctive parts." The philosopher tries to "see great significance in the changes which time works in the patterns of human life."[15]

This view differs in several respects from traditional metaphysics of history. It is not synoptic history; it is not the pronouncement of one ultimate purpose; and no one law is claimed to hold. If this interpretation is successful, what might emerge is "a standard of evaluation of history." We would be led to conceive of the good life, in Cohen's case with high stress on reason, and to judge human success in achieving it. Given such a standard, one might, as did Kant, offer a "general plan from which all the

[11] Patrick Gardiner, *The Nature of Historical Explanation*, Oxford University Press, London, 1952, p. x.
[12] *Ibid.*, pp. x–xi.
[13] *Ibid.*, p. ix.
[14] Maurice Mandelbaum, *op. cit.*, p. 319.
[15] M. R. Cohen, *The Meaning of Human History*, The Open Court Publishing Co., La Salle, Illinois, 1947, p. 9.

details have been omitted," and avoid the epistemological attack on metaphysical schemes.[16]

Many alternatives have emerged in our generation. Cohen finds history "tragic": there is so much irrationality which man fails to overcome. Reinhold Niebuhr's alternative is to make God's perfect justice and love the standard for mankind. Human history by this criterion is "sinful." The task of such men as Cohen and Niebuhr is said to be to show what attitude men ought to adopt toward the events of the past or of their own time, or toward the possibilities of the future.[17] Section VII, Moral Philosophies of History, will show further alternative answers to moral questions about the historical process.

IV. Fallacies of Historical Belief

It may seem ungracious to working historians when a philosopher sets forth the errors he discovers in some historical reasoning. A more serious objection is that philosophers who consider argument primarily as proceeding from premise to conclusions have imposed criteria of deductive reasoning upon reasoning that moves from particular fact to particular proposition. If historical narrative were empirical in this sense, surely there is no argument at all, hence no formal error in reasoning. But a working historian, and one of very high standing at the present time, has produced a book on the fallacies of historical belief. No historian could object if philosophers pay Herbert Butterfield's The Whig Interpretation of History the compliment of considering it a valuable contribution to philosophy of history. Its value lies in establishing a good case for considering historical discourse as more than a string of episodes.

Begging the Question. The idea of progress has dominated much writing of modern European and American history. Progress is taken to refer to achievements such as universal education, parliamentary government, the factory economy, which England and America now enjoy. The movements that account for these achievements are claimed by some to be the Protestant Reformation and the revolutionary movements called collectively "Whig." One American counterpart of this argument is to ascribe progress to religious and political "liberals."

Butterfield's criticism is shocking to many readers, particularly those who consider these claims to be conclusively established by the facts. He

[16] Michael Oakeshott, *op. cit.,* p. 155. Oakeshott comments that "the result may possibly be philosophy," in contrast to a metaphysical survey of universal history, such as Hegel's, which he regards as a kind of history no philosopher should attempt to write.

[17] Maurice Mandelbaum, *op. cit.,* p. 320.

does not argue primarily that these statements are false, but that they should be regarded as conclusions of arguments. If they are conclusions, then we may ask whether the evidence adduced to support them is adequate. How does the historian select from the past? Consider the vast range of particular facts of European history of the past four centuries. Butterfield says that the more macroscopic our point of view, the more narration is guided by some preconceived framework. The "facts" used are the facts selected because they fit into the framework.

We might object that if this is the case, it demonstrates mere bias. Some historians have decided, writes Butterfield, "to praise revolutions provided they have been successful" and to "produce a story which is the ratification and the glorification of the present."[18] But the mere expression of likes and dislikes is not necessarily fallacious reasoning. No fallacy is committed if a historian writes that he dislikes Catholics and Tories; indeed, like the rest of us, he brightens his discourses by taking sides in past and present controversies. What, then, is fallacious in some historical writing?

The sin in historical composition is the organization of the story in such a way that bias cannot be recognized, and the reader is locked along with the writer in what is really a treacherous argument in a circle. It is to abstract events from their context and set them up in implied comparison with the present day, and then to pretend that by this 'the facts' are being allowed to 'speak for themselves'.[19]

Most historians would grant that this procedure is fallacious, and not merely circular reasoning, but vicious. But this fallacy might be discoverable only in general history, such as students study in textbooks. Would it be pertinent to the research done by a specialist on some narrow area, such as Connecticut in the 1640's? Butterfield's argument is that such a small unit of study is taken to fit into some larger preconceived framework of the whole.

To sum up the arguments thus far, we may say that historical reasoning is inferential. Inference proceeds from premises to conclusion. But if the conclusion is asserted in the premises, the fallacy is our old logical trap called begging the question or *petitio principii*. Much history-writing, according to The Whig Interpretation of History, is the production of a "gigantic optical illusion."

When we read history books we are often led to believe that we receive

[18] Herbert Butterfield, *The Whig Interpretation of History*, George Bell and Sons, Ltd., London, 1951, p. v.

[19] *Ibid.*, p. 105.

infallible certainties about the course and direction of events. But in reality the arguments are not even "inferences made from the past but . . . inferences made from peculiar series of abstractions from the past— abstractions which by the very principle of their origin beg the very questions that the historian is pretending to answer."[20]

In fact, the question the historian poses at the beginning of his inquiry may be misleading and yet go uncriticized. For example, Butterfield discovers that many of his fellow historians set out to answer, "To whom do we owe our religious liberty?" His point is that this question is on a logical level with "When did you stop beating your wife?" As the proper questions prior to this last one are "Do you have a wife?" and "Did you ever beat her?" so the proper prior questions in historical inquiry are "Have we religious liberty?" and "How did religious liberty arise?"[21]

To summarize in a way useful for an inquiry into the logic of historical reasoning, the fallacy of hypostatization will be added to the fallacy of begging the question; then examples of casual fallacies and fallacies of evaluational argument will be supplied. This fourfold division is not made by Professor Butterfield, but it does seem faithful to his major emphases, and all of his examples fit into this classification.

Hypostatization. Fallacies of hypostatization occur when we talk about concepts as though they were things, or about ideas and words as though one could find objects in the world to which these ideas or words refer. The author of The Whig Interpretation assumes that liberty, capitalism, and Protestantism are ideas, not independent agents. This is a metaphysical assumption and debatable. But few would assert that liberty or capitalism or Protestantism are real agents in the sense that Martin Luther, for example, was.

Hence when we meet such expressions as Butterfield adduces, we may suspect a fallacy.

"Capitalism is the social counterpart of Calvinist Theology."[22] " 'But for Luther' this liberty would never have come down to us as it did come. . . ."[23] Neither capitalism nor Calvinism is a "Thing, a fixed and definite object. . . ." Our first example does not explicitly make the claim that they are; yet when a historian goes on to assert that "the changes of the 16th century can be accounted for . . . by the nature and essence of Protestantism," he is using an abstraction as though it were causally efficacious. Butterfield does not deny that a metaphysician might discover

[20] *Ibid.*, pp. 29–30.
[21] *Ibid.*, p. 43.
[22] *Ibid.*, p. 51.
[23] *Ibid.*, p. 43.

how an essence produces changes, but no historian who claims to argue from historical facts is entitled to this assumption.

There may be an essence of Protestantism . . . that lies at the root of the matter, but there is no essence of the history of the Reformation, no formula that can take the place of the whole story. . . . [Why? Because historical knowledge is incapable of finding] the essence apart from the accidents.[24]

Men have a tendency to personify such ideas as liberty, or to treat them as "self-standing agencies in history." Whatever liberty is, it is not the sort of thing that can be passed on from hand to hand. Yet these examples of historical discourse make this idea appear as "a fixed and definite object."

These fallacies of hypostatization may seem rather innocuous, but the analyses we have suggested are not yet complete. For any given fallacious argument is rarely guilty of only one type of error. Hypostatization is generally coupled with some form of causal fallacy. Hence we continue to examine the same cases.

Causal Fallacies. There is another fallacious aspect of the historical statement "But for Luther this liberty would never have come down to us as it did come." This is an instance of making one among innumerable conditions a single sufficient cause. To

. . . disentangle from the present one fact or feature that is required to be traced back into history, the historian is faced with more unravelling than a mind can do . . . the network of interaction [is] so intricate, that it is impossible to point to any one thing in the sixteenth century as the cause of any one thing in the twentieth. It is as much as the historian can do to trace with some probability the sequence of events from one generation to another. . . . Any action which any man has ever taken is part of that whole set of circumstances which at a given moment conditions the whole mass of things that are to happen next. . . . We do not know where Luther would have been if his movement had not chimed with the ambitions of princes. We do not know what would have happened to the princes if Luther had not come to their aid.[25]

Butterfield discovers in such an argument other fallacious aspects.

In reality we can no more work out what religious liberty owes to Luther than we can calculate what proportion of the price of a man's suit in 1930 ought to be divided between the inventor of the spinning-jenny, the inventor of the steam-engine, and the firm which actually wove the cloth. . . .[26]

[And again] It is meaningless to trace liberty along a line which goes back to

[24] *Ibid.*, pp. 68–69.
[25] *Ibid.*, pp. 19–20.
[26] *Ibid.*, p. 44.

Luther merely because Luther at one time and in a world of different connotations put forward some principles of freedom, from which as a matter of fact he shrank when he saw some of the consequences that we see in them.[27]

There is another fallacious aspect of the argument "The changes of the 16th century can be accounted for . . . by the nature and essence of Protestantism." The causal fallacy here is making a logical relation, such as what a belief implies, seem like a dynamical relation, such as what a person holding a belief does. Unfortunately either may be called a "consequence." Butterfield puts it this way: historical mediation or transition is "much less like the procedure of a logical argument and perhaps much more like the method by which a man can be imagined to work his way out of a 'complex'."[28] He sees in historical argument a tendency to ignore the concrete events. "Principles [are] caught amongst chance and accident. . . ."[29] The fallacy is then produced by an attempt to make a story into a deductive system.[30]

A purely causal fallacy, in contradistinction to the two mixed examples of fallacies of both cause and hypostatization, is: A "line . . . leads through Martin Luther and a long succession of Whigs to modern liberty." The metaphorical line is only a device of serial organization. Yet it is taken to be a series of causes and effects. If the analyses quoted above are correct, namely, that no historian can disentangle a single line of causes and effects linking events over four centuries, then it follows that the historian who claims to prove such a chain is committing a fallacy. Butterfield has a psychological explanation of how a historian comes to deceive himself. When a historian "is not careful he begins to forget that this line is merely a mental trick of his; he comes to imagine that it represents something like a line of causation."[31]

The cumulative effect of these fallacious ways of thinking and arguing can be seen in this final example: "Without Martin Luther there would have been no Louis XIV." This argument does depend on hypostatization because Protestantism is taken to be a "Thing," or a "fixed and definite object that came into existence in 1517." Then its nature and essence are made to explain the sixteenth century, and indeed the whole modern period, and this is taken to be characterized essentially as "the rise of the secular state." Then in this fallacious chain, Protestantism is identified with Martin Luther, and Louis XIV with the modern secular state. Hence

[27] *Ibid.*, pp. 44–45.
[28] *Ibid.*, p. 46.
[29] *Ibid.*, p. 66.
[30] *Ibid.*, p. 76.
[31] *Ibid.*, p. 12.

Martin Luther is one great origin, referred to as "a watershed of history." The great optical illusion is to

. . . seize upon it as a source, a cause, an origin, even of movements that were taking place concurrently . . . as though Protestantism itself had no antecedents, as though it were a fallacy to go behind the great watershed, as though indeed it would blunt the edge of our story to admit the workings of a process instead of assuming the interposition of some direct agency.[32]

Fallacies of Evaluational Arguments. Our analysis of fallacies of historical argument began with the fallacy of begging the question and proceeded through hypostatization to various fallacies of a causal nature. To recapitulate Butterfield's argument, reflect on the initial misleading question: "To whom do we owe our religious liberty?" The assumptions are that by describing events factually we can reach conclusions about the individuals and movements that are to be praised, and the individuals and movements that are to be blamed. Several prior questions are involved. First, can the historian claim on the basis of facts alone to deduce moral consequences of praise or blame? Second, can the historian find the same praiseworthy and blameworthy sides in the struggles of past men that he finds among his own contemporaries? Third, can the historian legitimately employ his own moral standards to judge which struggles of a past age were trivial and which were important? Fourth, can the historian validly indicate in the light of subsequent events which institutions of the past were good or bad? Butterfield answers all these questions negatively.

It is only fair to add that he is far from denying that the historian ought to take his moral responsibilities seriously. Those who care to examine this line of his argument should read Christianity and History. Use is made of this book in the last section of this chapter. The point is very simple: Unless one admits explicitly some moral premise in an argument, no moral conclusion can follow validly. The following fallacies are examples in historical discourse of what was called by G. E. Moore, also of Cambridge University, "the naturalistic fallacy." Rather than dealing only with the predicate "good," Butterfield considers the moral tone of such predicates as "reactionary," "irreproachable," "Protestant," "Catholic," "great powers," etc. That these *appear* to be simply factual and non-moral encourages fallacious use of them in some moral sense.

A historian may say of a character in his narrative that "though a reactionary," he "was irreproachable in his private life." The fallacy is, in

[32] *Ibid.*, pp. 51–52.

part, that this occurs in narrative context as if it were just another factual statement. But the invalidity of the argument rests on a level deeper than discourse. The "original unconscious fallacy" is to organize the story on the assumption that men are "good and evil, progressive and reactionary, black and white." Then we claim that the story written on these moral lines is the evidence that proves that the enemies of progress are defeated by the friends of progress. The origin of this muddle is the assumption that it is factually true that the "present" world of the historian is the best. Hence the past, surveyed from the historian's present height, is less than best, and indeed the rising ground that leads up to the present. This

. . . interpretation of history . . . studies the past with reference to the present. . . . Through this system of immediate reference to the present-day, historical personages can easily and irresistibly be classed into the men who furthered progress and the men who tried to hinder it; so that a handy rule of thumb exists by which the historian can select and reject, and can make his points of emphasis. . . .[33]

[Thus] The total result of this method is to impose a certain form upon the whole historical story, and to produce a scheme of general history which is bound to converge beautifully upon the present—all demonstrating throughout the ages the workings of an obvious principle of progress, of which the Protestants and whigs have been the perennial allies while the Catholics and tories have perpetually formed obstruction.[34]

The value of this analysis is that it bears not only on the reasoning used to construct historical beliefs, but also upon one of the major modern metaphysical types of belief about history. The general point is that we should beware of sets of values or systems of evaluational norms masquerading as empirical truths. This is most pertinent also to moral philosophies of history.

The other examples can be given briefly. That they are fallacious can be seen also from the context of what the historian is able to construct from the facts. It seems simply factual to write "Protestant fought Catholic in the 16th century." Is this not as true a generalization as we can make? What fallacy could be involved? When the context describes Luther as "the founder of religious liberty" and sanctifies him as "the apostle of religious liberty," we are led to read back into the parties of four centuries ago "our own feelings concerning liberty." Hence "we draw out of history the very things we go to look for."[35] Telling a story of the break-up of the medieval world in this way implies that Catholics were fighting for the

[33] *Ibid.*, p. 11.
[34] *Ibid.*, p. 12.
[35] *Ibid.*, p. 27.

past, hence against progress. This reading of our feelings back into the past is called *anachronism*, or making others seem to feel as we do—"The historian's 'pathetic fallacy'."[36]

That the net logical result of begging the question in this way is ignorance of the past can be seen in the next example.

Historians who tell the story of great figures of the fourth century after Christ may slip in a sentence: "Arius and Athanasius . . . quarrel about a diphthong."[37] This seems to be a simple factual statement about the words "homoousios" and "homoiousios." Not so, argues Butterfield. For the historian, who is in a position to find out what mattered to men of fifteen centuries ago, tells us rather that he considers their quarrel merely verbal and hence trivial. He has failed to help us understand "that that diphthong was bound to be the most urgent matter in the universe to those people."[38] And more grave than cheating us by masking the historian's evaluation in pseudo-empirical language, is the question whether it is within the historian's competence to pass judgment on a theological issue. If the relation between God and Christ is not a factual issue, history books should not contain judgments upon it.[39]

It might seem factual to write that "the Inquisition was in some way responsible for reducing Spain from the ranks of the great powers." But this statement may contain in context no amplification that the same institution once gave Spain "prestige and power."[40] More seriously, if the historian thinks he has proved the Inquisition "was fatal to happiness," he begs the question as to what is "the good life." Has the historian access to the premise that to be a subject of a great power is the ultimate moral criterion? Is it not an error to expect historical facts to give us such "judgments of value"?[41]

These are only a few of the many logical pitfalls historians encounter. We must learn to read history as critically as we should write it. This involves not merely questioning the facts, but also the organization and interpretation of the facts.

V. *Problems of Historical Knowledge*

What shall I believe about past human events? This question was first asked explicitly by Herodotus, and we too are often confronted by con-

[36] *Ibid.*, pp. 30, 36.
[37] *Ibid.*, p. 17.
[38] *Ibid.*
[39] *Ibid.*, p. 73.
[40] *Ibid.*, p. 74.
[41] *Ibid.*, p. 105.

flicting stories about past events. Consider his case, and the decision he made. The Persians believed that Io, daughter of a Greek king, was kidnapped. The Phoenicians believed that Io fell in love with a ship's captain and ran away with him. Herodotus found it impossible to assert consistently both that the girl was willing and unwilling. If it is logically impossible to be both, then if one statement is true the other is false. But this historian chose to believe nothing about Io. He reasons that he cannot infer the existence of Io from legends about her. We would add that if Io never existed, then there are no positive facts to be known, hence no predicative propositions capable of being true or false. If a poet or novelist allows his fancy to produce tales about Io, we can never say he errs or judges incorrectly. By contrast, Herodotus begins his history with a person whose existence he claims to know, Croesus, King of Lydia.[42]

If the epistemology of Herodotus is correct, we should distinguish historical statements from legend and myth on the grounds that history tells of persons who actually existed and what they actually did. The implicit test of truth would then be direct confrontation with Croesus and observation that he behaves as a King of Lydia. But if this is a necessary basis for belief in his existence, then only those contemporaries, who came into close spatial proximity to him, have adequate grounds for believing that he existed. Shall we believe that Herodotus, who was born two or three generations after the reign of Croesus, can mediate between the real concrete King and us? If we have no direct confrontation with this entity called "Croesus King of Lydia," we must admit that our knowledge rests upon the hypothesis that Herodotus made a correct inference from evidence that survived, or that he trusted witnesses whose testimony was based upon accurate memory judgments.

There seem to be several worthwhile lines of epistemological inquiry to establish the possibility of historical knowledge.

The first way is to examine the methods employed by the historian in getting his facts and constructing his story. The claims made by Thucydides, the successor of Herodotus, will be examined.

The second way is to ask whether a historian can know past events directly. To exemplify this line of investigation, the realistic versus the idealistic alternatives will be suggested.

The third way is to examine the language of historical discourse. Here there are two alternative methods advanced by philosophers in the twen-

---

[42] *History of the East and West*, Book I, quoted by A. Toynbee, *Greek Historical Thought*, New American Library, Inc., New York, 1952, pp. 29–31.

tieth century, one defending the language of working historians, the other recommending to them a language that claims to make history a science.

These three ways help us to focus upon the judgment of historians, the object of historical knowledge, and the language of historical discourse. The first and third ways seem to avoid explicit metaphysical commitment, but the second way inevitably raises questions about what there is to know, and some of the different views will be discussed. Also at stake are the contrasted criteria of truth that accompany idealism and realism. The issues that motivate inquiry are: First, can one know the existence of persons, events, or situations that have perished? Second, can one know facts of past persons, events, or situations directly? Third, if one grounds beliefs in past events only on faith in some witness or on inference from present traces of the past, should one ever claim certainty for the inferences?

Historical Method. Let us consider the first question. "Thucydides of Athens has written the history of the war between the Peloponnesians and the Athenians." These are the opening words of his work. His second sentence assures us that the basis of his belief is observation of the events that took place as he wrote, that is, there is a minimal trust in memory. "He began to write as soon as the war broke out. . . ."

Why should we believe what Thucydides says? His claims for himself should be read in his own language, particularly when he says that before the war began he had predicted that the preparations by Athens and Sparta would produce "the greatest upheaval ever experienced by Hellas." The History of the Peloponnesian War, then, in part confirms the author's hypothesis. He proves that his fellow Athenians, who had predicted a short war with victory for Athens, failed to understand the course of events they initiated. But why should we accept this interpretation? It is based, Thucydides insists, upon as unbiased a report of men's thoughts, words, and deeds as is possible.

The rules Thucydides followed seem to be these: First, get as much as possible firsthand. Second, if you summarize a speech, state the general sense without distortion from the original context. Third, if you condense the facts, preserve a maximum of detail. Fourth, if you depend on other witnesses, take the version that is given by the man with the most accurate memory and the least confusion between his desires or wishes and the events themselves. Whether Thucydides succeeded will ever be debated by professional historians. "I have tried," he assures us, "to produce a permanent contribution to knowledge. . . ."[43]

[43] *Ibid.*, p. 41.

Historical statements generated by the method of Thucydides are largely particular propositions. The subject matter of these propositions is individual men or groups of men, and a certain thought, word, or deed is predicated of them. The sentences we read are "Nicias, throughout his speech, had estimated the requirements of the campaign at a high figure." "It was midsummer when the expedition to Sicily set sail." These statements of fact have existential import. That is, if they are true, the ground of their truth is the concrete happening of unique events. The sentences are not universal and are not hypothetical. Statements of a higher order of generality, such as "all Athenians make speeches," or "if any Athenians sail, they do so in midsummer," are rare. Hence, if Thucydides gives us a fair sample of historical beliefs and historical discourse, we may say that history stands in great contrast to mathematics. We may say epistemologically that the truth of historical claims could not be deducible from definitions and axioms.

But are historical statements true because they copy or correspond to events? Here we encounter difficulty, for Thucydides explains certain overt actions by making them effects of covert causes. At least, it seems difficult to observe a man's mind or his feelings or his thoughts. The Athenians set sail in 100 warships. Why? Because they were moved by "passion" and believed that such a number could not be defeated. They did not restrain their acts, even though Nicias had warned them of the consequences. "The Athenians, however, were not cured of their eagerness for the expedition by the burdensomeness of the armaments entailed, but felt the impulse more strongly than ever, and the result of Nicias' speech was the exact opposite of his intention."[44]

Although it was said that most historical beliefs are particular propositions with a singular object describing a concrete event happening at some given time and at some given place, there is in Thucydides' account one great exception. Perhaps in every history there is one implicit principle or law. This is made explicit in the History of the Peloponnesian War: Wars, such as this one, "are destined approximately to repeat themselves in all human probability."

The question is, do the details of Thucydides' account give us knowledge of more than one Greek war in the fifth century B.C.? By knowing this one sequence, do we know something about all human behavior? That is, do we have a law, which says that although two political powers are of approximately equal strength, men flushed with confidence are inclined to ignore the sober advice that neither side can win easily? If this law is

[44] *Ibid.*, p. 100.

true, we might have the explanation of why great imperial political orders go down to defeat. It has seemed appropriate to apply this law to Napoleon and Hitler. But if it is a law, does it apply to every instance? If history could give us knowledge with predictive power, this might be invaluable in guiding the affairs of men. We should then have a general ground for historical inference, and a hypothesis subject to verification.

Even if the rules Thucydides adopted are in general those that historians have continued to trust in generating "objective" accounts of events, they do not say what it is that historians know. Thucydides claims to know both events in the spatio-temporal world and ideas in the minds of men. Realists stress the former, and idealists the latter. The following paragraphs will examine a proponent of each type of epistemology. One applies the correspondence theory of truth, the other the coherence theory of truth.

Realism vs. Idealism. Now what about question two, that is, whether knowledge of the past can be direct? The common point shared by realists and idealists in epistemology is the assumption that something must be known directly. If there is no direct knowledge, historians can have no warrant for their claims to know the historical past. But what is this direct knowledge? R. G. Collingwood will represent the idealistic view that we now know minds and thoughts of the past. M. R. Cohen will represent the realistic view that we now know past events and the connections between them that have continued into the present. For the idealist, knowledge is identity of the historian's thought with, say, in F. H. Bradley's famous example, the thought of Julius Caesar.[45] For the realist, knowledge is the conformity of the structure of the historian's propositions to the structure of the events themselves.[46]

That some form of idealism is the epistemology and metaphysics required for a sound conception of historical knowledge is the main thesis of Collingwood's The Idea of History. His argument involves the most complete available survey of the whole course of epistemological dialectic as it bears on our knowledge of the past. Unless the philosopher is an idealist, he either ignores history or relegates it to an insignificant place compared with the eminence of the natural sciences. Collingwood was himself a historian and tended to make historical knowledge the supreme type; even the natural sciences, which change through time, he regarded as aspects of history. What there is to know ultimately are minds. And all

[45] F. H. Bradley, "What Is the Real Julius Caesar?" *Essays on Truth and Reality,* The Clarendon Press, Oxford, 1914, pp. 409–427.
[46] Maurice Mandelbaum, *op. cit.,* especially pp. 184–186.

there is to know of a past human agent is his thought. "Of everything other than thought, there can be no history."[47]

Collingwood's case will be presented by quotations that picture the historian working as a detective from clues, thereby reconstructing the past sequences of events by re-enacting the acts of others, affirming and justifying the claim that he takes up into his own thought the very act of a past person.

When a man thinks historically, he has before him certain documents or relics of the past. His business is to discover what the past was which has left these relics behind it. For example, the relics are certain written words; and in that case he has to discover what the person who wrote those words meant by them. . . . Suppose, he is reading the Theodosian Code, and has before him a certain edict of an emperor. Merely reading the words and being able to translate them does not amount to knowing their historical significance. In order to do that he must envisage the situation with which the emperor was trying to deal, and he must envisage it as that emperor envisaged it: Then he must see for himself, just as if the emperor's situation were his own, how such a situation might be dealt with; he must see the possible alternatives, and the reasons for choosing one rather than the other.[48]

Collingwood has laid down what is required of the historian. The satisfaction of the requirement is what the historian does. ". . . He is re-enacting in his own mind the experience of the emperor; and only in so far as he does this has he any historical knowledge. . . ."[49] Although the circumstances of the twentieth century differ from those of the fifth century, something in the acts of Theodosius and our historian is identical. But can the historian claim more than to have tried by sympathetic imagination to enter into the situation? Can he claim to do more than to have inferred the existence of a mind with impulses expressed in the words we now read? Collingwood must answer this difficulty to sustain the idealistic analysis.

To think at all about that past activity of thought, I must revive it in my own mind, for the act of thinking can be studied only as an act. But what is so revived is not a mere echo of the old activity, another of the same kind; it is that same activity taken up again and reenacted. . . .[50]

How can one justify these claims? The word "thought" may mean an argument from premises to conclusion as well as the experience of think-

---

[47] R. G. Collingwood, *The Idea of History*, The Clarendon Press, Oxford, 1946, p. 304; the historical achievement of this philosopher is *The Archaeology of Roman Britain*.

[48] *Ibid.*, pp. 282–283.

[49] *Ibid.*, p. 283.

[50] *Ibid.*, p. 293.

ing. The former is often distinguished from the latter as the logical over against the psychological. It is the use of the former that justifies our claim to understand some past event. Collingwood uses as an example what goes on in studying Plato's Theaetetus.

> In its immediacy, as an actual experience of his own, Plato's argument must undoubtedly have grown up out of a discussion of some sort, though I do not know what it was, and been closely connected with such a discussion. Yet if I not only read his argument but understand it, follow it in my own mind by re-arguing it with and for myself, the process of argument which I go through is not a process resembling Plato's, it actually is Plato's, so far as I understand him rightly. The argument simply as itself, starting from these premises and leading through this process to this conclusion; the argument as it can be developed either in Plato's mind or mine or anyone else's, is what I call the thought in its mediation.[51]

In going from the first to the last quotation, we pass from what almost no one doubts to what almost no one can affirm. It is left to the good critical sense of the reader to examine the steps of argument; it is suggested that the uses of the key term "identity" should be examined carefully.

The only account of knowledge that can do justice to historical knowledge is, according to Morris R. Cohen, realism. What is essential to knowledge is reference to something other than knowing, called "events." From this first point of realism, Cohen's argument will be developed by quotations from The Meaning of Human History. The threads of the argument, comparable to Collingwood's alternatives, are: First, historical propositions are true or false; second, therefore the historian refers to something that is or is not the case; third, if we affirm or deny any connection between events, the truth of the proposition depends on whether these connections can be objectively discovered in the events.

> The word "past" does point to or indicate something about which true or false propositions can be asserted. It must therefore have some sort of being or be a phase of true existence. This, of course, does not mean that the snow of last year is now on the ground or that the man who died long ago is still living. That, indeed, would be to make false assertions in denying that certain events did occur, to wit, the melting of the snow or the death of that man in the past.[52]

In spite of the fact that events have happened, the world is such that no event is ever done with.

> The past literally continues into the present. Past conditions, such as old ideas and habits, buildings, fields, and laws, continue to operate. Inertia is the first

[51] *Ibid.*, p. 301.
[52] M. R. Cohen, *The Meaning of Human History*, The Open Court Publishing Co., La Salle, Illinois, 1947, p. 6.

law of history, as it is of physics. Every event is an integral part of a larger segment of history, and the task of tracing causal connections is the task of discovering those elements that persist through, and despite, the arbitrary cuts by which we mark off the event we are at the moment seeking to explain.[53]

It then follows that the sort of event called "the American Revolution" is present in our twentieth-century world as its past, and that we cannot know the present America without discovering causal connections by which America came to be. The war of independence is "a series of causal connections between the affair at Lexington and Concord, the Declaration of Independence, and the surrender of Cornwallis. And no doubt the connections are there, and perfectly objective."[54]

We might doubt whether the connections are "there" to be known directly. Indeed the idealists affirm that only thoughts can survive. Our realist is eager to show us by what criteria we test whether we are or are not referring to events. If we grasp the relevance of one event to another, then from knowledge of one we know another. But this knowledge can be had only when the conditions are both necessary and sufficient for the occurrence of some event.[55] Since "accidents," or the meeting of "two relatively independent streams of causality," would render historical knowledge impossible, Cohen postulates or assumes that all human events follow "determinate patterns."[56] Now if this is the case, our knowledge of the present would give us knowledge of future as well as of past events. Since we cannot, for example, return to the American Revolution and predict the Civil War, the best we can now do is to try to predict our own future. This Cohen attempted in the summer of 1939. He knew "a war would break out sooner or later, and, in the summer of 1939, there was much evidence to support the expectation that its outbreak would come very soon. But there was also evidence on the other side and even a day before its outbreak there seemed nothing inevitable about it."[57]

Some might be tempted to assert that the course of history is not determined. But that would imply, for Cohen, that history is not knowable. Hence, to defend the truth and falsity of historical beliefs, he admits that our knowledge is not yet sufficiently objective "to tell what a given individual or a nation will do in a specific situation."[58]

Again, in realism as in idealism, we pass in steps from what almost no

[53] *Ibid.*, p. 107.
[54] *Ibid.*, pp. 107–108.
[55] *Ibid.*, pp. 110, 124.
[56] *Ibid.*, p. 123.
[57] *Ibid.*, p. 110.
[58] *Ibid.*, p. 123.

one doubts to what almost no one can affirm. Again the argument is left to be assessed by the reader. It is suggested that the various claims that events, past, present, and future, are "there" to be known deserve critical attention.

Historical Language. Let us now look to the third question. Philosophers who have grown sceptical of the possibility of talking about what there is may shift the focus of philosophical inquiry from minds or events to the language men use. This has happened in the mid-twentieth century, and in the following paragraphs are discussed linguistic epistemologies of history.

It should have become evident that answering questions about metaphysical assumptions is very troublesome. It may be that the metaphysical assumptions of both realism and idealism are unnecessary, and indeed hampering to our understanding of historical knowledge. Why should we suppose that the task of the historian is to get the very event itself or to get the very mind behind the event? Why must the historian satisfy the demand of realism that a belief should correspond to a past event? Or why satisfy the demand of idealism that the thought of the historian should be identical with the thought of some past mind? It may well be that these dogmatic and a priori requirements imply that historical knowledge is impossible. Many practicing historians are in theory uncertain that any historical belief is more than an opinion, conditioned by the circumstances under which the historian works, and not ever true or false as such.[59] However paradoxical it sounds, it may be that metaphysical scepticism could rescue us from epistemological scepticism. Before we determine to reformulate realism or idealism we should consider abandoning them altogether. Thereby we can discover whether we need to assume minds and events apart from their being talked about in either the ordinary language of historians, or some language formulated in terms shared with the natural and the social sciences.

Linguistic epistemologies of history have been referred to because there is a sharp difference in method which is one of the great philosophic issues of our age. The first type of linguistic analysis considers the language actually in use to be normative. In epistemology of history, this line is ably taken by Patrick Gardiner in The Nature of Historical Explanation,[60] which is a good source in which to examine the much-debated Oxford method of analysis. It fits well into the development given here, since on at least four distinct points he denies realistic assumptions, such as those

[59] Maurice Mandelbaum, *op. cit.*, Part 1.
[60] Patrick Gardiner, *op. cit.*

presented from Morris Cohen. The second type of linguistic analysis is that of logical positivism. This position holds that all meaningful propositions are subject to empirical verification. These propositions must be formulated in a language shared by all theoretical sciences. Although both schools are extremely hostile to metaphysical philosophies, and would purge language of all "meaningless" sentences, there are several differences. On the one hand, Oxford analysis, at least in Gardiner's version, does not seek certain knowledge. Historical knowledge is not either true or false. But logical positivism, represented by Ernest Nagel, Carl G. Hempel, and Morton White, does seek for history the kind of certainty achieved in physics. Gardiner is as hostile to any program that would attempt to formulate laws applicable to the course of human events as he is to speculative schemes; indeed the positivists' unity of science program is another illusory effort to know what cannot be known.[61] And the positivists are as convinced that the ordinary language of historians should be overhauled as Gardiner is convinced that it is as satisfactory for its purposes as the language of physics is for its purposes. These statements may at this stage seem obscure, but the exposition will make the positions clear.

Since these two versions of linguistic epistemology of history are in rather early stages of development, the literature is filled with polemic against realism and idealism. A sketch of what Gardiner denies in realism, and a sketch of what the three logical positivists deny in idealism will therefore be presented here.

The ordinary language epistemology of history denies that when we claim to "know" a historical event that "know" is a verb taking a direct object.[62] This was a point shared by idealism, and it leads to an attempt to get at some event or mind "behind" the acts of people. Second, Gardiner denies that historical propositions are either true or false.[63] This, as we saw, was the premise from which Cohen argued to the existence of past events in present reality. Third, ordinary language epistemology gives up the hope of getting at connections in the facts to which connections in our language correspond or fail to correspond. What are causal connections apart from our talk about them? Cohen's necessary connections of "deterministic patterns," are, for all Gardiner knows, only made by language. Fourth, these three errors of realism add up to what Gardiner regards as a muddle. In his own language:

[61] *Ibid.*, p. 96.
[62] *Ibid.*, p. 109.
[63] *Ibid.*, p. 96.

A postulated historical explanation is not, as a rule, justified (or challenged) by demonstrating that a given law implied by it does (or does not) hold; far less by showing such a law to follow (or not to follow) from an accepted theory or hypothesis, or to be confirmed (or falsified) by experiment; nor, again, by pointing out that the case under consideration does (or does not) satisfy in the required respects the conditions exactly specified in the formulation of the law.[64]

The grounds for Gardiner's strong denials and affirmations are based on a knowledge of how historians actually do explain human behavior. If one examines the language of Thucydides, as has been done, it is apparent that the historian explains, as all of us do, in common language. Gardiner affirms that we all know what we mean when we say we *"know* what someone else is thinking. . . ."[65] So Thucydides knew what Nicias thought when he heard him estimate that the cost of the Athenian expedition would be high. There is no metaphysical mystery here that calls for either realism or idealism. "The patterns are familiar to us both from experience of our own behavior and from experience of the ways other people behave; and it is in virtue of this that we are able to make the inferences and provide the explanations in question."[66]

The language of historians helps us to "see" a situation, and the effort is successful when the connections in language are made correctly or according to usage.[67] To make this clear, Gardiner shows what he means by describing what a historical explanation of a situation is like. It is analogous to

. . . judgments that are made in the face of situations demanding a practical decision. Generals before launching an offensive, statesmen before initiating a policy, are said to 'appreciate the situation' in which action is contemplated. A particular decision taken, or course of action embarked upon, is said in general to be justified if the agent is able to produce reasons describing factors in the situation confronting him which . . . strongly *suggest* or *support* the conclusion that the course of action he contemplates will be successful in achieving the end he desires.[68]

If this is the story of historical explanation, and all that need be said about it, then the epistemology of realism and the epistemology of logical positivism are quite unacceptable. First, realists maintain that knowing is a relation such that an object can be found somewhere in either present or past to which each word corresponds. "The root misconception is . . .

[64] *Ibid.,* p. 96.
[65] *Ibid.,* pp. 126–127.
[66] *Ibid.,* p. 125.
[67] *Ibid.,* p. 69.
[68] *Ibid.,* p. 94.

the theory of meaning which maintains that language mirrors, copies, or pictures reality."[69] Second, scientific realism and, as we shall shortly see, positivism, which propose a scientific language for historical knowledge, are equally in error. Situations, argues Gardiner, can be expressed only in vague terms and the rules used in judging are never precise. Further, he argues, if they were in precise terms, judged by exact rules, historical explanation would be less illuminating.

The ultimate philosophic conclusion is that by linguistic analysis we can know that metaphysical philosophies of history are based on mistakes. Those historians who write history from, for example, the Marxist perspective, import a doctrine of matter as the real cause of every event. Those historians who write history from an idealist perspective import a doctrine of mind as the real cause of every event. But it is a linguistic mistake to distinguish a human being into body and soul. That is, if we think of "body" and "soul" as more than words. Hence, it is worthless to wonder whether a man is one or the other, or whether history is explained by one sort of causes rather than another. "Human beings are not 'really matter' or 'really mind': they are human beings. Different ways of talking about them, dictated by different interests, have been hypostatized into different ingredients."[70]

If Gardiner's philosophy of history is complete and adequate, there would be absolutely no good reason for a section on the traditional philosophies that are metaphysical. Before making a decision, the student should examine these speculations to discover whether they are thoroughly mistaken. Gardiner cannot dissolve "different interests" into linguistic errors. But the positivists claim that their program would, if carried out, completely eliminate them from historical knowledge.

As a parallel to the discussion of ordinary language epistemology of history, steps of analysis from a series of interrelated papers by logical positivists are now presented. As Gardiner rejected realism as useless metaphysics, so Nagel, Hempel, and White reject idealism as dangerous metaphysics. Collingwood's position gives the kind of central target aimed at by the positivists' destructive criticism.

First, does the historian reconstruct the past sequence of events by re-enacting the thought of past minds? The assumption is that the knower and known must be of the same kind. This is an error and a dangerous one. According to Ernest Nagel's "The Logic of Historical Analysis," the blunder is as obvious as supposing that "only a fat cowherd can drive

[69] *Ibid.*, p. 55.
[70] *Ibid.*, p. 139.

fat kine."[71] That many, if not most, historians do in practice write history as though they were participants, is a worthless argument for Nagel. It might be a sound argument for Gardiner. But the result is a "crude error . . . that one cannot inquire into the conditions and consequences of values and evaluations without necessarily engaging in moral or aesthetic value judgment."[72] Why is this dangerous? Because value judgments are not empirically verifiable and hence not knowledge of any sort. Since there is no way to determine the truth or falsity of an interest, historians conclude that they may give free rein to their personal bias or social loyalties. If history is to be knowledge, no matter how the historian has become concerned with the facts, the facts must be stated as though no one were interested in them. (An attack on this position will be considered in Section VII, Moral Philosophies of History.)

Second, what does "cause" mean in historical explanation? Collingwood provided one meaning: that a man takes thought and does what he has intended. Gardiner left historians free to suggest this, provided they do not believe "minds" stand "behind" the events. But the positivists hold that men know empirically only that events of a certain kind accompany regularly events of another kind. This is called the constant-conjunction theory of causation. Causal connections are introduced by human language. Logically, we say that given certain initial conditions, we may deduce the effect as a conclusion. But obviously we can do this only when we have a law or universal hypothesis.

Have historians a body of formulated laws? The point of Carl G. Hempel's "The Function of General Laws in History" is that historians do not seem to explain events in this way.[73] This is only because historical research is scientifically primitive. Historians now produce what Hempel calls the "explanation sketch." Not all the conditions are stated, nor are all hypotheses formalized. "Such a sketch consists of a more or less vague indication of the laws and initial conditions considered as relevant, and it needs 'filling out' in order to turn into a full-fledged explanation."[74]

But the social sciences have made progress toward a more explicit and concrete explanation of human behavior.[75] And in becoming more scientific, a direction is pointed out for historians. Negatively, historians

[71] Herbert Feigl and May Brodbeck (eds.), *Readings in the Philosophy of Science,* Appleton-Century-Crofts, Inc., New York, 1953, p. 692.
[72] *Ibid.,* p. 692.
[73] Reprinted in Herbert Feigl and Wilfrid Sellars (eds.), *Readings in Philosophical Analysis,* Appleton-Century-Crofts, Inc., New York, 1949, pp. 459–471.
[74] *Ibid.,* p. 465.
[75] *Ibid.,* pp. 402–403.

should also eliminate all empirically meaningless terms. Those that are quite common now in historical explanation have reference to the historical destination of a certain race, or appeal to a principle of historical justice. Such terms make it impossible to "indicate the type of investigation that would have a bearing upon those formulations, and that might lead to evidence either confirming or infirming the suggested explanation."[76] Positively, when historians use only empirical terms, history may become a science.

But should history explain as does a science? Hempel answers affirmatively, because whenever historians do explain genuinely, by Hempel's criterion, they appeal to what he regards as scientific laws. This seems to be a circular argument, but its point is the common ground occupied by history and the sciences. Doubtless idealistic metaphysicians ignored the truth in this claim.

But it may be worth mentioning here that those universal hypotheses to which historians explicitly or tacitly refer in offering explanations, predictions, interpretations, judgments of relevance, etc., are taken from *various* fields of scientific research, in so far as they are not pre-scientific generalizations of everyday experiences. Many of the universal hypotheses underlying historical explanation, for instance, would commonly be classified as psychological, economical, sociological, and partly perhaps as historical laws; in addition, historical research has frequently to resort to general laws established in physics, chemistry, and biology. Thus, e.g., the explanation of the defeat of an army by reference to lack of food, adverse weather conditions, disease, and the like, is based on a—usually tacit—assumption of such laws. The use of tree rings in dating events in history rests on the application of certain biological regularities.[77]

Third, if a "history" is a linguistic entity, what sort of discourse is it? Morton White in "Analytic Philosophy of History" set out to answer this question. It is, he answers, a sequence of sentences, that is, "true declarative sentences," written down in connective order. Each statement sums up "all the things happening to y or characteristic of y at the time in question."[78]

We find two classes of terms. Some of these are very general, such as "history" itself, which ought to be defined, and such predicates as are defined for many other branches of science: law, explanation, true, cause. These are words of a higher type or higher generality, hence part of what White calls a "metalanguage of history," or for short, "metahistory."[79]

[76] *Ibid.*, p. 466.
[77] *Ibid.*, p. 470.
[78] Marvin Farber, *op. cit.*, pp. 705–726.
[79] *Ibid.*, p. 710.

Since these are also terms used in the natural and social sciences, to have a clear notion of how they are used in history is to unify history theoretically into the sciences. The second class is that of names for individual things. Historians talk about Julius Caesar, the Dark Ages, etc. These are "physical objects . . . things that exist and change in time."[80] Hence these terms constitute the "object language of history." The more general terms of the metalanguage are largely predicates.

If this is all that needs saying by philosophers, a startling consequence follows. Since the connections between events are logical inferences, and "a history contains true statements about the whole course of an object's existence," whether the time specification is past or future makes no theoretical difference. "True statements about the future of the object will be as much a part of its history as true statements about its remote past."[81] All knowledge is based on observation of the given object, and "inference from the present to the past that is no longer subject to direct observation or memory is in principle similar to the inference from the present to the future."[82]

It will become apparent in the succeeding sections that most conceptions of history rest upon assumptions radically different from those of logical positivism. History as knowledge is believed to be itself a historical object. Men are commonly held to be responsible for what they do because they know they produce effects by planning actions and carrying them out. Most conceptions of history assume the irreversibility of the temporal and historical sequence, which implies a basic difference between inference from past to present and from present to past. Further, if the past is the sum of events that were actual, and the future the sum of events that are now only possible, their modality (actuality-possibility) is different. These four anti-positivist positions are metaphysical.

VI. Metaphysical Philosophies of History

It has been mentioned a number of times that there are metaphysical types of philosophy of history. Now we should be ready to consider these, remembering that we may not look for finalities, but we may continue to seek for possibilities. Some of these possibilities historians and philosophers have defined and explored are: First, the *cyclical* view of the early Greeks; second, the *providential* view dominant in the Middle Ages; third, the *progress-evolutionary* position of the eighteenth and nineteenth centuries; and finally, the *pluralistic-scientific* interpretation of the twentieth

[80] *Ibid.*, p. 712.
[81] *Ibid.*, p. 718.
[82] *Ibid.*, pp. 719–720.

century. This particular classification has in its favor the fact that each was peculiarly characteristic of a certain age. These, of course, are not absolutely unmixed periods. We are speaking now of the dominant tendencies only.

The Cyclical Theory of History. This view of history is as old as ancient Greece, though it has also had more recent adherents. Simply stated, it is the belief that time moves in never-ending circles, that there are eternally repeatable rhythms and recurrences in events. Anaximander, one of the earliest Greek philosophers, thinks everything must return again and again to the original stuff from which it came and then again be reproduced. There are innumerable worlds succeeding one another in time, but each is a reduplication of the dying past. The Pythagoreans, too, hold this theory of cyclical recurrence, insisting that only a numerical distinctness separated the unending rebirth of universes. And the Stoics also think of the world as arising in time and then returning to an original fire whence it came, only to appear again as life and rationality, cycle after cycle, world without end. One of the classic statements of this position comes from the Meditations of Marcus Aurelius. Speaking of the rational soul, he says,

It traverses the whole universe, and the surrounding vacuum, and surveys its form, and it extends itself into the infinity of time, and embraces and comprehends the periodical renovation of all things, and it comprehends that those who come after us will see nothing new, nor have those before us seen anything more, but in a manner he who is forty years old, if he has any understanding at all, has seen by virtue of the uniformity that prevails all things which have been, all that will be.[83]

In the nineteenth century Nietzsche revived the cyclical theory and called it the doctrine of eternal recurrence. According to his view there is a limited amount of energy in the universe and an infinite time in which the energy works. Thus the number of states, changes, and combinations is limited.

Consequently the present process of evolution must be a repetition, as was also the one before it, as will also be the one which will follow. And so on forwards and backwards! Inasmuch as the entire state of all forces continually returns, everything has existed an infinite number of times.[84]

More recent writers, notably Spengler, interpret the events of history in large, rhythmic, cyclical movements with more or less definite stages to be

---

[83] Marcus Aurelius, *Meditation*, XI, 1. In: (Whitney J. Oates, ed.), *The Stoic and Epicurean Philosophers*, Random House, New York, 1940, p. 571.
[84] F. Nietzsche, *The Eternal Recurrence*, George Allen & Unwin, Ltd., London, n.d., Vol. XVI, p. 237.

passed before the cycle is complete. In Spengler these stages are called infancy, adolescence, maturity, and senescence. History, therefore, takes on the appearance of progress or decline, depending upon which stage is reached.

It cannot be denied that there are recurrences in our world. Birth and death with persistent cadence mark out the limits of experience; planets and seasons in precise measure give us the comforting assurance that things will be as they have been. But it must be seriously doubted that this is sufficient evidence to establish the theory of cyclical transformation in history. In the first place, it contravenes common sense. We have no consciousness of having existed in some earlier state, thus at least this present consciousness is novel. Moreover, if everything must recur, why should one accept any moral responsibility for one's actions? What has happened will happen and one is an impotent pawn behaving only according to the rules laid down by previous games.

There are other difficulties that make it impossible to adopt this view. Morris Cohen has put them clearly:

> In the first place, the notion of a governing life-cycle of civilizations assumes that external influences cannot change the course of a civilization. But even the path of a planet can be changed by external occurrences, and there is no reason to suppose that the paths of societies are more immutable. It is true that the order of the periods of human life span cannot be changed. But the analogy between the individual life cycle and the life cycle of civilization is very far-fetched. We know the factors that bring about the hardening of the arteries, decreasing oxygenation, etc. Do we know the factors that break up and change the character of a civilization? The whole idea of the life of a civilization is neither clear nor definite. The test whether a man is or is not still alive is definite enough, but when did Greek civilization fall?
>
> A second difficulty in the way of any cyclical conception of history lies in the fact that historically no two known civilizations have gone through the supposed cycle in the same way, for no two civilizations have started at the same point. Later civilizations have learned from the experience of others.[85]

The Providential View of History. The opening words of the Old Testament contain the central doctrine of the providential theory of history. "In the beginning God created the heaven and the earth." It is only necessary to add that His creation is according to plan and that His continued sway is manifest in all succeeding events which are fulfilling, and will eventually bring to completion the entire design. History is not the working out of man's purposes, except on a limited scale, but of God's. Man may be a

[85] M. R. Cohen, *The Meaning of Human History*, The Open Court Publishing Co., La Salle, Illinois, 1947, p. 263.

historical agent created by God, but his role is to function as a vehicle for accomplishing the purposes of the Deity. For the most part, one cannot say how any given event, war, pestilence, revolution, or discovery fits into the providential scheme. There is no preserving the sense of universal history except by faith. Generally those who accept this position are optimistic about the final end. Whatever intermediate turmoil and pain must be endured, God is in His heaven, and though all may not be right with the world now, He will see it through to its designed goal—presumably some kind of justice and felicity. Neither the final fulfillment nor the successive stages can be verified as the purposes of God. Thus history in this sense can never be a science, but may be a powerful check on immorality, for if God is at work in the world, to oppose Him is to become lost, but to think and act in concert and concord with Him is to be saved.

The classic statement of this view is to be found in the thought of St. Augustine expressed in his great work, The City of God. As history moves toward a definite purpose and goal, it cannot be merely a matter of cyclical transformation. There is a moral as well as a theological reason for the rejection of the argument for eternal recurrence:

> On the basis of an everlasting revolution of definite cycles, we could expect only a blind rotation of misery and happiness, that is, of deceitful bliss and real misery, but no eternal blessedness—only an endless repetition of the same but nothing new, redemptive, and final. The Christian faith truthfully promises salvation and everlasting blessedness to those who love God, while the godless doctrine of futile cycles paralyzes hope and love itself. If everything were to happen again and again at fixed intervals the Christian hope in a new life would be futile.[86]

The City of God in general works out the details of the cosmic drama of man's salvation and God's ultimate triumph. Two cities are in conflict, the City of God and the City of Man. These are not actually existing institutions as, for instance, the Church and State, but two mystical societies representing two different types of men. The City of Man is governed by expediency, pride, and ambition. It is mortal, that is, existing in a time which was created by God. It can be maintained only by natural generation. The City of God, on the other hand, is governed by self-sacrifice, obedience, and humility. It is eternal and immortal. Its citizens live by and for the love of God even to the extent of contempt for self. This city owes its being to supernatural regeneration.

Although no single event, except the uniqueness of Christ's birth, death, and resurrection, is taken as empirical proof or evidence for God's pres-

[86] Karl Löwith, op. cit., pp. 163–164.

ence in history, yet Augustine tries to show the periods or stages through which history moves towards the expected final triumph of His city over the city of sinful man.

It is clear that the providential view of history depends upon the truth of the proposition: God exists. If this is not true, the whole theory is either shattered into nonsense or relegated to the land of fairy tale or mythological speculation. On the other hand, if the proposition is true, it does not seem unreasonable to expect that this God will be a determining factor in both the contemporary historical processes and the ultimate fulfillment. But no historian can use the truth or falsity of this idea in his methodology without running the risk of a devastating criticism of his objectivity. To say of event *A* that it is compatible with the purposes of God, while event *B* is not, is to claim a knowledge which seems far superior to anything we ordinarily find in fallible man. History, in short, does not teach only one lesson; it sometimes teaches many, and at other times none at all. If it is difficult to tell what happened, it is certainly more so to tell why it happened or to what end it happened. If God's existence is a matter of faith, then the providential theory of history is a matter of faith. But how can such a faith be serviceable in the discovery and interpretation of events without running the danger of subjectivity and distortion? As Santayana has remarked,

In truth, whatever plausibility the providential view of a given occurrence may have is dependent on the curious limitation and selfishness of the observer's estimations. Sheep are providentially designed for men; but why not also for wolves, and men for worms and microbes?[87]

The Progressive-Evolutionary View of History. It is not until the eighteenth and nineteenth centuries that civilizations were judged as good or bad depending on their degree of progress. Earlier conceptions of progress were fragmentary and undeveloped. It had not become, in Bury's phrase, a "controlling idea." But when the idea was accepted as the key to events, it dominated most of the historical thinking for two centuries. One of the great representatives of this view was Condorcet, whose magnificent faith in the progressive perfectibility of man is matched only by his courage in writing about it while hiding from Robespierre and other revolutionary leaders who were seeking to kill him, though he had befriended their cause. For him there are no fixed limits to man's improvement except the duration of the physical earth and the constancy of its laws. He antici-

[87] George Santayana, *The Life of Reason: Reason in Science,* Charles Scribner's Sons, New York, 1932, p. 56.

pated, however, that man's life itself will be indefinitely extended and death postponed if no accidents occur. But it will not be an empty prolongation of existence. There will be moral and intellectual progress too and a vast accumulation of learning for the human race, due to the stride in education. Wars will vanish, not only because weapons will be immensely improved, but because man's natural goodness will assert itself. The goal of history is nothing short of human perfection.

For the present it is unnecessary to examine the many variations on this theme. In general the idea seems clear enough. The events of history are the signs of a movement from a relatively disordered, evil, and undesirable condition to an ordered, perfect, and extremely felicitous state. Let us scrutinize the position more carefully.

We have first the problem of definition. There seems to be no agreement on the meaning of progress. Does it mean bringing order out of chaos; or reducing the amount of evil and increasing the goods of this world; or a state of happiness; or the achievement of so much control over the environment that living becomes highly efficient; or the lessening of human suffering, physical and psychical; or the reduction of labor and the attainment of comfort; or moral enlightenment and human brotherhood; or a gradual march toward human reasonableness and rationality? These questions are not answered in the same way by the advocates of the progressive view of history. Perhaps the best we can say is that progress is movement away from, or out of, a distressing unwanted plight to a less distressing, more desirable situation. But this leads immediately to the second problem.

Every statement about what is progress and what is not involves a value judgment. How do we know that our present state is any better than that of previous generations? And again, better in what sense? Moreover, is it intelligible to say that civilization did, does, and will continue to grow in a desirable direction? For this to make sense we would have to know the destination. And that cannot be known. Would it not be enormously difficult or even impossible to prove that contemporary civilization is much preferable to any preceding age? Certainly there are many living today who would gladly exchange dates—and perhaps some who would preserve the comfortable present, unwilling to take a chance on what may be the next disruptive mood of progress. Whether or not there is progress, in short, seems to depend on the range of our perspective. If we look at the astonishing control over nature and the comprehension of its laws, there has been enormous advance in this direction since the inclined plane of Galileo. It is certainly not as clear that man has similarly risen to intellectual and moral heights. If we look backward two thousand years we are impressed by the progress toward health and freedom from excessive labor. But who will judge that modern man's time and energy serve to make him a happier individual than his ancestors?

There is a third difficulty in many of the progress theories. It amounts to a central inconsistency in the doctrine. Let us put it this way: All progress views regard the universe as being in a condition of perpetual movement toward an ideal. But if the end is attained, this must lead to the cessation of movement and change, which are therefore temporary states of being and not of its essence. This is the paradox that closes Bury's famous study, The Idea of Progress.

But if we accept the reasonings on which the dogma of Progress is based, must we not carry them to their full conclusion? In escaping from the illusion of finality, is it legitimate to exempt that dogma itself? Must not it, too, submit to its own negation of finality? Will not that process of change, for which Progress is the optimistic name, compel 'Progress' too to fall from the commanding position in which it is now, with apparent security, enthroned? . . . A day will come, in the revolution of centuries, when a new idea will usurp its place as the directing idea of humanity.[88]

Progress philosophers stand between those philosophers of history who find the golden age in the past and those who anticipate the salvation of man in the future Heavenly City. The former wait with resignation the revolving cycles that will restore the glorified past. The latter turn with hope to the promise of a new life. Between the two are the progressive points of view that work with confidence, regenerating the present to get away from it, as quickly as possible. Santayana puts it neatly when he writes, "Singular doctrine of progress, that the present, so magnetic when it was the future, should always prove merely an incentive to escape into something else, and to turn itself into a portion of that dreadful past, from which, forever, we must flee."[89]

Progress theories, in short, as all other theories, are made plausible only by a careful selection of the data, only by maintaining a particular perspective. Increase the data or widen the perspective and we bring into view the irrational surds, the incalculable shifts and vacillations, the burdens of meaningless suffering. They are the constant elements of the human predicament. They cannot be theorized out of existence. This simply

[88] J. B. Bury, *The Idea of Progress*, Macmillan and Co. Ltd., London, 1921, pp. 351–352.

[89] George Santayana, *Dominations and Powers*, Charles Scribner's Sons, New York, 1951, pp. 334–335.

means that no Law of Progress can be formulated and verified that fits the whole range of historical experience. On the other hand, in some matters man seems able to advance if he really puts his mind to it. Failure to establish a law need not mean an abandonment of hope, a slackening of effort, or a disparagement of the ideal.

Before leaving the progressive or evolutionary philosophies of history, we must consider a view that in some sense belongs to this classification and in another sense does not. We shall call it the dialectical interpretation of history and develop briefly the position of its two major exponents, Georg Wilhelm Friedrich Hegel and Karl Marx. The full force and meaning of Hegel's view is extremely difficult to summarize, largely because his philosophy of history is an organic part of his metaphysics. Moreover, the language of this philosopher is notoriously ill-defined, vague, and complex. But perhaps the key beliefs can be made relatively clear. At any rate we must try, for the barriers of language and complexity of thought did not prevent Hegel's philosophy from becoming enormously influential.

Let us begin with a metaphysical belief basic to Hegelian thought: the real is the rational and the rational is the real. This suggests a form of idealism and gives us the first step in orientation. For Hegel mind alone is real; ideas, thoughts are real too, for they constitute mind. What happens when the mind thinks? It takes a certain position and then tries to develop this to the utmost. But in this process the original position is so modified as to be contradicted or negated. The tension now appearing is irrational and a third step must be taken which draws into itself the contradictions and resolves them. This then becomes a new position and the process begins again. Thus thought moves from thesis to antithesis to synthesis. This is the dialectic.

Now, because the real is rational, that is mind, and dialectic is the way in which rationality manifests itself, we should expect to find the dialectic at work in nature and in human events. This Hegel insists is the case. Historical processes then assume the pattern of the dialectic. It is Reason that governs the world and consequently history. In history, Reason is becoming self-conscious and the more self-conscious it becomes the greater freedom it acquires. For it is by becoming self-conscious that we achieve freedom. If this is a hard notion to get, try thinking of it this way: A man who has become fully conscious of, say, the German language, is free to use it, he is not limited by it. But not to be fully conscious of it is to be restricted, bound by his limitations. "World history," says Hegel, "is the progress of the consciousness of freedom." The driving power of history is Reason seeking self-consciousness, but the form by which Reason accomplishes this end is the irrevocable beat of thesis, antithesis, and synthesis, until all the categories have been marched through and the Absolute, that is, Reason fully self-conscious, is reached.

The problems associated with this view are severe enough to lead to its rejection. For example, how does the thesis produce the antithesis, or give rise to it? May not the antithesis arise by one's critical attitude toward the thesis? If so, the opposed tendencies are not found in events, but in our attitude toward events. Moreover, does the conflict between thesis and antithesis always result in a synthesis? Are there not many futile struggles in history which end in nothing being settled? And finally, what is the guarantee that the synthesis preserves the better, more reasonable parts of the thesis and antithesis? May they not mutually destroy each other?

And yet, is there not something very plausible in Hegel's conception? It stresses the fact of conflict, struggle, opposition, and tension, and these are observable features of human existence. Furthermore, when faced with opposition we frequently seek to find a reasonable way out by a compromise that prevents the situation from being a total loss to each. And how often it is remarked that one movement is a reaction against another.

However, though this is undoubtedly true, it is not the same thing as Hegel's logical juggernaut, which rolls on relentlessly, generating negations and negations of negations until the Absolute is reached. Not all of the conflicts we must reconcile are describable as logical negations. For example, consider the opposition of democracy and monarchy. Is one a contradiction of the other? Not at all, for both may be present in a democratic monarchy, such as in the government of Great Britain. That it is possible to explain some historical events as a kind of reaction between extremes does not argue the view of Hegel, for what is psychologically or sociologically or politically demonstrable need not be metaphysically necessary.

The philosophy of history associated with the names of Karl Marx and Friedrich Engels has been called dialectical materialism. The first term suggests their agreement with Hegel and the last their opposition. This, in fact, is the case. The Marxists have accepted a form of the Hegelian dialectic, but rejected its idealistic metaphysics. Precisely what is meant by "materialism" is not sufficiently clear, but it seems to refer to the fact that man must work with the materials of nature to satisfy his needs. But this puts him in relation not only to nature but to other men. All these relations in their totality constitute the economic structure of society. Moreover, these relations determine the social, political, moral, and intellectual bases of life. Thus mind, as it is in Hegel, is not an effective causal agent.

Changes are brought about in society because of the changes in the ways of production and economic exchange. Here, for example, is a statement by Engels:

The materialist conception of history starts from the principle that production, and with production the exchange of its products, is the basis of every social order; that in every society which has appeared in history the distribution of the products, and with it the division of society into classes or estates, is determined by what is produced and how it is produced, and how the product is exchanged. According to this conception, the ultimate causes of all social changes and political revolutions are to be sought, not in the minds of men, in their increasing insight into eternal truth and justice, but in changes in the mode of production and exchange; they are to be sought not in the *philosophy* but in the *economics* of the epoch concerned.[90]

In Marxist theory history is divided into four main epochs, which are to be superseded by the final and permanent stage. Each has its peculiar characteristics, but each is subject to the dialectic and is therefore unstable. Thus beginning with primitive communism, we move through the successive stages of ancient slavery, medieval feudalism, capitalism, and finally pure communism. When this is reached, the dialectic ceases to operate.

The steps in Marx's argument seem to be somewhat as follows: An increase of production and of the means of production leads to the wealth of the few and the wretchedness of the many. Thus a small class of owners becomes opposed to a large class of workers. Revolution results in which the victory goes to the workers with the consequent elimination of all classes and "in place of the old bourgeois society with its classes and class antagonisms we shall have an association in which the free development of each is the condition for the free development of all."[91]

Although this position is called dialectical materialism, it does not provide an unambiguous theory of matter. Matter is defined as that which acts on our sense organs in such a way that it produces sensations. This is obviously unclear, and would, for example, be subject to a Berkelian interpretation. Furthermore, matter too is said to change dialectically. Change is not the mere mechanical rearrangement of original stuff, but the result of dynamic development.

This view of history, too, cannot withstand serious criticism. Its theory of dialectical development is not empirically verifiable and can be read into historical events only with distortion and a failure to consider all fac-

[90] Friedrich Engels, *Anti-Dühring* (Emile Burns, tr.), Marxist Library, Vol. 18, International Publishers Co., New York, 1939, p. 292.
[91] Karl Marx, *Communist Manifesto*.

tors involved, which is strange when we remember the emphasis put upon totality and the interrelatedness of things. The view is so deterministic that little, if anything, can be accomplished by the individual. He is himself the result of the economic structure of society and really cannot cope with a blind driving dialectical fate. Again, on Marxist grounds it would be impossible to have philosophical, religious, aesthetic, or political reasons for affirming beliefs. One can hold them only for economic reasons. It is certainly doubtful whether the complex processes of human existence can be interpreted without distortion by a single, unverifiable factor. Finally Marx seems not to have considered the possibility of designed inner modification or change which does not require a dialectical opposition. Thus the capitalism of his own day, without doubt needing reformation, achieved its reforms by a gradual awareness of its weaknesses and not by a revolution of the working classes.

Pluralistic-Scientific View of History. Contemporary historians and philosophers are less inclined to look for single causes or all-pervading patterns in history. This does not mean that there is no interest in a metaphysical philosophy of history or that there are no brave attempts to construct a grand view within which local events get their meaning. But it seems generally recognized that to produce an over-all pattern one must appeal to something beyond history, or to religious and metaphysical speculations. Historians, in particular, being zealous to maintain the scientific spirit in history, tend to shy away from these speculations. A recent statement of this spirit maintained that it

. . . is characterized by (1) awareness of the existence and nature of problems that may be treated historically; (2) recognition of functions and limitations of the historical method in the treatment of historical problems; (3) readiness to collect and to submit to careful selection, in accordance with the established rules of historical method, the available evidence necessary to support the statements made in any piece of written history and to sustain the context of the historical construct; (4) willingness to give proper weight to the various pieces of evidence thus selected; (5) acknowledgment of one's own socioeconomic and other biases and the effort to eliminate their effects; and (6) determination to make only such conclusions or inferences as are justified by the evidence.[92]

The determination not to go beyond the evidence prevents the modern historian from engaging in speculative enterprises that take him too far from the security of his facts. Yet, unless he is a mere chronicler he cannot escape interpretation, and this brings him near the borders of a phi-

[92] *Theory and Practice in Historical Study:* A report of the Committee on Historiography, Social Science Research Council, Bulletin 54, New York, 1946, p. 134.

losophy of history, into a philosophy of social science or ethics or anthropology and so on. He does not claim to have discovered "the laws of history" as the scientist may discover "the laws of nature," but he does feel the need of searching for valid generalizations based on evidence and as comprehensive a view as is possible. Thus it is not a pattern in history that is stressed, but a pattern in inquiry.

The emphasis upon method and the demand for evidence is reflected also in the interest modern historians have taken in the language of written history. There is constant criticism of the terms to be used and a stricter requirement for precise definition. This is certainly a healthy and necessary move, for philosophies of history are freighted with vague and ambiguous terms. Consider the following as representative instances: Cause, progress, chance, dialectic, culture, civilization, force, fact, law. The list could be enlarged, for historians and philosophers share many terms.

Finally, we may mention the tendency of recent views to admit a plurality of causes in history and to regard an account or explanation inadequate until the geographical, economic, biological, political, climatic, and sociological data are in. This makes the problem of a philosophy of history, as well as history itself, enormously complex and difficult. Such, however, has not and will not deter man the questioner from asking for his place and its meaning in the concourse of events.

If no over-all pattern can be discovered that gives meaning to man's existence, this does not prevent him from establishing his own meaning and working it out if possible in cooperation with, but if necessary in defiance of, the natural world. If progress is not inevitable, that does not mean that it is not possible. If final destinations are not known, that does not mean that we must stand paralyzed, unable to choose a direction. If a rigorous law of historical development cannot be found, that does not mean that we are blind wanderers unable to say where we have been, or where we are, or where we would like to be. Man must rely on his knowledge. Because this is always fragmentary, his life, history, and his philosophy are full of adventure and risk. But this does not make them illusory, for partial knowledge is still knowledge.

VII. Moral Philosophies of History

Philosophers have not limited themselves to logical, epistemological, and metaphysical issues about history. Nor have historians been content with methods that insure the discovery of the maximum number of facts, from which is derived by the least dubious inferences the simplest ideal construction of some segment or whole of the human past. What other kinds of questions and answers are important? When we consider history (either in the first sense of human events or in the second sense of a causal account of these events in temporal sequence) can we avoid asking and trying to answer moral questions? Who has achieved good or acted rightly, and who has fallen into evil or acted wrongly? Who deserves credit or praise, who deserves reproach or blame, for what he has done? Which ordering of society and state and economy in the succession of historical stages can be judged to be the best? If the nature of man makes possible the achievement of alternative orders, which should I decide to prevent and urge others to avoid? There are strong arguments that we do most commonly regard history from the perspective indicated by these questions.

Although we may attempt in our writing of history and in our philosophizing about history to avoid these moral questions, it may be impossible and undesirable. Moral judgments are suspect among many philosophers because they are not decided by either common sense or scientific appeal to empirical data. They are suspect also as judgments because if they are deduced, at least one premise must be a moral premise, such as "War is evil," and this seems to be a mere opinion or expression of emotion, and not as such either true or false. Historians, exemplified by Herbert Butterfield in The Whig Interpretation of History, have reminded us of the danger to history of assumptions that there are good and bad men, that certain sides in human struggles are right or wrong, that one stage of the process is the best, and that the historian can do more solid work than to preach.

After having granted the cogency of these arguments, must we conclude that although most philosophy of history and history-writing have been strongly moral in approach, this is a mistake both for philosophy and for history? A contemporary logical empiricist, who has done the most considerable work in the field of philosophy of history, does not conclude that we can or should dispense with moral questions as irrelevant. Although the general consensus of opinion of logical positivists has been that moral judgments are meaningless and history should be value-free in order to achieve full status as a science, Karl Popper's The Open Society and Its Enemies is an impassioned plea for making moral issues central in both the writing of history and of the philosophy of history. This seems paradoxical, and we shall meet another paradox, namely the central place given to moral judgment in Herbert Butterfield's Christianity and History. These are two among many contemporaries who are now actively contributing to the field. They are selected to give considered answers to the four questions asked above, because they represent two dominant ethical tendencies in philosophy of history in the mid-twentieth century.

Popper regards moral judgments as based exclusively on human interests and justified by human knowledge and reason alone. In this sense he can be called a humanist. Butterfield regards moral judgments as based ultimately on the nature and work of God and justified by what God has revealed through the prophets of the Bible and what He will judge at the end of time. Butterfield can be called a theist. Other expressions of a humanist ethic of history can be found in Morris Cohen's Meaning in Human History and in various works of Lewis Mumford. Other expressions of a theistic ethic of history can be found in Reinhold Niebuhr's Nature and Destiny of Man, in works of Nikolai Berdyaev, Paul Tillich, and Arnold Toynbee.

The central ethical issue debated, often with great vigor, is whether man, of his own ability, is able to know what the good is and how to achieve it. The humanists as a group now allow the theists' point that man is capable of great evil. And the theists as a group allow the humanists' point that alleged knowledge of God is often illusory. The theists have attacked the doctrine of inevitable progress as a natural law of history. The humanists have attacked the doctrine that every event can be ratified as an act of divine judgment. But what motivates the concern of both camps with history are questions such as these: Can man achieve his good in a social process over long spans of time? What is the nature and extent of human responsibility for consequences of action? What are the plans for a better order of society? Are men able to fulfill them? The authors we have named would all agree that it is undesirable to evade these issues.

That moral judgment is integral to any conception of human society is the primary theme of Karl Popper's The Open Society and Its Enemies. His secondary theme will also be considered, that there are two basically contrasted types of moral judgment, one that encourages a closed, and one that encourages an open society. The first thesis may be true without the second. Unfortunately, most of the discussion has concentrated upon Popper's abuse of Plato and Hegel as fascists or authoritarians in political philosophy. The interpretation here will underplay the polemic side of Popper's book, so we may see his work as he intended it, a "critical introduction" to philosophy of history, here conjoined with sociology and politics.[93]

[93] K. R. Popper, The Open Society and Its Enemies, Routledge & Kegan Paul, London, 1952, Vol. I, p. v and Vol. II, p. 259. Used by permission of Routledge & Kegan Paul and the Princeton University Press.

We have raised four moral questions about historical process. Let us deal with them in the following order. First, can historical beliefs fail to express our interests? Second, can our historical beliefs fail to consider men responsible for their acts, and praise and blame them for the consequences of their acts? Third, can our historical beliefs be expressed without committing us to a judgment about the best age of man? Fourth, can our historical beliefs fail to urge men to act in a certain way prescribed by the view we take of interests, responsibility, and the best age of man? Popper's philosophy of history answers each of these questions in the negative.

1. *Can historical beliefs fail to express our interests?*

Let us assume with Popper that we do employ what he calls a "selective and organizing principle" to give structure to our historical beliefs. If this principle is not a law of nature such as the natural sciences discover, then it must be some principle that lies not in the subject matter itself but in the character of the person who organizes his experience in a certain way.[94] There is a variety of interpretations of historical data because the interests of historians vary. With succeeding generations historians shift their points of view because they share the "troubles and problems" of each generation. But this implies that there can be no one principle. Is historical objectivity then a vain delusion?

Popper's argument is that not only do we actually employ some moral criterion, but that we should introduce moral judgment into our accounts. If we are conscious of what we are about, and frankly disclose to the reader the standpoint we occupy, he will not then be deceived, but will know exactly how we organized our data. Hence frank subjectivity will aid in achieving more objective history. This sounds paradoxical. Popper resolves the paradox by postulating two historians. Each finds a principle within himself and applies it "consciously and critically to the problem" of human society.[95] One tells the story as a "history of progress," the other as a "history of retrogression." Since there are aspects of freedom and aspects of oppression, the stories do not necessarily conflict. Rather "they may be complementary to each other, as would be two views of the same landscape."

This program is in sharp contrast to the policy that no historian as an individual should introduce a moral judgment into his account. Yet the collective account compiled from various historians is expected to yield "the verdict of history."[96]

---

[94] *Ibid.*, Vol. II, pp. 264–265.
[95] *Ibid.*, Vol. II, p. 268.
[96] *Ibid.*, Vol. II, p. 255.

There are two absurdities Popper would avoid. The first is that even the most dispassionate spectator of historical process can be morally neutral. The second is that the sum-total of knowledge of past events will supply us with moral conclusions.

First, although Thucydides remains a model in refraining from overt moral judgment, Popper finds in his writings that the seemingly objective blame of "party spirit" is actually praise of the "pro-Spartan oligarchic party." Thucydides is not neutral between oligarchy and democracy. Although Popper believes him to be "the greatest historian, perhaps, who ever lived," yet he considers his moral judgment mistaken.[97]

Second, although most historians have taken over Thucydides' moral judgment as though it were a factual truth, this does not make this judgment "the official judgment of 'History'."[98] There is no sound basis upon which we can say that any moral judgment is "the verdict of history." Moral judgments are always personal. "For I hold that we cannot and must not evade deciding in such matters for ourselves; and that if we are not able to pass a verdict, neither will history."[99]

2. *Can our historical beliefs fail to consider men responsible for their acts, and praise and blame them for the consequences of their acts?*

Can we consider human action or the record of human action without placing responsibility somewhere? He argues that we cannot, and he analyzes traditional metaphysics to show that they do hold someone or something responsible. If holding someone or something responsible is a moral judgment, then all metaphysical philosophies of history are moral philosophies.

The common feature in four metaphysical alternatives is that the one held responsible for the historical process is not an individual human being. Some say "God is the author of the play performed on the Historical Stage." Others, Heraclitus in particular, say that what is responsible is a "developmental law as a law of nature." Hegel had a "law of spiritual development," and Marx a "law of economic development." It does not matter which of these four is adopted so far as the theoretical structure and practical application is concerned. Theoretically, one cannot change God's will or a metaphysical principle, hence one is never to blame. And the one obligation for the future is to do what one cannot help doing, to submit or to accept.[100] Since God or law has made some tribe or

---

[97] *Ibid.*, Vol. I, p. 178.
[98] *Ibid.*
[99] *Ibid.*, Vol. II, p. 255.
[100] *Ibid.*, Vol. I, p. 8.

race or nation "the instrument of destiny," there is but one supreme good, to act one's appointed role.[101]

Popper analyzes Hegel's position and Marx's position at length to prove that if these are typical metaphysical views, their prime failure is an attempt to transcend human moral judgment. The actual outcome is a theoretical amoralism and a practical immorality.[102] The alternative that he recommends is to allow individual men an ultimate place in planning and reviewing human action. To take this alternative is to avoid the mistake of confusing moral and natural law. With the latter there is no decision required whether to conform or not. But one may act in violation of a moral law, if one chooses to go against it.

To avoid making power into a norm, the course of events should not be the deciding factor in moral judgment. The only norm Popper can discover is the authority of personal conscience. In denying that "world history is a world court," Popper is making a moral judgment. His judgment is that "success should not be worshipped, that it cannot be our judge." And, consistent with his theory, he rests his case on no factual ground whatsoever, but takes full responsibility for its theoretical implications and practical applications.[103]

3. *Can we fail to make judgments as to which stage of society or which form of state is "best"?*

Popper argues that no history or philosophy of history fails to reveal some moral judgment of this kind. Since speculation about the succession of ages is a standard item in metaphysical philosophies of history, let us consider the moral import of various metaphysical alternatives. To say that the original form is best sets us the ideal of preserving the past from all change. To say that the present form is best is to accept all past changes, but to forbid any further alteration. To say that the future form is best is to encourage change as advance from something now imperfect. Roughly these three ideas, that the original is best, the present is best, the future is best, are abstractly the alternatives proposed by Plato, Hegel, and Marx.

Let those who attempt to restore some original best state be called "reactionaries." Let those who glorify the present and call it the best state be called "modernists." Let those who pin their hopes on what will become be called "futurists." Must one choose to be one or the other, or to combine aspects from these three? Popper's answer is in the negative.

[101] *Ibid.*, Vol. I, p. 9.
[102] *Ibid.*, Vol. II, pp. 74, 165, 191.
[103] *Ibid.*, Vol. I, p. 274.

There is a common error in talking of the "good old days" or the "glorious present" or the "best that is yet to be." The error is to confound factual and evaluative statements. The past was not factually as the conservative would have us believe. The present is not factually as the modernist would have us believe. The future will not be factually as the futurist would have us believe. Or to put the error in another way, are not these positions the result of equating the temporal distinctions with moral discriminations? Is it the same error of moral reasoning whether one says "past might is right," "present might is right," or "future might is right?" "In their theoretical structure there is no difference between moral conservatism, moral modernism, and moral futurism."[104]

There is another misleading aspect involved in speculations about the best state of society, namely the concealing of the moral judgment within a mass of factual data. Marx holds that the present state of society is full of "seeds of its own destruction," but that after the revolution, there will emerge a classless society, without poverty or inequality, hence without exploitation and war between classes. Since this is to come into being automatically, the good somehow happens without specific economic planning. Problems will simply solve themselves. This, of course, is a refusal to state one's moral ideal about what ought to be.

Marx's Capital is for Popper paradoxical. Although "largely a treatise on social ethics, these ethical ideas are never represented as such. They are expressed only by implication, but not the less forcibly on that account, since the implications are very obvious . . . Marx was reluctant to formulate his ethical convictions explicitly."[105] Popper's alternative to Marx, which will be discussed in the next paragraph, claims the rational right to urge men to follow a certain course of action. This Marx did as a revolutionist, but inconsistently if his premises are purely factual. The "irrational and apparently factual question (of Plato, Hegel, and Marx, is): 'Which way are we going? What, in essence, is the part that history has destined us to play?' " But the "rational question" Popper urges us to pose is: " 'What are we to choose as our most urgent problems, how did they arise, and along what roads may we proceed to solve them?' "[106]

4. *Can our historical beliefs fail to urge men to act in a certain way prescribed by the view we take of interests, responsibilites, and the best age of man?*

If a certain stage of society is the best, and a philosophy of history

---

[104] *Ibid.*, Vol. II, p. 206.
[105] *Ibid.*, Vol. II, p. 199.
[106] *Ibid.*, Vol. II, p. 268.

holds out the hope of achieving it, it is an application of moral philosophy. Actually the metaphysical schemes do call upon men to act in prescribed ways. But the assumptions required for imperative conclusions are certain moral judgments about the interests, responsibility, and the best age of man. In the previous three points, Popper has made these explicit as far as he is concerned. Hence he is rational in urging men to take specific measures to create "institutions to safeguard freedom, especially freedom from exploitation. . . ."[107]

To act in a certain way and to urge others to act cannot, according to Popper, be either logically deduced without assumptions or shown experimentally to be a body of knowledge. But how, then, can Popper call himself a rationalist? Does he not preach an irrational faith as did Plato, Hegel, and Marx? Popper admits that his faith is, as these previous faiths claimed to be, a "faith in reason."[108] But then how can one make a reasonable choice between alternative faiths?

The choice before us is not simply an intellectual affair, or a matter of taste. It is a moral decision. . . . [That is] arguments cannot *determine* such a fundamental moral decision. But this does not imply that our choice cannot be *helped* by any kind of argument whatever. On the contrary, whenever we are faced with a moral decision of a more abstract kind, it is most helpful to analyze carefully the consequences which are likely to result from the alternatives between which we have to choose. For only if we can visualize these consequences in a concrete and practical way, do we really know what our decision is about; otherwise we decide blindly.[109]

What can determine our decisions are the consequences. Although the outcome of any action cannot be now known in actuality, hence not experimentally, we "can confront its consequences with our conscience."[110] If this is obscure, an illustration may be presented from Shaw's Saint Joan. It may be too late if we wait for the consequences. We must anticipate them before they occur. Hence the Chaplain, who has demanded the Maid's death, seeing her at the stake, breaks down. "I meant no harm. I did not know what it would be like . . . I did not know what I was doing . . . If I had known, I would have torn her from their hands."

By analogy we can discover rational grounds for rejecting the practical programs of Hegel and Marx. The Nazis made efforts to restore an organic or tribal society. We are not in the dark about the outcome in prac-

[107] *Ibid.*, Vol. II, p. 143.
[108] *Ibid.*, Vol. II, p. 231.
[109] *Ibid.*, Vol. II, p. 232.
[110] *Ibid.*, Vol. II, p. 233.

tice of the doctrines of a closed society. The Russian Communists believed that a dictatorship would solve all problems; a free or open society, said Marx, could not. But this was not a scientific prediction. Call it rather "oracular prophecy." Marx's "withering away of the state" after the Revolution is a hope projected into the future. And the non-Communist world is actually doing what Marx claimed a society cannot do.

Has history any meaning? Popper answers yes and no. Yes, if we bring into connection our knowledge of events with moral judgments or decisions of conscience. No, if we expect our knowledge of events to supply a "verdict of history."

Popper's value premises that make history meaningful are:

[First, to use] not only intellectual activity but also observation and experiment. . . . [Second, to adopt] an attitude that seeks to solve as many problems as possible by an appeal to reason, i.e., to clear thought and experience, rather than by an appeal to emotions and passions. . . . [Third, to proceed on] an attitude of readiness to listen to critical arguments and to learn from experience . . . "I may be wrong and you may be right, and by an effort, we may get nearer to the truth." [Fourth, to guide one's self by the] belief that in the search for truth we need co-operation, and that, with the help of argument, we can in time attain something like objectivity.[111]

But without such statements of faith as these, what criterion of meaning could there be? The commonest criterion is power, which brings success. And indeed, says Popper, what most people learn of the past of mankind is the "history of political power."[112] But this, he thinks, is a mistaken moral judgment. The mistake is threefold. First, the decision to praise success leads us to approve of "the history of international crime and mass murder" as though men could do no better than they did. Second, because whatever meaning history has is found in the fulfillment of some specific human purpose of a given individual, the success of institutions is often destructive of individuals, and therefore of meaning. Third, if the criterion of meaning is power, then some process beyond men's control is made to judge men. Then we are robbed of our facility to make our own future, and reduced to mere prophets submitting to fate.

History may have a meaning if we learn from it what mistakes we ought never to make again, and to do things as well as we can, by our own lights.

And when we have dropped the idea that the history of power will be our judge, when we have given up worrying whether or not history will justify us,

[111] *Ibid.*, Vol. II, pp. 224–225.
[112] *Ibid.*, Vol. II, p. 270.

then one day perhaps we may succeed in getting power under control. In this way we may even justify history, in our turn. It badly needs such justification."[113]

If we adopt moral criteria and work out a moral philosophy of history to supplant the immoral and amoral metaphysical schemes, then concludes Popper, history will have meaning. It depends on our planning for a better world and acting according to our plans. Whatever "meaning" history has thus depends, in theory and in practice, on whether we "give it a meaning."[114]

Now we shall examine the answers of a contemporary Christian theist to these four questions. Herbert Butterfield's Christianity and History is comparable to Popper's Open Society and Its Enemies because it makes central the same moral questions about history. First, should the historian adopt moral criteria and write history in their light? Butterfield also answers yes. The criteria are those of the God of the Hebrews expressed in the Scriptures with the stress of Jesus on forgiveness of one's enemies. Second, these beliefs are said to make a man a more objective historian. This is so, according to Butterfield, because, in answer to the second question, a theist never makes his beliefs about human responsibility final. The Christian beliefs in Providence and Judgment express the truth that history as a process is too complex for a finite mind to fathom. Our judgments of praise and blame are unreliable and obscure. Third, can or should men engage in blueprinting the future best age? No, answers Butterfield, not even in the limited or piecemeal way suggested by Popper. The argument is that to do so is to act as though we could count on God, or the process beyond our control, to agree with our limited judgment and to help us out. But we should not so "presume upon Providence" and we know many human failures that spring from such presumption. Fourth, Butterfield also urges man to pursue wise policies, although he admits there is no best age in the future that fulfills human purposes and justifies history. Rather, he urges us to try to redeem past evil by accepting a present age as the only opportunity any generation has for its salvation.

1. Butterfield scorns such an attempt as Popper's to divide men into friends and enemies of freedom and progress. His logical objections have already been presented. His moral objection is that the historian ought not to "ratify old party cries but to find the unities that underlie the differences and to see all lives as part of the one web of life."[115] It is not merely that Butterfield considers it fallacious reasoning to call the Republic

---

[113] *Ibid.*, Vol. II, p. 280.
[114] *Ibid.*, Vol. II, p. 278.
[115] H. Butterfield, *op. cit.*, p. 3.

"Plato's *Mein Kampf*," a choice example of reading the present back into the past, but that the historian's interest is to extend sympathy even to his political enemies. Popper stresses only his own interests. Butterfield stresses human need to see our enemies' decisions in the light of their circumstances. Their decisions, as ours, express the "same human nature when it works under different conditions."[116]

The historian does not content himself with a simple picture of good men fighting bad, and he turns the crude melodrama that some people see in life into a more moving kind of tragedy. In the last resort he sees human history as a pilgrimage of all mankind, and human achievement as a grand co-operative endeavor, in which whigs and tories complement one another, both equally necessary to the picture. In the last resort even tories and socialists are to the historian only allies who happen to have fallen out with one another.[117]

This is an expression of a Christian to reconcile enemies. Popper, by contrast, drew battle-lines more sharply. Butterfield's belief fits a theistic faith that God is the father of all, but he insists that his moral decision can stand independent of supernatural religion.[118]

2. What would human responsibility for the consequences of acts mean in a philosophy of history? Given any act, perhaps some individual can be found to praise or blame. Or, perhaps only human beings as a whole can be praised or blamed for some total result. Either answer, argues Butterfield, is mistaken.

First,

. . . the pattern of history-making which we shall carry out will not be the product of my will or of yours or indeed of anybody else's, but will represent in one sense rather what might almost seem to be a compounding of these wills or at least of their effects—something which sometimes no single person will either have intended or anticipated. . . . Nobody ever sat down with a plan in his mind and said, "Go to—let us now produce a thing called the capitalist system."[119]

This author puts the point metaphorically: "History-making . . . goes on . . . over our heads."[120]

Second, it is true that "moral defects have something to do with the catastrophes that take place."[121] The moral meaning of historical process

[116] H. Butterfield, *Christianity and History*, G. Bell and Sons, Ltd., London, 1950, p. 31.
[117] *Ibid.*, p. 91.
[118] *Ibid.*, p. 46.
[119] *Ibid.*, p. 93.
[120] *Ibid.*, p. 94.
[121] *Ibid.*, p. 53.

is called "Providence," but the old doctrine often meant that only the guilty suffer and the innocent prosper. Butterfield disagrees, for there are no simply guilty or simply innocent men. But what is a common "moral defect" in which all share? Without an answer to this, we could have no content in the notion that "moral judgments . . . lie in the very nature of history. . . ."[122] Butterfield's illustration is that one-sidedness is a fault or vice or sin.

If men put their faith in science and make it the be-all and end-all of life, as though it were not to be subdued to any higher ethical end, there is something in the very composition of the universe that will make it execute judgment on itself, if only in the shape of the atomic bomb.[123]

But then, does something in the universe favor full human development as a higher end than technological progress? To affirm this is to rest an ethical doctrine on metaphysical grounds.

3. On the next moral point, Popper and Butterfield likewise differ sharply. The "best" age of man lies, according to the humanist, in the future which men make better than the past. History is a process justified, if at all, by what is accomplished in future time. History, then, could be justified only for our descendants. But meaning comes only if hopes are not yet fulfilled. Hence history has meaning only when it has no meaning.

Butterfield's alternative answer is that no generation of men has the "right to act as judges over others."[124] Moreover, the value of history is its part in "making personalities, ever . . . putting them through the mill. . . ."[125] Since the process produces "souls," and "each is of eternal moment," it follows that a historian should "look upon each generation as, so to speak, an end in itself, a world of people existing in their own right."[126]

And as for the "best" conditions for producing the "best" souls, Butterfield does not think we know enough even for Popper's "piece-meal social engineering," much less for utopian blueprints, which Popper also considers vicious. The plans of the French Revolution of 1789, which for Popper ushers in the open society, are for Butterfield one more effort to presume upon Providence. No man has yet invented "a form of political machinery which the ingenuity of the devil would not find a way of ex-

[122] *Ibid.*, p. 49.
[123] *Ibid.*, p. 60.
[124] *Ibid.*, p. 62.
[125] *Ibid.*, p. 76.
[126] *Ibid.*, p. 65.

ploiting for evil ends."[127] A corollary is that nothing is so evil that divine Providence cannot use it for good ends.

4. Should we take action and urge others to act in the light of imagined consequences? Popper answered yes, and considered this the only proper outcome of a moral philosophy of history. But for Butterfield, the main job of each generation is to "see what it can make of the mess left by its predecessors."[128] We may learn from experience, as Popper urged, but the central task, according to Butterfield, is to redeem errors. The point is that "the good life must be obtained now, no matter at what date in history you place the 'now'."[129]

Disasters of a given generation may be somewhat redeemed when, by a process of after-reflection, one people or another learns to profit by experience. The loss of our American colonies in the reign of George III taught this country [Butterfield is an Englishman] so to change her attitude to the question of overseas dominion that we were led to present the world with a new idea of empire. . . . [The] higher stage [is to] improve our relations with the universe if we conceive ourselves not as sovereign makers of history but as born to cooperate with Providence.[130]

When we reach this point, the disagreement of Butterfield with Popper is complete. The theist adopts an ethic on the basis of a metaphysics the positivist holds meaningless. Quite apart from his status as a historian, the general issue remains. Is man the only judge of good and evil, responsibility, the best age, and the future of mankind? Or must man take the universe into account? The question may be debated as long as history continues, and always be answered sometimes in contradictory and sometimes in complementary ways.

PROBLEMS FOR THOUGHT AND DISCUSSION

1. Consider the various theories of truth, for example, the correspondence, coherence, and pragmatic theories, with respect to historical judgments. Does any one theory fit the requirements of history better than another?
2. If all written history is selective and therefore from a point of view or perspective, in what sense can history be said to be objective?
3. Consider the following statement:

It is a rather widely held opinion that history, in contradistinction to the so-called physical sciences, is concerned with the description of particular events of the past rather than with the search for general laws which might govern those events. As a characterization of the type of problem in which some historians are mainly interested,

[127] *Ibid.*, p. 39.
[128] *Ibid.*, p. 105.
[129] *Ibid.*
[130] *Ibid.*, p. 99.

this view probably can not be denied; as a statement of the theoretical function of general laws in scientific historical research, it is certainly unacceptable.[131]

Would you defend or oppose the view that there are general laws in history? Would their presence or absence make a difference in whether or not history can be called a science?

4. A contemporary historian lists the following assumptions upon which he bases a work in history. Examine them carefully. Do you agree with him that they are all important and relevant? Would you take issue with any of them?

1. That the ideal of history, in the words of Morris Cohen, is "an imaginative reconstruction of the past which is scientific in its determinations and artistic in its formulation";
2. That history is more genuinely scientific in spirit as it takes into account the reasons why it cannot be utterly objective or strictly scientific in method;
3. That among these reasons is the necessity of dealing with a complex of factors—physical, biological, psychological, cultural—that cannot be measured, isolated in controlled experiments, or reduced to a single cause;
4. That among these factors is the force of human will—of mind and character, ideas and ideals;
5. That this force makes it necessary to pass ethical judgments on history, and that such judgments are in fact implicit in the works of the most resolutely amoral historians;
6. That our scientific, esthetic, and moral interests alike call for a world view, a kind of anthropological study of civilizations, as a perspective on our own civilization;
7. That in this perspective we can make out universals or underlying uniformities but cannot claim possession of the absolute truth about man and the universe, cannot hope for complete certainty about beginnings and ends; and
8. That this is not simply a depressing conclusion.[132]

5. In Oswald Spengler's famous book The Decline of the West, we find much of the argument based upon analogy. Examine the following carefully to find whether you think the analogy is imperfect, and if so, in what ways.

"Mankind," however, has no aim, no idea, no plan, any more than the family of butterflies or orchids. "Mankind" is a zoological expression, or an empty word. But conjure away the phantom, break the magic circle, and at once there emerges an astonishing wealth of *actual* forms—the Living with all its immense fullness, depth and movement—hitherto veiled by a catchword, a dryasdust scheme, and a set of personal "ideals." I see, in place of that empty figment of *one* linear history, which can only be kept up by shutting one's eyes to the overwhelming multitude of the facts, the drama of a *number* of mighty Cultures, each springing with primitive strength from the soil of a mother-region, to which it remains firmly bound throughout its whole life-cycle; each stamping its material, its mankind, in *its own* image; each having *its own* idea; *its own* passions, *its own* life, will and feeling, *its own* death. Here indeed are colours, lights, movements, that no intellectual eye has yet discovered. Here the Cultures, peoples, languages, truths, gods, landscapes bloom and age as the oaks and the stone-pines, the blossoms, twigs and leaves—but there is no ageing "Mankind." Each Culture has its own new possibilities of self-expression which arise, ripen, decay, and never return. There is not *one* sculpture, *one* painting, *one* mathematics, *one* physics, but many, each in its deepest essence different from the others, each limited in duration

---

[131] Carl G. Hempel, "The Function of General Laws in History," *Journal of Philosophy*, Vol. 39, No. 2, 1942, p. 35.
[132] Herbert J. Muller, *The Uses of the Past*, Oxford University Press, New York, 1954, pp. 29–30. Also in Mentor Books, The New American Library, New York, 1954, pp. 35–36.

and self-contained, just as each species of plant has its peculiar blossom or fruit, its special type of growth and decline. These cultures, sublimated life-essences, grow with the same superb aimlessness as the flowers of the field. They belong, like the plants and the animals, to the living Nature of Goethe and not to the dead Nature of Newton. I see a world-history as a picture of endless formations and transformations of the marvelous waxing and waning of organic forms. The professional historian, on the contrary, sees it as a sort of tapeworm industriously adding on to itself one epoch after another.[133]

6. According to Aristotle,

. . . the distinction between historian and poet is not in the one writing prose and the other verse—you might put the work of Herodotus into verse, and it would still be a species of history; it consists really in this, that the one describes the thing that has been, and the other a kind of thing that might be. Hence poetry is something more philosophic and of graver import than history, since its statements are of the nature rather of universals, whereas those of history are singulars. By a universal statement I mean one as to what such or such a kind of man will probably or necessarily say or do—which is the aim of poetry . . . by a singular statement, one as to what, say, Alcibiades did or had done to him.[134]

> Do you think this distinction between poetry and history is a valid one? Do you think the distinction would be more apt if applied to the natural sciences and history? Does Aristotle's distinction preclude any "historical explanation," or "prediction"?

7. A student of the American scene writes that "The use of history . . . is to rescue from oblivion the lost causes of the past. History is especially important when those causes haunt us in the present as unfinished business." What we inherit on this theory are missed revolutions, social changes that failed to substitute some designed social order in place of tradition, but succeeded only in disrupting tradition. Hence ambiguous values, or incompatible goals make it hard for the young to grow up.[135] What missed revolutions can you adduce to explain conflicts of value?

PERTINENT READINGS

Berlin, Isaiah, *The Hedgehog and the Fox,* Simon and Shuster, Inc., New York, 1953.

Gardiner, Patrick, *Theories of History,* The Free Press, Glencoe, Illinois, 1959.

Mandelbaum, Maurice, *The Problem of Historical Knowledge,* Liveright Publishing Corp., New York, 1938.

Meyerhoff, Hans, *The Philosophy of History in Our Time,* Doubleday Anchor Books, Garden City, New York, 1959.

Walsh, W. H., *An Introduction to Philosophy of History,* Hutchinson's University Library, London, 1951.

[133] Oswald Spengler, *The Decline of the West* (Charles Francis Atkinson, tr.), Alfred A. Knopf, New York, George Allen & Unwin Ltd., London, 1926, pp. 21–22.

[134] Richard McKeon (ed.), *The Basic Works of Aristotle,* Random House, New York, 1941, pp. 1463–1464, Aristotle, *De Poetica* (Ingram Bywater tr.), Clarendon Press, Oxford, 1924, 1451b, 1–11.

[135] Paul Goodman, "In Search of Community," *Commentary,* Vol. 29, No. 4, 1960, p. 315.

IX

Beliefs about Political Relations

I. The Problem of Political Relations

The opening words of the Declaration of Independence suggest the importance of the term "relations" in political thought: "When in the course of human events, it becomes necessary for one people to dissolve the political bands which have connected them with another", etc. The relations among human beings, by which society is constituted, may be analyzed logically. Any two persons, for example, may stand to each other in the relationship, among many others, of friend of, or slave of, or voter for. If A is a cousin of B, then B is a cousin of A. If A is a slave of B, then B cannot be a slave of A, but must be a master of A. If A votes for B, B may or may not vote for A. It is useful and worthwhile to apply the logical discrimination between symmetrical, asymmetrical, and non-symmetrical relations to our political beliefs.

There is a common belief that persons in society are better off when the relations among them are symmetrical. This is sometimes called mutuality. It describes the condition when A's respect for B's rights has the same form as B's respect for A's rights. It is further often believed that this mutuality of equals, if it is desirable, is impracticable in the political relationship of governing. We often express this: "Someone must be the boss." If A is the ruler or sovereign over B, then B cannot be ruler or sovereign over A. He must be ruled by or be the subject of A.

Political philosophers may defend or oppose this relation in

453

principle. It is a fact that some men believe there can be no lasting relation between persons unless the basis is inequality, whether the inequality be one of blood, caste, wealth, power, or divine favor. Others believe there can be no lasting relation unless the basis is equality. The latter stress the rights of each individual in the network of relationships, while the former emphasize the duties of subjects and their obedience to political authority. Here are two nicely opposed beliefs: A mutual relationship is thought to be free and just; a relationship of fixed subordination more orderly and stable and efficient.

Relations among human beings may also be considered with respect to transitivity. If *A* is ruler over *B* and *B* over *C,* then there are three possibilities. *A* must be ruler over *C,* or *A* cannot be ruler over *C,* or *A* may or may not be ruler over *C.* Consider the following case. It is a familiar, age-old belief that God is ruler and judge over earthly kings and magistrates, just as these are rulers and judges over their subjects. St. Augustine, for instance, stressed the transitivity of the relation of judging, although he did not give it this modern name. All human judges are themselves subject to judgment. This hierarchical concept of society answers Plato's question, "Who shall guard the guardians?" That is, the final term in such a chain is itself subject to no one. A common name for this term is Absolute. Here we may find a variety of current and often opposing beliefs. Some would prefer to see no human power considered an absolute, but leave the exalted place to God, or vacant. Others, for the sake of unquestionable law-making and administrative efficiency, ascribe this role to sovereign nations, their people, or their rulers. The United Nations did not and by its charter cannot make *A,* who is a citizen of the United States, a citizen of the United Nations. These two "associations" are not related to each other in the same way that a state, say New York, is related to the United States. In fact, much of the opposition in some quarters to the United Nations is based upon the reluctance and refusal to accept a transitive relation between it and the individual nations with respect to a particular area of power and authority.

Any theory of human relationships will be confronted with some very general questions, largely metaphysical in character. For example, consider the question: what are the basic units, entities, or "real things"? We might say that only individual human persons are real, and that all relations between individuals are attributes that cannot exist unless the individuals exist. Or we might say that no person can exist outside of relationships, like a child without parents or a man without a tribe or country. If the parents die, it is foster parents or death. If a man is exiled or deported, he must find some community to accept him. Under these circumstances we might say that the real entity is a community, small as a family or large as the human race, and that apart from these relations the individual is an abstraction, a thing thought but never found existing. We might, on the other hand, say that although there can be no individual without relations to others, that he is as real as a part can be and society is as real as a whole can be, still the truth is that neither can exist without the other. This third answer would deny absolute reality to either, but ascribe dependent reality to both.

Another metaphysical question is whether a society bears resemblance to an individual human being. The analogy, familiar in folklore, Plato, and fascism, is that society, in this case the state, is made up of members that resemble the physical parts or mental attributes of each man. We still talk metaphorically about heads of states and military arms of government. More modern myth-making developed in Hobbes, who compared individual man and the body politic to machines. If one calls an important leader of any group a wheel, imagination can lead to consideration of unimportant people as cogs. Other metaphors suggest vast speculations, for example, does each society live in the sense of developing through infancy, childhood, and youth, to maturity? Older societies and governments are said to hope that the American society and state will "mature."

This view that the state is an entity in the same sense that the individual human being is an entity has recently been challenged on linguistic grounds, that is, as a result of the misleading character of language. For example, consider these two statements, "England is brave" and "Socrates is brave." They look very much alike, but they behave linguistically in quite different ways, which can be brought out by analysis. The former means "Churchill is brave," "Eden is brave," "The pub-keeper on Madingley Road is brave," and so on for the great majority of Englishmen. Thus the "England" referred to in the first statement is not an entity or person but a shorthand expression for the multiple statements about individual Englishmen. So all statements of the form, "England loves," "England owes," "England trusts," "England respects," "England fights," "England votes," are really statements about what most or all individual Englishmen or their representatives do on certain occasions. The student will get some idea of how this analysis proceeds by reading Ryle's illustration of what he calls a category mistake.

A foreigner visiting Oxford or Cambridge for the first time is shown a number of colleges, libraries, playing fields, museums, scientific departments and administrative offices. He then asks 'But where is the University? I have seen where the members of the College live, where the Registrar works, where the scientists experiment and the rest. But I have not yet, seen the University in which reside and work the members of your University.' It has then to be explained to him that the University is not another collateral institution, some ulterior counterpart to the colleges, laboratories and offices which he has seen. The University is just the way in which all that he has already seen is organized. When they are seen and when their co-ordination is understood, the University has been seen. His mistakes lay in his innocent assumption that it was correct to speak of Christ Church, the Bodleian Library, the Ashmolean Museum *and* the University, to speak, that is, as if 'The University' stood for an extra member of the class of which these other units are members. He was mistakenly allocating the University to the same category as that to which other institutions belong.[1]

Although this analysis will apply to organizations of human beings, it fails when applied to men themselves. For one cannot say, "I have seen a snub nose, an enormous head, two bare feet, a shabby robe, and so on, so I have seen Socrates." For Socrates is something more than the parts of him that may be inventoried. The organization of the parts of a human being is not the same as the organization of the parts of a state, although it is not easy to bring out the differences. Mabbott has tried it in the following way:

When I say a State is happy, I mean that its citizens are happy; when I say a State is treacherous, I mean that its government is treacherous. But when I say a State is feudal or democratic or highly organized or well disciplined I do not mean that any particular persons have any of these characteristics. Here, however, analysis obviously reveals not *characteristics* of individuals but *relations* between them. For this reason it is again wrong to say that analysis treats a State or any other association as a mere aggregate. To say a state is feudal is to assert that there are certain relations between the individuals in it in virtue of their rank or status. There may, however, be a doubt whether relational statements completely eliminate a corporate unit. For example, it may be said that a human body is a unit as real as a cell and that cells behave as they do and are related as they are because they form part of a human body. The relations here may be held to be derivative and not ultimate. If, however, we apply this to organizational characteristics of an association, the parallel breaks down. Does the democratic character of a State account for the facts that its government is elected and keeps in touch with its people? Or is the statement that a State is democratic merely another way of stating these facts? Is it because an army is well disciplined that lower ranks obey orders unquestioningly? Or when we call an army well disciplined are we simply restating these relationships between higher and lower ranks? In each case the latter alternative is clearly the correct one. There is no further quality of democracy or discipline from which these

[1] From *The Concept of Mind*, by Gilbert Ryle, 1951, by permission of Hutchinson University Library, London, p. 16.

relationships are derived. Though a group of men united by such relationships is no mere aggregate, it is still not a new unit with curious characteristics of its own.[2]

It has been shown in these last few paragraphs how the analysis of language has recently been brought to bear on the problem of whether the State is an entity in addition to the units that make it up. It seems to be something more than a mere aggregate, that is, there are times when it makes sense to speak of its possessing certain characteristics that are not applicable to its parts. And yet it does not seem clear if we think of it as an entity in its own right. Each statement will require separate analysis, therefore, before we can say whether it does or does not apply to the kind of organization we call a state.

Some questions about human relations seem to be about matters of fact, answerable by knowing from experience the conduct of men. It is often debated whether a philosopher should attempt, as did Plato in the ancient world, and John Locke in the modern world, to engage in king-making and to make statements about the actual workings of society and state. Of course, we might say that there were no sociologists or political scientists when Plato lived, and that if he lived now he would be spared the descriptive work and could give his mind to pure philosophy. On the other hand, we could say that the question about the best ordering of society and the state is a moral and practical question to be answered from the actual workings of government. Political philosophy certainly runs grave risks either way. It may be on the one hand a poor substitute for professional work now done by the sciences of man, and on the other hand so remote from actuality that the speculations are irrelevant. There may be no ideal solution in programmatic form. But if the questions are about possible relations, then the philosopher may, as did Locke in his Letters On Toleration, hit upon a quite practicable scheme.

The most pertinent questions about human relations that are still the distinctive task of philosophers concern the definition of the nature of the state, considering its ends, and examining the meaning of the terms in the political vocabulary, which are largely moral, and in which we discuss the alternative beliefs. A convenient way to tie this up is to say that ancient and medieval philosophies of society attempted to define justice so that men could use this noun to clarify their beliefs about just and unjust laws, prices, and wars. Modern philosophers have tried to clarify the concepts of the rights of man and his liberty. The central notion that will be ex-

[2] From *The State and the Citizen*, by J. D. Mabbott, 1952, by permission of Hutchinson University Library, London, pp. 154–155.

amined here is obligation, that is, attention will be drawn to the question of why one should obey the state or any law of the state.

Section II attempts to show the need of, and the difficulties connected with the definition of certain key terms. Section III will deal with theories explaining political obligation. Section IV presents theories of the ideal state from four eminent political philosophers, each of whom wrote, in a different historical context, his conceptions of what the ideal state should be. The last section is a sketch of some logical barriers and pitfalls that prevent clear thinking on political matters.

II. Defining Key Political Terms

It is part of the task of political philosophers to define or clarify the key terms of their discourse. Aristotle's attention was directed to this problem by a dispute among his fellow Greeks. The question was raised whether a certain act was to be regarded as an act of the state or merely of its rulers. "What is a state?" he asks, and then offers a functional definition: A state is a composite made up of citizens, and a citizen is one who "shares in the administration of justice, and in offices." This definition states what the Athenian citizen actually did. But Aristotle was also the first to recognize some difficulties with this functional approach because, as he says, the citizens of some states "do not possess . . . such rights," they have "no legal right except that of suing and being sued." So when the definition is broadened to allow for more authoritarian kinds of government, we get the following: The state is "a body of citizens sufficing for the purpose of life."[3] This is of course so general that it would include among states associations such as the Church in medieval life, or the labor union in contemporary industrial society. Aristotle's difficulties in defining the state have proved perennial, and his comment, "At the present this is a disputed question . . . " is pertinent to most of the terms in a political vocabulary. But the prime value of political philosophy may be to urge men to inquire what they mean when they say, for example, "Nazi Germany was an unjust state," or "No citizen has a right to curtail the same freedom in others which he himself exercises."

Citizens whose legislators, executives, and judges hold their powers under a constitution, certainly believe there is value in defining the powers of the government and their own rights. It is extremely difficult to imagine how a government such as that of the United States could have been thought out apart from the discipline of political philosophy and a diligent

---

[3] Aristotle, *Politics* (B. Jowett, tr.), Modern Library, New York, 1942, pp. 125–127.

effort to define terms. As evidence we may cite the fact that in the political philosophers of the eighteenth century, notably in Montesquieu's Spirit of the Laws (1748), the powers of the state are classified as legislative, executive, and judicial, a pattern followed in Articles I, II, and III of the Constitution of the United States (1787). And Aristotle might well grant that in the Preamble there is expressed a fulfillment of his efforts, for the precise "purposes of life" that belong to the state are first put generally before their instrumentation in the articles.

We, the People of the United States, in order to form a more perfect Union, establish justice, insure domestic tranquillity, provide for the common defense, promote the general welfare, and secure the blessings of liberty to ourselves and our posterity, do ordain and establish this constitution for the United States of America.

Suppose we agree to give the name "state" to any association of men that does the kinds of things the United States does. That is, they are states if they can answer the following questions affirmatively: Do the people live as inhabitants of a geographical region within fixed boundaries? Does the government impose taxes, provide for defense, coin money, define and punish crimes, and in general regulate behavior by laws? Does it send ambassadors and in other ways establish relations with other governments? Is there an executive officer who makes appointments to offices not filled by election? Are there courts in which judges hear cases of controversy between citizens, and try those who have broken laws?

Not all of the tests will apply to every state, nor will those that are pertinent apply always in the same way or degree. But if we employed these criteria we should have little doubt that all members of the United Nations are states and exercise comparable powers, or have authority, as our constitution puts it.

It may be objected that the powers of some states are not derived from the people but from a belief that the processes of history coordinate to produce and justify them. This theory cannot be escaped on the pretence that it is merely speculative. It was held by Lenin. He thought that in the course of history, classes of men construct governments as instruments of economic power. When the middle class is supreme, the modern parliamentary states serve to protect private property and capitalism. But when the proletariat becomes supreme, the communist state will defend the corporate ownership of the means of production. The transition is made by meeting terror with terror. Such a state will not meet all of the tests we have suggested, but it will meet some, enough at least to be called a state.

This should make it clear to us that there is not a fixed number of characteristics that denominate a state. We can only agree on those that are obviously important, and then perhaps end every description with the abbreviation etc. Another way of accomplishing this is to distinguish between the defining characteristics of anything and the accompanying characteristics. The former are those characteristics without which the defined thing would not be named by a certain word. The latter are those characteristics without which the word or name would still be applied.

It would certainly be true to say that if one examines constitutional documents to find an answer to the question "What is a state?" one finds the question inextricably tied up with claims about "justice" and "right." The Colonists of 1776 did not deny that Great Britain was a state, but they did deny that its exercise of powers in the American Colonies was just and protected the rights of subjects. In the vocabulary of politics "These and other words of the same family are dependent on one another."[4]

Definitions of "Justice." Let us now consider the term justice. Certainly it is a key term in political thought and we will discover many alternative uses. We shall list and examine a number of these meanings and find that it is usually related to another term, rights.

It is sometimes said that a state is just—and men have rights—when it rules according to what is believed to be the will of God. The Declaration of Independence suggests this meaning in the words "endowed by their Creator with certain unalienable rights."

A related but sometimes independent doctrine is that the state is just and rights are protected when the state rules according to the laws of nature. These principles imply natural rights, that is, those rights any man, as man, can claim. The meaning is somewhat clarified if we remember that Socrates resisted the sophist reduction of justice to custom and the actual behavior of societies. His alternative was to consider some acts just even though no tradition had established them. They belonged to the nature of man, and he accused the sophists of being able to describe behavior while being ignorant of man's soul.

A state is sometimes said to be just and to respect men's rights when it governs in accordance with the established rules of a society. The terms just and right are then nearly synonyms for legal. George III was called unjust and a "usurper of rights" for depriving the Colonists "in many cases, of the benefits of trial by jury," and again, "for abolishing the free system of English laws. . . ."

[4] T. D. Weldon, *The Vocabulary of Politics,* Penguin Books, London, 1953, p. 45.

A state is sometimes called just and governing with respect to citizens' rights when punishment is meted out to fit the crime. The Colonists who drew up the Declaration of Independence regarded themselves punished for no crime at all. "He has called together legislative bodies at places unusual, uncomfortable, and distant from the depository of their public records, for the sole purpose of fatiguing them into compliance with his measures."

A state is sometimes called unjust and the rights of citizens invaded when acts are committed with partiality and not on the merits of the case. Thus the Colonists protested that the armed troops of Great Britain were protected by a "mock trial, from punishment for any murders which they should commit on the inhabitants of these States."

A state may be called unjust and a violator of rights when promises are not kept. In legal language we say that a contract has been broken or that one party has tried to escape some term of a contract unilaterally. This meaning too may be found in use by the writers of the Declaration of Independence. "He has forbidden his governors to pass laws . . . unless suspended in their operation till his assent should be obtained; and when so suspended, he has utterly neglected to attend to them." No doubt the sovereign felt he had not promised or contracted, but the Colonists felt he had. Perhaps apart from these subjective features of opinion, a more objective judgment of breach of contract is this: "For taking away our charters, abolishing our most valuable laws, and altering fundamentally the forms of our governments."

Failure to do what one ought to do and to provide what one ought to provide, that is, what is *due to* other persons, is also used as a definition of unjust. If one supposes that a ruler ought to protect his subjects and owes protection to their persons and property, then another allegation in the Declaration of Independence can be interpreted according to this meaning: "He has abdicated government here, by declaring us out of his protection and waging war against us. He has plundered our seas, ravaged our coasts, burned our towns, and destroyed the lives of our people."

Unjust may be a word used to condemn the interference in the achievement of what people regard as a good, or the prevention of reaching certain satisfactions. This meaning would probably interpret correctly the following: "He has endeavored to prevent the Population of these States; for that purpose obstructing the Laws for Naturalization of Foreigners; refusing to pass others to encourage their migrations hither, and raising the conditions of new Appropriations of Lands." And again, "For cutting off our trade with all parts of the world." Surely, if being just includes achieving some good, and a means to this is commerce, then the Colonists were right in their accusation.

If to be just means also to be merciful, as Christian philosophers insisted, then the Colonists were right in denouncing the following acts as unjust: "He has constrained our fellow-citizens taken captive on the high seas to bear arms against their country, to become the executioners of their friends and brethren, or to fall themselves by their hands. He has excited domestic insurrections amongst us, and has endeavored to bring on the inhabitants of our frontiers the merciless Indian savages, whose known rule of warfare is an undistinguished destruction of all ages, sexes, and conditions."

A final meaning of the word just to be mentioned is that found in Plato's Republic. His views will be discussed more extensively in Section IV, but this much may be presented here. Suppose that a state is made up of men who have various special abilities. Some, for example, produce more houses and clothes and shoes than they can themselves use. (Others need these things because they cannot produce enough.) Then there are others who have courage and training sufficient to defend the state. And still others are wise in the ways of ruling. A state that will provide the satisfactions for all these different abilities is just. Hence justice means the harmony and completeness of the whole society.

We have not tried to explore all the possible meanings of the terms just and right. But the student should see by now the difficulties of settling on any one meaning. From some of these meanings, political structures have been elaborated. Although the point of departure was the Declaration of Independence, it would be possible to find other political documents that accept as basic one or more of these interpretations.

Definitions of "Free." Another term of great importance for political philosophy is free and its relatives freedom and liberty. To illustrate its various uses in political theory we shall take the classic speech of Edmund Burke on "Conciliation with America." The very words tend to rouse in us such passion that we are prepared either to rise against an enemy, or to sneer that free means "capricious" and that freedom and liberty are "lawless license" or "sheer anarchy." In precisely what respects are men or governments free? What do we mean when we use these words in the statements of political beliefs? These questions point to a significant function of political philosophers.

Edmund Burke usually dealt with concrete issues as they came for decision to the British Parliament, and except for a work in aesthetics, took pride in meddling "with no theory." One of his classic speeches, however, is not only a model of rhetoric, but the work of an able logician. That is, if we can call a man a logician who tries to specify the various meanings of ambiguous words. The speech on Conciliation with America has been almost too popular in America, giving the generations that followed the Revolution the satisfaction of believing their cause justified by the most eminent political philosopher of his age and nation. Let us turn to this speech to illustrate from only one document the many possible definitions of political freedom.

The term free is sometimes used to refer to a quality of mind as in the phrases "spirit of liberty," or "love of freedom," which Burke ascribes to the "character of the Americans." This seems to refer to enterprise and courage in seeking the fulfillment of their ambitions.

The term free also applies to choice, as in the phrase "of their own election." We say, as Burke did, "I do not choose" when we are confronted with alternative acts and wish to reject one in favor of the other. In his case there seemed to be two courses open, war or peace. He chose the latter. Human history is not regarded as strictly determined, which makes it possible for man's actions and judgments to play an important role. The concept of choice is basic to the governmental notion of election of representatives, which also implies the power of refusal, or the ability to say no.

Certain acts of persons or associations of persons are sometimes designated as free. The negation of a free act is one done under "coercion and restraint" where we may be put under pressure to do what someone demands. This is the condition of those who are, says Burke, "captivated." The opposite of acting under restraint is acting by consent, or as we sometimes say, voluntarily. Burke points out that the Colonies had "the power of granting their own money" and although they might have granted none, they were more generous than when taxes were levied upon them.

The term free applies not only to minds, choices, and acts but to those who are not in a condition of servitude or slavery. Of the citizens of Virginia and the Carolinas, Burke says, "Freedom is to them not only an enjoyment, but a kind of rank and privilege." There are, as Burke recognizes, economic and cultural differences between masters and slaves, but the legal difference is that the slaves lack enfranchisement. They cannot be owners of themselves. This is clearly another use or meaning of freedom.

Systems of laws may also be considered free. Indeed, Burke refers to "laws and liberties." This may seem confused because free often means unlimited or uncontrolled behavior, while law suggests restraints. Burke, always concrete, refers to the Welsh who were "free" in their resistance to the laws of England that prohibited arms. But then "an Englishman traveling in that country could not go six yards from the high road without being murdered." These laws were, says Burke, "penal regulation." Parliament, however, granted the Welsh a "share in the fundamental security of these liberties," the "rights and privileges of English subjects." The Welsh participated in enacting the laws, and Burke's criterion is now clear. A law to be genuine is one that the inhabitants of a land have a part in enacting, or have the opportunity to amend or repeal. Then there is freedom. Lawless relations produce both anarchy and tyranny; anarchy because no one is regularly obeyed, tyranny because the strongest rules by strength alone. Man can be free yet obedient when the system of laws rests on consent.

Governments, as well as laws, may be considered free. Burke, for example, contrasts "free government" to "military government." The question seems to be one of authority and power. If one supposes that government depends solely upon coercion and that the authority to govern implies sending agents from an established state to rule over a colony, then says Burke, another source of authority is missed. "Until very lately, all authority in America seemed to be nothing but an emanation" from the British Parliament. But "this new government has originated directly from the people." "Obedience is what makes government. . . ." But why do men obey? Burke suggests that "all government is founded on compromise and barter. We balance inconveniences; we give and take; we remit some rights that we may enjoy others; and we choose rather to be happy citizens than subtle disputants." Free government does mean for Burke that the price is not too high, that is, at the cost of a man's soul, "all his essential rights, and all the intrinsic dignity of human nature." But free government does not mean a government that can be achieved without the sacrifice of some natural or civil liberties. Exactly what liberties are to be sacrificed, and for what, Burke fails to specify. But the principle is clear—if every man is to be protected from murder, then all must be prohibited from murdering.

The relations between governments and their peoples may be designated free. That is, there is a sense in which acts of government can be free toward citizens, and citizens free toward government. The state may be the supreme or sovereign authority but as such it may grant "privilege and immunities," "exemption . . . from the ordinary exercise of supreme authority." Burke's point is that the ideal is to "accede to the desires of

. . . discontented subjects," to remove "causes of dissatisfaction." Such generosity establishes a "mutual relation." The citizens then enjoy privileges and identify "civil rights" with the state. The attachment people have to the government springs "from the deep stake they have in such a glorious institution. . . ." The obedience is then "liberal." The word free in this case seems to mean giving better than one receives and more than could be bargained for. In this sense a free act is gracious, in doing more than the legal minimum and demanding less than the legal maximum. Burke's central point is that a wise state employs conciliation and avoids force.

The people may be referred to as free. Burke speaks, as we do, of "the free community" and a "free country." He seems to have three criteria by which to distinguish "a people sensible of freedom" from the opposite. First, each man has a "deep stake" in a nation's wealth and political institutions. He notes "that sense of dignity and that security to property, which ever attends freedom, has a tendency to increase the stock of the free community," and that "the voluntary flow of heaped-up plenty" in the economic aspect is paralleled by willingness to serve in governmental institutions. Second, since "whatever is got" in a free country is not "got by acts of absolute power," therefore among the citizens who contribute to the common stock there is no single plan for dividing rewards. Political "parties must ever exist in a free country." Third, Burke uses the term to designate a people's whole way of life. What they love and worship creates bonds and ties in the community that cannot be manufactured by law or external governmental control. But without good intention, "the cement is gone, the cohesion loosened, and everything hastens to decay and dissolution."

Finally, we find Burke using the word free with reference to the relations between countries. Two countries may be in the relation of absolute subordination, one to the other, where one commands and the other obeys, as against the relationship of "undivided unity." Burke calls free the relationship of "separate but not . . . independent." His criterion is that the mother country may grant liberty to the superintended country when the latter develops in its own way the capability to exercise its own authority. The implication is that there may be freedom and liberty of countries within an empire short of complete severing of the bonds. The notion of separate parliamentary governments with a common head or sovereign foreshadows the change from the British Empire to the Commonwealth of Nations. The Dominion of Canada differs from the United States of

America on precisely this point. The former is based on the doctrine that a country may be free without being independent, the latter that it cannot be free without being independent.

These various meanings of the term free found in one great political document certainly do not exhaust all the possible uses of the word. But this should be sufficient to show how necessary it is to refrain from using it loosely and to spell out carefully and distinctly what it means in any given context. It also should make clear that there is not a God-given or single definition of the term. Its meaning is given by men who use it to call attention to certain features of their beliefs. What these features are must be determined in each case, else we do not know what we believe or what we are talking about. There is a great deal of loose speech about freedom, and because it is loose it appeals to the emotions rather than to the intellect. Clear thinking requires that we specify what aspects of human experience we wish to achieve or avoid before we engage in controversy or warfare about abstract "freedom."

Before leaving this term, we should call attention to a distinction often found in ordinary language between "free from" and "free to." Even in Burke's oration this distinction can be discerned. To be free from something certainly suggests that whatever it is we are free from, our situation is improved when that something is absent or lacking. For example, we speak of being free from disease, or poverty, or worry. This particular expression also fits references to things, for example, a detergent is said to be free from irritants, or a house is free from termites. In these cases, aims, purposes, choices, are not thought to be present in the things. But the expression "free to" carries the connotation of understanding and real choice between alternatives. It seems applicable only to beings with minds. And yet to be "free to" does not ordinarily mean the absence of those relations that make any choice effective. In short, if we are to be free to do some act, or to decide between alternatives, we must also recognize that a certain order of relationship is required if the event is to be actualized. Freedom to does not imply an existence apart from the very relations necessary to make the intended act or choice possible. Therefore, it seems to make sense to say that in our political beliefs we must retain the meanings of both "free from" and "free to," which means that purpose, creativity, intention, value, and ideal are also vital terms in political theory. They cannot all be dealt with here, and the discussion must be limited to the critical term obligation. This will be treated separately because it will enable us to deal with some important theoretical questions and lead directly into some relevant historical considerations.

III. Theories Explaining Political Obligation

It has been said that when people live in the same time and share the same places, where "places" refers to certain geographical boundaries, there is established among them a variety of relationships, some of which give to one or more individuals a position of leadership, authority, and responsibility over some aspects of the lives of all persons within the defined geographical limits. Let us use the term sovereign to cover all such instances of authority at the political level. Then we may ask the question, "Why do we have any obligation to obey a sovereign, in whatever institution that sovereignty lies?" or "Why should we accept a situation in which the relations between us and some other person restrict our liberty or freedom?" The beliefs people hold in answer to these questions constitute their attempts to explain political obligation.

1. *The Social-Contract Theory.*

One family of such beliefs is known as the social-contract theory. This theory is as old as Plato and has a long history through the Middle Ages into the Modern era. Its fullest development, perhaps, came in the seventeenth and eighteenth centuries, with the work of Locke, Hobbes, and Rousseau. Let each speak for himself. Locke writes in the Treatise of Civil Government:

Men being, as has been said, by nature all free, equal, and independent, no one can be put out of this estate, and subjected to the political power of another, without his own consent, which is done by agreeing with other men to join and unite into a community for their comfortable, safe, and peaceable living one amongst another, in a secure enjoyment of their properties, and a greater security against any that are not of it.[5]

Hobbes in the Leviathan writes:

That a man be willing, when others are so too, as farre-forth, as for Peace, and defence of himselfe we shall think it necessary, to lay down this right to all things; and be contented with so much liberty against other men, as he would allow other men against himselfe. . . .[6]
The mutual transferring of Right, is that which men call *Contract*.[7]

And Rousseau in The Social Contract:

Now, since men can by no means engender new powers, but can only unite and control those of which they are already possessed, there is no way in

---

[5] John Locke, *Treatise of Civil Government and a Letter Concerning Toleration*, Appleton-Century-Crofts, Inc., New York, 1937, p. 63.
[6] Thomas Hobbes, *Leviathan*, Cambridge University Press, Cambridge, 1904, p. 87.
[7] *Ibid.*, p. 102.

which they can maintain themselves save by coming together and pooling their strength in a way that will enable them to withstand any resistance exerted upon them from without. They must develop some sort of central direction and learn to act in concert.

Such a concentration of powers can be brought about only as the consequence of an agreement reached between individuals.[8]

It is clear that a contract is an agreement, sometimes called a covenant, between at least two parties, although it is not always clear what the two parties are. Thus the contract may be between first, the people and the government; second, individuals with other individuals; or third, both together. In any case the idea of the contract implies a transaction in which something of value is exchanged at a cost. D'Entrèves puts it this way:

"Formally," the contract is a manifestation of individual will with the object of establishing a relationship of mutual obligation which would not otherwise exist by the law of nature. "Substantially," the content of the contract is the "natural right" of the individual, which is exchanged against a counterpart of equal or greater value—the benefits of society and the security of political organization. The social contract may effect a complete transformation of the original right, as is the case with Hobbes and Rousseau. Or it may leave that right unaltered, and have no other purpose than to secure it, as Locke was anxious to maintain. But in all cases the contract is the necessary pattern of all legal and political obligations.[9]

In each case the contract theory is related to two other important ideas, namely, a theory of human nature, and a theory of natural law and rights. When men are thought to be by nature belligerent and savage, then they may be brought around to decent behavior by realizing that mutual destruction will occur if they follow their natural tendencies. By compact they may agree to respect each other's rights and give over some of their claims to a sovereign, whose function it is to protect the people and keep order. Or, on the other hand, if men are naturally virtuous and charitable, then a contract might be unnecessary, except that a few have grown away from a state of original friendliness and become the attackers. From these society needs protection, and the contract is the way to it.

No adequate grasp of the contract theory is possible if one forgets that it is supported by beliefs about human nature. No less basic, however, is the notion of natural law and natural rights. It is not easy to say just what men believe in when they believe in natural rights. There seem to be many

[8] J.-J. Rousseau, *The Social Contract,* Oxford University Press, London, 1948, pp. 179–180.
[9] A. P. D'Entrèves, *Natural Law,* Hutchinson's University Library, London, 1951, p. 57.

traditions in which the same term is used, but that does not indicate a common meaning. We may find it less difficult to say what natural law is not than to say what it is. For example, it is not law in the sense that any human being has promulgated it, or passed upon it. Nor is it law in the sense of physical law as used in the sciences; natural law is strictly concerned with human conduct but, its origin is non-human, that is, in God or nature. At the very least we can say that when men have believed in natural law they have been trying to express two convictions—first, the universe is such that it provides a common moral basis for human action; and second, that there is a relation between law and morality. It is this relationship that is stressed in some of the great documents of political history, for instance, the American Declaration of Independence, the French Declaration des Droits de l'Homme, and the United Nations Declaration of Human Rights.

The contract theory of political obligation is one of those theories in human history that persists despite the difficulties of the view, and the severe criticisms with which it has been charged. Moreover, like other theories, it has had actual political effects, that is, men have behaved *as if* there had been a contract established. It is frequently thought a critical blow against this theory to point out that at no time in history was any contract made, that the contract is mythological in origin, and that it would be ridiculous to look for an original document. But this criticism seems to miss the point. It is certainly doubtful if any of the contract theorists ever thought that there was a time in history when a contract was signed; or that they even regarded such a historical event as relevant to the theory. The contract idea is a kind of analogy drawn from human experience to give a basis for understanding political obligation. In essence it says that the *kind of relationship* we establish between two parties in a contract is similar to the relationship we have as individuals to the government. A better form of criticism, therefore, would be to spell out the relationships that we know exist between two parties of a contract, and compare them with what we think are our relationships to the state or government, and see what the similarities and differences are. The contract theory, for example, is certainly one way of saying that the relationship between governed and government is not asymmetrical, that is, there may be instances when the breaking of the contract by one of the two parties is justifiable. This can happen when either one of the parties fails to conform to its agreement. Even Hobbes releases the individual from obligation to the state if the state is unable to provide and maintain his security.

2. The State as a Higher Entity.

The social-contract theory is not the only theory of political obligation. Another view to be found in the literature interprets the State as a system of law and order which represents the "higher" self: My incompleteness is completed in the State; my "real" will finds expression in the State and is opposed to my egocentric will; my individuality finds a greater value in the whole State than it does in the separate parts which compose it. Here the relations that tie the parts together form an organism in which the sum of the parts cannot be identified with the whole.

Again let us turn to the words of three political theorists for a description of this position. The first is from Burke.

Society is indeed a contract. Subordinate contracts, for objects of mere occasional interest, may be dissolved at pleasure; but the state ought not to be considered as nothing better than a partnership agreement in a trade of pepper and coffee, callico or tobacco, or some other such low concern, to be taken up for a little temporary interest, and to be dissolved by the fancy of the parties. It is to be looked on with other reverence; because it is not a partnership in things subservient only to the gross animal existence of a temporary and perishable nature. It is a partnership in all science; a partnership in all art; a partnership in every virtue, and in all perfection. As the ends of such a partnership cannot be obtained in many generations, it becomes a partnership not only between those who are living, but between those who are dead, and those who are to be born. Each contract of each particular state is but a clause in the great primaeval contract of eternal society, linking the lower with the higher natures, connecting the visible and invisible world, according to a fixed compact sanctioned by the inviolable oath which holds all physical and moral natures, each in their appointed place.[10]

The second is from Hegel.

The state is the actuality of the ethical Idea. It is ethical mind *qua* the substantial will manifest and revealed to itself, knowing and thinking itself, accomplishing what it knows and in so far as it knows it. The state exists immediately in custom, mediately in individual self-consciousness, knowledge, and activity, while self-consciousness in virtue of its sentiment towards the state finds in the state, as its essence and the end and product of its activity, its substantive freedom. . . .

The state is absolutely rational inasmuch as it is the actuality of the substantial will which it possesses in the particular self-consciousness once that consciousness has been raised to consciousness of its universality. This substantial unity is an absolute unmoved end in itself, in which freedom comes into

[10] Edmund Burke, *Select Works* (E. J. Payne, ed.), The Clarendon Press, Oxford, 1898, Vol. II, pp. 113–114.

its supreme right. On the other hand this final end has supreme right against the individual, whose supreme duty is to be a member of the state.[11]

The third is from Bernard Bosanquet.

We have seen that Self-Government can only be explained if the centre of gravity of the self is thrown outside what we are continually tempted to reckon as our individuality, and if we recognise as our real being, and therefore as imperative upon us, a self and a good which are but slightly represented in our explicit consciousness, at its ordinary level. . . .[12]

Thus, we have seen that the mind, and society or the State are identical in the characteristic of being organisations, each composed of a system of organisations, every superior and subordinate grouping having its own nature and principle which determines its members as such, and everyone, consequently, tending to impose upon its members a peculiar capacity or point of view, which, in so far as a given system is active, tends to put all other systems out of sight. . . .[13]

We thus see once more that the given individual is only in making, and that his reality may lie largely outside him. His will is not a whole, but implies and rests upon a whole, which is therefore the true nature of his will.[14]

This is not to suggest that all of these views of the state are identical, but they do have in common a theory of political obligation based on the concept of a state as an entity superior to the individual to which the individual has a moral duty. The vagueness of the language, the kinds of terms used to describe the state, and the emotional appeal to one's better or "higher" self, make it extremely difficult to say just what this superior being is, and what precisely is the nature of our duty toward it. It is not much help to be told that my moral duty is one which my "real" self sets up for myself. I know a good deal about my empirical self; at least I know how to go about getting the information. But how do I acquire knowledge about this "higher" self? Not by any of the fairly well-established methods of procedure. This looks as if I would have to be blessed by some knowledge gained in some unusual way.

But is the state as a superior organism an object of knowledge at all? Are not the terms organism, superior being, higher self, convenient metaphors, hence very misleading if taken literally? For example, if the state is an organism in the sense that, say, a horse is an organism, would any government be needed? That is, all the necessary vital parts would appear in

[11] G. Hegel, *Hegel's Philosophy of Right* (T. M. Knox, tr.), The Clarendon Press, Oxford, 1945, pp. 155–156.

[12] Bernard Bosanquet, *The Philosophical Theory of the State*, Macmillan and Co., Ltd., London, reprinted 1930, p. 145.

[13] *Ibid.*, p. 158.

[14] *Ibid.*, p. 165.

the natural processes of growth, and one part would not quarrel with another.

What these views are trying to express may be put this way: The relations men have with each other are internal rather than external. But again the language is unclear. There are various meanings of internal and external when applied to relationships.

However, at least this much is being said, namely, that my relations to others, and their relations to me are such that the characteristics I possess and they possess could not possibly occur without these relations. But although this could certainly be established for some characteristics, it seems patently false for others. For example, the fact that I have friendly relations with someone is not at all determined by the fact that this person lives exactly 200 miles east of me. Friendship does not determine distance, nor distance friendship.

Furthermore, the view of the state as an exalted and sublime being is difficult to reconcile with a theory of the importance of man's individuality and his freedom. To be a slave of any kind, willing or unwilling, moral or immoral, is repulsive. A state that rides over me as a tyranny or absorbs me in the relations of an organism, is denying me something men have tried to save on the long, tortuous road out of the wilderness. This something, vague as it is, is the belief in the dignity and liberty and self-direction of the individual man.

3. *The Theistic Theory of the State.*

Two other theories of political obligation will be mentioned briefly. The first affirms that man is bound to the state because he is bound by a higher law and a supreme being—the eternal law of God. Although the state exists for the good of individuals, this good is impossible to obtain without some relations of authority and obedience. The ultimate authority and source of power is God. Under his providential care we are governed by an eternal law that makes for our happiness. But God delegates by divine command certain functions to rulers to enable them to help the members of society arrive at their proper places and realize their proper ends. The best illustration is from St. Thomas Aquinas:

Now wherever there are movers ordained to one another, the power of the second mover must need be derived from the power of the first mover, since the second mover does not move except in so far as it is moved by the first. Therefore we observe the same in all those who govern, namely, that the plan of government is derived by secondary governors from the governor in chief. Thus the plan of what is to be done in a state flows from the king's command to his inferior administrators; and again in things of art the plan of whatever is to be done by art flows from the chief craftsman to the under-craftsmen who work with their hands. Since, then, the eternal law is the plan of government in the Chief Governor, all the plans of government in the inferior governors must be derived from the eternal law. But these plans of inferior governors are all the other laws which are in addition to the eternal law. Therefore all laws, in so far as they partake of right reason, are derived from the eternal law. Hence Augustine says that *in temporal law there is nothing just and lawful but what man has drawn from the eternal law.*[15]

This belief concerning men's political obligation rests, of course, upon another belief in a Supreme Governor or Providence. To this Power we have not only a moral duty but a religious duty also, that is, to know and love Him. This is our highest fulfillment and our true end. If any ruler, who receives his authority from God, fails to carry out the divine commands and becomes unjust, or makes it impossible for his people to actualize their final ends, such a ruler may be deposed. But this would be an extreme case. For the most part, the state and all its administrators are conceived not as merely human creations, but as products of Divine Reason to which all creatures owe submission.

This theory, although briefly sketched, obviously depends upon a belief in a God. If such a belief collapses, so does the theory. It is not possible to deal here with problems concerning God's existence, although they will be discussed in Chapter X. It is sufficient to point out now that any theory that interprets man's political obligations in terms of a non-human power will tend to justify the *status quo* and make it difficult for individual men to speak out against their governors when the governors have been unable to distinguish between themselves and God. Nor is it clear why some final, ultimate end of man is required in order to make sense out of his political obligations. Our political life is an earthly affair and its concerns have to do with the needs of this life. If God has man's existence fixed in detail, then there can be no meaning to obligation; if He has not, then our relations in society are our affairs, freely reasoned, and freely chosen. When these relations fail to fill our needs, it is our failure; when they succeed, this is our reward.

4. The Utilitarian Theory.

Another view that will be discussed very briefly is known as the utilitarian theory. The representative statements, will be drawn from the works of two British philosophers, David Hume and Jeremy Bentham. The former writes as follows:

[15] From *Basic Writings of Saint Thomas Aquinas* (ed. by Anton C. Pegis) Copyright 1945 by Random House, Inc. Reprinted by permission.

Had every man sufficient *sagacity* to perceive, at all times, the strong interest which binds him to the observance of justice and equity, and *strength of mind* sufficient to persevere in a steady adherence to a general and a distant interest, in opposition to the allurements of present pleasure and advantage; there had never, in that case, been any such thing as government or political society, but each man, following his natural liberty, had lived in entire peace and harmony with all others. What need of positive law where natural justice is, of itself, a sufficient restraint? Why create magistrates, where there never arises any disorder or iniquity? Why abridge our native freedom, when, in every instance, the utmost exertion of it is found innocent and beneficial? It is evident, that, if government were totally useless, it never could have place, and that the sole foundation of the duty of allegiance is the *advantage*, which it procures to society, by preserving peace and order among mankind.[16]

Bentham took from Hume the name for his general principle, and wrote the following:

Nature has placed mankind under the governance of two sovereign masters, *pain* and *pleasure*. It is for them alone to point out what we ought to do, as well as to determine what we shall do. On the one hand the standard of right and wrong, on the other the chain of causes and effects, are fastened to their throne. They govern us in all we do, in all we say, in all we think: every effort we can make to throw off our subjection, will serve but to demonstrate and confirm it. In words a man may pretend to abjure their empire: but in reality he will remain subject to it all the while. The *principle of utility* recognizes this subjection, and assumes it for the foundation of that system, the object of which is to rear the fabric of felicity by the hands of reason and of law. Systems which attempt to question it, deal in sounds instead of sense, in caprice instead of reason, in darkness instead of light.[17]

The utilitarian view of the state is a pragmatic justification of political obligation as long as the state provides the means and the goods for the satisfaction of one's numerous impulses and desires. In Bentham's terminology, the state must be ordered in such a way as to preserve the greatest happiness for the greatest number. If the state fails to do this one is entitled to rebel.

The simplicity and plausibility of this view, though deceptive, is certainly in its favor. It is not until we ask for criteria of happiness; or whether all human motivation is adequately explained by the principles of seeking happiness and avoiding pain; or whether it follows that one is justified in obeying all the laws of the state even if all his impulses are satisfied; or whether the state could possibly provide the conditions for

---

[16] David Hume, *An Enquiry Concerning the Principles of Morals*, The Open Court Publishing Co., La Salle, Illinois, p. 39.

[17] Jeremy Bentham, *An Introduction to the Principles of Morals and Legislation*, Hafner Publishing Co., Inc., New York, 1948, pp. 1–2.

all one's innumerable desires, that doubts begin to arise. It may be objected that these questions fail to bring out that it is the social good, not the individual good, that the utilitarians stress. But this is only partly true. Strictly, it is the individual that is happy, not the community. And when the social good is stressed, we have the further difficulty of trying to say what this good is that should be promoted by the state. The position suggests that the state is like an organization with a definite object in view, which it alone can provide. But when this object or aim is given as one principle, for example, happiness, much confusion arises.

5. *A Theory of the Common Good.*

A recent attempt to say more carefully what the state can do and what one's obligation is appeared in a splendid volume by J. D. Mabbott.[18] His position may be stated as follows: Though we speak of the social or common good, there are situations in which there is something good and common, but this does not give a basis for community. And yet there is a sense in which the phrase social or common good can be used meaningfully, namely, when

. . . the good itself at last ceases to be private in its nature but is a state of affairs involving relations between individuals, a state of affairs intrinsically social. Here the social relations are not means or machinery for the production of good but themselves the good at which men aim. If five men co-operate to help a sixth it is probable that he will be helped more efficiently, but besides this advantage there will come into existence the condition of willing co-operation, which is itself intrinsically good. . . .[19] [But still a word of caution is necessary.] Here we seem to find the clearest case of all for a 'common good'. Yet even here we must insert our safeguards. There need in these cases be no 'community,' wherever A and B trust each other, C and D show mutual sympathy, E and F co-operate, these states of affairs are all intrinsically good. So 'common good' (if it means the good of the community) is still a phrase with no application. It may well be true that the existence of an association, by providing a permanent basis for them, may heighten and diversify these good human relationships, yet the association is still only a means to the production of good.[20]

Mabbott's defense of political obligation, then, turns upon his belief that there are certain intrinsic values that the state, as an association whose law is supported by force, can provide. He does not define "intrinsic value" although he names some of those about which he is sure, for example, friendliness, sympathy, cooperation, and health. Moreover, Mabbott does not deny that these values may be achieved by human beings in

[18] From *The State and the Citizen*, by J. D. Mabbott, 1950, by permission of Hutchinson University Library, London.
[19] *Ibid.*, pp. 91–92.
[20] *Ibid.*, p. 92.

other associations or without membership in any association. But the state can aid in the achieving of these ends and it can also provide other values not easily gained in any other way.

What are these? Mabbott thinks there are at least six. Briefly, they are:

1. Security of life.
2. Social conduct, usually fixed by law or even generally accepted principles of courtesy.
3. Settlement of disputes either by law or by arbitration.
4. Provision of the conditions for health, transportation (roads) and education.
5. Economic action in relation to some individuals, that is, for those who cannot support themselves—the old, infirm, children, and unemployed.
6. Economic action in relation to certain industries.

There may also be occasions that justify state action with reference to agriculture, manufacturing, and so on. No a priori grounds for state action can be established, and each case must be based on factual inquiry. But *laissez faire* is ruled out.

Mabbott, then, justifies political obligation on moral grounds, for the state can be the means to intrinsic values. When this is possible, sacrifice for the state is morally right.

6. *Summary.*

It is important to see that in this discussion of political obligation it has been assumed that we can ask not only, "Why should we obey *this* law?" but that this leads us to another question we can significantly ask, namely, "Why should we obey *any* law?" But this gets us into serious difficulty. Recent work in philosophy has brought out the nature of the problem.[21] We can understand clearly enough how to apply a criterion to any given law or state, but to ask for criteria for *any* law or *any* state is to misuse language.

If after applying the tests for any particular law and finding that in each case the test is successful, that is, we find some basis for obligation, or we do not, but we still ask whether or not we have political obligation in general, then we do not know what we are asking. For suppose we ask why we should pay income tax. We may answer that it is a law passed by a government to which we have at least indirectly given our consent. Or we may answer that the tax enables the government to provide goods otherwise unobtainable. And so on for any given law. But if from this we

---

[21] For example see Margaret Macdonald, "The Language of Political Theory." In: Antony Flew, ed., *Essays on Logic and Language*, First Series, Blackwell, Oxford, 1951, pp. 167ff.

continue to ask for the basis of political obligation as such, then the distinction between law and non-law breaks down in the language, and we are left without a significant term to describe even the income-tax situation. In short, attempts to reduce political obligation to a single formula cannot succeed, for the language becomes too vague and ambiguous. The role of the political philosopher, in moments of particular crises, therefore, is not to give general information about political obligation, but to call our attention to criteria that in the present circumstances are forgotten, overlooked, or denied, but which must be acknowledged if the values associated with liberty, justice, and good-will are to be achieved.

It is not suggested that the social-contract theory, or the organic view of the state, or the utilitarian conception of the state's function are entirely useless, and certainly it is not the intention of the authors to mark them as false, nor, it should be added, as true. Each tries to bring to our understanding some aspect of human relationships that are politically important and that we need, as the occasion requires, to recognize and defend. For example, with the contract theory we keep alive the idea of the consent of the governed, with the organic view the idea of our interdependence is held before us, and utilitarianism will not let us forget that the state must meet some of the needs of individuals, and is better thought of as a means rather than an end.

IV. Theories of the Ideal State

Aristotle begins Book Two of his Politics with this sentence: "Our purpose is to consider what form of political community is best of all for those who are most able to realize their ideal of life." This leads him to a detailed comparison of the constitutions of various states. In this chapter a rather less ambitious project is attempted. The beginning student ought to know something about the great classic systems that have been constructed to define an ideal state, but it is not possible to deal adequately here with the extensive literature on utopias. Therefore, three views have been selected, each of them a product of one of the three periods we have used to divide the history of philosophy. Each is also expressed in a document that has become a classic in the field. The first is from ancient philosophy, Plato's Republic; the second from medieval philosophy, Dante's De Monarchia; and the third belongs to the modern period, Kant's Perpetual Peace. We have also included a brief statement from Hobbes' Leviathan.

That men have become engaged in building ideal states is not strange. There is always before us the contrast of the "is" and the "ought." Any actual world is burdened with pain and deprivation from which we would escape if possible. One way of escaping is to think out an ideal condition for men which not only eliminates evils but brings positive goods. We may never be able to achieve the better world we desire, but at least it will help us to improve the one we can do something about. "Without vision the people perish." It would take a long, difficult, empirical study to determine the extent to which "ideal states" have actually influenced the practical sciences of improving our lot. But it is probably safe to say, without making such a study, that their effect and power have been active in every generation.

A. Plato's Republic

This magnificent achievement of the creative intellect is so filled with insights and issues and arguments that it might serve as an introductory text in philosophy as well as a document needing mature and advanced minds for analysis. Here practically all the great questions of philosophy, religion, ethics, politics, sociology, education, and so on are raised and given an answer. This indeed is a consequence of Plato's view. It must not be thought, however, that Plato's theories have been free from attack. He has his detractors as well as his defenders. But the details of controversy will be left to the experienced. The present task is largely descriptive, after which, a few critical comments will be in order.

It will perhaps reinforce the contention that the contrast between the "is" and the "ought" is one reason for the construction of ideal states, if we remember that Plato was a young man when Athens was defeated by Sparta. He was also an Athenian aristocrat occupying a highly favorable position in society. The great cultural flowering of his city gave promise of even a more magnificent future, when the unbelievable occurred—the physical, brute power of another city crushed the life of his beloved Athens. Thus there comes the problem, how such tragedy could be avoided, not only for Athens, but for any state. What must any state do to be assured of its survival and still be able to provide the life best for the individuals? Plato's answer is the Republic. But in his Seventh Letter he recalls the pessimism and bitterness he felt when Athens' leaders failed to take the course that would provide for a good life and lead to her recovery.

When, therefore, I considered all this and the type of men who were administering the affairs of State, with their laws too and their customs, the more I considered them and the more I advanced in years myself, the more difficult appeared to me the task of managing the affairs of State rightly. For it was impossible to take action without friends and trusty companions; and these it was not easy to find ready to hand, since our State was no longer managed according to the principles and institutions of our forefathers; while to acquire other new friends with any facility was a thing impossible. Moreover, both the written laws and the customs were being corrupted, and that with surprising rapidity. Consequently, although at first I was filled with an ardent desire to engage in public affairs, when I considered all this and saw how things were shifting about anyhow in all directions, I finally became dizzy; and although I continued to consider by what means some betterment could be brought about not only in these matters but also in the government as a whole, yet as regards political action I kept constantly waiting for an opportune moment; until, finally, looking at all the States which now exist, I perceived that one and all they are badly governed; for the state of their laws is such as to be almost incurable without some marvelous overhauling and good-luck to boot. So in my praise of the right philosophy I was compelled to declare that by it one is enabled to discern all forms of justice both political and individual. Wherefore the classes of mankind (I said) will have no cessation from evils until either the class of those who are right and true philosophers attains political supremacy, or else the class of those who hold power in the States becomes, by some dispensation of Heaven, really philosophic.[22]

Plato's early disgust and disappointment with politics did not keep him from taking part in reform and king-making at a later date, nor did it turn him away from the more abstract task of setting forth a theory of human relationships and of a government that can be called an ideal republic or state.

It is perhaps best to begin with what many people of his own day, as well as ours, think is his most absurd proposal, namely that philosophers should be rulers, and rulers philosophers. Before laughing this out of court we ought to ask what he means by philosopher. Certainly not a college professor. In his Dialogues Plato presents a number of different conceptions of the philosopher, but from the Republic the following description is derived: It begins with the statement that "only the man who has a taste for every sort of knowledge and throws himself into acquiring it with an insatiable curiosity will deserve to be called a philosopher." Then follows a more complete delineation of his characteristics; he must be thorough, learn to apprehend the eternal and unchanging, manifest a desire to know the whole and not only the parts, have a love of truth and a corresponding hatred of falsehood, show no love of money or the things money can buy, possess a certain largeness of mind that keeps him from being petty and mean so that he can contemplate all time and existence, exhibit no fear of death, be quick to learn and blest with a good memory,

---

[22] Reprinted by permission of the publishers from the Loeb Classical Library edition, Translated by R. G. Bury, Plato, Timaeus, Critias, Cleitophon, Menexenus, Epistles, Vol. 7, Harvard University Press, Cambridge, Mass., 1929, Seventh Letter, p. 481.

endowed with measure, grace, and proportion so that he can see every reality in its true light, display no contentious spirit, but seek to remove gently the prejudices of men, and reproduce in his own soul the divine order he contemplates. At the end of the description, Plato candidly admits that "everyone would agree that a nature with all the qualities we require to make the perfect philosopher is a rare growth seldom seen among men."

One may think that such a creature as Plato describes would be so unbearable that it's a good thing he is rarely encountered. But at least these are high aims to which no superficial dilettantism can aspire. The conception of the philosopher and his task has been variously set forth since Plato, but few have drawn the dimensions with such generous disdain for diminutive minds and shapeless character. Incidentally, in all his discussions of the philosopher and ruler, Plato assumes that women too may attain this status.

The philosopher, then, is one who has special knowledge and superior qualities as a human being. He has acquired these both by heredity and education. By proper control over the procreation of children, Plato thinks a higher type of individual can be produced. This must become therefore a concern of the state. Superior men will be permitted to mate only with superior women at times designated by the state. Their children are to be taken away from them and educated by the state. In this way is guaranteed the perpetuation of a class able to carry on the complex tasks of the guardianship of the state. No family life is possible for this group.

But why should they rule? The argument has the following pattern: It is well known that professional men, for example, doctors, lawyers, engineers as well as farmers, generals, skilled mechanics, all have a special kind of knowledge which makes them experts and authorities in their fields. In matters of health the doctor rules, in matters of the law the lawyer rules, and in matters of military strategy the general rules. Therefore, it would seem to be reasonable to think that in matters of the state someone should rule who has a special knowledge and capacity for whatever is required. How is such knowledge and training acquired? This, says Plato, is the function of education. In the ideal state the years up to seventeen will be devoted to literature, music, and elementary mathematics. From seventeen to twenty will be a period of physical and military training. Then, for a rather select few who show promise, the next ten years, twenty to thirty, will be given to higher mathematics. A further selection will be made then and these will study dialectics and the ultimate principles of morality for the next five years. By this time those who have survived the rigorous years will be fit to serve in subordinate posts in the state. This they will do for fifteen years, that is, from thirty-five until fifty. After fifty they divide their time between study and serving the state as supreme councillors. They will live an austere life, eliminating from their existence all personal interests, such as private property, money, extra food, family life, and so on. Their interests are totally identified with the interests of the state, and they never act against it.

Even within this superior group there will be distinctions based on natural capacities and attainments. Some will never be able to reach the knowledge necessary for rulership. These will become the army, a professional military group whose duties are to defend the state and carry out the orders of the rulers. All persons excluded from these two classes constitute the third class of craftsmen, which is primarily responsible for the productive aspects of the state.

In this way Plato thinks he has created both a secure and a just state. It is just because responsibilities and duties are distributed according to abilities. But it is not necessarily permanent. Even the best state, which Plato calls an aristocracy, will decline and ultimately decay. In the Eighth Book of the Republic he writes, "Hard in truth it is for a state thus constituted to be shaken and disturbed; but since for everything that has come into being destruction is appointed, not even such a fabric as this will abide for all time, but it shall surely be dissolved. . . . " The destruction of the state, however, is not a sudden, catastrophic experience but a process in which definite stages can be marked, each stage representing a state of less order and virtue. Thus the aristocratic state falls away into the timocratic state, in which the rulers are military men; this gives way to the oligarchic state in which the government passes to the hands of a wealthy few; but this also cannot last, and the next stage in decline is the democratic state in which the masses get control. Finally, the last and worst stage appears, namely tyranny, a state in which the ruler is master and all the rest slaves. For each of these states, Plato draws an analogy to a particular type of personality. Thus, there is an aristocratic man, and likewise a timocratic, oligarchic, democratic, and tyrannical man. Each has his peculiar virtues and vices which will eventually bring him to disaster.

Plato's description of an ideal state has seemed attractive to some and appalling to others. It is just as unwise, however, to discredit him completely as it is to accept him uncritically. In a brief sketch such as this his many insights cannot be transmitted, so the reader is urged to read for himself one of the greatest documents in Western civilization.

One point emerges clearly in Plato's view, namely, that political theory cannot be separated from moral theory. The secure state is not only strong in a military sense, but also unassailable in its moral life. For a complete justification of this, one would have to consider the whole range of Plato's metaphysics and the contributions he has made to politics and morals in other works, such as the Gorgias, the Politicus, and the Laws. This cannot be done here. But certainly his belief in the reality of moral values, and the insistence that these must become the standards by which all behavior, including political behavior, is to be ordered, directed, and judged, is at the heart of his ideal state. In short, a state that does not make its people better, instead of merely happier, has missed its true aim, and a statesman who ignores the moral ends of existence is a dangerous failure. If this emphasis is lost in modern politics it will not be because we have not had an ideal set before us.

But there are a few major difficulties to be mentioned. Let us remember that the philosopher-king is supposed to have special knowledge that fits him for his task. What is this knowledge? Here Plato is never clear, or able to say with any precision. In Chapter II the distinction between forms and particulars was mentioned, and this knowledge the ruler must have. But Plato thinks there is still a higher form, called the Good, which in some mystical way must become the possession of the ruler. Nowhere are we told what this knowledge is, nor what the Good is. There are many suggestions, but these seem inadequate in the light of the insistence that anyone without such knowledge is unfit to rule.

Furthermore, is the analogy between the engineer or doctor, and the ruler, a good one? Without question, the former has a definite body of knowledge to acquire. But has "ruling" an object of knowledge in the same sense? Is it a similar type of activity? Plato cannot justify the analogy without appeal to some transcendent universal.

Finally, there is the danger of creating an elite class. In spite of the philosopher-king's devotion to the commonwealth, it constitutes, as a special group, the source of all the psychological tensions, prestige jealousies, and violent rivalries that accompany such distinctions.

In his book on Platonism, A. E. Taylor has pointed out that certain portions of Plato's Republic have had almost no influence on serious political thinking, for example, the rule of the philosopher-king and the abolition of family life and property for the rulers. But, says Taylor,

What he really cares about is chiefly the abolition of the political influence of mere wealth and rank, the connection of political power with proved character and wisdom, the elimination of jobbery from public life, and the imposing of public duties on those who are fittest to bear them, independently of sex.[23]

[23] A. E. Taylor, Platonism, Marshall Jones Co., Boston, 1924, p. 90.

B. Dante's De Monarchia

Dante is but one of many political philosophers between the ancient and the modern worlds. Perhaps in this period of a thousand years between the decline of the Greek city-state and the rise of modern nations came the most influential thinkers of our tradition. The ideal remains "justice," as Plato and Aristotle had proclaimed it, but the person who claims reward and punishment according to principle is no longer an Athenian, such as Socrates, under the laws of Athens, but any human being under the laws that are everywhere valid.

The Stoic philosophers proclaimed the universe their city. Dante's native city was Florence, but he considered that less important than his membership in the human race. He professed the idea of a citizen of the world. Should we believe ourselves indebted to the "whole of mankind" and obligated to it? We should, argues Dante, because man's "proper function," intellectual growth, "can not be achieved by any single man, or family, or neighborhood, or city, or state."[24] It is instructive to observe that although modern scholars proclaim the author of the Divine Comedy the greatest genius of Italian poetry, and perhaps, as Santayana argued, the most successful poet-philosopher, his own attention was fixed on the failure of mankind to enjoy one human civilization under one world government.

But may we not carry on the arts while we live in independent kingdoms? The great destroyer of the work of mankind is war, and it is this work that Dante values as "almost divine." And there will be war as long as there are kings who acknowledge no supreme ruler. For kings are never satisfied with their possessions. The vice of many rulers is greed or avarice, and this vice blinds each of them to the rightful claims of others. The argument for the establishment of one authority in each city to mete out impartial judgment is as valid between existing states as within each state. So long as mankind is divided into many states, men fail to make justice itself the greatest power, and by attempting to settle contentions by war rather than the appeal to reason, they deprive themselves of the greatest good "to live in peace." Further, they are carried into slavery, deprived of the privilege of liberty, that is, of living by the judgment of what is "for their own sake." Kings who make war consider that citizens exist for king and country, and not that king and country exist for citizens. (The student will notice shortly that four centuries later, Kant similarly deplores the perversion of government.)

[24] Dante, *De Monarchia*, The Liberal Arts Press, New York, 1950, p. 4.

The next problem is whether mankind, divided under many governments, might yet live under common law and in peace. Dante has no difficulty in conceiving of universal norms, springing from God, revealed through Moses and other prophets, and discovered by Greek philosophers. He is very clear that such universal law or laws of nature allow for local customs. Some tribes may live "where the excessive heat makes clothes unendurable." The customs of Esquimaux would not apply to naked Hottentots! Dante is rather vague in his formulation of universal norms or principles, but they have the logical status of higher or more general premises. The implicit major premise that clothing, or the lack of it, should be appropriate to the climate, is more reasonable than any appeal to traditional decency or modesty, and might be subsumed under Dante's higher principle that "laws should bind men together for their mutual benefit."

Laws are useful and right when they preserve society. Could there be concord between persons of different states "formally united," in agreement about some goal that benefits each and every will? Dante does not question that the single goal is "happiness" or "salvation," and he accepts Christ as the human symbol in time, of mankind enjoying "the blessing of human peace and tranquillity." Salvation is unity of men in mutual love, in freedom from greed and strife. Cannot religion in some form supply this formal agreement among all mankind, and establish universal law for nations, and hence peace? This is a common belief. Dante accepts fully the view that the ills of mankind spring from vices and that the power of religion is to inculcate virtue.

Further, the power of God was granted by Christ to the successors of Peter. Since spiritual power concerns eternal blessedness, should not temporal power that concerns only things in time, be subjected to the religious institution? In medieval language, should not the powers of the emperor be granted to the pope? Apart from the arguments about interpretation of the Scriptures, tradition, analogy, and history, there is a reasonable distinction between institutions, one claiming supernatural authority and the other resting on "human right." They have different functions, hence "different species of power." To paraphrase the argument, what would make a man a good pope might make him a bad emperor. There are, for example, distinct demands upon the wealth of one following Christ, namely, to give it to the poor. An emperor has no such obligation. Hence for one man to be both pope and emperor involves a self-contradiction. He would be obliged both to give money away and to spend it for value received. Therefore the problem of relations between states remains one that should be settled as a problem of the temporal order.

How is the common law to be enforced? Dante conceives of only one way in which mankind can live for its proper end. This requires the elimination of war, the establishment of one single supreme judiciary, the exemplification of one common goal, and the enforcement of a common set of principles. The emperors of Rome did for a time eliminate violent struggles between nations. Under the Romans there was set up a system of courts throughout the Empire, which Dante identified with humanity. As for a common goal, Dante seems to have regarded the conversion of nations to Christianity as a goal achieved by the Romans. And the Corpus Juris is so close to being a common set of principles that Dante regarded it as inspired by God.

But even if it were true that the only solution to the strife of nations is an empire embracing all nations under one temporal head, has Dante proved that it must be Rome in the fourteenth century? And if an empire, as that of Caesar Augustus, has eliminated all opposition, does the establishment of peace justify the bloodshed of nations reduced to impotence? And what if, in fact, "the world-ruler is the purest among mortal wills"? May not supreme power attract the baser sort to rebel by seizing power? On Dante's theory God would provide a universal emperor, so just that "he can have no enemies." But what if this "single, dominant will" should live not as a Marcus Aurelius, for the common good, but as a Nero, for personal fame?

Thus the argument of Dante rests, in the end, upon premises most difficult to establish: that divine Providence has given to the Romans the right to rule, that Dante knows that God can give to no other people the right to rule, that Dante knows that the Romans did everything for the common good of mankind and nothing for their own profit. All these propositions are debatable in principle and on the basis of historical fact. Does God give any people the privilege of being the one imperial people, even for a century, much less for all time? What would Dante now say of the efforts of Frenchmen, say Louis XIV and Napoleon; of Englishmen, say Victoria; of Germans, say William II and Hitler; of Italians, say Mussolini, to play the Roman role in subsequent history? And why cannot the ideal of peace be pursued by internal changes within nations and agreements between nations without a supreme personal ruler? And should not the danger of universal tyranny give us pause before we transfer sovereignty to one supreme head? May it not be that whatever universal principles get to be accepted by all the nations, they will have to be worked out by the cultures of six continents rather than adopted from the precedents of one culture and the arguments of one philosophic tradition?

How would this scheme of world government fit the cultures of non-Roman Catholics, non-Europeans? Perhaps it would be as unworkable as an attempt to make a Chinese emperor the world ruler and to ask American civil servants to memorize Confucius.

In spite of all these obvious objections, the problem of solving international conflicts is about as unsolved in the twentieth century as it was in the fourteenth. We have, however, more reason to press the argument that wars have continued to destroy the work of man. The necessity of thinking of humanity is a vital ideal for a century that failed to produce an effective League of Nations, and has had to devise a new scheme for the unification of nations. The poet Dante has voiced a cry as appropriate for us as for his war-torn age:

> O race of men, how many storms and misfortunes must thou endure, and how many shipwrecks, because thou, beast of many heads, strugglest in many directions! Thou art sick at heart and sick in mind, both theoretical and practical! No irrefutable arguments appeal to thy theoretical reason, and no amount of experience to thy practical intelligence, and even thine emotions are not moved by thy sweet, divine persuasiveness which sounds to thee from the trumpet of the Holy Spirit: 'Behold how good and how pleasant it is for brethren to dwell together in unity. Why have the nations raged, and the people devised vain things?'[25]

C. Hobbes' Leviathan

Hobbes' Leviathan was "occasioned by the disorders of the present time."[26] He took the occasion of the civil wars of seventeenth-century England, as had Plato the occasion of fourth-century Athens, and Dante the occasion of fourteenth-century Italy, and as will be shortly seen, Kant the occasion of eighteenth-century Europe. Hobbes wrote precisely of the causes of the struggle between Puritans and Cavaliers.

But this concerns us less than what he considers of philosophic value: "the Constitution, Nature, and Right of Soveraigns . . . the Duty of Subjects, derived from the Principles of Naturall Reason."[27] He hopes that his ideal of the commonwealth "will fall into the hands of a Soveraign," but he fears his labor will be as useless as the Republic of Plato. Surely Hobbes is correct in thinking that the modern world with its nation-states supplanting the medieval order renders the ideal of the ancient Greek polis strictly inapplicable. Athens was not torn by claims of rival Protestant and Catholic sects. Further, Hobbes is anxious to bring to the solution of the

---

[25] *Ibid.*, pp. 20–21.
[26] Thomas Hobbes, *Leviathan*, Cambridge University Press, Cambridge, 1904, p. 528.
[27] *Ibid.*, p. 268.

problem of his age a fresh observation of human nature and the methods he thinks central to the new natural philosophy of Galileo and Descartes.

No brief introduction to Hobbes' Leviathan can hope to do justice to his epistemology, metaphysics, and Biblical criticism as well as to his political philosophy. With the hope that the force and trenchancy of one line of argument will excite curiosity, the "Theoremes of Morall Doctrine"[28] will be examined to see whether he has proved them.

Let us assume that the passions of man, "what he doth, when he does *think, opine, reason, hope, feare,* &c, and upon what grounds," are so similar that if a man reads one character he gains a key to decipher all.[29] Each of us can discover two things: first, that weak as I may be, I claim what is another's, and second, I have "strength enough to kill the strongest."[30]

The implication from the unlimited and boundless claims each man makes, is that no man can be secure in his enjoyment. The potential threat to battle defines the state of war. What Hobbes deduces from his principle of the desire and ability to kill can be known by any one from experience.

Let him therefore consider with himselfe, when taking a journey, he armes himself, and seeks to go well accompanied; when going to sleep, he locks his dores; when even in his house he locks his chest. . . . Does he not there as much accuse mankind by his actions, as I do by my words?[31]

If we do this when there is a government, with laws and power to keep us all in line, what must life be with no government? This brutish state is approached by the degeneracy into civil war.

To this warre of every man against every man, this also is consequent; that nothing can be Unjust. The notions of Right and Wrong, Justice and Injustice have there no place. Where there is no common Power, there is no Law: where no Law, no Injustice. Force, and Fraud, are in warre, the two Cardinall vertues. . . . It is consequent also to the same condition, that there be no Propriety, no Dominion, no *Mine* and *Thine* distinct but onely that to be every mans, that he can get; and for so long, as he can keep it.[32]

Reason suggests an answer to the ill condition of war in the form of articles of peace. First is the right of each man "to use his own power, as he will himselfe, for the preservation of his own Nature; that is to say, of his own Life. . . . " But this liberty of natural right does not restrain our claims. Hence to prevent war, a law is required, which is, "every man

[28] *Ibid.*
[29] *Ibid.*, pp. xix–xx.
[30] *Ibid.*, p. 81.
[31] *Ibid.*, p. 84.
[32] *Ibid.*, p. 85.

ought to endeavour Peace." This takes precedence over self-defense, which is permitted only when we cannot obtain peace. What is peace but using no more liberty against another than you grant him against you? This implies renouncing our natural claim to everything.[33]

When parties renounce rights, or transfer rights to each other, then the mutual transferring is called a contract. This may involve keeping a promise, and one is obliged to give what is due another. But "the words are too weak to bridle men's ambitions, avarice, anger, and other Passions, without the fears of some coercive Power. . . . " It is this power that makes the difference between nature and the civil estate. The only motives that are strong enough are "fears of the consequences of breaking their word . . . or Pride in appearing not to need to break it." The fear of gods is not strong enough.

Hence it follows that to have obligations carried out there must be coercive power. Here "the names of Just, and Unjust can have place." Justice is the keeping of covenant, and "he that breaketh his Covenant, and consequently declareth that he thinks he may with reason do so, cannot be received into any society, that unite themselves for Peace and Defence. . . ."

The benefits of society cannot be had without submission to coercive power. Hobbes denies that man can be naturally social. The contract among men establishes society. Therefore society is artificial. "The only way to erect such a Common Power . . . is, to conferre all their power and strength upon one Man, or upon one Assembly of men, that may reduce all their Wills, by plurality of voices, unto one Will. . . . " The strength of all is to be used for the peace of all. The common power is called sovereign. Everyone else a subject.

The right to revolt against the sovereign, or to depose the sovereign is not in the ideal order, for either it means bringing back anarchy or plunging people into the miseries and calamities that accompany a civil war. Hobbes has reduced the possibilities to two, sovereignty and anarchy. Sovereignty cannot be less than unlimited or "absolute." Although evil as a consequence of unlimited power may occur "yet the consequences of the want of it, which is perpetual warre of every man against his neighbour, are much worse."

There is one limitation upon the power of the sovereign to command obedience of a subject. This goes back to the right of each man to preserve his own life. It involves not only the rightful refusal of a subject to kill himself at the sovereign's command, but to do "any other thing, without which he cannot live; yet hath that man the liberty to disobey?" Simi-

[33] *Ibid.*, p. 87.

larly, he is not bound to accuse himself. He may refuse, in some cases, to risk his life as a soldier.

D. Kant's Perpetual Peace

Hobbes planned carefully in theory to make civil war impossible. Many rulers of the seventeenth and eighteenth centuries made themselves absolute over the minds of their subjects, discouraging by force and fear of force dissent from the sovereign. And the contract of Hobbes' Leviathan denied the right of citizens to rebel against a tyrant. Although Immanuel Kant, a subject of Prussia, had the opportunity to enjoy civil order, this did not convince him that it was also right, for the price of the intellectual and moral freedom of the individual was far too high. Kant belonged to the generation that witnessed the American and the French revolutions. He was in sympathy with both because a great moral issue was at stake. The revolutionists had certainly broken laws, but not the moral law. When the rights of a nation are violated by a tyrant, one does no moral wrong in dethroning him.

Hobbes' premises imply the conclusion that absolute sovereigns are not subject to the laws they make. There is only one kind of restriction upon them, namely, they may not destroy the lives of the citizens. But in this theory no law protects a non-citizen. Thus it is not wrong to kill or injure a foreigner; no act against him can be called unjust. Furthermore, in Hobbes' theory sovereigns cannot limit their power in relation to other sovereigns. If they did they would cease to provide an absolute guarantee against civil war. And there is no other power over them to force obedience to a treaty. Hence a guarantee to another state to respect its territory is void, or in the language of later rulers, "a scrap of paper." Here in Hobbes' theory is an insurmountable difficulty—if international war is inevitable, and if it is as destructive of life and civilization as is civil war, which the Leviathan admits, then the very fulfilling of the ideal implies anarchy and barbarism and devastation.

Kant rejects Hobbes' premises and his conclusions. For Kant war is not inevitable. It is a moral obligation to create a society where the conditions that give rise to war never occur. And if it is a duty, then it is within human capacity to achieve it. Ought implies can. In short, for Kant, men ought and can guarantee to each other perpetual peace.

But this is more than moral dreaming or hoping for Kant. He has his vision fixed on an ideal, but he also accepts the responsibility for working out a practical way to realize the ideal. The result is the powerful and original statement published in 1795 under the title Perpetual Peace. In this Kant's ethical thought is brought to bear on a political and historical problem. Its basic conviction is that no international peace can be maintained if there is a divorce between politics and morals. These two can be united only by the idea of right or law.

For Kant the full development of the autonomous personality is the goal of civilization, and this goal cannot be reached except through the establishment of a universal rule of law, that is to say, a scheme of organization which would guarantee universal and eternal peace.[34]

The brevity of Kant's statement should not deceive one into thinking that it is hasty, ungrounded in rigorous thought, or feeble. Its roots are deep in Kant's ethics, epistemology, and metaphysics; but here only a summary of its major features will be presented. The document is divided into two sections, the first called Preliminary Articles, the second, Definitive Articles. Following these are two brief supplements and two appendices.

The whole essay defends the idea that men and nations can establish relations with each other that gradually lead to the fulfillment of the ideal of eternal peace. Each student ought to read it completely. This epitome can serve as an introduction.

a. Preliminary Articles

1. "No treaty of peace shall be held to be such which is made with the secret reservation of the material for a future war." Any reservation as to future conduct is beneath the dignity of man and makes the treaty mere casuistry. It would be only a truce, a suspension, not a cessation of hostilities.
2. "No state having an independent existence, whether it be small or great, may be acquired by another state, through inheritance, exchange, purchase, or gift." The point here is that a state is a kind of moral person—not a thing—and must be so treated. It is not something to be bargained for on the market as an object of merchandise. Hence troops must be forbidden to march through one state in war against a third state which is not a common enemy.
3. "Standing armies shall gradually disappear." They constitute a menace; excite to armed action; are a source of great expense; and frequently

[34] Reprinted by permission of the publishers from Carl J. Friedrich, *Inevitable Peace*, Harvard University Press, Cambridge, Massachusetts, copyright 1948 by the President and Fellows of Harvard College, p. 29.

cause hostilities merely with a view of being delivered from an oppressive burden. Moreover, being paid to kill or be killed is to be reduced to a machine or instrument in another's hand. This is incompatible with one's natural right—to be treated and to treat oneself as a person.

4. "No debts shall be contracted in connection with the foreign affairs of the state." Such debts, contracted to maintain the interests of the state abroad, set the stage for aggrievances and economic exhaustion.

5. "No state shall interfere by force in the Constitution and government of another state." The autonomy of all states must be certain. Intervention by a foreign power is a violation of the right of independence. Kant, however, does suggest that in case of civil war assistance may be given to restore unity.

6. "No state at war with another shall permit such acts of warfare as must make mutual confidence impossible in time of future peace: such as the employment of assassins, or poisoners, the violation of articles of surrender, the instigation of treason in the state against which it is making war, etc." All of these are dishonorable and Kant believes that even during war one must have confidence in the principles of the enemy. He concludes from this that a "war of extermination, in which destruction may come to both parties at the same time, and thus to all rights too, would allow eternal peace only upon the graveyard of the whole human race. Such a war, therefore, as well as the use of the means which might be employed in it, is wholly forbidden."

b. Definitive Articles

1. "The civil constitution of each state shall be republican." This represents Kant's opposition to despotism; a republican constitution is required in a state where there is freedom under law. Under this constitution the assent of every citizen is necessary to decide whether war shall be declared or not. This involves the decreeing of calamities against themselves which citizens will be reluctant to do. Republicanism is the political principle according to which the executive power is separated from the legislative. It alone makes possible representation.

2. "The law of nations should be based upon a federalism of free states." Kant does not think that this will guarantee prevention of war, but it is far better than bitter nationalism. If it were possible to have a united world government we would be nearer a real solution, but Kant doubts that the people will accept a comprehensive world state, which, of course, may lead to world-wide despotism.

3. "The Cosmopolitan or World Law shall be limited to conditions of a universal hospitality." The world order must be such that anyone has the right to visit foreign countries, but not the right to subject them.[35]

In the supplements and appendices Kant develops briefly the following ideas: First, there is a kind of guarantee of perpetual peace in the rigorous order of nature. "Nature's mechanical course evidently reveals a teleology; to produce harmony from the very disharmony of men even against their will." Second, "the maxims of the philosophers concerning the conditions of the possibility of public peace shall be consulted by the states which are ready to go to war." Kant thinks philosophers should be heard. They are enlightened men, incapable of betraying the truth, have no vested interests, and cannot be guilty of being mere propagandists. Third, morality and politics are not contradictory. To have an idea of duty that cannot be fulfilled is to annihilate the very idea of duty. There is a need for moral politicians, that is, statesmen who act according to the principles of morality, not political moralists who adapt morality to their own interests. Finally, Kant offers a formula for measuring the actions of statesmen: "All actions which relate to the right of other men are contrary to the right and law, the maxim of which does not permit publicity." If a statesman must keep his purposes secret he is suspect.

Kant's statement is by no means an adequate blueprint for world organization and peace. There are many weaknesses that do not make it fit contemporary civilization. On the other hand, few men have given such sober and rigorous thought to the theoretical and practical problems of improving the relations among men so that they may live in a moral and honorable peace.

V. Some Common Fallacies of Political Belief

All human interests that have to do with values, desires, hopes, and aims are constantly confronted with the dangers of crooked thinking. Our political beliefs are in this category. It is a mark of shame and weakness that where so much is at stake there has been so much unwisdom and downright folly. It seems to be peculiarly difficult for men to seek calmly and deliberately for the best reasons for holding their political beliefs, and to subject these beliefs to critical analysis. They are more likely to be dogmatically asserted in a loud voice, than quietly examined or tentatively expressed. Here, too frequently the brain gives way to the blood. "Wir denken mit unserem Blut," said Hitler. And as history so often reveals, when the rulers think with their blood, some one else is expected to

[35] Taken from the translation by Carl J. Friedrich in his *Inevitable Peace, op. cit.,* pp. 245ff.

sacrifice his blood. What all this points to is the need for more hard, persistent thought, and less emotional eruption than has been usually given to our political beliefs. It is largely the <u>emotional tension in which our beliefs are discussed that makes us easy victims of fallacious thinking</u>, even, for example, preventing us from giving the time and effort to the adequate definition of terms. This alone would do much to straighten out our political thinking. It is elementary that failure to define terms leads to a breakdown in communication, and in political relations may bring on catastrophe.

Suppose a Russian diplomat says, "The present state in Poland is a people's democratic government." To which a representative of the United States may reply, "When will you permit free elections in Poland?" "The people are free," answers the Russian, "and Poland is ruled by the party that represents the proletariat." "But your Government failed to keep its pledge to restore Polish democracy." "You do not know what true democracy is. All of your parties are tools of the ruling bourgeois class." "And your party representatives are dictators, hence you are the one who does not know what true democracy is."

It is obvious in this hypothetical interchange that the word democracy is assumed by each disputant to have one and only one meaning, and that to each the meaning is completely different. No wonder that each one drawing inferences from the other's words produces what seems absurd to both. The trouble is certainly in part verbal and can be resolved only when each recognizes the need for definition. Defining will not resolve all their differences, of course, but it may get them on a basis where communication is possible.

A deeper source of misunderstanding, however, lies in the assumption that there is a "true" or "essential" meaning of democracy, by which all instances of democracy are to be measured and judged. It is forgotten that the word democracy is *given* a meaning by men, and that this meaning may become common or customary but it does not become true or false. <u>"Democracy" like all other political words is extremely</u> vague. If we are going to use it effectively we need to give it a fairly precise meaning, that is, we must state the conditions and relationships under which we propose to live, or which we are willing to defend. "Democracy" then becomes a shorthand symbol for these preferred conditions.

In this connection it is useful to see that persuasive definitions often operate in political beliefs.

In any "persuasive definition" the term defined is a familiar one, whose meaning is both descriptive and strongly emotive. The purport of the definition is to alter the descriptive meaning of the term, usually by giving it greater precision within the boundaries of its customary vagueness; but the definition does *not* make any substantial change in the term's emotive meaning. And the definition is used, consciously or unconsciously, in an effort to secure, by this interplay between emotive and descriptive meaning, a redirection of people's attitudes.[36]

Consider the following remarks:

1. To be free means that no one has the right to force me to do anything, or to go anywhere, or think in any certain way, against my wishes. Whenever restrictions are placed on me my freedom is attacked. Of course, I can't be totally free, that's nonsense, but at least I can try to be as free as possible, that is, achieve as much independence from external coercion as I can.
2. But that is not true freedom. True freedom has nothing to do with restrictions, or chains. It is rather of the spirit. A man is free, even if a slave, when he possesses a certain quality of mind which enables him to rise above the annoyances of his temporary limitations. He finds his resources within himself and nothing can mar his inward life. This is real freedom.

Here we see each person disagreeing about the cognitive or descriptive meaning of the term freedom, but wanting to attach a laudatory and emotive value to his favored description. When words have a favorable emotive meaning, people tend to refuse to give this to another's cognitive meaning. In this way no new facts are brought out, but an effort is made to redirect people's attitudes. We are not suggesting that persuasive definitions have no use or that they are peculiarly vicious, but in political discussions we should be on guard against them, for they sometimes purport to give new data when they indicate only differences in attitudes. But sometimes they lead to actually fallacious argument, as illustrated in the following:

Citizen A: I can't support Mr. X for the Presidency because he is not a religious man and what this country needs more than anything else is Christian leadership.
Citizen B: But Mr. X is the most profoundly religious man I know. In the truest sense of the term, to be religious is to have a deep respect for human personality and to place moral values above all others. Although Mr. X is not and never has been a devotee of any narrow sectarian religious cult, he has always had a high regard for human dignity and rights, and no one can question that his ultimate values are those moral principles taught by the founder of the Christian religion.

[36] C. L. Stevenson, *Ethics and Language*, Yale University Press, New Haven, Connecticut, 1944, p. 210.

Citizen A: Well, I guess you are right. I hadn't thought of it in that light. What you said about Mr. X is certainly true. I have always considered him to be a man of high moral principles.

Citizen B may be charged with arguing by persuasive definitions. Citizen A has a favorable emotive reaction to any person whom he believes to be religious. He began by having an unfavorable attitude toward candidate X because he believed him to be nonreligious. Citizen B, however, led him to have a favorable attitude toward Mr. X without in any way changing any of his beliefs about the candidate. Citizen A had always considered Mr. X to be a man of moral principle. He had not been against him because he believed that he was immoral, but because he believed that he was not religious. He ends up with the same factual beliefs about Mr. X with which he began, and yet with quite a different attitude toward him simply because through redefinition of the term 'religious' he applied the term to Mr. X and thus directed the attitudes evoked by the term toward him. The emotive power of the term 'religious' was unaltered by the redefinition, so that Citizen A felt the same way about any person to whom the term applied on the basis of the new definition as he did toward the persons to whom it applied on the basis of its former meaning.

Arguments of this kind are fallacious. The fallacy becomes evident when we recast the thinking of Citizen A in this manner: First he reasoned: A religious man should hold this office. Mr. X is not a religious man. Therefore, he should not hold this office. After discussing the matter with Citizen B he reasoned: A *religious man₁* should hold this office. Mr. X is a *religious man₂*. Therefore, Mr. X qualifies for this office. The term 'religious man₁' is clearly quite different from 'religious man₂'. However, Citizen A does not notice this fact because of his emotive response to the term.[37]

C. D. Broad is distressed, and rightly so, about the low level of political and social discussion. He has pointed out, and aptly illustrated, some of the common fallacies in political thinking.[38] To be aware of these hazards is the first step toward learning how to avoid them. So let us look briefly at Broad's analysis.

There is a very natural tendency for a person to base his judgments about present trends and future prospects on the quite recent history of a quite small part of the world, in particular on what has happened in his own country during his own and perhaps his parents' lifetime. Now the features which he notices in this restricted segment of space-time, and which he makes the basis of his political and social judgments, may depend on a concatenation of circumstances which have seldom occurred before, are unlikely to happen again, and perhaps never existed outside a small area. This may well lead to an unjustified optimism

[37] E. M. Adams, *The Fundamentals of General Logic,* Longmans, Green & Co., Inc., New York, 1954, pp. 105–106.
[38] C. D. Broad, "Some Common Fallacies in Political Thinking," *Philosophy,* 1950, Vol. 25, No. 93. Used by permission of the author, *Philosophy,* and Routledge & Kegan Paul Ltd., *Religion, Philosophy and Psychical Research.*

or an equally unjustified pessimism, and in any case to ill-founded judgments.[39]

Broad gives a number of instances from British history to show that one cannot take as normal an exceptional and temporary state of affairs—even if the temporariness extends to a good many centuries.

A second group of fallacies is considered together under the name of causal fallacies. One of the most common of this type is the failure to distinguish between necessary and sufficient conditions.

. . . It will suffice for our present purpose to say that the statement that *C* causes *E* sometimes means that *C* is a *necessary* though perhaps not sufficient condition of *E*, sometimes that *C* is a *sufficient* though not perhaps necessary condition of *E*, and sometimes that *C* is a set of conditions which are *severally necessary and jointly sufficient* to produce *E*. Now popular talk about this causing that does not clearly distinguish these alternatives. It is very common, e.g., to start from the fact, which may be quite trivial and even tautologous, that *C* causes *E* in the sense that it is a necessary condition of *E;* then to take for granted that *C* causes *E* in the important and doubtful sense that it is necessary and sufficient to produce *E;* and then to infer various far-reaching practical conclusions from this.[40]

Those who argue, for example, that armaments cause wars are caught in this fallacy.

Another form of the causal fallacy is described by Broad in the following way:

It is alleged, rightly or wrongly, that if all the members of a certain class, e.g. all nations or all the individuals of a certain nation, were to act simultaneously in a certain way, certain very desirable results would follow. It is concluded that each member of that class ought to act in that way, regardless of whether the rest do so or not. This is crazy logic and crazy ethics. Often it is not enough that even a large majority of the members of the class could be relied upon to act in the way suggested if one or a few were to set the example. One of the greatest difficulties of social and political life is that the pace is inevitably so largely set by the most backward and most evilly-disposed individuals and communities. The existence of a single powerful aggressive fanatical nation, like pre-war Germany or present-day Russia, is enough to make it suicidal for other nations to reduce their armaments. And the existence of a comparatively small minority of criminals or lunatics or abnormally inconsiderate individuals within a community compels all its other members to take precautions and to support punitive and preventive measures which they would gladly do without.[41]

[39] *Ibid.*, p. 99.
[40] *Ibid.*, p. 104.
[41] *Ibid.*, p. 105.

A third causal fallacy Broad calls the extrapolation fallacy. It is described as follows.

It is known or reasonably conjectured that a change in a certain direction has produced predominantly good results. It is then uncritically assumed that further doses of change in that direction will produce still further predominantly good results, and that it is desirable to administer these additional doses as soon as possible. It is forgotten that almost any change involves at least some loss in some respects as well as gain in others, and that it often produces certain positive evils which would otherwise not have existed. The gains may well overbalance the losses, and the main positive goods may well be greater than the collateral positive evils, until the process has gone a certain length; but the losses and the collateral evils may begin to predominate if it is carried further. Again, even if it be desirable on the whole to continue a certain process further in the same direction, it is often most undesirable to do so with the maximum possible speed. People who would benefit from a slow development, to each phase of which they had time to adapt themselves or to adapt their children, may be merely bewildered and demoralized if the pace becomes too hot for them.[42]

It is this fallacy that threatens those who argue, for example, that as some machines are good the complete mechanization of living will lead to a high level of social felicity. Citizens of the United States might relate this type of thinking to problems of their own history such as prohibition and racial desegregation.

A fourth causal fallacy is the familiar *post hoc ergo propter hoc.*

From the nature of the case it is extremely difficult to say with any high degree of reasonable confidence whether a certain factor did or did not contribute to an important extent to cause a certain other factor in social or political phenomena. This is because it is practically impossible to isolate the facts to be investigated, to find really parallel cases, to devise and perform experiments intended to answer definite questions, and so on. But fools cannot be restrained from rushing in where logicians fear to tread; and, if some fairly outstanding social phenomenon *A* immediately preceeded some other fairly outstanding phenomenon *B* in some part of the world at some period in history, they will promptly generalize and conclude that *A* is necessary and sufficient to produce *B*. . . .

I have heard it cited as an instance of the truth of Karl Marx's economic theories that they enabled him to prophecy [sic] that great wars would happen with frequency in the Western world, that they would be increasingly destructive, and so on, and that we have seen this prophecy abundantly fulfilled. As if wars had not been a regular occurrence in the history of Europe and the rest of the world throughout recorded time; as if they had not always been waged with the maximum resources available at the time to the belligerents; and as if those resources had not enormously increased through industrialization and ap-

[42] *Ibid.,* pp. 105–106.

plied science. <u>How can any particular theory be verified by foretelling what could have been foretold with confidence on almost any theory or no theory at all?</u>[43]

Finally, there is a causal fallacy which leads to blaming or praising unfairly certain governments or individuals.

Suppose that there is a critical situation in which a government or a leading statesman has a choice of one or other of a comparatively few practically possible alternative courses of action, A, B, and C, including among these the possible alternative of doing nothing and letting events take their course. Alternative A is chosen, and we will suppose that the state of affairs which ensues is admittedly much worse that that which immediately preceded the decision. Then it is very common to hold that a wrong decision was made, and to blame severally the individual or the government which made it. Now of course such a judgment may be justified in some cases. But in most cases a whole nest of fallacies is involved. In the first place, even if a different decision would have had a more fortunate sequel, it does not follow that the maker of the actual decision was blameworthy. Before we can decide this we must know whether, in the situation in which he was placed and with the information which was available to him at the time, he might reasonably have been expected to see that the consequences would be much worse than those of some other alternative which he might reasonably have been expected to contemplate as possible. The mere fact, if it be a fact, that *we* can see all this *after* the event may have very little bearing on this question.

Secondly, the mere fact that a state of affairs which followed, the choice of alternative A was much worse than that which preceeded it is not sufficient evidence that the decision was mistaken. It may be that the ensuing state of affairs would have been much worse than the preceding *whichever* of the alternatives had been adopted, and that the results of adopting any other would have been still worse than those of adopting A. <u>Men find it very hard to admit that there are situations in which *all* possible alternative developments will be changes for the worse, and where the wisest decision that can be made would do no more than minimize the inevitably ensuing evil.</u> Suppose that we tacitly and unjustifiably assume that there are no such situations. Then we shall automatically conclude that there *must* have been some alternative open to the maker of the decision which would have averted the evils which in fact ensued and would not have been followed by still greater evils. And so we shall judge that the actual decision was mistaken. But there is no reason whatever to accept this premise, and therefore there is no reason to accept any such judgment as a conclusion from it.[44]

The last fallacy considered by Broad is of a different type, but very common. He describes it in the following way:

A citizen of country A condemns some contemporary public action or institution in another country B. Thereupon a fellow-citizen gets up and says 'We did

[43] *Ibid.*, p. 109.
[44] *Ibid.*, p. 111.

the same', and produces in support of his assertion some public action which was taken or some institution which existed at some time in the history of their common fatherland. This is supposed by many to provide some kind of answer to the criticism on this action or institution in the foreign country. At any rate it is often felt to be relevant and embarrassing by the critic himself, and the fear that such remarks might justifiably be made often prevents scrupulous persons from condemning publicly incidents in foreign countries which they cannot but deeply disapprove in private.

It is obvious that there must be a number of suppressed premises at the back of such an argument, and when one tries to make them explicit one sees that it is so hopelessly confused that nothing coherent can be made of it. I think we should all admit that a person ought to feel, and very often will feel, uncomfortable, if it can be shown that at the same time he strongly condemns x and approves or tolerates y when the only relevant difference between x and y is that the former occurs in a foreign country and the latter in his own. Even this, however, would not show that he is mistaken in condemning x. The fact that a man is inconsistent in his judgments or his emotions does not show that a particular one judgment is false or a particular one emotion is misdirected. Sin is not less sinful when it is Satan who condemns it; and he has the advantage of expert knowledge. But suppose, that as is very often the case, that a man not only condemns x in the foreign country but also quite consistently condemns similar actions and institutions in the history of his own country. Why on earth should the fact that something similar to what he condemns in another country exists or has existed in his own be thought to show that it is not worthy of condemnation? And, if he equally condemns similar acts or institutions in the history of his own country, why on earth should he feel embarrassed or diffident in publicly condemning them when they exist in a foreign country? Is bestial cruelty in contemporary Russian labor-camps any less evil because there was bestial cruelty in English slave-ships in the eighteenth century? And must an Englishman, who deplores that incident in English history and whose ancestors abolished that evil after a long and arduous Parliamentary struggle, hang his head in embarrassed silence and refrain from calling slavery and cruelty by their name when practiced on a vast scale by foreign countries which claim to be the moral leaders of mankind?[45]

There has been no intention of trying to present all the innumerable ways in which faulty thinking is responsible for foolish, ineffective, absurd, and even dangerous political beliefs. But some of the pitfalls to be avoided have been shown, not merely because bad thinking is offensive wherever it appears, but also because in political life there is often a grim practical necessity to think clearly. We need to learn how to detect fact from fable, to assess the evidence in disputes, to discount the effects of emotion and prejudice, to discipline ourselves for precise definition, to distinguish between the relevant and irrelevant in critical issues, and to submit our

[45] *Ibid.*, pp. 112–113.

beliefs to the known tests of logical procedure. But as all men are sinners, we cannot expect any to be gods. We must therefore be always alert. Thinking is a privilege that is often ignored. As a certainty it is often misused.

PROBLEMS FOR THOUGHT AND DISCUSSION

1. Following is one of the most famous statements in political philosophy. It is found in Book Five of Plato's Republic:

Until philosophers are kings, or the kings and princes of this world have the spirit and power of philosophy, and political greatness and wisdom meet in one, and those commoner natures who pursue either to the exclusion of the other are compelled to stand aside, cities will never have rest from their evils,—no, nor the human race, as I believe,—and then only will this our State have a possibility of life and behold the light of day.[46]

Plato does not mean by "philosopher" a college professor of philosophy, but he means, in part, a man who has knowledge and wisdom. Do you think Plato's ideal is relevant to contemporary political problems?

2. Immanuel Kant wrote:

That kings should become philosophers, or philosophers kings, can scarce be expected; nor is it to be wished, since the enjoyment of power inevitably corrupts the judgment of reason, and perverts its liberty. But that kings, or people-kings, that is to say, the people who govern themselves by laws of equality, should not suffer that the class of philosophers be reduced to disappear, or to maintain silence, but, on the contrary, should permit them to be freely heard.[47]

Is Kant right when he says that the enjoyment of power inevitably corrupts the judgment of reason? What kind of role can philosophers take in matters of government? Is thinking about political philosophy too unrealistic to be really effective? What do you think is the relation between thought and action?

3. Contemporary political science is caught in a relativistic dilemma.

Either it will be tempted to take flight in a subjective dogmatism that identifies the perspective and preferences of the observer with objective, general truth—thus becoming the ideology of a particular view of society, reflecting particular social interests—or else it will surrender the very concept of objective, general truth, concluding from the subjectivity of its own insights that there is nothing but opinion and that one opinion is as good as another, provided society does not object to it.

If nothing that is true regardless of time and place could be said about matters political, political science itself would be impossible.[48]

Do you agree that subjectivism is dogmatic or merely opinion? Or that having a perspective necessarily means that one opinion is as good as

[46] Plato, *The Republic* (B. Jowett, tr.), Third Edition, The Clarendon Press, Oxford, 1888, pp. 170–171.
[47] Immanuel Kant, *Perpetual Peace*, Columbia University Press, New York, 1939, p. 39.
[48] Hans J. Morgenthau, *Education in an Age of Science* (Brand Blanshard, ed.), Basic Books, Inc., New York, 1959, p. 135.

another? What objective, general truths that are true "regardless of space and time" could you point to in political thought?

4. Consider the following statement from Benito Mussolini:

The foundation of Fascism is the conception of the State, its character, its duty, and its aim. Fascism conceives of the State as an absolute, in comparison with which all individuals or groups are relative, only to be conceived of in their relation to the State. The conception of the Liberal State is not that of a directing force, guiding the play and development, both material and spiritual, of a collective body, but merely a force limited to the function of recording results: on the other hand, the Fascist State is itself conscious, and has itself a will and a personality—thus it may be called the "ethic" State.[49]

Is my duty to my country the same as my duty to my state or government? Can you think of possible duties overriding those toward the state? What obligations may the individual have that are stronger than his political obligations? Do you think there may be some danger to human welfare in an exaggerated insistence on a duty to one's country or state?

5. A student of the political theories used in justifying British rule in India distinguishes

. . . four distinct strands: the Burkean doctrine of imperial trusteeship; the Benthamite theory of state activity as propagated and modified by the two Mills; the Platonic conception of a ruling elite that would act as wise guardians; and the Evangelical zeal to spread the Christian gospel so as to save the souls of a perversely unresponsive people. All four theories formed part of the English intellectual climate of the time. . . .

Each was distorted, under stress: the Burkean into Prussian pride in military power, the Benthamite into Hobbesian coercion and concentration of power, the Platonic into the conception of a chosen people or caste. The Christian ideal fortunately required the believer to consider his own sins also. One might think that there could be a grand symphony. ". . . Burke provided a moral code, Bentham a programme, Plato an attitude of mind, and Wilberforce a transcendental sanction." But Gandhi challenged the whole amalgam. Can one nation be a trustee for another? If only results are considered in moral judgment, as Bentham and the Mills tell us, is not any means acceptable? If men are equals, as the liberal element of utilitarianism affirms, why should one caste be guardians? And what has evangelicalism produced but a revulsion from Christianity? Further, if any of these theories is true, the Indians themselves can thereby justify their own power, and not Britain's. Hence, to conclude the argument, the British Empire in India came to an end "by the very application of their doctrines."[50]

To what extent do Americans justify their power by arguments as incoherent as those of Victorian England? If our political thought is a mere

---

[49] B. Mussolini, *The Political and Social Doctrine of Fascism* (Jane Soames, tr.), The Hogarth Press, London, 1933.

[50] Raghavan Iyer, "Utilitarianism and Empire in India," *The Listener*, Vol. LXIII, No. 1617, 1960, pp. 526–527.

amalgam, not a consistent theory, will it also bring about the decay of our world power? Is there any coherent and consistent theory, that will not spell its own ruin?

6. To what extent are party arguments a tissue of fallacies? Can you identify those alleged misleading arguments in the following? Are they characteristic of political thinking?

Of all the hazards which beset the republican form of government, surely one of the least recognized is the practice of holding regular national elections, every two years, and especially if the presidency happens to be at stake, the good judgment, good temper, if not indeed the sanity of the voter is assailed by a barrage of partisan debate, loaded with what has been described as truths, half-truths and statistics. Thus a Democratic hopeful views with alarm the terrifying Soviet lead in ballistic missiles; in the next breath, however, he urges a continued ban on atomic weapons tests. "Our leaders talk of freedom and embrace dictators," charges another Administration foe, in casual disregard of what went on at Potsdam and Yalta. "The facts are," cries a third candidate in a remarkable display of political data processing, "that seventeen million Americans go to bed hungry every night."

On the other hand, the Republican officials release

. . . not just the straight facts and figures, for whatever they might be worth, but also a series of soothing official explanations. As a consequence, the country lately has been lulled into the belief that nothing is wrong with business that the belated advent of spring won't cure. This may or may not be true. . . . Around the year-end, to illustrate, Department of Commerce spokesmen hopefully labeled a sudden, largely artificial spurt in exports as a major turn in the adverse U. S. balance of payments; their exuberance was quenched only by an extraordinary rebuke from [the] Secretary of the Treasury. . . . In mid-March the Secretary of Commerce hailed a moderate increase in proposed outlays for capital goods as proof positive . . . in his glowing words, would be "the best year of our lives." . . . By the same token, unfavorable news either has been played down or explained away. The big jump in unemployment . . . has been blamed on "savage late-winter storms." . . . A surprisingly large vacancy rate was coupled with a belittling reference to the likelihood of sampling errors and statistical flukes.[51]

PERTINENT READINGS

Collingwood, R. G., *The New Leviathan, or Man, Society, Civilization and Barbarism,* The Clarendon Press, Oxford, 1947.

Laslett, Peter, *Philosophy, Politics and Society,* The Macmillan Co., New York, 1956.

Sabine, George H., *A History of Political Theory,* Henry Holt & Co., Inc., New York, 1937.

Santayana, George, *Dominations and Powers, Reflections on Liberty, Society and Government,* Charles Scribner's Sons, New York, 1951.

Weldon, T. D., *The Vocabulary of Politics,* Penguin Books, Harmondsworth, Middlesex, 1953.

[51] "State of Business: It's Not as Sturdy as Washington Pretends," *Barron's National Business and Financial Weekly,* Vol. 40, No. 17, 1960, p. 1. Copyright 1960, Barron's Publishing Co., Inc.

X

Religious Beliefs

I. Preliminary Statement

Religious beliefs seem to arouse such a high degree of emotional response, it is difficult to discuss them objectively. A further difficulty, however, is the vagueness of the language in which the beliefs are expressed. And finally there is the tendency among the pious to shy away from the examination of religious beliefs because of a fear that their beliefs may be weakened. None of these, nor all of them together, is sufficient reason to refrain from a critical analysis of those statements by which we express our religious beliefs.

Are all the basic religious beliefs matters of faith? Are all of them attitudes that may be explained psychologically or sociologically? Are some of them expressions of demonstrable knowledge? Piety is not itself an excuse for poor thinking. We cannot therefore refuse to examine our religious beliefs merely because they are religious. And this brings us at once to a problem. What is it that makes a belief religious?

Let us ask a parallel question about a scientific belief. What makes a scientific belief scientific? Here the answer would probably be that a scientific belief is a belief, the truth of which could be established by well-defined logical and empirical processes. It belongs strictly to a cognitive situation. But it is often thought that this is not the case with religious beliefs, that their distinctive quality is due to the fact that they are about a special object or a special state, for example, God, or heaven, or salvation. Nevertheless, they too claim to be cognitive, that is, to give us information about their subject matter, even though the methods of empirical veri-

503

fication, so necessary for scientific beliefs, cannot be used.[1] In other words, religious beliefs belong to that class of beliefs which claim to be true or false on some ground other than the empirical methods of science.

It is certainly doubtful whether the mere use of terms common to religious discourse is sufficient to designate a belief as religious. Thus, "Jesus of Nazareth was born in 4 B.C." is a scientific statement of belief which has the possibility of being verified by historical methods. It is probably not a statement of religious belief. On the other hand, "Jesus Christ is the Saviour of mankind" is a religious belief and not amenable to any known methods of empirical proof, although given certain premises, it may be deduced. Both statements contain terms common to religious language, but that does not make them both religious beliefs. We say the former is *probably* not a statement of religious belief; though it is conceivable that it might be. One cannot tell from the isolated statement alone. And perhaps this suggests a distinction between religious and scientific beliefs. The former seem always to belong to a larger context than the latter, and perhaps cannot be fully understood except in this context, which includes emotions, needs, attitudes, dispositions, values, that have no place in scientific beliefs.

Not only do religious beliefs provide a realm of beliefs for philosophers to analyze; philosophers are often themselves strongly influenced by religious beliefs. Sometimes a philosopher—in this case, a theologian—adopts the beliefs of a religious community and uses philosophy to attempt an orderly explication of some creed; or he may attempt to justify religious dogma on philosophical grounds. The distinguishing work of theology is, very roughly, the expression of faith in some revelation and tradition.

Greek philosophers, particularly Plato, Aristotle, and the Stoics, did not trust the traditional poetry of their people that contained stories of the gods and the relations of men to these gods. On the whole, the philosophers agreed on two points. The first was that these gods of the poets were the work of human imagination. "Aethiopians have gods with snub noses and black hair, Thracians have gods with grey eyes and red hair." Xenophanes added that if horses drew pictures they would draw their gods as horses. Moreover, Xenophanes also pointed out that the poets attributed to gods "all things that are shameful and a reproach among man-

---

[1] So says A. J. Ayer of immortality against Moritz Schlick.
See V. C. Aldrich "Messers Schlick and Ayer on Immortality," *The Philosophical Review*, Vol. 47, No. 278, 1938. Herbert Feigl and Wilfrid Sellars (eds.), *Readings in Philosophical Analysis*, Appleton-Century-Crofts, New York, 1949, pp. 171–174.

kind: theft, adultery, and mutual deception."[2] Socrates was accused of not believing in the gods of the city of Athens. But he protested that by no means was he therefore an atheist. What nearly all the Greek philosophers did was to redefine the concept "god." These redefinitions were the achievement of beliefs that were not, in their opinion, the projections of human imagination, and not the exaltation of base moral characteristics, but respect for what is good in the universe, and exemplified in the rational nature of man.

But, we may ask, will not reason in turn destroy philosophic religion by using the same rational tools that debunked the tales of Homer and Hesiod? Xenophanes described the sea as water, but not as Poseidon; the sun as the source of heat, but not as Phoebus Apollo; the rainbow as a cloud in which colors appear, but not as Iris. All this we should call scientific belief, or the crude common-sense naturalism which was historically the metaphysical basis of scientific knowledge. The ancient philosophers were not satisfied with answers to questions about water, heavenly bodies, meteorology. They asked more ultimate questions, those we call metaphysical, e.g., "What accounts for the whole world and its order?" The answers were called *theology* by Plato and Aristotle, but this theology did not make the kind of appeal that a Jew or a Christian makes to the revelation and tradition of his community. It became known later as *natural theology*, a group of questions about the nature of things. Philosophy, in other words, is a subject that includes such questions as "Does God exist?" "Why is there evil?" "Is man immortal?" Associated with these questions is always the problem of meaning as well as truth. What do we mean by "god," "evil," "immortal"? Even if one does accept a revelation, there is still a great area of philosophical analysis. One may then analyze the meaning of terms that occur persistently in religious beliefs without believing that they convey information, or are true in any other sense. One may analyze the meaning of "truth" as it occurs in the beliefs of religious men and theologians who claim that they have the true faith and that their faith is in the one true God.

When Xenophanes expresses his vision of the relation between the world and god, how should we know whether this view is true or false?

There is one god, among gods and men the greatest, not at all like mortals in body or in mind.
He sees as a whole, thinks as a whole, and hears as a whole. But without toil he sets everything in motion, by the thought of his mind.[3]

[2] K. Freeman, *Ancilla to the Pre-Socratic Philosophers*, Blackwell, Oxford, 1952, p. 22.
[3] *Ibid.*, p. 23.

If we are theologians in the first sense, appealing to revelation, we should set these passages from a philosopher side by side with passages from the Scriptures. The principle is that whatever agrees with divine revelation is true. Certainly it is no feat of scholarship to find passages on the uniqueness, the total knowledge, and the creative power of God. From a Hebrew prophet of roughly the same period we read:

To whom will ye liken me, and make me equal, and compare me, that we may be like?
For as the heavens are higher than the earth, so are my ways higher than your ways, and my thoughts than your thoughts.
Mine hand also hath laid the foundations of the earth, and my right hand spanned the heavens: when I call unto them, they stand up together.

But what if we find teachings in revelation that are not paralleled in philosophy? Examples of these are the doctrines that man sins against a God who lays down rules for human conduct, and that it is man who can be forgiven by God when man is penitent.

Seek ye the Lord while he may be found, call ye upon him while he is near: Let the wicked forsake his way, and the unrighteous man his thoughts: and let him return unto the Lord, and he will have mercy upon him; and to our God, for he will abundantly pardon.[4]

In what sense could it be "true" that God forgives the penitent sinner? One philosopher-theologian answers that we can speak of this only in parable, figuratively rather than literally. Truth is not found in a general proposition about God but in a typical action of God himself. How do we know the redemption of the sinner? Apparently by allowing the action of God to "work out in us."[5] But then could one who has not had this experience say truthfully that God forgives sinners? Evidently not. And apparently he would not know what the parables were about.

Other philosophers have endeavored to state religious beliefs in a more public and less private way. And many theologians have accepted the philosophic task as necessary when attempting to communicate with members of a different faith. We shall examine shortly the approach of St. Thomas Aquinas, who uses the Aristotelian physics and metaphysics shared by Jews and Moslems with Catholic Christians of the thirteenth century.

But many of the great philosophers have professed a private religious inspiration. A noted recent idealist of Cambridge, McTaggart, accepts a

[4] King James Version of The Holy Bible, Isaiah 46:5, 55:9, 48:13, and 55:6–7.
[5] Austin Farrer, Introduction, *The Core of the Bible*, Harper & Brothers, New York, 1956, pp. 10–11.

religion found in Plato, Spinoza, and Hegel: "an emotion resting on a conviction of a harmony between ourselves and the universe at large."[6]

The difference between such an emotion and the faithful piety of a
church theologian is that the philosopher claims that his affirmation is the
result of investigation and proof. What sort of inquiry? Not scientific in
the sense that such a proposition is derived from the observation of particular things that we can sense. These questions of religion are both
existential and evaluative: whether a God exists, whether the universe is
more good than bad, whether it becomes better or worse, whether we survive bodily death. Such beliefs determine men's attitude toward reality.
How can we call them "true"? The only justification McTaggart knows is
that they fit a coherent system of propositions. That is, the nature and test
of religious truth is coherence. If we have ruled out correspondence as the
nature and test of religious truth, are we limited to espousing coherence?
It would seem not. For religious philosophers of the churchly and non-
churchly type both stress the difference religious beliefs make in the conduct of men. This stress opens the way to a pragmatic interpretation of
religious truth:

It will depend on those beliefs, whether we shall consider the universe as
determined by forces completely out of relation with the good, or whether, on
the contrary, we may trust that the dearest ideals and aspirations of our own
nature are realized, and far more than realized in the ultimate reality. It will
depend on them whether we can regard the troubles of the present, and the
uncertainties of the future, with the feelings of a mouse towards a cat, or of a
child towards its father. It will depend on them whether we look on our
pleasures as episodes which will soon pass, or on our sorrows as delusions which
will soon be dispelled. It will depend on them whether our lives seem to us
worth living only as desperate efforts to make the best of an incurably bad
business, or as the passage to a happiness that it has not entered into our hearts
to conceive.
Are there any questions which affect our welfare more than these? It is true
that what primarily affects our welfare is the truth on these matters and not our
knowledge of the truth. But a belief that things are well with the world brings
happiness, a belief that things are ill with the world brings misery. And this
involves the intense practical importance of our belief on the problems of
religion.[7]

The pragmatic step is to say that the distinction between the truth of a
belief and believing something true is without objective difference. Many
persons have unwittingly accepted the pragmatist strategy by saying that

[6] G. L. Dickinson, *J. McT. E. McTaggart,* Cambridge Univesity Press, Cambridge,
1931, p. 129.
[7] *Ibid.,* pp. 130–131.

a true religious belief is one that is strongly affirmed: If someone believes firmly enough, and acts accordingly, then the belief is true, that is, true for him.

It is not possible to deal with all the religious beliefs men hold. It is enough for us to know that many men have what they call religious beliefs, and that they hold them to be true, although few make the attempt to establish their truth. It certainly could safely be said that no one would hold a religious belief if he were convinced of its falsity. But more, there have been some attempts to defend and demonstrate rationally some of the major beliefs in religion. To these we now turn.

II. Belief in the Existence of God

It can be said that a central belief of religion is that God or gods exist. Few would deny the centrality of this belief, although there may be some who claim to be religious and yet do not affirm the existence of a God or gods. It is extremely difficult to say what it is one believes when one believes that there is a God. If someone asks, "Do you believe there is a God?" what can one answer when it is not clear what is being asked? Suppose one says yes, then what does the questioner know? Certainly not that they both have the same conception of God. Suppose one says no, what has he denied that can be adequately described? In short, this, as with so many questions in religion, is not *one* question, but many, and it must be unpacked before anything significant about belief can be said. As it stands it may be possible to answer it with neither a yes nor a no, but with a yes and no.

To unpack the question thoroughly will not be attempted. But a part of the job must be done at least, in order to have some idea of what is sometimes meant by the word God. More often than not the word is used to mean a being who is the supreme perfection of all those qualities men value but possess only imperfectly themselves. Thus God is said to be morally, intellectually, spiritually perfect, and perfect in power. But there are others who would modify a part of this conception, and mean by God a morally, spiritually, and intellectually perfect being who must encounter something not himself, which in certain respects places a limitation upon his power and activity. This is the idea of a finite God, found in Plato, John Stuart Mill, and some contemporary philosophers. Others may use the word God to mean either those tendencies in man that fashion and fulfill ideals, or the total ideal realm itself. And finally, though this does not exhaust the possibilities, the term God may be used to refer to a being whose existence and ideally perfect qualities are gradually emerging or coming to be.

What are the sources of this belief in a being signified by the word God? Only four will be suggested here. First, one may acquire the belief through what is thought to be a direct, or immediate, or intuitive experience of God. One "senses" his presence. This is central to the mystical experience, and more will be said about it later. Second, one may believe because one accepts the authority of a book such as the Bible, or an institution, such as the Church, or a person, such as a priest, friend, or parent. Such acceptance is of little philosophical interest and we shall not examine it further. A third way of coming to a belief in God is through the experience of need and the pragmatic satisfaction the belief gives. We will want to look more deeply into this. Finally, men believe in God because the proposition "God exists" is the conclusion that follows from an argument. This is the way of reason, and it must certainly be explored in greater detail. In fact, it will be best to begin with this.

A. Belief in God Derived From Rational Argument

1. *St. Thomas Aquinas.*

Perhaps the most famous effort in Western philosophy to demonstrate by rational argument the truth of the proposition "God exists" was made by St. Thomas Aquinas. It is probably best to let him speak for himself. He offers five ways by which he thinks the existence of God can be proved.

The first and more manifest way is the argument from motion. It is certain, and evident to our senses, that in the world some things are in motion. Now whatever is moved is moved by another, for nothing can be moved except it is in potentiality to that towards which it is moved; whereas a thing moves inasmuch as it is in act. For motion is nothing else than the reduction of something from potentiality to actuality. But nothing can be reduced from potentiality to actuality, except by something in a state of actuality. Thus that which is actually hot, as fire, makes wood, which is potentially hot, to be actually hot, and thereby moves and changes it. Now it is not possible that the same thing should be at once in actuality and potentiality in the same respect, but only in different respects. For what is actually hot cannot simultaneously be potentially hot; but it is simultaneously potentially cold. It is therefore impossible that in the same respect and in the same way a thing should be both mover and moved, i.e., that it should move itself. Therefore, whatever is moved must be moved by another. If that by which it is moved be itself moved, then this also must needs be moved by another, and that by another again. But this cannot go on to infinity, because then there would be no first mover, and, consequently, no other mover, seeing that subsequent movers move only inasmuch as they are moved by the first mover; as the staff moves only because it is moved by the hand. Therefore it is necessary to arrive at a first mover, moved by no other; and this everyone understands to be God.

The second way is from the nature of efficient cause. In the world of sensible things we find there is an order of efficient causes. There is no case known (neither is it, indeed, possible) in which a thing is found to be the efficient cause of itself; for so it would be prior to itself, which is impossible. Now in efficient causes it is not possible to go on to infinity, because in all efficient causes following in order, the first is the cause of the intermediate cause, and the intermediate is the cause of the ultimate cause, whether the intermediate cause be several, or one only. Now to take away the cause is to take away the effect. Therefore, if there be no first cause among efficient causes, there will be no ultimate, nor any intermediate, cause. But if in efficient causes it is possible to go on to infinity, there will be no first efficient cause, neither will there be an ultimate effect, nor any intermediate efficient causes; all of which is plainly false. Therefore it is necessary to admit a first efficient cause, to which everyone gives the name of God.

The third way is taken from possibility and necessity, and runs thus. We find in nature things that are possible to be and not to be, since they are found to be generated, and to be corrupted, and consequently, it is possible for them to be and not to be. But it is impossible for these always to exist, for that which can not-be at some time is not. Therefore, if everything can not-be, then at one time there was nothing in existence. Now if this were true, even now there would be nothing in existence, because that which does not exist begins to exist only through something already existing. Therefore, if at one time nothing was in existence, it would have been impossible for anything to have begun to exist; and thus even now nothing would be in existence—which is absurd. Therefore, not all beings are merely possible, but there must exist something the existence of which is necessary. But every necessary thing either has its necessity caused by another, or not. Now it is impossible to go on to infinity in necessary things which have their necessity caused by another, as has been already proved in regard to efficient causes. Therefore we cannot but admit the existence of some being having of itself its own necessity, and not receiving it from another, but rather causing in others their necessity. This all men speak of as God.

The fourth way is taken from the gradation to be found in things. Among beings there are some more and some less good, true, noble, and the like. But more and less are predicated of different things according as they resemble in their different ways something which is the maximum, as a thing is said to be hotter according as it more nearly resembles that which is hottest; so that there is something which is truest, something best, something noblest, and, consequently, something which is most being, for those things that are greatest in truth are greatest in being. . . . Now the maximum in any genus is the cause of all in that genus, as fire, which is the maximum of heat, is the cause of all hot things. . . . Therefore there must also be something which is to all beings the cause of their being, goodness, and every other perfection; and this we call God.

The fifth way is taken from the governance of the world. We see that things which lack knowledge, such as natural bodies, act for an end, and this is evident from their acting always, or nearly always, in the same way, so as to obtain the best result. Hence it is plain that they achieve their end, not fortuitously, but designedly. Now whatever lacks knowledge cannot move towards an end, unless it be directed by some being endowed with knowledge and intelligence; as the arrow is directed by the archer. Therefore some intelligent being exists by whom all natural things are directed to their end; and this being we call God.[8]

An examination of these five arguments quickly shows that they all have a similar structure. There is first an appeal to experience, that is, to some observable fact or event such as this motion, this effect, this existent, this judgment of perfection, this purpose. Yet no fact is self-explanatory. Therefore in each case the problem is to find an explanation, that is, logically compelling reasons for the existence of the fact. But if the antecedents were other facts, then the same problem occurs with respect to them and we become involved in an infinite regress which would prevent us from accounting for the intermediate facts. And if we did not have the intermediate facts we would not have this present observable one. Nevertheless, we have it. The conclusion derived is that one must step outside the infinite series to solve the problem and then affirm the existence of an Unmoved Mover, an Uncaused Cause, a Necessary Being, a Perfect Being, and a Supreme Intelligence. All these names refer to the same being whom we call, says St. Thomas, God.

The arguments too have been given names, and the beginning student might as well learn them, for he will undoubtedly meet them again in other connections. The arguments from motion and cause are usually coupled and called the *cosmological argument;* the fourth, the *argument from degrees of perfection;* and the fifth is either the *argument from design* or the *teleological argument.*

Now let us look more closely at these arguments to be sure we understand what they are trying to do. Here, let us say is a case of motion, for instance a ball thrown into the air. Its motion is imparted to it by another motion; say that of the wrist, and that of the wrist by that of the arm, and that of the arm by that of the body, and that of the body by some previous motion, and so on, to where? Since motion can come only from motion there seems no stopping short of infinity. If we number these motions, e.g., 1, 2, 3, 4, 5, . . . 18, . . . 50, . . . 100 . . . to infinity, then we cannot have motion 1, the observed motion, until we have 2, nor 2 until we have 3, nor 3 until we have 4, and so on. But if this goes to infinity we will

---

[8] Anton C. Pegis (ed.), *Basic Writings of St. Thomas Aquinas*, Random House, New York, 1945, Vol. I, pp. 22–23.

never have motion 4, or 3, or 2, and consequently not 1. But we do have it. It was just observed. So an infinite series composed of actual events is impossible. The infinite series that is possible is of non-actual entities, that is, pure numbers. If the actual series is finite, and inexplicable within itself, we may explain it in terms of something else. This something else, its ground, is called the First Mover.

This is the structure that is present in all the arguments. No more will be said about cause, for it clearly fits the pattern. But perhaps some help may be needed for the argument from necessary and contingent being. Anything is contingent if three things may be said of it, first, there was a time when it did not exist, second, there is a time when it exists, and third, there will be a time when it will not exist. Consider this piece of chalk. It is contingent according to this definition. If everything is contingent, there would be a time when there was nothing, because being can come only from being and there would be no intermediate beings if we are involved in an infinite regress. In this case there would be nothing now, which is absurd, because here is the chalk. Thus we are forced to accept a necessary being which cannot not exist, that is, whose being is not derived from any previous being.

The argument from degrees of perfection also has the same pattern, and leads to the affirmation of the most perfect being whose perfection is the standard by which every other imperfection is judged, but whose own perfection cannot be judged since there is nothing superior to him.

The argument from design, or the teleological argument, is perhaps regarded by most people as the strongest of all. Hume and Kant, who were scornful of the other arguments, felt deep respect for this one. It certainly makes an appeal to common sense. It should be considered in greater detail, but briefly it amounts to something like this. Wherever we find order and adaptation in human experience, we find mind at work and responsible. But it is not only in deliberately arranged human works that we respond to harmony. The vast order of nature requires something great enough to account for its precision, regularity, and order. This cannot be a finite human mind. Thus we are led to an Infinite Intelligence.

Before going on to other arguments we ought to comment on these. For many laymen and theologians they constitute a powerful, rational support of faith, giving that faith the same degree and kind of certainty found in logic or mathematics. Some philosophers and many theologians are unanimous in rejecting the arguments as they are offered, namely, as "proof." The following points in criticism of the arguments can be made.

First, it is not clear from all these ways that the highly eulogistic terms

of moral and religious experience can apply to an Unmoved Mover, a *etc*
First Cause, a Necessary Being, and so on. Nor is it clear that the Unmoved Mover is the same being as the First Cause or the Necessary Being.
Thus the arguments require further demonstration for what is frequently
thought of as a personal deity, that is, one to which the following predicates may be applied, wise, good, loving, just, etc. The conception of a
personal deity is certainly vague and requires careful scrutiny.

Second, it is not immediately obvious that the cause of things must be
one and not many. This suggests, e.g., that the cosmological argument is
marred by the fallacy of composition, that is, because the things, persons,
and events we know have antecedent and determinable causes, therefore
the universe as a whole has an antecedent and determinable cause. This
does not necessarily follow, for we have seen that one cannot argue with
certainty that because something is true of the parts it is also true of the
whole that composes the parts. Similar objections can be made to the
other arguments.

Third, a further objection is sometimes raised from a study of the history of science. St. Thomas argued within the context of Aristotelian
physics in which matter is passive and the motion of a thing can be
explained only by a form, and ultimately by the pure form of the First
Mover. But, as a contemporary critic says:

Modern science is built on a dynamic rather than a static foundation. It assumes that the realities of the world are by their very nature in process rather
than at rest; one of its basic principles is Newton's first law of motion, according
to which every moving body continues to move in the same direction and with
the same velocity unless external forces prevent. This means that motion as such
needs no explanation; it is only change in the velocity or direction of motion
that requires to be accounted for. The same assumption is implied in the more
recent theory of evolution.[9]

Thus according to this objection, to agree with St. Thomas is to espouse
a physics that is as antiquated as alchemy and astrology.

Last, another possible objection to St. Thomas' proof is that from the
assumption that the world is an effect it argues to an unobservable cause.
The relationship between God and the world cannot be merely contingent;
which is to say the relationship must be necessary. Some philosophers
claim we are hampered in thinking of cause as a kind of productive agency.
An alternative view is possible, namely, cause as regular sequence. By this
stroke Hume and his followers thought they had banished any logical

[9] Edwin A. Burtt, *Types of Religious Philosophy*, New York, Harper & Brothers,
New York, 1939, pp. 96–97.

necessity of a first or ultimate cause. Moreover, if God is a necessary cause of the world, then the relation is reciprocal, for how could God be a necessary cause, that is, the Creator unless there were a world? Hence God could not be without the world. From this would follow the eternity of the world, and many other heresies that St. Thomas sought to avoid.[10]

The strongest appeal these arguments have is that they start with the fact that something exists. The mind confronted with this existent may be led in at least three different directions: First, it may find that the existent is self-explanatory; this seems not to occur universally, for there are so many disagreements about what the explanation is. Second, it may simply accept the fact without asking questions; this seems not to occur in any mind able to perform its highest function, namely, rational inquiry. Third, it may seek for an explanation in something other than the thing itself. This seems intelligent. Therefore, although the arguments fall short of proof, it cannot be said that they are utterly foolish. At least what is foolish about them must be brought out by careful analysis. And the final word has perhaps not yet been said.

2. *The Teleological Argument.*

The argument from design, or the teleological argument is regarded by many as the most compelling of all. It deserves special attention. The general nature of the argument is simple enough to grasp immediately: at the human level where there is order, organization, adaptation, in short, the fitness of one thing for another, there is present a mind or intelligence that intends or plans these arrangements. Therefore, wherever there is order and adaptedness and interrelatedness in the natural and cosmic dimensions, there is presumably a directing, intelligent agent responsible. The argument in its weakest form is a crude analogy: watch—watchmaker; world—worldmaker. David Hume had little trouble in dispatching it with his devastating criticism in which he reminded its proponents that though they had experience of both watches and watchmakers, they had none of universemakers.

Our common speech often reflects our conscious or unconscious belief that nature is a realm of ends or goals in which activity is goal-directed. We may say, for example, "birds have wings in order to fly"; or "fruits are often brightly colored in order to attract animals"; "plants grow toward the light because light is needed for photosynthesis." The phrase "in order to" is usually the sign of teleological thinking, that is, of referring purpose

[10] *Ibid.*, p. 98.
See also V. Burnwood Evans, "The Aquinate Proof of the Existence of God," *Philosophy*, Vol. 7, No. 27, 1932, pp. 305–306.

or plan to nature. The question is now, is purposing and planning a real or only apparent feature of the natural world of living beings?

Probably most biologists reject a teleological account of their science. It is not for them a useful hypothesis. All biological explanations, it is said, can be given without assuming teleology and thus even on the basis of Ockham's razor or the law of parsimony it is repudiated. Some even claim that teleology can be positively disproved in their science, but this is almost certainly going too far. It is one thing to show that an activity can be explained without reference to purpose—it is quite another to show that an alternative account is clearly impossible either logically or empirically.

Though denying purpose, some biologists admit direction in evolutionary process. Here, for example, are the words of Huxley:

> The ordinary man, or at least the ordinary poet, philosopher, and theologian, is always asking himself what is the purpose of human life, and is anxious to discover some extraneous purpose to which he and humanity may conform. Some find such a purpose exhibited directly in revealed religion; others think that they can uncover it from the facts of nature. One of the commonest methods of this form of natural religion is to point to evolution as manifesting such a purpose. The history of life, it is asserted, manifests guidance on the part of some external power; and the usual deduction is that we can safely trust that same power for further guidance in the future.
>
> I believe this reasoning to be wholly false. The purpose manifested in evolution, whether in adaptation, specialization, or biological progress, is only an apparent purpose. It is just as much a product of blind forces as is the falling of a stone to earth or the ebb and flow of the tides. It is we who have read purpose into evolution, as earlier men projected will and emotion into inorganic phenomena like storm or earthquake. If we wish to work towards a purpose for the future of man, we must formulate that purpose ourselves. Purposes in life are made, not found.
>
> But if we cannot discover a purpose in evolution, we can discern a direction —the line of evolutionary progress. And this past direction can serve as a guide in formulating our purpose for the future. Increase of control, increase of independence, increase of internal co-ordination; increase of knowledge, of means for co-ordinating knowledge, of elaborateness and intensity of feeling—those are trends of the most general order. If we do not continue them in the future, we cannot hope that we are in the main line of evolutionary progress any more than could a sea-urchin or a tapeworm.[11]

This statement probably represents the sentiments of most modern biological scientists. They do not deny that adaptation is real or that there is progression and direction. But the process is regarded as wholly natural

[11] Julian Huxley, *Evolution: The Modern Synthesis,* Harper & Brothers, New York 1943, pp. 576–577.

and mechanical in its operation. It is true that some admit the possibility of an Initiator of the process and its laws who employs mechanistic methods to accomplish his plans, but they immediately shy away from this problem as being too deep and not one upon which the scientist, as a scientist, can speak.[12]

The philosopher certainly may not contradict the biologist who says that he has no need of a hypothesis of teleology in his biological explanations—it may just be the case that biology as such is not furthered by the concept of a Planner and a Purpose. On the other hand, the philosopher may object if the biologist concludes from his evidence from particular events that purpose is not to be found at any level. At any rate, whether purpose is present at any level is not a scientific problem but a philosophical one, which must be solved in the context of a more inclusive philosophical perspective. If the biologist rejects teleology he must give another account or explanation.

R. B. Braithwaite has made an interesting attempt to explain goal-directed activity, that is, action with a direction but not a director, with the concept of the "plasticity" of this activity.[13] This calls attention to the fact that it is not the end or goal as such that is the distinctive feature of goal-directed activity, but it is the *persistence* of the activity in the face of obstacles. The organism, in short, can attain its goal under different circumstances by alternative forms of activity and by using different causal chains, and thus a teleological explanation of its achievement is not required. For a clear and full account the student is advised to read Braithwaite's work.

But the full force of the teleological argument is not disposed of by mere biological considerations. More recent attempts to give the argument vitality admit that no particular case of adaptedness, nor even a multiplicity of them, is sufficient to establish its validity, rather it is "in the conspiration of innumerable causes to produce, by their united and reciprocal action, and to maintain, a general order of Nature," that its real strength lies.[14]

The newer statement of the argument does not depend upon bad analogies, but seeks to establish a belief in God by deriving it inductively from certain facts. This, of course, cannot give the conclusion logical cer-

[12] See, e.g., G. G. Simpson, "The Problem of Plan and Purpose in Nature," *Scientific Monthly*, Vol. 64, No. 6, 1947, p. 495.
[13] R. B. Braithwaite, *Scientific Explanation*, Cambridge University Press, Cambridge, 1953, pp. 329–330.
[14] F. R. Tennant, *Philosophical Theology*, Cambridge University Press, Cambridge, 1930, Vol. II, p. 79.

tainty. But for many it does permit a highly reasonable belief. Tennant has suggested the following instances of adaptedness upon which many teleological arguments rest:

First, the adaptation of thought to things, that is, the knowability of the world, which has made science possible. Second, the internal adaptedness of organic beings when the various parts and organs are interrelated and dependent. Too much stress here can lead to absurdities, as satirical critics are not slow in pointing out—for example, one contemptously says, "How nice it is to have ears just back of the eyes so our glasses will stay on—there must be a God"; another is driven to express his distaste over the superficiality of the argument by saying, "How fortunate it is that the holes in a cat's hide correspond with his eyeballs, else the cat could not see out." These, of course, are not philosophic criticisms, but they do indicate the rejection of any explanation in terms of design when the principles of evolutionary change are sufficient. Third, the fitness of the inorganic to minister to life, that is, the world seems prepared or equipped to maintain life; its chemical, physical and thermal conditions are just right, a condition which seems to many thinkers inexplicable on the basis of mere coincidence. Fourth, the presence of aesthetic values in nature, which do not necessarily contribute to survival nor have other utilitarian functions. Nature, it is said, is radiant with beauty and elicits an aesthetic sentiment wherever it is observed, which adds little or nothing to man's knowledge, but much to his happiness. The beauty is a gift and therefore *intended* for man. Fifth, the instrumentality of nature to the realization of moral ends. Here it is pointed out that nature is not only not antipathetic toward man's moral aims, but positively both a promoter of them and an instrument by which they may be attained. Its uniformity, for example, is the condition for many values and the development of character. In fact, this point has given rise to an argument for God's existence that deserves separate consideration. It is called the Moral Argument and it will be dealt with later. Finally, the teleologists often insist that the evolutionary processes in nature, culminating in a rational and moral being, also give evidence of a supervisory mind. It is suggested that it is more difficult to accept a view that claims that a non-intelligent universe can produce intelligent beings, than it is to accept the view that the presence of intelligent beings presupposes an intelligent source.

The teleologist has offered an impressive case. The evidence he brings forth cannot be denied. But it may still be asked whether the evidence proves his conclusion. As strict proof the argument fails; on the basis of an inductive accumulation of evidence the only conclusion possible is a

518 / Philosophy: The Study of Alternative Beliefs

probable one. The reader will have to think carefully here and decide whether he must accept some teleology, or remarkable and perhaps inexplicable coincidence.

3. *The Ontological Argument.*

One of the most extraordinary and interesting arguments for the existence of God was first formulated in the eleventh century by Anselm (1033–1109). It is extraordinary because in spite of what some thinkers consider its downright logical fallaciousness, other philosophers have attempted a restatement to avoid the charge. Among these latter are Descartes, Spinoza, Hegel, and a battery of authorities as able as St. Thomas, Kant, and Hume. It is interesting because of its long history, which reveals that each proponent is aware of objections by equally competent philosophers who claim to have finally exposed it. Often it is abandoned with contempt at one period and is found attractive at another. Even St. Anselm was not always sure about the validity of his own argument. Bertrand Russell, writing of his student days at Cambridge when studying philosophy under men greatly influenced by Hegel, says,

I remember the precise moment, one day in 1894, as I was walking along Trinity Lane, when I saw in a flash (or thought I saw) that the ontological argument is valid. I had gone out to buy a tin of tobacco; on my way back, I suddenly threw it up in the air, and exclaimed as I caught it, "Great Scott, the ontological argument is sound."[15]

Whether Russell was referring to the use of the ontological argument for God is not clear, but if he was, it is a certainty that he has long since revised his opinion.

Now let us look at this strange argument as it was first stated by Anselm. We must be as fair as possible and therefore not fail to say that Anselm did not offer the argument to convince an unbeliever, rather he thought it would give rational support to one who already believed on faith. The argument, for Anselm, must be seen in the context of one of his major principles, namely, "I do not seek to understand that I may believe, but I believe in order to understand. For this also I believe,—that unless I believed, I should not understand."[16] So, already believing in God on nonrational grounds, he searches for a way in which reason may also sustain his belief. The argument then appears as follows:

First, a definition: God is a being "than which nothing greater can be conceived." Then a categorical proposition that asserts existence is an at-

---

[15] Paul Arthur Schilpp (ed.), *The Philosophy of Bertrand Russell*, Library of Living Philosophers, Tudor Publishing Co., New York, 1951, p. 10.

[16] St. Anselm, *Proslogium; Monologium; An Appendix in Behalf of the Fool by Gaunilon; and Cur Deus Homo* (Sidney N. Deane) The Open Court Publishing Co., La Salle, Illinois, 1951, p. 7.

tribute of perfection. And finally the conclusion which presumably follows, namely, "God exists." As it stands it is scarcely in strict logical form, but before putting it in proper form, let us see if we can understand what he is trying to say. The first statement tells us that we have an idea of a perfect being, so perfect, in fact, that no other being more perfect can be conceived. If we analyze this idea, which it is said we have, then we find that it includes the idea of existence. Suppose you begin to conceive of a God. Give him all the attributes you think a perfect being ought to have. But remember this is only a construction of your mind. Now can you conceive still a greater being? Yes, one that has all the attributes you first described but that now is outside your mind, namely, that has existence. In short, a being cannot be perfect no matter how many attributes it possesses to perfection, if it lacks the attribute of existence. This is the heart of all attempts to restate the ontological argument.

C. D. Broad has tried to put it in a plausible form with the following result:

Anything that lacked existence would lack a positive property which it might conceivably have had. Nothing which lacked a positive property which it might conceivably have had would be a most perfect being; for it is logically possible that there should be something superior to it, *viz.* a being which resembled it in all other respects but had the additional property of existence. Therefore no most perfect being would lack existence. Therefore, all most perfect beings exist.[17]

When it is put this way, the argument is a valid syllogism in the fourth figure, the structure of which may be shown as follows:

Things lacking P also lack M;
Nothing lacking M lacks S;
Hence no S lacks P.

The conclusion is obverted to produce "All most perfect beings exist."

But this presents difficulties. The universal affirmative proposition may be interpreted as a hypothetical or conditional proposition, that is, "All S is P" may mean, "If anything were an S it would be a P." But this does not say that there actually is an S. If "All S is P" is interpreted to mean "There are some S's and none lack P" then the logical principle is broken that it is fallacious to draw an existential conclusion from non-existential premises. This means that the above premises cannot lead to the conclusion that there is a perfect being, for this conclusion would require an existential premise. Thus all that can really be legitimately drawn from

[17] C. D. Broad, *Religion, Philosophy, and Psychical Research*, Harcourt, Brace & Co., New York, 1953, p. 180.

the premises is, "If anything were a most perfect being it would not lack existence," which, as Broad says, is trivial and useless. If the conclusion is interpreted existentially then another difficulty appears, namely, that the sentence is a pleonasm, that is, in "There are most perfect beings and none of them lack existence" one adds nothing to "There are" by saying "none of them lack existence."

There are further logical problems that make the argument highly suspicious, but they cannot be dealt with now. If the student would like to try out his philosophical wits let him ask himself whether existence is a quality or attribute, such as red or square, that can be predicated of anything. Thus, for example, one can intelligibly say, "Apples are red" which means "If anything exists as an apple then it is red." But if we say "Apples exist" do we mean, "If anything exists as an apple then it exists"? This is nothing but a tautology. "Existence" may function grammatically as a predicate but not logically. As least some philosophers think so and reject the argument on these grounds. Our concepts of anything, including that of a perfect being, are non-existential.

But these difficulties have not discouraged some philosophers from making further attempts to rescue the argument and to give it a new life. Let us put it in another context and look at a reformulation of the argument from a different point of view.

What are called ontological arguments are very intimately bound up with the doctrine of self-evident truth in epistemology and a rationalistic metaphysics. Each of these has been previously discussed, and to avoid repetition, it would be well if the student examined these theories in the earlier chapters.

Recall that one cannot affirm without contradiction that "A triangle has two sides" or "A triangle has four sides." It lies in the nature of a triangle to have three and only three sides. The definition demands this, and if a person fails to see the necessity, anyone who knows geometry—specifically Euclidian plane geometry—may well conclude that this person does not know what he is talking about when he talks of the possibility of two-sided or four-sided triangles. This is the method of the great rationalists Descartes, Spinoza, and Leibniz. The student may resume his acquaintance with them in studying ontological arguments. That we can argue ontologically is a proposition defended by nearly all philosophers called rationalists and denied by nearly all philosophers called empiricists.

Before criticizing any ontological argument, one should see it first from a rationalistic perspective. The rationalistic method begins with a concept that is clear and expressed in what we commonly call a real definition, that is, a definition that claims to do more than stipulate how a word is to be used. A real definition attempts to say what the entity is, thus we should limit ourselves to its necessary and sufficient characteristics. A model of this is the definition of triangle as "a plane closed figure of three straight lines." From the concept of an entity, expressed in a definition, can we deduce anything about its reality? Rationalists point out quite correctly that almost no one expects to meet a triangular shape with two sides or with four. Practically no one has any hesitancy in saying that there cannot be triangular shapes with more or less than three sides. The principle is that what is self-contradictory in the realm of thought is impossible in the realm of reality. Here is the simplest principle and example of an ontological argument.

If from a real definition we can make a reasonable conclusion about the impossibility of some entities, round-squares, cubic-spheres, etc., we can also make a reasonable conclusion about the possibility of other entities. There is no self-contradiction in the concept of round cheese, a square of aluminum, a red cube, a blue sphere. Whether there actually is a square of aluminum we may not know, but there may be. If we use this method in the case of "God," what we should do is to define God and to consider whether the characteristics are incompatible or compatible. An easy example is to consider the characteristics "being a spirit or mind" and "having a long white beard." Could there be a God who is a spirit with a long white beard? If minds are not hairy things, they are neither clean-shaven nor hirsute. We may ask of a man whether he is clean-shaven or wears a beard, and we may observe his features. But since we cannot observe divine characteristics, nor arrive at divine characteristics by abstraction from particular observations of other things, we are even more dependent upon the judgment of logical non-contradiction and coherence.

A possible thing can be defined without contradiction. But is the coherence of a concept any index of more than possibility? Those philosophers who use some version of the ontological argument in arguing for the actuality or necessity of God's being, evidently believe that logical coherence is such an index. But philosophers differ as to which concept of God is the most coherent. St. Anselm's God is much like St. Thomas' God, a ground of being on whom all depends for its creation and preservation, the standard of thought as Truth itself, the standard of creation as Beauty itself, the standard of human conduct as Goodness itself, moreover the Judge of every human act who punishes disobedience and who rewards obedience; yet coupled with perfect Justice is the mercy of perfect Love. St. Anselm sets out to demonstrate that all things must depend upon this

Perfect Being, yet God Himself depends in no whit upon anything else. Descartes finds in himself the concept of infinite being. All finite things depend upon the infinite, and Descartes makes sense of his concept only by believing that it is derived from God and refers to God. But Spinoza rejects the traditional distinction between God and the world as creator and creature. Rather God is the infinite whole of which each thing is a part or aspect. But if reality is in process then, argued Hegel, God should not be seen under the aspect of eternity, but rather under the aspect of logical change. In short, Anselm, Descartes, Spinoza, and Hegel all employ a version of the ontological argument with more or less variation as to how they conceive ultimate reality or God.

In order to avoid as far as possible an arbitrary choice between the versions of various philosophers, it will be best to quote a contemporary claim deliberately constructed to combine the insights of the philosophers mentioned above.

The ontological argument is generally supposed to have been refuted. Theologians are as ready to accept this verdict as philosophers. A professor of divinity has recently declared that the argument cannot be given formal or syllogistic statement without revealing a fallacy. This challenge can be met by the following double syllogism.

Major Premise: Whatever is coherently conceivable is *either* actual *or* an unactualized (but real, more than merely "logical") potency.

Minor Premise: God, or Perfect Being, is coherently conceivable.

Conclusion: God is *either* actual *or* an unactualized potency.

Third Premise: God is *not* an unactualized potency ("potency of perfection" being meaningless or self contradictory).

Conclusion: God is actual.

Where is the fallacy? True, one may question the premises; but if an argument can be refuted by showing that its premises are not absolutely indubitable, then what philosophical argument, for no matter what conclusion, can stand? Furthermore, the premises are capable of rational support.[18]

The logical form of this argument might be stated abstractly:

$$A \text{ is } B_1 \text{ or } B_2$$
$$\underline{C \text{ is } A}$$
$$C \text{ is } B_1 \text{ or } B_2$$
$$\underline{C \text{ is not } B_2}$$
$$C \text{ is } B_1$$

If there is no formal fault, then we should proceed to examine the truth of the premises.

[18] Charles Hartshorne, "The Formal Validity and Real Significance of the Ontological Argument," *The Philosophical Review*, Vol. 53, No. 3, 1944, p. 225.

If we are to use the major premise, we should be clear about its assumptions. When we talk of possibility, we mean logically that there is no contradiction in the concepts. But this means a reference to possible being, which is called *ontological potentiality*. This is in contrast to those categorical propositions that refer to actual existence. "An idea stands in relation to the actuality, or if not the actuality, then the possibility, of that which it means. . . . "[19] The order of thought and the logical order then depend upon the order of being. There are modes of thought and logical modes because there are ontological modes.

Some philosophers have balked at this assumption. But Hartshorne's case is strengthened by calling attention to our meaningful statements about the future. If I intend to write the following sentence, it is not yet. But by fulfilling the necessary conditions, I make it actual now. Hence we can talk of *real potency*.

Hartshorne denies that actuality can be deduced from logical or "mere possibility" and also that existence is a predicate found in the mere concept "perfection."[20]

The minor premise is "God is coherently conceivable." This means, according to Hartshorne, that "perfection can be meaningfully defined in terms that . . . do not yield incompatible consequences." The concept "perfection" is employed in thinking in logic and ethics. We are well aware of ignorance and error, of fallacy and sophistry, hence we have some absolute norm of "perfect knowledge." So also of "perfect good will" in ethics.[21]

Hartshorne does not mean that because perfection can be defined coherently that "the most usual definitions are so." The incoherent concepts are of a timeless absolute. The concept of perfection allows process or "increase in value." The former would imply that omniscience includes completed knowledge of the future and therefore of potential events as though already realized. Omniscience in the latter concept is knowledge of whatever can be known at some time. Hence it is defined relative to whatever has so far occurred.

Why does omniscience, thus defined, belong to God together with a "perfect good will," qualified by saying that "the contrast good-evil falls within God"? Apparently supremacy of one sort implies or requires supremacy of the other sort. It is difficult to see that anything could know without knowing values, or could know values without knowing what is.

[19] *Ibid.*, p. 226.
[20] *Ibid.*, pp. 227–228.
[21] *Ibid.*, pp. 228–229.

So all that remains to discuss is the second minor premise, "that there can be no such thing as the potency of perfection. *Perfection is existent or nothing*. This is Anselm's great discovery."[22]

Hartshorne's defense is:

If real potentiality means a capacity of nature or reality to produce something, then if there be potentiality of perfection there is productive capacity sufficient to produce a perfect (unsurpassable) being. But such capacity must itself be unsurpassable in its productiveness, and it seems that it could not be distinguished from the perfect being it is to be able to produce. And also, as Anselm points out, a productive being, *were* it produced, could not be perfect. It would be surpassed in duration by a conceivable being posited as produced still earlier, or as lasting to a later date, or both—unless a produced being could be immortal. Nor does it seem that a produced being could be omniscient, such that no more knowing being other than itself is conceivable. An unsurpassable being, if such is conceivable, must surely be conceived as eternal in the sense of having no beginning or end in time; potentiality means that a transition is conceivable from potential to actual existence; but what can be meant by an eternal transition, or a transition to eternality, to the status of never having come to be?[23]

A speculative philosopher like Hartshorne, formulating the ontological argument for God in the twentieth century, takes advantage of the criticisms offered against older formulations. Hartshorne grants that previous versions have been found wanting on some logical point or other. He invites the reader to answer the following:

1. Has he attempted to deduce actuality from possibility?
2. Is his concept of perfection a mere "regulative ideal"?
3. Has he employed the premise that "existence is a predicate"?
4. Has he begged the question by merely restating in the conclusion what was stated in the premises?
5. Has he made an illegitimate leap beyond possible experience to a non-entity?
6. Has he employed an argument that might be used in pretended demonstrations of perfect islands or a perfect devil?
7. May not "perfection" refer to a whole series or system of possibilities, rather than a single actuality or potentiality?

The best way to conclude this stage of our discussion is to present the problem as an ontologist sees it:

I . . . challenge anyone to show, from generally accepted principles, that the ontological argument is without force—the kind of force a philosophical argu-

[22] *Ibid.*, p. 231.
[23] *Ibid.*, pp. 231–232.

ment is capable of having. If I am in plainly demonstrable error, will not some-one point this out? If not, then should not philosophers alter some of their ways of teaching and writing upon this ancient subject?[24]

4. *The Moral Argument.*

The attempt to make a hidden God disclose himself in a rational argument has turned men not only to the evidence that can be gleaned from nature, but also to the evidence thought significant in man's moral experience. This has been called the moral argument. It consists in asserting the existence of God from the facts of morality, that is, our moral sentiments and aspirations cannot be accounted for except by resort to a supernatural cause. One of the most famous statements is Immanuel Kant's, and the student is advised to reread what was said in Chapter II in which we presented Kant's argument that God is a postulate of the practical reason, that is, He must exist if the moral order is to be intelligible. According to Kant's scheme of things, God is to bring about a proportionate correspondence between virtue and happiness, without which there is no moral universe.

There are many forms of the moral argument, but perhaps one of the best was formulated by Rashdall. It is worth quoting in full.

An absolute Moral Law or moral ideal cannot exist *in* material things. And it does not (we have seen) exist in the mind of this or that individual. Only if we believe in the existence of a Mind for which the true moral ideal is already in some sense real, a Mind which is the source of whatever is true in our own moral judgements, can we rationally think of the moral ideal as no less real than the world itself. Only so can he believe in an absolute standard of right and wrong, which is as independent of this or that man's actual ideas and actual desires as the facts of material nature. The belief in God, though not (like the belief in a real and an active self) a postulate of there being any such thing as Morality at all, is the logical presupposition of an 'objective' or absolute Morality. A moral ideal can exist nowhere and nohow but in a mind; an absolute moral ideal can exist only in a Mind from which all Reality is derived. Our moral ideal can only claim objective validity in so far as it can rationally be regarded as the revelation of a moral ideal eternally existing in the mind of God.[25]

The argument declares that our moral experience implies an absolutely perfect moral standard and that this standard is not found in any individual mind and therefore must exist in a supreme Mind or God.

But again the argument has flaws. It is true that our moral experience involves or presupposes ideals and norms, but it is not certain or obvious

[24] *Ibid.,* p. 245.
[25] Hastings Rashdall, *The Theory of Good and Evil,* The Clarendon Press, Oxford, 1907, Vol. II, p. 212.

that they presuppose an absolutely perfect norm or ideal. Moreover, the argument is full of vague and ambiguous terms, for example, consider the use of the term exist with reference to such phrases as "in material things" and "in the mind." One might also ask whether existence "in the mind" requires existence in actuality, that is, outside the mind. Again, if the moral argument intends to say that only those who ground their morality in a supernatural being can really lead morally acceptable lives, the argument is refuted in history again and again.

5. *Concluding Remarks.*

We can conclude from an examination of these arguments only that the existence of God has not been "proved" by reason; of course, other arguments may be found. Often the acceptance or rejection of the argument centers around the question of what a proof really is. But it does not follow from this failure that there is no such being as the religious consciousness often affirms. It is interesting to try to disprove the existence of God by rational argument. Although many philosophers think reason incapable of demonstrating the non-existence of God, some attempts have been made.

It is not only the logical weaknesses of the arguments that should make us suspect the competence of reason on this matter, but there is also a serious objection, raised by some theologians, to any attempt to find God in the premises of a valid syllogism. Paul Tillich has stated it well in these words:

> God can be proved, or again he can be refuted, by rational methods. But an idea which can be proved by means of arguments that are more or less convincing cannot give me a foundation for my existence in face of eternity. Arguments for the existence of God presuppose the loss of the certainty of God. That which I have to prove by argument has no immediate reality for me. Its reality is mediated for me by some other reality about which I cannot be in doubt; so that this other reality is nearer to me than the reality of God.[26]

B. Mysticism, the Direct and Immediate Experience of God

The mystic claims to know God, not by rational discourse, but by a direct and immediate experience of His reality. This knowledge, of which he has a strong degree of assurance, is peculiarly private and incapable of being adequately communicated. He knows *that* God is because of his experience, but he can only say *what* God is by the use of analogy, metaphor, and other types of figurative language, often highly colored by words drawn from intense sensory experiences. In order to know what he knows one

[26] Paul Tillich, "The Religious Situation in Germany To-day," *Religion in Life*, Vol. III, No. 2, 1934, p. 167.

is required to have the experience which ranges from the milder forms of religious worship to the extreme state of ecstasy. Thus God is beyond the intellect's reach. We may have communion with Him but not communication. Usually the mystic does not claim that the experience brings him any information, rather it leads to an enrichment of his life and a heightened conviction of the reality of God. And yet he is often led to make certain doctrinal assertions on the basis of his experience. For example, the sole reality of God which he learns in his experience teaches him also that all that is not God is essentially unreal. Thus the world of space and of time, of finite selves, and of evil is said to be unreal.

We must not identify the mysticism of the West with that of the East. The Christian mystic claims to have a cognitive experience of God, a being usually thought of as personal, while the object of non-Christian mysticism is largely impersonal in character. But in each there is an insistence on a moral preparation or discipline before the response of the divine to the human can occur. The vision of God comes only to the pure in heart. In general we can say that the mystic has a sense of the presence of the One, or of God; of the awareness of union with this Object and a kind of illumination of his life following the experience. Often accompanying the experience is an emotional state of varying degrees of intensity and the feeling of being utterly unable to communicate the content of the experience. Ordinarily these experiences, if intense, do not come frequently nor endure, although the milder forms are not nearly as transient as the extreme. Furthermore, in many mystics the experience, or its effect, is felt throughout the whole of life, so that it becomes reorganized and strengthened and useful.

What can be said about this way to a belief in God's existence? There is very little that the philosopher can say about the experience itself. It is only when knowledge-claims are made that he may raise certain questions. But even here he is uncomfortable because of the mystic's insistence that his real knowledge is ineffable, so the philosopher must have the experience before he can judge the mystic. At least some philosophers would shy away from this as a method, and some others would deny that they have any religious feelings at all so they could not possibly have the experience. It may also be said that frequently the mystic's knowledge-claims conflict, and this seems strange if what they possess can really be called knowledge. There is, of course, the further difficulty of verifying the knowledge-claim. The verification is a very private affair, but usually we require our knowledge-claims to be publicly verifiable. The mystic's vision, in short, is not itself a criterion of truth. Scientists and philosophers are right in being suspicious of the mystic's way of knowing and of his doctrine, else we cannot be protected from illusion. But is it right to deny categorically that there are no other ways to knowledge except by reason and science? Ought we not to leave open the possibility that the human consciousness may be enhanced or made sensitive to conditions and situations ordinarily obscured by the methods of the pure intellect? The reader should consider the matter carefully after having read, not about mysticism, but some of the mystical literature itself.

C. The Experience of Need and the Pragmatic Satisfaction of Belief

1. *James.*

Another source of belief in God's existence is to be found in man's experience of need and the pragmatic satisfaction arising when the gaps, which interrupt the sense of completeness or continuity of life, are filled. An appeal is no longer made to the mere intellect nor to an immediate and intuitive discovery of God, but rather to the service a profound affirmation of belief may provide for a better, happier, personal life. Instances of those who take this road to belief could be narrated again and again, but we shall present only two classic cases, namely, William James and Blaise Pascal. Let us now turn to James.

In a famous essay called The Will to Believe James set out to defend a man's right "to adopt a believing attitude in religious matters," even though the logical considerations may not be favorable. But first certain distinctions must be made. It is best to let James speak for himself here.

Let us give the name of *hypothesis* to anything that may be proposed to our belief; and just as the electricians speak of live and dead wires, let us speak of any hypothesis as either *live* or *dead*. A live hypothesis is one which appeals as a real possibility to him to whom it is proposed. If I ask you to believe in the Mahdi, the notion makes no electric connection with your nature,—it refuses to scintillate with any credibility at all. As an hypothesis it is completely dead. To an Arab, however, (even if he be not one of Mahdi's followers), the hypothesis is among the mind's possibilities: it is alive. This shows that deadness and liveness in an hypothesis are not intrinsic properties, but relations to the individual thinker. They are measured by his willingness to act. The maximum of liveness in an hypothesis means willingness to act irrevocably. Practically, that means belief; but there is some believing tendency wherever there is willingness to act at all.

Next, let us call the decision between two hypotheses an *option*. Options may be of several kinds. They may be—1, *living* or *dead*; 2, *forced* or *avoidable*; 3, *momentous* or *trivial*, and for our purposes we may call an option a *genuine* option when it is of the forced, living, and momentous kind.[27]

[27] William James, *The Will to Believe*, Longmans, Green & Co., Inc., New York, 1923, pp. 2–3.

Now to this we must add one more statement.

Our passional nature not only lawfully may, but must, decide an option between propositions, whenever it is a genuine option that cannot by its nature be decided on intellectual grounds. . . .[28]

James has pointed out that on all the great questions of philosophy and religion there is much disagreement, which comes not at the beginning of the mind's work but at the end. In short, even when the intellect is pushed to its concentrated best, some questions remain unresolved, that is, we cannot judge from the evidence which hypothesis is to be preferred. When this happens, says James, we need not be doomed to hang dissatisfied between the alternatives, rather we can turn to our "passional nature" and risk a belief in that hypothesis which is "live enough to tempt our will."

The religious hypothesis, say belief in God's existence, confronts us with a genuine option, that is, one that is forced, living, and momentous. The intellect fails to find sufficient evidence for either the possibility of proving or denying God's existence; therefore we must turn to our passions for support, that is, we must take the chance that our passional need to take the world religiously may be right. In this way all the good of religious belief may be preserved and the amelioration of life be achieved.

This is one of the ways James defended a belief in the existence of God. How adequate is the defense? In order to appreciate the full force of his argument the whole essay should be read, but one also ought to look for the difficulties in this condensed account. Some may be suggested here, but the reader is urged to try to think of others. Are the following difficulties avoided by James?

1. May it not be wiser to suspend judgment when evidence is lacking?
2. May not the pragmatic principle be used to justify whatever one wants to believe?
3. May not our passional natures also conflict? Then how resolve these incompatibilities?

In short, James desperately wanted to believe in God's existence. He thought a man was a better man when he did believe. Man needs God, therefore God must exist. Is this sufficient ground for belief?

2. *Pascal.*

More briefly we must consider Pascal's "religious wager." It was an attempt to encourage belief in God's existence because there is everything to gain from such a belief, if it is true, and nothing to lose, if it is false. Here are his own words:

[28] *Ibid.,* p. 11.

Yes, but wager you must; there is no option, you have embarked on it. So which will you have? Come. Since you must choose, let us see what concerns you least. You have two things to lose: truth and good, and two things to stake: your reason and your will, your knowledge and your happiness. And your nature has two things to shun: error and misery. Your reason does not suffer by your choosing one more than the other, for you must choose. That is one point cleared. But your happiness? Let us weigh gain and loss in calling heads that God is. Reckon these two chances: if you win, you win all; if you lose, you lose naught. Then do not hesitate, wager that He is.[29]

Let us suppose that one is convinced that the evidence for the existence of God is no more conclusive than the evidence against. Furthermore, let us suppose that so much is at stake that not to decide might have consequences as momentous as deciding one way or the other. More might be lost if one did not decide. Then the prudent man would have to make up his mind. But again suppose that deciding is not a function of knowledge, or at least not wholly a function of knowledge, that is, the act expressed as "I believe . . . " does not follow from premises alone. In this case deciding might be a function of our interests, discovered by contemplating probable consequences. But if an act of faith depends upon our knowledge of probable outcome, then it is a matter in which there can be evidence. Either the evidence is available to everyone or it becomes common knowledge through the reporting of human experience, or it is reserved for a future life and knowledge about it *now* comes only through revelation. James took the former alternative, Pascal the latter.

Arguments similar to this are frequently found in popular appeals to religious faith. They cannot, however, be said to carry much weight. Religious belief is too complex a matter, in its moral, logical, and psychological dimensions, to be treated so simply. Furthermore, we must raise the question of intellectual honesty. Can one make a wager of the kind required, if the intellect rebels, and should one expect happiness at the price of reason's abeyance? Finally, one may ask whether one has the right to believe solely on these grounds, unless one has first emerged from the trials of doubt? However questionable the religious and spiritual bases of Pascal's position, it is certain that the argument in no way can stand as a proof of God's existence.

3. *Concluding Remarks.*

We have gone as far as we can here on the problem of belief in God's existence. The result in part seems to be that philosophy can offer to the religious consciousness no completely satisfying grounds for establishing

[29] *Pascal's Pensées* (H. F. Stewart, tr.), Routledge & Kegan Paul, Ltd., London, 1950, p. 119.

such a belief. It can neither prove nor disprove. It can only point to the shaky foundations of the arguments on both sides. But men will probably continue to have feelings of deep assurance that the God of their beliefs exists, even when all ways to certainty end before that goal can be reached. Most philosophers would probably be unwilling to believe in God's existence on religious grounds alone. When they do believe it is usually because the belief is a necessary part of a larger system of belief, which we have described as metaphysics. Similarly, when the philosopher disbelieves it is usually because his metaphysics does not permit the belief.

Perhaps the student will reject the somewhat narrow interpretation of proof the philosopher often demands. He may wonder whether it would not be truer to say that God's existence is proved in a more acceptable way when the belief arises from a more complete or total experience of religious devotion which satisfies the needs not only of the intellect but also of the emotions, desires, and hopes of men. Belief in the existence of God may then serve to order and evaluate the details of human experience. This undoubtedly gives the belief a useful purpose, but does it make it true?

III. Beliefs Concerning the Presence of Evil

Very few people need to be told that there is evil in the world, for very few escape its ubiquitous threat. But its presence does bring a problem of both theoretical and practical dimensions. The former is crucial largely for those who accept a belief in an all-powerful and all-good God. The latter concerns all those who face pain, suffering, terror, or death, and who must find a way to deal with these facts.

Consider first the theoretical difficulties. David Hume wrote that the old questions posed by Epicurus were still unanswered in his day. They remain so in ours. "Is he (God) willing to prevent evil, but not able? then is he impotent? Is he able, but not willing? then is he malevolent? Is he both able and willing? whence then is evil?"[30]

It is usually thought necessary and helpful to distinguish the kinds of evil in the world. This does not solve any problems, but it may reduce the complexity so that one issue can be dealt with at a time. Some philosophers have named four kinds, *physical* evil, which includes all pains of the body and those brought about by nature in her wild and destructive adventures; *psychological* evil, that is, all those unhappy conditions that lead to mental suffering, such as grief, fear, terror, suspicion, and hatred; *moral evil*, which describes any choice of a lesser or lower good in preference to a higher, or

[30] David Hume, *Dialogues Concerning Natural Religion*, Hafner Publishing Co., Inc., New York, 1948, p. 66.

some forms of what has been called sin; and *metaphysical* evil, which is morally neutral and emerges from our human limitations or finiteness. It is obvious that these classifications are not mutually exclusive but may overlap in many ways on many different occasions. Bodily pains, for example, may bring on mental agony which may lead to moral evil, for instance, revenge.

A number of theories have been proposed to account for evil in the world. None, of course, succeeds in explaining away any particular case, nor for that matter do they succeed in making evil less harsh or more pleasant. But each points to certain facts, which if acknowledged, may make it possible for the victims of evil to endure it or perhaps to overcome its effects.

1. *Partial Evils, Total Good.*

It is sometimes said that evil is really necessary to the "good of the whole." If one lives, as Spinoza recommended, seeing things *sub specie aeternitatis,* then all that is, including therefore evil, has its necessary place in the totality of nature. This theory has many different expressions but they all tend to come to the same thing, namely, a denial that evil is ultimate, or even that evil is evil. Thus it may be said that evil is illusory, that it is good in disguise, or that it is something like the shadows in a picture, ugly when seen out of relation to the entire picture, but positively contributing to the beauty of the whole object. This view makes evil an appearance not a reality. Evil, it is claimed, arises because of man's limited perspective and narrow-visioned outlook on his existence.

The difficulties of this view are quite apparent. It is not at all clear, in the first place, just what "the good of the whole" is. Certainly it seems to be a highly formal and abstract good not intimately related to the immediate demands and conditions of our present consciousness. But it is precisely to this present consciousness that the evil of the world seems unbearable and inexplicable. To tell the victims of concentration camps, or those suffering from the indescribable pain of an invading malignancy, that this horror is necessary for some unknown, abstract, total good, may for a very few reconcile them to its presence, but it does not change its immediate revolting character. In short, but one cannot dispose of evil by calling it something else.

2. *God's Goodness Saved by Limiting His Power.*

Those who believe in the existence of a perfect and all-powerful God sometimes try to account for evil along similar lines. Thus it is said that conditions or events are only evil from man's perspective, but from God's all things are seen to be good and in harmony. This can scarcely be acceptable as a solution, for even if evil is a good from God's perspective it is still atrocious from man's and it is with human perspectives that we have to deal. Moreover, could the religious consciousness ever worship a God who actually brings about evil for man in order that He may enjoy a greater good? Faced with such a dilemma some philosophers have revised the conception of deity and developed the idea of a finite God who is relieved of the responsibility for evil.

The idea is as old as Plato. In the Republic, for instance, he suggests that a good God is

. . . not the author of all things, as the many assert, but he is the cause of a few things only, and not of most things that occur to men. For few are the goods of human life, and many are the evils, and the good is to be attributed to God alone; of the evils the causes are to be sought elsewhere, and not in him.[31]

Furthermore, God is not the creator of the eternal forms which are the models or patterns according to which He fashions this cosmos. Any deity who must take account of something outside himself not of his own making is finite.

John Stuart Mill also thinks the logic of belief in God's existence should lead to the conception of his finiteness. Mill argues that the indications of design in the world point away from the omnipotence of God because they suggest the need for contrivances, that is, the employment of means to secure desired ends. But to use contrivances is to admit a limitation of power. An all-powerful God would find His word alone sufficient to accomplish his ends.

The evidences, therefore, of Natural Theology distinctly imply that the author of the Kosmos worked under limitations; that he was obliged to adapt himself to conditions independent of his will, and to attain his ends by such arrangements as those conditions admitted of.[32]

God is limited, however, not only in power but also in knowledge. He is, therefore, not omniscient, although His knowledge is far in excess of that of any human being. In fact, says Mill, this limitation is evident when some of the contrivances of God are seen not to be the best possible. There are defects in the human body, and a slowness in development as if there were some unsureness and fumbling.

If the Creator, like a human ruler, had to adapt himself to a set of conditions which he did not make, it is as unphilosophical as presumptuous in us to call

[31] Plato, *Republic*, Book II (B. Jowett, tr.), Clarendon Press, Oxford, 1888, p. 62.
[32] John Stuart Mill, *Three Essays on Religion*, Henry Holt & Co., Inc., New York, 1847, p. 177.

him to account for any imperfections in his work; to complain that he left anything in it contrary to what, if the indications of design prove anything, he must have intended. He must at least know more than we know, and we cannot judge what greater good would have had to be sacrificed, or what greater evil incurred, if he had decided to remove this particular blot.[33]

William James defended the view that God works in an external environment and that He therefore has limits and enemies. "It is quite true," says James, "that there is very little outside God, but there is enough to make him a relative being."[34]

The most thoroughgoing exposition of the idea of a finite God among recent philosophers is to be found in the work of Edgar S. Brightman. He concludes that there is in God an eternal and uncreated nature which furnishes problems and obstacles for Him. Brightman calls this the Given. Both moral and religious experience give the grounds for belief in a finite God.

Moral experience thus leads us to a finite God, that is, to one who does not create the real, as distinguished from the apparent, evils of life, or the surplus evils, as distinguished from the disciplinary ones. In the presence of such a God we can feel a profounder religious satisfaction than the older view allowed. Of real evils, we may say: First, God did not create them; his will is present in them, but their surplus evil aspect was no act of his creative choice; it was due to a necessity, an uncreated "Given" in his nature, which he did not produce, but is a factor with which, as a part of his very existence, he always has to deal. Secondly, while God did not create any of these evils, he can cure all of them. His cure is slow and evolutionary rather than sudden and absolute. Even divine power cannot do away with all the consequences of evil; but God can so transform and overrule them that no evil is an ultimate barrier to his power for goodness, no disaster a final failure, no death an end.[35]

And again:

What sort of God, then, is the God to whom religious experience leads? In the nature of the case, it must be a finite God. No possible experience could reveal unlimited and absolute power. The God who has worked throughout man's religious history has been sufficient to save those that called upon him; but he could not demonstrate omnipotence if he would. Every demonstration to a finite being like man must assume a finite form.[36]

This notion of a finite God certainly has its usefulness and appeal. It does to some extent "solve" one aspect of the problem of evil, that is, we

[33] *Ibid.*, p. 180.
[34] William James, *A Pluralistic Universe*, Longmans, Green & Co., Inc., New York, 1909, pp. 124–125.
[35] Edgar S. Brightman, *The Finding of God*, The Abingdon Press, New York, Cincinnati, 1931, pp. 91–92.
[36] *Ibid.*, p. 115.

escape the dreadful alternative that God is responsible for evil and therefore malicious. Insofar as God is a spirit struggling against obstacles, we may feel a closer kinship with Him because of our own frequent ordeals and frustrations. None of the proposers of this idea seem to think a finite God is unworthy of worship, because although limited, He is incomparably superior to His creatures.

And yet, is there not in part the substitution of one mystery for another —or better, the multiplication of mysteries? For if God is even as powerful as these philosophers admit, ought He not to be both able and willing to modify much of the world's evil? Moreover, if their beliefs are to be accepted are we not then confronted with the problem not only of God's existence, but of the existence of the "not-God" which is as real as God, but which opposes Him, or at least places restrictions upon Him?

3. *Evils as Challenging Tests.*

Let us consider a third theory. We are reminded by some people that risk, hostility, opposition, hardship, bereavement, pain, and many other forms of adversity are often a means to the development of character; that salutary effects, even though delayed or remote, may follow what seems to be unquestionably evil. There is, without doubt, some psychological truth to this view. Men have been known to emerge magnificently from the cruel, devastating, and undeserved afflictions brought upon them by their own kind or by an indifferent nature.

But there are others too who have been unmade by evil. They have not been able to stand against its sudden violence or the long-drawn-out consequences of irrevocable misfortunes. They cannot overcome it, they are overcome by it. So such facts are indecisive for a theory of evil. Furthermore, one may always ask whether all the evil that is present in this world is required to produce staunch character. Would less not do the job just as well? Although it seems true that some evils are warnings against greater perils, as is the case with certain pains, yet do we need the great excess of pain to accomplish this end? And again, although suffering is sometimes a just punishment for folly and vice, and may be conducive to good ends, yet is there not more than is necessary as a contrast to pleasure, because a lesser pleasure itself would do? A world with a little evil in it offers man adventure, risk, exhilarating moments of triumph, and the opportunity of sympathetic concern for his fellows. True. But the problem of evil is not only why any evil at all, but why evil on such an enormous scale?

Thus this view of evil, namely, that it heightens our sense of danger and adventure and produces a better man, is highly romanticized and unrealistic. It treats evil too much as a game and deprives it of its genuine seriousness and makes all sufferers into "poor sports."

F. R. Tennant certainly does not regard evil in a romantic way, but he does insist that a merely happy world would stagnate; that a world most worthy of God and man must be a moral order, a forum where the moral life may be worked out. This means that there must be a world in which the risk of moral evil is possible, depending on man's choice, for a moral agent cannot be a mere automaton or puppet. Doubtless there is wisdom in this view, but it does not account for evils of a non-moral nature nor does it explain why much evil is so overpowering that it leads to moral discouragement and dismay rather than to freedom and enlightenment.

4. *Evil as the Privation of Being.*

Another theory of evil may be found in the history of thought, in which evil is regarded as the absence or privation of being; it is the lack of a good that ought to be present in a thing or person, much as blindness is an absence of a good in a man and is therefore evil. Jacques Maritain puts it this way:

> That does not mean that evil does not exist, or is merely an illusion, or that we need only deny its existence, as do the Christian Scientists, to make it disappear. Evil does exist in things, it is terribly present in them. Evil is real, it actually exists like a wound or mutilation of the being; evil is there in all reality, whenever a thing—which, in so far as it is, and has being, is good—is deprived of some being or of some good it should have. Thus evil exists *in good*, that is, the bearer of evil is good, in so far as it is being. And evil works *through good*, since evil, being in itself a privation or non-being, has no causality of its own. Evil is therefore efficacious not by itself, but through the good it wounds and preys upon as a parasite, efficacious through a good that is wanting or is deflected, and whose action is to that extent vitiated.[37]

This theory of evil rests upon at least two basic beliefs, first, that anything that exists is by the very fact that it exists, and to the degree that it exists, a good; in short, existence itself is a value. Thus to the extent that anything lacks existence proper to it, there is evil. A second basic belief affirms that a perfect universe requires inequality in things so that all levels of goodness can be represented. Thus a perfect universe requires some beings at lower levels and some who can fall to lower levels. The whole is better if there are some beings who lack good. And this is the kind of universe God actually creates. Thus the presence of evil gives God an opportunity to derive a good which would be lost if there were not some evil, that is, a universe in which all levels of goodness and

[37] J. Maritain, *St. Thomas and the Problem of Evil*, The Aquinas Lecture, Marquette University Press, Milwaukee, Wisconsin, 1942, pp. 1–2.

being are represented is better than one in which there are gaps, even if it means for the lower levels the absence of good, that is to say, the presence of evil.

It is obvious that this theory of evil belongs in a much wider metaphysical context than we have been able to present here. In fact, it is probably distorted when removed from this context. It depends not only on a metaphysical context but also upon one of religious faith. If this is not accepted the theory itself is certainly obscure. Even within the context, it is not fully intelligible as Maritain seems to admit when he says that the problem of evil is "in truth not a problem but a mystery."[38]

But there are other troubles. Does this view mean that it is evil for a dog to be a dog and act like a dog, just because there is a higher being, man? It makes sense to say that it is evil for a man to act like a dog, but this certainly switches the meaning of the word evil. Moreover this view does not satisfactorily account for the positive characteristics of evil, that is, its actual hostility and force in human affairs. Granting that a lack of being may be a form of evil, why must that bring to many persons such excruciating pain, which seems to add nothing good to the fullness of being?

5. *Good in Overcoming Evil.*

For those who do not accept a belief in the existence of an all-powerful, all-knowing God, the theoretical problem of evil is considerably lessened. But, of course, they are still faced with the problem in its practical aspects. Here a number of alternatives are open. One can take the way of resignation, submitting or yielding without lament to the unconquerable forces that determine discomfort, pain, and unhappiness. But such passive resistance solves no problems and certainly offers little intellectual satisfaction. Moreover, by refusing to move positively against evil one may increase its actual destructiveness. Or again, one may quietly endure the evil that comes or that one finds active in the world, and by a kind of heroism simply defy its threat, but at the same time engage in a crusade against all those evils that can be lessened by one's efforts. Other attitudes, of course, are possible but it is not necessary to explore them all here.

What we actually do about evil may be more of a reflection of our philosophy than we think. Thus the theoretical and practical aspects of the problem, though distinguishable, cannot really be separated. Can a theory of evil make pain less painful, death more welcome, cruelty more benign? Certainly not. But if it gives some explanation to the agonized "Why?" it may make the evil easier to endure.

[38] *Ibid.*, p. 14.

Neither religion nor science nor philosophy has in itself "solved" the problem of evil. Probably no solution can be achieved except within the framework of a more complete system of philosophy. Certainly the presence of evil and its power brings man sharply to an awareness of his limitations and impotency. At least some of these evils are, however, within his power to modify or to overcome. He is utterly incapable of preventing the earthquake, the cloudburst, or the tornado, but he can strengthen his buildings, plan flood-controls, and give radar warnings of the terrifying wind. Evil, in short, gives man something to overcome; it offers him the permanent possibility of triumph. Is it not better to think of the world itself as neither good nor evil, but providing the conditions for either, depending on man's deliberate or impulsive decisions?

IV. Beliefs in Immortality

Belief in immortality is often said to be the most widely held of all religious beliefs. It may be found in some form in the thought of primitive man as well as in the thought of contemporary and sophisticated persons. But we have certainly learned by now that the universality of belief is insufficient evidence for the truth of any belief. Moreover the fact that the belief is common to so many ages and generations may make us forget that there has also been a long line of unbelievers, and their number does not seem to be diminishing. But as such statistical evidence is silent with respect to the falsity as well as the truth of the belief, we may as well refuse to pursue this course any further. Whether primitive man had some vague, ill-defined idea of his personal survival may be anthropologically interesting but it is logically useless as evidence for his actual post-life existence. On the other hand, the mere fact that a scientist or philosopher has made it perfectly clear to his contemporaries that he could not possibly accept such an absurd belief is also useless if it is taken as proof that the belief is false. Both of the cases may be causes for belief or disbelief. They are not properly reasons for believing or disbelieving.

It is difficult but necessary to separate man's hopes and wishes from a consideration of the question, although it seems to be the case that immortality is almost universally desired. Both ancient and modern men have sought ways by which they could hold onto existence, if not in this world then in some other world. Of course there are exceptions. Santayana once wrote in a letter that "if some angel without a carnal body appeared to me and assured me that he was perfectly happy on prayer and music, I should congratulate him, but shouldn't care to imitate him."[39] And in another connection he made it quite clear that a certain form of immortality was not only undesirable but utterly repulsive.

And the prospect of awakening again among houses and trees, among children and dotards, among wars and rumours of wars, still fettered to one personality and one accidental past, still uncertain of the future, is not this prospect wearisome and deeply repulsive? Having passed through these things once and bequeathed them to posterity, is it not time for each soul to rest?[40]

Santayana's position is taken against a particular kind of immortality, and the argument may not hold against other forms. Moreover, some writers would place the belief in immortality in a moral context which is foreign to Santayana's argument. Thus, D. C. Macintosh is not impressed by the fact that some people do not desire immortality.

It will be seen that from the point of view of moral optimism the question as to whether the individual desires a future life is comparatively unimportant. Whether we desire immortality or not, the conservation of every person whose will is actually or even potentially moral is as imperative as the value of every such person is absolute. We may not want to live again; but as it is our duty to act morally whether we want to or not, so it is our duty to want to live again and to do in a future existence whatever good it may then be possible for us to accomplish. The desire to live forever is not a selfish or unworthy desire, if the extension of existence is not desired for unworthily selfish purposes. If to live is in itself better than not to live, to continue to live is similarly better than not to continue to live. It could never be right to refuse or not to desire further opportunity to develop and express the good will, and any adequate appreciation of the moral ideal with its categorical imperative must be accompanied by desire amounting to an absolute demand for opportunity progressively to realize that ideal.[41]

It is certainly not always clear just what the content of a belief in immortality really is, but it would not be unfair to say that in the minds of most believers death is the cessation of one form of experience and immortality the beginning of another without the loss of the identity of the experiencer. Even this is not fully clear, for some people believe that the identity includes not only personal memories and awareness, but the

[39] George Santayana, *The Letters of George Santayana,* Charles Scribner's Sons, New York, 1955, p. 250.
[40] George Santayana, *Reason in Religion,* Charles Scribner's Sons, New York, 1913, p. 245.
[41] D. C. Macintosh, *The Reasonableness of Christianity,* Charles Scribner's Sons, New York, 1926, p. 68.

original body, revised and changed. But let us not get bogged down with this difficulty now. If we take the above statement as a tentative description of the most common content of a belief in immortality, then we can discuss a number of substitutes that have been proposed, after which we will return to the first problem.

A. Non-Religious Beliefs in Immortality

1. *Continuity of the Germ Plasm.*

We may often find a person arguing for immortality on the basis of the continuity of the germ plasm. Life is passed on within the species from parent to offspring, and though all of the possibilities are not realized there is an uninterrupted transmission and a constant protection of whatever it is that grows into the human subject.

Although there may be grounds for biological optimism here, it is certain that such continuity is not what the religious believer holds when he believes in immortality. There is no moral worth to such persistence, no personal continuity, no opportunity for individual fulfillment. Moreover, the continuity of the germ plasm itself has a hazardous existence, and in our day we are faced with the possibility of its extinction, if not by an act of God, or of nature, then by man himself. Thus even its immortality is highly conditional.

2. *Continuous Effects of Every Life.*

Another way in which the belief in immortality is defended by changing its meaning is to insist that one lives on in the effects that follow from one's life. No one lives without producing a multitude of effects, and these go on indefinitely producing further effects and thus one has an influence on the future. This influence is one's immortality.

Here again, however, this substitute will hardly satisfy the man who gives his belief a religious character. Effects may be good or evil, significant or insignificant, and these must be distinguished, for the immortal life is not thought to be a mere continuous reverberation of any stupid, inane, and malicious decisions that have been made during one's life. But if only the good effects echo through the long reaches of time, it is still not our particular being that endures, and this is what the believer clings to.

Related to this view is another, which affirms that a man's achievements of good or evil may be so extraordinary that his name is kept alive through extended periods of history. There is no question about the truth of this statement, but a name, no matter how revered or condemned is still a name and not a being. To be kept, as a name, printed between the covers of a book, or carved in the side of a monolith, or cherished in the memories of men, is still a poor substitute for surviving as a person. The desire for immortality is not satisfied by knowing that there will be devices that remind the living that you too once lived.

3. *Ideal Immortality.*

George Santayana has described a view which, though in some respects similar to the above, must yet be distinguished from it. He calls it *ideal immortality*. Nothing in the past can really be destroyed, and a life once lived is an eternal part of the history of the world. But ideal immortality is not the same thing as a future life. The former is simply the name for the fact that the truth and value of a life never die, that it will always be true, no matter what happens, that this life was and added to the eternal glory of the universe. The two fine expressions of this ought to be given in his own words.

Existence is essentially temporal and life foredoomed to be mortal, since its basis is a process and an opposition; it floats in the stream of time, never to return, never to be recovered or repossessed. But ever since substance became at some sensitive point intelligent and reflective, ever since time made room and pause for memory, for history, for the consciousness of time, a god, as it were, became incarnate in mortality and some vision of truth, some self-forgetful satisfaction, became a heritage that moment could transmit to moment and man to man. This heritage is humanity itself, the presence of immortal reason in creatures that perish. Apprehension, which makes man so like a god, makes him in one respect immortal; it quickens his numbered moments with a vision of what never dies, the truth of those moments and their inalienable values.[42]

And in another place these exquisite words are found:

When a man's life is over, it remains true that he has lived; it remains true that he has been one sort of man, and not another. In the infinite mosaic of history that bit has its unfading colour and its perpetual function and effect. A man who understands himself under the form of eternity knows the quality that eternally belongs to him, and knows that he cannot wholly die, even if he would; for when the movement of his life is over, the truth of his life remains. The fact of him is a part forever of the infinite context of facts.[43]

Although there is an appealing truth in Santayana's view, it does not express the deeper hopes of those who believe that not only will the *fact* of their existence be eternally true, but that their *existence* will be eternally a fact. The arguments proposed by religious thinkers to justify a belief in

[42] George Santayana, *Reason in Religion*, Charles Scribner's Sons, New York, 1922, pp. 262–263.
[43] George Santayana, Introduction, Spinoza, *Ethics*, Everyman's Library, E. P. Dutton & Co. Inc., New York, 1938, p. xviii.

immortality are not constructed with a view to prove that they once lived, but rather to demonstrate the reasonableness of believing that they will continue to exist even after the body's dissolution. Santayana's *ideal* immortality may be all we can expect or deserve, but we cannot be satisfied with it until we examine the claims of those who argue for a *real* immortality.

4. *Persistence.*

The advance of science which has extended man's life expectancy suggests another possible substitute for the more common belief in immortality, namely, the persistence of life for long periods of time—perhaps indefinitely—through the use of medicine, a thorough understanding of the body's chemistry, and by the replacement, or restoration of vital parts. Thus survival, or future life, would simply mean never dying. This, of course, is highly speculative and it contains scarcely any substance of the religious and moral meaning of immortality. Even if a man lived as long as the reputed age of Methuselah his years are as nothing compared to the timeless existence enjoyed by the "immortals."

B. Religious Beliefs in Immortality

We come now to the arguments sometimes used to defend the belief that men survive the death of the body and continue to live on another plane, or in another world. In general, the authors think it fair to say that no argument of philosophy or science or religion, and no evidence brought forth by its advocates or its deprecators, is sufficient to prove either the reality or unreality of this future life. It is possible and conceivable, but not yet demonstrable. One may find dogmatic statements on both sides, and those eager to prove or disprove have been guilty of wishful thinking. The arguments usually fall into three major classifications, those that are primarily *ethical* in character; those that are *metaphysical;* and finally those that are *empirical.*

1. *Ethical Grounds.*

The ethical grounds for the arguments to immortality are often stated in different ways, but essentially they come down to this: If God is an ethically perfect being he would respect the moral aspirations of the personalities he has created, and this means he must have provided for the infinite preservation of the values of human life and consciousness. Tennant puts it in the following way:

The righteousness which theism must ascribe to God consists rather in provision of adequate opportunities for the development of all that is potential in God-given personality, conservation of the valuable, and love such as precludes the mockery of scheming that a rational creature's guiding light through life shall be a Will o' the wisp.[44]

From this point of view, belief in God and belief in immortality stand or fall together.

It is clear that the belief in this case rests upon a prior belief and can be no more certain than the basic belief. As we have not been able to find any logical certainty of God's existence, so we cannot accept this argument based on his existence as certain. On the other hand, it is certainly not inconsistent to accept a belief in God and from his nature to arrive also at a belief in immortality.

The argument is often put in such a way that an appeal to rationality is evident. Thus E. W. Barnes writes:

We are forced to assume that the Universe is rational. The assumption is largely confirmed by our experience and, unless it were true, the Universe would be unknowable. In that case God's works and ways would be unintelligible and experience would not lead to any understanding of Him. Now if, on the contrary, the character of the ordering of all that happens is for our thought rational, we are forced to conclude that God would not have allowed the majority of human beings to have lives, so wretched and incomplete as we observe them to be, were it not that earthly existence is but the first part, a mere beginning, of the complete life of the human spirit.

We may put the same consideration somewhat differently and say that, if Christian theism be true, we must create an understanding of man's place in the scheme of things which shall not be out of harmony with the nature of God as revealed by Christ. But such a harmony cannot exist unless this life is a probation or, more probably, an education for another which shall be both fuller and better. If the Universe be rational, man's potentialities must have opportunities of realisation; and on earth such opportunities do not come to the majority of men.[45]

This argument too is based on assumptions that may be questioned. It is not at all clear that there is a necessary connection between the rationality of the world, in the sense that it is an intelligible object of knowledge, and the preservation of whatever is ethically valuable. That is, it is possible to believe consistently in a rationally ordered nature and also in the temporary or transient character of human ideals. A rational universe alone cannot guarantee the persistence of either the values held by a person or the person's life itself no matter how high its worth. The laws that define the rationality of the world are *descriptive* in character. The

---

[44] F. R. Tennant, *Philosophical Theology*, Cambridge University Press, Cambridge, 1929, Vol. II, p. 272.

[45] E. W. Barnes, *Scientific Theory and Religion*, Cambridge University Press, Cambridge, 1933, p. 645.

"laws" that define the ethical behavior of man are *prescriptive* in character. Only confusion results if we do not keep these distinct. It makes sense to speak of breaking or obeying prescriptive laws, such as those forbidding assault, murder, or driving on the wrong side of the street, but one does not break or disobey a law of nature. These laws are not given, they are formulated after prolonged observation of repeated events. Thus the lawfulness of the universe, in a descriptive sense, does not guarantee the lawfulness, in a prescriptive sense, of man's ethical life. Of course, it may be that men are actually better off politically, socially, and psychologically when they believe that their values are permanent. But this is not in itself evidence for immortality.

2. *Metaphysical Grounds.*

The metaphysical arguments in general center around the belief that immortality cannot be maintained or supported except by arguments that belong to a synthesis constituting a philosophy. Thus even Christian philosophers argue that the belief depends upon an inclusive philosophy called ethical theism. Of course, some types of metaphysics are more compatible with a belief in immortality than others. Particularly hospitable to the belief is the metaphysics that defends the separability and independence of mind and body. If mind is a distinct substance and can function without the body, then presumably it can survive whatever shock the body endures at death.

But again the arguments are inconclusive. Our experience tells us over and over again how intimate the relation is between mind and body. We know that serious injury and pain, or too much in the way of drugs, impair the mind's activity. On the other hand, we know that "by taking thought" the body, within limits, can be made to respond as we wish. And no final answer is given if we look to the history of thought. Men of great intellectual stature have disagreed on this problem and for everyone who insists that the mind is inseparable from and totally dependent on the body, we may find another whose belief is just the contrary. A belief in immortality is not the basis upon which a metaphysics is constructed, rather it emerges as a defensible conviction from a metaphysics. It is not possible here to examine completely different types of metaphysics and to judge whether belief in immortality is justified or implied by the metaphysics. But the student may recall the work of Chapters VI and VII and ask himself which type would be compatible with the belief.

William James offered a theory to answer those who claimed that thought is only a function of the brain. He distinguished different kinds or meanings of function. The brain, he says, does not produce thought as steam is produced by a teakettle, or light by an electric current, but rather the brain may have a *transmissive* or *releasing* function. Here are his words:

Admit now that *our brains* are such thin and half-transparent places in the veil. What will happen? Why, as the white radiance comes through the dome, with all sorts of staining and distortion imprinted on it by the glass, or as the air now comes through my glottis determined and limited in its force and quality of its vibration by the peculiarities of those vocal chords which form its gate of egress and shape it into my personal voice, even so the genuine matter of reality, the life of souls as it is in its fulness, will break through our several brains into this world in all sorts of restricted forms, and with all the imperfections and queernesses that characterize our finite individualities here below.[46]

You see that, on all those suppositions, our soul's life, as we here know it, would none the less in literal strictness be the function of the brain. The brain would be the independent variable, the mind would vary dependently on it. But such dependence on the brain for this natural life would in no wise make immortal life impossible,—it might be quite compatible with supernatural life behind the veil hereafter.[47]

It is obvious that James' view is highly speculative and does not constitute a proof of immortality. Indeed, he does not offer it as such. All it may be said to do is to match one theory against another, making neither the exclusive alternative.

In an interesting article Paul Weiss has argued that men are immortal in at least six different ways.[48] First they are immortal *metaphysically*, in the sense that as an individual being a man is a meaning which is negated or rejected by the rest of the universe. The essence of the person is preserved by all other beings in the sense that it is negated, that is, as a being from which others must forever distinguish themselves. And this fact makes him necessary to the universe itself. This is true not only for man but for all other beings as well—every being is immortal as an essence or bare meaning—it could not possibly be or mean anything else and is therefore forever what it is.

Second, we are immortal *cosmologically*, by which Weiss means that our energy-matter does not cease to exist—it becomes dispersed in other forms—but it cannot become non-being, unless destroyed by an all-powerful God. This too is true of all existence and ignores the individuality of man.

[46] William James, *Human Immortality*, 2nd ed., Houghton, Mifflin, Co., New York, 1899, p. 17.
[47] *Ibid.*, p. 18.
[48] Paul Weiss, "Immortality," *The Review of Metaphysics*, Vol. I, No. 4, 1948.

In a third way, namely, *existentially*, men are immortal. Here Weiss points out that our acts and natures delimit the acts and natures of others. We make a difference to all that is by the very fact of our existence, and if this is a real difference it is a permanent one. "We are immortal in that we set limits to the places, actions, distributions of all that is, and thereby forever leave the mark of our presence on all existence."

Fourth, we are *temporally* immortal because our present becomes a permanent part of all time. It will always be true that what I say, think, or do is something that I said, or thought, or did. Here Weiss comes close to Santayana's conception of ideal immortality.

Fifth, we are *causally* immortal. We are embodied in a chain of effects through all time. "The future will forever bear testimony to our having been and done. It will always show traces of our having lived, acted, made, and marred, since the future will in part be as it is because of what we are and do today."

Finally, we are immortal *socially*. In all the relations we have with families, communities, and institutions we produce changes that make a difference that is permanent. This differs from causal immortality by taking account of the values men hold—thus it is peculiar to man and not shared by other beings.

Weiss is aware that something is missing in all these arguments. He writes:

> If the only immortality which is possible to us is an immortality of one or more of these six, we must in all honesty say to ourselves that we are not in fact immortal in the sense in which we normally understand the term. Immortality must be an immortality of an existent, vital individual man or not be a true immortality.

With this in mind he formulates his own theory of a self, which is neither body nor mind, but a "self-identical, responsible being with a capacity to will and an essential concern for values which are richer and deeper than those pertinent to my body or mind." It is this self, which is the "unchanging, activating, unifying, private core" of a man that could continue after death. The self is not a mere body, because it often controls, drives, checks, and forces the body in ways not native to the body. It is not mere mind for similar reasons. But the body gives the self a location and the opportunity to act.

We are capable of immortality because our selves are beings which are distinct from and beyond the reach of bodily corruption. But we are not now immortal; our selves do not now function as permanent substances. Our immortality is something achieved, beginning on the day of death. On that day each of us is forced to actualize the independent existence of which our selves are capable, but which during our life times we did not exercise. Instead of being destroyed on the occasion of death, each of us thus engages in the adventure of making his self be his entire substance. Each gives up an old way of existing for a while in a body, for a new way of existing apart from the body.[49]

It is not clear whether Weiss leaves grounds for the immortality of children, or infants. If our survival depends on the achievement of a self, can they be expected to engage in the adventure of making their selves into an entire substance when they have scarcely had opportunity to make much of themselves as a body? Are there not also some difficulties with respect to the most unfortunate instances of feeblemindedness? Will they be able to go it alone, that is, without the body? Although Professor Weiss' arguments are probably as strong as any arguments yet made for immortality, it is evident that they are far from conclusive. Every term needs careful definition; every proposition requires logical analysis. This is the only way to prevent our being carried away by personal wishes or fond hopes.

3. *Empirical Grounds.*

If all argument fails to establish immortality, then perhaps empirical methods will disclose it. This is the approach of those who base a belief in immortality on the phenomena investigated by the societies for psychical research. But after many years of effort nothing has been established that in any way demonstrates that there are spirits in another world trying to communicate with friends or relatives in this world. Certainly there is much that is strange and so far inexplicable, but the most that can be said is that for highly intelligent people the evidence is at least sufficient to keep the question of spirit-communication an open one. The utter triviality and inanity of so-called messages from this other world is in itself a barrier to much credibility of the claims. A. E. Taylor put the point succinctly:

The life which would be disclosed by such revelations . . . would rather be one of intellectual and moral idiocy. I do not think it too much to say of the most harmless of these 'messages from beyond the tomb' that, if they are what they claim to be, we can only hope that the unseen world, like the seen, has its homes for the feebleminded, and that it is with their inmates that our occultists are in communication.[50]

It is true that in some philosophies immortality means also pre-existence, notably in Plato and in certain forms of Eastern thought. But this is not

[49] *Ibid.*, p. 98.
[50] A. E. Taylor, *The Christian Hope of Immortality*, The Centenary Press, London, 1938, pp. 19–20.

the Christian conception. Here we find the interesting and daring idea that something that has come into existence, that is, had no past, will have an unending future. We have been unable to find any argument or evidence sufficient to establish unquestionably the truth of this belief. If it is held at all, it is because one is willing to go beyond the evidence or to accept it as a possible implication from a more inclusive system of belief. At the present time we must have the courage or the faith to meet the inevitable and the unknown with as much tranquillity as possible, a condition probably more fully attained if this life has not been marked by a persistent concern for one's personal satisfactions and happiness at the cost of another's deprivation.

However, for those who argue that if after death there is no survival, then we should "live it up" now, we will let Professor Broad have the last word. It should be sufficient and final.

If a man wishes to provide himself with sources of pleasure that will ensure a quiet but strong happiness over the greater part of his life, rather than a few spasms of enjoyment in the earlier part of it followed by years of boredom, he will be most unwise to adopt the 'fleeting-hour' plan even if he believes himself to be mortal. His wisest course will be, not indeed to neglect bodily pleasures in the earlier years of his life, but at any rate to indulge in them only to such an extent as will not interfere with the acquirement of sources of quieter but more permanent happiness which can be enjoyed when gout has forbidden port and a failing digestion has vetoed oysters. . . .

But of course the mere fact, if it be a fact, that we are mortal has no tendency to make it right to consider only our own pleasure. Suppose that I and all other men are mortal, this will not alter the fact that, so long as they and I are alive, some states of mind, such as the appreciative hearing of good music, are better than others, such as enjoyment of another's pain. Nor will it alter the fact that it largely depends on our present actions whether I, my contemporaries, and a long series of successors shall experience the one kind of state or the other. Whether we are mortal or not it will still be our duty, I suppose, not to produce a worse state when we can produce a better; not to treat our own pleasure, simply because it is *ours*, as more important than the pleasure of others; and not to show favouritism in the distribution of those materials for a good life which are at our disposal.[51]

No area of human interest and concern is so susceptible to unsound thinking as that which has to do with man's religious beliefs. There are, as was indicated earlier, at least two major causes for this: First, our religious beliefs have often become so imbedded in our emotional life that we are unable to separate, for purposes of candid examination, our feelings from

[51] C. D. Broad, *The Mind and Its Place In Nature,* Routledge & Kegan Paul Ltd., London, 1925, pp. 493–494. Used by permission.

the content of our beliefs; and second, it is commonly thought that religious beliefs are largely a matter of faith, and therefore are not amenable to the methods of investigation and evaluation we require to judge other beliefs. But as philosophers we must learn to distinguish between the emotional aura and the conceptual content of our beliefs, although not denying a priori that feelings and emotions may have a significant role in cognition. The content of our beliefs must somehow come out, get expressed, else we have little or no idea of what we may be asserting or denying. This is not to claim that religious beliefs can attain the preciseness and clarity that is possible in mathematics and the sciences, but it is to demand something more of the believer than increased pulse rate or mere diaphragmatic activity.

V. Concluding Remarks

It has not been possible to examine all of the major religious beliefs. There are others related, for example, to worship, such as prayer and ritual; and others related to knowledge, such as revelation and tradition; and still others related to an institution, such as the church. Although they cannot be dealt with now, it should be emphasized that it is the work of philosophy to examine the possible alternatives here too.

It is not the business of a philosopher either to defend or attack a believer, whether in religion or science or any other matter of human concern, but it is his business to look out for conceptual disorder and confusion wherever beliefs become expressed. A belief may be "lived" as well as expressed. With the former a philosopher has almost nothing to do; as a philosopher he is not a judge of man's activity and conduct. He is a judge only of those beliefs that are formulated into propositions and systems. If religious beliefs are not conceptually clear and ordered, this may or may not be a serious weakness to the believer, but then at least their characteristics in this respect must be brought to light.

PROBLEMS FOR THOUGHT AND DISCUSSION

1. Pascal wrote:

I look round and see naught but darkness everywhere. Nature offers me nothing that is not cause for doubt and unrest. Did I see no sign of a God, I should decide against him; did I see everywhere marks of a Creator, I should believe and be at peace. But, seeing too much evidence against, and too little in favour, I am in a pitiable state, and I have a hundred times prayed that if Nature is upheld by a God she would declare it unequivocally; and that, if the signs she gives of Him are deceptive, she would finally suppress them: that she would say all or nothing, so that I might see which side I ought to take. Whereas in my present state, not knowing what I am or what I ought to do, I know neither myself nor my duty.[52]

[52] *Pascal's Pensées* (H. F. Stewart, tr.), Routledge & Kegan Paul, Ltd., 1950, p. 169.

What ways would you suggest to end Pascal's perplexity? Do you think it can or should be ended? If you substitute "history" or "man" for nature does this lessen or increase the perplexity?

2. It is sometimes said that religion is not primarily argument, nor ritual, nor meditation, but rather a response, a free commitment of the whole self to a reality apprehended as divine, that is, unsurpassably great and good. What do you think of this way of speaking? Does it put the problems of religion beyond the reach of rational consideration?

3. In what sense or senses can the truth of religious propositions be established and tested?

4. We have discussed only three areas of religious belief, namely, God, evil, and immortality: what other problems occur to you about which a philosophical examination is possible?

5. C. A. Strong wrote:

Another proof that the universe is not a spiritual being is the observed character of things and events. The wind blows and the waves dash without a reason. Let a man note what happens through the years—earthquakes, floods, pestilence, wars—and ask himself whether it is conceivable that a world in which such things are possible was created by or proceeded from a mind: he must in honesty answer, No. Let him ask the same question regarding specific human ills. Insanity—how can goodness or intelligence have produced that cruellest and most debasing of inflictions? The different forms of disease, the innumerable varieties of insects in tropical forests, the sea which covers far more of the earth's surface than the land, the stars that are so beautiful to look at but so devastating to think of, the vast desolation of interstellar space— all prove that the universe was not made for man or by a being like a man, but *is what it is, an ever burning fire.*[53]

What kind of a proof is this? Do you think there are suppressed premises? If so, see if you can supply them.

6. W. H. Auden writes ironically of both those who deny God and those who profess to prove God:

> What reverence is rightly paid
> To a Divinity so odd
> He lets the Adam whom He made
>   Perform the acts of God?
>
>   . . .
>
> All proofs or disproofs that we tender
> Of His existence are returned
>   Unopened to the sender.
>
> Now, did He really break the seal
> And rise again? We dare not say;
> But conscious unbelievers feel
>   Quite sure of Judgment Day.[54]

Have you found any plain answers to questions about God? If so, would you deny that "*All* proofs or disproofs . . . are returned unopened to the sender"?

[53] C. A. Strong, *A Creed for Sceptics*, Macmillan and Co. Ltd., London, 1936, pp. 93–94.

[54] From *Homage to Clio,* by W. H. Auden. © Copyright 1955, 1956, 1957, 1958, 1959, 1960 by W. H. Auden. Reprinted by permission of Random House, Inc. and Faber & Faber Ltd., London.

7. Religious beliefs are commonly said to have pragmatic value in helping man to overcome fear. But if belief in God came from man's ignorance of the unknown, it seems to some critics of traditional religions based on faith, that only increasing knowledge could remove such fear. And if knowledge were our salvation, we would have no need of God in whom to put our faith. And faith in God would not then help man to overcome fear, but rather preserve or even intensify it. Is this theory of the origin of religion tenable? Is this theory of the value of religion tenable?

8. A contrary belief is that religion is man's courage in facing non-being, the threat of meaninglessness and death. And if you boggle at non-being, Paul Tillich points out that when every fearful apprehension of some particular threat is taken care of by insurance against every loss, there remains still anxiety. And what can be the basis of anxiety? Nothing. And since all knowledge is knowledge of something in particular, knowledge cannot supplant anxiety with courage. But religious faith can. Since ours is called an age of anxiety, can you understand in these terms the much heralded revival of religious belief?

9. Sir Julian Huxley, who places a high value on religious experience, believes it misconstrued as testimony of God. "For my own part the sense of spiritual relief which comes from rejecting the idea of God as a supernatural being is enormous. I see no other way of bridging the gap between the religious and the scientific approach to reality."[55] Is humanistic and naturalistic religion, such as Huxley's, in better position to link the "apprehension of sacredness in existence" to man's reason and "desire for right action"? On Huxley's basis, does morality need to be sanctified and itself made a sacrament?

10. What do you think of Paul Tillich's statement "Science can conflict only with science, and faith only with faith; science which remains science cannot conflict with faith which remains faith?"[56] Would you accept this at the price of putting your beliefs in compartments?

11. There is a familiar claim that religion and science cannot conflict, religion is the worship of Truth and science the search for truths, and truths cannot conflict with Truth. Indeed truths can be only because there is Truth, and Truth can be worshipped by discovering truths. Apart from the usefulness to religious movements, which thus have license to discard outworn dogma that seems false, what do you think of this formulation?

12. Somewhere Nietzsche protested that behind the shield of revelation "it is a matter of complete indifference whether something is true, while it is of the greatest importance whether it is believed to be true." Does religious faith sometimes mean not wanting to know what is true? Do the faithful make knowledge sin? Is the doubter made into a sinner to protect dogmas that will not bear examination?

13. An interpreter of certain Platonic strains of thought, Plotinus, claimed that the One is beyond subject and predicate, or any other kind of duality. But divine intelligence contains all things known. And the world soul is the "unity in which all souls are bound." "All beings are beings through the

[55] Julian Huxley, *Religion without Revelation*, New American Library, Inc., New York 1958, p. 32.

[56] Paul Tillich, *Dynamics of Faith*, Harper & Brothers, New York, 1957, p. 82.

One." One way of looking at such a doctrine is ontologically, as when we ask how the one emanated into plurality, which it yet contains. Another way is to regard such a philosophy as based on religious experience of unity underlying plurality.

Does all religious experience conform to this kind of mysticism? If not, do you see why some religions do not stress the unity of all things in God, but rather the gulf between things and God?

14. Are we enslaved by logic and ethics, which impose limits on thought and conduct? An interpreter of Zen Buddhism says that Zen is the search for the absolutely pure mind, the mind that thinks of no thing. Yet purity and non-purity, he says, are meaningless. This seems incoherent, even inconsistent to us, but Zen has no use for logic. Does it then seem appropriate to say that Western religions, such as Judaism and Christianity, attach great importance to logical system? What do you think of the advantages of a religion that cannot employ logic or be touched by any rational criticism? What do you think of the claim to break the tyranny of logic and thereby to deal with facts themselves? It would be difficult to assess Zen beliefs, for Zen claims to be beyond negation and affirmation.

15. Voltaire is quoted as saying "If there were no God, it would be necessary to invent Him." Why would anyone say this?

PERTINENT READINGS

Flew, Antony, and Alasdair MacIntyre, *New Essays in Philosophical Theology,* The Macmillan Co., New York, 1955.

Fromm, Erich, *Psychoanalysis and Religion,* Yale University Press, New Haven, Connecticut, 1950.

Hartshorne, Charles, and William L. Reese, *Philosophers Speak of God,* University of Chicago Press, Chicago, 1953.

Hume, David, *Dialogues Concerning Natural Religion* (Henry D. Aiken, ed.), Hafner Publishing Co., Inc., New York, 1951.

Huxley, Julian, *Religion without Revelation,* Mentor Books, New York, 1958.

James, William, *The Varieties of Religious Experience: A Study in Human Nature,* The Modern Library, New York, 1936.

Mascall, E. L., *He Who Is: A Study in Traditional Theism,* Longmans, Green & Co., London, 1958.

Mill, John Stuart, *Theism* (Richard Taylor, ed.), The Liberal Arts Press, Inc., New York, 1957.

Tillich, Paul, *The Courage to Be,* Yale University Press, New Haven, Connecticut, 1952.

Whitehead, Alfred North, *Religion in the Making,* The Macmillan Co., New York, 1926.

XI

Beliefs about Aesthetic Values

I. Some Common Aspects of Beliefs about Aesthetic and Moral Values

Philosophers often talk about "the True, the Good, and the Beautiful." We also dealt with the "true" when we asked what is meant by saying that a proposition is true or false. And we found that there are a number of alternative theories of truth. We defined a proposition as the content of a belief. It is common knowledge that men hold differing and sometimes conflicting beliefs about the goodness of acts. In the next chapter we shall consider moral beliefs. There are also beliefs about the beautiful or ugly character of certain objects, and to these we must now turn our attention.

A major difficulty immediately confronts us in ethics and aesthetics, for some philosophers have denied that we should say that such beliefs can be either true or false. If so, they cannot, of course, be propositions, because propositions deal primarily with what *is*, or *is not*, the case; but judgments of value, whether ethical or aesthetic, seem to deal only with what we believe *ought*, or *ought not*, to be the case, although many complex expressions include both a factual and an evaluative element. Sometimes we stress the continuity of the former with the sciences, while judgments of values are often claimed to be extra-scientific. This distinction between what we believe is the case and what we believe ought to be the case is common to many areas of our lives. On the witness stand one may be required to tell what he saw or otherwise came to know; but he may also be advised to stick

553

to the facts and not to evaluate them. A journalist may be asked by the editor to report what happened—"if anyone is to be blamed, leave that to me in an editorial." A clinical psychologist may assure a patient that he is absolutely free to tell about himself—"I will make no value judgment of your thoughts and actions." Moreover we are often told that the search for truth demands that a scientist consider only "cold facts" and "pure theory," and that he should be impersonal and disinterested, expressing no likes or dislikes. We are also told that he could not be a scientist unless he assumed that the truth was worth working for, and therefore he has presupposed that a body of data is worth his time and work to understand.

The student may become perplexed by these familiar beliefs. Is there nothing good or bad, beautiful or ugly, but thinking makes it so? Are propositions true because they report facts or conform to logical principles, but is there no arguing about taste? Are judgments of what one ought to do strictly private, a matter of "the little man inside" that moralists call conscience and Freudians the superego? If all aesthetic and moral preferences are private, do we tell only about ourselves when we utter them, and nothing about their objects at all? Are they then a matter of individual temperament, even mood, merely expressions of how we happen to feel? If they have no knowledge-content, then they might well be said to be emotive. Some philosophers who divide true and false beliefs into empirical and formal propositions find only the most superficial grammatical resemblance between "Crows are black" and "Crows are ugly." Very logically they suggest that the latter seems to convey no information about crows; it tells us only that the person who utters these words does not like to look at crows. Properly he should say "I don't like to see them." He may also mean "I hope you don't like them either," or even "I wish you would shoot them," or "Shoot them!" It is of great interest to note that the last paraphrase is an imperative rather than an indicative sentence. Propositions are normally expressed in an indicative sentence, and we are led to think of a fact to which it is true or false. But imperatives have invariably a future reference. Therefore an imperative cannot have a fact, unless a possible and future event, as an object. If what is not objective is subjective, this discussion has indicated how one may come to adopt a familiar theory of values, known technically as *subjectivism*.

But now consider the logical implications of the position that seems to be so plausible. If these judgments of value are merely subjective, what are we expecting when we ask in a practical art course "What should I make?" A common answer is "Make whatever expresses how you feel. If you feel angry, use an angry color and paint with angry brush strokes. Unless you do, you won't communicate to me. You'll leave me cold if you don't get that feeling on canvas." Does the artist know anything about the making of good paintings? If you accept his judgment as having validity of any sort, if you think this aesthetic belief is worth more because that artist has had experience in painting and that his criticism has been valuable, then something seems very wrong with subjectivism. Of course, something seems wrong also with saying, as some artists do, that crimson is an angry hue. Are we not reading into the color how we feel when we "see red" or are "mad enough to spill blood?" Is this not downright fallacious? Indeed, it is called the *romantic fallacy*, that is, ascribing to objects feelings that properly are predicated only of subjects.

Many philosophers have been intrigued with the general question: what does an artist do when he creates? Although we make aesthetic judgments of such natural things as sky and mountains, rivers and plains, it is man-made objects largely that occupy our attention: "A beautiful house on the Potomac," "An ugly slum near the Stock Yards," "A delicately-wrought sonnet," "A crude and bungled ballad," "A tune that makes us dance to its rhythm," "A symphony without melody and lacking rhythm is just so much noise," "That movie has a plot so tight that nothing could be omitted," "If you ran that play backwards, from scene 5 through scene 1, it wouldn't have less development." These statements are about the sorts of objects that are now collectively called art. We know what we mean, however difficult art is to define. And we seem to know very well what it is that seems aesthetically interesting or dull, pleasing or offensive, a success or a failure.

But there are so many different and various evaluations of what seems to be the same movie or song or building or sculpture. Subjectivism has an answer. Each of us has a set of emotions all his own and very private. Difference of taste is exactly what we should expect. But what we should not expect is agreement about the aesthetic qualities of things. Of course, some critics are like Anatole France who is commonly quoted as saying "Let me address you on myself on the subject of Shakespeare." If France disliked the tragedies and someone else, say A. C. Bradley, considered them well done, there would be no contradiction. Nor could there be agreement of belief, because if only propositions can be in logical relation to each other, and value judgments are not propositions, there could never be any rational dispute, or any evidence, or any proof, and no proposition common to two different acts of judgment.

Philosophers have therefore sought to understand what is commonly called appreciation of works of art. Only if we understand how we respond aesthetically can we appraise claims to know tragedies, skyscrapers, novels, and the like. You may already hold a firm belief about appreciation. Let us allude to one that will be developed later among alternatives. One person may say "I read a novel to forget myself. When problems become insoluble, I want to be quite free of worry and concern. A novel does this to me. The characters aren't real. They are only imaginary. I feel free when I merely observe all these events taking place—they are merely to be watched." Another may not hold this, and may say, "Some novels are like that. But a great one like War and Peace shows a mind grappling with the meaning of history. Tolstoy has a problem, namely, do individual men by their personal decisions control events? If they do, then a man is only to be praised or blamed for the consequences of a deliberate moral choice. Moreover, there is a real problem that some characters in War and Peace recognize, and others don't. Tolstoy personally decided that serfs ought to be freed, and knew how difficult it was to reform society. He later came to recognize that great art must communicate loving regard for every human being."

Some men formulate the doctrine that art is disinterested, others that it is purposive. Sometimes "escape" is tagged onto the first tendency, "propaganda" to the second. But these issues of the normative standards are not well dealt with by mere abuse. Can there be any satisfactory answer to the traditional question "What is the common characteristic of all beautiful things?" That is probably what was meant by the briefer question "What is beauty?" We might better ask, "Are there any standards applicable to all aesthetic objects?"

If there are applicable universal aesthetic standards, then subjectivism is quite misleading. Tolstoy thought he had discovered one. All good art, he claimed, teaches men to love one another. We may contrast two norms here, one of the content of art, the other of the form of art. This latter is a very ambiguous word, but we do often talk of the organization of an essay, of the structure of a symphony, and since we often complain about confusion from too many unrelated elements, or about monotony of unvaried repetition of the same element, the traditional unity in variety and variety in unity has great appeal.

Now to sum up questions that seem to demand answers about aesthetic value. Aesthetic questions are often said to cover the creation of works of art, their appreciation, and their criticism according to certain standards. First, men do make decisions in the process of producing aesthetic objects. If they did not, we should not have works of art to enjoy. There are various theories of creation, beginning with Plato and Aristotle. We do ask about our responses to works of art. There are various theories, largely formulated in the nineteenth century, of aesthetic experience. We also ask about standards of aesthetic value. These are more general than the particular theories of criticism that have been employed by critics of each of the arts.

Do questions about what is good and right, to which we shall devote the next chapter, also fall into a similar pattern? The first-person question "What should I do?" may be a moral one. Although the mere presence of alternatives does not make the question moral, it is a moral question when there are alternative courses of actions between which we may choose. That is the way we distinguish between conduct and behavior. Behavior may be involuntary or habitual, but conduct, for which we are held responsible, whether praised or blamed, is usually believed to be deliberate. That is, we think about the character of the act, why we do one thing rather than another, why we take other persons into account, and how our act affects them.

There are all kinds of answers given to a man who asks what he ought to do, for example: "Do what your mother (or father) tells you," "Do what other men (or women) do," "Do what the priest (or rabbi or minister) says God commands and expects," "Do what society says is your duty," "Do what is legal," "Do what Uncle Sam orders," "Do what a person of your upbringing is expected to do," "Do what the majority approves."

These answers are not very satisfactory. They all assume that some authority should be trusted to know what is right. And how can this be established? Of course, we would be in a very bad way if parents, friends, churches, courts of law, states, and societies with their traditions had utterly failed to pass on to us some results of their experience. We are not doomed to repeat their failures and may profit by their successes.

Amid this confusion philosophers have attempted to find evidence for the various beliefs. The peculiar feature of all attempts to reason to a conclusion about a moral choice is that the evidence may be factual or the ground may be purely rational. If the ground is not directly empirical, then we may have such a definition as "That action is right which produces pleasure rather than pain." It seems rather safe to assume that we can observe pleasures and pains, at least in our own bodies, and know what produces them. Then we may assume that other people feel pleasures and pains quite similar to our own, and we may, when confronted with a choice, select the one that will probably produce the most pleasure and the least pain to ourselves or to others. But this way of reasoning depends upon a definition; pleasure is good and pain is bad or evil, or pleasure characterizes results of actions that are right, pain characterizes the results of actions that are wrong. Hedonism, or the doctrine that moral quality is defined in terms of pleasure and pain, exists in many forms. When the pleasure and pain are one's own, we call this egoistic hedonism; when the pleasure and pain are others', we say, altruistic hedonism; when it is everyone's pleasure and pain we have in mind, then we may call this universalistic hedonism.

The important philosophical points to consider are epistemological and logical. Epistemologically, hedonists claim that pleasure and pain are knowable, directly in one's own experience, indirectly through others' observable behavior. It would unquestionably be a great improvement in clearly answering all questions of the type "What shall I do" if the replies were based on knowledge. Hedonists ask us to define moral good and right as productive of maximum pleasure and minimum pain. If there is real difficulty with this definition, the position is inadequate. Notice that one may say pain is evil and pleasure is good, without being a hedonist. To reason from these common beliefs to the conclusion that the good is the pleasant, is a simple fallacy. It would be like saying sensation is knowledge implies knowledge is sensation. Do you suspect any other weakness in hedonism?

Again we often say in condemnation of a man's actions that he is selfish. If to ignore the pleasure and pain of others is bad, is good to be defined as respect for others? Morality is often taught using some definition like this. Could there be any empirical proof of this belief: "You ought to regard the good of others as though it were your own." It is difficult to see what a verification of such a principle would be.

We certainly do often hear the belief that in principle one ought to do to others as one would be done by, and we usually condemn those who do to others what they would not wish done to themselves. Are we therefore to condemn as wrong an act that violates this principle? Are we to praise an act because the person does to another just what he does for himself or what he would wish another to do to him? These would be answers to the question "Which acts should be called right and which wrong?"

The important philosophical points of this second position are again epistemological and logical. How can we know this principle of equal treatment of all persons? If we cannot produce empirical evidence, then we might say that it is an axiom. One may employ it in judging actions, but upon what basis does it rest? Some have claimed a special faculty of moral insight called conscience. The most subtle version comes from Immanuel Kant, who developed a theory called formalism. There are certain universal principles such as, "Treat all men as ends rather than means," "So act that the motive of your act may become a universal law." The common belief that tests the moral rightness of an act is our willingness to allow anyone to do the same. Often we are asked "What if everyone would do as you have done?" In other words, can the maxim be universalized?

We shall develop the empirical answer to the question "What shall I do?" and the rational answer to the question "Shall I praise or condemn this act?" In the first alternative, hedonism, value judgments are true to the facts of pleasure or pain, that is, to the consequences of acts. In the second alternative, formalism, value judgments conform to logical principles that apply to the motives of acts. In either case moral judgments are true or false, that is, such propositions report facts or conform to logical principles employed in developing a self-consistent system of moral statements.

Just as in aesthetic questions we came to the problem of some final normative principle, so in ethics we sometimes demand more than facts and logical deductions. Traditionally, the question was asked "What is the utlimate good?" Beliefs about this good are common among us. Let us cite a few. "My ultimate goal is a just society where each man should work to the limit of his capacity, and each should be satisfied in every need." "Man's chief end is to glorify God and fully to enjoy him forever." We have quoted a typical humanistic doctrine and a typical theistic doctrine. You may have heard that Nietzsche considered the chief end of humanity to produce a being surpassing man in dignity, and that the final principle of morality is an imperative "Produce the Superman!" We shall look into the belief that the final purpose of mankind is the completest self-development of each member of the species in an all-encompassing organic whole. Plato's Republic sets forth this sort of perfect state and society. This ideal received its fullest elaboration in absolute idealism.

Now, before the artist has produced his work, it may be said to be both possible and future, while for the critic the work is both actual in its effects, and past in its causes. Thus the question, "What should I make" for the artist is properly answered by an imperative, while for the critic the question, "How do I appreciate this work" is properly answered by an indicative. Similarly, when we ask "What should I do" the question is answered, if answered at all, by an imperative. "Don't kill" cannot refer to a past murder, but to a future possibility. If murder has been committed, we would say "This ought not to have been done," "It was wrong of you to kill her." Is there any sense in tenseless, timeless beliefs about good and bad, right and wrong? Is there any sense in judgments about any act by any man, that is, in universal propositions about these acts? Some question the meaningfulness of "Thou shalt not kill." Some say it means, "If a man murders, he sins against God." Others say "If a man murders the crime ought to be punished by the state." Has this a meaning apart from any doctrine of God or functioning of political society?

Some philosophers are quite satisfied with subjectivism in both aesthetics and ethics. Others consider aesthetics to be a realm in which there can be no truths, either particular or general, but consider morality to be social, and demanding agreed-upon norms of conduct.[1]

If there are sharp differences between art and conduct, between works of art and deliberate acts, between aesthetic beliefs and moral beliefs, the conjoined field of value-theory would seem misleading. How can we defend this rather modern interest? We can say three things.

First, some philosophers have answered questions about the beautiful and the good in the same range of discourse. We will illustrate this from Plato's Gorgias where Socrates takes the position of a just judge trying to apply universal standards to reach as perfect a judgment as possible. This will illustrate the fact that the subjectivism that seems to us so modern was a problem with which the sophists confronted Socrates, Plato, and later, Aristotle.

Second, although Socrates approaches aesthetic questions with a basically moral attitude, men like Nietzsche have approached moral problems with a basically aesthetic attitude.

Third, since one may be objectivistic about aesthetic value or subjectivistic about moral value, there seems to be a common group of philosophic questions in the two fields. In philosophy we seek generality of method and the most general terms alone permit us to ask categorial questions. Hence we shall examine in the next section quotations from Socrates and Nietzsche that employ many of the terms used in a general theory of value.

II. Socratic Objectivism and Nietzschean Subjectivism

The just judge applies standards and gives as nearly perfect a verdict as possible. This is a central theme in the dialogues of Plato. Socrates calls

[1] S. Hampshire, *Aesthetics and Language* (William Elton, ed.), Basil Blackwell, Oxford, 1954, Ch. X.

attention to the fact that if we care about health and sickness, we turn to physicians who know what each state is. Medicine has a purpose, namely, to make the sick man well, and the art of medicine is a skill that may be successful or may fail, and we can judge the degree to which it fulfills its end or purpose. What is the good of the politician or statesman? Is it not to achieve justice, to punish the wicked and cure him of crime, to create health in society by giving to each man his due? Can we know whether this moral act succeeds or fails of its purpose? And what is the goal of the artist? Is it not to create beautiful things, things harmonious and orderly and therefore pleasing to the sight? Are we not able to distinguish beautiful things from ugly things? The arts that appeal to our faculties of knowledge are "fine" rather than merely "servile," as cookery, which only tickles the palate. Knowledge requires an understanding of forms, and in a Platonic sense, cooking does not turn the mind to these ideal patterns.

Socrates argues in the Gorgias that what is ugly is also morally bad, and what is beautiful is morally good. Both problems are problems of what we mean when we evaluate. Beauty can be called positive aesthetic value; moral goodness, or rightness, or justice can be called positive moral value. Each has a negative, ugliness and badness. When we say that a thing is just, do we imply that it is not morally bad? Socrates seems to assume an act or thing is either one or the other as a whole, rather than a mixture of both.

To fix one possible position that we have called *value objectivism,* let us continue with Socrates. The philosopher expresses a belief that he claims is true, for example, "that to do wrong is worse than to be wronged and that not to be punished for wrongdoing is worse than to suffer punishment." Socrates is unwilling to allow that this belief is false just because most people if asked to vote would disagree. What the objectivist means by a true value judgment is not that it is commonly accepted. This would mean relativity to some climate of opinion, and make the belief subject to variation between groups within any given society. "Which is uglier; to do or to suffer wrong?" Polus answers, "To do wrong." Socrates argues, "Well, then it's worse since it's uglier." Polus denies that good and beautiful or bad and ugly mean the same thing. Socrates argues again that all beautiful things, such as bodies, colors, figures, and sounds can neither be judged well-ordered nor be well-ordered without reference to some standard. In the first place, for instance, when you say beautiful bodies are beautiful, is it not either with reference to some utility, some use to which they may be put, or with reference to some pleasure that produces delight from contemplation of them? Can one adduce any other points of reference in discussing the beauty of the body?[2]

The key word in the objectivist's belief is standard. The man whose judgment counts is the one who knows the principle, which is a general statement of the purpose to which an act is directed. The principle of medicine is to cure the sick; it is a "happier condition for a man's body . . . to be cured or never to be sick at all."[3] What is this health which is the standard by which we judge the worth of the physician's art, and which is the sole reason for our going to a physician when we suffer disease? The basic meaning is one so general that it applies to the soul as well as to the body. It is *order* or *harmony* that characterizes all persons who are happy and virtuous, and those who are unhappy and vicious lack integration or wholeness. Thus, a genuine art is a skill practiced with knowledge of such a principle as that of the physician.

The principle of the statesman's art, namely, that of governing, is justice. The principle of the poet's art is "a genuine attempt to make the souls of one's fellows as excellent as may be, a striving always to say what is best, whatever the degree of pleasure or pain it may afford the audience."[4] If the end were mere gratification, the pleasant or the painful would depend upon how particular persons happened to feel at the time. Thus there would be an object that could be at the same time both beautiful and ugly, both good and bad. But then we should say that one man finds a thing beautiful, another finds it ugly, and we should have no true propositions but mere opinions about the thing. The thing would *seem* different to different men or to the same man at different times. But Socrates wants to know whether a thing *really is* beautiful or ugly, irrespective of his opinion about it. Thus we have the problem: What characteristics can a thing or act possess that allow those who judge its value to know that they are saying something about it, and not merely expressing what they like or desire?

Consider: will a good man, whose speeches are for the maximum improvement of his fellows, say anything at random? Will he not always have some definite end in view? Just as all other craftsmen keep their eye on the task in hand and select and apply nothing at random, but only such things as may bring about the special form he is bent upon effecting. Consider, if you like, painters and architects, and shipwrights and any other craftsmen you please; each one of them disposes every element of his task in a fixed order and ad-

[2] Plato, *Gorgias* (W. C. Helmbold, tr.), The Liberal Arts Press, Inc., New York, 1952, p. 474.
[3] *Ibid.*, p. 478.
[4] *Ibid.*, p. 503.

justs the parts in a suitable and harmonious scheme until the whole has been constituted as a regularized and well-ordered object.[5]

Socrates affirms his belief that this principle allows one to judge even the worth of a house. If it has order or harmony, it is good, if it is in disorder it is bad. The standard applies also to a ship, a human body, a soul, or even a community of men who form a state. He adds two considerations that are sometimes, but not always, used as a metaphysical basis for objectivism. The first is that the universe is a *cosmos,* or an order, that things happen in a regular or patterned way. The second is that this universe contains perfect judges, that is the gods. Men may err when deceived by wicked souls, but the gods are not deceived.

The Socrates of Plato's Dialogues defends the classic claim to objectivity of moral and aesthetic judgment, through an understanding of absolute standards. The most defiant voice against the doctrine of a fixed abstract hierarchy is that of Friedrich Nietzsche.

Hitherto, moral values have been the highest values: does anyone doubt this? . . . If we bring down the values from their pedestal, we thereby alter *all* values: the principle of their *order of rank* which has prevailed hitherto is thus overthrown.[6]

Furthermore, in his attempt to get rid of Socratic objectivity, Nietzsche praises falsehood above truth and appearance above reality. Why? Because we men are "the *creators* of our valuations—we will thus be able to put sense into history . . . if there is anything at all that must be worshipped it is *appearance; that falsehood and not* truth is—divine."[7]

It follows, third, that with no impersonal order of rank among values and no truth that impugns some beliefs as false, our preferences must be the expression of some other factor. Nietzsche selects strength, and draws a consequence that was calculated to shock his conventional contemporaries. Who then can say that one thing is preferable to another? "It is only a question of power: to have all the morbid traits of the century, but to balance them by means of overflowing, plastic, and rejuvenating power. The *strong* man." The individual who is strong has no "feeling of sin," no submission to "traditional ideals," particularly Christian, no craving for equality with other men, no yearning for "antiquity," no stress on "gregarious instincts."

[5] *Ibid.,* p. 77.
[6] Friedrich Nietzsche, *The Will to Power, an Attempted Transvaluation of All Values* (A. M. Ludovici, tr.), Foulis, Edinburgh and London, 1913, Vol. II, p. 390. Nietzsche specialists disagree about the purity of this text.
[7] *Ibid.,* p. 393.

If we should generalize these beliefs, they boil down logically to a denial that right, good, ought, just have any genuine negate, either contradictory or contrary. They are not genuine concepts that can be defined, because they do no more than express the feelings of weak men; indeed they define what Nietzsche meant by weak men. Hence nearly all morality represents the plot of the weak to drag down the able and courageous to the level of the mediocre, hesitant, inhibited, and indecisive Caspar Milquetoasts or Aunt Sallies. This is far from all Nietzsche had to say, nor does it all cohere neatly into a system, but what has been here excerpted does show the purpose Nietzsche espoused. If it is the true account of values, it would effect a "transvaluation of all values." And it is philosophically most valuable since it challenges nearly all we have excerpted from Plato's Gorgias. In order to discredit the customs of the herd, Nietzsche, with Socratic irony, follows the Socratic injunction, "Know Yourself."

We saw earlier that both inductive and deductive logic, and the philosophies that employ them, encounter difficulties with judgments of value. The writings of Nietzsche enable us to grasp why this is so. Inductive logic delineates the form of the process of generalizing from particular cases and employs the resultant probability statement for prediction. But suppose with Nietzsche that value is misconceived when predicated of objects, and resides always and only in the creator and appreciator of some work. More specifically, high value is associated with the intoxication of the artist who creates and the lover who admires.[8] Hence if we should seek to describe which acts are good, or which things are beautiful, the inductive approach rests upon the mistake of reading into objects our own reactions. What we might study are the conditions under which men respond to creation. Hence remarks are scattered throughout Nietzsche's work on sickness and health, for he claimed to divide our reactions into sick and healthy.

The mistake of employing deductive logic in discourse about values is even more egregious, according to Nietzsche. At the very least there can be no deductive process without a general criterion or a principle whereby we may draw a valid conclusion. The critic who argues rationally then differs radically from the creator and appreciator, especially if these latter are in a state of intoxication. But no one can be disengaged when the question is one of value, and if men were disengaged, there would be no value.

[8] George Morgan, *Friedrich Nietzsche*, Harvard University Press, Cambridge, Massachusetts, 1943, pp. 209–211, 221.

The notion of a major value premise, or even one applying to all aesthetic objects or a principle of all moral acts is, according to Nietzsche, a mistake. We either get it from cases inductively, or we are said to grasp it a priori by intuition. He thought he had destroyed the former alternative. But the latter alternative rests, as in Plato, on locating the value norm in another realm, which, in Nietzsche's phrase, is "the de-naturalization of morals," "by treating morals in terms of abstract ideas and inventing another world for them to inhabit. . . . "[9] The whole basis of our values is very much in this world, indeed, as Nietzsche never tired of stressing, in physiology. He meant by this that value statements are meaningless apart from human life with its animal basis.

What of deducing validly some judgment of value? This is absurd, Nietzsche would say, because the distinction between valid and invalid, appropriate in mathematics and theoretical science, does not apply. Artists create and moral man makes choices and acts. But the process is a vital one, like a fight rather than an argument. An artist or a noble man has no premises and conclusions to join by implication.

What of aesthetic and moral judgments as conclusions to syllogisms? We would supply premises and defend the form of the argument only if we cared whether someone could see how the conclusion had been reached. And the only reason for such a method would be concern for the truth or falsehood of the conclusion. This certainly motivated the Platonic Socrates in his effort to make a science of aesthetic and moral judgments. But Nietzsche's subjectivism has given several reasons why this is a mistake. The charge he often preferred is that human beings belong to diverse cultures which change in time. Now if there is nothing eternal about truth-in-itself, goodness-in-itself, beauty-in-itself, the final argument of Plato's Gorgias gives away Platonism. It is a roundabout appeal to man to submit to God, generally identified with perfection itself. But for Nietzsche "God is dead." Nevertheless in the creation of art and in the nobility of the strong, man may find something divine to worship.

Socrates and Nietzsche display just how far and completely each of us may go in what we have spelled out as two dramatic cases of objectivism and subjectivism. Rather than moderate the struggle at this point by giving an exposition of positions somewhere in between, it seems wise to examine beliefs about the arts and aesthetic value. In neither aesthetics nor ethics is there any one established method. We have already given clues as to why philosophers working at the problems often devise new

_____
[9] *Ibid.*, p. 162.

logics and novel theories of knowledge. Perhaps we do not make choices or settle value conflicts by processes reducible to inductive or deductive form.

III. Beliefs about Artistic Creation

Fyodor Dostoevsky in his Brothers Karamazov permits us to overhear Ivan and Alyosha.

> ". . . Do you know, Alyosha—don't laugh! I made a poem about a year ago. If you can waste another ten minutes on me, I'll tell it to you."
> "You wrote a poem?"
> "Oh, no, I didn't write it," laughed Ivan, "and I've never written two lines of poetry in my life. But I made up this poem in prose and I remembered it. I was carried away when I made it up. You will be my first reader—that is, listener. Why should an author forgo even one listener?" smiled Ivan. "Shall I tell it to you?"
> "I'm all attention," said Alyosha.
> "My poem is called 'The Grand Inquisitor'; it's a ridiculous thing, but I want to tell it to you. . . ."[10]

How does a work of art come to be? It might seem necessary to define "work of art" before one proceeds to answer this question, but many thinkers find it necessary to introduce notions of creation when trying to distinguish works of art from other sorts of objects. The situation seems to be this: If one answers the question, "What is a work of art," one will presuppose an answer to "How does a work of art come to be?"

And if one answers the question, "How does a work of art come to be," one will presuppose an answer to the question, "What is a work of art?" How can we escape the circle?

It seems sound to say that works of art are differentiated from natural objects because human making is necessary to the former, but not to the latter. But not all artifacts, or things made by men, are considered works of art. So we may say that all art is making, but not all making is art. One common theory calls attention to two differentiating features of art as a process to explain the differences among works of art. Susanne K. Langer supposes it is obvious in spite of borderline cases, that works of art include poems and novels and dramas and other literary works, paintings, and sculpture and other things in spatial arrangement, songs and symphonies and other arrangements of sounds in temporal sequence. Why should we group together such obviously different things? Her answer is: "Art is the creation of forms symbolic of human feeling." All things

[10] Fyodor Dostoevsky, *The Grand Inquisitor* (Constance Garnett, tr.), Haddam House, New York, 1948, p. 9.

that men make are arrangements of parts or "a modification of a natural object to suit human purposes." But are all pots and pans artistic creations, or all barns works of architecture? No, she answers, for "creation of forms symbolic of human feeling" requires man's "utmost conceptual power, imagination." She does not require a work to be "the invention of original turns, nor the adoption of novel themes," but one might define creation in just this way. Nor does she consider very highly the theories of creation found in Plato and Aristotle, namely that artists are inspired, which Plato stressed, or that artists imitate nature, which Aristotle stressed.[11] You may not think Mrs. Langer's definition in the least controversial. But some philosophers of art consider novelty essential to any aesthetic creation, although they may stand with her against imitation and inspiration. Other thinkers stress expression and say that to make the arrangement of physical parts essential is to bring the artist too close to the craftsman. And still others claim that only imagination is essential and consequently deny that forms can be symbolic of feelings.

It is sometimes said by philosophers of art that knowing how any work of art comes to be is helpful in appreciation and criticism. Psychologists, and particularly depth-psychologists, are interested in the process of creation in order to gain access to mental acts that are difficult to reduce to any simple stimulus-response pattern. A psychologist, or a literary critic, may tackle the problem in order to confirm or to refute some psychological theory. Thus, the approach in this section may include psychological data, but these cases are only illustrative.

Although it may be a mistaken belief, indeed a form of the intentional fallacy, it is frequently held that if one knows how an artist creates, one is then better able to approach works of art and to judge their worth. It is common in the arts to report something of the lives of, e.g., Wordsworth the poet, Dickens the novelist, Leonardo the painter, O'Neill the dramatist, Nijinsky the dancer, Beethoven the composer, Michelangelo the sculptor, Frank Lloyd Wright the architect. Philosophers have, throughout the history of philosophy, framed theories so general that they might apply to any artist. The task of a critical reader is to ask whether the general statements hold true of all or only of some particular arts. Do such theories apply to all artists within a group, say the visual arts, but are less true or misleading of the non-visual arts?

As a first step we shall show how a mind might move from one theory to another. Two Greek theories formulated classically by Aristotle and

[11] Susanne Langer, *Feeling and Form: A Theory of Art Developed from Philosophy in a New Key,* Charles Scribner's Sons, New York, 1953, pp. 40, 76.

Plato are called *imitation* and *inspiration*. Surely almost everyone has considered such a belief as: "This painting is of maple trees in autumn." What did the artist do in representing the appearance for us? Did he simply copy it as does a photographic camera? Or did he say something like the following: "I had a brainstorm. I don't know where the impulse and idea came from. It came to me as from outside. I felt inspired." Is this an illusion or a delusion, or is it an irreducible basic fact of how pictures, songs, or poems come to be?

Two modern theories are not often sharply distinguished. They are called *imagination* and *expression*. Kant in the eighteenth century explained works of art as imaginative. One sees a painting of angels in a presentation of the Nativity story and asks, "Is this the artist's representation of what he has seen in nature, or merely what he has thought abstractly?" Certainly not the first, and certainly not the second either, for by definition an angel is pure mind or a bodiless soul. Do not artists, then, picture the imperceptible, and even the ordinarily inconceivable? Or one may be puzzled by students who write poems or verse for a magazine. Some of them may express the exquisite delights of love or the excruciating pain of being refused or jilted. Anyone may ask "Why were these words put together," and answer "He or she felt so strongly that those passions had to be expressed."

A. Imitation

The artist, according to Plato and Aristotle, is an imitator. The arts, writes Aristotle, in the Poetics, spring naturally from the "instinct for imitation," and what distinguishes one art from another are "materials of imitation." For example, "dancing imitates character, emotion, and action by rhythmical movement." Music imitates by harmony and rhythm alone. Poetry and prose represent men by words. As to portraits, "we must represent men either as better than in real life, or as worse, or as they are." The artist is free to choose between different objects. When writing a tragedy, one selects "action that is serious, complete, and of certain magnitude." When writing a comedy, one selects for imitation "persons inferior," though not fully bad. Tragedy represents men as "better than in actual life"; comedy "as worse." There are principles governing the style appropriate to each form. But all forms of imitation are for the purpose of learning and taking pleasure in the execution of the imitation.[12]

Although Plato sometimes spoke of imitating as though it were mere

[12] Aristotle, *On the Art of Poetry* (S. H. Butcher, tr., M. C. Nahm, ed.), The Liberal Arts Press, Inc., New York, 1948, pp. 1–8.

copying of nature, he stressed, as did Aristotle, the factors of interpretation and organizing skill that are involved. The strength of the theory is that Plato had defined a relationship so general that the visible universe could be regarded as an imitation of the eternal forms. Aristotle, we have seen, regards the forms to be in things, and the artist makes things by borrowing these forms. Such metaphysical doctrines of form enable us to explain the capacity of works of art to impress us with their importance. They convey knowledge of the forms, as well as expressing human evaluation of them. Since the forms are common, art deals with the universal, but embodies the universal in sensuous matter. "Poetry is more philosophical than history" said Aristotle, for history deals only with particular events.

This accordingly means that poetry is truer than history. Of particular things we have only opinions, while of the general we can have knowledge.

No theory of artistic production has a longer development and more varied interpretations.[13] It is defended today by a celebrated Thomist, Jacques Maritain. It is important to notice that he does *not* mean by imitation the production of an illusion, as a painted landscape. Nor does Maritain agree with some Platonic texts in which art is taken to be a means of knowledge. According to Maritain, Aristotle means by imitation "copying only in the primitive elementary case." Imitation is not essentially the reproduction of things, rather it is a manifestation of form. The knowledge of forms is presupposed by the mind enjoying these symbols of "something over and above such symbols."[14]

In spite of these qualifications, there are a number of objections a defender should be prepared to answer.

First, if imitation is a constant relation between every work of art and its object, we should always be able to say what a work is "about." We can do this with pictures of concrete things. "Gilbert Stuart painted this portrait of George Washington." "Wordsworth wrote a poem about Grasmere and Lake Windermere." But does it make sense to say "The Empire State Building is about American enterprise"? To use Maritain's language, what is the "something" symbolized by a building? It would seem that an imitation theory is plausible for literature and pictorial art, but becomes unintelligible when applied to architecture.

Second, even if there were no non-representative art forms, such as

[13] Richard McKeon, "Imitation and Poetry," *Thought, Action, and Passion,* University of Chicago Press, Chicago, 1954, pp. 102–227.
[14] Jacques Maritain, *Art and Scholasticism* (J. F. Scanlan, tr.), Charles Scribner's Sons, New York, 1930, pp. 42–45.

architecture and music, it still remains a question whether imitation is the essence of creation even when the symbols are "about" something. We want to learn "about" something. But is art primarily an effort to learn and to teach? It was Plato, as we shall shortly see, who did not regard the artist as a scholar. In a word, the theory stresses cognition, which may be very unimportant in art forms. Most movies are for entertainment, and one does not go to Tea House of the August Moon to learn of Okinawa. The writers of a musical comedy are not trying to produce a documentary.

Third, some philosophers have followed Plato in considering a work of art a copy. The original form, being the model, has greater dignity. But why should we impugn a work on the ground that its origin is once, twice, thrice, removed from reality? This presupposes a metaphysical scheme, and we could just as well say that the form is merely abstract, a possibility for actualization, and that the work of art, which is concrete, has fuller reality and dignity. The imitation theory may therefore introduce a fallacious way of reasoning, namely, genetic evaluation. We certainly should not reason that Ralph Bunche is servile because his grandparents were born in slavery. The whole question of derivation distracts us from what the thing is.

Last, imitation theories seem to pay no attention to the novel aspects of reality produced in the arts. If there are forms in nature or forms transcendent to nature, why should we duplicate them? In music we may be creating formal patterns that cannot be found in bird songs. Some artists have stressed the depth of imagination or the intensity of emotion. These alternatives, which we shall shortly examine, are not dominated by the dependence of art on nature.

B. Inspiration

Why should anyone believe that the power moving the poet to sing is divine rather than human or simply natural? The most famous argument for this belief is contained in the shortest of Platonic dialogues, named the Ion, for an interpreter of Homer who came to Athens. Socrates supposed that the acknowledged power of Ion to interpret the meaning of Homer's words was derived from a knowledge of the principles of poetry. These would be general criteria by which one could discriminate good from bad workmanship. But Ion has no such knowledge, and the evidence for this is that he has absolutely no ideas about any other poet than Homer. Since everyone agrees that Ion has great power not based on knowledge, Socrates is asked to explain how this is possible. The explanation is one of the famous Platonic myths.

This gift which you possess of speaking excellently about Homer is not an art, but . . . an inspiration; there is a divinity moving you, like that in the stone which Euripides calls a magnet. . . . This stone not only attracts iron rings, but also imparts to them a similar power of attracting other rings; and sometimes you may see a number of pieces of iron and rings suspended from one another so as to form quite a long chain: and all of them derive their power of suspension from the original stone. In like manner the Muse first of all inspires men herself: and from these inspired persons a chain of other persons is suspended, who take the inspiration.

The evidence for this doctrine is that artists often do say that they are no longer their ordinary selves while they create. Some say that they seem to be instruments through which something else is singing, or painting, or writing. The Greeks called it ecstasy. "Are you not carried out of yourself, and does not your soul in an ecstasy seem to be among the persons or places of which you are speaking, whether they are in Ithaca or in Troy or whatever may be the scene of the poem?"[15] The question is, must we say these phenomena are produced by divinities? Should we not avoid explaining the obscure by the more obscure? Before we think about psychological doctrines of imagination and expression, let us pause to consider what the defender of inspiration owes us.

Again as with imitation, the inspiration theory has been expressed by a great name in twentieth-century art. James Joyce in A Portrait of the Artist as a Young Man puts it this way. "The artist, like the God of creation, remains within or behind or beyond or above his handiwork, invisible, refined out of existence, indifferent, paring his fingernails." The artist is godlike, and resembles the Father, making a world out of nothing or reshaping chaos into a harmonious universe. He corresponds also to the Son or Logos, who from pity of the world, becomes flesh. The creative process is also like the procession of the Spirit, the conception, gestation, and reproduction from "the virgin womb of the imagination."[16] Of course one may defend the analogy of the artist to God without defending either a Trinitarian aesthetic or a Trinitarian theology.[17]

This theory does appeal to some creative artists, and for a very good reason. It frees the artist from any bondage to rules. His poetic license is a divine privilege, and in the case of Joyce, public opinion, the law, the church, publishers, economic realities, none of these were to tell him what or how to write.

[15] Plato, *Dialogues* (B. Jowett, tr,), Random House, New York, 1937, p. 289, p. 290.
[16] James Joyce, *A Portrait of the Artist as a Young Man*, The New American Library, Inc., New York, pp. 163, 168, 169.
[17] Milton C. Nahm, *The Artist as Creator*, Johns Hopkins Press, Baltimore, 1956.

In spite of this claim, which the student may wish to support in just this way, if he espouses the belief in inspiration, he should be prepared to defend it on several scores.

First, the inspiration theory rests upon either an argument from effect to cause or on a priori assumption of divine activity. Either way may be challenged just as are arguments for the existence of God. If this is not what the theory means, then perhaps "divinely inspired" means "excellent." It may be a way of saying that a work of art can be produced by simple adherence to rule, as easily as a school can produce a genius. Very well, then, what seems an explanation is really a confession of ignorance. Say the work is surprisingly good, and it will not be misleading. If we do not really know, our explanation is *ad hoc,* giving merely the semblance of an explanation.

Another objection is that the inspiration theory tells us so little of the process. One critic puts this well:

Theories of inspiration are usually unintelligible not because of insistence upon divine influence, but because there is no aesthetic passage from the divine influence to the work of art, and certainly in and of itself art becomes no more clearly understood by reason of theological arguments which affirm divine impetus to creation.[18]

A third objection is that although the inspiration theory would have us believe that the artist is free from rules, he may be less free on that account. Rules at least suppose that a man who knows what he is making can shape material and deliberately choose between symbols. But to be unaware of what he is doing would mean the "greater bondage . . . of being a mere instrument for a divine will."[19]

C. Imagination

Theories of artistic creation that make imagination central stand in contrast to imitation and inspiration theories. The imagination is a human capacity, variously defined, and this explanation of creation leaves natural forms and divine afflatus to one side. Aristotle was primarily concerned with differentiating art from nature. Plato was primarily concerned with relating ideals and men. The birth of modern philosophy made man's knowing central. Hence Bacon, Descartes, Hobbes, and particularly Kant in his Critique of Judgment set out to distinguish a faculty called imagination from perception and understanding.

[18] Bertram Morris, *Aesthetic Process,* Northwestern University, Evanston, Illinois, 1943, p. 55.
[19] Milton Nahm, *op. cit.,* p. 45.

Imagination varies in definition from philosopher to philosopher. The issue between Hobbes and Kant is whether the imagination that accounts for works of art is passive or active. If imagination means "sense . . . fading, old and past," then says Hobbes it may be identified with memory. Then works of art reproduce what has been seen. But works of art as mere observation are inferior to works of science. Why prefer a fuzzy memory to a sharp description of present experience? It would be a paradox for Hobbes' theory if people preferred reading a biography based on recollection to reading a day-by-day journal. Hence we may say that more than accuracy makes the worth of such a work of art. Goethe called his autobiography Dichtung und Wahrheit. What accounts for the worth of poetry as against truth? The poet is not primarily concerned with observing and reporting. He uses his imagination, according to Kant. It is the "autonomous inventive powers of the artist." Hence the artist gives us something we could not observe in nature.

In works of art there are images of many things not found in nature. Sir Herbert Read reminds us of Indian gods with six arms, genii of the Arabian Nights, and the like. Sir Herbert is aware, as are all of us some of the time, of the phantasies in dreams. This helps us to appreciate works of art.

Some of the attraction we find in works of art is due to the presence in the work of art of primordial images which have found their way from the unconscious levels of the mind. Both the artist in creating the work of art, and we who look at the work of art, are penetrating more or less deeply into the world of dreams. From that world the artist derives what he calls his "inspiration"— his sudden perception of an image or a theme—and into that world and in the very act of perception, the spectator—the person enjoying a work of art—brings a new image. . . . We must think of the unconscious mind of the spectator as a sort of carnival into which a strange figure suddenly strays. All the merrymakers turn towards the newcomer and welcome him; he joins in their dance, and the fun goes all the faster.[20]

There is as much unknown in the unconscious levels as in the divine levels. It may be that the image of Hamlet owes its power to Shakespeare's Oedipus complex.[21] All a philosopher can say about this theory of artistic imagination is that the most common forms of it have been pushed to the point of absurdity.

Something like this has been claimed by Benedetto Croce and R. G.

[20] Quoted in M. Rader, *A Modern Book of Esthetics*, Henry Holt & Co., New York, 1952, pp. 41–42.
[21] Ernest Jones, *Hamlet and Oedipus*, Doubleday & Co., Inc., Garden City, New York, 1949.

Collingwood. Both denied that artistic production in any way requires techniques or materials or conscious purpose or should be subjected to any objective criticism. Why do Croce and Collingwood deny these? Because "a work of art may be completely created when it has been created as a thing whose only place is in the artist's mind."[22] Collingwood's best example is music, which involves so little stuff and has so little utility. But is it true of all art that we create "for ourselves" and that art is unconditionally free or subject to no external condition?[23]

Many conclude that this theory, like others, is not false, but an exaggeration. We may have to exaggerate in order to call attention to a neglected factor. So long as men confuse works of art with science or morality, just so long the exaggeration of Croce has value.

D. Expression

If the imagination theory is most plausible when we think of a lonely genius without an audience, the expression theory is most plausible when we take into account a social transaction. Some artists manage to communicate and wield great power to sway their audiences. Since they commonly convey so little information, we wonder what they do communicate. Well, emotions can be communicated. A brave Churchill can address a nation when the military facts spell defeat, and magnificently call upon blood, sweat, and tears to win victory. A good actor can make you ready to fight at one moment or to tremble with fright at another. An artist may use fact or fancy, but the central point of this belief about producing works of art is to make them media through which men are moved.

The most noted proponent of the doctrine is Leo Tolstoy.

Art begins when one person, with the object of joining another or others to himself in one and the same feeling, expresses that feeling by certain external indications. To take the simplest example: a boy, having experienced, let us say, fear on encountering a wolf, relates that encounter; and, in order to evoke in others the feeling he has experienced, describes himself, his conditions before the encounter, the surroundings, the wood, his own lightheartedness, and then the wolf's appearance, its movements, the distance between himself and the wolf, etc. All this, if only the boy when telling the story, again experiences the feelings he had lived through and infects the hearers and compels them to feel what the narrator had experienced, is art.[24]

[22] R. G. Collingwood, *Principles of Art,* The Clarendon Press, Oxford, 1950, p. 130.
[23] Milton Nahm, *Aesthetic Experience and Its Presuppositions,* Harper & Brothers, New York, 1943, pp. 227–228.
[24] Leo Tolstoy, *What is Art?,* quoted by M. Rader. In: *A Modern Book of Esthetics,* Henry Holt & Co., Inc., New York, 1935, pp. 101–102. See also World's Classics Series, Oxford University Press, 1905 translation by Aylmer Maude.

This may be most pertinent to story-telling and dramatic art. But can we generalize, as Tolstoy does, from story-telling to all works of art? The following points may be raised.

First, what of emotions expressed in music? Can we say of them that they had been experienced in circumstances prior to their production in certain arrangements of sounds?

Second, direct face-to-face relation between actor or story-teller and audience enables him to communicate emotion. But how is it done between an architect and a spectator? Suppose an architect is proud with his patron's pride. He builds a tall and huge house. Will every spectator join him in an emotional response on seeing that house? No. The spectator may pity the children overwhelmed by such luxury. Or he may take it as an example of conspicuous waste, and be filled with loathing.

Third, how can one's "own feelings" be transmitted to others? This has to be allowed if we are ever to speak of "one and the same feeling." Perhaps Tolstoy should have said that the artist stimulates in his audience a similar feeling. But how does one discover this?

Last, is it true that "the stronger the infection the better the art?" Tolstoy adds to the theory of art as infection the normative judgment "and not only is infection a sure sign of art, but the degree of infectiousness is also the sole measure of excellence in art." The only alternative is to judge the subject matter. The subject matter is "feelings," and the "kinder" these feelings, the better, for the purpose of art is to make people feel love towards one another. By this standard of feeling, the greatest prose work written in English would probably be Dickens' Christmas Carol. If the student suspects that something has gone wrong with Tolstoy's theory, he will not be the first.

E. Summary

In the previous section we have used the words creative, creation, creator, and creativity in many different senses. It is worth our while to make clear some alternative meanings.

To create may mean to make. Thus we may substitute "He made a nuisance" for "He created a nuisance." Do we mean by "creative" merely that an agent has produced a certain result? Then every man would be an artist and every production a work of art. This is too broad to be at all helpful in recognizing artistic or aesthetic value.

To create may mean to give form to materials. Thus we may substitute for "poet" the phrase "those who express their words in rhythmic patterns sometimes with rhyme, always with attention to sounds and images as well as to the sense." This certainly helps us to narrow our meaning for art. But do we intend to include all craftsmen indiscriminately? A carpenter is one who gives form to lumber, making useful wooden objects. A door may be indispensable and excellent but it is of a different sort of excellence from a sonnet.

To create may mean to give form to materials with the intent of conveying the impression of something else. Hence we should always be able to say of an artistic creation, e.g., a poem, a painting, or song, that it is, for example, "about a tree." We certainly cannot say this of a door. We can say what a door is for, but it is not as such a symbol of something else. But a door may be a sign, when closed, of retreat from society, or when open, a sign of hospitality. And is a work of architecture "about" something else? So this definition is both too narrow and too broad for artistic creation.

To create may mean to use some image original to the artist. This is sometimes our meaning when we say that poets have expressed their love for women by such phrases as "O my love is like a red, red rose." Perhaps this spells out what we mean when we say that Robert Burns created love poetry. But we also may want to distinguish Burns from sheer gush, and this definition will not do if we mean by "create" to produce forms of worth.

To create may mean to express intense feelings that would otherwise remain unknown to us. Sometimes we say "St. Augustine created the autobiography," and we mean by it, "It was St. Augustine who showed men of our tradition how one may discover himself by reflecting intensely upon the stages of one's career." But applied to all the arts, such events are quite rare, and there are certainly other approaches, for example, depth-psychology, that would be classed as works of art if this alone is what characterizes artistic creation.

To create may mean to make something new, in the sense of unpredictable from past events. In this sense, artists may surprise us by their freshness and originality, and religious men praise God for "a new heaven and a new earth." In this sense we wonder at military and political geniuses like Alexander who create empires out of city-states and kingdoms. Hence this meaning is a special one for "genius" although some works of art may not have this quasi-magical power. But is all becoming in the universe only the production of particulars that have not existed before? Some metaphysicians mean just this, and that only some events are predictable, and then only in a general way and not in full concrete actuality. Most philosophers of process have appealed to creation and have constructed systems to account for novelty.

Four slight sketches of the meanings of imitation, inspiration, imagination, and expression, do not convey adequately the great variation of theory
in one philosophic discipline. Those we have stressed are prominent attempts to reduce the ambiguity of a key term. Aristotle's Poetics seems the
clearest case for an imitation theory, and it has been historically of prime
importance. For an inspiration theory Plato's Ion has had many a follower.
Kant's Critique of Judgment makes an excellent case for imagination. And
for expression of feeling Croce's Aesthetic has had followers among both
artists and critics.

IV. Beliefs about Aesthetic Appreciation

There is much ancient precedent for discussing aesthetic value in
terms of the human response to works of art. Correlative to the creation
of an aesthetic object is the experience of it. In his account of tragedy,
Aristotle wrote: "It imitates actual deeds, not by means of narrative; and
by pity and fear effects the purgation of such emotions." This has been
one of the most suggestive lines in all aesthetics. In a standard work of a
generation ago, about sixty versions and paraphrases were listed; and some
have been added since.[25]

Medieval philosophers did not neglect an analysis of the beautiful. St.
Thomas Aquinas defined the beautiful in his terse Latin as *id quod visum
placet* (that which being seen pleases). Maritain comments:

The four words say all that is necessary: a vision, that is to say *intuitive
knowledge,* and a *joy.* The beautiful is what gives joy, not all joy, but joy in
knowledge; not the joy peculiar to the act of knowing, but a joy superabounding
and overflowing from such an act because of the object known.[26]

But it is among modern thinkers that we find elaborate theories of
beauty and the nature of art that dwell upon one or another aspect of our
responses. Consider the following definitions:

"Beauty is pleasure regarded as the quality of a thing."[27]

"The more we endow an object with human attributes, the less we
merely know, and the more we realize it, the more does it approach the
work of art."[28]

"There is a fine art of passion, but an impassioned fine art is a contra-

[25] E. F. Carritt, *Philosophies of Beauty,* Oxford University Press, New York, 1931, p.
33.
[26] Jacques Maritain, *op. cit.,* p. 19.
[27] George Santayana, *Sense of Beauty,* A. & C. Black, London, 1896, p. 49.
[28] Bernard Berenson, quoted from *Tuscan Painters* in I. A. Richards, C. K. Ogden,
and James Wood, *Foundation of Aesthetics,* Lear Publishers, [New York, 194–?], p. 67.

diction in terms, for the infallible effect of the beautiful is emancipation from the passions."[29]

"When he [the artist] can do all this, he opens out to others the way back [from phantasy] to the comfort and consolation of their own unconscious sources of pleasure, and so reaps their gratitude and admiration; then he has won—through his phantasy—what before he could only win in phantasy: honor, power, and the love of women."[30]

Often enough in a thoughtless way we say "It's pleasant, that is, it pleases me and I like it. It's beautiful. Say it anyway you like. All these mean the same thing." Some philosophers make the identity explicit in a definition, and also give the position a name. The agreed-on name is *hedonism*. We shall explore the position further.

Sometimes we note the identification of a person's physiological and psychological reaction to a work of art. We may believe this to be the criterion of appreciation. A cartoon shows a little girl playing a piano for her grandfather. The caption, "If you *really* enjoyed it, you'd be tapping your foot." That is an empathetic response, sometimes called, because of the central place given it by German psychological aesthetics, *Einfühlung*.

Often it is believed that works of art help us to "escape." "Let's go to the movies. We've got to get away from it all." Or one hears, "It's a good novel. You get lost in it, so absorbed that you forget yourself." This is sometimes called a *contemplative* view, in contrast to active and practical. Some theorists have explained the semblance to action as a feature of play. Other theorists appeal to our "distancing" of experience. That is, we are sometimes too much concerned with getting a job done to watch and listen and feel. But at other times we are unconcerned with a job, and then we are free for aesthetic delights.

In contrast to contemplation, there are theories that first insist on identifying the interest satisfied in some work of art. Sometimes we call these theories *voluntaristic*. The most common form is known as wish-fulfillment. One aesthetician expresses the belief that playing with dolls is an expression of the wish to have babies.

Each theory, or rather some statement of it, will be examined in turn. Each has been held to explain all cases of aesthetic appreciation. Each has been said to analyze the meaning of "enjoy" and each has been employed as a norm of criticism. As is commonplace with theories, each is

[29] Friedrich Schiller, quoted by M. Nahm, *Aesthetic Experience and Its Presupposition*, Harper and Brothers, New York, 1946, p. 461.
[30] Sigmund Freud, *Introductory Lectures on Psychoanalysis*, quoted in M. Rader, *Modern Book of Esthetics*, Henry Holt & Co., Inc., New York, 1935, p. 72.

illuminating in some cases, misleading in others, and each makes explicit some aspect of aesthetic experience. Whether any one of them is the "right" theory seems a naive question.

A. Pleasure

One of the most celebrated hedonistic theories of beauty and appreciation is that of George Santayana. He does not identify aesthetics with the study of the nature and conditions of all pleasures and pains; that would be too broad. But some pleasures are signs of beauty when they are immediately evident to us "in contemplation." There is a pleasure in getting what we want, a pleasure in knowing something to be a means to an end. Also we distinguish physical pleasures from those that are moral or purely intellectual. In the case of physical satisfactions we cannot forget the specific bodily organs through which our needs are satisfied; in the case of intellectual values we are always concerned with facts, with what is, and with that which is useful to know; in the case of moral values we are always concerned to avoid evil. Aesthetic pleasures are, then, contemplative, transcending immediate and positive bodily needs. But the important differentia is that "beauty" is a "pleasure of ours, which nevertheless we regard as a quality of things." There is no beauty unless there is pleasure to somebody; " . . . a beauty to which all men were forever indifferent is a contradiction in terms." To maintain the distinction between objective knowledge and aesthetic sensation and perception, Santayana says coherently that the qualities known to science are in objects, but the qualities the artist and critic are concerned with are imputed to objects. To maintain the distinction between moral and aesthetic value, he adds that moral evil is real, that is, what ought not to be, but aesthetic ugliness is "nothing but the absence of good. . . . Moral values are generally negative, and always remote. Morality has to do with the avoidance of evil and the pursuit of good: aesthetics only with enjoyment."[31]

Santayana himself later recognized four defects in this theory.

The first is that the theory assumes that all qualities are either objective or subjective. This is a mistake.

Nothing is subjective in experience except experience itself, the passing act of intuition or feeling; the terms distinguished during that experience, such as specific qualities of color or pleasure, are neither objective nor subjective, but neutral. . . .[32]

[31] George Santayana, "The Nature of Beauty," *The Sense of Beauty,* A. & C. Black, London, 1896, pp. 14–52.
[32] Melvin M. Rader, *op. cit.* 1st edition, p. 147, footnote.

In other words, "objective" and "subjective" are further specifications of experience, and not basic or ultimate.

The second defect is that if pleasure is as much an object of experience as color, it follows that it makes no sense to say that beauty is pleasure objectified.

Pleasure . . . does not need to be objectified in order to be fused into an image felt to be beautiful: if felt at all, pleasure is already an object of intuition; and the beautiful image is never objective in any other sense.[33]

Third, the classification of values as cognitive, moral, and aesthetic is an artificial division of the whole life of man.

I can draw no distinction—save for academic programmes—between moral and aesthetic values: beauty, being a good, is a moral good; and the practice and enjoyment of art, like all practice and all enjoyment, fall within the sphere of morals—at least if by morals we understand moral economy and not moral superstition. On the other hand, the good, when actually realized and not merely pursued from afar, is a joy in the immediate; it is possessed with wonder and is in that sense aesthetic.[34]

And last, a supreme achievement of beauty is tragedy, but the beauty of tragedy is hardly in the pleasure of its theme or in the avoidance of pain. Rather pains are compensated by the general truthfulness to human life, and the moral qualities of those who endure them. Thus aesthetic experience testifies against hedonism.

There is a scene in King Lear where the horror of the storm is made to brood over at least four miseries, that of the king, of the fool, of Edgar in his real person, and of Edgar in his assumed character. The vividness of each of these portrayals with its different note of pathos keeps the mind detached and free, forces it to compare and reflect, and thereby to universalize the spectacle. Yet even here, the beautiful effect is not secured without some touches of good. How much is not gained by the dumb fidelity of the fool, and by the sublime humanity of Lear, when he says, "Art cold? There is a part of me is sorry for thee yet"?[35]

In the discussion of empathy, we shall again be concerned with objectification. But an empathy theory attempts to explain aesthetic delight in a far more precise manner. Pleasure is much too general a term. It invites the theoretical obscurity of lumping together desire and preference and

[33] *Ibid.,* pp. 147–148.
[34] George Santayana, "A General Confession," *The Philosophy of George Santayana* (P. A. Schilpp, ed.), Northwestern University, Evanston and Chicago, Illinois, 1940, p. 20.
[35] George Santayana, *The Sense of Beauty, op. cit.,* p. 229.

satisfaction, and fails to give us a critical vocabulary with the distinctions we need to describe what we experience.[36]

B. Empathy

The student may believe that the appreciation of any work of art is dependent on his feelings. And the more deeply he feels, the greater the enjoyment. The feeling, according to some, is the emotion that the creative artist managed to embody in the materials. His aim is to get more feeling into the work, and to give the work an emotional unity that we can experience. A great idealist, Bernard Bosanquet, asks us to

. . . suppose a tribe or a nation has won a great victory; "they are feeling big, and they want to make something big. . . ." That, I take it, is the rough account of the beginning of the aesthetic attitude. And according to their capacity and their stage of culture, they may make a pile of their enemies' skulls, or they may build the Parthenon. The point of the esthetic attitude lies in the adequate fusion of body and soul, where the soul is a feeling, and the body its expression, without residue on either side.[37]

The emotive theory in its extremest form states that the expression of any feeling is beautiful; ". . . all beauty is the expression of what may be generally called emotion, and that all such expression is beautiful."[38] All beauty is emotional response, signified by "it moves me." Hence there is no difference between the creation and appreciation of works of art, and what passes for criticism is an autobiographical statement of the sort "this work moves me."[39]

How precisely can we conceive of a "fusion of body and soul"? How precisely are we moved by works of art? To these questions a theory of empathy attempts an answer. There are two reasons for its great prevalence. The first is that it takes as a problem the persisting feeling of identity between man and nature, even when the two have been believed to be as different as a living mind and a dead machine. The second is that psychologists verify the body's motor responses when reacting to music and dance, dramatic action and sports, architecture and perceived shapes.

In early versions, the term sympathy was used. Hume was puzzled by the fact that he was pleased with the balance of a sturdy standing figure, but disliked a figure that conveyed the suggestion of falling. In his Treatise he reported that a

[36] See S. Pepper, in P. A. Schilpp, *op. cit.*, pp. 226–228.
[37] Bernard Bosanquet, *Three Lectures on Aesthetics*, 1915, quoted in Rader, *op. cit.* 2nd edition, pp. 243–244.
[38] See E. F. Carritt, *The Theory of Beauty*, Methuen, London, 1914, p. 296.
[39] See E. F. Carritt, *Introduction to Esthetics*, Hutchinson's University Library, London, n.d.

. . . figure which is not justly balanced is disagreeable; and that because it conveys the ideas of its fall, of harm, and of pain: which ideas are painful, when by sympathy, they acquire any degree of force or vivacity. Add to this that the principal part of personal beauty is an air of health and vigor, and such a construction of members as promises strength and activity. This idea of beauty cannot be accounted for but by sympathy.

We now use "empathy" because "sympathy" is limited to feeling with another man or animal. Empathy may be felt in any sort of object, as when we say, "we are lost in the object." Empathy is feeling "into," while sympathy is feeling "with." When watching a game, there is a tensing of muscles as though one were ready to act. Something like this is going on when one looks at a print showing great waves heave over a tiny boat. "We enter into its upwelling movement, we feel the tension between its heave and the force of gravity, and as the crest breaks into foam, we feel that we ourselves are stretching angry claws against the alien objects beneath us."[40] The same sort of analysis has been applied to our enjoyment of music, dancing, architecture, and landscape. Detailed analyses can be found. These say much that is relevant both with respect to the objects we enjoy and the causes of our exaltation through works of art.

The only objection brought against the empathy theory by one critic is that, however true, it fails to account for the mood of freedom, or the "emancipation from the passions."[41] It should also be added that however true the theory is as an explanation of a great number of responses to works of art, it does not provide an adequate norm for the aesthetic value of different works. For many superb tragedies, such as King Lear, are not the sort of objects to which the body responds empathetically. But an auto crash is something to which we do so respond. If the strength of response were taken as an index of aesthetic worth, we should rank King Lear low and an auto accident high. There must be some other sort of response to aesthetic objects. The following types of theory are endeavors to make clear the cognitive and voluntaristic factors.

C. Contemplation

It has commonly been believed that for an object to be beautiful it need not be useful for any particular purpose, nor a means in any steps of practice, nor even the satisfaction of a desire. Many theories have been devised to account for this. One is that aesthetic experience is like play when we are free from work. We may appear to take the symbols

[40] Sir Herbert Read, The Meaning of Art, Penguin Books, Harmondsworth, Middlesex, 1949, p. 30.
[41] Milton C. Nahm, op. cit., 461–462.

of war seriously, but in a war game, we have the illusion of battle with no anxiety that we may really lose our lives, fortune, or honor. We are enabled by art to be consciously deceived. A noted English psychologist, Edward Bullough, has called this *psychic distance*. The moment our contemplation of such a scene as a fog at sea becomes anxiety for our safety, we cease to enjoy the scene, and the experience is no longer aesthetic. Bullough's example has convinced many readers.

Imagine a fog at sea: for most people it is an experience of acute unpleasantness. Apart from the physical annoyance and remoter forms of discomfort such as delays, it is apt to produce feelings of peculiar anxiety, fears of invisible dangers, strains of watching and listening for distance and unlocalized signals. The listless movements of the ship and her warning calls soon tell upon the nerves of the passengers; and that special, expectant, tacit anxiety and nervousness, always associated with this experience, make a fog the dreaded terror of the sea (all the more terrifying because of its very silence and gentleness) for the expert seafarer no less than for the ignorant landsman.

Nevertheless, a fog at sea can be a source of intense relish and enjoyment. Abstract from the experience of the sea fog, for the moment, its danger and practical unpleasantness, just as everyone in the enjoyment of a mountain climb disregards its physical labor and its danger (though, it is not denied that these may incidentally enter into the enjoyment and enhance it); direct the attention to the features "objectively" constituting the phenomenon—the veil surrounding you with an opaqueness as of transparent milk, blurring the outlines of things and distorting their shapes into weird grotesqueness; observe the carrying-power of the air, producing the impression as if you could touch some far-off siren by merely putting out your hand and letting it lose itself behind that white wall; note the curious creamy smoothness of the water, hypocritically denying as it were any suggestion of danger; and, above all, the strange solitude and remoteness from the world, as it can be found only on the highest mountain tops; and the experience may acquire, in its uncanny mingling of repose and terror, a flavor of such concentrated poignancy and delight as to contrast sharply with the blind and distempered anxiety of its other aspects.

The contrast, then, between aesthetic and non-aesthetic consciousness is that the former is characterized by "the marveling unconcern of a mere spectator."[42]

There have been several attacks on this theory.

First, some critics have found fault with this formulation on the ground that the "distance" is neither spatial nor temporal, but metaphorical. Indeed have no other way of talking about the mind in this state of contemplation. Bullough sometimes calls it "detachment," at other times "a putting of the object out of gear with our practical needs and ends."

[42] Melvin M. Rader, *op. cit.*, 1952, pp. 402–403.

Other critics have quarrelled with the notion that the aesthetic attitude is "impersonal." Indeed it may not be the satisfaction of a particular need, but a need that may be expressed in a symbolic way. Susanne Langer re-interprets "psychical distance" as "the experience of apprehending through a symbol what was not articulated before."[43]

Another criticism from the same author is that Bullough gives a theory that is perfectly valid for problems of drama, but not universally applicable. She does not see how we can apply it to ceramic art or to music.

The most violent attack upon theories of this sort was launched by Friedrich Nietzsche. Nietzsche granted that there is an art of repose and harmony. This is an art form that worships Apollo. But there is also Dionysus, god of drunkenness and passion. One worships Dionysus not by escape from the interests of life, but rather by intensifying these interests. This too is art, and its mode of aesthetic appreciation deserves exploration.

D. Voluntarism

Convincing as Bullough's account of aesthetic appreciation is, we can easily think of works of art that it fails to account for. Men celebrate their achievements by works of art. The Northwest Indians erect totem poles telling of the greatness of the family. The pharaohs of Egypt erected pyramids over their remains and great temples to the gods of the Nile. These are examples of conscious and deliberate purpose dominating creation. Appreciation also should take purpose into account, so say aestheticians who are called voluntarists. Easily the most provocative theory of the last century was Friedrich Nietzsche's, and of this century, Sigmund Freud's.

The precise connection between Nietzsche's theory and Freud's theory is that, according to both, what we really desire may be expressed only in dreams and artistic fantasy.

. . . Our *dreams* have this very value and meaning to *compensate* to a certain degree this accidental lack of 'nourishment' during the day. Why was the dream of yesterday full of tenderness and tears, that of the day before jocular and exuberant, a former one adventurous? . . . Why do I enjoy in this one indescribable beauty of music; why do I float and fly in another with the rapture of an eagle up towards distant mountain peaks? These fictions, which give play to, and permit the discharge of, our drives of tenderness or jocularity or adventurousness, or our demand for music and mountains—and everybody will have his own better examples at hand—are interpretations of our nerve stimu-

---

[43] Susanne Langer, *Philosophy in a New Key*, Mentor Books, The New American Library, Inc., New York, 1948, p. 181.

lation during dreams, *very free,* very arbitrary interpretations. . . . the inventing reason *imagines* such various *causes* for the same nerve stimulations today and yesterday—this is due to the fact that the prompter of this reason was a different one today than yesterday; another *drive* wanted to satisfy, exert, exercise, refresh, and discharge itself—today one drive is at its high tide, and yesterday it was another. Waking life does not have this same *freedom* of interpretation as in dreams. . . .[44]

What is the profundity of art? According to Nietzsche and Freud, in art we may express in images what society ordinarily forbids. Freud's favorite example was Oedipus. In ordinary life it is forbidden to kill one's father and to marry one's mother. But Sophocles could deal with this desire, which is, according to Freud, a universal one in all males. Since reality frustrates this desire, the artist finds satisfaction in dreaming of it. What characterizes the artist is a "powerful capacity for sublimation and . . . a certain flexibility in the repressions determining the conflict." The artist is in an unusual position with regard to our forbidden pleasures. He can both elaborate them in his day-dreams, yet express them in a way that is not forbidden; he can both conceal their prohibited sources, yet lead us to recognize our own unconscious pleasures; he can both turn away from reality to phantasy, yet lead us back to reality through phantasy. Freud speaks here in intriguing paradox. Do his paradoxes explain why the artist wins through phantasy what he had previously only in phantasy: honor, power, and love?[45]

One of the problems with a voluntaristic theory of unconscious drives is that it is difficult to criticize. The theorist tells us what we are ordinarily unable and unwilling to recognize, but if we say that it has been exaggerated, he can reply that this is evidence of our repression.

It certainly is the case that in works of art we find themes of criminal and sexual irregularity. If a voluntaristic theory offers to explain this, we should be grateful. A hedonistic theory might be extended to account for forbidden pleasures. An empathetic theory might hold that we respond to themes of conflict and find ourselves stimulated. A theory of disinterested contemplation and a theory of expressed interests genuinely exclude each other.

V. Beliefs in Aesthetic Criticism

If one would discover in the simplest way why artists, critics, and philosophers are deeply concerned with aesthetic form, one may sit down at a piano. Sound any note over and over again. There is a limit to the

[44] Quoted in Walter Kaufmann, *Nietzsche,* Meridian Books, New York, 1956, p. 156.
[45] M. Rader, *op. cit.,* 1st Edition, pp. 71–72.

number of times one can endure its monotony, but even a single note upon an instrument is indeed generally considered more pleasant than a simple rap upon the table. The note is a relatively pure sound in contrast to what we commonly call noise. The first formal principle of beauty was called by St. Thomas Aquinas *clarity*. But one element does not make a recognizable song. Nor do we commonly regard a single color tone as a picture. The unity involved in C-sharp being C-sharp or sky blue being sky blue is insufficient for complex aesthetic pleasure.

Two colors that clash may be put together; or at the piano two notes may be struck simultaneously or in succession—some do not sound well together, and you may have enough training in physics to formulate the ratios of the lengths of strings that produce harmonic sounds. To the ancient Pythagorean philosophers this suggested that in the nature of things there are mathematical principles that explain beauty. We may state as a formal principle that we find pleasing a combination of elements that are neither too close together nor too different. It is not easy to explain what is better in the juxtaposition of yellow and blue of the same intensity and value rather than of red and purple, but in spite of the idiosyncrasies of different cultures, some need of variety and contrast for pleasurable aesthetic experience is evident in all. Thus the principle of *harmony* is illustrated.

A third point to experiment with at the piano, or with patches of color, is the duration and tempo of the notes or the size and shape of the chips. The duration may be equal. The size and shape may be the same. It may be pleasing to group the sounds, or to stress one, and the little patches of color may be grouped, doubling the size of one as against another. Thus the formal feature called *rhythm* begins to emerge. We talk of patterns of sound as well as of colors. The variations may increase if three or four elements are grouped together. However, if a group of, say, ten elements is attempted, confusion sets in. The patterns are there, but we may fail to find a certain "unity in variety" that has often been set forth as the norm of the aesthetically good. There may be sound psychological reasons for three or five act plays, and we may be better able to comprehend a plot when we are not confronted with ten scenes.

Next, let us suppose that we know just enough about "America" to pick out the melody with one finger. We play the note of the first space twice, then the note of the second line; it is followed by a rising series; when we play the note of the second space twice, and then of the third line, these notes are followed by a descending sequence, giving us a kind of balance. We know the words "My country, 'tis of thee/Sweet land of liberty." But it is rare that we have identical halves on either side of a central axis like two windows on either side of a door, which we should call symmetry. We know in many subtle ways how to *balance* objects on a table, or in a room, or in taking a photograph.

But we also know more than how to balance elements. If we continue to pick out notes of "America," we conclude the balanced pair of twelve notes with three quarter notes and a dotted half, the sounds to which "Of thee I sing" are fitted. There seems to have been some *development*, and we end on the very note with which we began. Now we are ready for something different, and we play a sequence repeated a second time one note lower. We have the emphasis of four identical notes and again a regular descent from it step by step. These regular descents we have met before, but the theme has been developed. Something has been evolved out of those sequences. "Land where my fathers died/Land of the pilgrim's pride." The words hardly develop episodes in a story, but they seem to thicken the original sentiment.

What can we add to clarity, harmony, rhythm, balance, and development? Just one thing seems to make our little tune complete. It is reaching a *climax*. There is a bit more excitement in eighth notes followed by a final dotted half. The words clear up the main thought we are to be left with. We might have wondered whether it was "liberty" or "ancestors." It is the former theme apparently, and ancestors are associated with country because they loved liberty, "From every mountain side,/Let freedom ring."

There are many lists of formal principles. Some aestheticians boil them all down to "unity in variety, and variety in unity." Some call this normative principle *organic unity* and analyze it into six aspects as we have done. The precise number of principles is quite inconsequential.

The important point is that no account has been able to analyze away some formal aspect of creation, appreciation, and criticism of works of art. If creation is not composition or arranging or shaping, then it is not artistic creation. The ground of difference between theories of creation is whether what is composed is material stuff, or concepts, or emotions. If appreciation is not sensing and perceiving and apperceiving (forming a more integrated grasp of percepts) what has pattern or shape or design, then it is not aesthetic appreciation. The ground of difference between theories of appreciation is whether what has design is material stuff, or concepts, or emotions. In a sense, then, the issues of alternative theories of creation and appreciation come into focus when we consider aesthetic form.

It is about aesthetic form that artists, critics, and philosophers disagree most vehemently. Are these "forms" the patterns we discover in natural objects? This is the kind of form intended by Aristotle. They are what is intelligible to us. Art and nature both reveal to us the splendor of an ordering divine thinker.

> All order and proportion . . . are the work of the mind. So, to say with the schoolmen that beauty is the *splendour of form shining on the proportioned parts of matter* is to say that it is a lighting of mind on a matter intelligently arranged. The mind rejoices in the beautiful because in the beautiful it finds itself again: recognizes itself, and comes into contact with its very own light. This is so true that they especially perceive and particularly relish the beauty of things who, like St. Francis of Assisi, for example know that they emanate from a mind and refer them to their Author.[46]

A contrasted metaphysical view is Platonism. Forms for Platonists are ideals, only partly revealed in nature. Art therefore has the function of revealing a more perfect world that we might not otherwise know, except through mystic intuition of the divine realm of forms. A typical statement of this is from Keats:

> "Beauty is truth, truth beauty,"—that is all
> Ye know on earth, and all ye need to know.

Form, according to Aristotle, is necessary along with matter for anything to be. In Platonism form is sufficient in itself to be perfect apart from the imperfect world of change.

Even if it is only a phenomenalistic analysis that is given of beauty, some philosophers analyze their experiences of forms with either an Aristotelian or a Platonic stress. Most aestheticians deny that they are committing themselves to an ontology of either the Platonic or Aristotelian type, yet continue to talk of "form" and "content." Their problem is: Is the form an integral aspect of the work of art? Then there is no experience of "form" without "content." But other critics decry the dependence of form on content as a characteristic of poor art or mistaken appreciation of good art. Form, say those who would separate form from content, must be regarded independently. A colloquial way of putting this is: "Pay no attention to what the artist says, all that counts is how he says it." In our own age two critics of aesthetic experience debated the issue of whether the content cooperates with and enhances the form, or whether it rivals it and detracts from the formal beauty.[47]

[46] Jacques Maritain, *op. cit.*, p. 20.
[47] Roger Fry and I. A. Richards, In Morris Weitz, *Philosophy of the Arts,* Harvard University Press, Cambridge, Massachusetts, 1950, p. 16.

People often have strong beliefs about whether an artist *ought* to be primarily concerned with form. We may say that the highest art is produced by the painter who never paints a portrait or a landscape, in short, who never descends to mere illustration. Or we may say that a painter should show us what he sees, a novelist what he knows and believes. On the one hand, we may follow abstractionism; on the other hand, we may follow representationalism. The abstractionist regards all reference to something outside a work of art as an impurity; the representationalist regards some reference beyond the work as an enrichment.

Perhaps the student is acquainted with the issue of pure music versus program music. A purist regards the music as self-sufficient, and any consideration of a story to be told, a nation to be celebrated, etc., as a blemish. The point here is that the purist musician will talk in technical terms about the composition. There is another school that talks of the emotions of the composer, his life, his problems, and how the music is trying to communicate something to us.[48]

The term "form" has so many different meanings it is almost impossible to keep them clear or to settle on any one. Here are some of the alternatives. The problem may be stated as the contrast between *how* something is said and *what* is said. Is it true that aesthetic value depends entirely on how something is said and not at all on what is said? This question is still ambiguous, for the "what" may be a *content* within the work of art or it may be an *objective reference* beyond it. One interesting consequence of purism or formalism or abstractionism is that works of art that are representational are condemned, but non-representational exalted.

Form is also contrasted to emotion in much contemporary discussion. The forms of literature and music, such as the sonnet in poetry and the sonata in music, are distinguishable patterns not especially related to emotion. Again there is the form that we are told "ought to follow function". This is a different usage. We also speak of a musician being in "good form" much as we would say this of an athlete or a horse. In spite of the variety of meanings it is worth noticing that any one of them signifies something that can make a work or a performance hang together coherently.

We have then an ambiguous word, "form." It is necessary to examine carefully the context to be sure we know which interpretation to use. The term has been used pejoratively, as in Milton's contemptuous references to religious form, or making worship into etiquette. Romantics thought of

[48] John Hospers, *Meaning and Truth in the Arts*, The University of North Carolina Press, Chapel Hill, 1946, Ch. IV is excellent on this controversy in music, painting, and literature.

forms as the intellect's shackling of the heart's impulses. But the very fact that it is both a descriptive and an evaluational term has been the basis of many versions of aesthetic objectivism. If one is talking of something there in the work to be judged, and if unity of the work is a norm of good art, then judging one work to be more completely integrated is not a mere personal reaction.

Consider, for example, the statement that the tune "America" begins and ends on the same note and maintains three-four rhythm throughout, and that the melody uses only seven notes, usually in sequence. This is as true as statements are in any science. Does it explain the music itself as the cause of our unified apperception? It certainly is far less subjective than the contrasted associations an Englishman might have. He would associate "God Save the Queen" with a coronation and Buckingham Palace. Our American might hear the music in Hong Kong and grow homesick thinking of the Golden Gate Bridge, or the British subject might be a Greek-speaking Cypriot and have the urge to desecrate the Union Jack. Could we safely say that these subjective reactions are accidental to the worth of the tune as music? We might say that a music critic who told us his private associations was speaking irrelevantly. That there is more than private feeling we know, because a listener to music can be taught to hear the theme and its variation, the dissonance and harmonic resolution, the development of a melodic line toward a climax that makes it feel finished.

How can an aesthetic theory be verified? One plausible answer is by stating the grounds of our appreciation of works of art. There have been two other attempts to verify theories of aesthetic form. One of these is by mathematicians; the other by psychologists.

A word upon mathematical form. There are distinguished mathematical analyses in contemporary literature. George Birkhoff's Aesthetic Measure (1934) applied geometry largely to painting. Jay Hambridge's Dynamic Symmetry (1920) analyzed the rectangles he plotted from the silhouette shapes of Greek vases. However, critics are not sure that the principles he found are more than "a studio-tradition or rule of craftsmanship belonging to a very limited period of artistic creation." Moreover, of two vases with the same mathematical symmetry ". . . to the trained aesthetic judgment the shapes reproduced vary in their degree of aesthetic excellence." Third, the aesthetic vase is the vase as seen, and it is not perceptions that are measured, so the measuring isolates one factor that in experience is not separable.[49]

[49] H. Osborne, *Theory of Beauty*, Routledge & Kegan Paul, Ltd., London 1952, pp. 198–200.

German psychologists of the past century thought of making aesthetic norms a problem of laboratory experiment. People were given rectangles of different proportions, and then reported which was the most pleasing. Various choices were averaged to yield a norm of good taste. This attempt was a theoretical failure. Some preferred cards of 3×5 size, others of 5×8. Choices were grouped, but the average corresponded to no preference. Why make such a choice? No purpose was ever stated. The attempt to isolate the geometrical factor from color, etc., seems to make the results irrelevant.[50] American psychologists have turned to critics' appraisals and have sometimes found a surprising agreement about balance, rhythm, symmetry, and unity.[51]

Formal analysis might not take a strictly mathematical analysis. It is the work of art as experienced that is enjoyed, and should be judged, hence some critics approach works of art as perceptual configurations. A critic of architecture would teach us to ask whether the "effect of the whole" building "predominate[s] over that of the parts," whether the "disposition of the whole . . . conform[s] to our sense of powerfully adjusted weight," whether "the several parts of a building . . . [are] kept in proper 'scale.' Scale, in any design, is that relation of ornament (or minor features) to the larger elements, which controls our impression of its size."[52]

Whereas mathematical aesthetics would state an alleged perfect ratio, of the sides of a rectangle as a "necessary and sufficient condition of aesthetic beauty," the theory of aesthetic configuration would not expect any one absolutely pleasing proportion.[53]

A third view, while stressing formal properties as apperceived by a listener or viewer, would insist upon including appropriate emotions. G. E. Moore's theory of organic wholes is famous.

It is perhaps the case that all aesthetic emotions have some common quality; but it is certain that differences in the emotion seem to be appropriate to differences in the kind of beauty perceived: and by saying that different emotions are *appropriate* to different kinds of beauty, we mean that the whole which is formed by the consciousness of that kind of beauty *together with* the emotion appropriate to it, is better than if any other emotion had been felt in contemplating that particular beautiful object. . . . All of these emotions are essential elements in great positive goods; they are *parts* of organic wholes, which have

[50] *Ibid.*, pp. 179–181.

[51] N. C. Meier, *Art in Human Affairs*, Whittlesey House, New York, 1942, p. 67.

[52] Geoffrey Scott, *The Architecture of Humanism*, Doubleday & Co., Inc., Garden City, New York, 1954, pp. 172–173.

[53] H. Osborne, *op. cit.*, pp. 175–179. The alleged ratio roughly satisfied by 8:13 or 21:34.

great intrinsic value. But it is important to observe that these wholes are organic, and that, hence, it does not follow that the emotion, by *itself*, would have any value whatsoever, nor yet that, if it were directed to a different object, the whole thus formed might not be positively bad.[54]

At the very outset of our discussion of aesthetic form we notice disagreements in method. If we think of form, for example of a bathing beauty, in the first way we might limit the judges to taking measurements. The problem would be no more difficult than merely finding such proportions as 36″–27″–38″; it would involve relation of circumference of limbs to length and relations of various curves to each other. Practicing artists of the Italian and German Renaissance took just this approach. Rules were based on geometry.

Proponents of perceptual form as essential to artistic creation and aesthetic judgment do not care to be confused with mathematical artists and critics. Against the latter the student has perhaps heard the belief that one may follow all the rules strictly and produce uninspired "academic" work, and on the other hand, one must deviate from strict regularity to make an interesting work. The same defender of perceptual form elaborates his case.

We cannot . . . lay down fixed proportions of space as architecturally right. Space value in architecture is affected first and foremost, no doubt, by actual dimensions; but it is affected by a hundred considerations besides. It is affected by lighting and the position of shadows: the source of light attracts the eye and sets up an independent suggested movement of its own. It is affected by colour; a dark floor and a light roof give a totally different space sensation to that created by a dark roof and a light floor."

One may imagine from experience other facts of lines, vertical and horizontal, the way space is cut by domes and cornices, etc.

Nothing, therefore, will serve the architect but the fullest power to *imagine* the space-value resulting from the complex conditions of each particular case; there are no liberties which he may not sometimes take, and no 'fixed ratios' which may not fail him. Architecture is not a machinery but an art; those theories of architecture which provide ready-made tests for the creation or criticism of design are self-condemned. Nonetheless, in the beauty of every building, space-value, addressing itself to our sense of movement, will play a principal part.[55]

[54] G. E. Moore, *Principia Ethica,* Cambridge University Press, Cambridge, 1954, p. 190.
[55] G. Scott, *op. cit.,* pp. 170–171.

There are many reasons why artists, critics, and aestheticians have not cared to identify themselves with mathematical and perceptual formalism. The most impressive of these is that we cannot, either in composing the work or in the work itself and our enjoyment of it, distinguish what is called its form from its content, or form from matter, or design from ideational or representative elements. At least the distinction may seem artificial whether in creation, appreciation, or criticism. Some paintings are representational. Should standards appropriate to non-representational architecture impugn all portraits as "impure"? Language is never wholly a matter of sound. Should standards appropriate to orchestral music, music without words or dramatic plot or program, be imposed upon poetry? Further, if one asked whether a building's design is good, why not ask what the building is for? A well-designed library may be a very bad apartment house. Function may unify the design.

If it is organic form that is to be defined as distinctively valuable in works of art, we should then go beyond the emotions appropriate to the form. There might well be coherence of reference as a unifying factor. What holds together illustrations by Hogarth is his picturing of the seamy side of London life, with its rakes and trollops. What holds together Degas' paintings and sculpture is his picturing of girls dancing, bathing, ironing clothes, always doing something and not artificially posed. What holds together the New York sky line is that the only way to get more space on Manhattan was to build up. What holds together novels by Hemingway is not simply the economy of the short sentences, but also men having their strength and luck tested. Hence we might say that there are many ways of achieving unity in variety and variety in unity other than by strictly mathematical means.

If beauty is not measurable, does it follow that our standards are subjective, and that we must conclude "there is no disputing about taste?" Two aestheticians who have analyzed the organic forms of works of art deny that this follows.

But because objective beauty is not measurable we are not driven back to a subjective theory of beauty. We know that beauty is a quality of perceptual configurations of a special kind, but it is not constituted either by 'normal' emotional reactions or by the vagaries of individual emotional taste. The very argument by which beauty is shown to be unmeasurable is based upon the presuppositions that beauty is objective.[56]

One objective criterion of good art, then, according to the organic theory, is this principle of integration: the working together of all the elements is

[56] H. Osborne, *op. cit.*, p. 200.

aesthetically good, and the working against each other of some or all of the elements is aesthetically bad. Part of the reason some art is good is that it integrates its many elements, and part of the function of evaluative criticism is to determine what the elements or constituents are and whether or not they do work together.

A critical judgment that is based upon this criterion is aesthetically more cogent than one that is founded upon, let us say, the criterion of duration or the cost of an art work. It is objective in the sense that no evaluative criticism is possible without it. The alternative to the acceptance of this sort of principle as at least one aesthetic, critical principle is the denial of evaluative criticism altogether from which it follows . . . that any criterion (the ability of a work to put me to sleep or to keep me from scratching myself or to get me to think about the valleys on the other side of the moon) is as aesthetically valid as any other.[57]

VI. Aesthetic Fallacies

Of all fallacies discussed in the literature of aesthetics, none has received such widespread attention as the *pathetic fallacy*. It was so named by the artist-critic John Ruskin. Critics have made it so common that we rarely turn back to Ruskin's Modern Painters to grasp what he was attacking, namely, ascribing human feelings to natural objects.

Examine the point in question,—namely, the difference between the ordinary, proper, and true appearances of things to us; and the extraordinary, or false appearances, when we are under the influence of emotion, or contemplative fancy; false appearances, I say, as being entirely unconnected with any real power or character in the object, and only imputed to it by us. . . . So long as we see that the *feeling* is true, we pardon, or are even pleased by, the confessed fallacy of sight which it induces: we are pleased, for instance, with those lines of Kingsley's—

> They rowed her across the rolling foam—
> The cruel, crawling foam

not because they fallaciously describe foam but because they faithfully describe sorrow. But the moment the mind of the speaker becomes cold, that moment every such expression becomes untrue, as being forever untrue in the external facts. And there is no greater baseness in literature than the habit of using these metaphorical expressions in cool blood.[58]

Ruskin's question is relevant to the enjoyment and criticism of works of art. The question is whether some quality is external or internal to the perceiver, or, as we say, "in" the object or "in" the subject. An analyst of language, O. K. Bouwsma, has considered this a central puzzle of the way

[57] Morris Weitz, *op. cit.*, p. 197.
[58] John Ruskin, *Modern Painters*, IV, xii, §.4. quoted in E. F. Carritt, *Philosophies of Beauty*, Oxford University Press, New York, 1931, p. 179.

we talk about music. One character, Octave, says "It was lovely, wasn't it? Very sad music though." The other fellow, Verbo, "Sad music? How can music be sad? . . . It can't, of course." Bouwsma's conclusion is that we hear the sadness in the music. We may say this without error, as long as we know what we are talking about, namely the *expressive* character sounds have for us.[59] If one thinks that the music *unheard* would be "sad" or "sweet," then there would be an error into which language might lead us by our talk of something in the object itself. Perhaps the error lies in the assumption that values, for example, are either "inside" or "outside," either "in the subject" or "in the object." If so, either the formulation of a value objectivism or a value subjectivism begins with an untenable assumption.[60] Therefore the solution to the problem would seem to be a relativistic theory of knowledge, that is, that all knowledge is from some perspective, but is not therefore deprived of the status of objective truth.

Paul Edwards has reformulated the problem raised by the pathetic fallacy. The assumption has been made that the sadness of the music, for example, is "some simple quality over and above" the other qualities. That this cannot be found does not imply that it is misleading to say "The music is sad." The pathetic fallacy calls attention to the confusion between what is presumed to be subjective and what is presumed to be objective. Ruskin thought this to be a fallacy of the poet, but as we have seen, it may be generalized for any value judgment.[61]

The student may find it easier to think of alleged aesthetic fallacies if he begins with the question "What is strictly relevant to the appreciation and criticism of a work of art as an aesthetic object?" Certainly, as was said in the last section on aesthetic form, it is possible not to concentrate on the music, but to allow one's attention to wander over all manner of associations. Doubtless we may argue that the rich and many-sided content offers ample opportunity for wool-gathering. Our daydreams, however, demonstrate, when we reveal them, that they may be highly private and irrelevant to the object. But is it also irrelevant to report the intentions of the artist, that is, to account psychologically for the creation of the work? Is it also irrelevant to report our reaction to the work?

In a way the *intentional fallacy* and the *affective fallacy*, which have been analyzed by the joint efforts of a literary scholar and a philosopher, are applications of what we will meet in ethics as the *naturalistic fallacy*.

---

[59] W. Elton, *Aesthetics and Language*, Blackwell, Oxford, 1954, pp. 72–73, 95, 99.
[60] S. Toulmin, *Reason in Ethics*, Cambridge University Press, Cambridge, 1950, pp. 44–45.
[61] Paul Edwards, *The Logic of Moral Discourse*, The Free Press, Glencoe, Illinois, 1955, pp. 75–76.

G. E. Moore protested against confusing the meaning of "good" with the meaning of "pleasant," or "more evolved," or "according to the will of God." So W. K. Wimsatt and Monroe C. Beardsley protest against confusing a poem, for example, with its alleged psychological causes, the poet's intentions, or with our reactions to the poem. Much discourse in the literature about the arts is biographical and confession of private association. Therefore these are irrelevant.

> The Intentional Fallacy is a confusion between the poem and its origins, a special case of what is known to philosophers as the Genetic Fallacy. It begins by trying to derive the standard of criticism from the psychological *causes* of the poem and ends in biography and relativism. The Affective Fallacy is a confusion between the poem and its results. . . . The outcome of either Fallacy, the Intentional or the Affective, is that the poem itself, as an object of specifically critical judgment, tends to disappear.[62]

How could we confuse the writing of a poem with the poem? One is obviously a process, the other a product. We do not eat baking nor give rules for a cake. But some critics have held that the meaning of a poem is the "intention" of the poet, and some aestheticians have said that there is no poem other than the intention of the artist. Then when we ask, "Is this a bad poem?" the only answer possible is whether the poem successfully expresses what the poet set out to do. Hence the critic could judge only if he knew the artist's intentions, and the poem is forgotten. The result is that only the artist's biography now matters. But the artist may not be available; he may not remember what he intended; he may have had nothing at all in mind. To say that it therefore follows that we can say nothing of the value of the poem is to commit the intentional fallacy.[63]

How can we confuse the poem with our responses to the poem? We certainly do not confuse the contents of a bottle with a headache. If we say there's a Katzenjammer in the bottle, we are whimsically transferring the effect of drinking too much to what may not be drunk at all. But if we begin with an opposition between cognitive and emotive meaning, we may say that a poem has only the latter. This would be to commit the affective fallacy. But then how can we judge a poem? We cannot, really. We can only set up a criterion of our responses. Among the great variety of affective responses can there never be one that is appropriate or fitting to an object? Wimsatt and Beardsley find this conclusion fantastic. They illustrate their position thus. There is a reason for some emotion. The emotion may be appropriate to an object. Macbeth says, "Light thickens,

[62] W. K. Wimsatt, Jr., *The Verbal Icon,* University of Kentucky Press, Lexington, 1954, p. 21.
    [63] *Ibid.,* pp. 3–18.

and the crow makes wing to the rooky wood." This is spoken by a tormented murderer; it is appropriate to the horror of having murdered his king.[64]

Geoffrey Scott, in The Architecture of Humanism, has called attention to what he calls the *romantic fallacy,* the *ethical fallacy,* the *mechanical fallacy* and the *biological fallacy.* Each involves a principle that pays attention either to one feature only of a building or to a feature that the author claims is irrelevant to its aesthetic value. Is the value of a building found solely in our associations with its symbolism? If we argue this way we commit the romantic fallacy. Is the value of a building solely a function of conditions under which it was built? If we argue this way, we commit the ethical fallacy. Is the value of a building solely its formal construction? If we argue this way we commit the mechanical fallacy. Is the value of a building solely a function of the history of style? If we argue this way we commit the biological fallacy. For example, let us invent an argument that is a monstrosity by these standards. Suppose we say that the Cathedral of Chartres is beautiful because its spires direct men's attention to the Virgin in heaven, and because all the people of Chartres built it with common joy in the service of God, and because Gothic is a marvel of engineering skill and knowledge of thrust and balanced weight, and because it was built before the style degenerated. None of these reasons is relevant to the aesthetic object, claims Scott, and as stated singly, they distract our attention from the cathedral.

Certainly buildings are complex, and the symbolism, the process of building, the structural composition, and the history of style are each singly one aspect of their complexity. Hence we might say that Scott calls our attention to the fallacy of substituting a consideration of a part for the whole. We might therefore regard them as illustrations of the fallacy of composition.

Why the romantic fallacy? "The essential fallacy of romanticism was . . . that it treated architectural form as primarily symbolic. Now there is evidently no reason why an art of form . . . should have its meaning limited to an *aesthetic* reference." Scott refers to thinking of Gothic style as valuable solely for the "aspiring" quality of its "soaring" spires and pinnacles.[65]

Why the ethical fallacy? Scott calls attention also to the reasoning that concludes that a building is bad because its builders were bad. We might argue that the architects made slaves of the workmen, and built ostentatiously. Moral judgment properly applies to men, but these

[64] *Ibid.,* pp. 21–39.
[65] Geoffrey Scott, *The Architecture of Humanism, a Study in the History of Taste,* Doubleday & Co., Inc., Garden City, New York, 1954, pp. 100, 85.

judgments imply nothing as to the value of buildings. To think and argue that they do is to commit the ethical fallacy.[66]

Why the mechanical fallacy? This is to argue that the essence of good architecture is found in its structural laws, in which the only feature that is to count is "truthful construction." This mechanical fallacy is based upon a description of a few architectural forms and the ignoring of contrary cases or other features.[67] Surely these arguments could be identified as fallacies. It is possible for a building, say a railway station, to be a truthful construction but not beautiful in the sense of giving delight. Since construction is a matter of fact, delight a matter of value, we have in aesthetics a variation of the naturalistic fallacy.

Why the biological fallacy? Equally misleading, claims Scott, is to argue that because a building is said to have a style coming last in a sequence of styles that therefore it is decadent. The epithet "decadent" belongs properly to biology, and the analogy is irrelevant. What is misleading is to evaluate one stage in art development "by reference to another stage." This would be like complaining that the Dialogues of Plato do not tell a story of war as do the epics of Homer.[68]

What, then, is the upshot of these exposures of the intentional, affective, romantic, ethical, mechanical, and biological fallacies? All of them are rejections of certain kinds of evidence as irrelevant to aesthetic judgment. All of them are therefore formulated from a perspective that lays down a principle of what is relevant. Obviously Wimsatt and Beardsley, considering poetry, cannot rule out symbolism as Scott does in considering architecture. Therefore we cannot, without closer inspection, apply these fallacies generally.

In conclusion, then, we suggest that when a fallacy is alleged of an aesthetic argument, we inquire of the critic exactly why the argument misleads. The alleged error lies in the nature of art or a specific art. A clear statement of this point comes from an essay attacking the realistic fallacy. This fallacy is the notion that a specific art, in this case literature, expresses a higher degree of reality than the real world.

Dante claimed that the world of the *Divine Comedy* was the truly real world. Cervantes meant his *Don Quixote* to rehabilitate the true sense of reality in his readers' minds. In the literary debates of the eighteenth century in Germany, Shakespeare was held up before the adolescent poetical genius of the nation as the supreme example of realistic insight. Yet it was these two 'realists,' Cervantes and Shakespeare, that the early German romantics regarded as essential luggage when they prepared their desperate bid for the freedom of the imagination. . . .

[66] *Ibid.*, p. 99.
[67] *Ibid.*, p. 85.
[68] *Ibid.*, pp. 137–139.

The question is, then, whether works of literature are to be interpreted as philosophies, that is, as alternative representations of the structure of reality. Now if, as the author insists, Balzac's novels and Homer's epics are equally works of imagination, the mistake is to ignore the essential make-believe quality of works of art. The chief offender in confusing poetry with philosophy and both with science is Hegel. If everything becomes an expression of a universal spirit, how does poetry retain its unique and specific nature?

Neither reality nor literature, neither the world nor the word has yet recovered from this strange exertion. For nothing is more exhausting than the effort of proving fallacies true. After these extreme achievements of literature we may have to be realistically modest in our aesthetic expectations. The economy of the world cannot support forever the expensive households of so many creators competing with creation itself.[69]

VII. Concluding Remarks

This chapter has not solved specific problems in aesthetics, nor has it provided a theory that accounts for the whole range of aesthetic experience. Instead it has presented a somewhat full, but still introductory and incomplete series of alternative beliefs about some of the major problems of value judgments when these judgments have to do with either the creating of art objects, or the appreciation of art objects, or the criticism of art objects. In each case we have found interesting and plausible theories, but we have also found that each fails to be comprehensive enough to explain all the phenomena. This may mean that no universal account is possible and therefore we should be content with a pluralism of principles and viewpoints. In this case we can give our attention to the exploration and analysis of specific issues in special cases—for example, to this poem or to poetry, to this picture or to painting, to this symphony or to music, to this building or to architecture—and not feel compelled to reach conclusions that will fit all literature, painting, music, and architecture. Or it may mean that men have simply failed so far to discover an all-comprehensive theory that will save the full range of aesthetic phenomena, in which case we may be led by excitement and hope to continue the search. The liveliness of such an aim should not be discouraged—no one has yet shown that it is a priori impossible.

PROBLEMS FOR THOUGHT AND DISCUSSION

1. Experiencing art aesthetically is sometimes characterized as "willing suspension of unbelief." This could mean that in reading a novel or seeing a

[69] Erich Heller, "The Realistic Fallacy," *The Listener*, Vol. 53, No. 1368, 1955, pp. 888–889.

play we are not believing that things really are happening as they are portrayed, but that we are willing to enter into the course of events *as though* they were real. Is all art characterized by an appeal to our willing acceptance of illusion?

2. We speak commonly of a "good" sonnet as well as of a "good" will. Although we say that the first is aesthetically good, and that the second is morally good, is there a clear distinction between an aesthetic and a moral judgment? Some philosophers have claimed that the aesthetically bad, or ugly, is also inevitably morally bad, or evil, and the converse. Certainly we also say that one "ought to appreciate" something, or at least that one "ought" to respond to a work of art in a given way. Is this similar to or identical with a moral "ought"?

3. It is sometimes said that a work of art is beautiful because it is "true." But if we ascribe truth only to propositions, then only literature could qualify as beautiful. This hardly seems satisfactory. Moreover, poetry is not commonly in propositional form or ordered to conclusions, nor is fiction accurate reporting of fact. Could there be some special meaning of truth in "aesthetic truth"? For example, some critics say that Paul Klee's "Heron" reveals the essence of heron, or what it means to be a heron. Have you any critical point and/or experience that leads you to accept or reject such a theory?

4. An English philosopher named Sidgwick once said, "No one would consider it rational to aim at the production of beauty in external nature, apart from any possible contemplation of it by human beings." Another English philosopher, G. E. Moore, took issue with this statement, and argued that a beautiful world in itself is better than an ugly one. See if you can construct an argument to support Moore. Then read his own in Principia Ethica (pp. 83–85 1954 Edition). If beauty were a quality intrinsic to an object, then the object would be beautiful even if no one were enjoying it. If beauty were a relation to an observer then it could not be beautiful without the observer. Discuss.

5. Art frequently deals with ugly themes. And although we are more familiar with nudes of ideal proportions not uninfluenced by sexual desire, some painters, such as Rouault, painted prostitutes of monstrous proportion. And these figures suggest depravity of spirit as well as of the flesh. Is it relevant in the case of Rouault to recall that he was disaffected from secular materialistic society, and deeply Catholic? Rouault, writes a critic, chose to communicate

. . . this belief through the nude. He has done so precisely because it gives most pain. It has hurt him, and he is savagely determined that it will hurt us. All those delicate feelings, which flow together in our joy at the sight of an idealized human body . . . are shattered and profaned. The sublimation of desire is replaced by shame at its very existence; our dream of a perfectible humanity is broken by this cruel reminder of what, in fact, man has contrived to make out of the raw material supplied to him in the cradle. . . ."[70]

[70] Kenneth Clark, *The Nude: A Study in Ideal Form,* Doubleday & Co., Garden City, New York, 1959, p. 445.

Are there beliefs implicit in non-literary works of art?

6. Books, paintings, and dramatic performances often are condemned, and sometimes even banned or restricted in audience because they seem to be obscene or pornographic or sometimes merely in bad taste. What makes a work of art "obscene"? Is it the subject matter as such, the way the subject is handled, the intention of the artist, the reaction of readers? Sometimes nudity as such is condemned in paintings. Sometimes it is the use of four-letter words in novels. Sometimes artists are said to pander to men's sensuality for its own sake. Sometimes immature readers are said to read a novel for occasional unconventional passages while ignoring the aesthetic whole. Can there be any resolution of the problem to satisfy all the parties that interest themselves in such an issue? If not, whose interests should be paramount?

7. An interesting test case of subjectivity is whether, as is commonly held, "obscenity exists only in the minds and emotions of those who believe in it and is not a quality of a book or picture."[71] Grant that persons do differ in their definitions, that they disagree in response to the same object, do you see how a case can be made that within a given context, a judgment can be relatively objective?

8. Examine a review of a book, or a drama, or an exhibition of paintings to discover the procedure of the critic. To what extent are his claims factual? Can you verify any of them? Do you think there can be scientific art criticism? If criticism is not factual, in whole or in part, are there non-factual principles? Does the praise or blame follow from these principles logically? How would you characterize the language and logic of criticism?

9. Some philosophers have claimed that "aesthetic" characterizes a type of life different from the "ethical" or "religious." Kierkegaard's "aesthetic stage" is typified by the detached man who seeks pleasure only in utter disregard for the welfare of other people, and maliciously preserves his detachment from and non-involvement in practical concerns. Some men, like Santayana, have indeed said of themselves that they see both sides of every conflict and choose neither. Does it seem fair to you to say that aesthetic men are aesthetes, living, as they suppose, above ordinary affairs? In terms of Kierkegaard's categories, does some art show penitence or a sense of guilt? Does some art express despair? Does art commit itself in an attitude of faith? If so, art would not be in Kierkegaard's sense, "aesthetic." Is this paradoxical?

10. Some music critics stress the structure of a composition. They insist that the right way to listen is to get everything going on in the music: the texture of the sounds, the themes, rhythm, and a succession of tensions and resolutions that go to make up a total work. To the objection that formal analysis ignores emotion, these critics sometimes claim that without concentration on the complex and unified structure, we are merely indulging in subjective emotional states, and that musical form is like logic in discourse; we commonly may ignore it, but only because it is familiar. Hence the identifica-

[71] Abraham Kaplan, "Obscenity as an Esthetic Category." In: Sidney Hook (ed.), *American Philosophers at Work*, Criterion Books, Inc., New York, 1956, pp. 397–416.

tion of artistic expression with emotion ignores what is basic and necessary to art as art. How could one side persuade the other of erroneous exaggeration?

11. Is commercial art, a common adjunct to advertising, inferior to fine art? Some have claimed that its inferiority springs from the low aim of advertising, that is, to sell a product or a service. Others have claimed that a commercial artist works under severe limitations of his intelligence and imagination, that is, he must pretend there is no comparable cigarette and must imagine that this one smoke is the goal of life. Others have claimed that he must cynically appraise what the reader and viewer already likes and believes, and pander to his preconceptions and prejudices. Are men of insight justly insulted by advertising? Can you then make any case for advertising as art? Robert Frost and a few astute critics have confessed that the advertising in the *Scientific American* is of great artistic merit. How could this be if the charges above are relevant and adequate?

12. What is the difference between a craftsman and an artist, or better, since the question is not really about a person who may be simultaneously or subsequently both, what is the difference between a work of mere craftsmanship and a work of art? Have both products been deliberately aimed at and designed? Have both some structure or pattern? Have both the ability to communicate belief and emotion? Does one and not the other have a life of its own? These have been suggested as questions that lead us to make a sharp distinction between a work of craftsmanship and a work of art. How well can you distinguish between the two?

13. On one hand, we are given the picture of artists as long-haired Bohemians, talking a private language to which only other artists will listen. On the other hand, we are given the picture of artists as public heroes, worthy, as evidence of civilization, of being in the company of great statesmen, saints, and thinkers. It has often been claimed that artists in their lifetime are ridiculed, and even feared because they satirize or at least see life in a highly personal perspective, yet after they are dead and everyone has heard their works praised, they become, with statesmen, saints, and thinkers, the pinnacle of a nation's worth. How would you explain the ambiguity of the artist's position? Is there any way to preserve artists' freedom without the extremity of the Beatnik's rejection of the "squares"? Or, is there any way to secure artists' loyal participation in public life without a stifling academic conformity and censorship? It is often said that between a commercial society with freedom of expression and a totalitarian society with state-enforced propaganda through the arts, there is a clear· but not certain advantage to the former. What policies could be devised to resolve the conflicts and give a proper place to the arts in society?

14. Some philosophers have claimed that tragedy makes clear to us the human situation. Hegel claimed that it is the conflict of sides, not right against wrong, but right against right. This is commonly applied to the American Civil War. Schopenhauer claimed that by displaying the rotten state of human life, tragedy teaches us the most important of all truths, that in resignation man can overcome the will or desire. Nietzsche claimed that men and civilizations are as Greek tragedy reveals to us, basically detached

(Appolonian) or engaged (Dionysian). Can you justify the extension of the tragic from literary art to life in general? If you can, does this justify art as aiding man's understanding of himself in real life? Other categories have also been extended, the comic, the ironic, the classic, and romantic. Do any of these extensions puncture the notion that art and life are divorced and that art makes men indifferent to practical concerns?

15. John Stuart Mill claimed that "Nature [is] a scheme to be amended, not imitated, by Man."[72] It is certainly coherent, then, to say that art is a triumph over nature. "All praise of civilization, or Art, or Contrivance, is so much dispraise of Nature."[73] How does this view of nature and art differ from the imitation theories of Plato or Aristotle?

16. Sometimes objects are sharply divided between useful things and things of beauty. This we presuppose when we say "It's not much to look at, but it serves the purpose." You cannot be ignorant of the belief that many things designed to do their job efficiently, without any decoration, seem to merit high esteem for their aesthetic value. On this basis many very simple old things made by pioneers bring high prices as antiques, and very elaborate things from the subsequent age of Victorian opulence are junked. The doctrine of "form follows function" is a consequence. Is the movement sometimes called "modern," explicable on the basis that if things are designed solely to do their jobs efficiently, they will inevitably achieve unity of form?

PERTINENT READINGS

Aristotle, *On Poetry and Style* (G. M. A. Grube, tr. and ed.), The Liberal Arts Press, Inc., New York, 1958.

Carritt, E. F., *Philosophies of Beauty from Socrates to Robert Bridges, Being the Sources of Aesthetic Theory,* Oxford University Press, New York, 1931.

Collingwood, R. G., *The Principles of Art,* The Clarendon Press, Oxford, 1950.

Gilbert, Katharine Everett, and Helmut Kuhn, *A History of Esthetics,* The Macmillan Co., New York, 1939.

Heyl, Bernard C., *New Bearings in Aesthetics and Art Criticism: A Study in Semantics and Evaluation,* Yale University Press, New Haven, Connecticut, 1943.

Hospers, John, *Meaning and Truth in the Arts,* University of North Carolina Press, Chapel Hill, 1946.

Langer, Susanne K., *Feeling and Form,* Charles Scribner's Sons, New York, 1953.

Pepper, Stephen C., *The Basis of Criticism in the Arts,* Harvard University Press, Cambridge, Massachusetts, 1945.

Pepper, Stephen C., *Principles of Art Appreciation,* Harcourt, Brace & Co., New York, 1949.

Prall, D. W., *Aesthetic Judgment,* Thomas Y. Crowell Co., New York, 1929.

Santayana, George, *The Life of Reason: Reason in Art,* Charles Scribner's Sons, New York, 1924.

[72] J. S. Mill, *Three Essays on Religion,* Henry Holt & Co., Inc., New York, 1874, p. 41.

[73] *Ibid.,* p. 21.

XII

Ethics: Beliefs about What One Should Do

I. Introduction

It would be silly indeed to argue or quarrel about the height of a tree, the weight of a stone, or the distance of a mountain from a certain point. The answer is never won in the triumph of a debate, but rather by the simple steps of measurement. When men do dispute, it is frequently about some problem of moral value. Is this act proper, right, desirable, good? Or is it improper, wrong, undesirable, evil? Surround these questions with different points of view and you have the possibility of vigorous controversy. Certainly one of the reasons for disagreement is that there is no one common, simple, practical method for the resolution of the difficulties. But another is the presence of unclear, ambiguous, and vague words which succeed in keeping the disputants from knowing what they are talking about. And finally there is usually a deep emotional involvement which muddies both the issue and the intellect, leaving the arguers exhausted and the argument untouched.

Philosophers are expected to surmount these obstacles in some degree, and to bring to these problems reasonableness, insight, detachment, and perhaps even the ability to provide answers. Again we face the problem: Can any one set of beliefs be certain or final? Here, as elsewhere, we are confronted with alternatives. This chapter will try to introduce some classic criticisms. When the student has seen these beliefs from the inside he may be better fitted to get outside and establish his own. Let us proceed to the alternative an-

604

swers to the question "What should I do?" Four views will be presented and examined: hedonism, formalism, self-realization, and emotivism.

II. Hedonistic Answers

Hedonism as a basic belief about what a person should do has probably been as widespread as any other. Charles Darwin once argued that when we were infants, we lived by the implicit principle that pleasures are to be sought and pains avoided. The adjective from which the Greek word for pleasure, *hedone*, was derived, meant "sweet." We know what we mean when we say that food tastes good. We also know that the delight is more intense when we are hungry. Hunger may be called a need, or a desire, and one formulation of the hedonistic principle is, "satisfy your present desire." All hedonists refuse ever to say that enduring pain is good except on those occasions when suffering is a means to other pleasure or happiness.

But are all pains and pleasures bodily? Epicurus finds the most widespread pains to be fears and frustrations. Among those fears he thinks most painful is the fear of death, which is not a sickness of the body. His whole philosophy is argued from a materialistic metaphysics implying that the soul cannot be punished in an after-life, nor will the gods be concerned with us. He tries to reconcile men to their extinction. But before death, we make ourselves unhappy by seeking to satisfy unnecessary and unnatural desires. Among unnecessary desires is sexual lust. Root out desires of the flesh, and happiness will not depend upon finding a sex partner. Among unnatural desires are the love of money, and desire for fame, and desire to excel other men in any way. A famous maxim applies Epicurus' theory of the happy life: "If you wish to make Pythocles rich, do not give him more money, but diminish his desires."[1]

Epicurus lays down many positive maxims as rules of "the art of making life happy." Although these were taken as dogmas by his followers, he claimed a factual basis, a rational method, and a general theory of value based upon the good that each man could achieve. It is naturalistic in the negative sense of denying that good has any connection with the nature and will of the gods. It is naturalistic also in the positive sense of drawing imperatives from experience. In part we should characterize these experiences as aesthetic. "I know not how I can conceive the good, if I withdraw the pleasures of taste, and withdraw the pleasures of love, and withdraw the pleasures of hearing, and withdraw the pleasurable emotions

---

[1] Cyril Bailey, *Epicurus*, The Clarendon Press, Oxford, 1926, p. 127.

caused to sight by beautiful form."² On this basis many things can be known to be intrinsically good: friendship, self-sufficiency, wisdom, and justice. For if one has enemies, or is dependent, or is ignorant, or has committed crimes, one must fear the consequences. One is not "free from trouble" if people are hostile, or if there are other people to consider, or unsolved mysteries in the universe, or punishments from the state. These hypotheses may be as true as such generalizations can be, but what makes it true that the one and only end of human life is "peace of mind"?³

The Stoics objected to the doctrine because it fails to account for the satisfaction that comes to man when he acts as he feels a man ought to act, and a man ought to act, said the Stoics, in harmony with the purpose of the universe. Fulfilling this obligation made a man virtuous, and pleasures and pains had no bearing upon the happiness and peace of mind of men who were just, courageous, temperate, and wise.

The question is then: Can a happy life be conceived as made up of pleasures or based upon pleasures? Put negatively, is not a happy life conceivable quite independently of pleasures? Epicurus makes his defense against a stoic answer of no to the first and yes to the second question by identifying virtues as higher mental pleasures, enjoyable in and of themselves. Friendship is one of the virtues that involves a "compact not to harm or to be harmed," and that ends our fear of being forgotten. "Sweet is the memory of a dead friend." It is historically irresponsible to characterize Epicurus' view as "Eat, drink, and be merry, for tomorrow we die."

The form of hedonism that has made the greatest theoretical and practical impact in the modern world is called *utilitarianism*. The "principle of utility" of Jeremy Bentham was an ideological tool designed at the time of the French Revolution to reform the institutions of England. The English utilitarians were politically active. They did not withdraw into a garden, as did Epicurus, but forced their programs into the market places and debating halls. Theoretically they opposed the conception that the best life is one of inner contentedness.

The usual answers to the question, "What should I do?," were dictated by custom or tradition, and specifically a tradition that identified rights as established by God's will. But Bentham needed an alternative answer. Hence, he appeals to the naturalism of Epicurus. The bishops proclaimed that the divine Will rewarded men in an after-life, but experience pro-

² *Ibid.*, p. 123.
³ *Ibid.* The Greek word is *ataraxia*. A derivative in English names a drug to reduce anxiety. It is translated "impassiveness, coolness, calmness, tranquillity."

claims pleasures and pains in this life. If pleasures of the mind are exalted above pleasures of the body, it might be said that certain men were capable of enjoying a higher happiness, and that other men existed to permit these few aristocrats to enjoy themselves. Hence Bentham's case for democracy could be made only by considering every pleasure and pain a unit of equal value.

Utilitarianism, therefore, is called *universalistic hedonism.* Each man is to count for one; no man for more than one. What should I then do? Do whichever of two acts will produce a maximum of pleasure and a minimum of pain. Notice that this answer can only be given if we know the probable effects of an act on everyone, and if pleasures and pains can be added and subtracted.

Often we still appeal to the "greatest happiness of the greatest number." It is to Bentham's credit that he tried to make this slogan precise. Pains and pleasures are "greater or less, according to" their

1. Intensity.
2. Duration.
3. Certainty or uncertainty.
4. Propinquity or remoteness.
5. Fecundity, or "the chance it has of being followed by sensations of the *same* kind; that is, pleasures, if it be a pleasure; pains, if it be a pain."
6. Purity, "or the chance it has of *not* being followed by sensations of the *opposite* kind; that is, pains, if it be a pleasure; pleasures, if it be a pain."
7. Extent, "that is, the number of persons to whom it *extends.* . . ."[4]

If every pleasure is $+1$ and every pain -1, then an act that results in exact balance has zero value. However, are pleasures and pains opposites of this sort? Is the total value of an act an exact sum like one million dollars, the net worth of a company with two millions of assets and one million of liabilities? Is the net worth only in the results, and in no way dependent upon the intent and will of the agents? Do we take into account the pains and pleasures of others only because they are pains and pleasures exactly like our own? Should we ignore all qualitative differences between values that cannot be stated quantitatively?

Ethical reflection since Bentham has pressed the proponents of hedonism with these difficulties. John Stuart Mill was sympathetic to the objections

[4] Jeremy Bentham, *The Principles of Morals and Legislation,* Hafner Publishing Co., Inc., New York, 1948, pp. 29–30.

that some philosophers made, namely, that the Benthamite calculus is a wooden mechanism. That is, there is no place at all in it for what Mill called "self-devotion" and "beauties of character." Yet Mill continued to defend "the multiplication of happiness . . . [as] the object of virtue. . . ."[5]

Let us now examine rather closely the assumptions Mill asks us to accept and the implications he claims to follow from these assumptions.

His first assumption is that whether one should or should not do a certain act, or should do one thing rather than another, depends upon the consequences of the act. In Mill's words "all action is for the sake of some end." The second assumption is that there is "one fundamental principle or law at the root of all morality."[6] The third assumption is that the "morality of an individual action is not a question of direct perception, but of the application of a law to an individual case." Now how can this "end" and "principle" be discovered? Either it is a priori, known intuitively, or it is a posteriori, known from experience. Mill elects to try the inductive method, in the face of the difficulty that "questions of ultimate ends are not amenable to direct proof." The fourth assumption is that things are good because they produce pleasure, and "pleasure is good."[7] A consideration, in lieu of proof, is that past moral authorities have used this criterion of pleasure.

An interesting point to observe here is that Mill does not offer to define pleasure. Probably he thought no definition necessary or possible. John Locke had held that pleasure and pain "like other simple ideas, cannot be described, nor their names defined; the way of knowing them is . . . only by experience."

Mill's statement is:

> The creed which accepts as the foundation of morals 'utility' or the 'greatest happiness principle' holds that actions are right in proportion as they tend to produce happiness, wrong as they tend to produce the reverse of happiness. By happiness is intended pleasure, and the absence of pain; by unhappiness, pain, and the privation of pleasure. To give clear view of the moral standard set up by the theory, much more requires to be said; in particular, what things it includes in the ideas of pain and pleasure; and to what extent this is left an open question. . . . All desirable things (which are as numerous in the utilitarian as in any other scheme) are desirable either for the pleasure inherent in themselves, or as means to the promotion of pleasure and the prevention of pain.[8]

[5] John Stuart Mill, *Utilitarianism*, The Liberal Arts Press, Inc., New York, 1949, pp. 17, 20, 21.
[6] *Ibid.*, pp. 2, 3.
[7] *Ibid.*, pp. 2, 3, 4.
[8] *Ibid.*, p. 7.

Apparently we can perceive directly whether a thing is pleasurable, and whether a desire is satisfied or fulfilled. There is, then, from these assumptions no doubt about the morality of a student who enjoys reading because he is certainly satisfying his need when he settles down to some book to his taste. Should the student read? The hedonistic answer would be "He enjoys it," and "He harms no one by reading." In reading the pattern of words give sensuous gratification and this coincides with the satisfaction of the need to think. According to Mill's definition, this student's reading is good and right.

But now let us suppose that members of the student's family are engaged in some project, say, moving into a new house. And, let us say, that one person sitting down quietly when everyone else is hauling furniture and packing goods is so highly irritating that it demoralizes their work. They are overworked and frustrated, and robbed of the sensuous gratification of reasonable exertion. Then it is bad and wrong for one person to be satisfied at the price of several dissatisfactions.

How then could there be an identity between the pleasure and good of the student reading and the family moving? Mill assumes between individuals and society such an identity that society wants the individual's happiness and the individual wants other people's happiness. Only on this assumption can we have a universalistic hedonism. "The idea of pleasure of another is naturally pleasurable." Of course people are generally happier when they are with happy people. And members of a family do often devote themselves to satisfying each other's needs. But how could we overcome such conflicts as we have supposed? Could it be only if we desire what others find pleasurable? This principle is quite different from pleasures and pains in a hedonistic calculus. Mill encourages "a feeling of unity with our fellow creatures." He is more explicit: "So long as they are co-operating, their ends are identified with those of others; there is at least a temporary feeling that the interests of others are their own interests."[9]

Pleasure in the pleasure of others would seem to be a higher sort of pleasure than pleasure of one's own. Hedonism may be formulated altruistically rather than egoistically. But is any act good simply because we can deduce that it benefits someone else? Mill rejects this; " . . . The bare enunciation of such an absurdity as this last renders refutation superfluous."[10]

How are we to decide between different immediate pleasures and different desires? The decision is not simply the quantity of pleasure, immediate

[9] *Ibid.*, pp. 28, 34.
[10] *Ibid.*, p. 12.

or consequent upon an act, whatever "quantity" means. Quality is also to be considered. " . . . Some kinds of pleasure are more desirable and more valuable than others."[11] Mill knows only one way to find out which of two pleasures is "higher." "Of two pleasures, if there be one to which all or almost all who have experience of both give a decided preference, irrespective of any feeling of moral obligation to prefer it, that is the more desirable pleasure." "Desirable" evidently means ought to be desired, not merely can be desired.[12]

The sort of man Mill trusts to discriminate the quality of pleasures is like Socrates and other "wise" men. Is it better to pursue wisdom even though such a life involves "a greater amount of discontent"? Mill's conclusion is that the superior being is "happier." In this case "happiness and content" (we now say contentment) are "two very different ideas." Earlier, happiness and pleasure were identified. Mill does not prefer animal satisfactions available to pigs, in contrast to satisfactions peculiar to human animals. Apparently some desires are to be preferred even if not satisfied.

It is indisputable that the being whose capacities of enjoyment are low has the greatest chance of having them fully satisfied; and a highly endowed being will always feel that any happiness which he can look for, as the world is constituted, is imperfect. But he can learn to bear its imperfections, if they are at all bearable; and they will not make him envy the being who is indeed unconscious of the imperfections, but only because he feels not at all the good which those imperfections qualify. It is better to be a human being dissatisfied, than a pig satisfied; better to be Socrates dissatisfied than a fool satisfied.[13]

We have recognized a sensuous and intellectual pleasure in reading. We might also suppose that members of the student's family get pleasure from knowing he is getting an education. But what if the student has the desire to know all there is to know? Surely this is higher than easy satisfaction with less knowledge, and just as surely such a student will be dissatisfied! So Mill leaves us with a paradox that what is better, defined as satisfying desires, often inevitably leads to frustration.

We have recognized sensuous pleasure of an infant taking its milk. There is certainly a pleasant tone in the experience of hunger satisfied. A mother may desire her infant to delight in her nourishment, and thus also find relief from its hunger cries, and also keep it from starving to death. But where is the pleasure of a desire that cannot be satisfied? It is exceedingly paradoxical for a hedonist to believe that the quality of a desire outweighs the painful consequences of frustration.

[11] *Ibid.*, p. 8.
[12] *Ibid.*, p. 9.
[13] *Ibid.*, p. 10.

Now let us look more carefully at Mill's assumptions. The first is ambiguous. It can mean that all men act to secure pleasures. Psychologists sometimes say that all behavior is directed toward relieving tension. This may be quite true, but a question of another order is: What ought men to do? Which tension should I relieve? If, as the second assumption indicates, Mill is trying to find a principle that will discriminate right acts from wrong, a psychological explanation of all behavior could not serve. The psychological thesis is that all men satisfy desires. The normative ethical principle is that some desires ought to be satisfied rather than others. In discovering the principle of what ought to be done Mill attempted to find the answer from what is done. Hume warned us against the leap from propositions with the copula "is" to propositions with the copula "ought." G. E. Moore named this the *naturalistic fallacy*. A further difficulty pointed out by Moore is that Mill makes the definition "pleasure or happiness is the nature of the good" seem like a statement of ordinary fact, but Mill's evidence for this is that men regard pleasure as a criterion of the good. This difficulty parallels that in theories of truth. Because something is a sign of something, the thing is not the same as what signifies it.

Mill began by assuming one end of all human action. Since by definition this end is pleasure or happiness and they are the nature and criterion of the good, whatever is good, such as the search for wisdom, must somehow be shown to be pleasant. If Mill had said that there were bad pleasures or things good though unpleasant, he would have had to revise his assumptions. If he had said that to be wise is a higher end than to be happy, he could have secured coherence only by revising his assumptions. Or if he would have admitted that Socrates' decision to seek wisdom was something quite different from an empirical generalization, he would have had to revise his assumption of right method. Although Mill called such a decision a conclusion drawn from "experience," this would seem to get the cart before the horse. For how could one gain experience in seeking wisdom without the prior choice to seek wisdom?

If one cannot, from the evidence of sensuous pleasure, reach the conclusion that to seek wisdom is better than to gratify the senses, why did Mill think he could bridge this gap? The most plausible explanation is that the terms are fearfully ambiguous. "Pleasure" means sometimes an immediate sensuous gratification; sometimes the satisfaction that accompanies the fulfillment of a biological need; sometimes the tone of relief when a task is done; sometimes an aesthetic delight as in music; sometimes a delight because someone else is spared pain or in any of the above ways gratified; sometimes it is happiness or a way of life in which there may be much sorrow as well as joy but having aspects of what Mill calls a beautiful character; sometimes a state of society to which "love of music" and "desire of health" are parts of a concrete whole; sometimes the abstract character of being thought desirable or pleasant; sometimes an ideal of a society in which each member has his equal claim to happiness recognized. When Mill wants to show his loyalty to his father, an associate of Bentham's, he identifies all these meanings with pleasure undefined. At other times, showing his liberation from dogma, he distinguishes between simple sensuous gratification and complex states of mind, character, and society.

A second very ambiguous term, identified in thought and experience with pleasure, is desire.

Desiring a thing and finding it pleasant, aversion to it and thinking of it as painful, are phenomena entirely inseparable or rather two parts of the same phenomenon; in strictness of language, two different modes of naming the same psychological fact; that to think of an object as desirable (unless for the sake of its consequences) and to think of it as pleasant are one and the same thing; and that to desire anything except in proportion as the idea of it is pleasant, is a physical and metaphysical impossibility.

To this we may say simply that as a psychological fact, masochists seek to have pain inflicted upon them, and others may desire to know what is true, however painful it may be, just because it is true. However, desirable as it is that one's beliefs be true, it is difficult to think that pleasure or pain has any bearing upon truth or falsity. What is desire? Although it seems to have a dozen shades of meaning, two stand out. In one sense, apparently it is simply an urge or drive. In another it is a purpose with a conscious goal. In one sense, we can say that there are good and bad desires. In another sense, there are no bad desires, since the goal is happiness, which is the meaning of good. Hence sometimes "desirable" means simply, as a matter of psychological fact, what is needed by the organism. And sometimes "desirable" means what ought to be sought rather than what ought not to be sought, a matter of moral discrimination.

In a celebrated passage Mill attempts to pass logically from one to the other.

The only proof capable of being given that an object is visible is that people actually see it. The only proof that a sound is audible is that people hear it; and so of the other sources of our experience. In like manner . . . the sole evidence it is possible to produce that anything is desirable is that people do actually desire it.[15]

[14] *Ibid.*, pp. 41–42.
[15] *Ibid.*, p. 37.

Mill admitted earlier that a fool might desire to be a pig satisfied rather than Socrates dissatisfied, but he could scarcely think that because people do desire to be pigs they ought so to desire. Desirability is not established by the fact of being desired. "Desirable" is a word like "credible" or "believable." Men believe many incredible superstitions, and deny many believable propositions.

We shall present a thoroughgoing criticism of Mill's position from another point of view in Section IV.

III. Formalistic Answers

There are many approaches to be taken in judging the morality of an action. We may condemn a man because his policy led to failure. In this case wrong means having some bad consequence. Yet we may praise a man because he acted out of kindness. In this case right means having some worthy motive. Over and beyond motive and consequences we may consider the customs of his society. He did what persons are expected to do and what is approved among his people. Some customs become laws and their violations are crimes punished by civil authority. We may bring a man to trial by accusing him, and a court may hear a defense and render a verdict. We are sometimes told that a man did wrong by custom, though he was not legally a criminal, or right by custom, though he was condemned by law. Which should be supreme? Sometimes men believe that legislatures and courts must impose upon a society a stricter code than what is customary. Sometimes men believe that legislatures and courts should not do more than formalize what in a given society is acknowledged to be "the thing done." Or, again, men may identify right and wrong with what some power sanctions or condemns. Is this authority the will of the majority, the will of the most powerful class or individual, or the will of a transhuman metaphysical entity called God?

Although men often justify their conduct by claiming that what they did was their duty, who is to say what a man's duty is? A person may have believed it his duty to give a lethal dose of morphine to a patient suffering from incurable cancer, insisting that he owes it to a human being to prevent needless and useless pain. He may declare that it seemed right. On the other hand, editorials may ask whose life is safe if society allows an individual to decide who is to be put out of the way and sermons will be preached saying that life and death are in God's hands, and that "thou shalt not kill" brands the act as murder. The courts may say that there is no procedure whereby a person may permit another to take his life, and until there is a law, it has no alternative but to condemn. The medical society will point out that a physician takes an oath to do all in his power to preserve life. But a humanitarian group may defend euthanasia as a more enlightened moral policy, and may contend that when the motive is solely to prevent pain, there are only beneficial consequences.

We have said enough to indicate that there are conflicting beliefs about duty and right and wrong. Many philosophers have attempted to find a theory that will set in order our confused, vague, and conflicting opinions, and of these no philosopher of the past two hundred years has made a deeper impression upon his successors than Immanuel Kant. His ethical system was the only one that John Stuart Mill recognized as an alternative to be refuted. Still today moral philosophers commonly take as the most fundamental choice, that between basing *ought* statements on *is* statements or holding that ought statements are independent and autonomous. Kant defended the latter alternative.

Earlier, in Chapter IV on truth, we acknowledged that truth-telling is considered a duty or an obligation. If we follow Kant's analysis of what this obligation is, we shall easily see his central assumptions and principles that enable us to use clearly the predicates "right" and "wrong."

"It may well be that not all is true that a man considers so; but in all that he says he must be truthful. . . . The trespassing against this duty of truthfulness is called lying. . . . " Kant includes not only an "outer" lie to one's fellow man but an "inner" lie to oneself or to God. A lie is not an error, for the person may believe true what is false; nor is a lie ignorance, one may simply not know. To lie is to maintain that something is true that one knows to be untrue. Kant extends the notion of lying to philosophers who maintain as certain what seems uncertain. No man has any exemption from the rottenness in human nature.[16]

How does this law or principle, "Thou shalt not lie," differ from other laws or principles? Is it like a physical law? The natural sciences are based upon observation of events and give us knowledge of what happens. A moral law is not based upon observation, and it may tell us what ought to happen, even if it never does. In short, a moral law is prescriptive rather than descriptive. Kant defends an analogy between moral law and a logical canon. As in logic we discover forms of reasoning that enable us to discriminate valid argument from fallacious, so in morality we discover forms enabling us to discriminate right from wrong.[17]

[16] Carl Friedrich, *Inevitable Peace*, Harvard University Press, Cambridge, Massachusetts, 1948, p. 23.
[17] *Kant's Critique of Practical Reason* (T. K. Abbott, tr.) Longmans, Green & Co., Inc., New York, 1927, pp. 2–4.

To what does such a moral law as "Thou shalt not lie" apply? It cannot apply to things for two reasons; first, things do not tell the truth or lie, and second, they have no freedom. A moral law is applicable only to rational beings, such as persons who are capable of knowledge and of deliberation and choice. Why does Kant say "rational beings" rather than man? Because he wishes to stress the universality of a genuine rational law. A law by its nature applies to any act of any creature who satisfies the definition of rationality and freedom. We should speak nonsense if we said to a creature who does not know the difference between true and false that he should not lie, and it would be also nonsense if he does not have the opportunity to be either honest or dishonest. To will to deceive or to will not to deceive are traits of character.[18]

How can we tell when a man has acted morally, in this case telling the truth? He would not have done a morally right act if he told the truth because it suited his inclinations. If one told the truth only when the truth was flattering to one's ego, or secured for oneself a pleasure, this would require only a hypothetical maxim. A moral principle is not genuinely universal if it depends on certain other conditions and it would lose the moral force called obligation if it were made dependent upon empirical fact. The moral act is not done merely in conformity to principle, but out of respect for principle itself. On the basis of the nature of a moral act, we can devise a criterion for telling when a man has acted morally.

The test is a logical one. If the maxim is genuinely moral, then it can be willed to become a universal principle. If the maxim is not moral, then when universalized we have an absurdity.

May I when in distress make a promise with the intention not to keep it? I readily distinguish here between the two significations which the question may have: Whether it is prudent, or whether it is right, to make a false promise? The former may undoubtedly often be the case. I see clearly indeed that it is not enough to extricate myself from a present difficulty by means of this sub-terfuge, but it must be well considered whether there may not hereafter spring from this lie much greater inconvenience than that from which I now free my-self, and as, with all my supposed *cunning*, the consequences cannot be so easily forseen but that credit once lost may be much more injurious to me than any mischief which I seek to avoid at present, it should be considered whether it would not be more *prudent* to act herein according to a universal maxim, and to make it a habit to promise nothing except with the intention of keeping it. But it is soon clear to me that such a maxim will still only be based on the fear of consequences. Now it is a wholly different thing to be truthful from duty, and to be so from apprehension of injurious consequences. In the first case, the very notion of the action already implies a law for me; in the second case, I

[18] *Ibid.*, p. 4.

must first look about elsewhere to see what results may be combined with it which would affect myself. For to deviate from the principle of duty is beyond all doubt wicked; but to be unfaithful to my maxim of prudence may often be very advantageous to me, although to abide by it is certainly safer. The shortest way, however, and an unerring one, to discover the answer to this question whether a lying promise is consistent with duty, is to ask myself, Should I be content that my maxim (to extricate myself from difficulty by a false promise) should hold good as a universal law, for myself as well as for others? and should I be able to say to myself, "Every one may make a deceitful promise when he finds himself in a difficulty from which he cannot otherwise extricate himself"? Then I presently become aware that while I can will the lie, I can by no means will that lying should be a universal law. For with such a law there would be no promises at all, since it would be in vain to allege my intention in regard to my future actions to those who would not believe this allegation, or if they over-hastily did so, would pay me back in my own coin. Hence my maxim, as soon as it should be made a universal law, would necessarily destroy itself.[19]

A "deceitful promise" is not a promise at all. For "I promise" implies "I will to keep my promise," but the deceitful intent implies "I won't keep my promise." Intrinsically and a priori, we can know the logical self-contradiction of the concept "deceitful promise." A man who does what is wrong may be then said to commit a moral absurdity. The contradiction of an absurdity is a necessary truth. For example, if "nothing exists" is absurd, then "something exists" must be true. Hence it is a priori true that "All promises ought to be kept."

Kant's point is also given a somewhat different interpretation. If everyone were to borrow money, promising to repay it when this is known to be impossible, this "would necessarily contradict itself." A promise here means "whatever one pleases." In such a case "no one would consider that anything was promised to him, but would ridicule all such statements as vain pretenses."[20] Thus we must know more than the meaning of promise in this case, namely, what the consequences would be, to see the alleged self-contradiction. In such a case the law is not purely a priori.

A third account considers the person to whom a "deceitful promise" is made.

He who is thinking of making a lying promise to others will see at once that he would be using another man *merely as a mean*, without the latter containing at the same time the end in himself. For he whom I propose by such a promise to use for my own purposes cannot possibly assent to my mode of acting towards him, and therefore cannot himself contain the end of this action.[21]

[19] *Ibid.*, pp. 18–19.
[20] *Ibid.*, p. 40.
[21] *Ibid.*, pp. 47–48.

A person to whom a promise is made has as a rational being the right to claim in principle that the promise be kept. And "I promise" can be made only to a rational being. Hence the intent not to keep a promise implies that the other person is but a thing without reason and right. Hence a "deceitful promise" implies an absurdity in transgressing "the rights of men," and the law is then a priori when another principle is included.

It now becomes possible to state the relation between "good" and "happiness."

Nothing can possibly be conceived in the world, or even out of it, which can be called good, without qualification, except a Good Will. Intelligence, wit, judgment, and the other *talents* of the mind, however they may be named, or courage, resolution, perseverence, as qualities of temperament, are undoubtedly good and desirable in many respects; but these gifts of nature may also become extremely bad and mischievous if the will which is to make use of them, and which, therefore, constitutes what is called *character,* is not good. It is the same with the *gifts of fortune.* Power, riches, honor, even health, and the general well-being and contentment with one's condition which is called *happiness,* inspire pride, and often presumption, if there is not a good will to correct the influence of these on the mind, and with this also to rectify the whole principle of acting, and adapt it to its end. The sight of a being who is not adorned with a single feature of a pure and good will, enjoying unbroken prosperity, can never give pleasure to an impartial rational spectator. Thus a good will appears to constitute the indispensable condition even of being worthy of happiness.[22]

This passage is not altogether clear. Kant restricts morally "good" to "will." "Will" signifies *"nothing but practical reason."* This is called also "a faculty to choose that only which reason independent of inclination recognizes as practically necessary, i.e. as good." What the will ought not to choose is pleasure, which Kant calls subjective. Yet a will that chooses what is "objective" deserves to be happy or to obtain pleasure. Since every will does not in this life obtain happiness in proportion to its goodness, Kant postulates immortality so that God may reward the will worthy of happiness. Further, the judgment of who deserves happiness could only be safely left to God. God's will is "holy," for there is no possibility of his being swayed by impulse, and thus being partial. Happiness, which Kant finds so "indefinite" that he does not define it, is only a reward for choosing maxims that conform to an objective moral principle. Happiness is not an end, and can only be wished or hoped for. What the content of a happy life in "all future circumstances" is, only an "omniscient" knower could know.[23]

[22] *Ibid.,* p. 9.
[23] *Ibid.,* pp. 31, 35.

It is not yet clear how we can know the principle by which God judges the maxims by which human wills may choose morally right acts. Kant conceives of a moral world composed of autonomous wills. Each will is sovereign. This can be so only if there is one and the same moral law or categorical imperative. Since it is this law that each person wills when he reasons correctly by his own inherent standard, each will is autonomous, and not subject to the will of another.

There are various formulations of the supreme moral principle. From the perspective of an individual will making a choice, one may say *"Act only on that maxim whereby thou canst at the same time will that it should become a universal law."*[24] From the perspective of a human observer judging the rightness or wrongness of any act one may say *"So act as to treat humanity, whether in thine own person or in that of any other, in every case as an end withal, never as means only."*[25] From the perspective of a sovereign laying down commandments for all others one may say *"Act as if the maxim of thy action were to become by thy will a universal law of nature."*[26]

Kant claimed that these were three formulations of the same principle. The problem is often therefore raised whether the others follow from any formulation of the principle. If they do, then one might expect that any formulation logically follows from any other. The student should examine them to see whether they are identical in this sense. Further, Kant claims that all moral laws can be deduced from this principle. Yet, if we should say that a man may take his own life in case of useless suffering, or allow another to take it, we would universalize the maxim, but this Kant regards as immoral in content. Critics, however, have failed to see any formal contradiction.

The standard criticism is that Kant from the beginning has divorced man as a moral will or practical reason from man as an animal acting in nature. Are there two realms, one of freedom, the other of necessity? If there are, how does pure practical reason ever actually motivate an observable act? A man may never be able sharply to detach his will from his inclination, may never know the exact mixture of reason and inclination that enters into his act. For this reason Kant was pushed into saying that we can be sure of a moral act only if it goes against all interest, liking, and consideration of consequences. He can save the theory by claiming only to be dealing with an element that never exists purely but is abstracted

[24] *Ibid.*, p. 38.
[25] *Ibid.*, p. 47.
[26] *Ibid.*, p. 39.

conceptually. Yet to give the theory some semblance of applying to actual conduct, Kant introduces an element of feeling into motivation, namely respect for law and esteem for every rational being.

We might also object that Kant's exclusive attention to motives and maxims implies that in judging the rightness or wrongness of an act we are asked to know another man as only God can know him. Since we are not omniscient and cannot search the heart as God is said to do, how can we judge morally the act we observe? Further, the actual deed cannot be sharply distinguished from its circumstances and consequences. If we must leave all judgment to God, then we are deprived of ever using Kant's formalistic system as the basis for punishing and rewarding in actual human affairs. We should not strictly approve or disapprove any man's conduct. Yet this Kant himself does, when he applies his system to human conduct in international relations in his essay on Eternal Peace.

A third objection is that our concern may be to judge moral behavior as that which conduces to the complete good of men in this life. The good is not complete unless all people worthy of happiness actually are made as happy as they ought to be. Hence Mill's attention to human institutions, such as education, economy, and government. If we could be assured that all wrongs will be punished, all rights rewarded by God, then we might ignore human institutions in our metaphysic of ethics. But God and immortality, and freedom also, are in Kant's system postulates only.

In the fourth place, we may doubt what Kant assumes, namely, that each human act is either right or wrong, if not right then wrong, if not wrong then right. Is every act done out of respect for moral law or not? If merely in conformity to moral law, is it as bad as if it were done in defiance of law? If acts are done other than out of respect for the moral law, why should they be worthless morally? Kant's absolutism seems to presume that ethical principles are not capable of being variously formulated according to different ideals. His own ideal, viewed historically, seems to us to have been formulated with many aspects borrowed from Stoicism, Christianity, and the ideals of the American and French revolutions. To assume that this is the one absolute set of principles does violence to our knowledge of the influence of temporal and local circumstances.

In spite of all these criticisms, Kant contributes something very worthwhile to our understanding of moral judgment. The formal principle has been restated by a contemporary:

> It is first of all in many cases a clear test of wrongness: a person whose act violates a principle which he wills to be a universal law is acting wrongly. Moreover, if, unlike Kant, we admit the possibility of alternative moral codes,

the principle helps us to distinguish moral codes from a-moral codes of behavior, i.e., from those which, like codes of fashion, have nothing to do with morality. Unless a code of rules contains the formal principle of morality, it is not a moral code.[27]

IV. Answers of Self-Realization

We may on the one hand attempt to calculate the consequences of our acts, but since the consequences are never fully known, whether an act is right or wrong can be only a probability statement, or merely a prediction that it will bring pleasure. On the other hand, we may attempt to state the rightness or wrongness of an act by judging how it squares with a principle. But however validly we make our deduction, it can be no truer than the assumed principle. Is it only good to produce consequences that satisfy our desires? Is it only good to make self-consistent judgments or judgments consistent with the judgments of a wise man? Just as in the ancient world Epicureanism chose one answer, Stoicism the other, so in the modern, Mill's utilitarianism chose one, leaving Kant to systematize the other. Yet if both the consideration of consequences of acts and the judgment of maxims of acts are helpful in conceiving of morality, might there not be a principle which determines the goodness of a life that achieves happiness and is lived in obedience to moral law? Since Kant and Mill there has been an eminent assessment of both together suggesting a more inclusive good, which each is too one-sided to make clear. This is the view of F. H. Bradley, whose Ethical Studies examined Mill's Utilitarianism in a chapter called "Pleasure for Pleasure's Sake," and Kantian formalism in a chapter called "Duty for Duty's Sake." The basis of Bradley's criticism is that neither position did justice to man as a member of society and a participant in the changing circumstances of historical process. Man's moral obligations cannot be concretely stated unless one considers the social nature of morality.

Man is a social being, he is real only because he is social, and can realize himself only because it is as social that he realizes himself. The mere individual is a delusion of theory; and the attempt to realize it in practice is the starvation and mutilation of human nature, with total sterility or the production of monstrosities.

Bradley's position counters individualism, a belief that is still widely held among us, with the belief that society is an organism of which we are functions. The thesis we are to examine is this: must we think of man

[27] S. Körner, *Kant*, Penguin Books, Harmondsworth, Middlesex, England, 1955, p. 140.

organically to give a credible account of man's complete good? A second question is also pertinent: can we better conceive of man's complete good if his end is said to be neither happiness nor duty alone, but his self-realization?

Let us consider first the precise grounds Bradley states for considering that happiness alone, or duty alone, is less than man's complete good. It is out of criticism of partial truths that a dialectical thinker professes to develop a truer position. Although Bradley was influenced by Hegel, we shall have to examine his claim that he did not reduce the "ought" to the "is" of human society.

Bradley's first point in criticism of Mill expresses what has come to be called the *hedonistic paradox*. That is, happiness or pleasure when consciously and deliberately sought proves to be illusory, but when one engages in some positive task, happiness may ensue as a by-product of success. This psychological fact, if it is a fact, would not refute the conception of the good in terms of pleasure, but it would refute the notion that happiness can be found by pursuing it apart from all other considerations. The common belief Bradley rephrases bears on the practicability of hedonism. ". . . If you want to be happy in the sense of pleased you must not think of pleasure, but taking up some accredited form of living, must make that your end. . . ."[28]

Bradley's second point is equally conventional, i.e., that the "end" or goal used by utilitarianism as a guide conflicts with moral consciousness. What is meant is that the moral world is constituted by "the family, society, and the State; and the work of the individual in them, and again, on its internal side of moral feeling and belief."[29] Mill had claimed that utilitarianism could employ every sanction to which other ethics appeal, but Bradley's attack is on the basis of things "we should choose even if no pleasure came from them."[30] As to the family, Bradley refers to the demand for loyalty to a single spouse. "Thou shalt not commit adultery" might well be indefensible on utilitarian grounds.[31]

The third point Bradley presses against Mill is that it is mistaken to apply the logical principle of the excluded middle to the two theories expounded by Mill and Kant. Mill advanced his theory by claiming to refute Kant's intuitive theory. There are two assumptions Bradley thinks, one unproved and the other false: "The first is that there must be some existing theory which is a sufficient account of morals . . . the second is that the

[28] F. H. Bradley, *Ethical Studies,* The Liberal Arts Press, Inc., New York, 1951, p. 31.
[29] *Ibid.,* p. 33.
[30] *Ibid.,* p. 32.
[31] *Ibid.,* p. 48.

disjunction, that the either-or of intuitive and utilitarian is complete and exhaustive. . . ."[32]

The fourth point against Mill is that those who know the range of human desires do in fact sometimes envy the beasts.

There doubtless are hours . . . when all that is called progress seems so futile and disappointing that we bitterly feel "increase of knowledge" is indeed "increase of sorrow," and that he who thinks least is happiest; when we envy the beasts their lives without a past or a future, their heedless joys and easily forgotten griefs; and when for ourselves, and if for ourselves then for all others, we could wish to cease or be as they are. . . .[33]

The fifth point, based on the fourth, is that even when the "pleasure of advance is counted in," human progress rests upon a decision to resist the gain of pleasure in leading what Mill called the "lower" or easier life. Therefore, deduces Bradley, moral men make what is an immoral choice, if hedonism is morality.[34]

The sixth point is that Mill's effort to rescue hedonism by discriminating "lower" from "higher" pleasures qualitatively is a failure. It is a failure because right must still be determined by "that which is most 'grateful to the feelings' of connoisseurs in pleasures, who have tried them all."[35] Bradley's point is that this is "absolutely irreconcilable with ordinary moral beliefs." A virtue is not a virtue in ordinary morality if a person has his eye on wages or perquisites, or anticipated feelings of pleasure.[36]

The seventh point is that pleasure gives us "no standard to work by and no end to aim at, no system to realize in our lives." One reason is that pleasures "are as they are felt to be," and as merely subjective tell us nothing about reality. Another reason is that although Mill claimed that happiness is a "concrete whole," his reduction of happiness to pleasure was an interpretation of the real in terms of an abstraction. Pleasure, claims Bradley, is nothing but a "general name." If pleasure, or pain, is the common quality shared by an infinite series of perishing moments, there is no sense at all in attempting to sum the series. It is meaningful to "get some one pleasure," but to "get happiness" means to "get a general name" and to imagine the infinite series to be finite. Against Mill's own claim that he provided an ideal for each man, that is, a "concrete whole," Bradley proposes an answer. "Happiness for the ordinary man neither means a pleasure nor a number of pleasures. It means in general the finding of

[32] *Ibid.*, p. 33.
[33] *Ibid.*, p. 34.
[34] *Ibid.*, p. 35.
[35] *Ibid.*, p. 36.
[36] *Ibid.*, p. 37.

himself or the satisfaction of himself as a whole, and in particular it means the realization of his concrete ideal of life."[37]

The eighth point is that men cannot meaningfully set out to realize something unattainable. In the utilitarian calculus the stress is on the pleasures which other persons have and not on one intense moment of our own, or delights we choose by the way. When then can anyone be said to have achieved his end? We are never able to say that happiness has been attained. We are not only always putting off "present certainty for the sake of a doubtful future," but we do not know who is to judge the probabilities of this future, nor whether it is terminated by a hedonistic judgment day.[38]

The ninth point is that morality is the consciousness of laws that are "not to be departed from." People are aware of some principles which they take for certain. But utilitarians cannot account for the conscience that is unwilling to accept every principle as a mere rule or questionable policy that may be departed from. "The moral consciousness is the touchstone of moral theories, and that moral consciousness, I appeal to it in every man, has laws which are a great deal more than rules." Hence a utilitarian has no basis for his purported standard "that the end is the maximum surplus of pleasure in the sentient world." There is no basis because the hedonist's "ought to be" is a matter of private opinion. What Bradley is thinking of is behavior like that of prostitution. He claims we may know it to be wrong, even if it increases "the surplus of pleasant sensations." Hence to demand that one prove that it actually diminishes this surplus is to over-throw established moral standards.[39]

The tenth point is logical. How does Mill reason from the desire of each man for his own happiness to the desirability of the general happiness? In Mill's words, "that each person's happiness is a good to that person, and the general happiness, therefore [is] a good to the aggregate of all persons." By parity of reasoning, Bradley suggests "it should follow that each pig, desiring his own pleasure, desires also the pleasure of all," thus quarrelling with the shift from the consideration of "each" as an individual member of a class, to "all" as a collective whole made up of members.[40]

Bradley's criticism further produces a *reductio ad absurdum.*

It is monstrous to argue thus: "Because (1) on psychological grounds it is certain that we can desire nothing but our own private pleasure; because (2) on some other grounds something *else* (whatever it may be), something not my feeling of pleasure, something other than my private self, is desired and de-

[37] *Ibid.,* pp. 38–39.
[38] *Ibid.,* pp. 43–44.
[39] *Ibid.,* pp. 51–52.
[40] *Ibid.,* p. 54.

sirable; therefore (3) this something else which is desired and desirable is the pleasure of others, since by (1), only pleasure can be desired." If we argue in this way, we may well go a little further to "(4) and therefore we can and do desire something not our own private pleasure, and therefore (1) is false, and therefore the whole argument disappears since it is upon (1) that the whole rests."[41]

In thinking of happiness as a sum of pleasures, and in thinking of general happiness as an aggregate, Mill was responsible for what Bradley considered another mistake. This is the notion that within our calculus of pleasures we can coherently introduce a standard of "higher" and "lower" pleasures. It is difficult to find out by what standard some pleasures can be judged in this way.

Higher and lower, as comparative terms, refer to degree. What is higher has a greater degree (or it has a greater number of degrees) of something definite; what is lower has a less degree or number of degrees. Their quality, as higher and lower, is referrable to quantity. So that, apart from quantity, apart from degree, there is no comparison, no estimation, no higher and lower at all.[42]

What this standard could be Mill does not tell us, but if there were a standard to estimate pleasures, saying which *ought* to be preferred, then it follows that hedonism has been abandoned.

Bradley summarizes his devastating refutation with a statement of about a dozen points of agreement. The standard should be palpable and objective. The end is not an abstract idea, for whatever is realized is concrete. The end is not "Heaven knows what or where, but is the end for us as men." Further it is to be found in what is "distinctively human." Actions cannot be separated from consequences. Bradley agrees that pleasure is *a* good; but not *the* good. ". . . Happiness is the end; and therefore we say pleasure is not the end." What is this happiness that conforms to what all men believe ought to be? It is "the self-evolution of ourselves and of humanity," not as measured by feeling but by some standard that judges functions of men. This standard is "self-realization."[43]

"Function" and "self-realization" may seem to be as abstract and ambiguous as happiness. Functions seem to be activities that help to achieve whatever actual men ought to aim at, and Bradley concedes that pleasure may be used as a test of function. "It shows whether function is impeded in discharge or not."[44] "If 'happiness' means well-being or perfection of life, then I am content to say that, with Plato and Aristotle, I hold happi-

[41] *Ibid.*, p. 55, footnote.
[42] *Ibid.*, p. 58.
[43] *Ibid.*, p. 65.
[44] *Ibid.*, p. 77.

ness to be the end; and, although virtue is not a *mere* means, yet it can be regarded as a means and so is 'useful.' "[45]

Bradley's method now calls for an examination of the "opposite" to hedonism.

In Hedonism we have criticized a one-sided view; we shall have to do here with an opposite extremity of one-sidedness. The self to be realized before was the self or selves as a maximum quantity or number of particular feelings. In the theory which awaits us, the self to be realized has a defect which is diametrically opposed to the first, and yet is the same defect. Its fault is the opposite, since for mere particular it substitutes mere universal. . . .

It is more difficult to see from the standard of self-realization what is erroneous in Kant's formalism. Kant's good is not feeling, but "something to be done."[46] It is something to be done by me, and the

. . . end does not fall outside the doer. I am to realize myself; and . . : I cannot make an ultimate end of anything except myself, cannot make myself a mere means to something else. . . . The end is the doing which is to be done; the activity is good in itself, not for the sake of a result beyond.

Bradley agrees that there is nothing good unless it be a good will. "A man is not called good because he is rich, nor because he is handsome or clever. He is good when he is moral, and he is moral when his actions are conformed to and embody a good will, or when his will is good."

Kant characterized, as we saw, the good will as universal, free, autonomous, and formal. Universal, in that the end is an end for all of us and absolutely without condition. Free, in that it exists for itself and is not determined by anything else. Autonomous, in that it wills its own law. Formal, in that the will is determined by the test of non-contradiction.

Bradley's objection to all this is that the self I have to realize is not a mere form. ". . . I am not a mere form; I have an 'empirical' nature, a series of particular states of the 'this me,' a mass of desires, aversions, inclinations, passions, pleasures, and pains, what we may call a sensuous self. It is in this self that all content, all matter, all possible filling of the form must be sought. . . ." If there were no particular sensuous self, there would be nothing to be commanded. "Ought" and "duty" have meaning only when something is commanded. Bradley then insists that unless we conceive of a self both formal and material, we have not the two elements in opposition required by meaningful issuing of commands.[47]

A second aspect of "duty" makes a difficulty for Kant's formalism. The

[45] *Ibid.*, p. 80.
[46] *Ibid.*, pp. 81, 82.
[47] *Ibid.*, pp. 84–85.

good will was defined as practical reason insofar as it never contradicted itself. But the ought as a command "expresses something which neither simply is or is not, but which both is and is not—something, in short, which is to be."⁴⁸ If a will commands that I do something, and the will that commands is not mine, then it is the sensuous self that is involved. In that case what can be done is not simply subject to formal principles of logic.

A third difficulty emerges. Duty is to be done for duty's sake. This comes to mean, in Kant, to act self-consistently. Why? For the sake of realizing self-consistency. But Bradley again is sharply critical of this. If formal self-consistency is the end, then there should theoretically be no command or duty, no ought applying to action. For to act is to "carry out into the world of fact" what was in mind only. What is thus realized is particular and concrete. But then the empirical self is the locus of morality. And how are particular acts commanded by purely formal principles? Further, by being realized, the act is no longer purely formal and cannot be judged solely as a universal.

In its simplest form the contradiction is this. "Realize noncontradiction" is the order. But "noncontradiction" = bare form; "realize" = give content to; content contradicts form without content; and so "realize noncontradiction" means "realize a contradiction."⁴⁹

Everybody knows that the only way to do your duty is to do your duties; that general doing good may mean doing no good in particular, and so none at all, but rather perhaps the contrary of good. Everybody knows that the setting out, whether in religion, morals, or politics, with the intent to realize an abstraction, is a futile endeavor; and that what it comes to is that either you do nothing at all, or that the particular content which is necessary for action is added to the abstraction by the chance of circumstances or caprice. Everybody suspects, if they do not feel sure, that the acting consciously on and from abstract principles means self-deceit or hypocrisy or both.⁵⁰

One individual then cannot possibly without contradiction do all the acts which are, in principle, right for anyone to do. For the sake of argument, assume that it is right to produce food and right to produce shoes and right to defend the community against enemies and right to sit in jurisdiction as a ruler. This is Plato's problem in the Republic. Justice is that each man should do his particular task, that of a farmer, or that of a workman, or that of a soldier, or that of a ruler. This is just because each man has the kind of self that fits him for each task. Whereas Plato held a theory that fitted each kind of self into some function of the social or-

⁴⁸ Ibid., p. 85.
⁴⁹ Ibid., p. 89.
⁵⁰ Ibid., p. 91.

ganism, Bradley begins with the social organism that somehow assigns to each man his specific "station." This will require examination.

Why does Bradley press this solution? The problem is that:

. . . in a given case I may have several duties, and that I may be able to do only one. I must then break some 'categorical' law, and the question the ordinary man puts to himself is, Which duty am I to do? He would say, "All duties have their limits and are subordinated one to another. You cannot put them all in the form of your 'categorical imperative' (in the shape of a law absolute and dependent on nothing beside itself) without such exceptions and modifications that, in many cases, you might as well have left it alone altogether. We certainly have laws but we may not be able to follow them all at once, and to know which we are to follow is a matter of good sense which cannot be decided any other way. One should give to the poor—in what cases and how much? Should sacrifice oneself—in what way and within what limits? Should not indulge one's appetites—except when it is right. Should not idle away one's time—except when one takes one's pleasure. Nor neglect one's work—but for some good reason. All these points we admit are in one way matter of law; but if you think to decide in particular cases by applying some 'categorical imperative,' you must be a pedant, if not a fool."[51]

An application of Bradley's appeal to "ordinary morality" will show us exactly where he comes out.

According to ordinary morality (the fact is too palpable to be gainsaid), it is quite right to speak falsely with intent to deceive under certain circumstances, though ordinary morality might add, "I don't call that a lie." It *is* a lie; and when Kant and others maintained that it must always be wrong to lie, they forgot the rather important fact that in some cases to abstain from acting *is* acting, is willful neglect of a duty, and that there are duties above truth-speaking, and many offenses against morality which are worse, though they may be less painful, than a lie. So to kill oneself in a manner which must be called suicide, *may* not only be right but heroic; homicide may be excusable, rebellion in the subject and disobedience in the soldier all morally justifiable, and every one of them clear breaches of categorical imperatives, in obedience to a higher law.[52]

What is the "higher law?" It is to "never break a law of duty . . . but only for the sake of a superior and overruling duty." This seems to be circular and very obscure, and to say that "circumstances decide" hardly helps.

In confuting Mill's hedonism Bradley appealed to the "moral consciousness" having categorical laws which are not merely rules. Now in confuting Kant's formalism, Bradley denies that "ordinary morality" has any principle that is absolute, that may not be broken under some circumstances.

[51] *Ibid.*, pp. 94–95.
[52] *Ibid.*, pp. 95–96.

Moreover, he reduces the meaning of "higher" and "lower" to quantitative units. In justifying exceptions to universal principles, he makes use of these same adjectives without definition or clarification. Moreover, he had scorned the fallacy of arguing from what is desired to what ought to be desired, but he attempts to confute Kant by insisting upon what is our concrete duty in society's organism as against what ought to be apart from circumstances. And, finally, in confuting Mill's hedonism, he made a great point about the endless ambiguity of "pleasure" and "happiness." Yet throughout this criticism and that of Kant, much mystery surrounds the meaning of "to realize," and "the self to be realized"; "self-realization" must be a permutation and combination of different definitions.

Dialectic in philosophy often appears to be the incoherent philosophic policy of having one's cake and eating it. To meet this charge of incoherence, Bradley contrasts two perspectives, the "higher" and the "lower." The former is absolute and real, the latter is partial and appearance. Although a given society seems to be partial and relative, nonetheless, Bradley does not wish to say that its moral claims are merely relative, for a finite or empirical self is expected to fulfill society's demands as though they were absolute. The self has its station and consequently its duties. But if the finite self is only an aspect of the Absolute, what kind of unrealized existence does it possess? How can this self be both real and unreal?

This is a contradiction, but a contradiction that forces one dialectically to correct this meaning. A self to be realized may then be conceived as an individual set of potentialities. An infant is potentially a man. What is his good? Clearly for him to develop those skills that make him a human being, to communicate in some language, to perform some useful tasks, and to take his place as a citizen. Self, if it refers to a complex, is many-sided. Hence realization of a self may mean to develop a harmonious whole in which the above characteristics do not conflict. Hence we may talk of the ideal self as our goal. The good may be to become the personality that most fully satisfies the ideal. But since, as in Donne's sermon, "no man is an island unto himself, but part of the main," that is, constituted in essence by relations to others, the most fully real self is an identification with society. It is "real" because one cannot be related to others only accidentally. Without others, I can neither be nor be realized. Hence Bradley says:

. . . if my self which I aim at is the realization in me of a moral world which is a system of selves, an organism in which I am a member, and in whose life I live—then I cannot aim at my own well-being without aiming at that of others. The others are not mere means to me, but are involved in my essence.[53] . . .

[53] *Ibid.*, p. 56.

Bradley says that there is "nothing better than my station and its duties." But may not society demand the wrong thing from me? And this may call the whole position into question. Where is any opportunity for dissent from custom? How could the system allow any judgment that although something is done, it ought not to be done? Every critic of Bradley and other self-realization theories has found something wrong with this conservative principle. And Bradley himself claims that "the content of the ideal self does not fall within any community," and is "in short *not* merely the ideal of a perfect social being."[54]

Yet if one holds a moral conception apart from the concrete realities of societies in temporal change, one has, according to absolute idealism, nothing real or palpable," only illusion and contradiction. Although at times Bradley's absolute seems to be a God, for whom everything is good, the ultimate vision is an amoral one. If everything is good, then bad and evil and wrong have lost their meaning. If they are only finite, and the infinite alone is real, then moral distinctions are unreal and mortality an illusion. This is a familiar conclusion of speculative mystics, but it is Bradley's merit to have reasoned to a conclusion to which others arrive less reasonably.

In spite of this rejection of Bradley's position, from internal and external criticism, we may conclude on a note of positive contribution.

Bradley's intensive logical and linguistic analysis of ethical theories has set the style of the more rigorous work of our century. What do I mean when I say that X is good, or X is right, or X ought to be? These are the questions Bradley's successors ask.

Second, apart from the form of moral questions, the questions of the self and personality are issues that lay implicit in Mill and Kant. To make explicit the problems of how a self is developed in society and how a self seems to transcend any given society are puzzles to which some psychologists, some sociologists, some philosophers, some theologians now address themselves.

V. Emotivist Answers

One of the most recent approaches to moral philosophy is often called *emotivism.* Two men, A. J. Ayer from the British Isles, and Charles Stevenson from the United States, have played important roles in its definition and development. The theory has been frequently associated with the point of view of logical positivism, but it cannot be said that all positivists are emotivists.

[54] See Henry Sidgwick and Alban Widgery, *Outlines of the History of Ethics,* The Macmillan Co., New York, 1946, p. 286.

It is important to remember the distinction between value judgments on the one hand, and factual judgments on the other. Only the latter are verifiable by empirical methods; thus they and tautological statements alone can properly be said to be true or false. According to Ayer, ethical systems are made up of four classes of propositions. These are propositions expressing definitions of ethical terms; propositions describing the phenomena of moral experience; exhortations to moral virtue; ethical judgments. Of these, says Ayer, only propositions of the first class constitute ethical philosophy. But the only propositions that can be said to be true or false are those of the second class, which are ordinary scientific statements belonging to the disciplines of psychology and sociology. If moralists do genuinely argue, they only demonstrate that they are confused about the proper task of ethics. Exhortations of the third class, of course, are not propositions but "ejaculations or commands which are designed to provoke the reader to action of a certain sort."[55] These, along with ethical judgments, do not belong to any branch of philosophy or science.

Ayer's purpose is to try to translate or reduce the whole sphere of ethical terms to non-ethical terms (and aesthetic terms to non-aesthetic terms). It is apparent that Ayer's emotivist theory develops out of G. E. Moore's intuitionist theory of the indefinable good.

We begin by admitting that the fundamental ethical concepts are unanalysable, inasmuch as there is no criterion by which one can test the validity of the judgments in which they occur. So far we are in agreement with the absolutists. But, unlike the absolutists, we are able to give an explanation of this fact about ethical concepts. We say that the reason why they are unanalysable is that they are mere pseudo-concepts. The presence of an ethical symbol in a proposition adds nothing to its factual content. Thus if I say to someone, 'You acted wrongly in stealing that money,' I am not stating anything more than if I had simply said, 'You stole that money.' In adding that this action is wrong I am not making any further statement about it. I am simply evincing my moral disapproval of it. It is as if I had said, 'You stole that money,' in a peculiar tone of horror, or written it with the addition of some special exclamation marks. The tone, or the exclamation marks adds nothing to the literal meaning of the sentence. It merely serves to show that the expression of it is attended by certain feelings in the speaker.[56]

Because the contrast between "stealing, horrors!" and "stealing, hooray!" is one of emotion and not of factual knowledge, we can follow Ayer's next step. It is to ascribe to all moral expression the function of arousing feeling and stimulating action in others. And we have a wealth of moral terms

[55] A. J. Ayer, *Language, Truth and Logic,* Dover Publications, Inc., New York, n.d., p. 103.
[56] *Ibid.,* p. 107.

to mark the degrees between commanding emphatically, recommending, and suggesting. Moreover, consider two men in a dispute. One says that thrift is a virtue, the other that thrift is a vice. Both may be making true statements insofar as one feels one way and the other a different way. But there are no arguments about feeling one way rather than the other. This is shown by the fact that, "When we come to deal with pure questions of value, as distinct from questions of fact, . . . we finally resort to mere abuse."[57]

Stevenson added to this a distinction between two kinds of agreement and disagreement. One is between beliefs, the other between attitudes. "The two kinds of disagreement differ mainly in this respect: the former is concerned with how matters are truthfully to be described and explained; the latter is concerned with how they are to be favored or disfavored, and hence how they are to be shaped by human effort."[58]

There have been a number of criticisms offered in opposition to emotivism. One of the commonest is against the sharp division assumed by emotivists between cognitive meaning and emotive meaning. We do very often say something like, "Frenchmen are afraid of German rearmament." Can we say exactly where the cognitive content of three wars in three generations ceases and emotions stirred by destruction begin? If we cannot, then it will not do to assume a sharp distinction between belief and attitude. Moreover, it may be that emotions are sometimes an asset to cognition, and not always a detriment. By no means do all philosophers agree that knowledge in general, or scientific knowledge in particular, is devoid of emotion. The debate is very complex, but the student should know that pragmatists, particularly William James, and metaphysicians, particularly A. N. Whitehead, defend a continuity and overlap of cognition and emotion. Furthermore, "emotion" has been an unanalyzed concept in some positivist systems. That is, whatever the positivist does not care to take seriously he calls emotive. Thus it becomes a wastebasket term, or more politely, a "bin."[59] If one is to base a philosophic theory on a distinction between terms, these terms should be made explicitly clear. Critics of emotivists find this lacking.

On the emotivist theory there are no moral propositions, and no contradiction between expressions. That is, moral judgments are equated with statements such as "I approve of" and "Join me in the approval." But are

[57] *Ibid.,* p. 111.
[58] Charles Stevenson, *Ethics and Language,* Yale University Press, New Haven, Connecticut, 1944, p. 4.
[59] Philip Blair Rice, *On the Knowledge of Good and Evil,* Random House, New York, 1955, p. 61.

moral judgments no more than what may be called propaganda and advertisement? If you think that some appeals do not merely arouse your desire to buy something or to vote for someone, but stir you to desire it for good reasons or to have a justified reason for voting for one rather than another candidate, then emotivism is not for you. Is there no difference between the most violent appeal by a dictator to hate an enemy and the best-reasoned discourse on a political problem? Emotivists usually regard such criticism as unfair. They do not like to think that their theory justifies unprincipled rhetoric. They are not, it is true, themselves irrationalists, but does the theory permit the distinction they wish to make?

Again, may we not say that if "good" means only "I approve" and "Please join me in approving," then we might conclude that a thing became good when approved. And if something were not approved it would not be good, or bad either. Some philosophers call attention to suffering with no known benefit to anyone, and ask, if this agony and pain were unknown would that make it neither good nor bad? Finally we may ask whether any theory that regards values as merely expressions of emotions adequately reflects or grasps the importance values have in life and civilization. In their eagerness to do away with all absolute standards, the emotivists seem to falsify our experience and to introduce implicitly other absolute standards, for example, of clarity, verification, and so on, of their own. Thus we cannot really expect from the emotivists any answer to the question, "What should I do?" except perhaps "feel as I do."

VI. Some Practical Suggestions for the Resolution of Moral Perplexity

It is possible that many readers will feel we still owe them something. After all, our central question was "What ought I to do?" and we really, it might be said, have not given an answer. We have examined a number of theories, but these are frequently disappointing not only because of their formal character but because the relation between the theory and actual moral practice is not illuminated. What is to be done when we are faced with an immediate, specific, morally confusing situation in which a definite decision must be made? Certainly such a question belongs to moral philosophy even though it is not the only question, and many a contemporary ethical theory would exclude such a problem as merely practical. If the student will think over carefully what has been said in this exposition and criticism, he will find a number of points that might be brought together as a series of steps in moral deliberation. They merely suggest a way of meeting moral dilemmas, and propose neither that the final decision is the only one possible; nor that it is universal, that is, acceptable to all; nor that it is necessary, that is, logically inescapable. Central to these suggestions is the view that a necessary condition for moral conduct is reflection.

It has often been suggested that a moral act is one that springs from instinct, such as maternal instinct driving a mother to defend her children. It has often been suggested that a moral act, such as heroic sacrifice for one's comrades, springs from sheer impulse. It has often been suggested that some feeling, such as love, leads men to regard all men as brothers, and this becomes the essence of the moral act. Many of these acts may indeed be right, or good, or just, and useful and humane. But surely instincts, impulses, and feelings that have these morally valuable results are too exceptional to be trusted generally, and further they do not seem to be necessary. Reflection upon the nature of our act is more essential to the moral economy. Hence we argue that reflection is necessary, but the situations in which we act are far from simple. Consequently we cannot formalize reflection into a rigid or simple pattern of a few premises which yield the concluding answer to our moral problems. But we can suggest thorough reflection upon at least seven elements. Some of these we are often likely to ignore.

The factors in moral deliberation may be summarized in this manner:

1. Knowing the facts relevant to a problem insofar as one is able to discover them.
2. Appreciating the alternative solutions insofar as one can imagine them.
3. Estimating the consequences insofar as one can foresee them. These consequences may be individual and social; immediate and ultimate.
4. Knowing the social customs, laws, and conventions and the determination of one's agreement with them.
5. Projecting oneself imaginatively into the context of those most critically affected by the decision, including one's later self.
6. Accepting critically a theoretical framework insofar as one is able to formulate its principles.
7. Submitting the problem to the attention of a respected critic.

The elements of moral deliberation are then, facts, alternatives, consequences, customs, projection, principles and criticism. Any solution to a moral problem that involves reflection in these areas may be said to be a moral solution, that is, the individual has acted in a moral way even if he could not obtain the approval of most other thinkers.

Let us consider each in turn.

1. If one is to act with deliberation when confronted with a moral problem the relevant facts must be discovered. To act without awareness of facts is no less perilous in ethics than in medicine or business. Accumulation of facts, of course, does not in itself resolve moral quandaries. But the factual data, in so far as one is able to obtain them, may show what solutions are feasible for this particular contingency. The "in so far, etc." is a necessary qualification, because, being ignorant fallible creatures some facts will escape us and others might be impossible to get. Acquiring facts, moreover, is an activity which in itself tends to prevent capricious behavior and is serviceable in creating the readiness to reflect. The opposite of moral deliberation is moral impulsiveness or thoughtlessness, the unhappy consequences of which are sufficiently evident. Furthermore, to labor for the facts forces attention upon the particularity of this morally troublesome event. It may be a decision never faced before, or the repetition of a former one, or it may be only similar in character to another moral struggle. Whatever the case, each ethical encounter has something fresh, something singular and idiosyncratic about it. Trying to make clear the factual picture of the dilemma will help to disclose its peculiarities and may prevent a judgment being made which ignores these features.

There is, of course, an inevitable question. When does one have enough facts to proceed with the deliberation? There is no final answer to this problem. Theoretically one fact might lead to another until the universe itself is inventoried. But most moral issues will not wait for the exhaustive cataloguing of facts. One must, therefore, act when he feels ready to act or prepared to do so. This is a highly personal matter and one for which the individual alone shall assume the responsibility.

2. Procuring the facts relevant to an instance of moral uncertainty is by no means sufficient alone to turn doubt into action. Moreover, the time has not yet arrived when action can appropriately be taken. With the facts at hand, however, we are prepared for the next stage in moral deliberation. This involves the appreciative understanding of the possible alternatives. We discover that very infrequently do the facts allow for only one course of action. Nor can we always narrow the courses to two. Neither are all moral questions commonly simple either-or questions, nor are the solutions simply all black or all white. It is quite reasonable to suppose that a number of solutions may be worked out—some more adequate than others—so far as the particular circumstances are concerned. To see and weigh these alternatives fairly requires a certain tolerance of mind able to distinguish differences in judgment without demanding the acceptance of only one as moral. Moreover, if the deliberation is genuine

and sincere, the alternatives ought to be clearly defined and not merely vaguely and indistinctly set forth.

But not all the alternatives are of equal moral worth, and some are very inadequate. Moral deliberation rules out the latter as unacceptable solutions. No one can be sure, of course, that he has marked out all the alternatives. In comparatively simple moral choices they may be quickly seen because few in number. But in complex problems where there are numerous entangling relationships, it will require considerable effort and time to delineate with precision the various options. It is true here, as in every step of moral deliberation, that the endeavor to frame the alternatives will itself tend to curb thoughtless and impromptu choices in matters of moral doubt. It is not meant that because one has worked out the alternatives that the decision to move in one direction rather than another follows automatically. Resolution of the perplexity does not come so freely. There is still an expenditure of will and work to be made.

3. The third element in the resolution of moral uncertainty is to estimate the consequences which presumably would follow the alternatives. Here again we must allow for human weakness and limitations, and admit that not all the possible consequences can be foreseen. One can only judge for oneself when penetration has been thorough enough. There are no universal rules that operate here. The ability to envision the consequences may depend on wideness of experience and depth of understanding plus an acuteness of intelligence. So perhaps we are morally obligated to enlarge these features of our existence if progress in moral insight is to be won. However, it seems reasonable to say that moral deliberation or reflection would require an anticipation of future events which might be consequents of the alternatives. This is the mark that distinguishes the facts from the consequences. The relevant facts are present events or realities; consequences are future or possible occurrences.

Every moral choice may have consequences in two dimensions, individual-social and immediate-ultimate. A thoughtful weighing of results will have to consider the immediate individual effects and the ultimate individual effects, as well as the immediate social and the ultimate social consequences. The aim to compute and appraise the consequences of a conceivable course of action tends to throw this action against a larger reference of ideas and relationships, which should prohibit a too narrow or mean-spirited judgment. In addition, it ought to forestall a reverberation of unpleasant and unfortunate surprises that so frequently call forth the self-excusing lament "I didn't think." Foreseeing the consequences, therefore, demands an intellectual projection of oneself into the future and into a more extensive sphere of personal and social connections. This should aid in revealing what action is to be preferred and selected. When a person engages in such considerations, along with those previously mentioned and those to be discussed, he can be said to be morally deliberating. If the action is chosen because of these deliberations, he can be said to be acting morally. Josiah Royce endorsed this principle and stated it admirably in these words:

In thy acts treat all the future as if it were present. Let not a consequence believed by thee to be probable, escape thy notice because it is so remote. Suppose that thou hadst to suffer all the consequences at once and at this very instant. What act wouldst thou then think most desirable? Consider and choose that.[60]

A contemporary philosopher puts the point strongly in the following way:

Whenever we are faced with a moral decision of a more abstract kind it is most helpful to analyze carefully the consequences which are likely to result from the alternatives between which we have to choose. For only if we can visualize these consequences in a concrete and practical way do we really know what the decision is about; otherwise we decide blindly. In order to illustrate this point, I may quote a passage from Shaw's *Saint Joan*. The speaker is the chaplain who had stubbornly demanded Joan's death; but when he has seen her at the stake, he breaks down: 'I meant no harm. I did not know what it would be like. . . . I did not know what I was doing. . . . If I had known, I would have torn her from their hands. You don't know. You haven't seen: it is so easy to talk when you don't know. You madden yourself with words. . . . But when it is brought home to you; when you see the thing you have done; when it is blinding your eyes, stifling your nostrils, tearing your heart, then—then—O God, take away this sight from me!' There were, of course, other figures in Shaw's play who knew exactly what they were doing, and yet decided to do it; and who did not regret it afterwards. Some people dislike seeing their fellow men burning at the stake, and others do not. This point (which was neglected by many Victorian optimists) is important, for it shows that a rational analysis of the consequences of a decision does not make the decision rational; the consequences do not determine our decision; it is always we who decide. But an analysis of the concrete consequences, and their clear realization in what we call our 'imagination,' makes the difference between a blind decision and a decision made with open eyes; and since we use our imagination very little, we only too often decide blindly.[61]

[60] Josiah Royce, "Tests of Right and Wrong," *Fugitive Essays*, Harvard University Press, Cambridge, Massachusetts, 1925, p. 209.

[61] K. R. Popper, *The Open Society and Its Enemies*, Routledge & Kegan Paul Ltd., London, 1949, Vol. II, pp. 219–220, Princeton University Press, 1950, p. 418.

4. As moral problems do not emerge in a vacuum free of facts, neither do they rise unrelated to the social conventions, customs, and laws of a given society. Acting intelligently with respect to moral choices would seem to require acquaintance (though not necessarily agreement) with these conventions. It is a commonplace that these customs differ from time to time and from place to place. Awareness of them may not solve one's personal difficulties but it may throw some light on the obscurities and reflect what is or has been the common opinion on these matters. This will give one some idea of what is expected, and perhaps reveal the seriousness of the situation in case he decides not to conform.

It is altogether possible, of course, that one's decision will be a criticism of existing customs and be antithetical to common practice. Historically progress has been attained in this way. Society has on many occasions been shocked out of its ethical complacence by the courage and insight of a singleminded individual in conflict with the rigid certainties of the group. There is doubtless much risk in such opposition. History records that society does not look with favor upon those who step out of line, even if motivated by high ethical aims. Moreover, the funded and condensed wisdom of the majority ought not to be casually treated by one seeking to work his way out of moral confusion. Such wisdom has been tested more than once on the long road from beast to man. To ignore it is a kind of moral myopia. And yet we must allow the freedom to question it, to redefine it, and to refashion it in such a way that it will yield to clearer vision. Thoughtful morality or moral deliberation will, therefore, consider it an obligation to know the commonly accepted and acceptable solutions to moral problems. Then if one wishes to protest against, or to stand in opposition to, or to modify the traditional responses, one is privileged to do so, having given this evidence of the sincerity of one's quest.

5. The next stage in moral deliberation may be described as the imaginative projection of the self into the circumstances and context of those most critically affected by the decision, including the later self. All moral action involves in some way another person or persons, or at least the same self taken at a later date. There is no escape from the relationship to this "other," but one may modify or change completely the nature of the involvement if one is able to appreciate the possible effects of one's actions upon another. This requires the capacity to rehearse imaginatively these effects within an emotional context that is similar to that which might be expected to occur in the life of the other persons. To act as if no other person is involved is to act blindly. To act in spite of other persons, without first seeking to discover the degree and nature of their involvement, is

to act impulsively. Moral deliberation therefore demands that we make an effort to stand in the shoes of those most nearly concerned with our decision, in order to apprehend clearly the possible effects, should action be taken.

To reflect in this way is to conduct a kind of moral experiment. Its aim is to take one out of oneself but not out of the context. It may call forth a feeling of sympathy, responsibility, and unity which could determine the ensuing action. Such imaginative projection is more than an intellectual grasp of the situation from the outside. It is an effort to *be* the other person for a period of time in order to appreciate the full concreteness of the results. Moreover, it functions as a brake on impulse and hasty, ill-considered behavior, thus preparing the way for critical reflection and making possible the development of a new attitude. This practice also is a way of avoiding the fallacy of special pleading. By putting oneself in the place of another, one manifests willingness to apply principles to oneself, and thus one prevents exceptions made in one's own case.

6. Moral action is moral because a principle is consciously applied to a particular case. This is a fundamental and necessary feature of moral deliberation. The principles may not be the same for every instance but where there is no attempt to relate one's action to an accepted principle ethical reflection has stopped short of completion. Thus, so far as practice is concerned, one may be a moral pluralist, that is, one may solve this problem on the basis of a certain principle, but another problem with the aid of a quite different principle.

Nevertheless, that quality of an act which gives it its moral character arises when the act is deliberately chosen because of its pertinence to a clearly formulated and an operative theory. In the history of ethics a number of principles have been proposed. Some of them may be summarily stated as follows:

So act as to fulfill that function which one is designed to perform (Aristotle). So act as to live in accordance with nature (the Stoics). So act as to make the maxim of the action a universal law (Kant). So act as to bring about the greatest amount of happiness to the greatest number (the utilitarians). So act as to be willing to have the act repeated forever (Nietzsche). So act as to be in accord with the will of God (Paley). There are others, but it is pointless to draw out the list. Each of these maxims involves a definition of the good. In the next section we shall consider G. E. Moore's objection to any definition of the good.

Now, after one has marshalled the facts, determined the alternative solutions, examined the consequences, considered the customs, projected oneself into the lives of those most affected by the act, one is prepared to take the next step in deliberation, namely, to formulate the principle or principles which move one to select this action rather than some other. Why is this an important feature of moral decision? First, because it lifts the act out of its particularity and relates it to a universal. It acquires thereby a reasonableness that can be defended. Its primary motive is made clear and personal bias or favor or wishful thinking has been rejected in the process. In the second place, the attempt to formulate the principle of one's action is a sign of one's sincerity, of a genuine effort to see one's problem and its solution in a larger context of relationship than those observable from the self alone, in this particular predicament. This means, moreover, that one is stating a conviction about the values basic to the decision, and also that one is determining one's will to abide by them.

When G. E. Moore considered the question of the relation of ethics to conduct in his classic study, *Principia Ethica,* he said some of the things we have been trying to say. After taking as his principle the following: So act that the action "will cause more good to exist in the universe than any possible alternative," he then says:

In order to shew that any action is a duty, it is necessary to know both what are the other conditions, which will, conjointly with it, determine its effects; to know exactly what will be the effects of these conditions; and to know all the events which will be in any way affected by our action throughout an infinite future. We must have all this causal knowledge, and further we must know accurately the degree of value both of the action itself and of all these effects; and must be able to determine how, in conjunction with the other things in the Universe, they will affect its value as an organic whole. And not only this: we must also possess all this knowledge with regard to the effects of every possible alternative; and must then be able to see by comparison that the total value due to the existence of the action in question will be greater than that which would be produced by any of these alternatives. But it is obvious that our causal knowledge alone is far too incomplete for us ever to assure ourselves of this result. Accordingly it follows that we never have any reason to suppose that an action is our duty: we can never be sure that any action will produce the greatest value possible.

Ethics, therefore, is quite unable to give us a list of duties: but there still remains a humbler task which may be possible for Practical Ethics. Although we cannot hope to discover which, in a given situation, is the best of all possible alternative actions, there may be some possibility of shewing which among the alternatives, *likely to occur to any one,* will produce the greatest sum of good. This second task is certainly all that Ethics can ever have accomplished: and it is certainly all that it has ever collected materials for proving; since no one has ever attempted to exhaust the possible alternative actions in any particular case. Ethical philosophers have in fact confined their attention to a very limited class of actions, which have been selected because they are those which most commonly occur to mankind as possible alternatives. With regard to these they may possibly have shewn that one alternative is better, *i.e.* produces a greater total of value, than others. But it seems desirable to insist, that though they have represented this result as a determination of *duties,* it can never really have been so. For the term duty is certainly so used that, if we are subsequently persuaded that any possible action would have produced more good than the one we adopted, we admit that we failed to do our duty. It will, however, be a useful task if Ethics can determine which among alternatives *likely to occur* will produce the greatest total value. For, though this alternative cannot be proved to be the best possible, yet it may be better than any course of action which we should otherwise adopt.[62]

7. Another feature of moral deliberation is placing the problem before the attention of a respected critic. To bring out the obscure relations and implications of a difficulty one may engage in a discourse in which the problem gets clearly stated and its unknown possibilities are revealed. In this way one may see the perplexity in a different way from a different point of view. The most forceful and convincing illustration of this can be found in the early Dialogues of Plato in which Socrates, by a method of thorough conversation, called dialectic, worked through many moral puzzles. Morality is not merely a matter of action, it is necessarily a matter of thought. Frequently our involvement is so deep we may not be able to think clearly. Not only may our conscious wishes and desires be too persistent, but now, according to Freud, we must take account of possible unconscious wishes and desires. These can scarcely be grasped in true perspective by our own insights. And once again we point out that such an effort, namely, to present the problem to an acceptable critic, will considerably reduce the hazard of rash and impulsive decision. Often enough in other matters, such as health, business procedures, legal questions, even in science when the solution to some abstruse problem eludes us, we seek the critical judgment of another. This is not to suggest that we turn to another for the answer, but rather that the joint probing and pondering may place the problem in a new perspective so that a decision may be made less blindly. Of course, this too may become an interminable process, and perhaps also be a way of seeking support for a judgment already decided upon but not disclosed. But these are risks that must be accepted. It is not merely approval that one seeks, for even after prolonged discussion it is conceivable that one could refuse to adopt the recommendations. Rather it is to get things as straight as possible so that the decision which

[62] G. E. Moore, *Principia Ethica,* Cambridge University Press, Cambridge, 1954, pp. 149–150.

ultimately must be made is not marred by ignorance nor by failure to take into account anything relevant to the problem.

It is evident that this discussion makes little sense unless we can accept the idea that our deliberative and reflective powers make a difference when we make choices. And this is all that we need mean by *free will*. The indeterminists and determinists have battled long, and often bitterly, about the actuality of free choice. The arguments strike one as full of vague and ambiguous terms but the authors have neither the inclination nor the space to review this persistent controversy. Some indeterminists have put themselves in the absurd position of saying, or implying, that our choices, moral or otherwise, have no relationship to our habits, character, or previous actions, so that every action comes as it were from out of the nowhere. Some determinists, in their zeal to show the absurdities of indeterminism, have put themselves in the equally questionable position of saying, or implying, that all human decision and choice is illusory, and that how a man thinks or feels is not a factor in the final choice. Some determinists find it convenient to forget Hume's argument against necessary connection in their eagerness to establish a science of man. It is true, of course, that Hume himself sometimes argues as though natural law predetermined results of any cause. They seem to accept uncritically the "causal uniformity of nature" and extend it hopefully to psychology and sociology. But does freedom mean exemption from causality? Must the indeterminist accept this from the determinist? We do not think so. All we wish to say is that among the factors leading to a decision is man's capacity to reflect on the facts, consequences, alternatives, and so on. That is, to think his way through.

When confronted by a choice we are aware of three things: First, that two or more courses of action may be taken; second, that all one's history, physiological, psychological, and social does not coerce or compel or drive one in any direction, although it may "tend" to move one, or "suggest" that we move in one way rather than another; third, that *no action will take place* unless we do decide. It is the third point that is so often overlooked. It cannot be denied that glandular secretions, past experiences, environmental conditions, and so on determine to some degree our conduct and the choices we make. All we wish to insist on is that thought, anticipations, imagination, and memory are also relevant to human behavior and may even dominate, in a given situation, the other influences, sufficiently to modify the outcome.

The free-willists make chaotic and capricious our moral life if they mean by free will some kind of mysterious force that has no antecedents whatever. They sometimes claim that without free will the moral life becomes unintelligible because the idea of responsibility collapses—and without this notion we cannot have morality. What is it then to be responsible? It is to acknowledge one's acts as one's own, and hence to be judged by them, either praised or blamed. A person, then, is accountable for all he has deliberately done. And every act can be ascribed to someone as its cause. This is a common presupposition, although certain exceptions are made in law for "acts of God." If this belief generally is acceptable, what must be supposed? That there is continuity in one's life such that at a later date it is the same person who did something the consequences of which have become apparent. Therefore responsibility is founded on the notion that I am the causal agent of my acts and that indirectly the consequences of my acts are mine also.

There must be some identity of each agent, sometimes called the "self." Otherwise a person might have indeed the continuity of a material substance, but as a person he would be only a bundle of associated reactions and thoughts, one reaction or thought constantly replacing another. But even on the level of physical behavior there is continuity in the learning process, such that what we have learned to do, up to a limit, we can do again with increasing efficiency. On the level of deliberated conduct, we formulate a similarly continuing pattern sometimes called character, or the disposition to make certain kinds of choices. Hence if moral acts spring from personal choice, they are not uninfluenced by learning and character, and indeed coherent choices depend on being made within a settled context. But this is not to say that the act is nothing but the result of prior habituation. For reflection, as we have argued, makes us aware of alternative responses, between which we may choose and thus strengthen the disposition to act. Therefore the act is a reasoned consequence. Sometimes a person who is blamed attempts to shift responsibility to external circumstances, his environment, even to his unknown impulses. But these are factors that contribute to the act, necessary but not sufficient to the act, and not the locus of praise or blame. The inadequacy of making any factor or all the factors the sufficient ground of a moral act is the sound point on the side of free will, and the point is made to explicate a precondition of moral action.

What has been said here by no means resolves the complexities of human moral freedom. There are far too many issues requiring careful analysis for us to have more than a tentative satisfaction with the above approach. There seems to be little doubt about the fact that we do at times *feel* free, and that we do at times act *as if* we were free; but it is hard to get these facts expressed without conceptual confusion.

To meet a moral problem in the ways suggested may not lead to sainthood, nor to popularity, nor perhaps, even to personal happiness. But it should place one in a situation where one can defend one's choice and action, and be less susceptible to unfavorable judgment and condemnation. One of the greatest moral maxims ever stated is: "Let him without sin cast the first stone." Too much of our moral life is given to blaming and judging the actions of another. But if a person has demonstrated that he was or is troubled, and it may be, tormented, by his ethical confusion, and has with care and deliberation sought to work his way out, then for all practical purposes he is a moral being and he ought to be welcomed into the society of reasonable people.

What is the consequence of our fallibility, our ignorance of all the relevant facts bearing on a problem, our failure not only to know all the alternative solutions, but our failure to come to terms with all the consequences, particularly those remote in time, and effects on persons unknown to us, some of whom do not now exist, and our ignorance of their good, and our ignorance of the limitation of our principles? The consequence is that however defensible our act, it may seem ultimately to have been wrong. Since we never know and imagine all we could, every act is one that convicts us of guilt. Therefore all men are guilty. And the tragic situation of man is that none of us can, in the light of consequences and hindsight, revert to a former temporal point, and take some alternative solution. Consequently all men must live with regrets and stand in need of forgiveness. These features of the human situation have been especially stressed by existentialists. Atheistic existentialists allow us to writhe with nausea in our imprisonment, from which there is no exit; theistic existentialists encourage us to throw ourselves on the mercy of God.

VII. Fallacies in Our Beliefs about Ethical Values

It is common in the ethics of our day to discuss the fallacies we are likely to commit in our process of arguing value judgments. It has indeed been proposed that there really is no argument involved in making a value judgment, and where there is no argument, there can scarcely be an invalid one. If this situation is confusing to one beginning a study of ethics, it is also a matter of perplexity to many who are old hands in this field. It is not a waste of time to learn why some philosophers have denied that reason plays any part in purely evaluative statements, and why other philosophers consider valid argument possible in this area. Surely if our search is for beliefs that can be defended empirically or deduced, we should know whether this is possible when we are dealing with the alleged value of acts. If these well-publicized errors in argument can be identified early in our consideration of any problem, we shall spare ourselves much fruitless time wasted by our predecessors. Further, such identification is generally considered an exceedingly powerful weapon both by the one who uses it and the one who finds his argument attacked.

Let us cite the most celebrated example in ethics. G. E. Moore in his Principia Ethica, 1903, and Ethics, 1912, attacked virtually all theories based upon defining good either in terms of the nature of God or of evolutionary progress. Indeed to identify good, in his special moral sense, with any other characteristic seemed to Moore the root fallacy of nearly all ethical systems. Earlier we considered his attack upon Mill and any identification of good with happiness. This effort to reduce the meaning of good to something else Moore called the *naturalistic fallacy*.

The student may be puzzled by the presentation in ethics of fallacies not included in the standard types named and illustrated earlier. The explanation offered by some Aristotelian philosophers is that the reasoning in morality concludes not with a proposition that is purely cognitive, but with knowledge of what ought to be done, or with the act of choosing and doing. Since the conclusion is what they call a judgment of moral conscience or a judgment of election, the syllogism is known as the *practical syllogism*. Examples are needed.

> Every evil is to be avoided. . . .
> Adultery is evil because prohibited by the law of God. . . .
> This act of adultery is to be avoided. . . .

This is from St. Thomas. It seems to draw a particular conclusion from universal premises. One may well wonder, however, whether the singular emphasis on "this act" is logically warranted by two universal premises. Indeed this is what Nietzsche attacked, because it removed morality from the circumstances that were called to attention in the preceding section. Moore also would of course object to an effort to ground moral decision in the law of God. Can good mean commanded by the law of God, and evil prohibited by the law of God? It would seem that God must then himself be good. But what would then be meant by God's being good? That God is commanded by the law of God? Rather than this mystery or tautology that God's will is God's will, it would seem preferable to establish a meaning of good independent of God. And indeed if we merely move from good to God and from God to good and from good back to God this kind of ethic would seem to be viciously circular.

Another example from St. Thomas:

I should not kill my father. . . .
This man is my father. . . .
I will not kill this man. . . .[63]

These examples show us at least that moral reasoning is not simply deductive or inductive. And in the last example there occurs "should" in the premise but "will" in the conclusion. This may be harmless, but some shifts seem vicious. David Hume was struck by the contrast between reasoning that joins terms with "is" (or "are")and reasoning that employs "ought."

I cannot forbear adding to these reasonings an observation, which may, perhaps, be found of some importance. In every system of morality, which I have hitherto met with, I have always remarked, that the author proceeds for some time in the ordinary way of reasoning, and establishes the being of a God, or makes observations concerning human affairs; when of a sudden I am surprised to find, that instead of the usual copulations of propositions, *is* and *is not*, I meet with no proposition that is not connected with an *ought*, or an *ought not*. This change is imperceptible; but is, however, of the last consequence. For as this *ought*, or *ought not*, expresses some new relation or affirmation, it is necessary that it should be observed and explained; and at the same time that a reason should be given, for what seems altogether inconceivable, how this new relation can be a deduction from others, which are entirely different from it. But as authors do not commonly use this precaution, I shall presume to recommend it to the readers; and am persuaded that this small attention would subvert all the vulgar systems of morality, and let us see that the distinction of vice and virtue is not founded merely on the relations of objects, nor is perceived by reason.[64]

Now if one looks back to the example suggested by St. Thomas, it will be seen that the major premise might be rewritten with no violence to meaning, "I ought not to kill my father." The rule, then, seems to be this: *at least one premise in an argument concluding with a moral judgment must itself be a moral judgment.* Perhaps this could be generalized, *if the evaluative conclusion validly follows in any argument, there must be some evaluative premise.* These rules are special cases of the principle that you cannot validly get in the conclusion what is not in the premises.

[63] Vernon J. Bourke, *Ethics,* The Macmillan Co., New York, 1953, pp. 222–227.
[64] David Hume, *Treatise of Human Nature,* Everyman Edition, E. P. Dutton & Co., Inc., New York, 1920, Vol. II, pp. 177–178.

Now we can apply Hume's principle to his great successor John Stuart Mill. In his Utilitarianism Mill argued as follows:

The only proof capable of being given that an object is visible, is that people actually see it. The only proof that a sound is audible is that people hear it; and so of the other sources of our experience. In like manner, I apprehend the sole evidence it is possible to produce that anything is desirable is that people do actually desire it.

This is the best advertised fallacy in moral philosophy. What is the fallacy? "Visible" means what can be seen, but does "desirable" mean what can be desired? The usual meaning of "desirable" is that something *ought* to be desired.[65]

If this is a fallacy, whenever we attempt to draw an evaluation from factual premises, we are reasoning invalidly. Suppose we say that Hitler and Stalin were good rulers because their nations gave them overwhelming majority support. That would not prove it. Suppose we reason from statistical surveys of sexual behavior, as is frequent in the Kinsey reports, that because such and such is done therefore it is "not the intellectually contrived perversion which it has sometimes been considered." This would not follow from the Kinsey statistics, though it might unquestionably from other and unstated premises. What would a value premise be like that would permit us to reason validly from statistical premises to value conclusions? Simply this, "Whatever happens in a majority of cases (or any other percentage) is what ought to happen."

Now the question becomes one of meaning. Do we mean by "good" or "right" or "ought" or "beautiful" or any other value term, simply that a certain number of persons has acted or chosen in a given way? If this were the case, all normative questions could be settled by a definition and sociological statistics. In this case all value terms may be replaced by factual terms. Then we may say quite logically that whatever happens in a majority of cases is what happens in a majority of cases. Presumably we know this tautology from logical principles alone.

But the move from this empty identity to any answer to such questions as "What ought I to do?" or "Ought this act to be praised or blamed?" or "What is the good?" is fallacious. To answer these questions one employs some value premise, and logicians who have taken evaluation seriously attack many chains of reasoning because they beg the question. "Because this is done by a majority, therefore it ought to be done" assumes "what is

[65] A claim has been made that Mill's argument is not fallacious. See, e.g., E. W. Hall, "Mill's Proof of Utility." In: Sidney Hook (ed.), *American Philosophers at Work*, Criterion Books, Inc., New York, 1956, p. 360.

done by a majority ought to be done"—which is what it pretends to demonstrate.

One application is of great interest. F. S. C. Northrop notes that the prevailing theory of law is that empirical methods can reveal what the legal norms are by discovering the existing social practices. Is an act legally right if all or most people do it? "This commits, of course . . . the same culturalistic fallacy of identifying the 'ought' for society with the 'is' of that society, which occurred in the case of the Hegelians and the Marxians."[66] The chapters in political philosophy and philosophy of history showed how common it is to identify the best state with some actual state, as Hegel did, and Fascists after him, or to identify the best state with some future state, as Marx did, and Communists after him.

The naturalistic fallacy of G. E. Moore is one of the most celebrated contributions to twentieth-century ethics. Almost every consideration of moral beliefs since Moore has devoted a chapter to it, and there are many subsequent attempts to redefine the fallacy or to show that it is no fallacy at all.[67]

Moore's question is "What, then, is good? How is good to be defined?" He does not wish a stipulation or a verbal definition; he wishes to state what he is thinking of when the word is used in its ordinary sense.

> But, if we understand the question in this sense, my answer to it may seem a very disappointing one. If I am asked 'What is good?' My answer is that good is good, and that is the end of the matter. Or if I am asked 'How is good to be defined?' my answer is that it cannot be defined, and that is all I have to say about it. But disappointing as these answers may appear, they are of the very last importance. To readers who are familiar with philosophic terminology, I can express their importance by saying that they amount to this: that propositions about the good are all of them synthetic and never analytic; and that is plainly no trivial matter. And the same thing may be expressed more popularly, by saying that, if I am right, then nobody can foist upon us such an axiom as that 'Pleasure is the only good' or that 'The good is the desired' on the pretense that this is 'the very meaning of the word.'[68]

Moore explains that he means by definition the enumeration of parts as, e.g., a horse is "a hoofed quadruped of the genus *Equus*." But that which is simple, having no parts, cannot be defined, for example, the notion of "yellow." Although "all things which are good are *also* something else, just

[66] F. S. C. Northrop, *Meeting of East and West,* The Macmillan Co., New York, 1946, p. 255.

[67] W. Sellars and John Hospers (eds.), *Readings in Ethical Theory,* Appleton-Century-Crofts, New York, 1952, II: "Moore and the Naturalistic Fallacy," III: "The Development of Ethical Intuitionism," IV: "The Naturalistic Rejoinder."

[68] *Ibid.,* p. 70.

as it is true that all things which are yellow produce a certain kind of vibration"; to name these other properties is not to define good or yellow.[69]

Moore's attack is aimed particularly against hedonism's definition that good means pleasure and pleasure means good. If that is the case, the hedonist says only that pleasure is pleasure. He cannot mean anything by "Pleasure is good" unless good means something other than pleasure. The same holds for those who say good means normal, or more evolved or according to God's will.[70]

What basis has Moore for his attack upon all these various forms of the naturalistic fallacy?

Whoever will attentively consider with himself what is actually before his mind when he asks the question 'Is pleasure (or whatever it may be) after all good?' can easily satisfy himself that he is not merely wondering whether pleasure is pleasant. And if he will try this experiment with each suggested definition in succession, he may become expert enough to recognize that in every case he has before his mind a unique object. . . .[71]

One important criticism of Moore is that the "fallacy" is not an error in reasoning. Professor W. K. Frankena asks us to consider this syllogism:

Pleasure is sought by all men.
What is sought by all men is good (definition).
Therefore, pleasure is good.[72]

There is no error in reasoning here. Therefore, since Moore's objection is to the second statement, the definition, Frankena names the error the *definist fallacy*. But is this a logical confusion, or an error? No, he answers, it is simply that the hedonist claims no awareness of any unique property "good" distinct from "pleasure." Therefore, what Moore attacked was "rather a kind of blindness, analogous to colour-blindness."[73]

We have raised the question whether the romantic or pathetic fallacy applies to all value judgments, that is, those of aesthetics and ethics. If the fallacy impugns all moral judgments, then it could be said that nothing is good or bad but feeling makes it so. If all moral judgment is the ascription of properties to things, which properly should be predicated only of persons, then indeed the judgment is fallacious. We would not be able to defend moral judgments as Ruskin defended poetic expression, for the moral judge is expected to be self-critical and deliberate rather than passionate.

[69] *Ibid.*, p. 73.
[70] *Ibid.*, pp. 74–75.
[71] *Ibid.*, p. 77.
[72] *Ibid.*, p. 107.
[73] *Ibid.*, p. 112.

But it is presupposed by those who impugn all moral judgments as cases of the pathetic fallacy that the moral quality is something "over and above," as Paul Edwards says, the natural qualities of a thing or person. Thus if it is said that "Hitler was a bad man" it is presupposed that in addition to all the characteristics that define him as a man, there is another quality, namely, his badness. Now if the charge of the pathetic fallacy is tantamount to the judgment that moral quality is something in addition to natural qualities, then one may conclude with Paul Edwards that the charge is not well-founded. For if we mean that Hitler's badness is integral to his character as a man, then the judgment that he was a bad man does not commit the pathetic fallacy. Of course, if goodness or badness or any other value quality is "over and above" other natural qualities, then the attack is justified.[74] We are thus brought around to the momentous choice between beliefs in value subjectivism and value objectivism with which this chapter began.

VIII. Concluding Remarks

The authors have not dealt in this chapter with all the great questions of ethical reflection. Rarely have we mentioned problems of right and justice, because we had considered these topics as central to political philosophy. Perhaps we have not committed ourselves morally, and seemed in the discussion of the alternative systems of Mill, Kant, and Bradley to do little more than stress wherein each feels the others' systems fail. Yet we included as an element in the ethical situation the critical acceptance of principles. Have we, then, come to the frustrated conclusion that the full range of problems is too much for us and that no one system will apply equally well in all cases, yet urged you to adopt some set of principles? We did just that, and in some ways this is a recognition that moral principles are inevitably dependent upon human beings who are potentially moral. Yet we have not excluded the possibility that an adequate ethics may be developed only in a larger metaphysical context, which may be a naturalism or a theism. You would do well to remember that many acute contemporaries adopt an ethics in the metaphysical tradition of St. Thomas Aquinas or Spinoza. But inevitably the affirmation of principles is also a matter of choice, and cannot be imposed from outside by society. Philosophy ought not to produce dogmatists. Since your moral beliefs are what you live by, these should come from the established patterns of choice, which we called character. Even the most critical linguistic

---

[74] Paul Edwards, *The Logic of Moral Discourse*, The Free Press, Glencoe, Illinois, 1955, Ch. III examines theories that draw this conclusion in ethics and in aesthetics.

analysis of the language of moral judgment, that of G. E. Moore, was elaborated by a man of singular honesty and rectitude. Examine, therefore, the alternative theories, in conjunction with some substantive study of man and society and commit yourself to what seems the best life. You may, in the light of the consequences, discover a preferable alternative. And remember, as of all beliefs, there are alternatives that should be respected and understood. Doubtless, minds aware of the variety of beliefs are better fitted to live in a world in military and economic rivalry, but increasingly in need of common understanding of alternative beliefs in order to avoid another war of fanatical creeds. We dare not hope for a peace based on universal agreement, nor would we wish one universal creed, particularly since this would rob men of individual freedom. But we dare to hope for a future in which true and beneficial beliefs will flourish on their merits and not on the basis of any authority imposing them. To this end we have written, and this hope of ours is too deeply founded in philosophy as the analysis of belief for us to wish to conceal it—and we hope it is worthy of wide acceptance.

PROBLEMS FOR THOUGHT AND DISCUSSION

1. Some philosophers have felt deeply the difficulty of escaping from ethical subjectivity, or basing one's judgments on a "moral sensitivity." Bertrand Russell, for example, has written:

I cannot see how to refute the arguments for the subjectivity of ethical values, but I find myself incapable of believing that all that is wrong with wanton cruelty is that I don't like it. I have no difficulty in practical moral judgments, which I find that I make on a roughly hedonistic basis, but, when it comes to the philosophy of moral judgments, I am impelled in two opposite directions and remain perplexed.[75]

Do you think there is a way out of relativism and subjectivity? Or any convincing arguments for the objectivity of moral judgments?
2. That there are wide differences in ethical beliefs, practices, and regulations is well known. Examine the account below. Does it seem to support the view that all matters of ethics are culturally relative? What kind of data and arguments would you offer in opposition to cultural relativism? What conflicts between the anthropological approach and that of Kant's and Mill's do you observe?

There are societies in which it is required that you eat your deceased friend or brother to show your respect for him; others in which a cannibal feast on an enemy is an everyday event, and supplying this special game for the larder a required mark of adult status. There are societies where to eat your own crops, grown in your own garden, or the game bagged by your own hunting efforts, is out of the question, wrong in all the ways in which stealing is wrong in our own morality—offensive to gods

[75] Bertrand Russell, "Notes on Philosophy," *Philosophy*, January, Vol. 35, No. 133, 1960, pp. 146–147.

and men, indicative of a generally bad character, ringed around with evil consequences both social and supernatural—in short, a form of wickedness so wrong that
for the average man it is not usually even an admitted temptation. And there are
other societies where a man will die of some compound of shame, guilt, remorse or
fear if he finds that he has carelessly eaten a guinea hen with a forbidden pattern of
markings on its feathers. There are societies where the young are permitted far more
sexual freedom than we would allow, but where no man may decently eat in the
presence of anyone but a very close relative. And others where extra-marital sex relations between mature adults are ordinarily of no moral import whatsoever—matters entirely of the desires and preferences of the parties involved—but become horrifying
scandals if they are engaged in at some disapproved time or place.

The same kind of variety that is found in peoples' rules of behavior is found in their
ideals of character, in their concepts of virtue and vice and in their goals of life.
Anger and shouting may be offensive, abominable to the gods and dangerous; or they
may be an admired demonstration of strength of character, pointed to for children
to emulate as a model of respected masculine behavior.

Plains Indian honors go to the young warrior brave enough to go through the lines
of an enemy encampment to steal a tethered horse. To a warrior in another part of
the world that would be foolhardy; his own bravery can include ambush, or sudden
treachery, and most certainly the good sense of running away from danger. Others
abhor fighting altogether and do all they can to minimize it. Among the Trobriand
islanders of the South Pacific a basic code of mutual obligation is so ingrained that
a man will abandon a day's highly paid pearl diving for a puzzled white trader in
order to do a day's fishing for an inland neighbor in return for a few yams or other
farm produce, because the obligations to a trading partner must always be fulfilled. But
their neighbors from the nearby island of Dobu who also live by a complicated system
of trade relations, consider any cheating one can actually get away with as a mark of
the greatest shrewdness, an admired stepping-stone to success. To have enough to eat,
to have sons, and to die in respected old age on one's own ancestral land, is the
conscious goal of some peoples' striving, while others are concerned with wealth or
glory or power, and will see such pursuits as the proper aim of a good life.[76]

3. The relation between morality and religion is not always clear. A recent
    writer has this to say:

> The view has often been advanced, firstly that there can be no morality in the
> proper sense unless worth and obligation are independent of our own inclinations and
> reactions, and secondly that there cannot be this independence in the way required
> unless our standards are imposed or established by God or in some other way due to
> Him. The attractiveness of this view is obvious. It provides for morality the firmest
> possible foundation, and, at the same time it gives to morality that central place in re-
> ligion which seems to be its due. Morality and religion we feel to be closely intertwined,
> and the account of them just noted seems best fitted to this justice.
>
> Nonetheless I think the argument a specious and misleading one.[77]

Do you also think the argument is specious? Why? In what senses is morality
independent of religion?

4. It is often said that perplexities concerning what should be done can be
    resolved by "listening to conscience," or "reading the Bible," or "asking the
    Pope," etc. What are the strengths and weaknesses of such answers?
5. Discuss the differences between the following pairs of statements: "You ought

---

[76] From May Edel and Abraham Edel, *Anthropology and Ethics*. Courtesy of the
authors and Charles C Thomas, Springfield, Illinois, 1959, pp. 20–21.

[77] H. D. Lewis, *Our Experience of God*, The Macmillan Co., New York, 1959, p.
265.

to keep your promises" and "You ought to change the oil in your car every thousand miles"; "It is wrong to cause unnecessary pain deliberately" and "It is wrong to wear a white tie with a dinner jacket"; "Hitler was a bad man" and "Hitler was a bad painter."

6. Consider the remark made by the co-pilot of the Enola Gay—the airplane that carried the atomic bomb over Hiroshima—"My God, what have we done." Do you think this is merely an ejaculation of disapproval, or perhaps of regret, or of horror? Is it merely an expression of his emotions? Or is there an implicit judgment of a different sort present?

7. A contemporary Protestant theologian and critic of political life bases his ethical system on what he calls the "perfectionism of Jesus' love ethic." He considers this relevant because it "sets itself uncompromisingly not only against the natural self-regarding impulses, but against the necessary prudent defense of the self, required because of the egoism of others." Since individual self-interest breeds social disharmony and violent class conflict, not to mention personal aggrandizement, there must be some "morality of impulse" as well as of reason to break through narrow vision and calculation of "what's in it for me." Do you find that moralities of self-interest lead to bad results? If so, do they justify Niebuhr's case for "the motive power of a love which transcends the impulses of nature . . . a combination of obedience to God and love of God?"

8. Since the rise of totalitarian dictatorship there has been in Europe and the United States a revival of "natural law" jurisprudence. Often an appeal to moral justice is identified, as in our tradition, with God. What do you think of the following position:

The idea of justice and the concept of divine law of justice are one and the same thing. That is not a philosophical theory nor a religious opinion which may be agreed to or dissented from. Whoever says with serious intent, 'That is just' or 'That is unjust' has, even though unwittingly, appealed to a superhuman, supreme or ultimate tribunal, to a standard which transcends all human laws, contracts, customs and usages, a standard by which all these human standards are measured.[78]

Is Brunner's position, as he claims, the only valid alternative to arbitrary government, that is, a system that justifies any claim by "reason of state"?

9. David Hume believed that a concept of justice "is absolutely requisite to the well-being of mankind and the existence of society." Men create the idea to keep society in order. The basic need, according to this theory, springs from private property. If everyone had enough property for his own needs there would be no litigation in which rules of justice are applied.

The necessity of justice to the support of society is the sole foundation of that virtue, and since no moral excellence is more highly esteemed, we may conclude that this circumstance of usefulness is, in general, the strongest energy and most entire command over our sentiments.

How does this theory of Hume's square with his attack on slipping from factual "is" to evaluative "ought"?

[78] Emil Brunner, *Justice and the Social Order*, Lutterworth Press, London, 1945, p. 47.

PERTINENT READINGS

Aristotle, *The Nicomachean Ethics* (D. P. Chase, tr.) Everyman Edition, E. P. Dutton & Co., Inc., New York, 1930.

Beauvoir, Simone de, *The Ethics of Ambiguity* (Bernard Frechtman, tr.), Philosophical Library, Inc., New York, 1948.

Broad, C. D., *Five Types of Ethical Theory*, Routledge & Kegan Paul, Ltd., London, 1956.

Hare, R. M., *The Language of Morals*, The Clarendon Press, Oxford, 1952.

Mandelbaum, Maurice, *The Phenomenology of Moral Experience*, The Free Press, Glencoe, Illinois, 1955.

Plato, *Gorgias* (W. C. Helmbold, tr.), The Liberal Arts Press, Inc., New York, 1952.

Rice, Philip Blair, *On the Knowledge of Good and Evil*, Random House, New York, 1955.

Scheler, Max, *The Nature of Sympathy* (Peter Heath, tr.), Routledge & Kegan Paul, Ltd., London, 1954.

Sellars, Wilfrid, and John Hospers, *Readings in Ethical Theory*, Appleton-Century-Crofts, Inc., New York, 1952.

Index of Names

655

Index of Terms

This index is designed to aid the reader in locating definitions in the text. Since we have included many alternative definitions, a glossary of reasonable length could not be prepared without arbitrarily stressing certain meanings and neglecting others. We have used a stroke "/," to indicate an important distinction, but the degree of opposition varies from case to case.

Faith *(Cont.)*
    scientific, 276
    in substance (Santayana), 353
Fallacies
    formal
        self-referential propositions, 270–271
        simple conversion or false conversion, 105–106, 170
    formal hypothetical syllogistic
        affirming the consequent, 116
        denying the antecedent, 116
    formal syllogistic
        four terms, 112
        illicit major, 112–113
        illicit minor, 113
        negative premises, 113
        undistributed middle, 112
    linguistic
        argument from definition, 213
        confusing predicational and existential propositions, 265
        equivocation, 123, 493–495
        extension of reference to unknown, 263–265
        in history, 408–409
        mistaking abstract for concrete terms (reification, hypostatization, misplaced concreteness), 268–270
        in politics, 493–495
    material
        a dicto simpliciter (accident), 124
        causal, in history, 409–411, *See also* post hoc ergo propter hoc, 124
        composition, 123–124
        division, 123–124
        evaluational
            in aesthetics, 594–599
            in ethics, 643–650
            in history, 411–413
            in politics, 498–499
        evaluational, types of
            affective, 595–596
            biological, 597–598
            culturalistic, 647
            definist, 648
            ethical, 597–598
            intentional, 595–596
            mechanical, 597–598
            naturalistic, 595–596, 644, 647–648
            pathetic, 594–595
            realistic, 598–599
            romantic, 597–598, 648–649
        false analogy, 497
        hasty generalization, 495–496
        ontologizing, 107, 266–268, 525–526, *See also* Ontological argument

petitio principii (begging the question, arguing in a circle), 124, 271–273
    in ethics, 646–647
    in history, 406–408
    post hoc ergo propter hoc, 124
    origin of (Bacon's account), 65–66
False, Falsehood, Falsity. *See* True, Truth, Theories of Truth
Falsify, Falsification. *See* Verification
Fascism (Mussolini's definition), 501
Feeling
    belief defined as a feeling, 76
Final cause, 52
Finiteness of God in power and knowledge, 532–535
First cause, 358
Form
    aesthetic, 585–594
    Aristotelian, 214–216, 588, *See also* Universals
    logical structure of argument, 94
    perceptual/mathematical, 592
    Platonic, 26–27, *See also* Universals
    various definitions, 588–589
Form/Matter, 50–51, 588
Formal cause, 52
Formal proof, 122
Formalism, an ethics of duty, 613–620
    criticized, 625–628
Free from/Free to, 466
Freedom, a family of meanings
    aesthetic, 582–583, 584–585
    moral, 641–643
    political liberty, 462–466, 494
Function
    theory of art, 593, 603
    theory of mind as, 320–321
Future, concern with, 392

Generalization, 205
Genetic fallacy, 262
God
    Aquinas' argument, 59, 509–514
    Aristotle's conception, 52
    Berkeley's conception, 74
    characterized as the One, 55
    Creator/Son/Spirit (Trinity), 571
    Duns Scotus, conception, 61
    existence of, 168, 508–531
    and government, 472–473
    Hebrew and Christian conception, 393–394
    Hume's difficulty, 531
    intellectual and emotional requirements (James), 295
    as limited in power (Plato, Mill, James, Brightman), 532–535

Infinite regress, impossible in a proof, 132, 171, 229, 509–512
Inspiration theory of art, 570–572
Instrumentalism, defined, 85
a theory of truth (Dewey), 165
Intentions, 217–218, 596
Interaction theory of mind, 319
Internationalism
Kant's ideal, 489–492
Intuition, 18
Bergson, 188
Northrop, 189
Spinoza, 71
Is, seven senses (Santayana), 252–253, *See also* Being
-isms, *See also* Systems
uninformative names, 285

Justice, a family of meanings, 460–462
conditions of (Kant), 490–492
ultimately divine/ultimately economic, 652–653

'Knowing'/'Believing,' 12–13
alternative distinctions, 40–41, 187–188
Kant's distinction, 12–13
Pasteur's distinction, 25
Plato's distinction, 26
Ryle's distinction, 12
Knowing, ways of, 64, *See also* Universals, Empiricism, Rationalism, Pragmatism
Bacon, 65–66
blood-knowing (D. H. Lawrence), 244
Descartes, 68–69, 127–129, 182–185
Galileo, 66–67
Spinoza, 69–70
Knowing how/Knowing that, 190
Knowledge, *See also* Knowing, ways of
a priori, 78
analytic and synthetic, 204–213
Aristotle's conception, 50
A. J. Ayer's definition, 192
of historical events, 413–427
C. I. Lewis' definition, 191
of material things, 193–199
mystical, 526–528
identity of knower and known, 55, 188–189
of other minds, 199–204
Plato's definition, 50
as practical and power, 65, 190
precludes doubt, 186
of relations, 226–239
relativist theory of, 239–243
requires classification, 50
requires measurement, 66–67
result of sense-perception, 53–54

of self (McTaggart), 364
of universals, 214–226
Knowledge/True opinion, 47

Language
descriptive phrase/names, 281
of historical discourse, 414–417, 421–427
literal/figurative, 179
logical or syncategorematic, 218
and metaphysics, 249–273, 352–353
moral, 411–413, 438–450
names, general/particular, 221–222
object-language, 280
objective-metaphysical, 173
ordinary, 421–424
ordinary/artificial, 175
parts of speech
philosophers neglect verbs and prepositions (Russell), 222–223
political and social, 455–457
scientific, 424–427
sign/referent, 173
sign/signal, 225–226
Law, Descriptive/Prescriptive, 544
Law
natural, 472–473, 483–486
obedience to, five theories, 467–477
rule of, 463–464
universal (Dante), 483–486, (Kant), 489–492
Laws
of history, 425–426
of logic, 205–206, *See also* Principles
of nature, 132
distinguished from probabilities, 285
Liberty, political, 462–466
Lie, 614–617, *See also* Truth-telling
Limitation, 379
of God's power, 533
Linguistic analysis, *See* Language, Analysis, Meaning
Logic, defined, 31
ambiguity of term, 92–93
as inquiry (Dewey), 85
and mathematics, 119, 73, 205
and Socrates, 47
subject-predicate/relational, 352
Logical positivism, 87–88
Love
McTaggart's conception, 366
Niebuhr's conception, 652

Man
as affective, 55
as aspect of reality, 70

Man (*Cont.*)
　body-soul distinction denied, 424, *See
　　also* Mind
　contradictory views in social sciences,
　　311
　distinguished by symbolism, 225
　fixed nature denied, 370–371
　humanist-theist views of, 440–450, *See
　　also* Progress, Providence
　immortal in six ways (Weiss), 545–547,
　　See also Immortality
　individual or social, 454–457, 620–629
　like a god, 541
　as rational, 51–52, 53
　revealed in despair, 89
　views of in social contract theories, 467–
　　470
　as voluntary, 53, 79–80, 81
　wisdom of, 610–613
Marxism, *See* Dialectical materialism
Material cause, 52
Material things, knowledge of, 193–199
Materialism, 321, 324–341
　ally of science, 332–336
　ancient atomism, 328
　anti-supernaturalism, 328
　and hedonism (Epicurus), 605
　matter only substance, power, or agency
　　(Santayana), 356–360
　modern evolutionary view, 332
　objections to (Whitehead), 340
　primacy of matter, 332, 334
　view of causal efficacy, 326
　view of derivation of mind, 326
　view of organization, 327
　view of society, 327
　view of substance, 325
　view of values, 327
Mathematics
　related to philosophy, 68, 184–185, 219–
　　221
　truths of, analytic or synthetic, 208–
　　210
Matter
　ambiguity of, 357
　analogical meaning (St. Thomas), 264
　common sense view clarified (Broad),
　　325
　field of action (Santayana), 358
　pure potency (St. Thomas), 59
　spatial extension (Descartes), 269
　unconscious monads, 71
　view of physics popularized (Russell),
　　326
Matter/Mind, 316–317, *See also* Mind
Meaning
　by agreement/by similarity, 217–218

　alternative modes of, 276
　empirical criterion of (Ayer), 259–260
　of historical process, 446–447
　of historical reference, 172
　natural/artificial, 217–218
　pragmatic theory of, 84
　question of, prior to question of truth,
　　165–166
　subject-matter of 20th century philos-
　　ophy, 88–89
　true meaning discovered through other
　　minds, 201
　words without natural meaning, 97
Meaningless
　abstract ideas, 219–220
　idealist-realist dispute (Ayer), 259–260
　the logically absurd, 162, 164
　question, 168
　self-reference, 178
　use of categories beyond experience
　　(Kant), 257
Mechanism,
　categories of, 327
　use of machine analogy, 264
Mercy, 462
Metaphysics, definitions of
　Aristotle, 246
　Ayer, 258
　Bergson, 248
　Blanshard, 249
　Bradley, 247, 251
　Hume and Kant, 256
　Kant, 258
　Montague, 248
　Whitehead, 248
　Wisdom, 249–250
Metaphysics, *See* Systems
　absolute presuppositions, 283–284
　attacked as fallacious, 263–273
　attitudes towards: dogmatism, scepti-
　　cism, indifference, criticism, 257
　beliefs about reality systematized, 251
　creation of unconscious, 261–262
　cyclical theory, 428–429
　defended as non-fallacious, 273–286
　descriptive/revisionary, 286
　of history, 427–438
　　rejected, 424–427
　hypotheses attested by experience, 279
　instinctive beliefs, 251, 280
　methods of, 311–315
　natural disposition (Kant), 300
　pathos of, 300
　pragmatic method, 84
　progressive-evolutionary theory, 431
　providential theory, 429–431

Society, *See also* City of God
  aggregate or organism, 456–457
  characterized by value judgments, 226
  Christian view (Butterfield), 447–450
  contract theories, 467–469
  Marxist view, 436, 459
  open (Popper), 438–447
  organic views, 470–472, 620–629
  Platonic view, 462
  theistic view (Thomas Aquinas), 472–
    473
  utilitarian view, 473–475
Solipsism, 204
Sophrosyne (temperance), 5
Soul/Body, 51, *See also* Mind, Matter
  distinction denied (Dewey), 84
  distinction modified (Aristotle),
    Neo-Platonic contrast, 54
Sovereignty, theories of, 467–492
Space and Time
  Absolute (Newton), 67
  categories of experience (Kant), 78
  relative theory (Augustine), 231–234
Speculative philosophy
  conception of (Whitehead), 310, *See
    also* System, Metaphysics
  repudiation of, 86
Spirituality (McTaggart), 364, *See also*
  Mind
Square of opposition, 107
State, 456
  Aristotle's definition, 458
  contractual views, 467–470
  as higher entity, 470–472
  ideals of, 477–492
    Dante's Monarchia, 483–486
    Hobbes' Leviathan, 486–489
    Kant's Perpetual Peace, 489–492
    Plato's Republic, 477–482
  Lenin's conception, 459
  theistic view, 472–473
  U. S. Constitution, 459
  utilitarian view, 473–475
Sub specie aeternitatis, 362
Subject-predicate logic, a stress on noun
  and adjective in language, 222
Subjective/Objective, 579–580, *See also*
  Objective/Subjective
Subjectivism of values, 554–566, 601, 650
  denied (Osborne and Weitz), 593–594,
    (G. E. Moore), 600
  Santayana on subjectivism of beauty,
    579–580
Subsistent being, 223, 254
Substance, ambiguity of term
  many (Democritus, Leibniz), 43, 71–72
  material

no real conception (Berkeley), 74
materialism/idealism, 351–369
modes and relations, 194
no real conception (Hume), 75
  and reply to Hume, 354–355
one (Plotinus, Spinoza), 54, 70–71
power (Locke), 194
question raised in ancient philosophy,
  42–44
self basic to concept (Tennant), 354
substratum of properties, 264–265
theory of mind, 319
various definitions, 353
Substances, hierarchy of, 59
Sufficient Reason, principle of, 72
Supernaturalism, revolt against (Hobbes,
    d'Holbach), 328
  universe self-existent, 336
  values of vs. concern with this world,
    337
Syllogism, 109–117
  alternative, 117
  categorical, 109–115
  hypothetical, 115–116
  mood and figure of, 112
  practical, 644
  rules of, 112–113
Synthetic, 207–209
Synthetic judgment a priori, 207–213
Systems
  adequacy and coherence, 310
  claim to completeness and finality, 305
  defined, 86
    revolt against in philosophy, 86
    truth attained only in, 81
  different because of temperament or eco-
      nomic interest, 314
    factual evidence, 312–313
  final, objections to, 382
  logically necessary, 312–313
  materialism/idealism, 351–369
  objections to, 387–389
  as perspectives, 380–386
  philosophic/scientific, 303
    alternatives, 304–315
    motivation, 303–304
    only one coherent, 158–159, 344
    open/closed, 272, 369–370, 380–386
    use, 305–306
  scientific
    partial, contrasted to philosophic
      system, 160
    sometimes considered final, 380

Tabula rasa, 74
Tautologies, 88, 206
Teleology, 510–511, 514–518